ORIENTALISM: EARLY SOURCES

T0352816

ORIENTALISM: EARLY SOURCES
Edited by Bryan S. Turner

ORIENTALISM: EARLY SOURCES

Volume III

The Caliphate: Its Rise, Decline, and Fall

Sir William Muir

London and New York

First published 1891
by the Religious Tract Society
Reprinted 2000, 2002 by Routledge

2 Park Square, Milton Park, Abingdon, Oxfordshire OX14 4RN
Simultaneously published in the USA and Canada
by Routledge
711 Third Avenue, New York, NY 10017
First issued in paperback 2014

Routledge is an imprint of the Taylor and Francis Group, an informa business

Transferred to Digital Printing 2007

British Library Cataloguing in Publication Data
A catalogue record for this book is available from the British Library

Library of Congress Cataloguing in Publication Data
A catalogue record for this book has been requested

ISBN 978-0-415-20898-7 (set)
ISBN 978-0-415-20901-4 (hbk)
ISBN 978-0-415-75783-6 (pbk)

Publisher's note
The publisher has gone to great lengths to ensure the quality of this
reprint but points out that some imperfections in the original book
may be apparent.

THE CALIPHATE

ITS RISE, DECLINE, AND FALL

FROM ORIGINAL SOURCES

BY

SIR WILLIAM MUIR, K.C.S.I., LL.D., D.C.L.

PH.D. (BOLOGNA)

AUTHOR OF 'THE LIFE OF MAHOMET,' 'MAHOMET AND ISLAM,' ETC.

THE RELIGIOUS TRACT SOCIETY

56 PATERNOSTER ROW, 65 ST. PAUL'S CHURCHYARD

AND 164 PICCADILLY

1891

PREFACE

THIS work was intended as an abridgment of the *Annals of the Early Caliphate*[1], with continuation to the fall of the Abbassides; but I found, as I went on, the matter less compressible than I had hoped. The result, therefore, is much larger than anticipated. I trust, however, that its length notwithstanding, the narrative may be found not uninteresting; and I now offer it as a contribution towards the history of a period for which there are, as yet, but scanty materials in the English language.

The authorities, excepting for the later portions, are purely Arabian; indeed, for the earlier there are no other. After Tabari, who died in the fourth century A. H., Ibn Athîr (d. 630), a singularly impartial annalist, has been my chief guide. Towards the close, and especially for the brief chapter on the Caliphate under the Mameluke dynasty, I have drawn largely on Weil's admirable *Geschichte der Chalifen*[2], which indeed has been my constant companion throughout. I gratefully acknowledge my obligations to the late Dr. Weil. The more his great history is studied in connection with the original authorities, the more one is

---

[1] Smith & Elder, 1883.
[2] Vols. I.-III. Mannheim, 1846-1851; IV. and V. Stuttgart, 1860-1862.

impressed with the vast research, the unfailing accuracy, and the dispassionate judgment of the author.

I should mention here that the materials out of which our story is woven differ entirely from those for the Biography of Mahomet. For that, every incident of his life, and every phase of his character, is illustrated by myriads of traditions of all degrees of credibility—authoritative, uncertain, or fabulous—each tradition separate and independent, generally short and complete in itself. At his death the curtain drops at once upon the lifelike scene. Tradition collapses, and the little that remains is curt and meagre. Of the chief 'Companions,' indeed, from their connection with the Prophet, we have sufficient notice, and special prominence is given to the lives of the first four Caliphs. But tradition, instead of being, as before, a congeries of separate statements, now assumes the form of connected narrative, and eventually the style of ordinary annals ; and though there is now and then an exception, as in the minute and profuse description of such battles as Cadesia, the Camel, and Siffin, the story as a rule becomes bald and jejune. These annals also are strictly divided by the year, the chapter for each year containing everything belonging to it, and as a rule nothing else. The continuity of subjects which extend often over a long series of years, is thus broken up, and some inconvenience and difficulty experienced by the historian in forming a connected narrative. But upon the whole, the materials are amply sufficient for the historian's purpose.

I may be permitted here to lament the want of any full and standard work in our own language on the Crusades, and on the Mameluke dynasty and its overthrow by the Osmanlies,—chapters not only deeply interesting in themselves, but bound up with the interests of the Eastern Churches, and development of the political relations of Europe, Asia, and Egypt. I venture to express the hope that some worthy pen may supply the want.

At first sight, ' the Caliphate,' as here treated, might appear somewhat beyond the scope of the *Religious Tract Society.* It really is by no means so. For if the contrast with Christianity is not immediately expressed it must constantly be inferred, and cannot but suggest itself at every turn to the thoughtful reader ; while some aspects of it have been specially noticed in the Review at the close of the volume.

The reader will bear in mind that the Moslem year, as purely lunar, is eleven days shorter than the solar, and consequently loses about three years in every cycle of a hundred. The lunar month has also this peculiarity, that while, like the Jewish, the date indicates the age of the moon, the month itself gives no indication of the season of the year. The dates have usually been given throughout, according both to the Moslem and the Christian notation.

The Mussulman months, being unfamiliar to the English reader, have been indicated, as I trust in a more intelligible notation, by Roman numerals in the margin thus : —

Moharram	. . . . i.	Shaban	viii.
Safar	ii.	Ramadhan or Ram-	
Rabi I	iii.	zan	ix.
Rabi II	iv.	Shawwal	x.
Jumad I	v.	Dzul Cada	xi.
Jumad II	vi.	Dzul Hijj	xii.
Rajab	vii.		

I have not been very strict, and possibly not always

consistent, in the rendering of proper names. Received
forms have ordinarily been adhered to. As a rule, trans-
literation of Arabic names has been as follows :—

ث = th   ز = z   غ = gh
ج = j   ض = dh   ق = c (or k)
ذ = dz   ظ = tz   ك = k

For the letter ع I have not in the present work assigned
any diacritical mark.

W. M.

EDINBURGH, *September*, 1891.

CONTENTS

THE CALIPHATE:

ITS RISE, DECLINE, AND FALL.

CHAPTER I.

DEATH OF MAHOMET, ELECTION OF ABU BEKR.

11 A.H.   632 A.D.

IT was Midsummer in the year 632 of our era, when the Prophet of Arabia passed away. He had been ten years at Medina, for it was now the eleventh year of the Hegira era, that is of the Flight from Mecca. Mahomet had reached the age of three-score years and three, and up to the time of his last illness, which lasted but thirteen days, had been hale and vigorous. His death fell as an unexpected shock upon Medina.

For some days before, a burning fever had weakened him grievously and confined him to his bed. All through Sunday of the fatal week he lay prostrate, and at times delirious. Monday morning brought temporary relief. It was the hour of early prayer, and the worshippers had assembled in the court of the Great mosque adjoining the chamber of Ayesha, in which she had been tenderly nursing her husband throughout his illness. Feeling stronger that morning, he rose from the couch, drew aside the curtain from the door, and moved softly into the court, where Abu Bekr (as commissioned by Mahomet when laid aside) was conducting the service in his place. When prayers were ended, Abu Bekr, seeing his master to all appearance better, obtained leave to visit his

B

A.H. 11. wife who lived in the upper suburb of the city. Then the Prophet, having spoken a few kindly words to his aunt and others crowding around him, was helped back into the chamber. Exhausted by the effort, his strength sank, and shortly after he breathed his last on the bosom of his favourite wife.

Abu Bekr's return ; scene in court of mosque.

It was yet but little after mid-day. Rumour spreading, the Mosque was soon crowded with a host of bewildered followers. Amongst them Omar arose, and in a wild and excited strain, declaimed that the Prophet was not dead, but in a trance from which he would soon arise, and root out the hypocrites from the land. Abu Bekr had by this time hurried back. He crossed the court, not heeding his impetuous friend, and entered into Ayesha's chamber. Stooping down he kissed the Prophet's face. ' Sweet wert thou,' he said, 'in life, and sweet thou art in death.' Then he went forth, and finding Omar still haranguing the people, put him aside with the memorable words : *Whoso worshippeth Mahomet, let him know that Mahomet is dead; but whoso worshippeth God, let him know that God liveth and dieth not.* So saying, he recited certain verses from the Coran, which no doubt he had long dwelt upon as signifying that Mahomet was mortal and would die as other Prophets had died before him. Recognising the sacred words to bear a meaning that had never struck him before, Omar was speechless. 'My limbs trembled,' he would say, when speaking of that memorable hour, 'and I knew of a certainty that Mahomet was dead indeed.'

Men of Medina meet to elect a chief.

The assembly in the court of the Mosque had now quieted down, when a messenger ran up breathless with a report that the citizens of Medina had assembled to choose a Ruler from amongst themselves. The moment was critical. The unity of the faith was at stake. A divided power would fall to pieces, and all might be lost. The mantle of the Prophet must fall upon one Successor, and on one alone. The sovereignty of Islam demanded an undivided Caliphate; and Arabia would acknowledge no master but from amongst the Coreish. The die must be cast, and at once. Such, no doubt, were the thoughts that occurred to the two chief

Companions of the Prophet on hearing this report; and so, A.H. 11.
accompanied by Abu Obeida, another leading chief, they
hurried to the spot, if haply they might nip the conspiracy
in the bud. On the way two friendly citizens, coming from
the excited conclave, warned them of the risk they ran in
entering it alone ; but, notwithstanding, they hastened on.
The men of Medina meanwhile, gathered in one of their
rude halls, were bent upon an independent course. 'We
have sheltered this nest of strangers,' they cried. 'It is by
our good swords they have been able to plant the Faith.
The Ruler of Medina shall be from amongst ourselves.'
They had already fixed their choice on Sad ibn Obada,
leader of the Beni Khazraj, who, sick of a fever, lay
covered up at the further end of the hall, when the three Met by
Companions entered. It was just in time; for had the Abu Bekr, Omar, and
citizens elected Sad and pledged their troth to him, Medina Abu
might have been irretrievably compromised. Omar, with Obeida.
his native vehemence, was about to speak, when Abu
Bekr, calm and firm, anticipated him thus : 'Every word,'
said he, 'which ye, Men of Medina, have uttered in your
own praise, is true, and more than true ; but in noble birth
and influence the Coreish are paramount, and to none but
them will Arabia yield obedience.' 'Then,' cried they, 'let
there be one Chief amongst you and one from amongst us.'
'Away with you!' exclaimed Omar ; 'two cannot stand
together ;' and even Sad from beneath his covering mut-
tered that to divide the power would only weaken it. High
words ensued. Hobab, on the side of Sad, cried out,
'Hear him not! Attend to me, for I am the *well-rubbed
Palm-stem* [1]. If they refuse, expel them from the city.'
'The Lord destroy thee !' cried Omar; and Hobab
returned the words. The altercation gaining heat and
bitterness, Abu Bekr saw it must be stopped at any risk ;
and stepping forward said, 'Ye see these two,' pointing to
Omar and Abu Obeida. 'Choose ye now which of them ye
will, and salute him as your Chief.' 'Nay,' answered these
both at once, ' *Thou* hast already, at the Prophet's bidding,

---

[1] Meaning a palm-trunk left for the beasts to come and rub themselves upon ;
metaphor for a person much resorted to for counsel.

A. H. 11. led the prayers, and art our Chief.   Stretch forth thine
hand.' He did so, and they struck their hand on his, as
is the Arab custom, in token of allegiance.   Others were
about to follow their example, when Hobab cried to a man
of the Beni Khazraj about to take the pledge, ' Wilt thou
cut thine own kinsman's throat ? ' 'Not so,' he answered ;
' I only yield the right to whom the right is due.' Whilst
they yet hesitated, the Beni Aus, jealous of the rival tribe
and of Sad its nominee, spake among themselves : ' If this
man be chosen, the rule will be for ever with the Beni

Abu Bekr
elected
Caliph.

Khazraj.   Let us salute Abu Bekr as our Chief.'   The
example set, group after group advanced to strike their
hand on that of Abu Bekr, till none was left but Sad, who
still lay covered in the corner.   Acknowledged thus by the
men of Medina, there could be no doubt of Abu Bekr's
acceptance by the Refugees.   He was one of themselves.
Moreover the Prophet, when laid aside, by appointing Abu
Bekr to take his place at the daily prayers, had in a
manner indicated him as his Vicegerent.   And so homage
was done on all sides to Abu Bekr.   He was saluted as the
' Caliph,' or ' *Successor* of the Prophet.'

Burial of
the
Prophet.

The night was occupied in preparing the dead for sepul-
ture.   The body was washed and laid out, and the grave
dug in Ayesha's apartment, where Mahomet had breathed
his last.   On the morrow the citizens, men, women, and
children, thronged the chamber to look once more upon
their Prophet's face.   And then the remains were reverently
committed to the dust.

Abu Bekr's
inaugural
address.

The funeral over, and the court of the great mosque still
crowded with the mourners, Abu Bekr ascended the pulpit,
and, sitting down, was acknowledged Caliph by acclamation.   Then he arose, and said : ' Oh people !   Now I am
Ruler over you, albeit not the best amongst you.   If I do
well, support me ; if ill, then set me right.   Follow the
True, wherein is faithfulness ; eschew the False, wherein
is treachery.   The weaker amongst you shall be as the
stronger with me, until that I shall have redressed his
wrong ; and the stronger shall be as the weaker, until, if
the Lord will, I shall have taken from him that which he

hath wrested. Leave not off to fight in the ways of the
Lord ; whosoever leaveth off, him verily shall the Lord
abase. Obey me as I obey the Lord and his Prophet;
wherein I disobey, obey me not. Now, arise to prayer,
and the Lord be with you !' The assembly stood up for
prayer, and Abu Bekr, for the first time as Caliph, filled
the place of Mahomet [1].

The supreme power thus passed, without let or hindrance, *Aly delays*
into the hands of Abu Bekr. Sad, chagrined at being *doing*
homage.
superseded, held aloof. Aly is also said to have refrained
from doing homage till after the death of Fatima his wife.
The Alyite party pretend that he looked to the Caliphate
himself. But there is nothing in his previous life, or in the
attitude of the Prophet towards him, that warrants any
such surmise. He had indeed a grievance, but of quite
a different kind. The day after her father's death, Fatima
preferred a claim to his share in the crown lands of
Kheibar. Abu Bekr disallowed the claim ; holding that
the revenues were destined, as Mahomet had himself
desired, for purposes of State. Fatima took the denial so
much to heart that she held no intercourse with the Caliph
during the short remainder of her life. And hence it
was only after her death that Aly recognised with any
cordiality the title of Abu Bekr to the Caliphate [2]. *Fatima* Fatima
was the last surviving child of Mahomet. His other *mother of*
Hasan and
three daughters, two of whom had in succession married *Hosein.*
Othman, were already some time dead. Khadija had
also borne him two sons, but both died in infancy at
Mecca. A third, the only child the prophet had at
Medina, and that by a slave-girl, died sixteen months old.
There was thus no issue surviving in the male line. But two

[1] Presidency at public prayer was ever in Islam the sign of chief command,
whether in civil or in military life.

[2] Tradition regarding Aly is coloured and distorted by the canvass of a
political faction, which in the end assumed a *divine* right of succession in Aly
and his descendants. There is not a shadow of proof that he made any such
claim himself, or that any claim was made by others for him, during the
Caliphates of Abu Bekr and Omar. It was not till the election after the death
of Omar that he became a candidate, and even then from his being one of the
chief men among the Companions, rather than from any supposed right in
virtue of his relationship to Mahomet and marriage with his daughter.

A.H. 11. grandsons, Hasan and Hosein, were left by his daughter
Fatima. They were now but six or seven years of age.

How far   With Mahomet ceased the theocratic power; but his
Abu Bekr's
election   kingly functions, as ruler over all Islam, descended.
formed a   According to Arabian notions, the ruler of a nation, like the
precedent.
           chieftain of a tribe, is the head and representative of his
people, and the nomination invalid till confirmed by their
homage. Omar, in after days, held that the irregular
election of Abu Bekr (referring apparently to the scene
enacted in the hall) should not be a precedent. It was,
he said, an event the happiest in its consequences for
Islam, but justified only by the urgency of the moment.
What might have been the issue if any son of Mahomet
had survived, it is useless to speculate. But certainly the
hereditary descent of kingly power was foreign to the
sentiment of Arabia. As matters stood, Mahomet seems
to have shrunk from anticipating the contingency of his
death, and made no preparation for what should follow.
But in so far as we may suppose him to have felt his
illness mortal and death impending, the nomination of
Abu Bekr to conduct the public prayers (acknowledged
mark of chief or delegated authority) may be held the
natural indication of his wish that he should succeed[1].
Apart from the pretensions of the men of Medina, which
immediately died away, there was in the election neither
doubt nor hesitancy. The notion of divine right, or even
of preferential claim, resting in the Prophet's family, was
the growth of an altogether later age.

Parties at   It may be necessary here to remind the reader not fresh
Medina.   from study of the Prophet's life, of the state of parties at
the present juncture. The *Men of Medina* are the old inhabitants of the city who had received Mahomet on his
escape from Mecca, and supported his cause[2]; they now
embraced practically the whole native population, as the
party that opposed him had gradually succumbed before
his growing power. They were divided into two tribes, the
Aus and *Khazraj*, jealous of each other. Beside these
were the *Refugees*, or those who had followed Mahomet in

---

[1] See *Life of Mahomet*, p. 499.   [2] Hence called *Ansar*, or Helpers.

exile from Mecca or elsewhere, and were now settled at
Medina. Again, *Companion* was a title of honour given to
all those who had enjoyed the friendship or acquaintance
of the Prophet A few words may also be added here
to revive the reader's recollection of the three Companions
who turned the scale at the election of the Caliph.

Abu Bekr, three-score years of age, was somewhat short Abu Bekr.
in stature, of spare frame, rounded back, and stooping gait.
His face thin, smooth, and fair, nose aquiline and sharp,
forehead high, eyes deep-seated and far apart. His hair
scanty; the beard, now for many years white, dyed red.
His countenance still in old age was handsome; the
expression mild, but wise and resolute. To him faith in
the Prophet had become a second nature, and, now that
his Master was gone, the disciple lived but to fulfil his
will. It was this that nerved a disposition naturally soft
and yielding, and made Abu Bekr, of all the followers of
Mahomet, the truest, firmest, and most resolute.

Omar, fifteen years younger, differed from the other both Omar.
in frame and temperament. Broad-shouldered and tall, he
towered above the crowd. Somewhat dark in complexion,
the face was fresh and ruddy. His head was now bald, and
beard dyed like his friend's; his stride was long, and his
presence commanding. Naturally hasty and passionate,
he would twist his moustache when angry and draw it downwards to his mouth. But time had mellowed temper; and,
beneath an imperious manner, he was bland and courteous.
Attachment to Mahomet had, on these two friends, an effect
exactly opposite. That which braced the soft nature of
Abu Bekr, served to abate the vehemence of Omar. Both
stood in a like relation to the Prophet. Haphsa, Omar's
daughter, was one of Mahomet's favourite wives ; but
Ayesha, the child of Abu Bekr, was queen in his affections
to the end.

On these two men at this moment hung the future of Abu
Islam. The third, Abu Obeida, was between them in age. Obeida.
He was thin, tall, and sinewy ; bald, and with little beard.
Mild, unassuming and unwarlike, he was yet destined to
take a leading part in the conquest of Syria.

CHAPTER II.

Expedition to Syrian Border.

11 A.H.   632 A.D.

ABU BEKR had soon an occasion for showing his resolve to carry out to the utmost the will of Mahomet in things both great and small.

Osama ap-
pointed by
Mahomet
to com-
mand the
force.
Just before he fell sick, the Prophet had given orders for an expedition to the Syrian border. It was to avenge the disaster which three years before had befallen the Moslem arms on the field of Muta. In that reverse, Zeid, the bosom friend of Mahomet, who led the army, fell; and now, distinctly to mark the object, his son Osama, though still young, was nominated by Mahomet to the command, and bidden to avenge his father's death. The camp, including all available fighting men, had been formed at Jorf, outside Medina, on the Syrian road. During the Prophet's sickness the force remained inactive there, uncertain of the issue. When the fatal event took place, Osama broke up the camp, and carrying back the banner received at the hands of Mahomet, planted it in the court of the great mosque, close by the door of Ayesha's apartment.

The day following his inauguration, Abu Bekr took up the banner, and restoring it to Osama, in token that he was still Commander, bade the army again assemble, and encamp at Jorf as it had done before; not a man was to be left behind. Obeying the command, the fighting men of Medina and its neighbourhood flocked to the camp, even Omar amongst the number. While yet preparing to

depart, the horizon darkened suddenly. Report of the Prophet's illness, soon followed by tidings of his death, had
spread like wildfire over the land. From every side came
rumours of disloyalty, and of resolve to cast the yoke of
Islam off. The sense of the army, and of Osama himself,
was strongly against leaving the city thus defenceless, and
the Caliph exposed to risk of sudden danger. Omar was
deputed to represent all this to Abu Bekr, and also to
urge (a request which Mahomet already had refused) that,
if the expedition must proceed, a more experienced general
should command. To the first request Abu Bekr replied,
calm and unmoved : ' Were the city swarming round with
packs of ravening wolves, and I left solitary and alone, the
force should go ; not a word from my Master's lips shall
fall to the ground.' At the second demand the Caliph's
anger kindled : ' Thy mother be childless, O son of
Khattab !' he said, seizing Omar by the beard :—' Shall
the Prophet of the Lord appoint a man to the command,
and I, deposing him, appoint another in his place ?' So
Omar returned, with neither object gained.

When all was ready for the march, Abu Bekr repaired to
the camp, and accompanied the force a little way on foot.
' Be mounted,' said Osama to him ; ' or else I will dismount
and walk by thee.' ' Not so,' replied Abu Bekr ; ' I will not
mount ; I will walk and soil my feet, a little moment, in
the ways of the Lord. Verily, every step trodden in the
ways of the Lord is equal to the merit of manifold good
works, and wipeth out a multitude of sins.' After a while
he stopped, and said to Osama : ' If it be thy will, give
Omar leave that he may return with me to the city, for
strength and counsel.' So he gave him leave.

He accompanies Osama a little way on foot.

The army then halted, to receive Abu Bekr's parting
words. ' See,' said he, addressing Osama, 'that thou avoid
treachery. Depart not in any wise from the right. Thou
shalt mutilate none ; neither shalt thou kill child or aged
man, nor any woman. Injure not the date-palm, neither
burn it with fire ; and cut not down any tree wherein is
food for man or beast. Slay not of the flocks or herds or
camels, saving for needful sustenance. Ye may eat of the

And gives his last instructions.

A.H. 11. meat which the men of the land shall bring unto you in
———   their vessels, making mention thereon of the name of the
         Lord.   And the Monks with shaven heads, if they submit,
         leave them unmolested.   Now march forward in the name
         of the Lord, and may He protect you from sword and
         pestilence!'

Osama re-   So Abu Bekr returned with Omar to Medina.   Osama
turns vic- marched by Wadi al Cora, in the direction of Duma and the
torious.
         highlands south of Syria.   The brunt of his attack fell upon
         the Beni Codhaa, and the semi-Christian tribes which, under
         the Roman banner, had discomfited and slain his father.
         That disaster was now avenged in fire and blood.   The
         land was ravaged far and near, and after an absence of two
         months, the army returned laden with spoil.

         Meanwhile stirring events had been transpiring at
         Medina.

CHAPTER III.

MEDINA THREATENED.

11 A.H. 632 A.D.

IN after-days Abu Bekr was used to look back with just pride upon the despatch, universal reclamation notwith- standing, of Osama's force. Public opinion was not long in justifying the act by results of essential benefit. His bold front struck the Bedouin mind with the stability of his rule. If the leaders at Medina had not been confident in strength at home they would not have sent away their army ; and the Arabs, reasoning thus, were restrained from much that they might otherwise have done. Still the position was critical, and at times alarming.

It was indeed a thing for the brave old Caliph to be proud of. 'The Arabs,' we read, 'were on all sides rising in rebellion. Apostasy and disaffection raised their heads ; Christians and Jews began to stretch out their necks ; and the Faithful were as a flock of sheep without a shepherd, their Prophet gone, their numbers few, their foes a multi- tude.' In face of all this Abu Bekr sent off beyond recall his only force, and left Medina open and apparently de- fenceless.

Towards the close of Mahomet's life, three rivals laying claim to the prophetic office had raised the standard of rebellion. In the south, insurrection was hardly quelled by the death of the 'Veiled Prophet' of Yemen, when, on tidings of the decease of Mahomet, it burst forth with redoubled violence. At the centre of the peninsula, again,

A. H. 11. Moseilama detached the powerful tribes around Yemama from their allegiance. To the north-east, nearer home, Toleiha, the third pretender, was now openly and dangerously hostile. From every quarter, in rapid succession, came news of spreading disaffection. Collectors of the tithe (an impost hateful to the Bedouin), Legates and Residents of Mahomet throughout the provinces,—all, in fact, who represented the authority of Islam, fled or were expelled. The faithful were massacred, some confessors suffering a cruel death. Mecca and Tayif wavered at the first; but in the end, through the strong influence of the Coreish, stood firm. They were almost alone. Here and there some few tribes, under loyal, or, it might be, temporising, chiefs, maintained the semblance of obedience; but they were hardly discernible amidst the seething mass of rebellion. Amru, hurrying back from Oman (whither he had been sent as ambassador at the Farewell pilgrimage), saw as he passed the whole of Central Arabia either in open apostasy or ready to break away on the first demand of tithe; and his report filled the citizens of Medina with dismay. In truth, Islam had never taken firm hold of the distant provinces; and as for the Bedouins, Mahomet himself had frequent cause to chide their fickleness. It was fear of punishment, and lust of plunder under the Prophet's banner, rather than attachment to the faith, which hitherto had held in check these wild sons of the desert. The restraints and obligations of Islam were ever irksome and distasteful; and now rid of them, they were again returning to their lawless life.

Danger of Medina.

As report after report came in of fresh defection, Abu Bekr could but instruct his scattered officers to hold together wherever able the loyal few, bravely trusting to tide over the crisis till Osama's force returned. For the immediate defence of Medina he took such measures as were possible. The faithful tribes in the neighbourhood were called in, and pickets posted at the various approaches to the city. The turbulent clans in the near desert eastward were the first to assume a threatening attitude. The Beni Abs and Dzobian massed there in such numbers 'that

the land was straitened by them,' and they parted into two
bodies, one at Rabadza, the other at Dzul Cassa, the first
station from Medina on the road to Nejd. The false
prophet Toleiha sent his brother to encourage the insurgents: but they still vacillated between his claims and
those of Islam. At last they bethought themselves of a
compromise. A deputation offered to hold by Islam and
its ritual, if only they were excused the tithe. The
strangers bearing the message were welcomed by the chiefs
of Medina, but by the Caliph their advances were indignantly rejected. He would relax not a tittle of the legal
dues. 'If ye withhold but the tether of a tithed camel,'
said Abu Bekr, sharply, 'I will fight with you for the
same.' With this refusal they retired, and also with the
intelligence that the city had but few defenders left. Now
was the moment, not for plunder only, but for a decisive
blow upon Medina. Abu Bekr, foreseeing this, redoubled
his precautions. He strengthened the pickets, and set over
them the chief men still remaining with him,—Aly, Talha,
and Zobeir. For the rest of the people he appointed the
great mosque a rendezvous. 'The land hath rebelled
against us,' he said, 'and they have spied out our nakedness and the weakness of our defence. Ye know not
whether they will come upon you by night or come upon
you by day, or which of you may be first attacked.
Wherefore be vigilant and ready.'

And so it came to pass. They tarried but three days,
when a surprise was attempted from Dzul Cassa. The
outposts were on the alert, and kept the assailants at bay
while the main guard was hurried up on camels from the
Mosque. The Bedouins, hardly prepared for so warm a
reception, fled back upon their reserves. They were pursued; but the insurgents, blowing out their water-skins,
cast them before the camels of the Moslems, which, unused
to the stratagem, took fright and fled back to the Mosque.
None were killed or wounded, but the rebels were emboldened by the discomfiture. Abu Bekr, anticipating
renewed attack, called out every man capable of bearing
arms, and spent the night in marshalling his force. Next

A. H. 11. morning, while yet dark, he led forth the little band himself in regular array with centre and two wings. The enemy were taken by surprise at early dawn, and as the sun arose were already in full flight. Abu Bekr drove them with slaughter out of Dzul Cassa, and, leaving a portion of his little force as an outpost there, returned to Medina.

Good effect of the victory.   The affair was small, but the effect was great. As failure would have been disastrous, perhaps fatal, to Islam, so was victory the turning-point in its favour. The power of the Prophet's successor to protect his city, even without an army, was noised abroad. And soon after, the spirits of the Moslems rose as they saw some chiefs appear, bringing in the tithes. The tribes whom these represented, to be sure, were few compared with the apostate hordes; but it was an augury of brighter days. The first to present their legal offerings to the Caliph were deputations from the Beni Temim and Beni Tay. Each was ushered into his presence as an embassy. 'Nay,' said Abu Bekr; 'they are more than that; they are Messengers of glad tidings, true men, and defenders of the faith.' And the people answered, 'Even so; now the good things that thou didst promise do appear.'

Saving of Islam due to Abu Bekr.   Tradition delights to ascribe with pious gratitude the preservation of Islam to the aged Caliph's faith and fortitude. 'On the death of Mahomet,' so runs our record, 'it wanted but little, and the Faithful had perished utterly. But the Lord strengthened the heart of Abu Bekr, and stablished us thereby in the resolve to give place, not for one moment, to the apostates; giving answer to them but in these three words—*Submission, Exile*, or *the Sword.*' It was the simple faith of Abu Bekr which fitted him for the task, and made him carry out the law of his Master to the letter. But for him, Islam would have melted away in compromise with the Bedouin tribes, or, likelier still, have perished in the throes of birth.

CHAPTER IV.

RETURN OF OSAMA. EXPEDITIONS SENT AGAINST THE APOSTATE TRIBES THROUGHOUT ARABIA.

11. A.H.   632 A.D.

OSAMA at last returned, his army laden with booty ; and Osama's return. vi. 11 A.H. Sept. 632 A.D. Medina, for two months unprotected, was at once relieved from further danger.   The royal Fifth (portion of the booty reserved by sacred ordinance for the State) was delivered to the Caliph, and by him distributed among the people.

Abu Bekr lost no time now in following up the advantage Expedition against Beni Abs and Dzobian. he had gained over the insurgents.   Driven back from Dzul Cassa, they had retired to Rabadza, and vented their anger in destroying by cruel deaths some faithful followers of the Prophet still left amongst them.   Deeply moved at their fate, Abu Bekr took an oath that 'he would by the like deaths destroy as many of them as they had slain, or even more.'

Leaving Osama in command of the city, and the army Abu Bekr chastises rebel tribes at Rabadza. also there for a little to recruit, Abu Bekr with a small force marched out towards Rabadza.   The chief men expostulated against his going forth to fight in person.   Were a commander killed in action, his place could easily be filled ; but if the Caliph fell, their head and master would be gone.   'Nay,' replied Abu Bekr ; 'but I will go forth, and will be your comrade even as one of your ownselves.' So they marched on, and coming up with the enemy, completely discomfited them, killing some, and taking others prisoners.   The Beni Abs and Dzobian fled to Toleiha, and

A.H. 11. joined his army at Bozakha. Thereupon Abu Bekr confiscated their pasture-lands, to be in all time to come a
reserve for the stud and camels of the State. The rebels
eventually tendered their submission, and then found ample
compensation in conquered lands beyond Arabia. Satisfied
with this success, the Caliph returned to Medina.

Islam must
be reim-
posed on
all Arabia.
The army by this time was refitted. The tithes had
begun to come in from the neighbouring tribes in token of
submission. Medina was no longer in peril, and the citizens
breathed freely. But a heavy burden still lay upon the
Caliph. Save a remnant here and there, faith had vanished,
and the Arabs had relapsed into apostasy. And yet Islam
was to be the faith of all Arabia ;—' Throughout the land
there shall be no second creed,' was the behest of Mahomet
upon his death-bed. False prophets must be crushed ;
rebels vanquished ; apostates reclaimed or else extermi-
nated ; and the supremacy vindicated of Islam. It was,
in short, the mission of Abu Bekr to redeem the dying
Prophet's words.

Eleven ex-
peditions
despatched
to different
parts of
Arabia.
With this great purpose, Abu Bekr went forth a second
time to Dzul Cassa, and summoned there the whole available forces of Islam and all the loyal chiefs. These he
divided into eleven independent columns, and over each
appointed a distinguished leader, to whom (following the
example of his Master) he presented a banner. Arabia
was parcelled out, and each detachment given a quarter to
reclaim, with marching orders, where to begin and what
course to take. Thus Khalid was to subdue Toleiha ; and
Ikrima with Shorahbil, Moseilama. Mohajir was sent to
Yemen ; Ala to Bahrein ; Hodzeifa to Mahra ; Amru
against the Beni Codhaa. And so by this great scheme,
in course of time, no spot would be left unconquered.
The troops retained at home were few; but few were
needed now.

Proclama-
tion to
apostates
to repent.
viii. 11 A.H.
Oct. 632
A. D.
Having despatched the various expeditions, Abu Bekr
returned to Medina. There his first concern was to publish
a summons to apostate tribes, commanding them everywhere to repent and submit themselves, on which condition
they should be pardoned, and received back into Islam.

Such as refused would be attacked, their fighting men cut to pieces, and their women and children taken captive. This summons was sent by the hand of envoys to every province and rebellious tribe. The Adzan, or call to prayer, was to be the test of faith: if that were heard and responded to, good and well; if not, the people were to be held as apostate, and punished to the bitter end.

Abu Bekr never again left Medina to lead his troops. Some say that he regretted this; but it is not likely that he did. Medina, the capital, was his proper place. From it, as a central point, he was able to direct the movement of his commanders all over the peninsula; and with operations in so many different quarters to control, he could not have been better placed.

It is not quite so clear why he failed to appoint the more distinguished Companions to any chief command. The same was afterwards the policy of Omar, who would say that he refrained partly because the liability to render an account to him would have implied subjection inconsistent with their dignity, but chiefly also to strengthen his own hands by having them about him as advisers. This latter reason no doubt also weighed with Abu Bekr, who used to take counsel on all important matters with the leading Companions. Still, it is singular that men like Aly and Zobeir, so prominent in the battles of Mahomet, should now altogether disappear from operations in the field.

CHAPTER V.

Recovery of Arabia. Campaign of Khalid.

11 A.H. 632-3 A.D.

The struggle of a year for Arabia's recovery. It was indeed time for decisive action. But a few weeks before, the entire Peninsula was submissive to the claims of Mahomet both as Prophet and as King. Now all was on a sudden changed ; and the Arabs abjuring Islam, were fast relapsing into apostasy and tribal independence. It took a year to reclaim the Peninsula, a year of hard fighting and obstinate resistance in every corner of the land. It was the indomitable spirit alone which had been breathed by Mahomet into his faithful followers that crowned their efforts with victory. The Arabs at last were forced back, in sullen mood and with unwilling step, to confess the faith of Mahomet and submit themselves to his successor.

Details meagre and hazy. A brief outline of the twelve-months' campaign will suffice ; for tradition, up to the Prophet's death clear and copious, suddenly at this point, becomes curt, obscure, and disconnected. The scene of confusion prevailing throughout the land is presented to us in meagre, dim, and hazy outline. While Islam struggled for very life, its followers thought only of the lance and sword ; and when the struggle at last was over, little remained but the sense of escape from a terrible danger. No date is given for the many battles fought throughout the year. We can only guess at the sequence of events.

Such being the case, we shall begin with the operations of Khalid on the north and east, and then take up the other Provinces in order as they lie around the coast from Bahrein on the Persian Gulf to Yemen on the Red Sea.

Campaign of Khalid.

I. *Against Toleiha.*

After Abu Bekr and Omar, the most prominent figure in the early days of Islam is without doubt that of Khalid, son of Welid. More to him than to any other is it due that the Faith recovered its standing, and thereafter spread with such marvellous rapidity. A dashing soldier, brave even to rashness, his courage was tempered by a cool and ready judgment. His conduct on the battle-fields which decided the fate of the Persian empire, and of the Byzantine rule in Syria, ranks him as one of the greatest generals of the world. Over and again, always with consummate skill and heroism, he cast the die, in crises where loss would have been destruction to Islam. From the carnage of his arms he was named *The Sword of God* ; and so little regard had he for loss of life, that he wedded the widow of his enemy on the field still sodden with his own soldiers' blood. He had already distinguished himself in the annals of Islam. Fighting on the side of the Coreish, the defeat of the Prophet at Ohod was due mainly to his prowess. After his conversion, Khalid's was the only column which at the capture of Mecca disobeyed by shedding blood ; and shortly after, the cruel massacre of an unoffending tribe brought down upon him stern reproof from Mahomet. On the field of Muta he gave signal promise of the future when, the Moslem army having been routed by Roman legions and its leaders one after another slain, he saved the shattered remnants from destruction by skilful and intrepid tactics. It was this Khalid whom Abu Bekr now sent forth against the rebel prophets Toleiha and Moseilama.

Khalid ibn Welid.

A.H. 11.

Khalid
marches
against
Toleiha.
His column, by far the strongest of the eleven, was composed of the flower of the Refugees, as well as of the native Citizens. To divert the enemy's attention, Abu Bekr gave out its destination as for Kheibar ; and, to strike the greater terror, that he himself would join it there with a fresh contingent. Khalid, however, was not long in quitting the northern route. Striking off to the right, he made direct for the mountain range, seat of the Beni Tai, and not distant from the scene of Toleiha's revolt among the Beni Asad.

Toleiha.
Of the doctrines of Toleiha, and the other pretenders to prophetic office, we know little, nor indeed anything at all to show wherein the secret of their influence lay. So far as appears, their worship was a mere travesty of Islam. Some doggrel verses and childish sayings are all that the contemptuous voice of tradition has transmitted of their teaching. That four pretenders (for Sajah the prophetess was also such) should have arisen in different parts of Arabia, and just then drawn multitudes after them, would seem to imply something deeper than senseless rhymes and more specious than petty variations of the Moslem rite. It is not unreasonable to assume that the spiritual sense of Arabia had been quickened by the preaching of Mahomet, and that his example had at once suggested the claims of others, and contributed to their success. Jealousy of Mecca and Medina, moreover, and impatience of the trammels of Islam, were powerful incentives for Bedouins to cast in their lot with these pretenders. Thus the Beni Ghatafan, who aforetime were in league with the Beni Asad, had recently fallen out with them and lost some pasture-land. Oyeina, chief of the Ghatafan, now counselled a return to their old relations with the Beni Asad. ' Let us go back,' he said, ' to our ancient alliance which we had with them before Islam, for never since we gave it up have I known our pasture boundaries. A prophet of our own is better than a prophet of the Coreish. Beside all this, Mahomet is dead, but Toleiha is alive.' So saying, Oyeina, with 700 of his warriors, joined the false prophet at Bozakha.

Bedouin
jealousy of
Mecca and
Medina.

On first hearing of the heresy, Mahomet had sent A.H. 11.
an envoy to rally the faithful amongst the Beni Asad <u>Beni Tai</u>
and crush the pretender. But the cause, gaining ground, reclaimed.
was now supported by the neighbouring Beni Tai, as
well as by the insurgents who flocked to Toleiha after their
defeat at Rabadza ; and so the envoy had to fly. The
great family of Tai, however, was not wholly disloyal,
for (as above mentioned) the legal dues had been already
presented to Abu Bekr on behalf of some of them. Adi,
their loyal chief, was therefore now sent forward by Khalid
to his people, in the hope of detaching them from Toleiha's
cause. He found them in no friendly humour. ' The
Father of the foal!' they cried (for such was the sobriquet
contemptuously used for Abu Bekr[1]), 'thou shalt not persuade us to do homage to him.' 'Think better of it,'
replied Adi ; 'an army approacheth which ye cannot withstand. Ye shall know full soon that he is no foal, but the
lusty stallion. Wherefore see ye to it.' Alarmed at his
words, they begged for time to recall their fellows who had
joined Toleiha ; ' For,' said they, 'he will surely hold them
as hostages, or else put them to death.' So Khalid halted
three days, and in the end they not only tendered submission, but joined him with 1,000 horse, 'the flower of the
land of Tai, and the bravest of them.'

Thus reinforced, Khalid advanced against Toleiha. On Battle of
the march his army was exasperated by finding the bodies Bozakha.
of two of their scouts, one a warrior of note named Okkasha,
who had been slain, and left by Toleiha to be trampled
on the road. The armies met at Bozakha, and the combat
was hot and long. At last the tide of battle was turned by
a strange utterance of Toleiha, who, in his prophetic garb
of hair, was on the field. Oyeina was fighting bravely with
his 700, when the situation becoming critical, he turned to
Toleiha, saying, ' Hath any message come to thee from
Gabriel?' '*Not yet,*' answered the prophet. A second
time he asked, and received the same reply. 'Yes,' said
Toleiha, a little after, 'a message now hath come.' 'And

---

[1] *Abu Bekr* means 'Father of the young camel ;' so they called him by the
nick-name *Ab ul Fasil,* ' Father of the foal.'

what is it?' enquired Oyeina eagerly. 'Thus saith Gabriel to me, *Thou shalt have a millstone like unto his, and an affair shall happen that thou wilt not forget.*' 'Away with thee!' cried Oyeina scornfully; 'no doubt the Lord knoweth that an affair will happen that thou shalt not forget! Ho, every man to his tent!' So they turned to go; and thereupon the army fled.

Toleiha's sequel.

Toleiha escaped with his wife to Syria. The sequel is curious. At the first he took refuge with another tribe on the Syrian frontier. When the Beni Asad were pardoned, he returned to them, and embraced Islam. Passing Medina soon after on pilgrimage to Mecca, he was seized and carried to Abu Bekr, who set him at liberty, saying, 'Let him alone. The Lord hath now verily guided him into the right path.' When Omar succeeded, Toleiha presented himself to do homage. At first Omar spoke roughly to him: 'Thou art he that killed Okkasha,' he said, 'and his comrade too. I love thee not.' 'Was it not better,' answered the quondam prophet, 'that they by my hand should obtain the crown of martyrdom, rather than that I by theirs should have perished in hell-fire?' When he had sworn allegiance, the Caliph asked him concerning his oracular gift, and whether anything yet remained of it. 'Ah,' he replied, 'it was but a puff or two, as from a pair of bellows.' So he returned to his tribe, and went forth with them to the wars in Irac, where, in the great struggle with Persia, he became a hero of renown.

Repentant tribes received back into Islam.

After the battle of Bozakha, the Beni Asad, fearing lest their families should fall into the conqueror's hand, submitted and were pardoned. Other important tribes in the neighbourhood which had stood aloof watching the event, now came in, and received from Khalid the same terms. They resumed the profession of Islam with all its obligations, and in proof brought in the tithe. A full amnesty was accorded, on but one condition that those who during the apostasy had taken the life of any Moslem should be delivered up. These were now (to carry out the Caliph's vow) put to the like death as that which they had inflicted. If they had speared their victims, cast them over

precipices, drowned them in wells, or burned them in the A.H. 11.
fire, the persecutors were now subjected to the same cruel
fate.

Khalid stayed at Bozakha for a month, receiving the Body of
submission of the people and their tithes. Troops of malcon-
horse scoured the country, striking terror into all around. comfited.
In only one direction was serious opposition met. A body
of malcontents from amongst the penitent tribes, unable to
brook submission, assumed a defiant attitude. They had
yet to learn that the gripe of Islam was stern and crushing.
These gathered in a great multitude around Omm Siml,
daughter of a famous chieftain of the Ghatafan. Her
mother had been taken prisoner and put to a cruel
death by Mahomet. She herself had waited upon Ayesha
as captive maid in the Prophet's household; but the
haughty spirit of her race survived. Mounted on her
mother's war-camel, she led the force herself, and incited
the insurgents to a bold resistance. Khalid proclaimed
a great reward to him who should maim her camel. It
was soon disabled; and, Omm Siml slain, the rout of the
rebel host was easy.

A few of the leading rebels were sent prisoners to Abu Oyeina
Bekr. One of them, Oyeina, a notable marauding chieftain, pardoned.
had often been the terror of Medina. When the city was
besieged by the Coreish, he offered his assistance on
certain humiliating terms, which the Prophet was near
accepting; and he was also one of the influential leaders
'whose hearts,' after the battle of Honein, 'had been
reconciled' by the Prophet's largesses. He was now led
into Medina with the rest in chains, his hands tied
behind his back. The citizens crowded round to gaze at
the fallen chief, and the very children smote him with their
hands, crying out, 'Oh enemy of the Lord, apostate!'
'Not so,' said Oyeina bravely; 'I am no apostate; I never
was a believer until now.' The Caliph listened patiently
to the appeal of the captives. He forgave them, and commanded their release [1].

---

[1] For Omm Siml's mother, see *Life of Mahomet*, p. 361; and for Oyeina,
ibid. p. 323, &c.

II. Discomfiture of the Beni Temim. Story of Malik ibn Noweira.

Khalid's advance, II A.H. (Nov. ?), 632 A. D.

Having subdued the tribes inhabiting the hills and desert north of Medina, Khalid bent his steps eastward, against the Beni Temim who occupied the plateau towards the Persian Gulf.

Beni Temim.

This great tribe, partly Christian and partly heathen, had from time immemorial spread its innumerable branches over the pasture-lands between Yemama and the mouth of the Euphrates. With the rest of Arabia, it acknowledged Mahomet and submitted to his claims. But the Prophet's death had produced amongst them the same apostasy as elsewhere. After Abu Bekr's first success some of the chiefs, as we have seen, came to Medina with the tithes. Meanwhile a strange complication had arisen which embroiled the Beni Yerboa (one of their clans, commanded by the famous Malik ibn Noweira) in hostilities with the rest of the tribe, and eventually brought Khalid on the scene.

Sajah, the prophetess, invades Central Arabia.

It was no less than the advent of the prophetess Sajah, at the head of a great host from Mesopotamia. Descended from the Yerboa, her family had migrated north, and joined the Taghlib, among whom in Mesopotamia she had been brought up as a Christian. How long she had assumed the prophetic office, and what were her peculiar tenets, we do not know. At the head of the Taghlib and other Christian tribes she now crossed into Arabia, hoping to profit by the present confusion, and was on her way to attack Medina. Reaching the seats of the Temim, she summoned to her presence the Yerboa, her own clan, and promised them the kingdom, should victory crown her arms. They joined her standard, with Malik ibn Noweira at their head. The other clans of the Temim refused to acknowledge the prophetess; and so, diverted from her design upon Medina, she turned her arms against them. In a series of combats, though supported by Malik, she was worsted. Then, having made terms and exchanged

prisoners, she bethought her of attacking the rival prophet,
Moseilama, and so passed onwards to Yemama.

As Khalid, flushed with victory, now approached, most Mâlik ibn
of the branches of the Temim hastened to tender their Noweira;
submission. At this critical juncture, the withdrawal of
Sajah left Malik ibn Noweira with the Yerboa tribe in
a position of some perplexity, and he was undecided how
to act. Conflicting views respecting Malik's loyalty divided
the Moslem camp. For some reason Khalid was bent on
attacking the Yerboa. The men of Medina were equally
opposed to the design, for which they alleged there was no
authority. It had been better for Khalid to have listened.
But he replied haughtily, 'I am commander, and it is for
me to decide. I will march against Malik with such as
choose to follow me. I compel no man.' So he went
forward and left the malcontents behind. These, however,
thought better of it, and rejoined the army. Khalid
marched straight upon the headquarters of Malik, but
found not a soul upon the spot. It was utterly deserted.

In fact, Malik had resolved on submission, though his Brought a
proud spirit rebelled against presenting himself before prisoner to
Khalid. He knew the ordinance of Abu Bekr, that none Khalid.
but they who resisted, and who refused the call to prayer,
should be molested. So he told his people that there was
no longer use in opposing this new way, but that, bowing
down, they should suffer the wave to pass over them.
'Break up your camp,' he said, 'and depart every man to
his house.' Khalid, still bent on treating the neighbourhood as enemy's land, sent forth bands everywhere to slay
and plunder, and take captive all who failed to respond to
the call for prayer. Amongst others, Malik was seized
with his wife and a party of his people. When challenged,
they had replied that they were Moslems. 'Why, then,
these weapons?' it was asked. So they laid aside their
arms and were led as captives to the camp. As they
passed by Khalid, Malik cried aloud to him, 'Thy master
never gave command for this.' '*Thy* master,' rejoined
Khalid, 'didst thou say? Then, rebel, by thine own
admission, he is not thine!'

The captors differed in their evidence. Some averred that the prisoners had offered resistance. Others, with Abu Catada, a citizen of Medina, at their head, deposed that they had declared themselves Moslems, and at once complied with the call to prayer. So the party was remanded till morning under an armed guard. The night set in cold and stormy, and Khalid, with the view (so he averred) of protecting them from its inclemency, gave command 'to *wrap* the prisoners.' The word was ambiguous, signifying in another dialect not 'to wrap,' but 'to *slay*;' and Dhirar, commandant of the guard, taking it in that sense, put the prisoners, and with them Malik, forthwith to the sword. Khalid, hearing the uproar, hurried forth; but all was over, and he retired, exclaiming, 'When the Lord hath determined a thing, the same cometh verily to pass.' But the fate of Malik was not thus easily to be set at rest. The men of Medina who had opposed the advance were shocked at his cruel fate. Abu Catada roundly asserted the responsibility of Khalid. 'This is thy work!' he said; and, though chided for it, he persisted in the charge. He declared that never again would he serve under Khalid's banner. In company with Motammim, Malik's brother, he set out at once for Medina, and there laid formal complaint before the Caliph. Omar, with his native impetuosity,

took up the cause of the Yerboa chief. Khalid had given point to the allegations of his enemies by wedding Leila, the beautiful widow of his victim, on the spot. From this scandalous act, Omar drew the worst conclusion. 'He hath conspired to slay a believer,' he said, 'and hath gone in unto his wife.' He was instant with Abu Bekr that the offender should be degraded and put in bonds, saying, 'The sword of Khalid, dipped in violence and outrage, must be sheathed.' 'Nay!' replied the Caliph (of whom it is said that he never degraded any one of his commanders); 'the Sword which the Lord hath made bare against the heathen, shall I sheathe the same? That be far from me.' Never-

theless, he summoned Khalid to answer the charge.

Khalid obeyed the call. On reaching Medina, he went straightway to the great mosque, and entered it in his rough costume, clothes rusty with his girded armour, and turban coiled rudely about the head with arrows stuck in it. As he passed along the courtyard towards the Caliph's chamber, Omar could not restrain himself, but seizing the arrows from his turban, broke them over his shoulders, and abused him as hypocrite, murderer, and adulterer. Khalid, not knowing but that Abu Bekr might be of the same mind, answered not a word, but passed into the Caliph's presence. There he told his story, and the explanation was accepted by Abu Bekr; but he chided him roughly for having taken his victim's widow, and run counter to Arab sentiment in incontinently celebrating his nuptials on the very field of battle. As Khalid thus relieved again passed by, he lightly rallied Omar in words which showed that he had been exonerated. Motammim then pressed his claim of blood-money for his brother's life, and release of the prisoners that remained. For the release Abu Bekr gave command, but payment he declined.

Omar, still unconvinced of Khalid's innocence, was of opinion that he should be withdrawn from his command. He persevered in pressing this view upon Abu Bekr, who would reply, 'Omar, hold thy peace! Refrain thy tongue from Khalid. He gave an order, and the order was misunderstood.' But Omar heeded not. He neither forgave nor forgot, as in the sequel we shall see.

But held guilty by Omar.

The scandal was the greater, because Malik was a chief renowned for generosity and princely virtues, as well as for poetic talent. His brother, Motammim, a poet also of no mean fame, commemorated his tragic end in many touching verses, which Omar loved to listen to, and used to say that, 'had he been himself a poet, he would have had no higher ambition than to mourn in such verse the fate of his own brother Zeid,' who shortly after fell at Yemama.

Scandal of the case.

The materials are too meagre for a conclusive judgment on the guilt or innocence of Khalid. But the scandalous marriage with the widow of Ibn Noweira whose blood was yet fresh upon the spot, if it gave no colour to darker suspicion, justified at any rate the indictment of shameless indulgence and reckless disregard of the proprieties of life.

III. *Battle of Yemama.*

End of A.H. 11. Beginning of 633 A.D.

Khalid's campaign against Moseilama. End of 11 A.H. Beginning of 633 A.D. But sterner work was in reserve for Khalid. In the centre of Arabia, some marches east, lay Yemama. The Beni Hanifa, a powerful branch of the great Bekr tribe, resided there. Partly Christian and partly heathen, they had submitted to Mahomet, but now were in rebellion, 40,000 strong, around their prophet Moseilama. It was against these that Khalid next directed his steps.

Moseilama. The beginning of Moseilama's story belongs to the life of Mahomet[1]. Small in stature, and of mean countenance, he yet had qualities which fitted him for command. He visited Medina with a deputation from his people, and it was pretended that words had then fallen from Mahomet signifying that he was destined to share with him the prophetic office. Upon this Moseilama advanced the claim, and was accepted by his people as their prophet. Summoned from Medina to abandon these pretensions, he sent an insolent reply, claiming to divide the land. Mahomet in anger drove the ambassador from his presence, and thereafter sent Rajjal, a convert from the same tribe, to counteract the heresy and reclaim his brethren; but Rajjal, like the rest, was gained over by the pretender. Moseilama, we are told, deceived the people by pretended miracles, counterfeited the language of the Coran, and instituted prayers like those of Mahomet. In short, his religion was but a poor travesty of Islam. Though strongly supported by his people both as their prophet and their ruler, he now felt that the meshes of Abu Bekr began to close around him. The Caliph's generals were steadily reducing the rebels along the coast of the Persian Gulf, and Khalid, whom he dreaded most, was not far behind. At this juncture came tidings that the Prophetess Sajah, worsted as we have seen by the Beni Temim, was coming with troops against him. In his perplexity he sent her a friendly invitation. She came, and their sentiments were so much

His marriage with Sajah, the prophetess.

———
[1] See *Life of Mahomet,* p. 490.

at one that the Prophet of Yemama took the Prophetess of Mesopotamia to wife, and celebrated their nuptials on the spot,—the dower being one half the revenues of Yemama. After remaining thus a few days, Sajah departed for her home in the north, and, like a meteor, disappeared just as she had startled Arabia by her advent. Parties of Mesopotamian horse still ranged over the land collecting her dues, when Khalid's approach changed the scene; and Moseilama, marching out with a heavy force to meet him, pitched his camp at Acraba.

Ikrima and Shorahbil, the commanders originally despatched by Abu Bekr to quell the rising at Yemama, had both already suffered at the hands of Moseilama from a hasty and ill-advised advance. The reverse was so serious that Abu Bekr wrote angrily to Ikrima, 'I will not see thy face, nor shalt thou see mine, as now thou art. Thou shalt not return hither to dishearten the people. Depart unto the uttermost coasts, and there join the armies in the east and south.' So, skirting Yemama, he went forward to Oman, there to retrieve his tarnished reputation. Shorahbil, meanwhile, was directed to halt and await the approach of Khalid. *Ikrima and Shorahbil's reverse.*

It was after this reverse that Khalid, on being summoned to Medina about the affair of Malik, received his commission to attack Moseilama. In anticipation of severe fighting, the Caliph sent with him a fresh column of veterans from amongst the men of Mecca and Medina. Thus reinforced Khalid returned to his camp at Bitah, and advanced in strength to meet the enemy. *Khalid sets out for Yemama.*

While yet a march from Acraba, Khalid surprised a mounted body of the Beni Hanifa under command of their chief Mojaa. They were returning from a raid against a neighbouring tribe, unaware of his approach. But they belonged to the enemy, and as such were put to the sword, excepting Mojaa, whom Khalid spared, in hope of his being useful on the morrow, and kept chained in his tent under charge of Leila, his lately espoused wife. *Mojaa taken prisoner.*

Next day, the armies met upon the sandy plain of Acraba. The enemy rushed on with desperate bravery. *Battle of Yemama.*

' Fight for your loved ones ! ' they cried, ' it is the day of
jealousy and vengeance; if ye be worsted, your maidens will
be ravished and your wives dragged to their foul embrace ! '
So fierce was the shock that the Moslems were driven back
and their camp uncovered. The wild Bedouins entered the
tent of Khalid, and, but for the chivalry of her captive,
who conjured his countrymen to spare a lady of noble
birth, Leila would have perished by their swords. ' Go,
fight against men,' Mojaa cried, ' and leave this woman ; '
on which they cut the tent-ropes and departed. There
was danger for Islam at the moment. Defeat would have
been disastrous ; indeed, the Faith could hardly have
survived. But now the spirit of the Moslems was roused.
To stimulate rivalry between the Bedouins and city Arabs,
Khalid made them to fight apart. On this they rallied
one the other. ' Now,' cried the sons of the desert, ' we shall
see carnage wax hot amongst the raw levies of the town.
We shall teach them how to fight ! ' Prodigies of valour
were fought all round. Tradition dwells with enthusiasm
on the heroic words and deeds of the leaders, as one after
another they fell in the thick of battle. Zeid, brother of
Omar, who led the men of Mecca, singled out Rajjal, and,
reproaching his apostasy, despatched him forthwith. A
furious south wind, charged with desert sand, blinded
the Moslems and caused a momentary check. Upbraiding
them for their slackness, Zeid cried out : ' Onward to those
that have gone before ! Not a word will I speak till we
drive these apostates back, or I appear to clear me before
my Lord. Close your eyes and clench your teeth. Forward
like men ! ' So saying, he led the charge and fell. Abu
Hodzeifa, with leaves of the Scripture stuck on the flag-
staff which he bore, and calling out ' Fight for the Coran,
ye Moslems, and adorn it by your deeds ! ' followed his
example and shared the common fate. His freedman
seized the banner as it fell, and exclaiming, ' I were a
craven bearer of the Sacred text if I feared death,' plunged
with it into the battle and was slain. Nor were the
Citizens of Medina behind. Their commander, when they
gave way, reproached them thus : ' Woe be to you

because of this backsliding. Verily, I am clear of ye, A.H. 11.
even as I am clear of these,' pointing to the apostate enemy,
amongst whom he flung himself and perished in their midst.
Animated thus, the rank and file charged furiously. Backwards and forwards swayed the line, and heavy was the
carnage. But urged by Khalid's valiant arm, and raising Enemy dis-
the battle-cry '*Ya Mohammedâ!*' the Moslem arms at comfited.
length prevailed. The enemy broke and fled. 'To the
garden!' cried Mohakkem, a brave leader of the Beni
Hanifa; 'to the garden, and close the gate!' Taking
his stand, he guarded their retreat as they rushed into
an orchard surrounded by a strong wall, and Moseilama
with them. The Moslem troops, following close, swarmed
round the wall, but found the entrance barred. At last The
one cried, 'Lift me aloft upon the wall.' So they lifted Garden
him up. For a moment, as he looked on the surging of Death.
mass below, the hero hesitated; then, boldly leaping down,
he beat right and left, until he reached the gate, and threw
it open. Like waters pent up, his comrades rushed in;
and, as beasts of the forest snared in a trap, so wildly
struggled the brave Beni Hanifa in the *Garden of Death.*
Hemmed in the narrow space, hampered by the trees,
arms useless from their very numbers, they were hewn
down, and perished to a man. The carnage was fearful,
for besides the 'thousands' (as tradition puts it) slain
within the walls, an equal number were killed on the
field, and again an equal number in the flight. The Moslems Terrible
too, despite their splendid victory, had cause to remember slaughter
on both
the 'Garden of Death,' for their loss was beyond all sides.
previous experience. Besides those killed hand to hand
in the garden, great numbers fell in the battle. The
Refugees lost 360 men, and the Citizens of Medina 300,
nearly 700 in all; while the slaughter amongst the Bedouins, though somewhat less, raised the gross number
over 1,200, besides the wounded. Amongst the dead
were nine and thirty chief Companions of the Prophet.
At Medina there was hardly a house, whether of Refugees or Citizens, in which the voice of wailing was not
heard.

A. H. 11.

Moseilama was slain by Wahshi, the negro warrior who,
swinging round his head a javelin, after the savage Ethiopian
style, had on the field of Ohod brought Hamza to the
ground. After the battle, Khalid carried the chief Mojaa,
still in chains, over the field to identify the dead. Turning
the bodies over, they came upon a stalwart figure. 'Look,
was this your master?' said Khalid. 'Nay,' replied Mojaa,
'this was a nobler and a better man.' It was the brave
Mohakkem, who fell covering the retreat, slain by the hand
of the Caliph's son. Entering the 'Garden of Death,'
among the heaps of mangled dead they stumbled on a
body of insignificant mien. 'This is your man,' Mojaa
said, as he turned it on its side; 'truly ye have done for
him!' 'Yea,' replied Khalid, 'or rather it is he which
hath done for you, that which he hath done.'

Moseilama among the slain.

The Mussulman horse now scoured the country, and
every day brought in bands of prisoners. Aware that
after their crushing defeat the Beni Hanifa were incapable
of resistance, Mojaa bethought him of a stratagem. He
represented the forts and fastnesses as held in force throughout the country, in proof of which he had their battlements
lined with the aged, the women, and even the children,
in disguise. Persuaded thus that the inhabitants would
fight to the last, and seeing his army wearied and anxious
to visit their homes, Khalid concluded a truce, more
favourable than he would but for Mojaa's artifice have
given. When it came to light, Khalid was angry; but in
the end excused him on the ground of patriotism, and
stood by the treaty. No sooner was it concluded, than
he received a despatch of unwonted severity from Abu
Bekr, who, to strike terror into other apostate tribes,
commanded that not a single fighting man of the rebel and
ungodly race be spared. Fortunately this the truce forbade;
the Beni Hanifa were received back into Islam, and a
portion only of the multitude were retained as prisoners.

Truce with the Beni Hanifa.

The campaign ended, Khalid sent a deputation of the
tribe to Abu Bekr, who received them courteously. 'Out
upon you!' said he; 'how is it that this impostor led you
all astray?' 'Oh Caliph!' they answered, 'thou hast heard

it all; he was one whom the Lord blessed not, nor yet his
people;' and they repeated to him some of the things he
used to say. 'Good heavens!' exclaimed Abu Bekr;
'what kind of words are these? There is neither sense in
them for good nor yet for evil, but a strange fatuity, to
have beguiled you thus.' So he dismissed them to their
homes.

Among the slain are not a few names familiar to the Many Com-
student of the Prophet's life. The carnage amongst the panions
'*Readers*'—those who had the Coran by heart—was so slain.
great, as to give Omar the first idea of collecting the Sacred
text, 'lest any part should be lost therefrom.' At the death
of his brother Zeid, who had shared with him the dangers
of the early battles of Islam, Omar was inconsolable.
'Thou art returned home,' he said to his son Abdallah,
'safe and sound; and Zeid is dead. Wherefore wast not
thou slain before him? I wish not to see thy face.' 'Father!'
was the reply, 'he asked for martyrdom, and the Lord
granted it. I strove after the same, but it was not given
unto me.' Such was the spirit of these Moslem warriors.

Khalid again signalised his victory by wedding a captive Khalid
maid upon the field. 'Give me thy daughter to wife,' takes Mojaa's
he said to Mojaa, the prisoner who had so faithfully daughter
defended his bride in the hour of peril. 'Wait,' replied to wife.
Mojaa; 'be not so hasty. Thou wilt harm thyself in
the Caliph's eyes, and me likewise.' 'Man, give me thy
daughter!' he repeated imperiously; so Mojaa gave her to
him. When Abu Bekr heard of it, he wrote him a letter
sprinkled with blood. 'By my life! thou son of Khalid's
father, thou art a pretty fellow, living thus at thine
ease. Thou weddest a damsel, whilst the ground beneath
the nuptial couch is yet moistened with the blood of twelve
hundred!' The reproof fell lightly upon Khalid. 'This
is the work,' he said, as he read the epistle, 'of that left-
handed fellow,' meaning Omar. The sentiment was Abu
Bekr's own; but the 'Sword of the Lord' could not be
spared.

We shall meet Khalid next in Chaldæa, by the banks
of the Euphrates.

CHAPTER VI.

APOSTASY AND REBELLION CRUSHED IN OTHER PARTS OF THE PENINSULA.

11 A.H. 632–3 A.D.

WHILE Khalid thus pursued his victorious career from the north to the centre of Arabia, the various columns despatched by Abu Bekr were engaged with the apostate and rebellious tribes in other parts of the Peninsula. The opposition was not less stubborn; and the success, though in many quarters slow and at times even doubtful, was in the end complete.

Beyond Yemama, and skirting the Persian Gulf between Catif and Oman, lie the two desert provinces of Hejer and Bahrein. Mondzir, their Christian chief, had adopted Islam, and recognizing the suzerainty of the Prophet, received Ala as Resident at his Court. Mondzir died shortly after Mahomet, and the province went into rebellion. Ala fled, but was sent back with a strong force to reclaim the apostate people. The brilliant campaign of Khalid had just then struck terror into the neighbouring country; and so, as he passed near the borders of Yemama, Ala was joined by contingents from many chiefs anxious thus to prove their loyalty. A scion of the Hira dynasty, hostile to Islam, had succeeded Mondzir, and Ala found him so well supported, that even thus strengthened he had to entrench his army, and content himself with single combats and indecisive skirmishes. At last, finding through his spies that the enemy were in a festive and drunken state, he overwhelmed them unexpectedly and took their prince a prisoner. The discomfited host fled by ship to Darin, an island near the coast, whither they were again pursued and put utterly to the sword. The spoil was prodigious, and so was the multitude of women and children taken captive.

After the Prophet's death tradition ceases to indulge in the miraculous. This expedition forms a singular exception. As the column marching from Medina reached the water-less zone of Dahna, it had nearly perished by long-protracted thirst; when in the last extremity, water suddenly shining in the horizon, man and beast hurried joyfully on to slake their thirst at an extensive lake. No spring had ever been seen in that wilderness before; nor was the miraculous lake ever found again. Shortly after, while pursuing the apostate host to the isle of Darin, a second miracle parted the waves, and the Moslems, after a wild invocation of the Deity, rushed on and crossed the strait as it had been a shallow beach. A pious bard has likened the passage to that of the Israelites through the Red sea, and a monk is said to have been converted by the double miracle of waters breaking out in the wilderness and waters drying up in the channel of the great deep. *Miraculous lake; and drying up of the sea.*

While thus engaged, Ala received material help from loyal followers along the coast. Amongst those who aided in this work was Mothanna, a chief of great influence amongst the Bekr clans. Following up the victory of Ala along the Persian Gulf, this warrior in his progress from Hejer upwards, reached at last the delta of the Euphrates, where he inaugurated a fresh movement that will shortly engage attention. *Mothanna.*

The reduction of the important province of Oman followed close on that of Bahrein. Its Prince had recently tendered allegiance to Mahomet. Amru was thereupon deputed as Resident, and the tithes were, by reason of the distance, given up to the local poor. Notwithstanding this concession, Mahomet was no sooner dead than the people, led by a rebel, who claimed to be a prophet, rebelled. The Prince fled to the mountains, and Amru to Medina. The task of reclaiming Oman and the adjoining province of Mahra was committed by Abu Bekr to Hodzeifa, a convert *Oman.*

A. H. 11. of influence in those parts. He was assisted by Ikrima, sent, as we have seen, by Abu Bekr to retrieve his reputation in this distant quarter. Arrived in Oman, they effected a junction with the loyal Prince. An engagement followed, in which the Moslems, hard pressed, were near to suffering defeat, when a strong column from the tribes recently reclaimed in Bahrein appeared on the field and turned the battle in their favour. The slaughter amongst the enemy was great, and the women, placed in the rear to nerve their courage, fell a welcome prize into the believers' hands. The mart of Daba, enriched by Indian merchandise, yielded a magnificent booty, and there was at once despatched to Medina the royal Fifth of slaves and plunder.

Battle of Daba.

Mahra.

Hodzeifa was left behind as governor of Oman. Ikrima, having thus reached the easternmost point of Arabia, turned to the south-west; and with an army daily swelled by levies from repentant tribes, pursued his victorious course to Mahra. This province was at the moment distracted by a breach between two rival chiefs. Espousing the cause of the weaker, who at once avowed the faith, Ikrima attacked the other and achieved a great victory. Among the spoil were 2,000 Bactrian camels and a vast supply of arms and beasts of burden. This quarter of the peninsula quickly subdued and restored to order, Ikrima now in great strength advanced, as he had been instructed, to join Mohajir in the campaign against Hadhramaut and Yemen. But we must first take note of how things stood after the death of Mahomet nearer home in the west and south of the peninsula.

The Hejaz and Tihama.

While the towns of Mecca and Tayif remained tolerably secure, the country round about was rife with violence and misrule. Hordes from the lawless tribes, ready as ever for plunder and rapine, hovered close even to the Holy City. They were attacked by the governor, and dispersed with slaughter. Order was restored by a body of 500 men quartered within the sacred limits, and by pickets throughout the neighbourhood. But from thence, all the way to Yemen, nothing was seen save turmoil and alarm. Troops of bandits, remnants of the false prophet's

army, ravaged Najran, and the loyal adherents of Islam A. H. 11.
were fain to fly to mountain fastnesses. The Tihama, or
long strip of land skirting the shore of the Red sea, was
overrun by bands of Bedouin robbers, stopping all communication between the north and south. An army at
length cleared the country of these robbers so effectually
that the roads became again for a time unpassable, but now
only from the offensive mass of carcases strewn upon them.

Peace in Yemen was not so easily restored. The Yemen
'Veiled Prophet,' Aswad, had been recently assassinated after Aswad's
by conspirators in the interest of Mahomet[1]. These were death.
Cays, an Arab chief, and two others of Persian descent,
Feroze and Dadweih, into whose hands the government
of Sanaa fell. The tidings reaching Medina just after
Mahomet's death, Abu Bekr appointed Feroze his lieutenant. The Arab blood of Cays rebelled against serving
under a foreigner, and he plotted to expel the whole
body of Persian immigrants. To effect this, he called in the
aid of Amr ibn Madekerib, a famous poet and influential
chief, who having like others cast off the faith, ravaged the
country with remnants of the false prophet's army. Dadweih was treacherously slain by Amr at a feast, but Feroze
escaped, and after much hardship secured his retreat with
a friendly tribe. For a time Cays carried all before him.
The family of Feroze was taken captive, and the Persian
settlers, pursued in every direction, fled to the mountains,
or took ship from Aden. Feroze appealed to Medina;
but it was long before the Caliph had any men to send. So
Feroze cast about for himself, and at length, by the aid of
loyal tribes, put the troops of Cays to flight, regained
possession of his family, and reoccupied Sanaa.

But more effectual help was now approaching. On one side Cays and
was Mohajir. Appointed by the Prophet his lieutenant in Amr defeated.
Hadhramaut, he had been detained sick at Medina, perhaps Yemen
also by inability earlier to obtain a following. Last of the restored. End of
commanders to take the field, it was probably ten or twelve 11 A. H.
months after the Prophet's death that he marched south, Spring, 633 A. D.
and joined on the way by loyal tribes neared the disturbed

[1] See *Life of Mahomet*, p. 492.

A.H. 11. country at the head of a substantial force. On the other
hand, Ikrima, with an ever-growing army, advanced from
the east. Hastening to meet Mohajir, he, for the present,
left Hadhramaut aside, and passed rapidly on towards Aden.
Alarmed at the gathering storm, Cays and Amr ibn Madekerib joined their forces to oppose Mohajir. But soon quarrelling, they parted, sending each other, after Arab wont,
lampoons in bitter verse. Opposition being now vain, Amr
sought by an unworthy stratagem to gain his safety. Making
a night attack on Cays, he carried him prisoner to Mohajir;
but he had forgotten a safe-conduct for himself. Mohajir,
therefore, seized both, and sent them in chains to Medina.
The Caliph was at first minded to put Amr to death
because of the murder of Dadweih; but he denied the
crime, and there was no evidence to prove it. 'Art thou
not ashamed,' said Abu Bekr to him, 'that following the
rebel cause, thou art ever either a fugitive or in bonds?
Hadst thou been a defender of the Faith instead, then had
the Lord raised thee above thy fellows.' 'So assuredly it
is,' replied the humbled chief; 'I will embrace the faith,
and never again desert it.' The Caliph forgave them both;
and his clemency was not abused, for we find the two
gallant but unscrupulous chiefs soon after fighting loyally in
the Persian war. After this, Yemen was speedily reduced
to order. And Mohajir was at liberty to pursue his march
to Hadharmaut.

Hadhra-
maut.
Ashath ibn
Cays

The government of the great southern province of Hadhramaut was held with difficulty, during the protracted
absence of Mohajir, by Ziad, who aroused the hatred of
its occupants, the Beni Kinda, by exacting from them the
tithe; but with the support of some still loyal clans was
able to hold his place. In one of his raids, Ziad having
carried off the families of a vanquished tribe, Ashath ibn
Cays, chief of the Beni Kinda, was moved by their cries; and,
having gathered a strong force, fell upon Ziad, and rescued
the captives. It is the same Ashath who, when he tendered
homage to Mahomet, betrothed to himself the sister of
Abu Bekr[1]. Now compromised, he went into active re-

[1] *Life of Mahomet*, p. 476.

bellion, and roused the whole country against Ziad, who,
surrounded by the enemy, despatched an urgent summons
for Mohajir to hasten to his deliverance.

By this time Mohajir and Ikrima, marching respectively
from Sanaa and Aden, had effected a junction at Mareb,
and were crossing the sandy desert which lay between
them and Hadhramaut. Receiving the message, Mohajir
set off in haste with a flying squadron, and, joined by Ziad,
fell upon Ashath, and discomfited him with great slaughter.
The routed enemy fled for refuge to a stronghold, which
Mohajir immediately invested. Ikrima soon came up with
the main body, and there were now troops enough both
to besiege the city and ravage the country around. Stung
at witnessing the ruin of their kindred, and preferring
death to dishonour, the garrison sallied forth, and fought
the Moslems in the plain. After a desperate struggle,
in which the approaches were filled with bodies of the
dead, they were driven back. Meanwhile, Abu Bekr,
apprised of their obstinate resistance, sent orders to make
an example of the rebels, and give no quarter. The
wretched garrison, with the enemy daily increasing, and no
prospect of relief, were now bereft of hope. Seeing the
position desperate, the wily Ashath made his way to
Ikrima and treacherously agreed to deliver up the fortress
if nine lives were guaranteed. The Moslems entered, slew
the fighting men, and took the women captive. When
Ashath presented the list of nine to be spared,—'Thy name
is not here!' cried Mohajir, exultingly; for the craven
traitor had forgotten, in the excitement of the moment, to
enter his own name;—'The Lord be praised, who hath
condemned thee out of thine own mouth.' So, having cast
him into chains, he was about to order his execution, when
Ikrima interposed and induced him, much against his will,
to refer the cause to Abu Bekr. The crowd of captive
women, mourning the massacre of their sons and husbands,
loaded the recreant as he passed by with bitter imprecation. Arrived at Medina, the Caliph abused him as a
pusillanimous wretch who had neither the power to lead,
nor yet the courage to defend, his people; and threatened

him with death. But at last, moved by his appeal to the terms agreed upon by Ikrima, and by protestation that he would thenceforth fight bravely for the faith, Abu Bekr not only forgave him, but allowed him to fulfil the marriage with his sister. Ashath remained for a while in idleness at Medina, and the Caliph would say that one of the three things he repented of, was having weakly spared the rebel's life. But afterwards Ashath went forth to the wars, and, as we shall see, effectually redeemed his name.

Peace universally restored.

Thus, in this, the last province of the peninsula, rebellion was finally crushed, and the reign of Islam completely re-established. Mohajir elected to remain in Yemen, where he shared the government with Feroze. Ziad continued to administer Hadhramaut.

Lady who had been betrothed to Mahomet.

A curious story is told of a lady whom Ikrima married at Aden, and carried with him in his camp. She had been betrothed to Mahomet, but the marriage had not been completed. The soldiers murmured, and questioned the propriety of Ikrima's marriage. Mohajir referred the matter to Abu Bekr, who decided that there was nothing wrong in the proceeding, as Mahomet had never fulfilled his contract with the damsel [1].

Two song-stresses mutilated.

I should not here omit to mention the fate of two song-stresses in Yemen, who were accused, one of satirising the Prophet, the other of ridiculing the Moslems, in their songs. Mohajir had the hands of both cut off, and also (to stay their singing for the future) their front teeth pulled out. The Caliph, on hearing of it, approved the punishment of the first; for, said he: 'Crime against the Prophet is not as crime against a common man; and, indeed, had the case been first referred to me, I should, as a warning to others, have directed her execution.' But he disapproved the mutilation of the other.

A free-booter burned to death.

As a rule Abu Bekr was mild in his judgments, and even generous to a fallen and submissive foe. But there were, as we have seen, exceptions. On one occasion the treachery of a rebel chief irritated him to an act of barbarous cruelty.

---

[1] *Life of Mahomet*, p. 404. She was brought to the Prophet for her beauty, who, finding some defect, sent her home.

Fujaa, a leader of some note, under pretence of fighting against the insurgents in his neighbourhood, obtained from the Caliph arms and accoutrements for his band. Thus equipped, he abused the trust, and, becoming a freebooter, attacked and plundered alike Moslem and apostate. Abu Bekr thereupon wrote letters to a loyal chief in that quarter to go against the brigand. Hard pressed, Fujaa challenged his adversary to a parley, and asserted that he held a commission as good as his. 'If thou speakest true,' answered the other, ' lay aside thy weapons and accompany me to Abu Bekr.' He did so, but no sooner did he appear at Medina, than the Caliph, enraged at his treachery, cried aloud : ' Go forth with this traitor to the burial-ground, and there burn him with fire.' So, hard by the graveyard of the city, they gathered wood, and heaping it together at the place of prayer, kindled the pile, and cast Fujaa on it. If the charges were well founded, which we have no ground for doubting, Fujaa deserved the fate of a bandit ; but to cast him alive into the flames was a savage act, for which Abu Bekr was sorry afterwards, and used to say,—' It is one of the three things which I would I had not done.'

CHAPTER VII.

REVIEW. SULLENNESS OF RECLAIMED TRIBES. CAM-
PAIGNS IN SYRIA AND CHALDÆA. DESPATCH
OF TROOPS REKINDLES ENTHUSIASM. DOMESTIC
EVENTS.

11 A.H. 632 A.D.

Review.
Reign of
Islam re-
established
in Arabia.
THUS, within a year of the death of the Prophet, the sway
of Islam, which for a time had clean gone, was re-established
throughout the peninsula. The circle of victory was now
complete. Begun, with the avenging expedition of Osama
in the north, it was followed up by Khalid's brilliant
achievements in the east and centre of Arabia. While
in the 'Garden of Death' the flower of the faithful
were deciding the fate of Islam, then trembling in the
balance, operations, as we have seen, languished elsewhere.
Eventually, the campaign was carried vigorously over the
other provinces, though in some quarters with limited
resource and varying fortune; till, in the end, Ikrima,
sweeping down the eastern coast, and joined by Mohajir
in the south, stamped out the last embers of apostasy.

The Arabs
sullen, till
roused by
war-cry
from with-
out.
The rebellion was suppressed, but the Arab tribes
remained sullen and averse. The Bedouin, wont to wander
wild and free over his pathless deserts, chafed at the demand
of tithe, and spurned obedience to Medina. Simply force
and fear as yet attached him to the Caliph. The question
occurs, what would have been the fortune of Islam had
no great impulse arisen from without? The prospect was
not encouraging. Convictions so shallow, and aspirations

so low, as those of the Bedouin would soon have disappeared; A. H. 11.
force and fear would not long have availed to hold together
such disintegrated materials as go to form the Arab
nation. The South was jealous of the North; Bedouins
of the desert scorned the settled population; each tribe
had cause of rivalry with its neighbour, and feuds were
ever arising out of the law of blood. Even in Medina,
cradle of the faith, the Aus were impatient of the Khazraj,
and both were jealous of the Refugees. The only authority
recognised by a Bedouin is that of his tribal chief, and even
that sits lightly. To him freedom is life; and dependence
on a central power most hateful. Had nothing external
supervened, he had soon shaken off the yoke of Islam, and
Arabia would have returned again to its primeval state.
But, fortunately for Islam, a new idea electrified the nation.
No sooner was apostasy put down than, first in Chaldæa
and then in Syria, collision with border tribes kindled
the fire of foreign war; and forthwith the whole Arabian
people, both town and Bedouin, were riveted to Islam by a
common bond—the love of rapine and the lust of spoil.

That the heritage of Islam is the world, was an after- Islam in-
tended for
thought. The idea, spite of much proleptic tradition, had Arabia;
been conceived but dimly, if at all, by Mahomet himself.
His world was Arabia, and for it the new dispensation was
ordained. The Revelation ran in 'simple Arabic' for the
teaching of its people[1]. From first to last the summons
was to Arabs and to none other. It is true that, some
years before his death, Mahomet called on certain kings
and princes to confess the catholic faith of Abraham; but
the step was not in any way followed up. Nor was it
otherwise with the command to fight against Jews, Christians, and Idolaters; that command announced to the Arab
tribes assembled at the Farewell pilgrimage, had reference
to Arabia alone, and had no immediate bearing on warfare
beyond its bounds. The Prophet's dying legacy was to
the same effect:—'See,' said he, 'that there be but the
one Faith throughout Arabia.' The seed of a universal
creed had indeed been sown; but that it ever germinated

---

[1] Coran xlii. v. 6; et passim.

A. H. 11. was due to circumstance rather than design. Even Omar, after his splendid conquests, continually dreaded lest his armies should proceed too far, and be cut off from succour. Therefore he set barriers (as we shall see) to the ambition of his people, beyond which they should not pass.

but spread at the call to conquer. Nevertheless, universal empire was altogether in accord with the spirit of the Faith. 'When a people leaveth off to fight in the ways of the Lord,' said Abu Bekr, in his inaugural address (and, so saying, struck the key-note of militant Islam), ' the Lord casteth off that people.' Thus, when the Rubicon once was crossed, the horizon enlarged in ever-widening circles, till it embraced the world. It was this that now turned the sullen temper of the Arab tribes into eager loyalty : for the brigand spirit of the Bedouin was brought thus into unison with the new-born spirit of Islam. The call to battle reverberated through the land, and was answered eagerly. The response began with the tribes in the north, the first reclaimed from apostasy. Later, in the second year of the Caliphate, the exodus spread to the south, and grew in magnitude year by year. At first the Caliph forbade that help should be taken from any that had backslidden. The privilege was reserved for such only as had remained steadfast in the faith. But, step by step, as new spheres opened out, and the cry ran from shore to shore for fresh levies to fill the ' Martyr ' gaps, the ban was put aside, and all were bidden. Warrior after

Teeming hosts go forth. warrior, column after column, whole tribes in endless succession, with their women and children, issued forth to fight. And ever, at the marvellous tale of cities conquered ; of rapine rich beyond compute ; of maidens on the very field, ' to every man a damsel or two ;' and at the sight of the royal Fifth set forth in order as it reached Medina,—fresh tribes arose and went. Onward and still onward, like swarms from the hive, or flights of locusts darkening the land, tribe after tribe issued forth, and hasting northward, spread in great masses to the east and to the west.

Discredit still attaching to apostasy. It must not, however, be overlooked that though apostasy was thus condoned, and in the blaze of victory almost lost sight of, a certain discredit still clung to the backslider.

His guilt was not like that of other men who had sinned
before conversion. The apostate, once enlightened, had
cast by his fall a deliberate slur upon Islam. Therefore
no leader who had joined the great apostasy was ever
promoted to a chief command. He might fight, and was
welcome, in the ranks,—allowed even to head small parties
of fifty or a hundred,—but to the last the post of honour
was denied.

The Arabs, thus emerging from their desert-home, Arabs the
became the aristocracy of Islam. Conquered nations, even nobility of
the Moslem
of higher civilisation, if they embraced the faith, fell into a world.
lower caste. Arabians were the dominant class, and they
alone, wheresoever they might go. It was only as 'clients,'
or dependants, that people of other lands might share their
privileges—crumbs, as it were, from off the master's table.
Yet great numbers of the Arabs themselves were at this
early period slaves, captured during the apostasy or in
previous intertribal war, and held in bondage by their
fellow-countrymen. Omar saw the inconsistency. It was
not fit that any of the noble race should remain in slavery.
When, therefore, he succeeded to the Caliphate, he decreed
their freedom. 'The Lord,' he said, 'hath given to us of
Arab blood the victory, and great conquests without. It is
not meet that any one of us, taken captive in the days of
ignorance, or in the recent wars, should be holden in cap- Slaves of
tivity.' Slaves of Arab descent were therefore all allowed Arab blood
set free.
their liberty on payment of a slender ransom, excepting
only bondmaids, who having borne children to their
owners, already held, as such, a place of privilege. Men
that had lost wives or children now set out in search, if
haply they might find and claim them. Strange tales are
told of these disconsolate journeys. But some of the women
captive at Medina preferred remaining with their masters.

This ascendency, social, military, and political, the Arab
nation maintained for upwards of two centuries. Then they
were gradually supplanted, as we shall see, throughout
the East, by Turks and Persians. Such as had settled
in the cities mingled with the people; the rest returned
to their desert wilds, and with them departed the glory of

A.H. 11. the Caliphate. This, however, was not the case in the
———   West; and so in Spain and Africa the prestige of Arab
        blood survived.

Medina.   The domestic history of Medina is at this early period
        barren of incident. As supreme judge in civil causes, the
        Caliph nominated Omar ; but warlike operations, first in
        the peninsula, and then opening out in foreign lands, so
        occupied men's minds, that for the time the office was a
        sinecure.

Pilgrim-   The presidency at the annual Pilgrimage is always
age.   carefully recorded by the annalists of Islam. The Caliph
        was too much engrossed with the commotion throughout
        Arabia to proceed himself to Mecca on this occasion,
        and the governor of the Holy City presided in his stead.

        So ended the first year of the Caliphate.

CHAPTER VIII.

CAMPAIGN IN CHALDÆA.

12 A. H. 633 A. D.

CHALDÆA and Southern Syria belong properly to Arabia. The tribes inhabiting this region, partly heathen, but chiefly in name at least Christian, formed an integral part of the Arab race, and as such fell within the immediate scope of the new dispensation. When these came into collision with the Moslem columns on the frontier, they were eventually supported by their respective sovereigns,— the western by the Kaiser, and the eastern by the Chosroes. Thus the struggle widened, and Islam was brought presently face to face in mortal conflict with the two great Powers of the East and of the West. _{Collision with border tribes led to conflict with Greek and Persian empires.}

It is important, especially in the early part of this history, to bear in mind that the only sources available to the student are Arabian. As for the West, Byzantine annals utterly disappear in the Saracenic cataclysm; and it is many long years before any help whatever is available from that quarter. On the other side, the Persian empire was swallowed up in the invasion of the Arabs, and consequently it is from the conquerors alone that we learn the events about to be told. Thus, both for East and West, we are entirely dependent on Arab tradition, and this, at the first, singularly brief and fragmentary; while the authorities being altogether one-sided, we are left, as best we can, to draw a narrative just and impartial to all concerned. _{History dependent on purely Arabian sources.}

A.H. 12.

Position of Greek and Persian empires.

In neither of the great Powers which Abu Bekr was about to try conclusions with, had the nerve and virtue of earlier days survived. Luxury, corruption, and oppression, religious strife and military disaster, had impaired their vigour and undermined their strength. Barbarous hordes, overrunning the Western empire, had wrested the farther provinces from Byzantine rule. Between the Kaiser and the Chosroes again, war had long prevailed. Syria and Mesopotamia,—scenes of the coming chapters,—being the prize, now of one, now of the other. By the last turn of fortune, Heraclius, marching from the Black sea, had routed the Persians on the field of Nineveh, and advanced triumphantly to the very gates of the enemy's capital.

6 A.H.
627 A.D.

Siroes, after putting to death his father and eighteen brothers, enjoyed but a few months the fruits of his parricidal crime ; and (as we are told by Gibbon) ' in the space of four years, the royal title was assumed by nine candidates, who disputed, with the sword or dagger, the fragments of an exhausted monarchy.' Such was the condition of Persia, its court imbecile and anarchy rampant, at the time when Abu Bekr was engaged in his struggle with the apostate tribes. Nevertheless, the Arabian armies met with a fiercer and more protracted opposition on the Persian than on the Syrian side. And the reason is that Islam aimed its blow at the very heart of Persia. Constantinople might remain, with Syria gone, ignobly safe. But if the Arabs gained Irac, Ctesiphon (Medain), close at hand, must fall, and Persia with it. To this quarter attention will be now directed.

Mothanna attacks Chaldæa.

Among the chiefs who helped to reclaim Bahrein, Mothanna has been named. Advancing along the Persian Gulf, he reduced Catif, and carried his victorious arms into the delta of the Euphrates. ' Who is this Mothanna ?' asked Abu Bekr, as tidings of success kept reaching Medina ; ' and to what clan doth he belong ? ' Learning that he was of the great Bekr tribe which peopled that vicinity, he commanded him to march forward, fighting in the ways of the Lord. The service was such as Bedouins love ; and his column was soon swelled to

8,000 men. But opposition gathered in front. The Chris- A. H. 12.
tian and heathen tribes were roused; and Abu Bekr,
anticipating the impending struggle, resolved that 'the
Sword of the Lord' should be again unsheathed, and so
Khalid was deputed to subdue Chaldæa.

By the beginning of the twelfth year of the Hegira, Troops
rebellion had been put down throughout Arabia, excepting to Irac.
the South, which was also in fair way of pacification. i. 12 A. H.
It was now Abu Bekr's policy to turn his restless Arab A. D.
columns to similar work elsewhere. He despatched two
armies to the north. One, under command of Khalid
joined by Mothanna, was to march on Obolla, an ancient
city near the mouth of the Euphrates, and thence, driving
the enemy up the western bank, to work its way towards
Hira, the capital of Chaldæa. Iyadh, at the head of the
other, was directed to Duma (midway between the heads
of the Red Sea and Persian Gulf), which had cast off its
allegiance; and thence to pass also on to Hira. Whichever first reached that city was to be in command of the
country [1].

Iyadh, hampered by the enemy, was long detained in Khalid
the neighbourhood of Duma. Khalid, meeting no such joins
Mothanna
obstacle, was joined on his march from Yemama to in Irac.
Irac by large bodies of Bedouins. These were of the
greater service, as his numbers had been thinned, not
only by the carnage at Yemama, but also by the free
permission given the army, after that arduous campaign,
of furlough to their homes. Nevertheless, the expedition
was so popular that when Khalid, after a flying visit to
the Caliph, rejoined his camp as it neared the Euphrates,
he found himself at the head of 10,000 men; and this
besides the 8,000 of Mothanna, who hastened loyally to
place himself under the great leader's command.

The country before them was, in some of its features, Mesopota-
familiar to the invading army, in others new and strange. mia and
the Syrian
desert.

---

[1] Tradition here probably anticipates the march of events. It is doubtful
whether the Caliph had the city of Hira yet in view; for the aims of Khalid
and his Master widened as victory led him onwards.

A. H. 12. From the head of the Persian Gulf across to the Dead Sea
stretches a stony desert, trackless and bereft of water. Advancing north, Nature relaxes; the plain, still wilderness,
is in season clothed with verdure, bright with flowers, in-
stinct with the song of birds and hum of winged life.
Such is the pasture-land for hundreds of miles between
Damascus and the Tigris. Still further north, the desert
gradually disappears, and, about the latitude of Mosul,
blends with the hills and vales of Asia Minor. Athwart
the plain, from Aleppo to Babylon, runs the Euphrates,
while the far east is bounded by the Tigris flowing under
the mountain range that separates Irac Araby[1] from Persia.
Between the two rivers lies Mesopotamia, full of patriarchal
memories. Over this great waste there roamed (as still
there roam) Bedouin tribes with flocks and herds. The
greater part had long professed the Christian religion.
Those on the Syrian side, as the Ghassan of Bostra,
owed allegiance to the Roman Empire; those on the
east were dependent upon Persia. But nomad life tends
to fickle loyalty and laxity of faith; and, not infrequently,
these northern Arabs were now led by affinity with their
brethren of the south, and by the lust of plunder, to desert
their ancient allies and ancestral faith, and cast in their lot
with the invading columns.

Chaldæa
and Delta
of the
Euphrates. The lower Euphrates—Irac Araby—is in striking contrast with the region just described. The two great rivers,
while yet far from the sea, approach each other; but,
instead of joining, still keep apart, and for some two hundred and fifty miles, running parallel, inclose the memorable
plain of Dura. The country is covered with long hillocks
and mounds marking the ancient channels of irrigation,
and strewed with fragments of brick and pottery, remnants of a dim antiquity. The face of the land was not
then, as now, a barren waste, but richly cultivated and
watered by canals. On the Tigris, a little below where
the two rivers approach, was Medain, 'the twin city' (so
called from Seleucia on the western bank and Ctesiphon

---

[1] Irac of the Arabs, as distinguished from *Irac Ajemy*, i.e. 'foreign' or
Persian Irac.

on the eastern), the capital of Persia. Fifty miles farther
south, a mass of shapeless mounds, looking down upon the
Euphrates from its eastern shore, mark the site of Babylon,
and from their summit may be descried the Birs Nimrud
(or 'Tower of Babel') rearing its weird head on the horizon
of the verdant plain. Thirty miles yet further south lay
Hira, capital of the surrounding Arab tribes. It stood
(like its successor Kufa) on a branch which issues from
the Euphrates by a channel in the live rock, cut by the
hand of man, but of unknown antiquity. Sweeping along
the west, the rival stream feeds many marshes, especially
the great lake called the 'Sea of Najaf;' and, after a wide
circuit, rejoins the Euphrates above its junction with the
Tigris. There was in olden times another branch called
the 'Trench of Sapor,' which, intended as a bar to Bedouin
incursions, and taking a yet wider range to the west,
returned into the parent river near Obolla. This is now
dry, but originally it carried a stream which, like the
other, helped materially to widen the green belt pressed
in upon by the farther desert. The lower delta again,
subject to tidal flow, alluvial, low, and watered with
ease, is covered with a sea of corn, and has been called
'the garden of the world.' Besides the familiar palm,
the country abounds with the fig, mulberry, and pomegranate. But the climate is close and oppressive; the
fens and marshes, always liable to inundation, were aggravated by the neglect of dams and sluices in those days
of anarchy; and the Arab, used to the sandy steppes
of the peninsula, gazed wonderingly at the luxuriant growth
of reeds and rushes, and at buffalos driven by the pest-
iferous insects to hide their unwieldy bodies beneath the
water, or splash lazily along the shallow waste of endless
lagoons. All Chaldæa, from the estuary upwards, was
cultivated, as now, by *Fellaheen*, or Arab peasantry, and
these were lorded over by *Dihcans*, or district officers of
the Persian Court.

Such then was the magnificent province lying between Khalid
the desert and the mountain range of Persia, the cradle summons
of civilisation and the arts, which now attracted the Moslem Hormuz.

A.H. 12. arms. The first to oppose them was Hormuz, Satrap of
the Delta, a tyrant, hated by his Arab subjects. To him,
as master of the tribes gathering in front, Khalid addressed
a letter in the haughty type of Moslem summons : '*Accept
the Faith and thou art safe; else pay tribute, thou and thy
people; which if thou refusest, thou shalt have thyself to
blame. A people is already on thee, loving death, even as
thou lovest life.*' Then placing Mothanna in command of
the advanced column, Adi, son of Hatim (the famous
chieftain of the Beni Tay), over the second, and himself
bringing up the rear, Khalid advanced on Hafir, the
frontier station of the Persian empire.

Battle of   Startled by the strange summons, Hormuz sent word
Chains.   to the Chosroes, and himself set out to meet the invader
Hormuz
slain.   with an army whose wings were commanded by princes
of the royal blood. He marched in haste, thinking to
have an easy victory over untrained desert tribes ; and
reaching Hafir first, took possession of the springs. Khalid,
coming up, bade his force alight, and at once unload their
burdens. 'Then,' said he, 'let us fight for the water forthwith ; by my life ! the springs shall be for the braver of
the two.' Thereupon Hormuz challenged Khalid to single
combat, and, though he treacherously posted an ambuscade,
was in the encounter slain. The Moslems then rushed
forward, and with great slaughter put the enemy to flight,
pursuing them to the banks of the Euphrates. The Arabs
had now a foretaste of the spoils of Persia. The share of
each horseman was a thousand pieces, besides great store
of arms. The jewelled tiara of Hormuz, symbol of his
rank, was sent to the Caliph with the royal Fifth. An
elephant taken in the field, and led as part of the prize to
Medina, was paraded about the town, much to the wonder
of the admiring citizens, but sent back as unsuitable to the
place. The action was called 'the Battle of the Chains,'
from a portion of the Persian soldiers being bound together (as tradition contemptuously tells us) to prevent
their giving way.

'The   The defeated army fled towards the capital, and Mo-
Lady's
Castle.'   thanna with his horse hastened after them. Crossing the

Euphrates, he came upon a fortress called 'The Lady's A.H. 12.
Castle,' held by a Persian princess. Leaving his brother
to besiege it, he advanced to a second fort defended by
her husband. This he took by storm, and put the garrison
to the sword; which, when the lady heard of, she embraced
Islam, and, forgetting her Persian lord, gave her hand to
Mothanna's brother.

The ardour of Mothanna was near to causing a disaster. Persians
When the message of Hormuz reached Medain, the king again de-
despatched another prince with troops to reinforce him.
Rallying the defeated army, this force met Mothanna, who
had been brought up by the great canal, or branch of the
Tigris, which runs athwart the peninsula, and placed him
with his small flying column in great peril. Khalid, apprised of the check, hastened to relieve his lieutenant, and
just in time. The field was fiercely contested. Again the
enemy fled; a prodigious number were either slain or
drowned; the remainder escaped in boats. The deep
channel stopped farther advance; but the spoil of the
enemy's camp was very great. Khalid scoured the country,
killing all the men fit for war, and taking their women
captive. But the Fellaheen, or unwarlike peasants, he left
unharmed.

The court was now thoroughly aroused. Arab invaders, Victory of
it was said, would best be matched by Arabs who knew Walaja,
their tactics; and so the king raised a great levy of the April,
Bekr and other loyal clans, under a famous warrior of their 633 A.D.
own. He also summoned Bahman, a veteran general, from
the east, to command the imperial troops. The combined
army, in imposing force, advanced towards the junction of
the two rivers. Leaving a detachment to guard his conquests in the delta, Khalid marched to meet the enemy.
The battle, long and obstinate, was won by the tactics of
the Moslem leader, who surprised the exhausted enemy by
ambuscades in their rear. The discomfiture was complete.
The Persians fled; and with them their Bedouin allies, but
not until several had been taken prisoners. Flushed with
success as he gazed at the scene around, Khalid thus ad- Khalid's
dressed his followers :—' Ye see the riches of the land. Its oration.

paths drop fatness, so that corn and oil abound even as do
the stones with us. If but as a provision for this present
life,—let alone merit of fighting in the ways of the Lord,—
it were well worth our while to battle for these fair fields
and banish care and penury for ever[1].' Khalid here struck
a chord delightful to the Bedouin heart. Now, also, the
inducements with respect to the other sex began to tell.
Persian ladies, both maids and matrons, ' captives of their
right hand,' were forthwith, without stint of number, and
by permission which they held divine, lawful to the conquerors' embrace ; and, in the enjoyment of this privilege,
they were nothing loth to execute upon the heathen ' the
judgment written.' Thus religious fanaticism grew along
with martial ardour, both riveted by motives native to the
Arab—fight and foray, spoil of war, and captive charms.

Battle of
Allis,
iii. 12 A.H.
May,
633 A.D.
The cup had but just touched their lips, and many
a chance might yet dash it from them. The great
family of the Beni Bekr was divided in the struggle,
part holding with Khalid and part with Persia. A bitter
feeling was aroused between the Bedouins of Mesopotamia
and the invaders, aggravated by defeat and the treatment
of those taken captive. Smarting under injury, the Christian
tribes roused their nomad brethren on both banks of the
Euphrates, and urged the Court of Persia to revenge.
Just then, Ardshir the king fell sick, and Bahman was
detained at court; but he sent an army across the Euphrates
to join the loyal Bedouins, who, from every side, flocked
to Allis, half-way between Hira and Obolla. News of this
great rising forced Khalid to fall back hastily, and recross
the Euphrates. Leaving a strong detachment at Hafir
to secure his rear, he boldly advanced to meet the enemy.
The Arab tribes first rushed to the attack, and Khalid slew
their leader. Then the Persians with a vast front came up,
and the Moslems were hard pressed as they had never been
before. The battle was fiercely contested, and the issue
at one time so doubtful that Khalid vowed to the Lord
that in event of victory the blood of His foes should flow

---

[1] Khalid's speech is quoted by Al Kindy, the Christian Apologist, S.P.C.K.,
1887, p. 85.

in a crimson stream. At last the Persians, unable to withstand the impetuous onset, broke and fled. To fulfil his savage oath, Khalid proclaimed that no fugitive should be slain, but all brought alive into the camp. For two days the country was scoured by the Moslem horse, and a great multitude of prisoners gathered. Then the butchery commenced in the dry bed of a canal, but the earth drank up the blood. Company after company was beheaded, and still the gory flux remained. At last, by advice of an Arab chief, Khalid had a flood-gate opened, and the blood-red tide redeemed his vow. There were flour-mills upon the spot, and for three days corn for the army was ground by the reddened flood. We may hope that tradition has magnified the details of this great barbarity; but its memory lived in the name of the 'River of Blood,' by which thereafter the ill-omened stream was called.

The 'River of Blood.'

The battle over, a sumptuous repast was found ready spread in the enemy's camp, to which the Persians, when surprised by Khalid, were about to sit down;—a novel experience for the simple Arabs, who handled the white fritters with childish delight, and devoured with avidity rich pancakes and other eastern delicacies. Khalid ate his supper leaning on the body of a stalwart hero, 'the equal of a thousand warriors,' whom, in single combat, he had but just cut down. Tidings of the victory, with choice portion of the spoil, a welcome earnest of the royal Fifth to follow, were at once despatched to Abu Bekr. The messenger, himself a brave warrior, described the heat and progress of the battle, the feats and prowess of its heroes, the multitude of captives and the riches of the spoil. The Caliph, overjoyed at his glowing tale, bestowed upon the envoy a beautiful damsel from amongst the captive maidens he carried with him.

A Persian supper on the field.

Abu Bekr's delight.

For the moment the spirit of the Persians was broken; but their Bedouin allies proved so troublesome to Khalid, and occupied a position from which they could so materially annoy his rear and communications with Medina, that he resolved on reducing the whole tract west of the Euphrates

The principality of Hira.

occupied by these tribes, together with Hira, its capital. The Lakhmite dynasty had long ceased to rule over this city, which now for many years had been governed by a Persian Satrap. Partly from its interests being akin to those of the Christian tribes of Mesopotamia, partly from its being a dependency of Persia, the influence of Hira had hitherto been little felt in Arabia proper. But recent events had shown that even the Beni Bekr might combine with the border capital to resist the invader; and to prevent the recurrence of such a danger, Khalid now directed his steps to Hira.

Amghisia sacked.

With this view he advanced rapidly up the western channel of the Euphrates, and surprised Amghisia, a town the rival of Hira in size and wealth. The inhabitants fled, and the booty was so rich that each horseman took 1,500 pieces. When the Fifth reached Medina, Abu Bekr was overwhelmed at the sight; 'Oh ye Coreish,' he exclaimed in ecstasy, 'verily your lion, the lion of Islam, hath leapt upon the lion of Persia, and spoiled him of his prey. Surely the womb is exhausted. Woman shall no more bear a second Khalid!'

Hira besieged capitulates.

Finding boats at Amghisia, Khalid embarked his infantry and baggage, and was tracking up the stream to Hira when, the Satrap having laid open the irrigating escapes above, the flotilla grounded suddenly. Apprised of the cause, Khalid hastened with a flying squadron to the canal-head, closed the sluices, and enabled the boats again to ascend. Then the army, having disembarked and taken possession of the beautiful palaces of the princes of Hira[1], encamped before the city walls. The Satrap fled across the river; but the city, defended as it was by four citadels, refused to surrender. The ramparts were manned, and the besiegers kept at bay by the discharge of missiles. A monastery and cloisters lay without; and at length the monks and clergy, exposed to the fury of the besiegers, induced the citizens to capitulate on easy terms embodied in a treaty. Then they brought gifts, which Khalid accepted, and despatched to Medina. Abu Bekr ratified

---

[1] *Life of Mahomet,* 1861. Vol. i. p. clxxi.

the treaty and accepted the presents, but desired that their A.H. 12.
value should be deducted from the tribute.

The men of Hira bound themselves to pay a yearly Treaty with Hira.
tribute, all classes, saving religious mendicants, being
assessed thereto. The Moslems, on their part, engaged
to protect the city from attack. The treaty, though
shortly set aside by the rising which swept over the land,
is interesting as the first concluded with a principality
without the peninsula. One strange condition may be
mentioned. The beauty of Keramat had been long
proverbial, and a soldier laid claim to her on the ground
that Mahomet, hearing him extol her charms, had promised
(so the story runs) that when Hira was captured she should
be his bride. Khalid insisted that the prophetic promise
should be now fulfilled. The thing was grievous to the
lady's household, but she took it lightly. 'Care not for
it,' she said, 'the fool saw me in my youth, and hath forgotten that youth remaineth not for ever.' He soon found
out that it was even so, and was glad to name a ransom,
which having paid, she returned to her people.

The occupation of Hira was the first definite step in the Hira remains Christian,
outward movement of Islam. Here Khalid fixed his head-
quarters, and remained a year. It was, in fact, the earliest 12 A.H. 633 A.D.
Moslem capital beyond the limits of Arabia. The administration was left with the heads of the city, who were
at the least neutral. Khalid, indeed, expected that, being
of Arab descent, and themselves long ruled by a native
dynasty, the citizens would actively have joined his cause.
Adi, grandson of the poet of that name, was one of the
deputation which concluded the peace. 'Tell me,' said
Khalid, rallying him, 'whether ye be of Arab or of Persian
blood?' 'Judge by our speech: doth that betray ignoble
birth?' 'True,' answered Khalid; 'then why do ye not
join our faith, and cast in your lot with us?' 'Nay,' answered the Christian, 'that we shall never do; the faith of
our fathers we shall not abjure, but shall pay tribute unto
thee.' 'Beshrew the fools!' cried Khalid; 'Unbelief is as
a trackless desert; and the wanderer in it the silliest of
mankind. Here are two guides, an Arab and a stranger;

A.H. 12. and of the two they choose the stranger!' The flux and reflux of Roman invasion had, no doubt, loosened their faith in Persia; but the court of Medain was near at hand, and, though in the last stage of senility, sufficiently strong to retain its hold upon a small dependency like Hira. The permanence of Arab conquest, too, was yet uncertain; the love of their ancestral faith was still predominant; and so the city chose to remain tributary. Several centuries later we find the inhabitants of the neighbourhood in considerable numbers still attached to the Christian faith [1].

Prayer, and Service of Victory.   Public prayer, outward symbol of the dominant faith, was now established; and the citizens might hear the cry of the Muedzzin, as, five times a day, beginning with the earliest dawn, it resounded from the adjacent camp. Khalid celebrated his success in a special *Service of Victory.* The occasion was memorable. Clad in a flowing robe girt loosely about the neck, he turned, when prayers were ended, to the assembly, and thus extolled their bravery: 'In the field of Muta, when fighting with the Greeks, nine swords were broken in my hand. But I met not any there to match the foes ye have encountered here; and of these none more valiant than the men of Allis.' The early campaign in Irac, however, is surrounded by tradition with a special halo; for the loss here on the Moslem side had not hitherto been great, and the fighting could hardly

The feeling of this Christian principality in losing first their native rulers, and then being swallowed up in the Moslem invasion, is well expressed in these verses sung by one of their poets. Mundzir and Noman were princes of the Lakhmite dynasty:—

Now that the Princes of the house of Mundzir are gone, shall I ever again behold the royal herd of camels returning at eve from the pastures of Khawarnac and Sedir?

Now that the horsemen of Noman are passed away, shall I ever again feed the young she-camel on the pastures between Mecca and Hafir?

Like a flock of goats on a stormy day, we are scattered by the Beni Maad (the invading Moslems), even as pieces of camels slaughtered for the feast.

Heretofore our homes were sacred, and we like the teats of a well-filled udder,
Yielding tribute at the appointed times to the Chosroes, and imposts in cattle and gold.

Alas! even so is the changeful wheel of the well of fortune. Now the day ascends with joy and gladness, and now it sinks into darkness and distress.

have compared with that of many a well-contested field A.H. 12. in the Prophet's time.

While Hira was left in the hands of its chief men, Adminis- summary rule was set up over the adjacent country. tration of the pro- The *Dihcans*—great landholders and imperial tax-gatherers vince. —had been waiting upon fortune. Seeing now that Khalid carried everything before him, many began to tender submission and enter into engagements for the revenue. Abu Bekr had wisely enjoined that the Fellaheen should be maintained in possession, and their rights as occupiers of the soil respected. The demand remained unchanged, with the addition only of a light poll-tax. In other respects, the terms, made with the consent and approval of the army, corresponded with those of Hira. Holding their ancestral faith, the people became *Zimmies*, or protected dependants. Khalid undertook to defend them, and they on their part pledged allegiance and bound themselves to give notice if danger threatened. Garrisons were quartered here and there, and the troops held ready in moveable columns. Thus the country west of the Euphrates was kept in check, and also the lower Delta to the east. Throughout this region none was secure from rapine but such as entered into engagements. Hostages were taken for the revenue; and a formal discharge given upon its payment. The tribute, as well as the booty, was all distributed among the army 'for the strengthening of the same.'

Persia meanwhile was hopelessly distracted. Male pro- Persia paralysed geny near the throne had been so ruthlessly massacred, that by internal no heir of royal blood could anywhere be found, and a rapid troubles. succession of feeble claimants was set up by the princesses left to form the court. Thus paralysed, the Persians did little more than protect Medain by holding in force the country opposite as far as the Nahr-shir, a deep channel, which, drawn from the Euphrates, flowed athwart the peninsula. This line was threatened by Mothanna; but Abu Bekr gave stringent orders that no advance should be made till all was secure behind. No tidings, moreover, had as yet been received from Iyadh at Duma, with whom co-operation was imperative. Khalid fretted at remaining thus inactive, 'playing,' as he complained, 'for so many months the woman's part.' But he curbed his ardour, and contented himself with inditing two letters, in imperious tone, one to 'the Princes of Persia,' the other to 'the Satraps and inhabitants at large.'

Anbar.   Towards the north and west, however, aggressive measures were continued. Siege was laid to Anbar, a fortress on the Euphrates some 80 miles above Babylon. The worn-out camels of the army were slain and cast into the deep fosse, which thus was crossed and the city captured. The Persian governor sued for terms, and was permitted to retire. Anbar and the well-watered neighbourhood thus

Ain Tamar. secured, the army attacked Ain Tamar, a fortress on the desert border three days' journey further west. The Persian troops were here supported by a great gathering of Arab tribes, and among them the same Taghlib levies which had followed their prophetess to Yemama. These met Khalid as he approached, but were repulsed, and the Persian governor, seeing the rout from the ramparts, fled and left the fugitives to defend themselves as best they could. Refused terms, they surrendered at discretion. The persist-

Khalid's severity. ent opposition of the Christian Bedouins now led Khalid into an unwise severity that embittered them against him. Their leader was beheaded in front of the city walls, and every adult male of the garrison led forth and put to death; while the women and children were made over to the soldiers or sold into slavery. In a cloister of the church, hard by, were forty youths, who in their terror barred the door upon the enemy. When the retreat was forced, they

Christian students. gave themselves up as students receiving instruction in the Gospel. Their lives were spared, and they were distributed among the leaders. The fate of these unfortunate youths, snatched from a Nestorian seminary to be brought up as captives in the Moslem faith, must have been common enough in the rude and sanguinary tide of Saracen invasion; the reason why tradition makes special mention of these, is that amongst them were progenitors of several distinguished men, such as Ibn Ishac, the historian, and Musa, the conqueror of Spain.

All this while, Iyadh, who ought long since to have A.H. 12.
joined Khalid, was battling unsuccessfully with enemies at Iyadh at
Duma. The Caliph, becoming anxious, sent Welid, who Duma.
had been deputed by Khalid to Medina in charge of royal
booty, to assist him. By his advice an urgent message for
help was despatched to Khalid. The courier reached just
after the fall of Ain Tamar; and Khalid, with no enemy
now in the field, replied in martial verse:—

> Wait, my friend, but for a moment, speedily shall help appear;
> Cohort upon cohort follows, waving sword and glittering spear.

Leaving Cacaa in command at Hira, and starting at once
with the flower of his force, he crossed the intervening
desert, and made good his word.

He was not a day too soon. Okeidar and Judi, chiefs of Duma
Duma, were supported by the Kelb and other tribes from stormed by Khalid,
the Syrian desert; and now the Ghassan were pouring down vii. 12 A.H.
from the north, under Jabala, Christian prince of Bostra. Sept.
The position of Iyadh, thus beset, grew day by day more 633 A.D.
critical. The advent of Khalid changed the scene at once.
His very name was a tower of strength. Okeidar had
already felt his prowess, having several years before been
taken by him prisoner to Medina[1]. Much afraid, he hastened
to surrender, but on the way was taken prisoner and beheaded. Then Iyadh on the Syrian side, and Khalid on
the nearer, attacked the hostile tribes and utterly routed
them. Jabala effected his flight to Bostra. But the helpless crowd that remained were hemmed in between the
two forces, and none escaped. The gate of the fort was
battered down, and the crowded inmates put promiscuously
to the sword. The women were sold to the highest bidder;
and the most beautiful, the unfortunate Judi's daughter,
bought by Khalid for himself. Celebrating thus fresh
nuptials on the field of battle, he enjoyed a short repose
at Duma, while the main body of the troops marching
back to Hira, were there received with timbrels and
cymbals and outward demonstrations of rejoicing.

But all was not going on smoothly in that vicinity. The
absence of Khalid encouraged the Persians and their Arab

---

[1] *Life of Mahomet*, p. 458.

A. H. 12.

Expeditions in Irac, viii. 12 A.H. Octr. 633 A.D.

allies, especially the Taghlib, still smarting under the execution of their leader, to resume offensive operations. Cacaa, though on the alert, was able to do no more than guard the frontier and protect Anbar from threatened inroad. At this news, Khalid hastened back ; and placing Iyadh in the government of Hira, despatched Cacaa across the Euphrates, while he himself appointed a rendezvous at Ain Tamar to attack the Taghlib tribe ; for he had vowed that thus he would crush the viper in its nest. On the eastern bank the Persians were routed and their leaders killed ; while on the western, by a series of brilliant and well-planned night attacks, the Bedouins were repeatedly surprised as they slept secure in their desert homes, cut to pieces, and their families carried off. Thus Khalid fulfilled his vow. Multitudes of women, many of noble birth, were distributed among the army. A portion also, with rich booty, were sent to Medina, and there disposed of by sale[1].

Battle of Firadh. Persians, Greeks, and Bedouins defeated, xi. 12 A.H. Jany. 634 A.D.

Following up his Bedouin foes, Khalid at last reached Firadh, on the Syrian border, and by the river rested his army during the fast of Ramadhan and for some weeks after. But the Byzantine garrison on the frontier, uneasy at the prolonged encampment and threatening attitude of Khalid, and making common cause with the Persian outposts and neighbouring loyal tribes, advanced in imposing force to chase the invader away. They challenged Khalid to cross the river ; but the wary general bade them rather come over to the eastern bank. A long and severe conflict ensued. The Moslems were victorious ; the cavalry pursued the fugitives, and the carnage must have been great, for tradition places it at the fabulous number of a hundred thousand.

Khalid's incognito pilgrimage, xii. 12 A.H. Feby. 634 A.D.

For the moment opposition was crushed, and no enemy anywhere in sight. The season for the Meccan pilgrimage being now at hand, Khalid formed the singular resolve of

[1] One was bought by Aly. He had recently taken into his harem another girl, one of the captives of Yemama ; she was of the Hanifa tribe, and the son she bore him hence called the Hanifite, whose descendants being thus of the stock of Aly, had a political *rôle* of which we shall hear hereafter. He also married in this year a granddaughter of the Prophet, the child of Zeinab and niece of his deceased wife Fatima.

performing it incognito, unknown even to his royal master. So, having recruited his army for ten days on the well-fought field, he gave orders to march slowly and by easy stages back to Hira. Then, making as though he remained behind, he set out secretly with a small escort on the pious errand. Without a guide, he traversed the devious desert route with marvellous sagacity and speed. Having accomplished the rites of pilgrimage, he retraced his steps from Mecca with like despatch, and entered Hira in early spring, just as the rear guard was marching in. So well had he kept his secret, that the army thought he had been all the while at Firadh, and now was journeying slowly back. Even Abu Bekr, who himself presided at the pilgrimage, was unaware of the presence of his great general. When, after some time, the secret visit came to his knowledge, he was much displeased. But the action which he took in consequence belongs to the succeeding year.

CHAPTER IX.

CAMPAIGN IN SYRIA. BATTLE ON THE YERMUK [1].

12–13 A.H. 633–4 A.D.

Khalid ibn Said posted on Syrian border, 12 A.H. 633 A.D.
THE campaign in Syria opened under a very different Khalid, son of Said. An early convert, and as such an exile to Abyssinia, he held high place as a confessor of the faith. Employed as envoy in the south, he was forced to retreat in the turmoil following the Prophet's death, and now claimed fresh command. Omar and Aly doubted his fitness, but Abu Bekr, overcome by importunity, sent him to rally the friendly tribes on the Syrian frontier; but unless attacked he was to take no forward step. The Byzantine garrisons, alarmed at his approach, summoned their Bedouin allies, and assumed a threatening attitude. Khalid was thereupon permitted to advance, yet cautiously, and so as to allow no danger in his rear. Proceeding onwards to the Dead Sea, he routed there a Syrian column; but finding himself so far away, called urgently for rein-

Ikrima sent to his support.
forcements. Just then the Moslem troops, having crushed apostacy in the south, were returning in great numbers to Medina, and so were available for any other service. Ikrima, with Dzul Kelaa and his Himyar followers, being the first to appear, were despatched in haste to support Khalid in the north.

Also Amru and Welid. End of 12 A.H. Jany. 634 A.D.
Two other Chiefs of note were despatched with a similar commission. These were Amru and Welid, who

[1] It is well again to remind the reader that our authorities are purely Arabian, the entire loss of Syria being recorded by the Byzantine authorities in but a few lines. Details, especially of the enemy's numbers, movements, &c., must be received simply as rumours handed down by tradition.

were away on a joint command, given them by the Prophet, A.H. 12-
13. in the country between Tayma and the Red Sea. Since the reduction of Duma, this tract having quieted down, Abu Bekr gave them the option either of remaining where they were, or of engaging in a work 'better for them, both in this present life, and in that which is to come.' To this Amru made answer: 'I am but an arrow in the quiver of Islam, and thou the Archer. It is for thee to pick out the fittest shaft, and whithersoever thou wilt, discharge it.' So they were despatched, Welid to join Khalid, and Amru to occupy Ayla and the tract south of the Holy Land.

Emboldened by these reinforcements, Khalid hastened in the early spring to gain the first laurels of the campaign. Forgetful of his master's injunctions, he was in his eagerness decoyed by the Byzantine general towards Damascus. He had reached as far as Marj Soffar, to the east of the Sea of Tiberias, when the enemy closed in upon his rear, and cut off his retreat. Discomfited, he fled, leaving his camp in the enemy's hands, and Ikrima to retrieve the disaster. That able leader rallied the retreating force, and with a sufficient remnant, including the brave Himyar band under Dzul Kelaa, took up a strong position on the frontier, until help should come. Khalid continued his flight, but was stayed on the road by a message from the indignant Caliph. 'By my life!' he wrote, 'thou shalt come no further; thou pratest bravely when secure, but in battle art a coward. I have no patience with thee!' To those about him, he said,—'Truly Aly and Omar knew the man better than I. Had I listened to them, this mishap had not been.' We hear no more of Khalid ibn Said.

Khalid
defeated at
Marj, near
Sea of
Tiberias.
Beginning
of 13 A.H.
March,
634 A.D

In the present emergency, it was fortunate for Abu Bekr Reinforce-
ments for
Syria that Arabia being now entirely pacified, he was able, as the columns returned, to hurry them off to Syria, there to retrieve the fortunes of Islam. Duly sensible of the gravity of the enterprise,—nothing short of measuring swords with the Kaiser,—the Caliph strained every nerve to meet it. He had thrown down the gauntlet, and was waging war, at one and the same time, with the potentates both of East and

West. The brigades now formed for this great enterprise
were pitched one after another at Medina on the plain of
Jorf, a little way on the Syrian road; and, as each was
ready to march, the Caliph walked (as nearly two years before
he had done with Osama) by the side of the mounted leader,
addressed and gave him thus his farewell command. 'Profession,' he
by Abu
Bekr.
would say, 'is naught without faith. The merit of a work
dependeth on the purpose of the worker. The reward promised in the Book of the Lord for such as fight in His
ways, is great. Set this ever before thee and before thy
men. But when thou haranguest them, be brief, for in the
multitude of words the foremost are lost in the hindermost.
So striving, ye will obtain the prize, riches and glory in
the present life, and in the life to come salvation.' Then
with a hearty ' Fare ye well,' he would retrace his steps and
return to his simple home.

Syrian
Army.
The force thus brought together differed altogether in
composition from the army of Irac. That in the main con-
sisted of Bedouin tribes, which flocked to the banners of
Mothanna and Khalid; the men of Mecca and Medina
were there comparatively few, for most had returned to
their homes after the battle of Yemama. In the Syrian
army, on the contrary, there are reckoned at least 1,000
Companions, men who had seen and conversed with the
Prophet, and no fewer than 100 of the famous Three
hundred of Bedr. These enrolled themselves at pleasure
under the chief of their choice; but, once enrolled,
they yielded to that leader implicit obedience; while he,
on his part, consulted their views and wishes on all occasions of importance. Sheikhs of renown, who but a few
years before had wielded the whole power of Mecca, and
haughty chieftains of high descent, now joined with alacrity
the column of any one, however young and inferior, into
whose hands the Caliph was pleased to present the banner
of command. And the whole force, thus formed in separate
detachments, held itself at the absolute disposal of the
Commander of the Faithful.

Four
battalions
Four such detachments were now despatched. *First*,
Shorahbil was appointed to supersede Welid, who shared

in the disgrace of Khalid. Rallying the scattered fragments A.H. 12-
13.
of the discomfited force, he took up the most advanced
position. *Second*, followed Yezid, son of Abu Sofian, with concentrated on
the Syrian
frontier.
a levy from Mecca, which included many chief men of the
Coreish roused by the Caliph's call and stirring news from
Syria. His brother Muavia shortly after joined him with
further remnants of the beaten army. Abu Obeida, trusted
Companion of the Prophet, led the *third* column, and
posted himself near Amru, who commanded the *fourth*, in
the Wady Araba, west of all the others. Many of the new
troops, specially the levies from the south, travelled after
Bedouin fashion with their families, ready to make the
north their home. For the marvellous conquests of
Khalid's army in Chaldæa suggested the venn more inviting
prospect of settlement in the 'Land of blessing and promise,' as it is called in the Coran, a land flowing with milk
and honey.

The four battalions thus gathered in the spring of the Their
advance.
year on the Syrian border numbered 30,000, besides a
reserve of 6,000 under Ikrima. In their first advance they
met with little opposition, and putting to flight such Arab
and Greek troops as occupied the country about the Dead
Sea, eventually took up ground in a sort of *échelon*,
threatening the garrisons in the south of Syria. Abu
Obeida, approaching Damascus, held a position the furthest
east, near to Ikrima and the recent scene of disaster. Next
came Shorahbil, overawing Tiberias and tth valley of the
Jordan. Yezid, in the Belcaa, threatened Bostra; and
Amru, in lower Palestine, Hebron. Each of these eventually found himself confronted by a Byzantine force.

For Heraclius was at last alarmed. A few years before Four
battalions
oppose
them.
he gloriously repulsed the Chosroes; but after that had
relapsed into inactivity. Tidings of the invasion, an irruption, it would seem, of barbarians from the south, now
roused him from his lethargy. Repairing to Hims, he
gathered an immense force, and sent it, in four divisions, to
stem the advancing tide. The largest, numbering (as tradition has it) 90,000 men, was commanded by his brother
Theodoric. The Moslems, startled at the formidable array,

A.H. 12-13.
___
Abu Bekr's command to draw together.

consulted how to meet it. Amru urged the commanders to gather into one body.—'For how,' he sent to say, 'can our scanty numbers, divided and apart, encounter these mighty hosts?' To this they agreed, and Abu Bekr, who had constant tidings, was of the same mind. 'Draw ye all together,' was his order, 'near unto the river Yermuk. Ye are the Lord's host, and shall surely put the enemy to flight. Such as ye, shall never be discomfited by reason of the fewness of your numbers. Tens of thousands are smitten in battle because of their sins. Wherefore, do ye eschew sin. Let every man stand close by his fellow. So shall the Lord give you the victory.'

The two armies at Wacusa on the Yermuk, ii. 13 A.H. April, 634 A.D.

Acting thus, the columns concentrated on a spot south of the Yermuk, near where it was crossed by the high road from Damascus. The Greeks, suiting their tactics, also drew together, and pitched their camp on the northern bank of the river. The place was singular. The Yermuk, taking its rise in the high lands of the Hauran, runs in a deep and rugged gorge far beneath the level of the land; and descending rapidly, falls into the Jordan below the Lake of Galilee. The battle-ground was probably some 30 miles above it. Here the stream, by fetching a compass, leaves on its northern bank a wide plain, the field of Wacusa, bounded on three sides by a sheer precipice; while the remaining part was shut in by a ravine which nearly closed the circuit. Only a narrow neck was thus left for entrance, across which the highway passing, formed the key of the position. The Greeks, tempted by the wide expanse, entered from the north, and spread themselves out upon the plain. Thereupon the Moslems crossed the river and encamped likewise on the northern bank, upon a spot abutting on the road, and thus threatening the exit of the enemy. Amru, seeing this, rejoiced and said: 'Be of good cheer, my friends; the Greeks are shut in, and few that are shut in escape.' A desultory warfare ensued, without definite result. The Byzantine troops often formed up in force, and as often were driven back; the ravine was to them a strong protection, and the Arabs gained no material advantage. In such indecisive skirmishing two

iii. iv. 13 A.H. May and June.

months passed away, and the armies remained still facing one another.

Abu Bekr became anxious at the delay, and the urgent appeals for reinforcements. It was not so much poverty in number, as lack of fire and military genius, that disquieted him. Abu Obeida was mild even to timidity; Amru an able counsellor, but lacking military dash. The mettle of the generals had not yet been fully tested; and their independence one of another, in the absence of a general-in-chief, was fatal to common action. When, therefore, the cry reached Medina for help, the Caliph exclaimed : 'Khalid is the man for this! By the son of Welid, with the help of the Lord, shall the machinations of Satan and of the Greeks be overthrown.' Accordingly, he sent this message to him :—' Depart and join thyself unto the armies of the Faithful in Syria, for they are downcast and forlorn. But beware (referring to his stealthy pilgrimage) that thou return not again to do what thou hast done. The Lord helping, thy removal shall not dishearten thy followers in Irac. Go forward, and high resolve attend thee! Fill up the measure of the Lord's benefits upon mankind, and He shall fulfil the same on thee. Have a care, lest the world and the flesh ensnaring thee, thou stumble and thy works perish. The Lord doth recompense!'

Khalid transferred to Syria.

This mandate disconcerted Khalid. He set it down to Omar, who, envying him the conquest of Irac, would thus snatch it from his hand. There was reason for the fear. But had Abu Bekr lived, it had been otherwise, for he continued thus :—' Take with thee half the army, and leave Mothanna half. When the Lord shall have given thee victory in Syria, then thou shalt return to thy command in Irac.' Reconciled by the assurance, and loyal to his Chief, Khalid began by selecting the Companions and flower of the force to accompany him. Mothanna insisted that the division should be equal, and was at last conciliated by securing a goodly portion of the veterans. The strength of either moiety was about 9,000. Mothanna accompanied to the border of the desert the great general whom he had served so loyally, and taking a last farewell, retraced his steps to Hira.

Sets out with reinforcements.

The Syrian desert lay between Khalid and his new
sphere of action.   He could not take the northern route,
because of hostile tribes and Byzantine garrisons; therefore,
turning south, he crossed a second time that waste and
tumbled sea of sand, the Nefud, and halted at Duma.
Thence he took the direct road to Syria, and keeping the
same, would in a few days have reached Bostra, but he
feared lest the enemy opposing him in that direction should
hinder his junction with the Moslem army.   He formed,
therefore, the bold design to strike north, right across the
waterless and pathless desert, and emerging at Tadmor, so
turn the Roman flank.   A council of war was held, and a
Bedouin guide brought in.   'There is but one way,' said he,
'a way so bare, and for five days so waterless, that even single
horsemen shun it, lest they perish on the road.'   'By the
same shall we go,' was Khalid's prompt resolve; and when
expostulated with on the wild and perilous attempt, he answered that, with divine aid and firm resolve, nothing was
wild and nothing perilous.   The words fired his followers,
and the project was by acclamation carried.   'Do this

then,' said the guide, 'if ye will.   Gather as many camels
as ye can; withholding water for a while; then let them
drink plentifully, and again a second time; afterwards, bind
their ears and slit their lips, so that they ruminate not.   So
haply may your water last.'   At each stage across the wilderness, ten such camels were slain for each troop of a hundred
lances.   The water drawn from their bodies, was mixed
with milk for the horses.   The men were given but a single
draught each day.   On the fifth day a shudder crept over
the host.   The supply was at an end.   They had reached
the neighbourhood where water should have been, but signs
were wanting, and the guide at fault.   After casting
anxiously about in all directions, he cried in despair—
'Search for the bramble bush; the bramble should be here;
if ye find it not, we are lost.'   So they searched all round.
At last they came upon a half-concealed root; and with
loud shouts of 'Great is the Lord!' rushed to the spot, dug
down into the ground, and found a plentiful supply of
water.

They were now on the Syrian side of the desert, about a hundred miles east of Damascus. Early next morning, Khalid fell on the astonished neighbourhood, scattering terror all around, and attacking Tadmor, which after slight resistance yielded. Then fetching a circuit, he skirted the Hauran within sight of Damascus, and emerged at Adzraat. Having achieved this marvellous journey in the course of a few weeks, and reopened communications with the south, he sent tidings to Abu Bekr of his safety, with the Fifth of spoil taken by the way; and, about midsummer, effected a junction with the army of the Moslems which still lay inactive on the Yermuk.

A.H. 12-
13.

and effects
junction
with Syrian
army,
iv.v.13A.H.
June, July,
634.

Fresh reinforcements had lately arrived and raised the flagging spirits of the enemy. They numbered 240,000, of whom a portion were felons released for the occasion, and others chained in line, that they might not fly, or in token rather of resolve to die. Such are the exaggerated, and it may be fanciful, rumours handed down as, no doubt, current in the Moslem ranks. But whatever abatement is made from them, so much we may readily accept, that the army with which Heraclius sought to stay the surging tide of Saracen invasion must needs have been very large. We may also believe that though devoid of union, loyalty, and valour, it was well appointed, and elated by its late achievements in the Persian war. In discipline and combined movement, and also in equipment, the Byzantine must vastly have surpassed the Arab force. But the Bedouin horse excelled in celerity and dash. Their charge, if light, was galling, and so rapidly delivered that, ere the surprise was over, the troop itself might be out of sight. The Byzantine army, it is true, had Bedouin auxiliaries as numerous, perhaps, as the whole Moslem army. But their spirit widely differed. The fealty of the Syrian Arab was lax and loose. Christian in name, the yoke of his faith sat lightly on him. Indeed, throughout the empire, Christianity was eaten up of strife and rancour. With the reinforcements came a troop of monks and bishops, who, bearing banners, waving golden crosses, and shouting that the faith was in jeopardy, sought thus to rouse the

The two
armies
compared.

passion of the army. The passion roused was often but the scowl of hatred. Bitter schisms rent the Church, and the cry of the Orthodox for help would strike a far different chord than that of patriotism in the Eutychian and Nestorian breast. Lastly, the social and ancestral associations of the Syrian Bedouin, alien from his Byzantine masters, were in full accord with his brethren from Arabia ; and of such instinctive feeling, the invaders knew well to take advantage. With this lukewarm and disunited host, compare the Moslem in its virgin vigour, bound together as one man, and fired with a wild and fanatic fervour to ' fight in the ways of the Lord,' winning thus at one and the same time heavenly favour and worldly fortune. For the survivors there was endless spoil, captive maidens, fertile vales, houses which they builded not, and wells which they digged not. Should they fall by the sword, there was the martyr's prize of paradise, and black-eyed Houries waiting impatiently for the happy hour. The soldiers' imagination was inflamed by tales of heaven opened on the very battle-field, and the expiring warrior tended by two virgins wiping away the sweat and dust from off his face, and with the wanton graces of paradise drawing him upwards in their fond embrace. Of an army, nerved by this strange combination of incentives, divine and human,—of the flesh and of the spirit, faith and rapine, heavenly devotion and passion for the sex even in the throes of death,—ten might chase a hundred of the half-hearted Greeks. The 40,000 Moslems were stronger far than the 240,000 of the enemy.

Moslem army paralysed by separate commands.
The Byzantine army, swollen by its reinforcements, began to overlap the Arabian camp and force it back into straitened quarters. But Khalid's energy soon caused things to mend. In a series of encounters, the enemy, worsted, retired behind the ravine in front. Still the prospect otherwise was not encouraging. The battalions of the Moslem host were separately pitched ; the conduct of public prayer (mark always of supreme command) was separate in each ; the attacks, delivered independently, from want of combination, failed. The issue hung fire. A month passed, and Khalid became impatient. To secure

success, authority must be vested in a single hand. He saw A.H. 12–13.
the fault, and set himself to remedy it.

Opportunity soon offered. Unusual movement on the Khalid obtains command in chief for the day.
Roman side led to a council of the Moslem chiefs, and
Khalid laid his views before them. The Caliph, it was
true, had commissioned them to meet each a separate
Byzantine army. But the enemy was now massed in one;
and Abu Bekr would surely under the altered circumstances approve the assumption of command by a single
general. The merit in the sight of the Lord would be the
same ; not less the merit in the Caliph's eyes. ' Come
now,' he said, to disarm their jealousy, ' let us vary the
supreme control, taking it each in succession for the day,
and, if ye will, let mine be first.' The proposal thus
adroitly made was by acclamation carried. All expected
that, with the emergency, the change would likewise pass
away : but once made, it proved itself so good, that the
supreme command in Syria was ever after held by one alone.

Meanwhile Khalid had sown dissension in the enemy's A Greek general gained over.
camp, and gained over one of its leading men. The facts
are obscure, and the episode strange. But so much
appears, that a general, Jareja by name, perhaps of Arab
blood and Bedouin sympathies, was persuaded to promise
that, at the decisive moment, he would leave the Byzantine
and join the Moslem side.

The powers conferred on Khalid were soon used to Disposition of Moslem army.
purpose. His first care was to reorganise the army. ' The
Greeks,' he said, ' are a vast host, and we but few to look
at. Now no disposition swelleth numbers to the eye like
that of squadrons.' So he divided the troops into forty
squadrons, each about a thousand strong under a trusted
leader. These he arranged so that one half formed the
centre, under Abu Obeida. Ten squadrons were assigned
to each wing, of which one was led by Amru, the other by
Yezid. Abu Sofian, now well stricken in years, went about
from troop to troop, and roused their ardour by martial
declamation.

It was soon manifest that the Byzantine captains were Greek army advances,
preparing to deliver a decisive charge. Issuing from their

defences, they advanced in volume, darkening both sides of the plain. A bystander, gazing at the moving field, exclaimed, ' How many the Greeks, how few the Moslems!' ' Nay,' cried Khalid, ' rather " How many the Moslems, how few the Greeks!" for, if ye count aright, numbers wax by the help of the Lord, but wane if He withdraw His face. Would that the Greeks were double what ye see, had I but under me my good Arab!'—for the hoofs of his favourite bay had been worn down by rapid marching from Irac. And still the Greeks kept rolling on in dense columns. The fate of Syria depended on the day.

Moslems advance; tidings from Medina.

As the enemy drew near, Khalid called upon Ikrima with his column, and Cacaa with the veterans from the east, to advance. Just then a messenger from Medina rode up in haste. To the inquiry of men who flocked around, he answered shortly :—' All is well ; reinforcements on the way.' But for the general's ear he had a secret message, and he also handed to him a letter which, hastily glanced at, Khalid slipped into his quiver. Then, unruffled by the startling tidings it contained, and bidding the messenger keep close by him throughout the day, he rode forth to meet Jareja.

Battle of Wacusa on the Yermuk, viii. 13 A.H. Sept., 634 A.D.

The defection of that general was a calamity for the Greeks, but at the first it caused an unexpected issue. Followed by his escort, the traitor rode forth from the Byzantine ranks to meet Khalid. The unexpected advance was at the first mistaken for an attack upon the Moslems; and a Syrian battalion hastened to its support with such energetic charge that the Arab front was broken and thrown into confusion. Ikrima stood firm. He who in the ' days of Ignorance' had measured arms even with the Prophet of the Lord, should he flee before the infidel! ' Who now,' cried he, ' will join me in the covenant of death ?' Four hundred, with his own son, and the hero Dhirar, took the fatal pledge. He charged, and the battalion which had created the surprise, bewildered now at the treachery of Jareja, fell back. The ground thus clear, Khalid ordered the whole line to move on. The Grecians too advanced, and both sides drew the sword.

All day the battle raged. Fortune varied; and the carnage amongst the Moslems, as well as in the enemy's ranks, was great. Ikrima's gallant company, holding their ground firm as a rock, bore the brunt of the day; they were slain or disabled almost to a man. So fierce were the Arabs, that even the women fought wildly in the field.

A.H. 12-
13.

Towards evening the enemy began to falter, and Khalid's quick eye perceived that their horse were declining from the infantry. Thereupon he launched his centre wedge-like between the two, and the cavalry, with nothing behind them but the precipice, made a fierce charge for their lives. The Moslem front opened to let them through, and so they gained the country, never to re-appear. The Arabs then drove down upon the remaining force hemmed in by the surrounding chasm; and thus, pressed right and left, the Byzantine columns were 'toppled over the bank even as a wall is toppled over.' The battle drew on into the night, but opposition was in vain. Those that escaped the sword were hurled in living mass into the yawning gulf. ' One struggling would draw ten others with him, the free as well as chained.' And so, in dire confusion and dismay, the whole multitude perished. The fatal chasm engulfed, we are told, 100,000 men. The Byzantine general and his fellow-captains, unable to bear the sight, sat down, drew their togas around them, and, hiding their faces in despair and shame, awaited thus their fate.

The Moslem victory.

Greeks driven over the chasm.

Morning found the Moslems in silent possession of the plain. They flocked into the Greek entrenchment, and Khalid took possession of Theodoric's pavilion. The camp and its rich equipage yielded a booty of 1,500 pieces to each horseman. More than this, the fearful fate of the army struck such terror into the Byzantine court as well as the people of the land, that the fate of Syria was sealed. The opposition that remained was poor and feeble.

Importance of the victory.

But the victory was purchased at a heavy cost;—three thousand buried on the field, besides a great multitude wounded, and among the fallen many a distinguished name. Of Ikrima's forlorn hope few survived. The famous Dhirar, badly wounded, recovered to signalise himself on other

Heavy loss.

fields. But Ikrima and his son sank under their wounds. In the morning, when near their end, they were both carried to the tent of Khalid. He laid the head of the father on his breast, and of the son upon his lap, tenderly wiped their faces and moistened their lips with water. As they passed away, he kept fondly saying : ' Alas, alas ! the father and the son ; who would have thought of a martyr's death for both !'

But Khalid was no longer in command. The messenger in the field had whispered in his ear the news of Abu Bekr's death ; and the letter slipt into his quiver brought the new Caliph's order that Khalid should deliver up command into the hands of Abu Obeida.

Date of
battle.
The battle was fought about the middle of A.H. 13, that is, towards the end of August, or beginning of September, A.D. 634, little more than two years after the Prophet's death.

Before narrating the sequel of this great victory, we must turn for a little to what was passing elsewhere.

CHAPTER X.

CAMPAIGN IN IRAC—NEED OF REINFORCEMENTS.
MOTHANNA FINDS ABU BEKR ON HIS
DEATH-BED.

FIRST HALF OF 13 A. H.   MARCH–AUGUST, A. D. 634.

BEFORE he left for Syria, Khalid, seeing that, with a Mothanna attacked by the Persians. diminished force, the situation in Irac would be somewhat insecure, sent away the sick with the women and children to their homes in Arabia. On his departure, Mothanna made the best disposition in his power to strengthen the line of defences towards the Persian capital. Fresh dangers threatened. A new prince had succeeded to the throne ; and he thought to expel the invaders by an army under Hormuz 10,000 strong. Mothanna at once called in the outlying garrisons ; but with every help, his force was in numbers much below the Persian. The king, confident of victory, wrote to Mothanna insultingly that ' he was about to drive him away by an army of fowl-men and swine-herds.' Mothanna answered : ' Thou art either a braggart or a liar. But if this be true, then blessed be the Lord that hath reduced thee to such defenders!' Having despatched this reply, he advanced to meet Hormuz. Leaving Hira, the little force crossed the Euphrates and encamped north of the shapeless mounds that mark the site of Babylon. There, some fifty miles from the capital, he chose the battle- Battle of Babylon. Summer, 13 A.H. 634 A.D. ground ; and, placing his two brothers in charge of either wing, himself at the head of the centre, awaited thus the attack of Hormuz. The Persian line was headed by an

A.H. 13. elephant, which threw the Arab ranks into confusion, and for a while paralysed their action. Mothanna, followed by an adventurous band, surrounded the great creature, and brought it to the ground. Deprived of this help, the enemy gave way before the fierce onslaught of the Arabs, who pursued the fugitives to the very gates of Medain. The praises of ' the Hero of the Elephant ' have been handed down in Arab verse.

Mothanna asks Abu Bekr for reinforcements. The king did not long survive this defeat. His son, succeeding him, was killed in a rebellion caused by the attempt to give a princess of the royal blood in marriage to a favourite minister. The princess, saved from dishonour, succeeded to the throne. From a court weakened thus by continual change and treachery, there was little, one might think, to fear, but Mothanna had to guard a frontier of great extent, and for the task his army was inadequate. The inhabitants were at the best indifferent; the Syrian Bedouins distinctly hostile. Victories might be won, but could not be followed up. The position, with so small a force, was full of risk. Accordingly, Mothanna urged upon the Caliph the pressing need of reinforcements. He also pointed out the ease with which they might be raised : ' Remove the embargo from the apostate but now repentant tribes,' he wrote ; 'they will flock to the war, and none more brave or eager. 'Answer being long delayed, Mothanna ventured to Medina, there to urge his suit

Abu Bekr on his death-bed desires Omar to order levy. in person. He found Abu Bekr on his death-bed. The aged Caliph knew that his end was near; but the mind was clear, and he at once perceived the urgency of the appeal. ' Call Omar to me,' he said (for he had already named him his successor) ; and he then addressed him thus :—' Command a levy for Mothanna. Tarry not. If I die, as I may, this day, wait not till the evening ; if I linger on to night, wait not till the morning. Let not sorrow for me divert thee from this service of the Lord. Ye saw what I myself did when the Prophet died (and there could be no greater sorrow for mankind than that); truly if grief had stayed me then from girding my loins in the cause of the Lord and of His Prophet, the Faith had fared badly ; the flame of rebellion had surely kindled in the city. And, list thee,

Omar! when the Lord shall have given victory in Syria, then send back to Irac its army; for they are the proper garrison thereof, and fittest to administer the same.'

Omar was touched by the delicacy of these last words, and the allusion they contained; 'For,' said he, 'Abu Bekr knew that it grieved me when he gave the command to Khalid; therefore he bade me to send back his army to Irac, but forbore to name the name of Khalid, or bid me send him back.' He listened attentively to the dying Caliph's words, and promised to fulfil them.

CHAPTER XI.

DEATH OF ABU BEKR.

AUGUST, A.H. 13. A.D. 634.

Abu Bekr
presides
over pil-
grimage,
xii. 12 A.H.
February,
634
AT the first yearly pilgrimage, Abu Bekr had been hindered by the pressure of rebellion from the journey to Mecca; but the following year he presided at the solemnity himself. As the party entered Mecca, the citizens hastened to tell his father, who, blind from great age, was seated at his door. On his son's approach, the old man arose to greet him. Abu Bekr made the camel on which he rode kneel down at the threshold, and alighting, embraced his father, who shed tears of delight, and kissed him between the eyes. The governor and other great men of Mecca approached and shook the Caliph by the hand. Then they did obeisance to him and to his father also, who said: ' These be our nobles; honour them, my Son, and make much of them.' 'Make much of them,' answered Abu Bekr,—' that I do; but (mindful of his Master's teaching) as for Honour, there is none save that which cometh from the Lord alone.' After bathing, he went forth in pilgrim garb, to kiss the Black stone, and encompass the Holy house. The people crowded round him; and as they made mention of the Prophet, Abu Bekr wept. It was but two years since Mahomet had been amongst them, celebrating the same rites, and how much of danger and deliverance had come to pass in that short space! And so they mourned his loss. At midday, he again went through the ceremonies of the Kaaba; then, sitting down under the

shadow of the Hall of assembly, he commanded the citizens that, if any had complaint to make, he should speak it out. All were silent; so he praised the people and their governor. Then he arose and celebrated the midday prayer. After a little, he bade them all farewell, and departed for Medina.

During the summer, Abu Bekr was busied with rein- forcements for the Syrian campaign. Simple and temperate in habit, he was now, though over three-score years, hale and hearty. In the autumn, bathing incautiously on a cold day, fever laid him low and obliged him to make over the presidency at public prayer to Omar. When the illness had lasted a fortnight, his friends became anxious, and said : ' Shall we send for a physician ? ' ' The Physician hath been to me already,' was the solemn answer. ' And what said he ? ' ' He saith to me, *I am about to do that with thee which I purpose to do.*' They understood his meaning, and were silent. Aware that the end was near, he made preparation for a successor. The choice was fixed on Omar ; but willing to fortify his own conviction by that of others, he first consulted Abd al Rahman, one of the Prophet's foremost councillors, who praised Omar as the fittest man, but withal inclined to be severe.—' Which,' responded the dying Caliph, ' is because he saw me soft and tender-hearted. When himself master, he will forego much of what thou sayest. I have watched him. If I were angry with one, he would intercede in his behalf; if over lenient, then he would be severe.' Othman, too, confirmed the choice. ' What is hidden of Omar,' said he, ' is better than that which doth appear. There is not his equal amongst us.' Talha, on the other hand, expostulated : ' If we have suffered this much from Omar, thou being yet with us, what will it be when thou art gone to thy Lord, there to answer for having left His people to the care of so hard a master ? ' ' Set me up,' cried the Caliph, much excited ; ' seekest thou to frighten me ? I swear that when I meet my Lord, I will say unto Him, " I have appointed as ruler over Thy people him that is the best amongst them." '

Thereupon Abu Bekr called for Othman, and dictated an

ordinance appointing Omar his successor. He fainted while it was being written. Recovering, he bade Othman to read it over. Satisfied now, he praised the Lord; 'for,' said he, 'I saw thee apprehensive lest, if I passed away, the people had been left in doubt.' Upon this, he desired the ordinance to be read in the hearing of the citizens, who had assembled in the court of the Mosque. Omar himself was present, and hushed the noise, that they might hear. Then, desiring to obtain their assent, the dying Caliph bade his wife Asma raise him to the window (for the Caliph's house looked out upon the court); so she bore him, in her tattooed arms, to the window, from whence, with a great effort, he called out: 'Are ye satisfied with him whom I have appointed over you? None of mine own kin, but Omar son of Khattab. Verily I have done my best to choose the fittest. Wherefore, ye will obey him loyally.' The people answered with one voice, 'Yea, we will obey.'

To the end, the mind of Abu Bekr was clear and vigorous. On his last day, he gave audience, as we have seen, to Mothanna, and, grasping the crisis, commanded Omar to raise, with all despatch, a levy for Irac. During his illness one repeated verses from a heathen poet supposed to be appropriate. Abu Bekr was displeased, and said: 'Not so; say rather (quoting from the Coran)—*Then the agony of death shall come in truth. This, O man, is what thou*

soughtest to avoid[1].' His last act was to summon Omar to his bedside, and counsel him at great length to temper severity with mildness. Shortly after, he expired with these words on his lips:—'Lord, let me die a true believer, and make me to join the blessed ones on high!'

Abu Bekr had reigned but two years and three months. According to his express desire, the body was laid out by the loving hands of Asma. He was wound in the clothes in which he died; 'for,' said he, 'new clothes befit the living, but old the mouldering body.' The same Companions that bore the Prophet's bier bore that of Abu Bekr: and they laid him in the same grave, the Caliph's head resting by his Master's shoulder. Omar performed

[1] Sura v. 18.

the funeral service, praying, as was customary, over the
bier. The funeral procession had not far to go ; it had only
to cross the open court of the Sanctuary; for Abu Bekr
died in the house appointed him by Mahomet opposite his
own [1].

During the greater part of his reign, he occupied that Character.
house. For six months, indeed, after Mahomet's death, he life at
continued to live partly as before in Al Sunh, a suburb of Al Sunh.
Upper Medina. There he inhabited a simple dwelling
with the family of the wife whom he married on coming to
Medina, and who shortly after his death gave birth to a
daughter. Every morning he rode or walked to the Mosque,
where Mahomet had lived and ruled, to discharge business
of the day, and to perform the public prayers, Omar presiding in his absence. For the more important service of
Friday, at which an address also was delivered, he stayed
in the early hours at home to dye his hair and beard, and
dress more carefully ; and so did not appear till midday
prayer. Here, as elsewhere, he preserved the severe simplicity of early life, and even fed and milked the household
goats. At the first he continued to maintain himself by
merchandise ; but perceiving that it interfered with the
burdens of State, he consented to forego all other occupation, and to receive a yearly allowance of six thousand
dirhems for household charge.

Finding Al Sunh too distant from the Mosque, where, Removes to
as in the time of Mahomet, public affairs were all transacted, the great
Mosque.
he transferred his residence thither. The exchequer was in
those days but simple. It needed neither guard nor office of
account. The tithes as they came in were given to the poor,
or spent on military equipage and arms; the spoil of war also
was distributed just as received, or on the following morning.
All shared alike, the recent convert and the veteran, male
and female, bond and free. As claimant on the Moslem
treasury, every believing Arab was his brother's equal.
When urged to recognise precedence in the faith as ground of
preference, Abu Bekr would reply, ' That is for the Lord ;
He will fulfil the reward of such, in the world to come.

[1] *Life of Mahomet,* p. 185.

G 2

A.H. 13. These gifts are but an accident of the present life.' After his death, Omar had the treasury opened; they found but a solitary golden piece, slipped out of the bags; so they lifted up their voices and wept, and blessed his memory. The Caliph's conscience troubled him for having taken even what he did by way of stipend from the people's chest; and on his death-bed gave command that certain lands, his private property, should be sold, and a sum equal to all received, refunded.

Mild and gentle.

In disposition Abu Bekr was singularly mild and gentle. Omar used to say there was no man for whom the people would more readily have laid down their life. He had long been called 'the Sighing,' because of his tender-heartedness. He was severe in his treatment of the apostate tribes; but excepting the solitary case in which he committed a brigand to the flames, no act of cruelty stands out against him; and for that he expressed his sorrow. 'It was one of the three things which he would wish undone.' The others were, that he had pardoned Ashath, when he deserved death; and that when Khalid was transferred to Syria, he had not at the same time sent Omar to Irac. 'Then,' said he, 'I should have stretched out mine arms, both the right hand and the left, in the ways of the Lord.'

Wives and family.

Unlike his Master, he contented himself with but few wives. Two he had at Mecca before his conversion. On arrival at Medina, he married the daughter of a Citizen, and, later on, Asma, widow of Jafar, Aly's brother, slain at Muta. By all he left issue. There is no mention of any other wives, nor of any slave-girls in his harem. Of his children, he loved Ayesha best, and, in proof thereof, gave her a property for her own. On his death-bed, troubled at the seeming partiality, he said to her, 'I wish thee, my daughter, to return that property, to be divided with the rest of the inheritance amongst you all, not forgetting the one yet unborn.' His father survived him six months, reaching the great age of ninety-seven.

Simple, diligent, wise, and impartial.

At his court, Abu Bekr maintained the same simple and frugal life as Mahomet. Guards and servitors there were none, nor anything approaching pomp and circumstance.

Diligent in business, he leaned upon Omar as his counsellor,
whose judgment had such weight with him, that he might
have been said to share the government. Abu Bekr never
spared himself, and he personally descended to the minutest
things. Thus, he would sally forth by night to seek for the
destitute and oppressed. Omar found him one night
inquiring into the affairs of a poor blind widow, whom Omar
had himself gone forth to help. The department of justice
was made over to Omar, but for a whole year 'hardly two
suitors came before him.' The seal of State bore the
legend, *God the best of Potentates*. The despatches were
chiefly indited by Aly. Abu Bekr made use also of Zeid
(the amanuensis of the Prophet and compiler of the Coran)
and of Othman, or any other penman at hand. In the choice
of agents for high office or command, he was altogether
free from partiality, wise and discerning in his estimate of
character.

But he had not Omar's strength and decision ; nor was Not so
his sense of justice so keen and stern. This is illustrated in strong as
the matter of the two Khalids. Upon the one, though warned Omar.
by Omar and Aly, he was prevailed to confer a command ;
the disaster in Syria was the consequence. Again, by
refusing to condemn the other Khalid for injustice, cruelty,
and the scandal of marrying Ibn Noweira's widow, he became
responsible for his evil deeds. Yet to this unscrupulous
agent is due, more than to any other, the survival and the
triumph of Islam. But Abu Bekr was not wanting in
firmness when occasion demanded ; for example, the
despatch of Osama's army when Medina lay defenceless,
and all around was dark, showed a boldness and steadfast-
ness of purpose that, more than anything else, helped to roll
back the tide of rebellion and apostasy.

Abu Bekr had no thought of personal aggrandisement. Faith in
Endowed with sovereign and irresponsible power, he used Mahomet,
it simply for the interests of Islam and his people's good. strength.
But the grand secret of his strength was faith in Mahomet.
'Call me not *the Caliph of the Lord*,' he would say, 'I am
but *the Caliph of the Prophet of the Lord*.' The question
with him ever was, What did Mahomet command ? or, What

A.H. 13. now would he have done? From this he never swerved a hair's-breadth. And so it was that he crushed apostasy, and laid secure the foundations of Islam. His reign was short, but, after Mahomet himself, there is no one to whom the Faith is more beholden.

Evidence of Mahomet's sincerity. For this reason, and because his belief in the Prophet is itself a strong evidence of the sincerity of Mahomet himself, I have dwelt at some length upon his life and character. Had Mahomet begun his career a conscious impostor, he never could have won the faith and friendship of a man who was not only sagacious and wise, but throughout his life simple, consistent, and sincere.

CHAPTER XII.

Accession of Omar—Reinforcements for Irac.
Campaign under Abu Obeid and Mothanna.

August to March, 13–14 A.H. 634–5 A.D.

On the morrow after Abu Bekr's death, Omar ascended the pulpit, and addressed the people assembled in the Mosque. 'The Arabs,' he said, 'are like a rebellious camel, and it pertaineth to the driver which way to lead him. By the Lord of the Kaaba! even thus will I guide you in the way that ye should go.'

Omar's accession, vi. 13 A.H. Aug., 634 A.D.

The first act of the new Caliph was to issue the despatch, already mentioned, deposing Khalid. The second was, in fulfilment of Abu Bekr's dying behest, to raise a fresh levy for Mothanna. A standard was accordingly planted in the court of the Mosque, and urgent proclamation made for soldiers to rally round it. Then followed the oath of fealty to Omar, taken by all who were in and around the city. Meanwhile, so great a fear of Persian prowess had fallen on the people, that none responded to the call. Seeing this, Mothanna, still at Medina, harangued them in stirring speech. He told of his victories, the endless plunder, the fair captives, and the fruitful fields of which they had already spoiled the enemy; 'and the Lord,' he added, 'waiteth but to give the rest into your hands.' Inflamed by his discourse, and stung by reproaches from Omar, men began at last to offer. The first to come forward was Abu Obeid, a citizen of Tayif; then, following him, numbers crowded to the

Fresh levies for Irac.

standard. When a thousand were thus gathered, they said to Omar: 'Now choose thee, either from the Coreish or from the men of Medina, one of the chiefest to be commander.' 'That I will not,' replied the Caliph; 'wherein lay the glory of a Companion but in this, that he was the first to rally round the Prophet? But now ye are backward; ye come not to the help of the Lord. Such as be forward to bear the burden, whether light or whether heavy, have the better claim. Verily I will give the command to none

Abu Obeid appointed commander.

other but to him that first came forth.' Then turning to Abu Obeid: 'I appoint thee over this force, because thou wast the first to offer; and in eagerness for battle is the Arab's glory.' With this emphatic declaration, he presented to him the standard; but, at the same time, earnestly enjoined upon him ever to take counsel with the other Companions, and associate them with himself in the conduct of affairs. So the force started for Irac. Now also Omar removed the ban against the employment of the once apostate tribes; and bade Abu Obeid to summon to his standard all, without distinction, who since their apostasy had made a good profession. Mothanna, with lightened heart, hastened back in advance of Abu Obeid, and re-entered Hira after the absence of a month.

Rustem rouses Persia against the invaders.

During this period further changes were transpiring at the unhappy court of Persia. Prince and princess succeeded one another amidst bloodshed and rebellion, till at last a royal lady, Buran, summoned the famous Rustem from Khorasan, and by his aid established herself upon the throne. Proclaimed supreme, the energy of Rustem soon was felt. The nobles rallied round him; great landholders rose against the invaders, and the whole country speedily cast off the Arabian yoke. Two columns were despatched from Medain, one under Jaban to cross the Euphrates and advance on Hira; the other under Narsa to occupy Kaskar on the nearer side. The people flocked to their standard, and the position of the Moslems grew precarious.

Abu Obeid's victory over the

Mothanna called in his forces, still all too few, abandoned Hira to the enemy, and falling back on the desert road to Medina, there awaited Abu Obeid. But he had

some time to wait. Swelled by Bedouin tribes on the A.H. 18-
way, and burdened by their families, it was a month before   14.
he came up. After a few days' repose, Abu Obeid took Persians,
command of the combined force, and, attacking Jaban, put viii. 13 A.H.
him to flight. Then crossing the Euphrates, he surprised 634 A.D.
Narsa, strongly posted by a royal date-grove near Kaskar,
routed his army and took his camp, in which, with much
spoil, was great store of rare dates reserved for royal use.
These were distributed among the army, as common food
for all. With the Fifth, Abu Obeid sent some of them
to Omar : ' Behold,' he wrote, ' the fruit wherewith the Lord
hath fed us, eaten only by the kings of Persia ; wilt thou
see the same with thine own eyes, taste it with thine own
lips, and praise the Lord for His goodness in giving us royal
food to eat ?' The unfortunate Delta, prey to alternate conquest and defeat, again acknowledged Moslem sway. The
neighbouring chiefs brought in their tribute, and, in proof of
loyalty, made a feast of good things for Abu Obeid. He
declined to partake of it, unless shared equally with his
soldiers. A further supply was furnished, and the army
sat down with him to the repast.

Enraged at the defeat, Rustem assembled a still larger Bahman
force under another great warrior, Bahman. The imperial advances
banner of panthers' skins was unfurled, and an array of against
elephants sent with the army. Before this imposing host, Abu Obeid.
the Arabian army again fell back, and, re-crossing the
Euphrates, took up ground on the western bank. Bahman
encamped on the opposite shore. The field of battle was
not far from Babylon, and a bridge of boats spanned the
river. Bahman, in his pride, gave Abu Obeid the option of
crossing unopposed, and thus of choosing either bank for
the impending action. His advisers sought to dissuade him
from quitting their more advantageous ground. But Abu
Obeid made it a point of honour ;—' Shall we fear death
more than they ?' he cried, as he gave the order at once to
cross. They found the ground upon the farther side confined ; and, though they were under 10,000, there was little
room to manœuvre, and nothing but the bridge to fall back
upon. The unwieldy elephants, with jingling bells and bar-

A.H. 13-
14.
baric trappings, spread confusion among the Arab cavalry.
The riders, however, dismounting, went bravely at them,
and tried, with some success, to cut the bands of the litters,
and drive them from the field. Abu Obeid himself singled
out the fiercest, a white elephant with great tusks, and
rushed at it sword in hand. Vainly endeavouring to
reach some vulnerable part, the huge beast caught him
with its trunk, and trampled him to death. Consternation seized the ranks at the horrid spectacle. One after
another, the captains whom Abu Obeid had named to take
command in case of disaster, were slain, and the troops

Battle of
the Bridge.
Abu Obeid
slain and
defeated,
viii. 13 A.H.
Octr.,
634 A.D.
began to waver. Just then a soldier, appalled at the fate
of his leaders, ran to the bridge, and crying,—*Die, as your
chiefs have died, or conquer,*—cut the first boat adrift. Exit
closed, the panic spread. The Moslems, hemmed in, were
driven back upon the river. Many leaped into the deep
swift stream, but few reached the other shore. At this
eventful moment Mothanna rushed to the front. Backed
by a few heroic spirits, among them a Christian chief of the
Beni Tay, he seized the banner, and, planting himself
between the enemy and the bewildered Arabs, called out
that he would hold the ground till all had passed over.
Then he chided the soldier, and commanded the bridge
to be restored. 'Destroy not your ownselves,' he cried ;
'retire in order, and I will defend you.' While thus bravely
holding the Persians at bay, the thrust of a lance imbedded
the rings of his armour in a deep and dangerous wound.
Heedless of it, he stood to his ground, endeavouring to calm
the panic-stricken force. But in vain. The confusion
increased, and before order could be restored, vast numbers
had perished in the river. At last, the bridge restored,
a remnant escaped across ; but 4,000 were swept off by the
flood, left dead upon the field, or borne wounded away.
Of the new levies, some 2,000, stung with remorse, fled from
the terrible field back to Arabia ; and Mothanna, again
assuming the command, was left with only 3,000 of his men.
After the battle, Bahman was on the point of crossing the
river to follow up his victory. Had he done so, it would
have fared badly with Mothanna and the disheartened

remnants still holding their ground on the opposite bank.
But fortunately at the moment, news reached Bahman of a
revolt at Medain; and so, relinquishing his design, he has- Mothanna
tened back to the distracted capital. Mothanna fell back retires with
upon Allis, farther down the river, and fixing head-quarters to Allis.
there, bravely defended his early conquests amongst a people
now not unfriendly to the cause. Jaban, unaware of Bahman's hasty recall, fell into Mothanna's hands, and with his
followers was beheaded. Things, no doubt, looked dark;
but a hero like Mothanna was not one to despair. As on
his first advance, so now he sought to recruit the diminished
ranks from kindred tribes about him; and, before long,
regained a firmer footing.

Omar received with calmness the unhappy tidings. Abu Omar's
Obeid's levies kept on their flight till they reached home; calm recep-
and some from Medina returning thither, covered their faces tidings.
with shame. The Caliph spoke comfortably to them thus:—
'Verily, I am a defence to every believer that faceth the
enemy and misfortune overtaketh him. The Lord have
mercy on Abu Obeid, and be gracious unto him. Had he
survived, and taken refuge on some sandy mound, I surely
would have been his advocate and his defender.' Muadz,
famous as a reciter of the Coran, was among those who fled.
Shortly after, in the course of recitation, he came to the
verse: 'Whosoever in the field shall give his back to the
enemy (excepting again to join in battle), or shall turn aside
unto another party, verily he draweth the wrath of God
upon him; his refuge shall be hell-fire—an evil end!' and
he lifted up his voice and wept. Omar addressed him
kindly:—'Weep not, O Muadz, thou hast not *turned aside
unto another party;* thou hast turned aside to none but
unto me.' Such was the spirit of these Moslem heroes,
even in defeat. The reverse had no effect but to nerve the Summons
Caliph to redoubled effort. The fresh cry for a levy *en* levy.
masse soon resounded over the peninsula. But reinforcements in response would have been too late to help
Mothanna if (fortunately for Islam) earlier succour had
not reached him.

For the previous call was still drawing. Levies, from

A.H. 18-
14.

Numerous
reinforce-
ments join
Mothanna,

all directions, daily reached Medina, eager—now the ban
against apostasy was removed—to show the sincerity of
their repentance, and share in the rewards of victory. Each
band as it came in besought Omar to send them to the
favoured land of Syria. But the late victory on the Yermuk
had made him easy in that direction; and every available
man must now be hurried forward to Irac. A brave levy
raised under the banner of Jarir, urged that their ancestral
relations were all with Syria; but Omar was firm, and, at
last, reconciled them to set out at once for Persia by the
promise that they should have one fourth of the royal Fifth
of booty taken there. The fugitives also hastened back,
seeking to retrieve their honour. But the most remarkable
of all was a Christian tribe of the desert, which, without
detriment to their faith, threw in their lot with Mothanna,
and brought a contingent to his help. Thus, rapidly reinforced, he was soon stronger than ever, and ready for
offensive movement. His troops were massed at first on
the edge of the Arabian desert, near Khaffan. The women
and children (for the practice was now common of carrying with them house and home) were placed in security
at a distance behind; some were even left with friendly
citizens in Hira, although, since the last retreat, the city
had been re-occupied by a Persian satrap. Mothanna had
also a trusty follower in hiding, to give him notice of what
was passing there.

who
advances
against
Persian
army.

From this spy, Mothanna now learned that, matters
having been settled at the Capital, a great army was in
motion against him. Sending an urgent message to Jarir,
now close at hand, to hurry on, he marched forward to
Boweib, on the western branch of the Euphrates, and there,
close by the future site of Kufa, and on ground approached
by a bridge, awaited the enemy. Omar had cautioned
him not again to risk his men by crossing the river before
victory was secure; so he suffered the Persian undisturbed
to defile his troops across the bridge. The Persians advanced in three columns, an elephant, defended by a company
of footmen, at the head of each, and all with tumult and
barbaric din. It was the fast of Ramadhan; but under

special dispensation the troops had been strengthened by a A.H. 13-14.
repast. Mothanna, on his favourite charger (humorously
called *the Rebel,* from its docility in action), rode along the
lines, and exhorted his soldiers to quit them like men :
' Your valour this day shall be a proverb. Be still as death,
and if ye speak one to the other, speak it in a whisper.
None amongst us shall give way this day. I desire not
glory for myself, but glory for you all.' And they answered
him in like words ; for he was beloved by his men.

The signal was the Takbir, or cry, *Great is the Lord,* Battle of
repeated thrice ; then, on the fourth, the general advance. ix. 13 A.H.
But Mothanna had barely shouted the first, when the Nov.,
Persian myrmidons bore down ; and the nearest column 634 A.D.
broke before them. Mothanna pulled his beard in trouble.
Calling an officer, he bade him hasten with this message to
the wavering corps : ' The Ameer sendeth greeting, and
saith, *Ye will not this day shame the Moslems!*' They gave
answer, 'Yea, we shall not!' And, as the broken ranks
closed again in serried line, Mothanna smiled approvingly.
The battle raged long and equally. At last, Mothanna,
seeing that a desperate onset must be made, rode up to the
Christian chief, and said : ' Ye are one blood with us ; come
now, and as I charge, charge ye with me.' The Persian
centre quivered before the fierce onslaught, and as the dust
cleared off it was seen to be giving way. The Moslem
wings, hitherto outflanked, now took heart, and charged.
Then the Persian army fell back, and made for the bridge.
Mothanna was before them. In despair, they turned on
their pursuers. But the fiery zeal of the Arabs, though a
handful in comparison, beat back the forlorn charge. ' The
enemy,' says an eye-witness, 'driven before us, were brought
up by the river, and finding no escape, re-formed, and
charged again. One cried to our leader to hold his banner
back ; *My work,* he answered, *is to move the banner on.* So
forward we drove, and cut them up, not one reaching even
to the river bank.' Mothanna reproached himself afterwards
with having closed the bridge, and caused useless loss of his
men. ' I made a grievous error,' he confessed ; 'follow not
my example herein ; it behoveth us not to close the way

A.H. 13-
14.
_____

Enemy
routed with
terrible
carnage.

against such as may be driven to turn upon us in despair.'
The carnage was almost unparalleled even in the annals of
Islam, and it went on into the night. A hundred warriors
boasted that they slew each ten men to his lance; hence
the battle has been called *The field of Tens.* No engagement left marks wider or more lasting. For ages bones of
the slain bleached the plain; and the men of Kufa had
here, at their very door, lasting proof at once of the prowess
and the mercilessness of the first invaders.

Victory
helped by
Christian
Arabs.

The victory is remarkable as gained in part by the
valour of a Christian tribe. And yet further, the gallantest
feat of the day was achieved by one of another Christian
clan; for a party of Bedouin merchants, with a string of
horses for sale, arriving just as the ranks were being
dressed, threw themselves into the battle on the Arab
side. A youth from amongst them, darting into the centre
of the Persians, slew the leader, and leaping on his richly
caparisoned horse, rode back amidst the plaudits of the
Moslem line, crying, as he passed in triumph: 'I am of the
Beni Taghlib. I am he that hath slain the chief.'

Moslem
loss.

The loss on the Moslem side was considerable. Mothanna
mourned the death of a brother, who, when borne from the
field mortally wounded, cried: ' Exalt your banners, ye
Beni Bekr, and the Lord will exalt you, my men; let not
my fall disturb you !' The Christian chieftain met a similar
fate. Mothanna affectionately tended the last moments of
both—the Christian and the Moslem—an unwonted sight
on these fanatic fields. He performed the funeral service
over his brother and the other fallen Moslems, and said in
his panegyric: ' It assuageth my grief that they stood
stedfast; they yielded not a step; and now here they lie,
the martyrs of Boweib.'

The spoil.

The spoil was great. Immense stores of grain and herds
of cattle were captured; and supplies sent to the families
in their retreat. As the convoy rode up, the women, mistaking it for a hostile raid, rushed out with their wild Arab
scream, and attacked it with stones and staves. The leader
soon made himself known, and praised their courageous
bearing. ' It well becometh the wives of such an army,'

he said, 'thus to defend themselves.' Then he told of the A.H. 13-
14.
victory; 'and lo,' pointing to the stores of grain, 'the first-
fruits thereof!'

The country was now ravished without let or hindrance Country re-
occupied.
to the very walls of Medain. The enemy's garrisons were
driven back; and Lower Mesopotamia and the Delta
occupied anew. Parties scoured the country higher up,
and many rich markets were ransacked. They penetrated
to Baghdad (then a mere village on the Tigris), and even as
far north as Tekrit. Great booty was gathered in these
plundering expeditions, to be divided in the usual way.

Mothanna lived but a few months after his last great
victory. He never entirely recovered from the wounds
received at the battle of the Bridge, and eventually succumbed. His merits have not been recognised as they
deserve. That he did not belong to the nobility of Islam
was the misfortune which kept him in the background.
Jarir, as we shall see, declined to serve under him, a common
Bedouin like himself, not even a Companion of the Prophet,
and complained accordingly to the Caliph. Omar listened
to the appeal; and eventually appointed another commander over both. But before entering on a new chapter
in the Persian war, we must revert to the course of events
in Syria.

The character of Mothanna, however, deserves more than Mothanna.
a passing notice. Among the generals who secured the
triumph of Islam, he was second only to one. Inferior to
Khalid in dash and brilliancy of enterprise, he did not yield
in vigour and strategic skill. Free from the unscrupulous
cruelty of that great leader, we never hear of his using
victory to gratify private ends. It was due alone to the
cool and desperate stand which Mothanna made at the
Bridge, that the Moslem force was not utterly annihilated
there; while the formation so rapidly afterwards of a fresh
army, by which, with the help of Christian tribes (rare mark
of Moslem liberality, in contrast with the bigotry of later
days), a prodigious host was overthrown, showed powers of
administration and generalship far beyond his fellows. The
repeated supersession of Mothanna cost the Caliphate much,

and at one time rendered the survival of Islam in Irac doubtful; but it never affected his loyalty to Omar. The sentiment of the day may have rendered it difficult for the Caliph to place a Bedouin of obscure origin in command of men who, as Companions, had fought under the Prophet's banner. But it is strange that no historian, jealous for the honour of the heroes of Islam, has regretted the supersession of one so distinguished in its annals, or sought to give Mothanna his deserved place as one of the great generals of the world.

CHAPTER XIII.

CAMPAIGN IN SYRIA.—TAKING OF DAMASCUS. BATTLE OF FIHL.

13–14 A.H.   634–635 A.D.

AFTER the terrible slaughter at Wacusa, we left the Moslem army on the banks of the Yermuk, burying their dead, tending the wounded, and dividing the spoil. *Army on the Yermuk.*

The country in which they were now encamped,—'the land beyond Jordan on the east,'—differed from any they had previously known. Away to the south were the pastoral tracts of the Belcaa, and again to the north the pasture lands of Jaulan. Between the two lay the hills and dales of Gilead, with fields of wheat and barley, dotted here and there with clumps of shady oak, olive, and syca-more, and thickets of arbutus, myrtle, and oleander. It was emphatically 'a good land, a land of brooks of water, of fountains and depths that spring out of valleys and hills.' The landscape, diversified with green slopes and glens, is in season gay with carpeting of flowers and melody of birds. From the green expanse above the Yermuk may be descried the blue waters of the Sea of Galilee sparkling in the west, and away in the north the snow-capped peaks of Lebanon and Hermon;—striking contrast to the endless sands and stony plains of Arabia. Not less marked is the contrast with Chaldæa. There the marshy delta displays a tropical luxuriance; while the plains abound with sites of cities that flourished in early cycles of the world, strewn with fragments of pottery and bricks of *Country east of the Jordan.*

H

strange device, mysterious records of bygone kingdoms. Here the pride of the Byzantine empire was yet alive. Skirting the Jordan were busy cities founded by the Romans, that boasted church and theatre and forum. Even naval contests of the naumachia might be witnessed in the land of Gilead. The country was populous and flourishing, inhabited by a mongrel race half Arab, half Syrian, who aspired to the privileges and aped the luxurious habits, without the chivalry or manliness, of the Roman citizen. It was altogether a civilisation forced and of exotic growth. No sooner was the western prop removed than the people returned to their Bedouin life, true sons of the desert ; the chariot and waggon were banished for the camel ; and nothing left of Roman rule but columns and peristyles, causeways and aqueducts, great masses of ruined masonry— which still startle the traveller, as if belonging to another world. But, at the time we write of, the age of so-called civilisation was still dominant there. Such was the beautiful country, strange to the southern Arab both in natural feature and busy urban life, which was now traversed by the Moslem armies, and soon became the beaten highway between Syria and Arabia.

Abu
Obeida
succeeds
Khalid,
viii. 13 A.H.
Sept.,
634 A.D.
Having achieved the victory of Wacusa, Khalid at once delivered to Abu Obeida the despatch from the new Caliph put into his hands at the commencement of the action, and with it surrendered the commission which he held from Abu Bekr. The other leaders were confirmed in their commands by Omar. The affront thus put upon Khalid did not damp his loyalty or zeal. He placed himself forthwith at the disposal of the new Commander, who published with reluctance the order of his deposition. Abu Obeida knew full well the rare military genius of Khalid ; and, himself of a mild and unwarlike turn, was wise and magnanimous enough to ask, and as a rule implicitly to follow, his advice. Khalid, nobly putting aside the grievance, devoted his best energies to the service of the State ; and, his supersession notwithstanding, remained virtually the chief captain of Islam in the west.

The course of Moslem victory in Syria advanced with

little let or hindrance. Persia's struggle was not for a limb, but for life itself. Here it was otherwise. Syria, indeed, contained the holy places and what was dear to the Greeks as the cradle of their faith. But, after all, it was, though fair and sacred, but an outlying province, of which a supine and selfish court could without vital injury afford the loss. There were no such mortal throes in Syria as on the plains of Chaldæa. *A.H. 13–14. Byzantine opposition faint in Syria.*

Leaving a strong detachment on the Yermuk to keep communications open, the invading army resumed its north-ward march. On the way news came that Damascus had been reinforced, and that in Palestine the scattered frag-ments of the defeated army had re-formed in the valley of the Jordan, thus threatening the Moslem rear. The moment was critical, and Abu Obeida wrote for orders to the Caliph. The answer was to strike a decisive blow at Damascus ; the citadel of Syria gained, the rest was sure. Accordingly, a strong column was sent back to hold in check the enemy on the Jordan, while the main body advanced by the military road upon Damascus. *Advance on Damas-cus.*

This city, the most ancient in the world, has, ever since the days of Abraham, survived through all vicissitudes the capital of Syria. The great plain on which it stands is watered by streams issuing from adjoining mountain ranges; and the beautiful groves and rich meadows around have given it (with more reason than the Chaldæan delta) the name of ' garden of the world.' An *entrepôt* of commerce between the east and west, it has been from age to age, with varying fortune, ever rich and populous. The city wall, twenty feet high and fifteen broad, still contains stones of cyclopean size that must have been builded in ages before our era. Over the gates and elsewhere there are turrets for defence, all of venerable structure. The traveller entering at the eastern gate may even in the present day pass through the narrow ' street which is called Straight,' as did St. Paul 1,800 years ago. The Cathedral of St. John the Baptist still rears its great dome, towering above all other buildings ; and besides it there were, at the time of which we write, fifteen churches in the city and its suburbs. Not *Damascus.*

A.H. 13–
14.

long before, Damascus had suffered severely from the alternating fortunes of the Persian war; but had now, in great measure, recovered its prosperity.

Damascus bursts in view of the invading army.

Such was the capital of Syria, ' Queen of Cities,' which, in all its radiance, surrounded far off by lofty mountains tipped with snow, now burst on the gaze of the Arab warriors. Some amongst them may perchance have visited it, trading to the north ; but, as a whole, the army had heard of it only by report; and in beauty, richness, and repose, fancy could hardly have exceeded the scene now stretched before them.

City invested, x. 13 A.H. Dec., 634 A.D.

The Arab force was strong enough to invest the city. Abu Obeida pitched his headquarters on the western plain. Khalid took ground at the eastern entrance, where the gateway was strengthened by the remains of an ancient temple. The other gates were similarly guarded. Battering-rams were drawn up against the walls ; but every attempt at a breach of the massive defences failed. At first the citizens, ignorant of the ardour and persistence inspired by the faith of Mahomet, regarded the attack as a desultory Bedouin raid, like many before it, and looked for succour. The city lies two thousand feet above the sea, and the severity of the cold in spring would, no doubt, drive away the Arab tribes, used to a more genial climate. But months passed, and the host still hung obstinately around the walls. The Emperor, indeed, from Hims, attempted a diversion; but Dzul Kelaa, posted with his Himyar horse to the north of the city, kept the enemy at bay ; and another column covered the siege from annoyance on the side of Palestine. The summer was coming on, and no relief appeared. The Moslems, instead of retiring, pressed their attack with increasing vigour; and the hopes of the Damascenes melted in despair.

Storm and capitulation. Summer, 14 A.H. 635 A.D.

On a certain day the Governor made a feast to the garrison. They ate and drank and, relaxing into merriment, began to quit their posts. Khalid knew of the entertainment, for nothing escaped his vigilance ;—' he neither slept himself, nor suffered others to fall asleep.' And so, reckoning upon the season of revelry, he settled with Abu

Obeida to seize it as the occasion for a general assault. A.H. 13-
The defences on Khalid's side were by far the most formid- 14.
able; the moat was deeper and the walls were stronger.
The garrison at the spot, holding it impregnable, were less
on the alert than elsewhere; and in their negligence Khalid
found his opportunity. In concert with certain daring
spirits, comrades from Irac, he planned an escalade.
Ladders were got in readiness, and scaling ropes with nooses
to catch the projections of the castellated wall. In the
darkness preceding dawn, they stealthily crossed the well-
filled moat upon inflated skins; then, casting up their tackle,
caught the battlements. The way thus silently secured,
others scaled rapidly. Right and left they surprised the
slumbering pickets and put them to the sword. The gate
from within was forced open, and the appointed cry '*Allah
Akbar!*' resounded from the walls to the expectant troops
without. The Byzantine soldiery, panic-struck, fled before
their assailants; and now through the gateway Khalid's
column poured in, slaying and sacking all around. They
had already penetrated near to the centre of the city, when
their progress was brought to an unwelcome end. For on
the other side a very different scene was taking place. The
Governor, seeing that resistance to a general assault was
hopeless, had issued from the western gate, and already
tendered his submission to Abu Obeida. Terms were made
upon the spot, and capitulation signed. The gates were
thrown open, and the Moslem force, unopposed, kept
streaming in from the western camp. As they advanced,
cries of despair and appeals to stay the carnage met the
ears of Abu Obeida, who no sooner heard what had transpired in the eastern quarter than he sent orders to stay the
onslaught. Khalid remonstrated that the city had been
fairly carried by assault, and was at their mercy; but in
vain. Abu Obeida, juster and more clement, pointed to the
treaty, and insisted that its provisions should be fulfilled.
Good faith was the best. as well as fairest policy. The
people were conciliated, and throughout Syria the capitulation of Damascus became the type of surrender.

One half of all property, both money and buildings,

Terms of
capitula-
tion.

private and public, was by this capitulation surrendered to
the conquerors. Besides the taxes levied under Byzantine
rule, the tribute of one golden piece was imposed on every
male adult who did not embrace Islam, and a measure of
corn taken from every field. In this way the Arabs gained,
not only large spoil and permanent revenue, without alienating
the people, and even with a show of moderation, but obtained
also possession of buildings sufficient for their own accommodation and for the conduct of public business. And so
this beautiful city, ' the Eye of the East,' passed from the
grasp of Heraclius into the hands of the Caliph, and became
' the Eden of Islam.'

Church of
St. John
turned into
a Mosque.

The churches of Damascus shared the common fate, and
were equally divided between the Christians and the conquerors. The Cathedral church of St. John the Baptist
was separated into two. In one half the rites of the ancient
faith were still celebrated, and the gospel of Jesus read ; in
the other half, carefully detached, the Coran was recited,
and the service of Islam observed; while from the dome
the Muedzzin proclaimed daily the supremacy of the Arabian prophet. For some 80 years the great Cathedral
continued thus to shelter under one friendly roof the symbols and practice of both religions. But that which was
reasonable in the first beginnings of Islam, became intolerable in the rapid advance of arrogance and bigotry. One
and another of the Caliphs sought, by offer of large payments,
to obtain surrender of the entire Cathedral ; but in vain. At
last Welid, about the 90th year of the Hegira, took the law
into his own hands, and summarily ejected the Christian
worshippers. They complained against the injustice, and
Omar II listened to their reclamation. But the doctors of
Islam declared it impossible to restore to Christian worship
a place once consecrated by the Idzan and prayers of
the Faithful ; and so at last the Christians consented to
take, instead, the churches of the city and its suburbs which
had been confiscated under the equal partition of Abu
Obeida. All that appeared Christian, therefore, in the
style or decoration of the Cathedral church was now removed or defaced. But this wonderful edifice retains to

the present hour marks of the different religions to which it has been devoted. In the massive foundations may be traced signs of a pagan Temple; these are surmounted by the architecture and embellishments of Byzantine art; and over the great entrance may still be deciphered the grand prophecy of the Psalmist, which may yet again be chanted within its walls, running thus :—

> THY KINGDOM, O CHRIST, IS A KINGDOM OF
> ALL AGES; AND THY DOMINION IS FROM
> GENERATION
>   TO GENERATION [1].

All through the siege, Abul Aur guarded the army from attack on the south. He was pitched in the valley of the Jordan, near Fihl (the ancient Pella), which lay on the eastern slope of the valley, a few miles below the Lake of Tiberias. Ruins still mark the site 600 feet above the river bed. The basin of the Jordan is here broad and fertile, and the stream in many places fordable. Opposite Fihl the vale of Jezreel, branching off from the plain of Esdraelon, falls into the Jordan valley. The broad opening is guarded on one side by the mountains of Gilboa, the scene of Saul's disaster, and on the other by the frowning eminence of Beisan, to the walls of which the Philistines fastened his body [2]. Mountain streams run along the valley, making it at times a sodden swamp. It was under the shadow of Beisan that the broken fragments of the Byzantine army took refuge, and were joined there by fresh supports. To secure their front, they dammed the streams, and so turned the whole vale into a marsh. At

---

[1] The following is the inscription, being the Septuagint version of Psalm cxlv. 13, with the addition only of the words, *O Christ:*—

H BACIΛEIA . COΥ X̄Ē BACIΛEIA . ΠANTΩN . TΩN
AIONΩN . KAI . H . ΔECΠOTEIA . COΥ . EN . ΠACH .
ΓENEAI
                          KAI ΓENEAI.

[2] 1 Samuel xxxi. 7, *et seq. Beth-Shan* by contraction *Beisan* (the ancient Scythopolis), once a noble city, the seat of a bishop and site of convents, the birthplace of Cyril and Basilides. Here Alexander had his interview with Cleopatra; and Pompey took it on his way from Damascus to Judæa. Pella has a special interest, as the refuge of the Christians when Titus attacked Judæa. Both Fihl and Beisan at the time of our history were populous and flourishing cities.

A.H. 18-
14.

first the Arabs chafed under the stratagem, for their horses were disabled in the yielding ground. But they soon discovered that the enemy had shut himself in from exit, as well as from attack. Abul Aur securely posted, with his rear open to the fertile vale of the Jordan from which the Greeks were cut off, was content to wait till the summer heat should dry up the quagmire. Meanwhile the enemy, 80,000 strong, was held in check, if not virtually blockaded.

Attacked
by main
army,
Summer,
13 A.H.
634 A.D.,

The summer was well advanced when the Arabs broke up their camp at Damascus. They were eager to attack Heraclius at Hims (Emessa); but Omar forbade advance so long as an army was in the rear. Leaving, therefore, Yezid with a garrison of Yemen levies as governor of Damascus, Abu Obeida hastened back with the rest of his army to Fihl. The province of the Jordan was in command of Shorahbil; to him, therefore, Abu Obeida committed the conduct of the campaign within his jurisdiction. Khalid led the van, Abu Obeida himself commanded one of the wings, Amru the other, and the famous warrior Dhirar (of whom romance tells so many marvellous feats) directed the cavalry. Retracing their steps, they crossed the Yermuk near the hot springs of Omm Keis (the ancient Gadara), and marching down the valley of the Jordan encamped under Fihl. Abul Aur, who had held the enemy so long in check, was now detached towards Tiberias, to prevent diversion from that quarter. The main army, taking his place before Beisan, continued patiently the blockade.

and routed.
Battle of
Fihl.

Reduced to straits, and mistaking inaction for remissness, the Byzantine army thought to fall upon the Arabs unawares. They little knew the vigilance of Shorahbil, who night and day was on the watch. Fetching a circuit, the enemy suddenly appeared on the Moslem flank. They met a warm reception, and there ensued a battle as fierce and obstinate as any that had yet taken place. All day the Greeks held their ground; but by nightfall the impetuosity of the Arabs had its way. The Byzantine captain fell, and his army broke and fled. The greater part were caught in the marsh, and few escaped the sword. ' Thus the Lord wrought for His people,' writes the pious annalist;

' and the morass which we thought a curse was turned into A.H. 13- a blessing.' The plain of Esdraelon again looked down 14. upon another great and sanguinary conflict, which, following on the defeat of Wacusa, decided for many a long century the fate of Syria. The Moslem loss was trifling; the immense booty served but to sharpen the Arab appetite for further victory.

No enemy now was left in sight. Omar, therefore, Khalid's contingent returns to Irac. remembering the behest of Abu Bekr, gave orders that the contingent of Khalid should return to Irac. Its ranks, thinned by hard fighting, were made up to former strength by transfer of volunteers from the Syrian army. Thus recruited, the troops (under command, not now of Khalid, but of Hashim, son of Otba) recrossed the desert just in time to take part in the great battle of Cadesiya. Abu Obeida, with Khalid, having now in view the advance on Hims, returned to Damascus. Shorahbil and Amru were left to reduce to order the province of the Jordan, and their Province of Jordan reduced. task was easy. The fire of patriotism had never burned brightly anywhere in Syria; and what there might have been was now extinguished by the listless cowardice of the Byzantine court. To the Bedouin race, weary of Roman trammels, the prospect of Arabian rule was far from unwelcome. Neither were the Jews and Samaritans unfavourable to the invaders; indeed, we find them not infrequently giving aid and information to the enemy. Even the Christians cared little for the maintenance of a government which by courtly and ecclesiastical intolerance had done its best to alienate their affection.

Beisan for some time held out; but the garrison, when Tiberias and district east of Jordan. their sallies had been repeatedly repulsed, at last capitulated. Tiberias followed, and both obtained the terms of Damascus. Jerash, Maab, Bostra, and other strongholds tendered submission. And so the whole tract from the Jordan eastward to the desert was brought under control, and safely garrisoned.

From Damascus Yezid extended his authority eastward Rest of Syria. as far as Tadmor. Toward the sea, his brother Muavia, meeting little opposition, reduced Sidon and Beyrut, and pushed his conquests to the north of Tripolis. Damascus itself, largely occupied by Arabs, quickly assumed the garb of a Moslem city.   Christian power and influence lingered longer on the coast.   Once and again, from seaward, Byzantine arms retook what the Arabs had gained.   It was not, indeed, until these had begun to cope with the naval forces of the Mediterranean, that their authority was riveted along the littoral, as it had long been in the interior.

Leaving Abu Obeida and Khalid to renew the campaign northward, we return for the present to stirring scenes on the plains of Chaldæa.

CHAPTER XIV.

Yezdegird succeeds to the Throne of Persia.
Battle of Cadesiya.

14 A.H. 635 A.D.

We left Mothanna, after the great battle of Boweib, ^{Yezdegird} ravaging at will the terror-stricken coasts of Chaldæa. But another wave of war was about to sweep over the unhappy land. A new movement was taking place at Medain. The Persian nobles, chafing under the weakness of Rustem and the feeble Queen, began to cry out that these were dragging the empire down to ruin. The ladies of the court assembled to search whether any king might not yet be discovered of the royal blood. And so Yezdegird was found, saved as a child from the massacre of Siroes, now a youth of twenty-one. He was placed upon the throne. Around the young King the nobles rallied loyally, and something was re-kindled of the ancient fire of patriotism. Troops were gathered, Mesopotamia reoccupied, and the cities as far as Hira strongly garrisoned.

The people returned to their allegiance; and Mothanna, finding his diminished army unable to cope with the rising which in the Spring assumed such formidable dimensions, again withdrew behind the Euphrates. He sent an urgent message to Omar of the new perils threatening all around. The danger was met bravely by the Caliph. 'I swear by the Lord,' was his emphatic word, 'that I will smite down the proud princes of Persia with the sword of the princes of Arabia.' It was clearly impossible permanently to hold

(marginal notes)

Yezdegird king of Persia.

End of 13 A.H. Dec., 634 A.D.

Revived military movement.

Mothanna again falls back.

A.H. 14.

Omar orders another levy.

Mesopotamia while it was dominated by the capital of Persia so close at hand. Medain must be taken at any cost, and a great army gathered for the purpose. Orders, more stringent than ever (as already told), went forth for a new and universal levy. 'Haste hither,' was the command sent everywhere, 'hasten speedily!' And forthwith Arabia again resounded with the call to arms. The tribes from the south were to assemble before the Caliph at Medina; those lying northward,—the demand being urgent and time precious,—

Goes on pilgrimage, xii. 13 A.H. Feb., 635 A.D.

were to march straight to Mothanna. So much arranged, Omar set out on the annual pilgrimage to Mecca. This accomplished, he repaired to the camp outside Medina, where the contingents as they came in were marshalled. There it was debated whether the Caliph, as he proposed, and as the people wished, should in person lead the army to Irac. The chief Companions were against it. Defeat, if Omar were on the field, might be fatal; seated at Medina, even at the worst, he could launch column after column on the enemy. Omar yielded; but the readiness he had thus shown to bear in his own person the heat and burden of the day added a new impulse to the movement.

Sad appointed commander in Irac.

Who now should be the leader of this great army in Irac? Mothanna and Jarir were but Bedouin chieftains. None but a peer could take command of the proud tribes now flocking to the field. The matter was at the moment under discussion, when there came a despatch from Sad, the Caliph's lieutenant with the Hawazin, reporting the levy of a thousand good lances from amongst that tribe. 'Here is the man!' cried out the assembly. 'Who?' asked the Caliph. 'None but the *Ravening Lion*[1],' was the answer, —'Sad, the son of Malik.' The choice was sealed by acclamation; and Omar at once summoned Sad. Converted at Mecca while yet a boy, the new Ameer of Irac was now forty years of age. He is known as 'the first who drew blood in Islam,' and was a noted archer in the Prophet's wars[2]. He took rank also as the nephew of Mahomet's mother. Short and dark, with large head and shaggy hair,

---

[1] A play upon the name *Sad*, or 'lion.'
[2] *Life of Mahomet*, pp. 63, 68.

Sad was brave, but not well-favoured. The Caliph gave A.H. 14.
him advice on the momentous issues of the campaign, and
warned him not to trust in his extraction. ' The Lord,' he
said, ' looketh to merit and good works, not to birth ; for in
His sight all men are equal.' Admonished thus, Sad set
out for Irac, with 4,000 men, the first-fruits of the new levy.
According to Arab custom, these marched now with their
wives and children.

As the levies kept coming in, Omar sent them on, one Sad with
after another, to join Sad. The numbers, swelling rapidly, the new
embraced the chivalry of all Arabia. Toleiha, the *quondam* marches
prophet, now an exemplary believer, and Amr ibn Made- to Irac.
kerib, went in command of their respective tribes ; and
Omar wrote that each alone was worth a thousand men.
Ashath, also, the apostate rebel of the south, now joined
the army with a column of his tribe. In short, Omar ' left
not a single person of any note or dignity in the land,
whether warrior, poet, orator, or chieftain, nor any man
possessed of horse or weapons, but he sent him off to Irac.'
Thus reinforced, Sad found himself at the head of 20,000
men ; so that, with the column now on its way from Syria,
the numbers were over 30,000—by far the largest force yet
mustered by the Arabs on the plains of Chaldæa. The
new levies, with the veterans of Mothanna, drew together
at Sheraf, on the borders of the desert, fifteen or twenty
miles south of Hira.

Before Sad reached the appointed rendezvous, Mothanna Death of
had passed away. His brother Moanna was just returning Mothanna,
from a mission to the Beni Bekr, whom the Court of Persia ii. 14 A.H.
were endeavouring to gain over. He went out to meet Sad April, 635.
with intelligence of his having frustrated the attempt, as well
as with the sad news of his brother's death. He delivered
also Mothanna's dying message to the new commander,
advising that the Arabs should hold to their ground on the
confines of the desert. ' Fight there the enemy,' was his
last behest ;—' Ye will be the victors ; and, even if worsted,
ye will have the friendly desert wastes behind : there the
Persians cannot enter, and from thence ye will again return
to the attack.' Sad, as he received the message, blessed

A.H. 14.   the memory of the great general. He also made the be-
⎯⎯⎯ reaved family his special care ; and, the more effectually to
discharge the trust, in true Arab fashion, took to wife his
widow Selma.

Sad mar-
shalls his   The army was marshalled by Sad anew. Companies
troops, were formed of ten, each under a selected leader. Warriors
of note were appointed to bear the standards. Columns
and squadrons were made up by clans and tribes ; and thus
by clans and tribes they marched, and also went into the
field of battle. Departments also were established for the
several duties incident to military service. The chief commands were given to veterans who had fought under the
Prophet's banner ; for in this army there were no fewer
than 1,400 Companions, of whom ninety-nine had fought
at Bedr. Following Mothanna's counsel, confirmed by
Omar, Sad marched slowly to Odzeib, still keeping to
the border of the desert. There he left the women and
children protected by a party of horse, and advanced to
and en-   Cadesiya, a great plain washed on its farther side by the
camps at
Cadesiya, inland channel of the Euphrates already described, and
Summer, bounded on the west by the Trench of Sapor (in those days
14 A.H. a running stream), with the desert beyond. The plain
was traversed by the highway from Arabia, which here
crossed the river on a bridge of boats leading to Hira, and
thence across the peninsula to Medain. Such was the
field of battle which was shortly to settle the fate of Persia.
Sad, keeping still to the western bank, fixed his head-
quarters at Codeis, a small fortress overlooking the stream
and a little way below the bridge. Here he encamped and
waited patiently the movements of his enemy.

The King,   Rustem would have played the same waiting game as
impatient,
orders Sad, had not the King become impatient. The Arabs
advance. were making continual raids across the river into Mesopotamia. The castles of the nobles were attacked, and their
grounds laid waste. A marriage procession was captured
near to Hira, and the bride, a satrap's daughter, carried
with her maids and trousseau into the Moslem camp. The
spring passed away, and the summer came ; but with it no
relief. Herds were driven from the pasture-lands, and

frequent forays served at once to furnish the Moslem army
with food, and punish their faithless allies. The people
grew clamorous ; and the great landlords at last made it
known that if help were delayed, they must go over to
the enemy. Moved by their cries, Yezdegird turned a deaf
ear to Rustem, and insisted on immediate advance.

Meanwhile, Sad kept up constant communications with   Sad gives
Omar. When asked for a description of the camp,—'Cade-   Omar description of
siya,' he told the Caliph, 'lay between the Trench of Sapor   field.
and the river ; in front was the deep stream, which on the
left meandered through a verdant vale downwards from the
town of Hira ; a canal led in like direction to the lake of
Najaf, and on its margin stood the palace of Khawarnac.
His right was guarded by an impassable swamp, and his
rear rested on the desert.' Omar, satisfied with the report,
enjoined vigilance and patience. But first, he said, Yezdegird must be summoned to embrace the Faith at the peril
of his kingdom. With this commission, twenty warriors of
commanding mien crossed the plain and presented themselves at the gates of Medain. As they were led to the   Deputation
royal presence, the rabble crowded round, and jeered at the   summons Yezdegird
rough habit of the Arabs, clad in striped stuff, and armed   to embrace
with rude weapons of the desert,—contrasting strangely with   Islam.
the courtly splendour of the regal city. 'Look!' they cried,
mocking, 'look at the woman's distaff,'—a Bedouin bow
slung over the shoulder,—little thinking of the havoc it was
soon to make amongst their crowded ranks. As the Chiefs
entered the precincts, the prancing and champing of the
beautiful steeds, and the wild bearing of the stalwart riders,
struck awe into the heart of the King and effeminate
nobles. Yezdegird demanded, through an interpreter,
wherefore, thus unprovoked, they dared invade his
kingdom. One after another the Arabian spokesmen
told him of the Prophet who had wrought a mighty
change in their land, and of the blessings and obligations
of Islam. 'Embrace the Faith,' they said, 'and thou shalt
be even as we ; or, if thou wilt, pay tribute, and come under
our protection ; which things if thou refuse, the days of thy
kingdom are numbered.' The king replied contemptuously:

A.H. 14. 'Ye are naught, ye are naught! hungry adventurers from
a naked land; come, I will give you a morsel, and ye shall
depart full and content.' The Arabs replied in strong but
modest words. 'Thou speakest truth; we are but poor
and hungry; yet will the Lord enrich and satisfy us; hast
thou chosen the sword? then between us shall the sword
decide.' The King's wrath was kindled. 'If it were not
that ye are ambassadors, ye should have been put to death,
all of you. Bring hither a clod of earth, and let the
mightiest among them bear it as a burden from out the
city gates.' The Arabs embraced the happy augury. A
stalwart horseman forthwith seized the load, mounted his
charger, and bearing it, rode away. Rustem coming up just
then, the King told him of the affront he had put upon the
simple Arabs. 'Simple!' cried Rustem, 'it is thou that art
simple;' and he sent in haste to get the burden back: but
the horseman was already out of sight. Hastening to
Cadesiya, he cast the clod before his chief, and exclaimed,
'Rejoice, O Sad! for, lo, the Lord hath given thee of the
soil of Persia!'

Rustem with great army advances slowly,
Rustem could no longer delay. Elephants and men had
been gathered from every quarter to swell the host, now
120,000 strong. Yet, notwithstanding, he marched slowly
and unwillingly. The auguries, we are told, boded some
great disaster. But he cherished the hope that the Arabs,
pinched in their supplies, would break up suddenly and
disappear; or that, wearied with suspense, they might
be drawn from their strong position across the river. After
great delay upon the road, he crossed the Euphrates below
Babylon. Advancing on Hira, he chided the people for
and encamps opposite Arabs, ix. 14 A.H. Oct., 635 A.D.
siding with the Arabs; but they replied that, deserted by
the King, they had no resource but to bow before the invaders. At last, having whiled away many weeks, he came
within sight of the Moslem force, and pitched his camp on
the opposite bank of the river.

Sad restrains his army.
During this long period of inaction, the impatience of
the Arabs was checked by the strong hand of Sad, to
whom as lieutenant of the Caliph they were bound to yield
implicit obedience. Excepting raids and reconnoitring

expeditions nothing was attempted. Some of these, how- A.H. 14.
ever, were sufficiently exciting. Toleiha, the *quondam*
prophet, entered alone the enemy's camp by night, and
carried off three horses. Hotly chased, he slew his pursuers
one after another; and single-handed carried off the last,
who embraced Islam, and thereafter fought faithfully by his
captor's side. As the enemy drew near, the Moslem host
lay couched like the tiger in its lair, ready for the fatal
spring.

The armies at last now face to face, Rustem had no Rustem gets three days' truce.
more excuse for putting off the decisive day. On the
morning after his arrival he rode along the river bank to
reconnoitre; and, standing on an eminence by the bridge,
sent for the Moslem officer guarding the passage. A
colloquy ensued; and Sad consented that three of his
captains should go to the Persian camp, and there explain
their demands to Rustem. One after another, these presented themselves. Each held the same language: *Islam*,
Tribute, or the *Sword*. Rustem, now contemptuous in his
abuse, now cowering under the fierce words of the envoys,
and scared by dreams and auguries, demanded time to consider. Three days' grace, they replied, was the limit
allowed by their Prophet; and that was given.

When the term was over, Rustem sent to inquire whether Throws dam across river,
he or they should cross for battle. Strongly pitched, as we
have seen, Sad had no thought of moving, and bade the
Persian cross as best he might. Rustem advanced, but
passage was denied. All night the Arabs watched the
bridge. But Rustem had another scheme; he meant to
cross the river by a dam. During the night his myrmidons
cast fascines and earth into the channel, and morning light
discovered a causeway over which it was possible to pass.

At early morn, Rustem, clad in helmet and double suit and crosses to field of battle.
of mail, leaped gaily on his horse. 'By the morrow we
shall have beaten them small,' he cried; but apart with his
familiars he confessed that celestial omens were against him.
And, indeed, previous mishaps, and the brave bearing of the
Arab chiefs, were sufficient, astrology apart, to inspire
grave forebodings. Crossing the dam unopposed, he

I

A.H. 14. marshalled his great host on the western bank, with its
centre facing the fortress of Codeis. Of thirty war elephants
on the field, eighteen supported the centre, the remainder
being divided between the wings [1]. On a canopied golden
throne by the river side, Rustem watched the issue of the
day. Messengers, posted within earshot of each other
across the plain to Medain, shouted continually the latest
news, and kept Yezdegird informed of all that passed.

Sad, disabled by illness, marshalls army from ramparts of Codeis. As the Persians began to cross, the advanced guard of
the Arabs fell back on Codeis, beneath which the main
body was drawn up. On its ramparts, Sad, disabled by
blains and boils, lay stretched upon a litter ; from whence
casting down his orders inscribed on scraps of paper, he
guided thus the movements of the day. The troops,
unused to see their leader in a place of safety, murmured ;
and verses lampooning him passed round the camp. That
he, the archer of renown, the ' first to shed blood in Islam,'
should be thus aspersed was insupportable, and Sad had
the ringleaders imprisoned in the fortress. He then descended, and discovered to the troops the grievous malady
which rendered it impossible for him even to sit upright,
much less to mount his horse. They accepted his excuse ;
for no man could doubt his bravery; but still a certain
feeling of discontent survived. Resuming his couch, he
harangued the army from the battlements, and then sent
his generals, with the orators and poets of the force, along
the ranks with stirring words to rouse their martial zeal.

Warlike texts recited before the Moslem host. At the head of every column was recited the revelation
of the thousand angels fighting on the Prophet's side, together with such texts as these :—*Stir up the Faithful unto*
battle. If there be twenty steadfast among you, they shall
put to flight two hundred, and a hundred shall put to flight
a thousand. The Lord will cast terror into the hearts of
the Infidels. Beware that ye turn not your back in battle ;
verily he that turneth his back shall draw down upon him

---

[1] These were distinct from the riding elephants of the court and nobles, and
must all have been imported from India. The elephant was not used by the
Assyrians in war. It rarely appears in their mural representations, and only
under peaceful associations.

the wrath of God. His abode shall be Hell-fire. The A.H. 14.
mention of the day of *Decision* at Bedr, with the Divine
command to fight, never failed to fire the souls of the
Moslem host; and here we are told, that upon the recital
'the heart of the people was refreshed, and their eyes
lightened, and they realized the divine peace that followeth
thereupon [1].'

The word passed round, that till midday prayer no one
should stir. The Commander-in-Chief would give the first
signal by the Takbir, or war-cry, ALLAH AKBAR, *Great
is the Lord!* and the host would take up the shout three
successive times from him. At the second and third shout,
they were to gird their weapons on and make their horses
ready. At the fourth, the ranks were to rush in one body
forward with the watch-word, *Our help is from the Lord!*
The order was deranged by the enemy, who, hearing the
first shout, advanced at once; whereupon impatient warriors
from the Moslem front stepped out, and challenging to single
combat, did prodigies of valour. The heroic feats of Bedr
were re-enacted on the field, and the spoil, stripped from the
fallen champions, was beyond description rich. Thus Amr
ibn Madekerib carried off triumphantly the bracelets and
jewelled girdle of a princely victim. Another, shouting
gaily the praises of his mistress [2], closed with Hormuz,
' a prince of the Gate,' and bore him with his diadem captive
to Sad. A leader of the Beni Temim, singing like verses,
pursued his adversary through the enemy's ranks; there
he seized a mule-driver, and carried him with his laden
beast to the Moslem lines; it was the king's baker with a
load of royal viands. More remarkable still is the story of
Abu Mihjan. A ringleader in the detraction of Sad, his
offence was aggravated by drunkenness. Bound a prisoner
in the fort, under charge of Selma, the general's wife, he

Margin notes: Battle of Cadesiya, ix. 14 A.H. Nov., 635. First day; called *Armath.* Abu Mihjan.

---

[1] Same word as *Shechina*, divine influence overshadowing the heart: Suras
viii and xlviii. The practice of reciting such Suras or portions of them
before battle has been handed down to the present day.

[2] His song, of the ordinary type, ran thus:—

The maid, with hanging tresses, milk-white breast and fingers tapering,
Knoweth full well the hero who will lay the warriors low.

was seized by an irrepressible ardour to join the battle. At
his earnest entreaty, and under pledge of early return, the
lady set him free, and mounted him on her husband's white
mare.   An unknown figure, he dashed now into the enemy's
host, and now in circuits round it, performing marvels of
bravery.   Some thought it might be the chief of the Syrian
contingent expected that day.   Others opined that it was
Al Khizr, precursor of the angelic band.   But Sad said,
'If it were not that Abu Mihjan is safe in durance under
Selma's care, I could swear it were he, and the mare my
own.'   According to promise, the hero, satisfied with his
exploits, returned to Selma, who reimposed his fetters as
before, and shortly after secured his release [1].   Now the
elephants bore down upon the Bedouin lines.   The brunt of
the onset fell upon the Beni Bajila.   The huge beasts swaying to and fro, 'their *howdas*, manned with warriors and
banners, like moving castles,' affrighted the Arab horses,
which broke away at the horrid sight.   The Beni Asad
diverted the attack upon themselves, and in the heroic act
left four hundred dead upon the field.   Then the elephants
attacked the wings, spreading consternation all around ; and
the enemy, profiting by the confusion, pressed forward.
The position was critical ; and Sad, as a last resource, bade
Asim rid them from the danger at whatever cost.   At once
that gallant chief chose a band of archers and of agile
skirmishers, who, drawing near, picked their riders from off
the elephants, and boldly cut the girths.   The howdas fell,
and the great beasts, with none to guide them, fled.   Thus
relieved, the Arabs regained their ground.   But the shades
of darkness were falling, and both armies retired for the
night.

*The
elephants.*

*Sad up-
braided by
his wife.*
          The Moslem force was downcast.   The uncertain issue

---

[1] He confessed to Selma that in his cups he had been singing these verses :—

'Bury me when I die by the roots of the vine ;
   The moisture thereof will distil into my bones ;
Bury me not in the open plain, for then I much fear
   That no more again shall I taste the flavour of the grape.'

But he pledged his word to her that he would not again indulge in drinking,
nor abuse Ameer.   Selma then obtained his release, and he joined his comrades
on the last great day.

added point to the invectives against Sad, and, what was
still harder for him to bear, the taunts of Selma. During
the day, as seated by her lord, they watched from the
ramparts the deadly conflict, she exclaimed, 'O for an hour
of Mothanna! Alas, alas, there is no Mothanna this day!'
Stung by the words, Sad struck her on the face, and pointing to Asim and his band, said, 'What of Mothanna?
Was he anything compared with these?' 'Jealousy and
cowardice!' cried the high-spirited dame, faithful to her
first husband's memory. 'Not so,' said Sad, somewhat
softened; 'I swear that no man will this day excuse me if
thou dost not, who seest in what plight I lie.' The people
sided with the lady ; but Sad was no coward, and he lived
the contumely down.

The morning was occupied with the wounded and the Second day;
dead ; and the day drew on before fighting recommenced. called
Aghwath.
Just then the first column of the contingent sent back from Return of
Syria came in view. It was led by Cacaa, who, leaving first Syrian
brigade.
Hashim to bring up the main body of five thousand on
the following day, hurried forward with a thousand men.
By skilful disposition Cacaa magnified his force, in the eyes
both of friend and foe. He arranged his men in squadrons
of a hundred, each at a little distance behind the other.
Advancing, he saluted Sad and his comrades, and bade
them joy of the coming help. Then calling on the rest to
follow, he at once rode forth to defy the enemy. The hero
of *the Bridge* accepted the challenge. Cacaa recognised
his foe; and crying out, 'Now will I avenge Abu Obeid
and those that perished at the Bridge,' rushed on his man
and cut him to the ground. As each squadron came up, it
charged with all the appearance of a fresh and independent
force across the plain in sight of both armies, and
shouted the Takbir, which was answered by the same
ringing cheer, *Allah Akbar*, from the Moslem line. The
spirits of the Arabs rose. They forgot the disasters of
yesterday ; and by so much the heart of the Persians sank,
who saw their heroes slain, one after another, at the hands
of Cacaa and his fellows. They had no elephants this day,
for the gear was not yet repaired. Pressed on all sides,

A.H. 14. their horse gave way, and Rustem was only saved by a
desperate rally. But the Persian infantry stood their
ground, and the day closed, the issue still trembling in the
balance. The fighting was severe and the carnage great.
Two thousand Moslems lay dead or wounded on the field,
and ten thousand Persians. All night through, the Arabs
kept shouting the names and lineage of their several tribes.
There was shouting, too, in the Persian camp. And so,
encouraging themselves, each side awaited the final struggle.

Third day; On the third morning, the army was engaged in the
called
Ghimas. mournful task of removing their fallen comrades from the
field. The space of a mile between the two lines was
strewn with them. The wounded were made over to the
women to nurse, if perchance they might survive—or
rather, in the language of Islam—'until the Lord should
decide whether to grant, or to withhold, the crown of
martyrdom.' The dead were borne to Odzeib, a valley in the
rear, where the women and children hastily dug graves in
the sandy soil. The wounded, too, were carried thither.
For the suffering sick it was a weary way under the burning sun. A solitary palm-tree stood on the road, and
under its welcome shade they were for a moment laid.
Its memory is consecrated in such plaintive verse as this :—

' Hail to the grateful palm waving between Cadesiya and Odzeib.
Around thee grow the wild sprigs of camomile and hyssop.
May the dew and the shower refresh thy leaves for evermore,
And let there never be a palm tree wanting in thy dry and heated plain !'

Fighting A day and a night of unceasing conflict were still before
resumed:
Syrian con- the combatants. The spirit of the Persians, whose dead
tingent lay unburied on the field, flagged at the disasters of the
comes up. preceding day. But much was looked for from the elephants, which, now refitted, appeared upon the field, each
protected by a company of horse and foot. The battle
was about to open, when suddenly Hashim came in sight
with the main body of his Syrian contingent. Sweeping
across the plain, he charged right into the enemy, pierced
their ranks, and reaching the river bank, turned and rode
triumphantly back, amidst shouts of welcome. The fighting
was again severe, and the day balanced by alternate victory

and repulse. Yezdegird, alive to the crisis, sent his body- A.H. 14.
guard into the field. The elephants were the terror of the
Arabs, and again threatened to paralyse their efforts. In
this emergency, Sad had recourse to Cacaa, who was achieving marvels, and had already slain thirty Persians in single
combat; so that the annalists gratefully acknowledge that
' had it not been for what the Lord put it into the heart of
Cacaa to do, we surely had been that day worsted.' Sad
now learned that the eye and trunk were the only vulnerable parts of the elephant: 'Aim at these,' he said, 'and
we shall be rid of this calamity.' So Cacaa with his brother
Asim and a band of followers issued on the perilous enterprise. There were two great elephants, the leaders of the The ele-
herd. Dismounting, Cacaa boldly advanced, and into the phants put
eye of one, the 'great White elephant,' he thrust his lance. to flight.
Smarting at the pain, it shook fearfully its head, threw the
mahout to the ground, and swaying its trunk to and fro,
hurled Cacaa to a distance. The other fared still worse,
for they pierced both its eyes, and slashed its trunk. Uttering a shrill scream of agony, the blinded and maddened
creature darted forward on the Arab ranks. Shouts and
lances drove it back upon the Persians. Thus kept rushing
wildly to and fro between the armies, and followed at last by
the other elephants, it charged right into the Persian line;
and so the whole herd of huge animals,—their trunks aloft,
trumpeting as they rushed, and trampling all before them,—
plunged into the river and disappeared on the farther
shore. For the moment the din of war was hushed as
both lines gazed at the portentous sight. But soon the
battle was resumed, and they fought on till darkness again
closed on the combatants with the issue still in doubt.

The third night brought rest to neither side. It was The Night
a struggle for life. At first there was a pause, as the of Clan-
light faded away; and Sad, fearing lest the vast host gour: fight
should overlap his rear, sent parties to watch the fords. ing.
There had as yet been hardly time for even momentary
repose when, early in the night, it occurred to some of the
Arab leaders to rally their tribes with the view of harassing
the enemy. The movement, made at the first without

A.H. 14. Sad's cognisance, drew on a general engagement in the
dark.   The screams of the combatants and din of arms
made *The Night of Clangour*[1], as it is called, without parallel
in the annals of Islam.   It could only be compared to 'the
clang of a blacksmith's forge.'   Sad betook himself to
prayer, for no sure tidings reached him all night through.
Morning broke on the two hosts, worn and weary.   Then
arose Cacaa, crying out that one more vigorous charge must
turn the tide, 'for victory is ever his that persevereth to
the end.'   Four-and-twenty hours long the Arabs had
fought unceasingly.   And now they issued with the freshness

Persians
routed and
Rustem
slain.
and alacrity of a new attack.   The Persian wings began to
waver.   A fierce onslaught shook their centre, which opened
and laid bare the bank with Rustem on his throne.   Tempestuous wind arose, and the canopy, no longer guarded,
was blown into the river.   The wretched prince had barely
time to fly and crouch beneath a sumpter mule.   The
chance blow of a passer-by brought down the pack and
crushed the prince's back.   He crawled into the river ; but
was recognised by a soldier, who drew him out and slew
him, and then mounting the throne, loudly proclaimed his
end.

Destruc-
tion of Per-
sian host.
No sooner was their leader slain, than rout and slaughter
of the Persian host began.   Some of the columns succeeded
in passing the dam ; but it was soon cut (probably to prevent pursuit), and swept away with a multitude by the pent-
up stream.   To the right and left, up the river bank and
down, the Mussulmans chased the fugitives relentlessly.
The plain, far and wide, was strewn with dead.   The fugitive
multitude, hunted into the fens and marshes, were everywhere put mercilessly to the sword.   But the army was too
exhausted to carry the pursuit far off.

Moslem
loss.
The Mussulman loss far exceeded that of any previous
engagement.   In the final conflict 6,000 fell, besides 2,500

---

[1] *Harir.* Each day had its name, as given in margin. The first and third
have no apparent meaning, perhaps names of places.   The second may refer to
the 'succour' brought by the Syrian contingent.   See C. de Perceval, vol. iii.
p. 481.   Gibbon (ch. li.) ignores the first day, and names the other three, as
Succour, Concussion, and Barking.

previously. No sooner was the battle ended, than the
women and children, with clubs and pitchers of water,
issued forth on a double mission of mercy and of vengeance.
Every fallen Mussulman, still warm and breathing, they
gently raised and wetted his lips with water. But towards
the wounded Persians they knew no mercy ; for them they
had another errand—to raise their clubs and give the *coup
de grâce*. Thus had Islam extinguished pity, and implanted
in the breasts of women, and even of little children, savage
and cold-blooded cruelty.

The spoil was great beyond all parallel, both in amount Vastness
and costliness. Each soldier had six thousand pieces, of booty.
besides the special gifts for veterans and such as showed
extraordinary valour. The jewels stripped from Rustem's
body were worth 70,000 pieces, although its most costly
portion, the tiara, had been swept away. The great banner of the empire was captured on the field, made of
panthers' skins, and so richly garnished with gems as to
be valued at 100,000 pieces. Thus did the needy Arabs
revel in the treasures of the East, the preciousness of which
exceeded almost their power to comprehend.

For the enemy, the defeat was fateful and decisive. Importance
Little more than thirty months had passed since Khalid of victory.
set foot in Irac; and already that empire, which fifteen
years before had humbled the Byzantine arms, ravaged
Syria, and encamped triumphantly on the Bosphorus,
crumbled under the blows of an enemy whose strength
never exceeded thirty or forty thousand Arabs rudely
armed. The battle of Cadesiya reveals the secret. On
one side there was lukewarm, servile following ; on the
other, an indomitable spirit, which after long and weary
hours of fighting nerved the Moslems for the final charge.
The vast host, on which the last efforts of Persia had been
lavished, was totally discomfited ; and, though broken
columns escaped across the river, the military power of
the empire never again gathered into formidable and
dangerous shape. The country far and wide was terror-
struck. The Bedouins on either side of the Euphrates
hesitated no longer. Many of them, though Christian, had

fought in the Moslem ranks. These came to Sad and said: 'The tribes which at the first embraced Islam were wiser than we. Now that Rustem hath been slain, we will accept the new belief.' And so, many of them came over and made profession of the faith.

Tidings, how received by Omar.

The battle had been so long impending, and the preparations on so grand a scale, that the issue was watched all over the country, 'from Odzeib away south to Aden, and from Obolla across to Jerusalem,' as about to decide the fate of Islam. The Caliph used to issue forth alone from the gates of Medina early in the morning, if perchance he might meet some messenger from the field. At last a camel-rider arrived outside the city, who to Omar's question replied shortly, 'The Lord hath discomfited the Persian host.' Unrecognised, Omar followed him on foot, and gleaned the outline of the great battle. Entering Medina, the people crowded round the Caliph, and, saluting, wished him joy of the triumph. The courier, abashed, cried out, 'O Commander of the Faithful, why didst thou not tell me?' 'It is well, my brother,' was the Caliph's simple answer. Such was the unpretending mien of one who at that moment was greater than either the Kaiser or the Chosroes.

CHAPTER XV.

EVENTS FOLLOWING THE BATTLE OF CADESIYA.
CAPTURE OF MEDAIN.

15–16 A.H.   636–7 A.D.

By desire of the Caliph, Sad paused for a while to let the weary troops refit. Fragments of the defeated host escaped in the direction of Babylon, and rallied there. After two months' rest, Sad, now recovered from sickness, advanced to attack them. On the march he reentered Hira. It was the third time the unfortunate city had been taken. Punishment for the last helpless defection, was the doubling of its tribute. Soon supplanted by Kufa, a few miles distant, the once royal city of Hira speedily dwindled into insignificance. But the neighbouring palace of Khawarnac, beautiful residence of a bygone dynasty, was still left standing by the Lake of Najaf, and was sometimes visited as a country seat by the Caliphs and their court in after days. *Sad reoccupies Hira, End of 14 A.H. Jan., 636 A.D.*

The scattered Persian troops rallied first at the Tower of Babel, and then, recrossing the Euphrates, under the great mound of Babylon. Driven from thence, they fell back upon the Tigris. Sad pitched a standing camp at Babylon, from whence he cleared the plain of Dura, fifty miles broad from the Euphrates to the Tigris. The territorial chiefs from all sides now came in, some as converts, some as tributaries ; and throughout the tract between the two rivers Moslem rule again became supreme. Several months passed ; and at last, in the summer, Sad found *Plain of Dura cleared.*

A.H. 15–
16.
himself able, with the full consent of Omar, now in the
second year of his reign, to advance upon Medain.

Medain,
capital of
Persia.
The royal city was built on both banks of the Tigris,
at a sharp double bend of the river, fifteen miles below
the modern Baghdad. Seleucia, on the right bank, was
the seat of the Alexandrian conquerors. On the opposite
shore had grown up Ctesiphon, residence of the Persian
monarchs. The combined city had for ages superseded
Babylon as the capital of Chaldæa. Repeatedly taken by
the Romans, it was now great and prosperous, but helplessly torn by intrigue and enervated by luxury. The
main quarter, with its royal palaces, was on the eastern
side, where the noble arch, the *Tak i Kesra*, still arrests
the traveller's eye as he sails down the Tigris. Sad now
directed his march to the suburb on the nearer side. On
the way he was attacked by the Queen-mother. Animated
by the ancient spirit of her race, and with a great oath
that so long as the dynasty survived the empire was
invincible, she took the field with an army commanded

Queen-
mother
discom-
fited.
by a veteran general, 'the lion of Chosroes.' She was
utterly discomfited, and her champion slain by the hand
of Hashim.

Sad then marched forward ; and, drawing a lesson from
the vainglorious boast of the vanquished princess, publicly
recited before the assembled troops this passage from the
Sacred text :—

'Did ye not swear aforetime that ye would never pass away? Yet ye inhabited the dwellings of a people that had dealt unjustly by their own souls ;
and ye saw how We dealt with them. We made them a warning and example
unto you.'—(*Sura* xiv. *v.* 44.)

Siege laid
to western
quarter.
Summer.
15 A.H.
636 A.D.
In this spirit, they came upon the river; and lo! the
famous Iwan, with its great hall of white marble, stood
close before them on the opposite shore. ' Good heavens! '
exclaimed Sad, dazzled at the sight; ' *Allah Akbar!* What
is this but the White pavilion of Chosroes! Now hath the
Lord fulfilled the promise which He made unto His Prophet.'
And each company shouted *Allah Akbar!* ' Great is the
Lord! ' as it came up and gazed at the palace, almost within
their grasp. But the city was too strong to storm, and Sad

sat down before it. Warlike engines were brought up, but they made no impression on ramparts of sunburnt brick. The besieged issued forth in frequent sallies ; it was the last occasion on which the warriors of Persia adventured themselves in single combat with the Arabs. The investment was strict, and the inhabitants reduced to great straits. The army lay for several months before the city ; but Sad was not inactive in other directions. Bands were despatched wherever the great landholders failed to tender their submission. These ravaged Mesopotamia, and brought in multitudes as prisoners; but, by Omar's command, they were dismissed to their homes. Thus, the country from Tekrit downwards, and from the Tigris to the Syrian desert, was brought entirely and conclusively under Moslem sway.

The siege at last pressed so heavily on the western quarter, that the king sent a messenger with terms. He would give up all dominion west of the Tigris if they would leave him undisturbed on the eastern side. The offer was indignantly refused. Not long after, observing the walls no longer manned, an advance was ordered. They entered unopposed; the Persians had crossed, and carrying the ferry-boats with them, entirely evacuated the western bank. Not a soul was to be seen. But the further capital with the river between, was still defiant and secure. So the army, for some weeks, rested, and, occupying the deserted mansions of the western suburb, enjoyed a foretaste of Persian luxury.

On Medain being threatened, Yezdegird had despatched his family, with the regalia and treasure, to Holwan, in the hilly country to the north : and now he contemplated flight himself in the same direction. The heart of Persia had sunk hopelessly; for otherwise the deep and rapid Tigris still formed ample defence against sudden assault. Indeed, the Arabs thought so themselves; for they were occupied many weeks in search of boats, which had all been removed from the western bank. Unexpectedly, a deserter apprised Sad of a place where the river could be swum or forded. But the stream, always swift, was then upon the rise, and they feared lest the horses should be carried down by the turbid flood. Just then, tidings coming of the intended flight of Yezde-

Western quarter evacuated, end of 15 A.H. Jan., 637 A.D.

Capture of Medain, ii. 16 A.H. March, 637 A.D.

gird, Sad at once resolved upon the enterprise. Gathering his force, he said to them :—' We are now at the mercy of the enemy, who, with the river at command, is able to attack us unawares. Now, the Lord hath shown unto one amongst us a vision of the Faithful upon horses, crossing the stream triumphantly. Arise, let us stem the flood!' The desperate venture was voted by acclamation. Six hundred picked cavalry were drawn up in bands of sixty. The foremost plunged in, and bravely battled with the rapid flood. Down and across, they had already neared the other shore, when a picket dashed into the water, and vainly endeavoured to beat them back. ' Raise your lances,' shouted Asim; ' bear right into their eyes.' So they drove them back, and safely reached dry land. Sad no sooner saw them safe on shore, than he called on the rest to follow ; and thus, with the cry—' Allah! Triumph to thy people; Destruction to thine enemies!'—troop after troop leaped into the river, so thick and close, that the water was hidden from view ; and, treading as it had been solid ground, without a single loss, all gained the farther side. The Persians, taken by surprise, fled panic-stricken. The passage afforded time barely to escape. The few remaining, submitted themselves as tributaries. The Moslems pursued the fugitives ; but soon hastened back to share the royal spoil. They wandered over the gorgeous pavilions of a court into which the East had long poured its treasures, and revelled in gardens decked with flowers and laden with fruit. The conqueror

Service of
Victory.
established himself in the palace of the Chosroes. But first he was minded to render thanks in a Service of praise. A princely building was turned for this end into a house of prayer ; and there, followed by as many as could be spared, he ascribed the victory to the Lord of Hosts. The lesson was a passage of the Coran which speaks of Pharaoh overwhelmed in the Red Sea ; and also this verse, thought peculiarly appropriate :—

> ' How many Gardens and Fountains did they leave behind,
>   And Fields of Corn, and Dwelling-places fair,
> And pleasant things which they enjoyed!
>   Even thus We made another people to inherit the same.'
> (*Sura* xliv. *v.* 25.)

The booty was rich beyond conception. Besides millions A.H. 15-
of treasure, there was countless store of silver and golden 16.
vessels, gorgeous vestments and garniture,—precious things Spoil of
of untold rarity and cost. The lucky capture of some Medain.
mules disclosed the unexpected freight of tiara, robes, and
girdle of the king. The Arabs gazed in wonder at the
crown, jewelled swords, and splendour of the throne; and,
among other marvels, at a camel of silver, large as life, with
rider of gold, and a golden horse, with emeralds for teeth,
its neck set with rubies, and trappings of gold. The precious metals lost their value, gold being plentiful as silver.
Works of art in sandal-wood and amber were in the hands
of every one, hoards of musk and spicy products of the
East. Camphor lay about in sacks, and was at first
by mistake kneaded with the cakes as salt. The prize
agents had a heavy task, for each man's share (and the army
now numbered 60,000) was twelve thousand pieces [1], besides
special largesses to the more distinguished. The army
despatched to Medina, beyond the royal Fifth, such rare
and precious things as might stir the wonder of the
simple citizens at home. To the Caliph they sent, as
fitting gift, the regalia of the empire, and the sword of the
Chosroes [2]. But the spectacle of the day was the royal
banqueting carpet, seventy cubits long and sixty broad.
It represented a garden, the ground wrought in gold,
and the walks in silver; meadows of emeralds, and
rivulets of pearls; trees, flowers, and fruits of sparkling
diamonds, rubies, and other precious stones. When the
rest of the spoil had been disposed of, Omar took counsel
what should be done with the carpet. The most advised
to keep it as a trophy of Islam. But Aly, reflecting on
the instability of earthly things, objected; and the Caliph,
accepting his advice, had it cut in pieces and distributed

---

[1] Say £400 or £500 sterling for each soldier; from which (in addition to the
Fifth) the entire value of the booty may be gathered. The treasure alone is
put at 1500 million pieces, a like sum having been taken away by Rustem for
the Cadesia campaign.

[2] Four other swords were taken: that of the Kaiser kept by Sad, and of
Bahram by Cacaa; a third, of the Khacan of the Turks; and a fourth, of the
'King of Hind.'

with the other booty. The part which fell to Aly's lot fetched twenty thousand dirhems.

Medain offering every convenience for the seat of government, Sad established himself there. The palaces and mansions of the fugitive nobles were divided amongst his followers. The royal residence he occupied himself. The grand hall, its garnishing unchanged, was consecrated as a place of prayer, and here, the Friday or cathedral service was first celebrated in Irac.

CHAPTER XVI.

BATTLE OF JALOLA.—REDUCTION OF MESOPOTAMIA.— KUFA AND BUSSORAH FOUNDED.

16 A. H.   637 A. D.

OMAR was satisfied, as well he might be, with the success Battle of Jalola.
achieved.   His old spirit of caution revived, and beyond
the plain skirted by the hilly range to the east, he strictly
forbade a forward movement.   Summer of the 16th year
of the Hegira was passed in repose at Medain.   The king,
with his broken troops, had fled into the Persian mountains;
and the people on either bank of the Tigris, seeing opposition vain, readily submitted to the conqueror.   In the Persian advance.
autumn, the Persians, resolving again to try the chance of
arms, flocked in great numbers to Yezdegird at Holwan,
about 100 miles north of Medain.   From thence part of the
force advanced to Jalola, a fortress held to be impregnable,
defended by a deep trench, and the outlets guarded by
chevaux de frise and spikes of iron.   With Omar's sanction,
Sad pushed forward Hashim and Cacaa at the head of
12,000 men, including the flower of Mecca and Medina;
and they sat down in front of the citadel.   The garrison,
reinforced from time to time by the army at Holwan,
attacked the besiegers with desperate bravery.   Fresh
troops were despatched from Medain, and the siege was
prolonged for eighty days.   At length, during a vigorous
sally, a storm darkened the air; and the Persian columns,
losing their way, were pursued to the battlements by Cacaa,

K

who seized one of the gates. Thus cut off, they turned in
Routed and
Jalola
taken.
End of
16 A.H.
Dec.,
637 A D.
despair upon the Arabs, and a general engagement ensued,
which 'was not surpassed by the *Night of Clangour*, excepting that it was shorter.' Beaten at every point, many
Persians in the attempt to flee were caught by the iron
spikes. They were pursued, and the country strewn with
corpses. Followed by the fragments of his army, Yezdegird
fled to Rei, in the direction of the Caspian Sea. Cacaa
then advanced to Holwan, and defeating the enemy, left
that stronghold garrisoned with Arab levies as the farthest
Moslem outpost to the north.

The spoil again was rich and plentiful. A multitude of
captive women, many of gentle birth, were distributed as a
welcome prize, part on the spot and part sent to the troops
at Medain. The booty was valued at thirty million dirhems,
besides vast numbers of fine Persian horses—a material
acquisition to the army,—nine falling to the lot of every
combatant. In charge of the Fifth, Sad despatched a
youth named Ziad, of doubtful parentage (of which more
hereafter), but of singular readiness and address. In presence of the Caliph, he harangued the citizens, and recounted
in glowing words the prize of Persia, rich lands, endless
spoil, slave-girls and captive princesses. Omar praised his
speech, and declared that the troops of Sad surpassed the
traditions even of Arab bravery. But next morning, when
distributing the rubies, emeralds, and vast store of precious
things, he was seen to weep. 'What!' exclaimed Abd al
Rahman; 'a time of joy and thankfulness, and thou shedding
tears!' 'Yea,' replied the simple-minded Caliph; 'it is not
for this I weep, but I foresee that the riches which the Lord
bestoweth on us will be a spring of worldliness and envy,
and in the end a calamity to my people.'

Ziad was also the bearer of a petition for leave to pursue
the fugitives across the border into Khorasan. Omar, content with the present, forbade the enterprise. 'I desire,' he
replied, 'that between Mesopotamia and countries beyond,
the hills shall be a barrier, so that the Persians shall not be
able to get at us, nor we at them. The plain of Irac sufficeth
for our wants. I would rather the safety of my people than

spoil and further conquest.' The thought of a world-wide A.H. 16. mission was yet in embryo ; obligation to enforce Islam by a universal crusade had not yet dawned upon the Moslem mind ; and, in good truth, an empire embracing Syria, Chaldæa, and Arabia, might have satisfied the ambition even of an Assyrian or Babylonian monarch. The equal mind of Omar, far from being unsteadied by the flush and giddiness of victory, cared first to consolidate and secure the prize already gained.

Nothing now threatening on the Persian side, the ambition of Sad and his generals, checked by the Caliph's interdict, was for the present confined to the reduction of Mesopotamia. For this end, troops were sent up the Tigris as far as Tekrit—a stronghold about a hundred miles above Medain, held by a mixed garrison of Greek troops and Christian Bedouins. These bravely resisted attack. After forty days the Byzantines thought to desert their native allies and escape by boat. The Bedouins, on the other hand, gained secretly over by the Moslems, seized the water-gate ; and so the Greeks, taken on both sides, were put to the sword. The column, joined by the newly converted allies, pressed forward to Mosul, which surrendered and became tributary. On the Euphrates, the Moslem arms met with equal success. The Bedouin tribes in Mesopotamia urged by the Byzantine court to attack the invaders then threatening Hims, Sad was charged by Omar to draw them off by a diversion from his side. The fortress of Hit on the Euphrates was accordingly besieged ; but was too strong to carry by assault. Half of the force being left before the town, the rest marched rapidly up the river to Kirkesia, at its junction with the Khabur, and took it by surprise. The garrison of Hit, when they heard of it, capitulated on condition of being allowed to retire. Thus, the lower half of Mesopotamia, from one river to the other, was reduced, the strongholds garrisoned, and the Bedouins either converted to the faith or brought under subjection.

From the junction of the two rivers also, downwards on either side of the Shat al Arab to the shores of the Persian Gulf, the rule of Islam was now thoroughly established. This

[Side notes: Operations in Mesopotamia. Hit and Kirkesia taken. Summer, 16 A.H. 637 A.D.]

A.H. 16. tract had been exposed, with various fortune, to Arab raids
Delta
occupied, ever since the invasion of Mothanna. Omar saw that, to
14 A.H.
635 A.D. secure Irac, it was needful to occupy the head of the Gulf
as far as the range of hills on its eastern side. About the
period, therefore, of Sad's appointment, he deputed Otba, a
Companion of note, with a party from Bahrein, to capture the
flourishing seaport of Obolla. The garrison was defeated,
and the inhabitants, chiefly Indian merchants, effected their
escape by sea. The Persians rallied in force on the eastern
bank of the river, and many encounters took place before
the Arabs succeeded in securing their position. On one
occasion, the women of the Moslem camp turning their veils
into flags, and marching in martial array to the battle-field,
were mistaken thus for fresh reinforcements, and contributed
at a critical moment to the victory. At last, in a great and
decisive action, the enemy was routed, and the girdle of the
leader, a Persian noble, sent a trophy to the Caliph. The
bearer, pressed by Omar's questions, confessed that the
Moslems were becoming luxurious in foreign parts :—' The
love of this present life,' he said, ' increaseth on them, gold
and silver dazzling their sight.' Concerned at this, the Caliph
summoned Otba, who came, leaving a Bedouin chief in
charge. The arrangement was highly distasteful to Omar :
' What!' he said, ' hast thou placed a man of the Desert
over the Citizens and Companions of the Prophet? That
may never be!' So Moghira was named in place of the
Bedouin, and became governor instead of Otba, who died
on the journey back. Thus early we see the spirit of
antagonism bred between the Bedouin chiefs and men of
Mecca and Medina.

Bussorah   On the ruins of Obolla arose a small town of huts confounded,
17 A.H. structed of reeds, with a Mosque of the same material.
638 A.D., The settlement grew in size and importance by constant
arrivals from Arabia. But the climate was inhospitable.
The tide rises close to the level of the alluvial plain, which,
irrigated thus with ease, stretches far and wide a sea of
verdure. Groves of pomegranate, acacia, and shady trees
abound ; and a wide belt of the familiar date-palm fringing
the river might reconcile the immigrant of the Hejaz to his

new abode.   But the moisture exhaled by so damp a soil   A.H. 16.
was ill-suited to the Arabian humour; pestilential vapours
followed the periodical inundations, and gnats everywhere
settled in intolerable swarms[1].   Three times the site was
changed; at last the pleasant spot of Bussorah, near the
river, which supplied a stream of running water, was fixed
upon; and here a flourishing city rapidly grew up.   It was
laid out about the same time, and after the same fashion,
as its rival Kufa.   But, partly from a better climate, partly
from a larger endowment of conquered lands, the sister
city took the lead, as well in numbers as in influence and
riches.

The founding of Kufa was on this wise.   The Arabs had   and Kufa,
been in occupation of Medain for some months, when a
deputation visited Medina.   The Caliph, startled by their
sallow and unwholesome look, asked the cause.   They
replied that the city air did not suit the Arab temperament.   Whereupon, he ordered enquiry for some more
healthy and congenial spot; such as, approaching nearer the
desert air, and well supplied with wholesome water, would
not be cut off from ready help in any time of need.   After
diligent search along the desert outskirts, they found no
place answering so well as the plain of Kufa, not far from
Hira, on the banks of the western branch of the Euphrates.
Omar confirmed the choice, and left it open for each man
either to remain at Medain, or transfer his habitation thither.
The new capital suited the Arabs well, and to it accordingly   x. 18 A.H.
they migrated in great numbers.   The dwellings, as at Bus-   Oct.,
sorah, were made at first of reeds.   But fires were frequent;   638 A.D.
and after a disastrous conflagration, the Caliph gave permission that both cities might be built of brick.   'The
flitting camp,' he wrote, 'is the warrior's proper place.   But
if ye must have permanent abode, be it so; only let no
man have more houses than three for wives and children,
nor exceed the modest exemplar of the Prophet's dwelling-
place.'   So the city was rebuilt, and the streets laid out in
regular lines.   The centre was kept an open square, in which

---

[1] The traveller of to-day still complains of the pest of musquitoes issuing
from the groves of the Delta in gigantic swarms.

A.H. 16. was erected a Mosque with a portico for shade, and for
ornament pillars of marble brought away from Hira. Sad
built himself a spacious edifice, and reared in front of it a
gateway, to prevent intrusion from the market-place hard by.

Omar bids The rumour of 'the Castle of Sad' troubled the simple-
Sad pull
down the minded Caliph, and he sent a Companion, ibn Maslama,
gateway of with a rescript commanding that the gateway should be
his palace.
pulled down. Arrived at Kufa, the envoy, invited by Sad
to enter his mansion as a guest, declined. Sad came forth,
and received this letter at his hands :—'It hath been reported to me that thou hast builded for thyself a palace,
and people call it *The Castle of Sad*; moreover thou hast
reared a gateway betwixt thee and the people. It is not
thy castle; rather is it the castle of perdition. What is
needful for the treasury, that thou mayest guard and lock;
but the gateway which shutteth out the people from thee,
that thou shalt break down.' Sad obeyed the order; but
he protested that his object in building the portal had been
falsely reported, and Omar accepted the excuse.

The Sawâd The settlement of the land was the next concern. The
settled
with the *Sawâd*, or rich plain of Chaldæa, having been taken, with
Fellaheen. some few exceptions, by force of arms, was claimed by the
Arab soldiery as prize of war. The judgment and equity
of Omar is conspicuous in the abatement of this demand.
After counsel held with his advisers at Medina, the Caliph
ordered that cultivators who had fled during the operations
in Irac, as well as those who had kept to their holdings
throughout, should be treated as *Zimmies*, or protected
subjects, and confirmed in possession on moderate tribute.
Royal forests and domains, lands of the nobles and of those
who had opposed the Moslem arms, and endowments of
Fire-temples, were confiscated; but the demand for their
division as ordinary prize was denied. Equitable distribution was impossible, and the attempt would but breed
bad blood amongst the people. The necessities also of the
great system of canals, and of the postal and other services,
as first charge upon the revenues, demanded that the
public lands should be kept intact. Such were the
ostensible reasons. But a cause more weighty underlay

the order. Omar would maintain the martial spirit of his
followers at any cost, and render it perpetual. With him
it was of first necessity that the Arabs should not settle
anywhere but in the field, or other place of arms; nor
engage at all in husbandry, lest becoming fixed to the soil,
the temper militant should wane. The people of Arabia must
in every land be men of arms, ready at a moment's notice
for the field, a race distinct and dominant. Therefore, much
to the army's discontent, not only were the confiscated lands
held undivided, but, from the border of the Syrian desert to
the mountain range of Persia, the sale of any portion of the
soil, whether confiscated or not, was forbidden. Thus there
arose a double protection to the native tenantry, who under
no pretext could be evicted from their lands. The country
also, remaining in the hands of its own cultivators, was
nursed, and became a rich and permanent source of revenue.

The confiscated lands scattered over the province were
administered by crown agents, and the profits shared between
the captors and the State. The prize domains of Kufa—
conquered by the armies of Khalid and of Sad—were much
more extensive than those of Bussorah. Shortly after its
foundation, the inhabitants of Bussorah sent representatives
to urge that their endowments should be increased, and
income made more adequate to their responsibilities.
'Kufa,' said their spokesman, 'is a well-watered garden
which yieldeth in season its harvest of dates, while ours is
brackish land. Part bordereth on the desert, and part upon
the sea, which laveth it with briny flood. Compared with
Kufa, our poor are many, our rich are few. Grant us,
therefore, of thy bounty.' Recognising the justice of the
plea, Omar made substantial addition to their endowments
from the Crown lands of the Chosroes. But, although Kufa
was richer, it had heavier obligations to discharge than the
sister city. Its government had a wider range; and the
charge of garrisons at various points, as Holwan, Mosul, and
Kirkesia, had to be provided from the resources at the
command of Sad.

Kufa and Bussorah, unique in their origin, had a singular

Crown lands and endow-ments of Kufa and Bussorah.

A.H. 16.

Influence
of the two
cities on
the future
of Islam. influence on the destinies of the Caliphate and of Islam
at large. The vast majority of the population were of pure
Arabian blood. The tribes which, scenting from afar the
prey of Chaldæa and Persia, kept streaming into Chaldæa
from every corner of Arabia, settled chiefly there. At
Kufa the races from the south of the peninsula predomi-
nated ; at Bussorah, from the north. Rapidly they grew
into two great and luxurious capitals, with an Arab population each of from 150,000 to 200,000 souls. On the
literature, theology, and politics of Islam, the two cities had
a greater influence than the whole Moslem world besides.
Service in the field was desultory and intermittent. The
intervals were spent in idleness. Excepting when en-
livened by the fruits of some new victory, secluded harems
afforded their lords little variety of recreation or amusement.
Otherwise the time was whiled away in the converse of
social knots ; and in these, while they discussed the pro-
blems of the day, they loved still more to live in the past,
to recall the marvellous story of their Faith, and fight their
battles over again. Hence tradition, and the two great
schools of Bussorah and Kufa. But the debates and gossip
of these clubs too often degenerated into tribal rivalry and
domestic scandal. The people grew petulant and factious ;
and both cities became hotbeds of turbulence and sedition.
The Bedouin element, conscious of its strength, was jealous
of the Coreish, and impatient at whatever checked its own
capricious humour. Thus factions sprang up which, con-
trolled by the strong and wise arm of Omar, broke loose
under weaker Caliphs, rent the unity of Islam, and brought
on disastrous days, that, but for its marvellous vitality,
must have proved fatal to the Faith.

CHAPTER XVII.

CAMPAIGN IN NORTHERN SYRIA.

15 A.H.   636 A.D.

To recover the thread of Syrian warfare we must go back *Abu* to the great victory on the banks of the Jordan. At the *Obeida's advance on* close of the 14th year of the Hegira, Abu Obeida, *Northern* leaving Amru to follow up the success in Palestine, and *Syria, 14 A.H.* Yezid as governor of Damascus, marched with the rest of *635 A.D.* his forces northward upon Hims,—the ancient Emessa,— where the emperor watched the progress of his enemies. Dzul Kelaa, who with his Himyar column had been ever since covering Damascus from attack on the north, now joined his chief. They had advanced but a little way, when they were stopped by two columns. Theodore, who commanded one of these, seeing Damascus no longer guarded, thought to make a sudden dash upon it. But Yezid, issuing with his garrison, assailed him in front ; and Khalid's flying column was immediately in pursuit. Taken thus before and behind, Theodore's army was cut to pieces. The other column was put to flight by Abu Obeida. Meeting no further opposition, the Arabs continued their march, storming Balbek by the way.

Abu Obeida advanced straight upon Hims, and closely *Hims* invested it. Heraclius, on the defeat of Theodore, retired *besieged. End of* hastily on Roha (Edessa), where he endeavoured to raise *14 A.H.* the Bedouins of Mesopotamia, and thus effect a diversion. *Jan., 636 A.D.* The effort (as we have seen) was defeated by Sad, who,

A.H. 15.   making an inroad on Kirkesia, recalled the tribes to the defence of their desert homes. The siege of Hims, prosecuted with vigour, was bravely resisted. But the expectation of succour died away; the severity of winter failed to make the Arabs retire, the sallies of the beleaguered garrison became less frequent, and their spirits fell. When the siege had been protracted many weeks, an earthquake breached the battlements. The governor, finding the position no longer tenable, offered to capitulate; and the Moslems, unaware of the full extent of mischief, readily gave the same terms as to Damascus. In answer to the despatch announcing the capture, Omar bade Abu Obeida press boldly forward; and promising further reinforcements, counselled him to gain the powerful tribes on the border, and strengthen thus his army.

*Capitulates.
Spring,
15 A.H.
636 A.D.*

*March
northward.
Antioch
taken.*

Leaving a garrison in Hims, Abu Obeida resumed his northward march. Hama, and other towns of inferior note, tendered submission. The fortified city of Laodicea alone showed an obstinate front; but the Arabs made a feint to withdraw, and then darting back in early morning through an open portal, seized the defences, and overpowered the garrison. Advancing still to the north, Khalid, with great slaughter, defeated the Greeks near Kinnisrin (Chalcis), which was seized and dismantled. Aleppo next fell, after a brief resistance; and then Abu Obeida turned his arms westward upon Antioch. In this famous emporium of merchandise, art, and luxury, the broken troops of the Empire rallied. And here, at length, within the great lines of circumvallation which ran along the surrounding heights, we might have expected Heraclius to make a bold stand. But no effort befitting the crisis seems even to have been thought of. A heavy battle, indeed, was fought on the wooded plain outside the walls; but the garrison was driven back, and the city, surrounded on all sides, capitulated. Such are the details, comprised within the space of a few lines, which tell us whatever we know of the loss of Northern Syria, from Damascus to the hilly range of Asia Minor.

*Northern
Syria
reduced.*

Eastward, the Greeks made a last but feeble attempt to regain their footing. They were again hopelessly beaten,

their leader slain, and great numbers taken prisoner. The
arm of the Empire was for the moment paralysed, and
Syria, from the Euphrates to the sea-shore, brought under
the sway of Islam.   The nomad tribes, as well as the
settled inhabitants, became tributary, and bound by engagements to keep the conquerors informed of any movements
by the enemy.   Before long time, the Bedouins, who have
ever sat loose to the trammels of religion, went for the most
part over to the Moslem faith.   But the urban population, Christian
as a whole, resisted the inducements to abandon Christi- population.
anity; and, although reduced, as the Coran demands, to
an humbled and degraded state, were yet treated with
moderation, their churches spared and their worship respected.   They either reconciled themselves to their unhappy fate, or retired unmolested into Byzantine territory.

When Heraclius beheld his armies, one after another, Heraclius
defeated, and his efforts to rally the Bedouin tribes end only Constan-
in secession and hostile risings throughout Mesopotamia, he tinople.
gave up Syria as lost, and fell back upon Samsat.   But he
was in peril even there.   For, after reducing Membij and
other fortresses within the Syrian frontier, Khalid made a
dash into Cilicia, and ravaged Marash and the surrounding
country.   The Emperor, alarmed at his line of retreat thus
threatened, retired altogether from the scene; and, relinquishing to the enemy the fairest and best loved provinces
of his realm, resolved to recross the Bosphorus.   Wending
his sad way westward, Heraclius (so the Arabian annalists
tell us) ascended an eminence whence might be had a last
glimpse of the wooded hills and sunny plains of Syria, now
vanishing in the southern horizon.   He turned to gaze:
' Peace be with thee, holy and blessed land!' he said,
' Syria, fare thee well!   There is for me no more returning
unto thee; neither shall any Roman visit thee for ever, but
in fear and trembling, until the accursed Antichrist shall
come.'   It was but ten years before that the same Emperor,
performing on foot a pilgrimage to Jerusalem through the
same lovely province, to commemorate the recovery of the
' true Cross,' and his own signal victories in the East, had
cast aside a rude missive from the Arabian Prophet

A.H. 15.
Jabala, the
Ghassanide
Prince.

demanding submission to Islam. What seemed then the wild phantasy of a maniac was now an accomplished fact [1]. A similar despatch from Mahomet had been at the same time received by Jabala, last Prince of the Ghassanide dynasty; who thereupon had asked the Emperor's leave to chastise the insolent Arab, but was bidden instead to swell the imperial train at Jerusalem. And now Jabala was to share his master's fate. At the head of the Ghassan, he had fought loyally on the Byzantine side, till now, disheartened by the flight of Heraclius, he turned to Abu Obeida, and embraced Islam. Thereafter, splendidly clad, and with a pompous following, he visited Medina, where the people, familiar with the illustrious name, received him with peculiar honours. Thence he accompanied the Caliph on pilgrimage to Mecca. There a Bedouin chancing to tread upon his flowing robe, caused him to stumble and fall. The haughty prince struck the offender on the face. To his amazement he was summoned before the Caliph, who ordered, under the law of retaliation, that the Bedouin should have his satisfaction by returning the blow. 'What!' cried Jabala; 'I, the Prince of the Ghassan, and he a common Bedouin of the desert!' 'Yea,' replied Omar; 'for in Islam all are equal.' Stung by the affront, Jabala retired at once to Constantinople. There returning to the Christian faith, he was hospitably entertained at the Byzantine court. The tale has been garnished by touches of romance such as that, pining after his old haunts, he offered again to embrace Islam, if Omar would give him one of his daughters to wife; but so much is certain that he died in exile, and left behind him at Constantinople a colony of Arab followers.

Exchange
of gifts
between
Empress
and Omar's
wife.

It is interesting to be told that friendly relations subsisted at times between the Caliph and the Byzantine Court. Omar's wife sent to the Empress a royal gift of frankincense, and precious things fit for the toilet of a lady; and the Empress in return sent her a beautiful necklace. Omar doubted

---

[1] *Life of Mahomet,* p. 383. The reader is again reminded that the history of the Byzantine war is taken exclusively from Arabian sources, and these fragmentary and brief.

whether the gift should be accepted, or whether it should
not rather be held public property.   Some said, 'The
Empress is not a subject ; she hath sent a present for Omm
Kolthum ; let her keep it ;' others said, 'It is but a gift
in return for a gift.'   But Omar replied : 'It was an embassy
at the cost of the Moslems, and they have got this in
return.'   So it was made over to the treasury ; but he gave
his wife the value of it from his privy purse.

In this campaign, the conduct and chivalry of Khalid Omar
made such an impression upon Omar that he received him reconciled
back into favour, and appointed him to the government of to Khalid.
Kinnisrin.   'Verily,' he said, 'Khalid hath proved himself
a prince among men.   Blessed be the memory of Abu
Bekr, for verily he knew mankind better than I.'   The
reconcilement, however, was not of long duration.

CHAPTER XVIII.

CONQUEST OF PALESTINE.

15 A.H. 636 A.D.

Territorial division of Palestine. PALESTINE, according to the Arabs, is the tract that lies west of the Dead Sea. A line drawn from that sea to Mount Carmel, would be its northern boundary. North of that, again, the country, with the valley watered by the river, is the province of the *Jordan*. Still farther north is *Syria* (*Shâm*), and to the east of Jordan, again, is the *Hauran*.

Palestine invaded. The first inroads of the Arabs were, as we have seen, on the Hauran. Issuing from Arabia, their northward course was the highway to Damascus, the pilgrim route of the present day, east of the Dead Sea. The base of operations throughout the Syrian campaign was at Jabia, a town on the high land to the east of the Sea of Galilee; from whence columns could be forwarded, by the great military roads, either to Damascus and the north, or westward to Tiberias, the Jordan, and Palestine. Soon after the siege of Damascus and battle of Fihl, the greater part of the province of Jordan fell rapidly under the arms of Amru and Shorahbil. In Palestine proper, with Egypt in its rear and Cæsarea open to the sea, the Byzantine power was still unbroken. Gaza, Ramleh, and Jerusalem, were heavily garrisoned. The Patrician Artabun, commanding in Palestine, guarded Jerusalem with part of his army. With the rest, taking his stand at Ajnadein, some distance to the west, he sought to hold the invaders advancing from Beisan in check. This

foolhardy general invited Amru to a conference, having laid A.H. 15.
an ambush on the way to slay him. But he was outwitted Battle of
by the wily Arab, and, before long, cut off from his com- Ajnadein.
munications, was defeated in a decisive engagement, which Spring, 15 A.H.
took place at Ajnadein. Of the details we know little, 636 A.D.
and are simply told that 'the battle of Ajnadein was fierce
and bloody as that of Wacusa.' After great slaughter,
Artabun was driven back on Jerusalem. Amru encamped
on the battle-field, his way being now clear to the holy
city. But he took the precaution first to secure his rear,
still bristling with garrisons. One after another, Gaza,
Lydda, Joppa, and other places, fell before his arms.
Jerusalem and Ramleh alone held out.

Towards Jerusalem, full of associations sacred to the Jerusalem
Moslems, Amru first directed his steps. On his approach, End of
Artabun retired with his army into Egypt. The Patriarch 15 A.H.,
sued for peace. One condition he made, that Omar should and of 636 A.D.
himself come to the Holy City, and there in person settle
the capitulation. The Caliph, braving the objections of his Omar's
court, at once set out, journeying direct for Jabia. It was a journey to Jabia
memorable occasion, the first progress of a Caliph beyond the
limits of Arabia. Abu Obeida, Yezid, and Khalid hastened
from the North to welcome him. A brilliant cavalcade,
dressed in rich Syrian stuff, and gaily mounted, they rode
forth to meet their Master on the border of Arabia. At
sight of all their finery, Omar's spirit was stirred within him.
He stooped down, and, gathering a handful of gravel,—
'Avaunt!' he cried, 'is it thus attired ye come out to meet
me, changed in two short years! Verily, had it been two
hundred, ye would have deserved this;' as he flung the
gravel at them. 'Commander of the Faithful!' they replied; 'this that thou seest is but the outside; beneath
it' (and they drew aside their robes) 'behold our armour.'
'Enough,' said Omar, still displeased; 'Go forward.' So
journeying onwards, they alighted at Jabia. Shortly after,
the camp was startled by the appearance of a strange troop
of horse. It was a deputation from the Patriarch of Jerusalem. Terms were soon settled, and the treaty, duly
witnessed, carried by the envoys back to their master;

whereupon the gates of Jerusalem, and of Ramleh, were thrown open to the invading force. Amru and Shorahbil, thus relieved, left their camp and presented themselves at Jabia. Omar rode forth to meet them; they kissed his stirrup, while he, dismounting, affectionately embraced them both.

Dismissing the other generals to their respective commands, the Caliph, with Amru and Shorahbil, crossed the Jordan below the Lake of Tiberias, and journeyed onward to Jerusalem. They gave him a palfrey to ride on, which pranced with jingling bells after the Syrian fashion. He disliked the motion. 'What aileth the animal?' he said; 'I know not who hath taught it this strange gait.' So he dismounted and rode upon his own horse again. Arrived at Jerusalem, Omar received the Patriarch and citizens with kindness and condescension. He granted the same privileges as to the most favoured cities; imposed an easy tribute, and confirmed possession of all the shrines and churches. Jerusalem was to the Moslem an object of intense veneration, not only as the cradle of Judaism and Christianity, but as the first *Kibla* of Islam, or sacred spot to which the Faithful turn in prayer; and also the shrine at which Mahomet alighted on the heavenly journey which he performed by night. At the crest of the sacred mount is a stony projection, which tradition marked as Jacob's pillow. The Moslems fondly fancy this to be the spot in the 'Farther Temple,' from which the winged steed of Mahomet took its upward flight; and the eye of faith still traces an outline of the Prophet's foot imprinted on the rock as he sprang into his airy saddle. It was here that Omar laid the foundation of the Mosque which, to this day, bears his name[1].

---

[1] Ali Bey, the traveller, tells us that when Mahomet stood upon it, the rock, 'sensible of the happiness of bearing the holy burden, depressed itself, and becoming soft like wax, received the print of his holy foot upon the upper part. . . . This print is now covered with a large sort of cage of gilt metal wire, worked in such a manner that the print cannot be seen on account of the darkness within, but it may be touched with the hand through a hole made on purpose. The believers, after having touched the print, proceed to sanctify themselves by passing the hand over the face and beard.' (*Travels of Ali Bey,* vol. ii. p. 220.)

The heavenly journey is thus referred to in the Coran: 'Praise be to Him,

Mahometan tradition gives no further detail respecting
this memorable visit. But Christian writers say that Omar
accompanied the Patriarch over the city, visited the various
places of pilgrimage, and graciously inquired into their
history. At the appointed hour, the Patriarch bade the
Caliph perform his orisons in the church of the Resurrection,
where they chanced to be. But he declined to pray either
there, or in the church of Constantine where a carpet had
been spread for him, saying kindly that if he did so
his followers would take possession of the church for ever,
as a place where Moslem prayer had once been offered
up. Omar also visited Bethlehem ; and having prayed
in the church of the Nativity, left a rescript with the
Patriarch, who accompanied him on the pious errand,
securing the Christians in possession of the building, with
the condition that not more than one Mussulman should
ever enter at a time. The stipulation was disregarded,
and a mosque was eventually erected there, as well as on
the site of the church of Constantine.

Whatever the truth in these traditions, Omar did not
prolong his stay in Jerusalem. Having settled the matter
for which he came, the only other duty he performed was
to divide Palestine into two provinces ; one he attached
to Jerusalem, and the other to Ramleh. He then returned
by the way he came back again to Medina.

Thus was Syria, from the farthest north to the border
of Egypt, within the space of three years, lost to Christen-

who carried His servant by night to the FARTHER TEMPLE, the environs of
which we have made blessed.' *Sura* xvii. (The 'Farther Temple,' in con-
tradistinction to the ' Nearer Temple,' i.e. the Kaaba.) Jerusalem was the
Kibla of Mahomet and his followers, up to the time of his flight from Mecca.
In the second year after settling at Medina, he was suddenly instructed while at
prayer to turn instead towards Mecca, and ever since, the Kaaba, and not
Jerusalem, has been the Kibla of the Moslems.

The *Haram* is the sacred inclosure on the S.E. corner of Mount Zion. The
Kubbet al Sakhra, or ' Dome of the Stone,' has been built polygonal, to meet
the shape of the 'Stone,' or Rock referred to in the text, which gives its name
to the Mosque. This rock rises to a height of six or seven feet from a
base, according to Ali Bey, 33 feet in diameter, or, according to others,
57 feet long and 43 wide. The architecture is Byzantine, and Greek builders
were no doubt engaged in its construction. There is probably little, if anything,
of Christian remains in the present Haram.

L

dom.   One reflects with wonder at the feeble resistance of
the Byzantine power, military and naval, and of its renowned
strongholds, to this sudden inroad.   The affinity of the
Syrian Bedouins to the Arabian nation no doubt facilitated
the conquest.   There was also an element of weakness in
the settled population; luxurious living had made the race
effeminate, and unable to resist the onset of wild and
fanatic invaders.   Still worse, they had no heart to fight.
What patriotic vigour might have still survived, was lost
in religious strife ; and rival sects rejoiced each in the
humiliation of its neighbour.   Loyalty was smothered by
bitter jealousies, and there are not wanting instances of
active assistance rendered by Jews and Christians to the
enemy.   There may have been even a sense of relief in
the equal though contemptuous licence which the haughty
conquerors conceded to all alike.   But there was a deeper
cause, the decrepitude of the Roman empire.   The vigour
and virtue to repel the shock of barbarian invasion
were gone.   And while northern hordes gradually amal-
gamated with the nations which they overran, the exclusive
faith and intolerant teaching of Islam kept the Arabs a
race distinct and dominant.

The Arabs
do not
settle in
Syria as in
Chaldæa.   The conquerors did not spread themselves abroad in
Syria, as in Chaldæa.   They founded no such Arabian
towns and military settlements as Bussorah and Kufa.
The country and climate were less congenial; though a
land of brooks of water, of vines and fig-trees, of oil-olive
and honey, yet it offered fewer attractions to the Arabian
than the hot and sandy plains of Irac, with its familiar
garb of tamarisk and date.   The Arabs came to Syria as
conquerors ; and as conquerors they settled largely, par-
ticularly the southern tribes, in Damascus, Hims, and other
centres of administration.   But the body of native Syrians,
urban and rural, remained after the conquest substantially
the same as before ; and through long centuries of degradation they clung, as the surviving remnant still cling,
to their ancestral faith.

We read in later days of the 'Ordinance of Omar,'
regulating the conditions of Christian communities through-

out Islam.   But it would be a libel on that tolerant Ruler
to credit him with the greater part of these observances.
It is true that the stamp of inferiority—according to divine
injunction,—*Fight against the people of the Book, Jews and
Christians, until they pay tribute with their hands and are
humbled*[1]—was branded on them from the first; but the
worst disabilities of the intolerant 'Ordinance' were not
imposed till a later period.   Introduced gradually, these
became, by use and habit, the law of the land.   At first
the exactions of the conquerors, besides the universal
tribute, were limited to the demand of a yearly supply
of oil-olive and other food, and the obligation to entertain
for three days Moslem travellers.   But when the Caliphate
was established at Damascus and Baghdad, its pride could
no longer brook even the semblance of equality, and hence
the badge of inferiority at every step;—the dress of both
sexes and their slaves must be distinguished by stripes of
yellow; forbidden to appear on horseback, if they rode on
mule or ass, the stirrups and knobs of the saddle must be
of wood; their graves level with the ground, and the
mark of the devil on the lintel of their doors; the children
prohibited from being taught by Moslem masters; and the
race, however able or well qualified, proscribed from
aspiring to any office of emolument or trust; besides
the existing churches spared at the conquest, no new
building to be erected for the purposes of worship; free
entry into all the holy places allowed at pleasure to any
Moslem; no cross to remain outside, nor any church bell
rung.   They must refrain from processions in the street at
Easter and other solemn seasons; in short, they must
abstain from everything, whether by outward symbol,
word, or deed, in rivalry or derogation of the royal faith.
Such was the so-called *Code of Omar*.   Gradually infringing
the just rights of Jews and Christians, and enforced with
more or less stringency in different lands and under various
dynasties, it was, and still remains, the law of Islam.   One
must admire the rare tenacity of the subject faith, which,
with but scanty light and hope, held its ground through

A.H. 15.

Humilia-
tion of
Jews and
Christians.

'Ordinance
of Omar,'
the growth
of time.

---

[1] *Sura* ix. 30.

L 2

A.H. 15.   weary ages of insult and depression, and still survives to
———   see the dawning of a brighter day.

East cut off   I have spoken of the loss of Syria as the dismember-
from the
West.   ment of a limb from the Byzantine empire.   In one respect
it was something more.   For their own safety, the Greeks
dismantled a broad belt on the border of hostile and now
barbarous Syria.   The towns and fortresses within this
tract were razed, and the inhabitants withdrawn.   And so
the neutral zone became a barrier against travel to and
fro.   For all ordinary communication, social, religious, or
commercial, the road was for generations closed.   The
East was severed from the West.

Silence of   'The abomination of desolation stood in the Holy place.'
Byzantine
annalists. The cradle of Christianity, Zion, the joy of the whole earth,
was trodden under foot, and utterly cut off from the sight
of its votaries.   And all is told by the Byzantine writers
in a few short lines.   The pen of the Christian annalist
might well refuse to write the story of cowardice and
shame.

CHAPTER XIX.

RISING IN NORTHERN SYRIA.

17 A.H.   638 A.D.

IN the sixth year of Omar's Caliphate, a desperate effort was made by the Greeks, at one moment not without some prospect of success, to shake off the Moslem yoke and recover possession of Northern Syria.

The movement is attributed to an appeal from the Christian tribes of Upper Mesopotamia, who besought the Emperor to save them from falling under the adversary's sway. Although the strongholds of Mesopotamia had fallen into the hands of Sad, yet these had little control over the wandering Bedouins, and many of the Christian tribes still looked for support to the Persian or Byzantine rule. The maritime power of the West was yet untouched. Cæsarea with its naval supports remained proof against landward attack; and the whole sea coast was kept unsettled by the fear, or by the hope that a fleet might at any time appear. The Emperor now promised the dwellers in Meso-potamia to second their efforts by way of the sea. An expedition was directed from Alexandria on Antioch, while the Bedouins gathered in great hordes around Hims. Thus seriously threatened, Abu Obeida called in his outlying garrisons. But finding the enemy too strong to be dispersed by the force at his disposal, he sent an urgent summons for assistance to Medina. Thereupon Omar ordered Sad immediately to despatch a strong column from Kufa under Cacaa for the relief of Hims; and likewise to effect a

A.H. 17. diversion in Upper Mesopotamia. Meanwhile the Greeks
——— landed from their ships. Antioch threw open her gates
to them ; and Kinnisrin, Aleppo, and other towns in the
north, were in full revolt. A council of war was called.
Khalid was for giving battle, but Abu Obeida, feeling too
weak to cope with the now combined forces of the Bedouins
and Greeks, retired to Hims, and there hemmed in by
enemies, awaited the succour advancing from Kufa. So
grave did Omar himself regard the crisis, that, quitting
Medina for the second time, he journeyed to Jabia, intending to march in person with the reinforcements northwards.
But while on his journey, a change had already come over
the scene. The vigorous diversion in Mesopotamia so
alarmed the Bedouins for the safety of their desert homes,

Abu
Obeida
puts enemy
to flight.
that they began to forsake the Emperor's cause. Seeing
now his opportunity, Abu Obeida issued from the fortress,
and after a severe engagement routed the enemy, who fled
in confusion, and before the arrival of Cacaa were already
totally dispersed. Omar returned to Medina, delighted at
the result. He specially commended the alacrity of the
Kufa column :—'The Lord reward them,' he wrote to
Sad, 'for their ready gathering and speedy march to the
succour of their beleagured brethren.'

Campaign
in Northern
Mesopo-
tamia,
17 A.H.
638 A.D.
It was the last effort of Constantinople to expel the
invader from Syria, and the yoke was now plainly not to
be shaken off. The diversion undertaken in Mesopotamia
had also the effect of reducing that province to its farthest
limits. Not content with this, the infant faith, becoming
conscious of its giant strength, began to stretch itself still
farther north. Success in Mesopotamia was followed up
by a campaign in Asia Minor ; and the name of Iyadh,
under whom even Khalid did not disdain to serve, begins
to figure as one of terror in the brief Byzantine record.
Nisibin, Roha, and other strong places on the frontier were
taken or recaptured, and part even of Armenia overrun.

Christian
tribes.
Beni Iyadh.
Most of the Bedouin tribes in Mesopotamia embraced
Islam. There were exceptions, and the story of the Beni
Iyadh is singular. They migrated to the north, and found
an asylum in Byzantine territory. But Omar, nettled at

their disappearance, and fearing lest they should remain a A.H. 17.
thorn in his side, demanded their extradition, on pain of
expelling all Christian tribes living under his protection.
The Emperor, unwilling to expose these to ill-treatment,
complied with the demand. Equally remarkable is the Beni
tale of the Beni Taghlib. They tendered submission to Taghlib allowed
Welid, who, solicitous for the adhesion to Islam of this to pay
famous race, pressed them with some rigour to abjure their tithe.
ancient faith. Omar was displeased ;—' Leave them,' he
wrote, ' in the profession of the Gospel. It is only within
the Arabian peninsula, where are the Holy places, that
none but a Moslem tribe is to remain.' Welid was removed
from his command ; and it was enjoined on his successor
to stipulate only that the usual tribute should be paid,
that no member should be hindered from embracing Islam,
and that children should not be educated in the Christian
faith. The tribe, deeming in its pride the payment of
' tribute ' an indignity, sent a deputation to the Caliph :—
They were willing, they said, to pay the tax, if only it were
levied under the same name as that taken from the
Moslems. The liberality of Omar allowed the concession ;
and the Beni Taghlib enjoyed the singular privilege of
being assessed as Christians at a ' double *Tithe*,' instead of
paying the obnoxious badge of subjugation.

The last place to hold out in Syria was Cæsarea. It fell Fall of
in the fifth year of Omar's Caliphate. Amru had sat long Cæsarea, 17 A.H.
before it. But, being open to the sea, and the battlements 638 A.D.
landward strong and well manned, it resisted his efforts ;
and although Yezid sent his brother Muavia with reinforcements from Damascus, the siege was prolonged for several
years. Sallies persistently made by the garrison, were
driven back with equal constancy: but in the end, the
treachery of a Jew discovered a weak point in the defences,
and the city was carried by storm, and with prodigious
carnage. Four thousand prisoners of either sex were
despatched with the royal booty to Medina, and there sold
into slavery[1].

---

[1] The Jew betrayed the town by showing the Arabs an aqueduct, through
which they effected an entrance. The population was mixed ; 70,000 Greeks;

A.H. 17.
___
Khalid
brought
to trial,
17, 18 A.H.
638–9 A.D.

The unfortunate Khalid again incurred Omar's displeasure. He came back from the campaign in the north to his seat of government, greatly enriched with the spoils of war. In hopes of his bounty, many old friends flocked to him at Kinnisrin. Amongst them was Ashath, to whom he gave the princely largess of one thousand pieces of gold. Again, at Amida, Khalid had indulged in the luxury of a bath mingled with wine, the odour whereof as he came forth still clung about his person. On both charges he was arraigned. About the second, there could be no question ; the use of wine, even in a bath, was a forbidden thing, and Khalid now forswore the indulgence. The other offence was graver in the Caliph's eyes. Either the gift was booty of the army ; or, if Khalid's own to give away, he was guilty of culpable extravagance. Either way he deserved to be deposed from his command. In such terms a rescript was addressed to Abu Obeida, and sent by the hands of a courier charged to see that the command was fully carried out. Khalid was to be accused publicly ; his helmet taken off ; his hands bound with his head-kerchief ; and so arraigned he was to declare the truth.

Arraigned
for malver-
sation be-
fore Abu
Obeida.

Abu Obeida had an ungracious task, seeing that to the degraded warrior he was beholden for all his victories in Syria. But Omar's word was law. And so he summoned Khalid from Kinnisrin, proclaimed an assembly in the Mosque of Hims, and, standing in the pulpit, placed Khalid in the midst. Then the courier put the Caliph's question —From whence the money given to Ashath came ? Khalid, confounded at the unexpected charge, made no reply. Pressed by his friends, still he remained silent. Abu Obeida himself embarrassed, a painful pause ensued. At last Bilal, privileged as the Muedzzin of the Prophet, stepped forth, and with stentorian voice cried, *Thus and*

30,000 Samaritans ; and 200,000 (?) Jews. It was a sad fate that of the captives. Multitudes of Greeks, men and women, pined miserably in strange lands in hopeless servitude. Amongst these must have been many women of gentle birth degraded now to menial office, or if young and fair to look upon, reserved for a worse fate—liable, when their masters tired of them, to be sold into other hands. No wonder that Al Kindy in his Apology inveighs, with scathing denunciation, against the proceedings of the Moslems in these early wars.

thus hath the Commander of the Faithful said, and it is incumbent on us to obey ; so saying, he unwound the kerchief from the head of Khalid, bound his hands therewith, and took his helmet off.　The great warrior, to whom Islam owed its conquests, stood as a felon before the congregation.　Bilal repeated the question, and Khalid at length replied, ' The money was my own.'　At once Bilal unbound his hands, and, replacing the helmet on his head, wound round the kerchief as before, and said, ' We honour thee still, even as we did honour thee before, one of our chiefest captains.'　But Abu Obeida was silent; and Khalid, stunned by the disgrace, stood speechless and bewildered. Abu Obeida had not the heart to proclaim his deposition ; but still spoke kindly to him as one who had his confidence. Omar, informed of what had passed, made allowance for Abu Obeida's delicacy, and summoned Khalid to Medina. Prompt to obey, though sore at heart, Khalid first returned to his seat of government ; and both there and at Hims, bidding adieu to his friends and people, complained of the ingratitude of the Caliph, who scrupled not to use him in times of difficulty, but cast him aside when, through his aid, he had reached the summit of his power.　Arrived in the Caliph's presence, he broke out in bitter reproach :—' I swear that thou hast treated despitefully a faithful servant to whom thou owest much.　I appeal from thee to the body of the Faithful.'　' Whence came that money ? ' was Omar's only answer.　The question was repeated day by day ; till at last, galled by the charge, Khalid made answer: 'I have naught but the spoil which the Lord hath given me in the days of Abu Bekr, as well as in thine own.　Whatever thou findest over 60,000 pieces, hath been gained in thy Caliphate ; take it if thou wilt.'　So his effects were valued, and the estimate reaching 80,000, Omar confiscated the difference.　But he still affected to hold the great general in honour and regard. Accordingly, he sent a rescript to the various provinces, announcing that he had deposed Khalid from his government, not because of tyranny or fraud, but because he deemed it needful to remove a stumbling-block out of the way of the people, who were tempted to put their trust in

A.H. 17.

Dies in
penury and
neglect,
21 A.H.
642 A.D.

an arm of flesh, instead of looking alone to the Giver of all victory.

So closed the career of Khalid. The first beginning of Omar's alienation was the affair of Malik ibn Noweira, followed by acts of tyranny in Chaldæa, which grated on his sense of clemency and justice. But these acts had long since been condoned ; and therefore his conduct now was both ungenerous and unjust. He used the 'Sword of God' so long as he had the need, and when victory was gained, he cast the same ungratefully away. Khalid retired to Hims, and did not long survive. His manner of life when in the full tide of prosperity, may be gathered from the brief notice that in the Plague, from which he fled with his family to the desert, forty sons were carried off. Soon after, in the eighth year of Omar's caliphate, he died. In his last illness he kept showing the scars which covered his body, marks of bravery and unflinching prowess. 'And now,' he said, 'I die even as a coward dieth, or as the camel breatheth its last breath.' His end illustrates forcibly the instability of this world's fame. The hero who had borne Islam aloft to the crest of victory and glory, ended his days in penury and neglect.

CHAPTER XX.

EXPULSION OF JEWS AND CHRISTIANS FROM ARABIA.—
REGISTER OF ARAB TRIBES.—CIVIL AND MILITARY
ADMINISTRATION.—THE CORAN.

14–15 A.H.   635-6 A.D.

WE must now revert to one or two matters of domestic Domestic events, 14–15 A.H.
interest.

Arabia, as the nursery of legions devoted to fight for Expulsion of Jews and Christians from Arabia.
Islam, must be purged of strange religions. So soon there-
fore as victory was secured in Syria and Chaldæa, Omar
proceeded to execute an act of harshness, if not of questionable equity.

In the centre of Arabia lies the province of Najran, Christian inhabitants removed from Najran,
inhabited from of old by a Christian people. Mahomet
concluded a treaty with their chiefs and bishops, which
on payment of a settled tribute secured them in the
undisturbed profession of their ancestral faith. Throughout the rebellion they remained loyal to their engagements,
and Abu Bekr renewed the treaty. Worthy descendants
of a persecuted race, they resisted the blandishments of
Islam ; and as a penalty they must now quit their native
soil, consecrated by the ashes of their martyred forefathers[1].
They were ordered to depart and take land in exchange
elsewhere.   Some migrated to Syria ; but the greater part

---

[1] For the story of persecution and martyrdom, under the tyrant Dzu Nawas,
a century before Islam, see *Life of Mahomet*, p. v. For the treaty of
Mahomet, p. 158.

settled in the vicinity of Kufa, where the colony of Najrania
long maintained the memory of their expatriation. The
rights conferred by the Prophet, so far as the altered circumstances might admit, were respected by successive
rulers ; and the tribute, with decreasing numbers, lightened
and Jews from time to time. Some years after, the Jews of Kheibar,
from Kheibar. a rich vale two or three days north of Medina, met a
similar fate. Their claim was not so strong ; for, conquered
by Mahomet, they had been left on sufferance with their
fields at a rent of half the produce. In lieu of this partial
right, they received a money payment, and were sent away
to Syria. Various pretexts are urged for the expatriation
in either case. But underlying is the dogma, founded on
the supposed dying behest of Mahomet,—*In Arabia there
shall be no faith but the faith of Islam.* The recruiting
field of Islam must be sacred ground[1].

Arabs share in spoil of war and revenues of conquered lands. The Arabian nation was the champion of Islam ; and to
fight its battles every Arab was jealously reserved. He
must be soldier, and nothing else. He might not settle
down in any conquered lands as owner of the soil ; while
for merchandise or other labour, a warlike life offered little
leisure. Neither was there any need. The Arabs lived on
the fat of conquered provinces, and subject peoples served
them. Of booty taken in war, four parts were distributed
to the army on the field, the fifth reserved for the State ;
and even that, after public obligations were discharged,
shared among the Arabian people. In the reign of Abu
Bekr this was a simple matter. But under Omar the spoil
of Syria and of Persia in ever-increasing volume poured
into the treasury of Medina, where it was distributed
almost as soon as received. What was easy in small beginnings, by equal sharing or discretionary preference,
became now a heavy task. And there arose, also, new
sources of revenue in the land assessment and the poll-tax of
conquered countries, the surplus of which, after defraying
civil and military charges, became equally with spoil of
war, patrimony of the Arab nation.

At length, in the second or third year of his Caliphate,

---

[1] *Life of Mahomet,* p. 503.

Omar determined that the distribution should be regulated on a fixed and systematic scale.   The income of the Commonwealth was to be divided, as heretofore, amongst the Faithful as their heritage, but upon rules of precedence befitting the military and theocratic groundwork of Islam. For this end three points were considered :—priority of conversion, relationship to the Prophet, and military service. The widows of Mahomet, 'Mothers of the Faithful,' took precedence with an annual allowance of 10,000 pieces each[1]; and so also all his kinsmen on a scale corresponding with their affinity.   The famous Three hundred of Bedr had 5,000 each ; presence at Hodeibia and the *Pledge of the Tree*[2] gave a claim to 4,000 ; those engaged in quelling the Rebellion had 3,000; those who had fought in the great battles of Syria and Chaldæa, and also sons of the men of Bedr, had 2,000; and such as took the field after the actions of Cadesiya and the Yermuk, 1,000.   Warriors of distinction received an extra grant of 500.   And so they graduated downwards to 200 pieces for the latest levies.   Nor were the households forgotten.   Women had the tenth of a man's share.   Wives, widows, and children had each their proper stipend ; and in the register, every new-born infant had a title to be entered with an allowance of ten pieces, rising with its age.   Even Arab slaves (so long as any of the blood remained in slavery) had their portion.

A.H. 14-15.

New rule of distribution.

Thus every soul was rated at its worth.   But the privilege was confined to those of Arab blood.   A very few exceptions there were of distinguished Persian chiefs ; but their mention only proves the stringency of the rule.   The whole nation, man, woman, and child of the militant Arab race, was subsidised.   In theory, the rights of all believers of what blood soever are the same.   'Ye are one brotherhood,' said Mahomet at the Farewell pilgrimage ; and as he spake placed two fingers of one hand upon the other, to enforce the absolute equality ruling in Islam.   But in point

All other races form a lower caste.

---

[1] Ayesha was allotted 2,000 extra, 'for the love the Prophet bare her,' but some say she declined it.   Mahomet's two slave-concubines were at first rated only at 6,000 ; but at the desire of the other widows were placed on an equality with them.   The grandsons had 5,000 each.

[2] *Life of Mahomet*, p. 368.

A.H. 14–
15.
__

of fact, the equality was limited to the Arab nation. The right of any brother of alien race was but a dole of food sufficient for subsistence, and no more.

Omar's rule disarms Arab jealousies.

A people dividing amongst them the whole revenues, spoil, and conquests of the state, on the basis of an equal brotherhood, is a spectacle probably without parallel in the world. The distinction also of early conversion was well conceived. In no other way could the susceptibilities of tribal rivalry have been reconciled. The proud chiefs of the Coreish, who did not join the Prophet till after the fall of Mecca, refused any allowance but the highest: 'We know of none nobler than ourselves,' they said; 'and less than other we will not take.' 'Not so,' answered Omar; 'I give it by priority of faith, and not for noble birth.' 'It is well,' they replied; and no reason but this would have satisfied them. There were two farther sources of danger: first, the rivalry between the Bedouin tribes and the 'Companions' or men of Mecca and Medina; and, second, the jealousies that sprang up between the house of Hashim (the Prophet's kinsmen) on the one hand, and the Omeyyads and other branches of the Coreish on the other;—jealousies which by-and-by developed into large proportions, and threatened the very existence of the Caliphate; but which, held in check by Omar, were now for a time allayed by assuming an acknowledged test as the ground of precedence.

Arabs the aristocracy of the Moslem world.

The blue blood of Arabia was universally recognised as the aristocracy of the Moslem world. Rank and stipend now assigned, and even rewards for special gallantry in the field, descended by inheritance. Implied in this inheritance was the continuing obligation to fight for the Faith: by it their martial genius was maintained, and employment perpetuated as the standing army of the Caliphate. A nation thus of ennobled soldiery, pampered, factious and turbulent, formed too often a dangerous element of sedition and intrigue. But, nevertheless, they were the real backbone of Islam, the secret of conquest, the stay of the Caliphate. Crowded harems multiplied the race with marvellous rapidity. The progeny of the Arab sire (whatever the mother) was kept sedulously distinct, so as never to mingle

with the conquered races.   Wherever Arabs went they
formed a class apart and dominant,—the nobles and
rulers of the land.   Subject peoples, even if they embraced
Islam, were of a lower caste ; they could aspire to nothing
higher than, as 'clients' of some Arab chief or tribe, to court
their patronage and protection.   Thus the Arabians were set
apart as a nation militant for the sacred task of propagating
Islam.   Even after the new-born zeal of the Faith had eva-
porated, the chivalry of the Arabs as a race wholly devoted
to arms was, owing mainly to Omar's foresight, maintained
in full activity for two centuries and a half.   The nation was,
and continued, an army mobilised ; the camp and not the city,
their home ; their business, war ;—a people whose calling it
was to be ready for warlike expedition at a moment's notice.

   To carry out this vast design, a Register was kept of
every man, woman, and child, entitled to a stipend from
the State—in other words, of the whole Arab race employed
in the interests of Islam.   This was easy enough for the
upper ranks, but a herculean task for the hundreds of
thousands of ordinary families which kept streaming forth
to war from the Peninsula, and which, by free indulgence
in polygamy, were multiplying rapidly.   The task was
simplified by the strictly tribal disposition of the forces.
Men of a tribe fought together ; and the several corps and
brigades being thus territorially arranged in clans, the Register assumed the same form.   Every soul was entered
under the tribe and clan whose lineage it claimed.   And
to this exhaustive classification we owe the elaborate and
to some extent artificial genealogies and tribal traditions
of Arabia before Islam.

   The Roll itself, as well as the office for its maintenance and for pensionary account, was called the *Dewan*
or Exchequer.   The State had by this time an income
swollen by tribute of conquered cities, poll-tax of sub-
jugated peoples, land assessments, spoil of war, and tithes.
The first charge was for the revenue and civil administration ; the next for military requirements, which soon
assumed a sustained and permanent form ; the surplus
was for the support of the nation.   The whole revenues

A.H. 14-
15.
of Islam were thus expended as soon almost as received ; and Omar took special pride in seeing the treasury emptied to the last dirhem. The accounts of the various provinces were at the first kept by natives of the country in the character to which they were accustomed—in Syria by Greeks, and in Chaldæa by Persians. At Kufa this lasted till the time of Hajjaj, when, an Arab assistant having learned the art, the Arabic system of record and notation was introduced.

Vastness of Arab exodus.
We are not told the number enrolled on the Dewan of Omar, but the population of Kufa and Bussorah may give us some idea of the vast exodus in progress from Arabia, and the rapid strides by which the crowded harems multiplied the race. Arab ladies, as a rule, married only Arab husbands; but the other sex, besides unlimited concubinage with slave-girls, were free to contract marriage with the women of conquered lands, whether converts or 'People of the Book.' And although wives of Arab blood took precedence in virtue of rank and birth, the children of every Arab father, whether the mother were slave or free, Moslem, Jew, or Christian, were equal in legitimacy. And so the nation multiplied. Looking also to the further drain upon Arabia to meet continuing war, we shall not greatly err if we assume that before Omar's death the Arabs beyond the limits of Arabia proper, numbered half a million, and before long doubled, perhaps quadrupled.

Provincial administration.
Civil administration followed close on conquest. In Chaldæa, the great network of canals was early taken in hand. The long-neglected embankments of the Tigris and Euphrates were placed under special officers. Syria and Irac were measured field by field ; and the assessment established on a uniform basis. In Irac, the agency of the great landholders was taken advantage of, as under the previous dynasty, for the maintenance of order and collec-

Reserves of cavalry.
tion of the revenue. In addition to the armies in the field, a reserve of cavalry was maintained at the headquarters of the several provinces, ready for emergency. The corps at Kufa numbered 4,000 lances, and there were eight such centres. Reserves for forage were also set apart.

The cost of these measures formed a first charge upon A.H. 14-- provincial revenue. 15.

The 'Collection' of the Coran, that is, the gathering Coran, how into one volume of the various ' Revelations ' of Mahomet, collected. belongs to the early years of this reign. It had been begun by Abu Bekr, at the instance of Omar himself, who seeing that many of the ' Readers,' or those who had the Coran by heart, perished at the ' Garden of Death,' feared that otherwise ' much of the Sacred text might be lost.' The duty was assigned to Zeid who, as well as others, had from time to time, taken down portions at Mahomet's dictation. Many such Suras, or chapters, were already used, as well in private as for the public services, in a complete and settled form. In addition, Zeid now sought out from every possible quarter, whatever had at any time emanated from the Prophet, in the way of revelation, from the earliest period of his ministry—' whether inscribed on date-leaves, shreds of leather, shoulder-blades, stony tablets, or the hearts of men.' Having gathered together exhaustively the diverse, and often fugitive materials, he carefully and with reverent hand dove-tailed them, as they were found, in continuous form. A certain regard to time and subject was no doubt observed in the pious task ; but still evidently with a good deal of haphazard collocation ; and to this may be ascribed much of the obscurity and incoherence that pervade the volume. The original manuscript was committed to Haphsa, Omar's daughter, one of the Prophet's widows ; and continued to be the standard text until the time of Othman.

M

CHAPTER XXI.

FAMINE AND PLAGUE.

18 A.H. 639 A.D.

THE fifth year of Omar's Caliphate was darkened by the double calamity of pestilence and famine. It is called 'The Year of Ashes,' for the dry air of the Hejaz was so charged with unslaked dust from the parched and sandy soil as to obscure the light by a thick and sultry haze.

In the northern half of the Peninsula the drought was so severe that Nature languished. Wild and timid creatures of the desert, tamed by want, came seeking food at the hand of man. Flocks and herds died of starvation, or became too attenuated for human food. Markets were deserted, and the people suffered extremities like those of a garrison long besieged. Crowds of Bedouins, driven by hunger, flocked to Medina, and aggravated the distress. Omar, with characteristic self-denial, refused any indulgence not shared with those about him. He swore that he would taste neither meat nor butter, nor even milk, until the people had food enough and to spare. On one occasion his servant obtained at great price a skin of milk, and another of butter. Omar sent both away in alms. 'I will not eat,' he said, 'of that which costeth much; for how then should I know the trouble of my people, if I suffer not even as they?' From coarse fare and oil-olive instead of milk and butter, the Caliph's countenance, naturally fresh and bright, became sallow and haggard.

Every effort was made to alleviate distress, and effective aid at last came from abroad. Abu Obeida brought 4,000

beasts of burden laden with corn from Syria, which he A.H. 18.
distributed himself amongst the famished people. Amru Grain im-
despatched food from Palestine by camels, and also by ship- ported from
ping from the port of Ayla. Supplies came likewise from Syria and
Chaldæa. The beasts that bore the burden were slain by elsewhere.
twenties daily, and served, together with their freight, to
feed the citizens of Medina. After nine months of sore trial,
a solemn assembly was called by Omar; and in answer (we
are told) to a prayer offered up by Abbas, the Prophet's
aged uncle, the heavens were overcast and rain descending in heavy showers drenched the land. Grass sprang
rapidly, the Bedouins were sent back to their pasture
lands, and plenty again prevailed. Out of the calamity
there grew a permanent traffic with the north, and the
markets of the Hejaz continued long to be supplied from
Syria, and eventually by sea from Egypt.

The famine was followed, but in a different region, by Plague in
an evil of still greater magnitude. The plague broke out Syria.
in Syria; and, attacking with special virulence the Arabs
at Hims and Damascus, devastated the whole province.
Crossing the desert, it spread even as far as Bussorah. Consternation seized every rank. High and low fell equally
before the scourge. Men were struck down and died as by
a sudden blow. Omar's first impulse was to summon Abu
Obeida to Medina for the time, lest he too should fall a
victim to the fell disease. Knowing his chivalrous spirit,
Omar veiled the purpose, and simply ordered him to come
'on an urgent affair.' Abu Obeida divined the cause, and,
choosing rather to share the danger with his people,
begged to be excused. Omar, as he read the answer,
burst into tears. 'Is Abu Obeida dead?' they asked. 'No,
he is not dead,' said Omar, 'but it is as if he were.' The Omar holds
Caliph then set out himself for Syria, but was met on the Council on
Syrian
confines by Abu Obeida and others from the scene of the border.
disaster. A council was called, and Omar yielded to the
wish of the majority that he should return home again.
'What,' cried some of his courtiers, 'and flee from the
decree of God?' 'Yea,' replied the Caliph, wiser than
they,—'if we flee, it is but from the decree of God unto the

A.H. 18. decree of God.' He then commanded Abu Obeida to carry the Arab population in a body out of the infected cities into the desert; and himself wended his way back to Medina[1].

Arabs fly to Hauran. Acting on the Caliph's wish, Abu Obeida lost no time in making the people fly to the high lands of the Hauran. He had reached as far as Jabia, when he too was struck down, and with his son fell a victim to the pestilence. Moadz, designated to succeed, died almost immediately after; and it was left for Amru to lead the panic-stricken folks to the hill country, where the pestilence abated. Not less than five-and-twenty thousand perished in the visitation. Of a single family which had emigrated seventy in number from Medina, but four were left. Such was the deadliness of the scourge.

Death of Abu Obeida.

Omar's journey to Syria, autumn, 18 A.H. 639 A.D. The country was disabled, and fears were entertained of an attack from the Roman armies. The terrible extent of the calamity showed itself in another way. A vast amount of property was left by the dead, and the gaps amongst the survivors caused much embarrassment in the claims of succession. The difficulty grew so serious, that to settle this and other matters, Omar resolved on making a progress through his dominions. At first he thought of visiting Chaldæa, and thence through Mesopotamia, entering Syria from the north; but he abandoned the larger project, and confining his resolution to Syria, took the usual route. The way lay through the Christian town of Ayla, at the head of the Gulf of Acaba; and his visit here brings out well the simplicity and kindly feeling which he evinced toward his Christian subjects. He rode on a camel with small pomp and following; and, minded to enter the village unrecognised, changed places with his servant, putting him in front.

Visits the Bishop of Ayla.

---

[1] During the discussion Abd al Rahman quoted a saying of Mahomet :—'If pestilence break out in a land, go not thither; if thou art there, flee not from it.' Omar's views were more reasonable, and he justified them by this illustration : 'Suppose that ye alight in a valley, whereof one side is green with pasture, and the other bare and barren, whichever side ye let loose your camels upon, it would be by the decree of God; but ye would choose the brow that was green.' And so he judged that in removing the people from the scene of danger into a healthier locality, he was making no attempt to flee from the decree of God.

'Where is the Ameer?' cried the eager citizens, streaming forth to witness the Caliph's advent. 'He is *before* you,' replied Omar, with double meaning, as the camel moved slowly on. So the crowd hurried forward, thinking that the great Ruler was still beyond, and left Omar to alight unobserved at the house of the bishop, with whom he lodged during the heat of the day. His coat, rent upon the journey, was given to his host to mend. This the bishop not only did, but had a lighter garment made for him, more suited to the oppressive travel of the season. Omar, however, preferred to wear his own.

Proceeding onwards, the Caliph made the circuit of Syria. He visited the chief Moslem settlements, gave instructions for the disposal of the estates of the multitudes swept away by the plague, and himself decided doubtful claims. As both Abu Obeida and Yezid had perished in the pestilence, Omar now appointed Muavia, another son of Abu Sofian, to the chief command in Syria, and thus laid the foundation of the Omeyyad dynasty. Muavia was a man of unbounded ambition, but wise and able withal; and he turned to good account his new position. The factions which glorified the claims of Aly and Abbas, and spurned the Omeyyad blood of Muavia, were yet unknown. Both Aly and Abbas had hitherto remained inactive at Medina. The latter, always weak and wavering, was now enfeebled by age. The former, honoured, indeed, as the cousin and son-in-law of the Prophet, and also for his wit and wisdom, was amongst the trusted counsellors of the Caliph, but possessed no special power or influence, nor any apparent ambition beyond a life of quiet indulgence in the charms of a harem, varied ever and anon by fresh arrivals. Neither is there any reason to suppose that the by-gone opposition to Islam of Abu Sofian and Hind, parents of Muavia, was now remembered against them. Sins preceding conversion, if followed by a consistent profession, left no stain upon the believer. It was not till the fires of civil strife burst forth that abuse was heaped upon the Omeyyad race for ancient misdeeds and enmity towards the Prophet, and political capital made of them. The accession, therefore, of

Omar in Syria.

Appoints Muavia governor.

A.H. 18.   Muavia at the present time to the chief command in Syria
—   excited no jealousy or opposition. It passed, indeed, as a
           thing of course, without remark.

Bilal per-   As Omar prepared to take final leave of Syria, a scene
forms office
of Muedz- occurred which stirred to their depths the hearts of the
zin.   Faithful. It was the voice of Bilal, the Muedzzin of the
           Prophet, proclaiming the hour of prayer. The stentorian
           call of the aged African had not been heard since the
           death of Mahomet; for he refused to perform the duty for
           any other. He followed the army to Syria, and there,
           honoured for the office he had so long discharged at
           Medina, lived in retirement. The chief men now petitioned
           Omar that on this last occasion, Bilal should be asked once
           more to perform the Call to prayer. The aged man
           consented, and as from the top of the Great mosque the
           well-known voice arose clear and loud with the accustomed
           cry, the whole assembly, recalling vividly the Prophet at
           daily prayers, was melted into tears, and strong warriors,
           with Omar at their head, lifted up their voices and sobbed
           aloud. Bilal died two years after [1].

Pilgrimage,   On returning to Medina, Omar set out on the annual
xii. 18 A.H.
Dec.,   Pilgrimage to Mecca, at which he presided every year of
639 A.D.   his Caliphate. But this was the last journey which he made
           beyond the limits of Arabia.

---

[1] For Bilal and his office of Muedzzin, see *Life of Mahomet*, p. 204.

CHAPTER XXII.

Conquest of Egypt.

19, 20 A.H. 640–641 A.D.

THE year following was one of comparative repose. Islam continued to push its way now steadily into Persia. Reserving the advance in that direction, we shall first narrate the conquest of Egypt.

The project is due to Amru.   After the fall of Cæsarea, he chafed at a life of inaction in Palestine.   On the Caliph's visit to Syria, he urged a descent upon Egypt, at once to enfeeble the enemy's power and augment the Moslem.   The advice was good; for Egypt, once the granary of Rome, now fed Constantinople with corn.   Alexandria, though inhabited largely by natives, drew its population from every quarter.   It was the second city in the empire, the seat of commerce, luxury, and letters.   Romans and Greeks, Arabs and Copts, Christians, Jews, and Gentiles mingled on common ground.   But the life was essentially Byzantine.   The vast population was provided, in unexampled profusion, with theatres, baths, and places of amusement[1].   A forest of ships congregated in its safe and spacious harbour, from whence communication was maintained with all the seaports of the realm.   Alexandria was a European, rather than an Egyptian, city.

---

[1] The male population alone is given at 600,000.   There were 70,000 (according to others 40,000) male Jews of an age to pay the poll-tax, and 200,000 Greeks, of whom 30,000 effected their escape by sea before the siege: 4000 baths, 400 theatres, and 12,000 vessels of various size.

A.H. 19–
20.
———
Egypt
disaffected
towards
Byzantine
rule.

It was otherwise with the rich valley beyond. Emerging from the luxurious city, the traveller dropped at once from the pinnacle of civilisation to the depths of poverty and squalor. Egypt was then, as ever, the servant of nations. The overflowing produce of well-watered fields served but to feed the great cities of the empire. And the people of the soil, ground down by exaction and oppression, were ever ready to rise against their rulers. Hatred was embittered here, as elsewhere, by the never-ceasing endeavour of the Court to convert the inhabitants to orthodoxy, while the Copts held tenaciously by the Monophysite creed[1]. Chronic disaffection pervaded the land, and the people courted deliverance from Byzantine rule. There were in Egypt no Bedouin tribes with Arabian sympathies; but elements of even greater danger had long been here at work.

Amru
invades
Egypt,
19 or 20
A. H.
640–1 A. D.

It was in the 19th or 20th year of the Hegira that Amru, having obtained the hesitating consent of the Caliph, set out from Palestine for Egypt. His army, even with bands of Bedouins, lured on the way by hope of plunder, did not exceed 4000. Soon after he had left, Omar, concerned at the smallness of his force, would have recalled him; but finding that he was already too far gone, sent Zobeir with heavy reinforcements after him. The army of Amru was thus swelled to an imposing array of some 15,000, many of them veterans and warriors of renown.

Reduces
Upper
Egypt.

Amru entered Egypt by Arish, and then turning to the left, passed onward through the desert, and so reached the easternmost estuary of the Nile. Along this branch of the river he marched towards Upper Egypt, where Mucoucus, the Copt, was governor—the same who sent Mary the Egyptian slave-girl and her sister as a gift to Mahomet[2]. On the way he routed several columns attempting to arrest the inroad; amongst them one commanded by his Syrian antagonist Artabun, who was slain in the encounter. Marching along the vale of the Nile, with channels from the swelling river, verdant fields, and groves of the fig tree and acacia, Amru reached at last the obelisks and ruined temples of Ain

---

[1] See Palmer's *Origines Liturgicæ*, vol. i. p. 82.
[2] See *Life of Mahomet*, p. 385.

Shems (Heliopolis).   There the bishop procured for Mucoucus a truce of four days.   At its close, an action took
place, in which the Egyptians, driven back into their city,
were there besieged.   The opposition was at one time warm,
for the Yemen troops gave way.   Reproached for their
cowardice, one replied, ' We are but men, not iron or stone.'
' Be quiet, thou yelping dog ! ' cried Amru.   ' If we are
dogs,' answered the angry Arab, 'then what art thou but
the Commander of dogs?'   Amru made no reply, but
called on a column of veterans to step forth ; and before
their fiery onset the Egyptians fled.   'What chance,'
said the Copts one to another, 'have we against men that
have beaten both the Chosroes and the Kaiser?'   And, in
truth, they deemed it little loss to be rid of the Byzantine
yoke.   The siege was of no long duration.   In a general
assault Zobeir, with desperate valour, had already scaled
the walls, when a deputation from Mucoucus obtained terms
from Amru.   A capitation tax was fixed of two dinars on
every male adult, with other impositions similar to those of
Syria.   Many prisoners had been taken ; and a fifth part
of these and of the spoil was sent to Medina.   The same
conditions were given to the Greek and Nubian settlers in
Upper Egypt.   But the Greeks, fallen now to the level of
those over whom they used to domineer, and hated by
them, were glad to make their escape to the sea-coast.

   Amru lost no time in marching on Alexandria, so as to   Marches
reach it before the Greek troops could rally for its defence.   on Alexandria,
On the way he put to flight several columns which sought
to hinder his advance ; and at last presented himself before
the city walls, which, offering on the land side a narrow and
well-fortified front, was capable of obstinate resistance.
Towards the sea also it was open to succour at the pleasure of the Byzantine court.   But during the siege Heraclius died, and the opportunity slipped away.   Some of
the outworks on the narrow isthmus were taken by storm ;
and, there appearing no prospect of succour, the spirit of
the garrison began to flag.   The Greeks took to their ships,
and pusillanimously deserted the beleaguered city.   At last
Mucoucus, who had retired to Alexandria, finding the place

A.H. 19–
20.

which
capitulates,
20 A.H.
641 A.D.

too weak for prolonged defence, offered to capitulate, on the terms given to Upper Egypt, and on condition that the prisoners taken throughout the campaign were set free. The Caliph was referred to, and readily agreed. 'Tribute,' he replied, 'is better than booty; for it continueth, whereas spoil soon vanisheth as if it had not been. Touching the captives, such as remain, saving those taken in battle, shall be restored.' And so the city escaped sack, and the people became tributary to the conquerors.

Fostat.

Amru wished to fix his seat of government at Alexandria, but Omar would not allow him to remain so far away from his camp. So he returned to Upper Egypt. A body of the Arabs crossed the Nile and settled in Ghizeh, on the western bank—a movement which Omar permitted on condition that a strong fortress was constructed there to prevent the possibility of surprise. The headquarters of the army were pitched near Memphis. Around them grew up a military station, called from its origin *Fostat*, or 'the Encampment.' It expanded rapidly into the capital of Egypt, the modern Cairo. And there Amru laid the foundations of a great mosque that still bears his name[1].

Soil left
with the
cultivators.

Zobeir urged Amru to enforce the right of conquest, and divide the land among his followers. Amru refused; and the Caliph confirmed the judgment. 'Leave it,' was his wise reply, 'in the people's hands to nurse and fructify.' As elsewhere, Omar would not allow the Arabs to become proprietors of a single acre. Even Amru was refused ground whereon to build a mansion for himself. He had a dwelling-place, the Caliph reminded him, at Medina, and that should suffice. So the land of Egypt, left in the hands of its ancestral occupants, became a rich granary for Arabia, even as in bygone times it had been the granary of the Roman empire.

Suez Canal

A memorable work, set on foot by Amru after his return

---

[1] An interesting history of the mosque with illustrations appears in the *Asiatic Journal* for October, 1890, p. 759. Amru (Amr) is there described, from a tradition of Makrizi, as 'a short thick-set man with a large head and black eyes, and a good-humoured expression.' The tradition adds a sermon given by Amru in this mosque, which of course is mere fiction.

to Fostat, facilitated the transport of corn from Egypt to the Hejaz. It was nothing less than the reopening of the ancient communication between the waters of the Nile in Upper Egypt and those of the Red Sea at Suez [1]. The channel left the eastern branch of the river at Belbeis, then turned to the right, and, striking the salt lakes near Timseh, reached the Red Sea by what is now the lower portion of the Suez canal. Long disused, the bed was choked with silt; but the obstructions could not have been very formidable, for within a year navigation was restored, and the Caliph, at Yenbo (port of Medina), witnessed vessels discharge their burdens which had been freighted under the very shadow of the Pyramids. The Canal remained navigable for some eighty years, when, choked with sand, it was again abandoned.

Finding that the Egyptians, used to delicate and luxurious living, looked down upon the Arabs for their frugal fare, Amru, famed for mother wit, chose a singular expedient to disabuse them. First he had a feast prepared of slaughtered camels, after the Bedouin fashion; and the Egyptians looked on with wonder while the army satisfied their hunger with the rude repast. Next day a sumptuous banquet was set out, with all the dainties of the Egyptian table; here again the warriors fell to with equal zest. On the third day the troops were paraded in battle array, when Amru thus addressed the crowds who flocked to the spectacle :—' The first day's entertainment was to let you see the simple manner of our life at home; the second to show that we can enjoy the good things of the conquered lands, and yet retain, as ye see this day, our martial vigour notwithstanding.' The Copts retired, saying one to the other, 'See ye not that the Arabs have but to raise their heel upon us, and it is enough!' Omar was delighted at his lieutenant's device,

---

[1] The attempt was first made by Pharaoh Nechos, and subsequently by Darius, who opened communication from Bubastis, on the eastern estuary of the Nile, to the head of the Red Sea. A second canal was made by the Ptolemies at Tel Fakhus, nearer to the Mediterranean. This took the line of lagoons (the modern fresh-water canal) to the Red Sea, and was too shallow to be of much use, excepting in high flood. One of these lines eventually, deepened by Trajan, remained navigable to the end of the third century of our era. It was the same canal, no doubt, now cleared out and deepened by Amru.

A.H. 19-   and said of him, ' Of a truth it is on wisdom and resolve, as
20.   well as upon force, that warfare doth depend.'

Fable of   A curious tale is told of the rising of the Nile.   The
maiden   yearly flood having been long delayed, the Copts, according
sacrifice
to Nile.   to custom, sought leave to cast into the river a maiden
beautifully attired, or rather, as we may suppose, the
effigy of such a one [1].   When referred to, the Caliph in-
closed this singular letter in a despatch to Amru :—

> ' The Commander of the Faithful to the River Nile, greeting.
> ' If in times past thou hast risen of thine own will, then stay thy flood ; but
> if by will of Almighty God, then to Him we pray that thy waters may rise
> and overspread the land.'

' Cast this letter,' wrote the Caliph, ' into the stream, and
it is enough.'   It was done, and the fertilising tide began to
rise abundantly.

Alexandria   Amru, with the restless spirit of the faith, soon pushed
retaken ;   his conquests westward, established himself in Barca, and
finally
reduced,   reached even to Tripoli.   The subject races were taxed in
25 A.H.   a fixed tribute of Berber slaves, thus early sanctioning in
646 A.D.   that unhappy land traffic in human flesh and blood.   The
maritime settlements received little aid from the Byzantine
fleets.   But, a few years after, in the Caliphate of Othman,
a desperate attempt was made to regain possession of
Alexandria.   The Moslems, busy with their conquests elsewhere, had left the city insufficiently protected.   The Greek
inhabitants conspired with the Byzantine Court ; and a fleet
of 300 ships, under command of Manuel, drove out the
garrison and took possession of the city.   Amru hastened
to its rescue.   A great battle was fought outside the walls :
the Greeks were defeated, and the town subjected to the
miseries of a second and a longer siege.   It was at last taken
by storm and given up to plunder.   To obviate the recurrence of similar mishap, Amru razed the fortifications,
and quartered in the vicinity a strong garrison, which twice
a year was relieved from Upper Egypt.   The Moslem court
was transferred to Fostat, and Alexandria ceased to be the
capital of Egypt.

---

[1] The tradition is not given by the earliest authorities, but may nevertheless
be grounded on fact, for Lane tells us it is the custom to cast year by year such
a figure into the river, calling it *The Bride of the Nile.*

CHAPTER XXIII.

ADVANCE ON THE SOUTH OF PERSIA.—HORMUZAN
TAKEN PRISONER.

16–20 A.H.   637–641 A.D.

TURNING once more to the eastern provinces of the Cali- Barrier
phate, we find the cautious policy of Omar still tending to $\frac{\text{fixed by}}{\text{Omar east-}}$
restrain the Moslem arms within the limits of Irac-Araby, ward.
or the country bounded by the western slopes of the Persian
range.   But they were soon, by the force of events, to burst
the barrier.

To the north of Medain, the Moslem border was securely Situation
defended by Holwan and other strongholds planted along $\frac{\text{in Lower}}{\text{Irac.}}$
the hilly range.   In Lower Irac, Otba had, after repeated
encounters, established himself at Bussorah, from whence he
held securely the country at the head of the Gulf.   But the
Persian satraps were still in strength at Ahwaz and Ram
Hormuz, within a hundred miles of him.

Hostilities in this direction were precipitated by a rash Governor
and unsuccessful raid upon Persepolis.   Ala, who had dis- $\frac{\text{of Bahrein}}{\text{attacks}}$
tinguished himself by crushing the rebellion in Bahrein, saw Persepolis.
with jealous eye the conquests in Irac of Sad and Otba.
Tempted by the nearness of the Persian shore across the
narrow strait, he set on foot an expedition to seize the
district lying opposite.   This was done, not only without
permission, but against the known unwillingness of Omar
to trust the treacherous element.   Success might have
justified the project; but it fell out otherwise.   The troops
landing on the Persian coast, met for a time with no check

A.H. 16–
20.
_____
Meets a
check, but
is relieved
from
Bussorah.

in their advance upon Persepolis. But before long they were drawn into a trap. Advancing all together, they had neglected to secure their base, and were cut off by the enemy from their ships. After a severe engagement, unable to disperse the gathering enemy, and turning as a last resource towards Bussorah, they found the road in that direction barred. Messengers were hurried to Medina, and Omar, incensed with Ala for his foolhardiness, despatched urgent command to Otba to relieve the beleaguered army. A force of 12,000 men set out immediately; and forming, not without difficulty, a junction with Ala, beat back the Persians, and then retired on Bussorah. The troops of Otba gained a great name in this affair, and the special thanks of Omar.

Campaign
in Khu-
zistan,
17 A.H.
638 A.D.

But the retreat, conducted with whatever skill and bravery, put heart into the hostile border. Hormuzan, a Persian satrap, had escaped from Cadesiya to his own province of Ahwaz, on the lower mountain range, at no great distance from Bussorah. He began now to make raids upon the Arab outposts, and Otba resolved to attack him. Rein-forcements were obtained from Kufa, and Otba was fortunate enough to gain over a Bedouin tribe, which, though long settled near Ahwaz, was by blood and sympathy allied to the garrison of Bussorah. Thus strengthened, he dislodged the enemy from Ahwaz, and drove him across the Karoon river. A truce was called; and Ahwaz, ceded to the Moslems, was placed by Otba in the hands of his Bedouin allies. A dispute as to their boundary shortly after arose between the Bedouins and Hormuzan; and the latter, dissatisfied with the Moslem general's decision, again

18 A.H.
639 A.D.

raised his hostile standard. He was put to flight by the Moslems, who reduced the rebellious province, and sought permission to follow up the victory by a farther advance. But Omar, withholding permission, bade them rather busy themselves where they were in restoring the irrigation works, and so resuscitate the deserted fields of Khuzistan. Hormuzan fled farther east, and was, for the second time, granted an amnesty.

Not long after, emissaries from Yezdegird at Merve were

found at work stirring the people up to fresh rebellion. The A.H. 16-
attitude of Hormuzan became once more doubtful ; and the 20.
Caliph, suspecting serious opposition, assembled a powerful Ram Hor-
army from Kufa and Bussorah, of which he gave command muz and
Tostar
to Noman. Hormuzan, with a great Persian following, again captured,
19 A.H.
routed at Ram Hormuz, fled to Tostar, fifty miles north of 640 A.D.
Ahwaz, a stronghold which, obstinately defended by the
Persians, kept the Moslems for several months at bay.   In
the end, but not without considerable loss, it was stormed,
and Hormuzan, with the garrison, surrendered at the discretion of the Caliph, to whom he was accordingly sent.

Siege was then laid to Sus, the royal Shushan of ancient Sus, or
memory; still a formidable city, it was planted between Shushan.
two rivers, on a verdant plain with snow-clad mountains in
the distance.   The army succeeded here in drawing over a
body of Persian nobles with a large native following ; these
were at once admitted to confidence, commands conferred
upon them, and the singular honour of a well-portioned
place on the tribal list.   Still, it was not till after a protracted siege and conflict that Sus was taken.   Omar gave Tomb of
orders for the reverential maintenance of the tomb of Daniel.
Daniel in this the scene of his memorable vision ' by the
river of Ulai ;' and here, to the present day, the pious care
of succeeding generations has preserved his shrine through
thirteen centuries of incessant change.

The important city of Jundai-Sabur, with surrounding Jundai-
country, was also reduced by Noman, and an advance Sabur.
threatened on Ispahan.   But events were now transpiring
in Khorasan, which at length opened the way to an advance upon the heart of Persia, and called that leader to
more stirring work.

The deputation which, along with the spoil of Tostar, Hormuzan
carried Hormuzan a prisoner to Medina, throws light upon spared by
Omar.
the reasons that weighed with the Caliph to withdraw the
long-standing embargo on a forward movement.   As they
drew near Medina, they dressed out the captive in his
brocaded vestments, to show to the citizens the fashion of
a Persian noble.   Wearied with the reception of a deputation
from Kufa (for in this way he transacted much of the pro-

vincial business), Omar had fallen asleep, whip in hand, on
his cushioned carpet in the great mosque. When the party
entered the precincts of the court, 'Where is the Caliph?'
asked the captive prince, looking round, 'and where his
guards and warders?' It was indeed a contrast between the
sumptuous palaces of the Chosroes, to which he had been
used, and the simple surroundings of the mightier Caliph!
Disturbed by the noise, Omar started up, and, divining who
the stranger was, exclaimed, 'Blessed be the Lord, who
hath humbled this man and the like of him!' He bade
them disrobe the prisoner and clothe him in coarse raiment.
Then, still whip in hand, he upbraided Hormuzan, and
(Moghira interpreting) bade him justify the repeated breach
of his engagements. The captive made as if fain to reply ;
then gasping, like one faint from thirst, begged for a
draught of water. 'Give it,' said the Caliph, 'and let him
drink in peace.' 'Nay,' said the captive, trembling, 'I fear
to drink, lest some one slay me unawares.' 'Thy life is
safe,' replied Omar, 'until thou hast drunk the water up.'
The words were no sooner spoken than Hormuzan poured
the contents upon the ground. 'I wanted not the water,'
he said, 'but quarter, and now thou hast given it me.'
'Liar!' cried Omar, angrily, 'thy life is forfeit.' 'But not,'
interposed the bystanders, 'until he drink the water up.'
'Strange,' said Omar, foiled for once, 'the fellow hath deceived me, and yet I cannot spare the life of one who hath
slain so many of the faithful by reiterated treachery. I
swear that thou shalt not gain by thy deceit, unless thou
embrace Islam.' Hormuzan, nothing loth, made profession
of the faith upon the spot ; and thenceforth, taking up his
residence at Medina, received a pension of high grade.

Deputation
urge re-
moval of
ban against
advance.
'What is the cause,' inquired Omar of the deputation,
'that these Persians persistently break faith and rebel
against us? Maybe, ye treat them harshly.' 'Not so,'
they answered ; 'but thou hast forbidden us to enlarge our
boundary ; and the king is in their midst to stir them up.
Two kings can in no wise exist together, until the one
expel the other. It is not our harshness, but their king,
that hath incited them to rise against us after having made

submission. And so it will go on until thou shalt remove A.H. 16-
the barrier and leave us to go forward and expel their 20.
king. Not till then will their hopes and machinations
cease.'

These views were also enforced by Hormuzan. The Omar begins to see this.
truth began to dawn on Omar that necessity was laid upon
him to withdraw the ban against advance. In self-defence,
nothing was left but to crush the Chosroes and take entire
possession of his realm.

CHAPTER XXIV.

CONQUEST OF PERSIA.

21–22 A. H. 642–3 A. D.

Persian campaign forced on Omar.

IT was not long before any lingering doubts of Omar were put an end to. He was compelled at last by the warlike attitude of the Persian court to bíd his armies take the field with the avowed object of dealing the empire a final blow.

Yezdegird gathers a great army, 20 A.H. 641 A.D.

Though forced to fly, Yezdegird may have buoyed himself up with the hope that the Arabs, content with the fertile plain of Mesopotamia, would leave his possession undisturbed beyond the mountain range. But the capture of Sus the ancient capital of Media, and the advance on Ispahan put an end to any such imagination. Arabian hordes still pressed upon the border; and their irruption into farther Persia was inevitable. The king, having resolved once more to stem the hostile tide, ordered the governors of provinces to gather their forces together for a vigorous attack. Many of these enjoyed a virtually independent rule ; but now their interests were knit together by the common danger. From the shores of the Caspian to the Indian Ocean, from the Oxus to the Persian Gulf, they rallied in vast numbers round the royal standard on the plain below the snow-capped peak of Demavend.

Force under Noman opposes them.

Tidings of the rising storm as they reached Sad were passed on directly to the Caliph. Each courier brought a

fresh alarm. A host of 150,000 was assembled under Firuzan; now encamped at Hamadan, now marching on Holwan,
they would soon be close to Kufa, at their very doors.
The crisis, no doubt, was serious. Any reverse on the
mountain border would loosen hold upon the plains below ;
and Chaldæa, even Kufa and Bussorah, might be wrested
from them. As on previous occasions of imminent danger,
Omar declared his resolve to march in person. Encamped
midway between these two cities, his presence would restore
confidence ; and while able from thence to direct the
movements in front, his reserve would be a defence to them
in the rear. But the old arguments again prevailed, and
Omar was persuaded to remain behind. Noman was summoned from the campaign in Khuzistan to take the chief
command. Leaving strong garrisons behind, troops were
pushed forward in two columns from Bussorah and Kufa.
The army at Sus, besides furnishing a contingent for the
main advance, renewed its attack upon Persepolis, and so
prevented the forces in that quarter from joining the Royal
standard.

Arrived at Holwan, Noman sent forward spies, who reported the enemy pitched in great force on the plain
bounded by the lofty peaks of Elwand, but that the road
thus far was clear. So they marched forward, and were soon
face to face with the Persians on the memorable field of
Nehavend. The Moslems were 30,000 strong, one fifth only
of the enemy ; weak in numbers, but strong in faith, and
nerved by the presence of veterans and heroes of former
fields. After two days' skirmishing, the Persians retired
behind their line of fortification, from whence they were able
at pleasure to issue and molest their adversaries. The Moslems at last, wearied by delay, resolved by artifice to draw
them out. At Toleiha's instance they fell back, and, on the
Persians following, wheeled round and cut them off from
their return. A fierce engagement followed, and in it Noman
was slain. But the Arabs achieved at last their wonted
success. Of the enemy 30,000 were left on the field ; the
rest fled to an adjoining hill, and there 80,000 more were
slain. Of the great army but shreds effected their escape

A.H. 21-
22.
—
Decisive
effect of
Moslem
victory.

The fate of Firuzan gave rise to a pious proverb. He fled towards Hamadan, but finding the mountain pass choked by a caravan of honey, and losing his way, was overtaken thus and slain. Hence the saying—'*Part of the Lord's host is the honey-bee.*' Hamadan fell into the hands of the victorious army; and the royal treasure and jewels, deposited for safety in the great Fire temple there, were delivered up. The chiefs and people of all Western Persia submitted and became tributary. The booty was immense; and amongst it two caskets of rare gems, which Omar at first placed in the treasury at Medina. Next morning, the courier was recalled, Omar having seen a vision of angels, who warned him of punishment hereafter if he kept the jewels. 'Take them hence,' he said; 'sell them, and let the price be divided amongst the army.' They fetched 4,000,000 dirhems.

Rei and
other con-
quests,
22 A.H.
643 A.D.

Omar had now embarked on an enterprise from which there was no returning. The proud Yezdegird refused to yield, and the Caliph no longer scrupled pursuing him to the bitter end. The warlike races south of the Caspian again gathered under Isfandiar, brother of the ill-fated Rustem, for the defence of Rei. The Moslems advanced to meet them; and another great victory placed the city at their mercy. Isfandiar retired to Azerbijan; again defeated, he was taken prisoner, and then, despairing of success, changed sides, and made common cause with the invading army. From Rei, Yezdegird fled to Ispahan; finding no shelter there, he hurried to Kerman, and thence retired to Balkh. At last he took refuge in Merve, whence he sought the aid of the Turks, and of the Emperor of China. The former espoused his cause; and for several years the contest was waged with varying success in the vicinity of Merve. But in the end the Turkish hordes retired, and with them Yezdegird, across the Oxus. The conflict was subsequently renewed, but Yezdegird never recovered his authority; bereft of his treasures and deserted by his followers, who in vain besought him to tender submission, he survived till the reign of Othman, when, as we shall see, he met with an ignoble death.

On the fall of Rei, the Arabs turned their arms against A.H. 21-
the various provinces.   Some of these, though subordinate 22.
in name, had been, in point of fact, their own masters; Persian
and now, even when the heart had ceased to beat, main- empire reduced.
tained a dangerous vitality. Six columns, drawn from Kufa
and Bussorah, and continually replenished by new Arabian
levies thirsting for rapine and renown, invaded as many
different regions, each falling under the government of the
leader who reduced it.   Thus, one after another, Fars,
Kerman, Mokran, Sejestan, Khorasan, and Azerbijan, were
conquered.   But the people would ever and anon rise again
in rebellion ;   and it was long before the invaders could
subside into a settled life, or feel secure away from the protection of garrisoned entrenchments.   But the privileges
enjoyed by professors of the faith were so great, that the
adherents of Zoroastrian worship were not long able to
resist the attraction; by degrees the Persian race came over,
in name at least, to the dominant creed, and in the end opposition ceased. The notices of Zoroastrian families, and of
Fire temples destroyed in after reigns, show indeed that in
many quarters the conversion was slow and partial[1].   But Persians
after the fall of the Court, the political and social induce- long held a subordinate
ments to bow before Islam were, for the most part, irresist- race.
ible.   The polished Persian formed a new element in Moslem
society. Yet, however noble and refined, he held for long a
place apart, and altogether inferior to that enjoyed by the
rude but dominant classes of Arabian blood.   Individuals
or families belonging to the subject peoples could only
gain a recognized position by attaching themselves to some
Arab chief or clan, as 'clients' or adherents ; and, thus dependent, might claim some of the privileges of the ruling
faith.   But neither here nor elsewhere did they intermarry
with the Arabs on equal terms, nor were they, in point of
fact, looked upon otherwise than as of inferior caste. Thus,
though in theory, on becoming Mussulmans, the con-

---

[1] The Zoroastrians were still numerous, especially in the outlying provinces,
even under the Abbassides.   The social and political inducements to profess
Islam,—a profession at first but superficial,—are well brought out in *The
Apology of Al Kindy.* See especially the speech of Al Mamun, pp. 29 and 84.

quered nations might enter the ' equal brotherhood ' of the faith, they formed, not the less, a lower estate. The race and language, ancestral dignity, and political privileges, of the Arabs continued for many generations to be paramount.

CHAPTER XXV.

THE LATER YEARS OF OMAR'S REIGN.—DOMESTIC EVENTS.

17-23 A.H.   638-44 A.D.

WHILE Moslem arms were thus rapidly reducing the East under the sway of Omar, the wave of conquest which had swept over Syria, and broken threateningly on the borders of Asia Minor, now for the time relaxed into a calm. After the death of Heraclius there was no longer spirit left in the empire to continue the struggle by either land or sea. Desultory attempts there were at intervals upon the coast, but followed by no lasting success. Muavia was busy meanwhile consolidating the administration of Syria, and, with sagacious foresight, strengthening his hold against the chances of the future. Elsewhere peace prevailed. Amru maintained firm rule in Egypt ; and, waging chronic warfare against the native tribes and Roman settlements on the coast, gradually extended westward the boundaries of Islam. Arabia, still pouring forth its restless spirits to fight abroad, was tranquil at home.

Besides the journeys into Syria already mentioned, Omar quitted his residence at Medina only for the annual pilgrimage. The governors of the various provinces used to visit Mecca for the same purpose ; and the Caliph was wont to improve the opportunity for conferring with them as they returned by way of Medina, on matters of provincial interest. Several years before his death, he spent three weeks

A.H. 17- at Mecca, and enlarged the space around the Kaaba. Dwell-
23. ings that approached too closely to the Holy house were
pulled down, and the first step taken to form a grand
square and piazza becoming the place of worship for all
nations. Some owners refused to sell their patrimony;
but the houses were demolished nevertheless, and the price
in compensation deposited in the treasury. The boundary
pillars of the *Haram*, or Sacred precincts around the city,
were renewed; and convenient halting-places constructed
at the pilgrim stations, for custody of which and care of
the adjoining springs, the local tribes were held responsible.

Disaster in   In the seventh year of Omar's reign volcanic fires burst
Red Sea,   from a hill in the neighbourhood of Medina. The Caliph
19 A.H.
640 A.D.   gave command to distribute alms amongst the poor, a pious
work in which the people joined; 'and so the volcano
stopped.' In the same year a naval expedition was sent
across the Red Sea, to check attacks upon the Moslems on
the Abyssinian coast. The vessels were wrecked, and the
expedition suffered great privation. The disaster led Omar
to vow that he would never again permit troops to embark
on an element so treacherous. It was not till some years
after his death that the Mussulmans gathered courage to
brave the risks of a naval encounter.

Moghira   In the governors appointed to control the turbulent cities
arraigned
on charge of Kufa and Bussorah, Omar was not altogether fortunate.
of adultery, Otba died at Bussorah shortly after rescuing the unfortu-
17 A.H.
638 A.D.   nate expedition to Persepolis. The choice of a successor
in Moghira was ill-advised. Of rude and repulsive aspect,
he had committed murder in his youth at Tayif, and Islam
had not softened his nature or improved his morals. A
harem of fourscore wives and concubines failed to satisfy
his vagrant passion. At Bussorah his movements were
watched by enemies, who through an intervening window
were witness to an intrigue with a Bedouin lady visiting his
house. When he came forth to lead the public prayer,
they shouted him down as an adulterer; and Omar
summoned him to answer the accusation. By any reasonable law of evidence, the crime had been established beyond
a doubt; but, under the strange conditions promulgated by

Mahomet on the misadventure of his favourite wife, there
was a flaw in the testimony of Ziad, the fourth witness [1].
The Caliph, with an ill-concealed groan at the miscar-
riage of justice, ordered the witnesses to be scourged
according to the ordinance, and the accused set free.
' Strike hard,' cried the barefaced Moghira, addressing the
unwilling minister of the law ;—' strike hard, and comfort
my heart thereby ! ' 'Hold thy peace,' said Omar ; ' it
wanted but little to convict thee ; and then thou shouldest
have been stoned to death as an adulterer.' The culprit
was silenced, but not abashed. He continued to reside in
Medina, a crafty courtier at the Caliph's gate.

As successor, Omar appointed Abu Musa to the govern- Abu Musa
ment of Bussorah, a man of very different stamp. Small governor of
Bussorah.
of stature, smooth in face, and of little presence, he had
yet distinguished himself at Honein, and had been employed as an envoy by the Prophet. He wanted strength
and firmness for the stormy times that were coming, but
was wise and sufficiently able to hold the restless Bedouins of
Bussorah in check. Belonging to a Bedouin tribe himself,
it was perhaps an advantage, in the jealousies now growing
up, to be outside the clique of Mecca and Medina citizens.
But feeling still the need of such support, he said to Omar:
' Thou must strengthen my hands with a company of the
Companions of the Prophet, for verily they are as salt in
the midst of the people ; ' and his request was granted,
for he took nine-and-twenty men of mark along with
him. But even Abu Musa was near losing his command, and
that in a way which curiously illustrates Omar's government.
After a successful campaign against the Kurds, he sent, as
usual, a deputation to Medina with report of the victory,
and the royal Fifth. Dhabba, a discontented citizen, being
refused a place upon it, set out alone to Medina, and there
laid charges against Abu Musa, who was summoned by

---

[1] The autoptic witness of four persons is necessary for conviction, the penalty
being death ; but if the evidence fail of full proof, the witnesses instead are·
scourged (*Life of Mahomet*, p. 313). Conviction therefore is, under ordinary
circumstances, practically impossible. Moghira felt beholden to Ziad for his
evidence in this matter, as we shall in the sequel see.

A.H. 17-
23.

Omar to clear himself. After some days of confinement, he was brought before the Caliph, face to face with his

Accused of
malversa-
tion,
23 A.H.
643 A.D.

accuser. The first charge was that a band of youths taken in the expedition were used by him as attendants. 'True,' said Abu Musa; 'they did me good service as guides; therefore I paid their ransom, and now, being free, they serve me.' 'He speaketh the truth,' answered Dhabba, 'but what I said was also true.' The second was that he held two landed properties. 'I do,' explained Abu Musa; 'one for the subsistence of my family, the other for the sustenance of the people.' Dhabba answered as before. The third was that the governor had in his household a girl who fared too sumptuously. Abu Musa was silent. Again, he was charged with making over the seals of office to Ziad; which was admitted by Abu Musa, 'because he found the youth to be wise and fit for office.' The last charge was that he had given the largess of a thousand dirhems to a poet; and this Abu Musa admitted, to preserve his authority from scurrilous attack. The Caliph was satisfied, and permitted Abu Musa to resume his government, but desired him to send Ziad and the girl to Medina. On their arrival, Omar was so pleased with Ziad, already foreshadowing his administrative talent, that he sent him back with approval of his employment in the affairs of state; but the girl was detained, perhaps because of her undue influence, in confinement at Medina. With Dhabba the Caliph was very angry. Out of malice he had sought to ruin Abu Musa by one-sided allegations. 'Truth perverted is no better,' said Omar, 'than a lie; and a lie leadeth to hell fire.'

Sad, gover-
nor of Kufa
deposed,
21 A.H.
642 A.D.

Kufa remained several years under its founder Sad, the conqueror of Chaldæa. At length, in the ninth year of Omar's reign, a faction sprang up against him. The Bedouin jealousy of the Coreish had already begun to work; and Sad was accused of unfairness in distributing the booty. There was imputed also lack of martial spirit and backwardness in the field, a revival of the slanderous charge at Cadesiya. He was summoned, with his accusers, to Medina; but the main offence proved against him was one

of little concern to them. In his public ministrations he
had cut short the customary prayers; and Omar, deeming
the misdemeanour to be unpardonable, deposed him. To
fill a vacancy requiring unusual skill, experience, and
power, Omar unwisely appointed Ammar, who, as a persecuted slave and confessor in the first days of Islam,
was second to none in the faith; but a man of no ability,
and now advanced in years [1]. The citizens of Kufa were
not long in finding out his incapacity; and, at their desire,
Omar transferred Abu Musa from Bussorah to rule over
them. But it was no easy work to curb the factious
populace. They took offence at his slave for undue influence in buying fodder before it crossed the bridge; and
for so slight a cause, after he had been governor for a year,
the Caliph sent him back to Bussorah. Omar was on the
point of making another nomination, when the artful
Moghira wormed the secret from him; and dwelling on the
burden of a hundred thousand turbulent citizens, suggested
that the candidate in view was not fit to bear it. 'But,' said
Omar, 'the men of Kufa have pressed me to send them
neither a headstrong tyrant, nor a weak and impotent
believer.' 'As for a weak believer,' answered Moghira,
'his faith is for himself, his weakness thine; as for a strong
tyrant, his tyranny injureth himself, his strength is for thee.'
Omar, caught in the snare, was weak enough to confer on
Moghira, his former scandal notwithstanding, the government of Kufa. With all his defects, Moghira was, without
doubt, the strong man needed for that stiff-necked city;
and he held his position during the two remaining years
of this reign.

About the same time, Omar appointed another early
convert of singular religious merit, Abdallah ibn Masud,
who had like Ammar been a slave at Mecca, to a post at
Kufa, for which, however, he was better fitted—the charge
of the treasury. He had been the body-servant of the
Prophet, who was used to call him 'light in body, but
weighty in faith [2]'. He was learned in the Coran, and had

Margin notes: A.H. 17-23. To Moghira appointed in his room. Abdallah ibn Masud.

---

[1] *Life of Mahomet*, p. 72.   [2] *Ibid.*, p. 64.

A.H. 17- a 'reading' of his own, to which, as the best text, he held
23.   persistently against all recensions.

Bussorah,   There was still considerable jealousy between Bussorah
additional
endow-   and its richer rival. The armies of both had contributed
ment.   towards the conquest of Khuzistan, and had shared accord-
          ingly. But Bussorah, with its teeming thousands, was
          comparatively poor; and Omar, to equalise the benefits of
          all who had served in the earlier campaigns, assigned to them
          increased allowances, to be met from the surplus revenues
          of the territories administered at Kufa.

Provincial   In the more important governments, the judicial office
officers,
civil, mili- was discharged by a functionary who held his commission
tary, and as Cazee immediately from the Caliph.   The control of
religious.
          other departments remained with the governor, who, in
          virtue of his office, led the daily prayers, and, especially
          on Friday, added an address which had often an important
          political bearing. Military and fiscal functions, vested at
          the first, like other powers, in the governor's hands, came
          eventually to be discharged by officers specially appointed
          to the duty. Teachers of religion were also commissioned
          by the State. From the rapidity with which whole peoples
          were brought within the scope of Islam, risk arose of error
          in respect both of creed and ritual, to the vast multitude of
          'New-moslems,' as they were called. To obviate the danger,
          Omar appointed masters in every country, whose business
          it should be to instruct the people—men and women sepa-
          rately—in the Coran and its requirements. Early also in his
          reign, he imposed it, as a magisterial obligation, that the
          people, both small and great, should all attend the public
          services, especially on Friday; and notably that in the
          month of Fast, the whole body of Moslems should be
          constant in the assembling of themselves together in the
          mosques.

Era of the   To Omar is popularly ascribed, not only the establish-
Hegira,
17 A.H.   ment of the Dewan or Exchequer, and Offices of systematic
          account, but also the regulation of the Arabian year. He
          introduced for this purpose the Mahometan era, commencing
          with the new moon of the first month (Moharram) of the
          year in which the Prophet fled from Mecca. Hence the

Mahometan year was named the *Hegira*, or 'Era of the A.H. 17–23. Flight[1]'.

Of the state of Mahometan society at this period we have not the materials for judging closely. Constant employment in the field, no doubt, tended to check the depraving influences which, in times of ease and luxury, relaxed the sanctions and tainted the purity of Bedouin life. But there is ample indication that the relations between the sexes were already deteriorating. The baneful influence of polygamy, divorce, and servile concubinage, was quickened by the multitudes of captive women distributed or sold among the soldiers and community at large. The wife of noble blood held, under the chivalrous code of the Bedouins, a position of honour and supremacy in the household, from which she could be ousted by no base-born rival, however fair or fruitful. She was now to be, in the estimation of her husband, but one amongst many. A slave-girl bearing children, became at once, as *Omm Walad*[2], free; and in point of legitimacy her offspring ranked with the children of the free and noble wife. Beauty and blandishment thus too often outshone birth and breeding, and the favourite of the hour displaced her noble mistress.

Deterioration of social and domestic life.

With the coarse sensualist, revelling like Moghira in a harem stocked with Greek and Persian bond-maids, this might have been expected. But it was not the less the case in many a house of greater refinement and repute. Some lady, ravished, it may have been, from a noble home, and endowed with the charms and graces of a courtly life, would captivate her master, and for the moment rule supreme. The story of Leila affords a sample. The beautiful Ghassanide princess was bought at Duma by Khalid from the common prize. The fame of her charms

Story of Leila.

---

[1] The calendar was already strictly lunar, as announced by the Prophet at the Farewell pilgrimage. But the *era*, and consequent numbering of the years, was introduced now. The lunar year is eleven days shorter than the solar, and so loses three years in every century of ours. There is this convenience in the lunar reckoning that the date given, you know the age of the moon; but also this serious want, that the month is no indication of the season of the year.

[2] I. e. 'Mother of his child.'

reached Medina, and kindled a romantic flame in the breast of Abd al Rahman, son of Abu Bekr. The disconsolate lover ceased not singing his mistress's praises, and his own unhappiness, in verses still preserved. At last he became her master, and she was despatched from the camp to his home. At once he took her to wife. His love was so great that, forsaking all other, he kept only to her, so long as her beauty lasted. She was the queen of his household. After a time she fell sick and began to waste away. The beauty went, and with it the master's love, and her turn came to be forsaken. His comrades said to him: 'Why keep her neglected and forsaken thus? Suffer her to go back to her people and her home.' So he suffered her. Leila's fate was happy compared with that of most. Tired of his toy, the owner would sell her, if still young and beautiful, to be the plaything of another; or if disease or years had fretted her beauty, leave her to eke out the weary, wistless, hopeless lot of a household slave.

Use of
wine.
Relaxation of manners is significantly marked by frequent notices of drunkenness. There are not wanting instances even of governors deposed because of it. Omar was rigorous in imposing the legal penalty. He did not shrink from commanding stripes to be inflicted, even on his own son and his boon companions, for the use of wine. At Damascus, the scandal grew to such a height that Abu Obeida had to summon a band of Citizens, with the hero Dhirar at their head, for the offence. Hesitating to enforce the law, he begged of Omar that the penitent offenders might be forgiven. An angry answer came: 'Gather an assembly,' he wrote in the stern language of his early days, 'and bring them forth. Then ask, *Is wine lawful, or forbidden?* If they shall say *forbidden*, lay eighty stripes on each; if *lawful*, behead them every one.' They confessed that it was forbidden, and submitted to the ignominious punishment.

Influence
of concu-
binage on
the family.
Weakness for wine may have been a relic of the days when the poet sang, 'Bury me under the roots of the juicy vine.' But there were domestic influences altogether new

at work in the vast accession of captive women, Greek, Persian, and Egyptian, to the Moslem harems. The Jews and Christians might retain their ancestral faith, whether as concubines or married to their masters. With their ancestral faith they, no doubt, retained much also of the habits of their fatherland; and the same may be said both of them and of the Heathen and Parsee slave-girls, even when adopting outwardly the Moslem faith. The countless progeny of these alliances, though ostensibly bred in the creed and practice of Islam, must have inherited much of the mothers' life and nationality who nursed and brought them up. The crowded harem, with its sanction of servile concubinage, was also an evil school for the rising generation. Wealth, luxury, and idleness were under such circumstances provocative of licence and indulgence, which too often degenerated into intemperance and debauchery.

For, apart from war and faction, Moslem life was idle and inactive. There was little else to relieve its sanctimonious voluptuousness. The hours not spent in the harem were divided between listless converse in the city clubs, and prayers at mosque five times a day. Ladies no longer appeared in public excepting as they flitted along shrouded beneath 'the veil.' The light and grace, the charm and delicacy, imparted by their presence to Arab society, were gone. The softness, brightness, and warmth of nature, so beautifully portrayed in ancient Arab song, were chilled and overcast. Games of chance, and such like amusements, were forbidden; even speculation was checked by the ban on interest for money lent. And so, Mussulman life, cut off, beyond the threshold of the harem, from the ameliorating influences of the gentler sex, began to assume the dreary, morose, and cheerless aspect ever since retained. But nature is not to be for ever thus pent up; the rebound too often comes; and in casting off its shackles, humanity not seldom bursts likewise through the barriers of the faith. The gay youth of Islam, cloyed with the dull delights of the sequestered harem, were tempted thus when they went abroad to evade the restrictions of their creed, and seek in the cup, in music,

A.H. 17-
23. games and dissipation, the excitement which the young
and light-hearted will demand. In the greater cities, intemperance and libertinism were rife. The canker spread,
oftentimes the worse because concealed. The more serious
classes were scandalised not only by amusements, luxuries,
and voluptuous living, inconsistent with their creed, but also
with immoralities not even to be named. Development of
this evil came later on, but tares were already sown even
under the strict regime of Omar [1].

Simplicity
of Omar's
domestic
life.
For the present such excesses prevailed only in foreign
parts. At home, the Caliphs, fortified by the hallowed
associations of Medina, preserved the simplicity of ancient
Arab life. Severe simplicity, indeed, was not incom-
patible (as in the case of Mahomet himself) with the
indulgences of the harem. But even in this respect, the
first three Caliphs, judged by the standard of Islam, were
temperate and modest. Omar, they say, had no passion for
the sex. Before the Hegira, he contracted marriage with
four wives, but two of these, preferring to remain at Mecca,
separated from him. At Medina, he married five more, one
of whom, however, he divorced. The last marriage was in
the eighth year of his reign, when near sixty years of age.
Three years previously, he had married a granddaughter of
the Prophet, under circumstances casting a curious light on
his domestic ways. He conceived a liking for Omm Kolthum, the maiden daughter of Abu Bekr, and sister of Ayesha,
through whom a betrothal was arranged. But Ayesha
found the light-hearted damsel with no desire to wed the
aged Caliph. In this dilemma she had recourse to the
astute Amru, who readily undertook to break the marriage
off. He broached the subject to Omar, who thereupon
imagined that Amru wished the maiden for himself. 'Nay,'
said Amru, 'that I do not; but she hath been bred softly
in the family of her father Abu Bekr, and I fear she may
ill brook thine austere manners, and the gravity of thy
house.' 'But,' replied Omar, 'I have already engaged

[1] For a description of the shameless demoralisation that prevailed in
Damascus and Baghdad, I must refer to the learned and elaborate work of
H. von Kremer, *Culturgeschichte des Orients unter dem Chalifen.*

to marry her ; how can I break it off?' 'Leave that to me,' said Amru ; 'thou hast indeed a duty to provide for Abu Bekr's family, but the heart of this maiden is not with thee. Let her alone, and I will show thee a better than she, another Omm Kolthum, even the daughter of Aly and of Fatima.' So Omar married this other maiden, and she bore him a son and a daughter.

A.H. 17-23.

Many of those whose names we have been familiar with were now dropping off the scene. Fatima, the daughter, and Safia, the aunt, of Mahomet, Zeinab one of his wives, and Mary his Coptic bond-maid, Abu Obeida, Khalid, and Bilal ; and many others who bore a conspicuous part in the great *rôle* of the Prophet's life, had all passed away, and a new race was springing up in their place.

Death of many familiar personages.

Abu Sofian survived till A.H. 32, and died 88 years of age. One eye he lost at the siege of Tayif, and the other at the battle on the Yermuk, so that he had long been blind. He divorced Hind, the mother of Muavia—she who ' chewed the liver' of Hamza at the battle of Ohod[1]. The reason for the divorce does not appear.

Abu Sofian and Hind.

[1] *Life of Mahomet*, p. 272.

O

CHAPTER XXVI.

DEATH OF OMAR.

23 A.H.   644 A.D.

Omar's last pilgrimage, 23 A.H. Oct., 644 A.D. — IT was now the eleventh year of Omar's Caliphate, and though some 60 years of age, he was full of vigour and vigilant in the discharge of the vast responsibilities devolving on him. In the last month of the year, he journeyed, as was his wont, to Mecca ; and taking the Widows of Mahomet in his suite, performed with them the rites of annual Pilgrimage. He had returned but a few days to Medina, when his reign came to a tragic and untimely end.

Abu Lulu, a slave, promises to make him a wind-mill. — A Persian slave, Abu Lulu, had been brought by Moghira from Irac. Made prisoner in his youth by the Greeks, he had early embraced Christianity ; and now, taken by the Moslems, his fate was to endure a second captivity as Moghira's slave. When the crowd of prisoners was marched into Medina from the battle of Nehavend, said to have been Abu Lulu's birth-place, the sight opened springs of tenderness long pent up ; and, stroking the heads of the little ones, he exclaimed : ' *Verily, Omar hath consumed my bowels !* ' He followed the trade of carpenter ; and his master shared the profits. Meeting Omar in the market-place, he cried out, ' Commander of the Faithful ! right me of my wrong, for verily Moghira hath assessed me heavily.' ' At how much ? ' asked the Caliph. ' At two dirhems a day.' ' And what is thy trade ? ' ' A carpenter and worker in iron,' he said. ' It is not much,' replied Omar, ' for a clever artificer like thee. I am told that thou couldest design for me a mill

driven by the wind.' 'It is true.' 'Come then,' continued
the Caliph, 'and make me such a mill that shall be driven
by the wind.' 'If spared,' said the captive in surly voice,
'I will make a mill for thee, the fame whereof shall reach
from east even to far west;' and he went on his way.
Omar remarked, as he passed, the sullen demeanour of
Abu Lulu:—'That slave,' he said, 'spoke threateningly to
me just now.'

Next day, when the people assembled in the Mosque for
morning prayer, Abu Lulu mingled with the front rank of
the worshippers. Omar entered, and, as customary, took
his stand in advance of the congregation, having his back
towards them. No sooner had he begun the prayers, crying
Allah Akbar, than Abu Lulu rushed upon him, and with a
sharp blade inflicted six wounds in different parts of his
body. Then he ran wildly about, killing some and wound-
ing others, and at last stabbed himself to death. Omar,
who had fallen to the ground, was borne into his house
adjoining the court, but was sufficiently composed to desire
that Abd al Rahman should proceed with the service. When
it was ended, he summoned him to his bedside, and signified
his intention of nominating him to the Caliphate. 'Is it
obligatory upon me?' inquired Abd al Rahman. 'Nay, by
the Lord!' said Omar, 'thou art free.' 'That being so,' he
replied, 'I never will accept the burden.' 'Then stanch my
wound,' said the dying Caliph (for life was ebbing through a
gash below the navel), 'and stay me while I commit my trust
unto a company that were faithful unto their Prophet, and
with whom their Prophet was well pleased.' So he named,
together with Abd al Rahman, other four,—Aly, Othman,
Zobeir, and Sad,—as the chiefest among the Companions,
to be Electors of his successor, and called them to his
bedside. When they appeared, he proceeded:—'Wait for
your brother Talha' (absent at the moment from Medina)
'three days; if he arrive, take him for the sixth; if not, ye
are to decide the matter without him.' Then, addressing
each in turn, he warned them of the responsibility attaching
to the duty now imposed upon them, and the danger to the
one elected of partiality towards his own clan and family. 'O

Aly, if the choice fall upon thee, see that thou exalt not the house of Hashim above their fellows. And thou, Othman, if thou art elected, or Sad, beware that thou set not thy kinsmen over the necks of men. Arise, go forth, deliberate, and then decide. Meanwhile Soheib shall lead the prayers.' When they had departed, he called Abu Talha, a warrior of note, to him, saying:—'Go, stand before the door, and suffer no man to enter in upon them.' After a pause he spoke solemnly to those around him :—' Tell it to him who shall succeed, as my last bequest, that he be kind to the Men of the city which gave to us and to the Faith a home; that he make much of their virtues, and pass lightly by their faults. Bid him treat well the Arab tribes; verily they are the backbone of Islam ; the tithe that he taketh from them, let him give it back unto the same for nourishment of their poor. And the Jews and Christians, let him faithfully fulfil the covenant of the Prophet with them. O Lord, I have finished my course. And now to him that cometh after me I leave the kingdom firmly stablished and at peace.' Then he lay down quietly and rested for a time.

Desires to be interred by the Prophet.
After a while he bade his son go forth, and see who it was that had wounded him. Told that it was Abu Lulu, he exclaimed :—' Praise be to the Lord that it was not one who had ever bowed down before Him, even once, in prayer ! Now, Abdallah, my son, go in unto Ayesha and ask her leave that I be buried in her chamber by the side of the Prophet, and by the side of Abu Bekr. If she refuse, then bury me by the other Moslems, in the graveyard of Backie [1]. And list thee, Abdallah, if the Electors disagree' (for he was to have a casting voice) ' be thou with the majority ; or, if the votes be equal, choose the side on which is Abd al Rahman. Now let the people come in.' Crowds had assembled at the door; and, permission given, they approached to make obeisance. As they passed in and out, Omar asked whether any leading man had joined with Lulu in conspiracy against him. ' The Lord forbid ! ' was the loud response, in horror at the very thought.

Among the rest, Aly came to inquire ; and as he sat by the

---

[1] For this burying ground outside the city, see *Life of Mahomet*, p. 208.

Caliph's bedside, the son of Abbas too came up. Omar, who A.H. 23.

dreaded the factious spirit of the latter, said : ' O Ibn Abbas, His death,

art thou with me in this matter ? '   He signified assent, 26 xii. 23

whereupon Omar added earnestly : 'See that thou deceive A.H. Nov.,

me not, thou and thy fellows. Now, Abdallah, my son, 644 A.D.

raise my head from the pillow, then lay it gently down
upon the ground : peradventure the Lord may in mercy
take me thus, this night, for I fear the horrors of the rising
sun.' A physician gave him to drink of date-water ; but it
oozed through the wound unchanged ; and so also with a
draught of milk. Which when the physician saw, he said :
' I perceive that the wound is mortal : make now thy testament, O Commander of the Faithful.' 'That,' said Omar,
' have I done already.' As he lay, his head resting on the
bosom of his son, he recited this couplet :—

> It would have gone hard with my soul, had I not been a Moslem ;
> And fasted and prayed as the Lord hath commanded.

And so, in a low voice, he kept repeating the name of the
Lord, and the Moslem creed, until his spirit passed away.
It was a few days before the close of the 23rd year of the
Hegira. He had reigned for the space of ten years and a
half.

So died Omar, next to the Prophet the greatest in the Achieve-
kingdom of Islam ; for it was all within these ten years that, ments of
by his wisdom, patience, and vigour, the dominion was phate.
achieved of Syria, Egypt, and Persia. Abu Bekr beat down
the apostate tribes ; but at his death the armies of Islam
had but just crossed the Syrian frontier. Omar began his
reign master only of Arabia. He died the Caliph of an
empire embracing some of the fairest provinces under
Byzantine rule, and with Persia to boot. Yet throughout
this marvellous fortune he never lost the balance of a wise
and sober judgment, nor exalted himself above the frugal
habit of the Arab chief. 'Where is the Caliph?' the
visitor would ask, as he looked around the court of the
Medina mosque ; and all the while the monarch might be
sitting in homely guise before him.

Omar's life requires but few lines to sketch. Simplicity Character.

and duty were his guiding principles, impartiality and
devotion the leading features of his administration. Responsibility so weighed upon him that he was heard to
exclaim, ' O that my mother had not borne me; would that
I had been this stalk of grass instead! ' In early life of a
fiery and impatient temper, he was known, even in the later
days of the Prophet, as the stern advocate of vengeance.
Ever ready to unsheathe the sword, it was he that at Bedr
advised the prisoners to be all put to death. But age, as
well as office, had now mellowed this asperity. His sense
of justice was strong. And excepting the treatment of
Khalid, whom he pursued with an ungenerous resentment,
no act of tyranny or injustice is recorded against him; and
even in this matter his enmity took its rise in Khalid's
unscrupulous treatment of a fallen foe. The choice of his
captains and governors was free from favouritism, and
(Moghira and Ammar excepted) singularly fortunate. The
various tribes and bodies in the empire, representing
interests the most diverse, reposed in his integrity implicit
confidence, and his strong arm maintained the discipline of
law and empire. A certain weakness is discernible in his
change of governors at the factious seats of Bussorah and
Kufa. Yet even there, the conflicting claims of Bedouin
and Coreish were kept by him in check, and never dared
disturb Islam till he had passed away. The more distinguished of the Companions he kept by him at Medina,
partly, no doubt, to strengthen his counsels, and partly (as
he would say) from unwillingness to lower their dignity by
placing them in office subordinate to himself. Whip in
hand, he would perambulate the streets and markets of
Medina, ready to punish offenders on the spot; and so the
proverb,—'Omar's whip more terrible than another's sword.'
But with all this he was tender-hearted, and numberless
acts of kindness are recorded of him, such as relieving the
wants of the widow and the fatherless [1].

---

[1] For example, journeying in Arabia during the famine, he came upon a poor
woman and her hungry weeping children seated round a fire, whereon was an
empty pot. Omar hastened on to the next village, procured bread and meat,
filled the pot, and cooked an ample meal; leaving the little ones laughing and
at play.

Omar was the first who assumed the title Ameer al
Momenin, or 'Commander of the Faithful.' '*Caliph* (Suc- First
cessor) *of the Prophet of the Lord*, was too long and called
cumbersome a name,' he said, 'while the other was easier, Commander
and fitter for common use.' of the
Faithful.

According to his desire, Omar was buried side by side Burial.
with the Prophet and Abu Bekr, in the chamber of Ayesha.
Soheib, as presiding over the public prayers, performed the
funeral service, and the five Electors, with the Caliph's son,
lowered the body into its last resting-place.

The Moslem annalist may well sigh as, bidding farewell Stormy
to the strong and single-minded Caliph, he enters on the prospect.
weak, selfish, and stormy reign of his successor.

CHAPTER XXVII.

ELECTION OF OTHMAN.

DZUL HIJJ, 23 A.H.—MOHARRAM, 24 A.H.
NOVEMBER, 644 A.D.

WHAT arrangements Omar might have made for a
successor, had his end come less suddenly upon him, it is
perhaps unnecessary to inquire.   But some more definite
choice he would, in all probability, have formed.   We know
that the perils of disunion hung heavily on his mind.
The unbridled arrogance of the Arabian tribes at Kufa
and Bussorah, flushed with the glory and spoils of war,
was already felt to be a growing danger; while family
rivalries amongst the Coreish themselves had begun to
weaken their hold upon the people.   So much is plain,
that (Abd al Rahman excepted) Omar saw no one
amongst them endowed with sufficient power and influence to hold the reins of government ; none, at least, so
prominent as to take the acknowledged lead.   Again, the
mode of nomination or election proper to Islam was yet
uncertain.   Abu Bekr on his death-bed appointed Omar
his successor; but the higher precedent of Mahomet himself, who when laid aside simply named Abu Bekr to lead
the prayers, was of doubtful meaning.   Had Abu Obeida
survived, Omar was known to say that he would have
chosen him ; but he was gone, and Abd al Rahman would
none of the post.   Weak and faint from the assassin's
dagger, the emergency came upon the dying Caliph un-
prepared.   So, relieving himself of the responsibility, he

fell upon the expedient of nominating the chiefest of the A.H. 23.
Companions, on one or other of whom he knew the choice
must fall, to be Electors.

Omar hoped, no doubt, that the successor thus chosen Their
would have the unequivocal support of those who elected character.
him. But he had not calculated on the frailty of human
nature ; and selfish ends proved more powerful than loyalty.
Abd al Rahman was the only real patriot amongst them.
Talha, Zobeir, and Sad, had none of them any special reason
to aspire to the Caliphate. Zobeir, indeed, was closely related
to the Prophet. Sad, also, was the nephew of Mahomet's
mother ; but his recall from Kufa had tarnished his fame
as conqueror of Medain. Aly, a few years younger, had
the strongest claim of kinship, whatever that might be ; for
he was at once the son of the Prophet's uncle, the widowed
husband of the Prophet's daughter Fatima, and the father
of his only surviving grandsons. He had hitherto, from
inactive temperament, remained passive at the Caliph's
court ; but, of quick and high intelligence, he had ever held
a distinguished place in the counsels of Omar. In the
absence of any leading competitor, his claim could now no
longer be left out of sight, or, without want of spirit, fail to
be asserted by himself. Othman was his only real rival.
Years carried weight with him, for he was now close on
seventy. Attractive in person and in carriage, he first gained
the hand of Rockeya, the Prophet's daughter; shortly after
her death, he married her sister Omm Kolthum ; and when
she, too, died, Mahomet used to say he loved Othman so
dearly that, if another daughter had yet remained, he would
have given her to him. But his character withal had vital
defects. Of a close and selfish disposition, his will was soft
and yielding. And of all the competitors, Othman probably
had the least capacity for dominating the unruly elements
now fermenting throughout the Moslem empire.

The Electors, when appointed by Omar, retired, and The
forthwith fell into loud and hot discussion. Omar, over- conclave.
hearing it, desired that they should wait till his decease.
So after the burial, Micdad, a veteran Citizen appointed by
the deceased Caliph to the duty, assembled the Electors in

A.H. 23. the treasury chamber adjoining Ayesha's house, Abu Talha
with a guard keeping watch at the door. Omar had ordered
that the choice should not be delayed beyond the third day,
so that his successor might be declared by the fourth at
latest ; and signified the utmost urgency by saying that if
the minority then resisted, they should be beheaded on the
spot. The Electors, when thus again assembled, pressed
hotly each the claim of his own party, and two days passed
in unprofitable wrangling. Abd al Rahman spent the
night in visiting the leading citizens, and the chief officers
from the provinces (who, having come for the yearly
pilgrimage, had not yet departed), and in sounding their
views. On the third day, Abu Talha warned the Electors
that he would allow no further delay, and that decision
must be come to by the morning. To bring the matter
to an issue, Abd al Rahman offered to forego his own claim,
if only the rest would abide by his choice. They all agreed
but Aly, who at first was silent, but at last said : ' First
give me thy word that thou wilt not regard kith nor kin,
but the right alone and the people's weal.' ' And I,'
rejoined Abd al Rahman, 'ask thee first to give me thy
troth that thou wilt abide by my choice, and against all
dissentients support the same.' Aly assented, and thus the
matter rested in the hands of Abd al Rahman.

Abd al
Rahman
as umpire.
That night Abd al Rahman, closeted with each of the
Electors in turn, did not close his eyes. The contest was
narrowed between the houses of Hashim and Omeyya,
in the persons of Aly and Othman ; and their influence
with the electoral body was fairly equal. Zobeir was in
favour of Aly ; how Sad voted is not certain. Talha had
not yet returned. With Aly and Othman, separately,
Abd al Rahman was long in secret conference. Each
pressed his own claim ; but each admitted the claim of
the other to be the next in weight. The morning broke
upon them thus engaged ; and now the nomination must
be made.

Othman
elected.
The courts of the Mosque overflowed with expectant
worshippers assembled for the morning service. Abd al
Rahman addressed them thus :—' The people think that the

governors, chiefs, and captains from abroad should, without
further waiting, return to their respective posts. Wherefore
advise me now in this matter.' Ammar, late governor of
Kufa, said : ' If it be thy desire that there be no division in
the land, then salute Aly Caliph!' and Micdad affirmed
the same. ' Nay,' cried Abu Sarh, ' if it be thy desire that
there be no division, then salute Othman!' and Abu Rabia
affirmed the same. Ammar turned in contempt on Abu
Sarh ; who, repaying scorn with scorn, said : ' And pray,
Ammar, how long hast thou been counsellor to the Moslems ? Let the Beni Hashim and Omeyya speak for themselves.' But Ammar would not be silent ; whereupon one
cried angrily, ' Thou passest beyond thy bounds, O son of
Someyya ; who art thou, thus to counsel the Coreish [1]?'
Sad, seeing the strife wax warm, said to Abd al Rahman :
' Finish thy work forthwith, or flames of discord will burst
forth.' ' Silence, ye people!' cried Abd al Rahman. ' Be
quiet, or ye will bring evil on yourselves. The determination
of this matter resteth with me.' So saying, he called Aly to
the front ;—' Dost thou bind thyself by the covenant of the
Lord, to do all according to the Book of the Lord, the example of the Prophet, and the precedent of his Successors ? '
' I hope,' responded Aly, ' that I should do so ; I will act
according to the best of my knowledge and ability.' Then
he put the same question to Othman, who answered un-
conditionally,—' Yea, I will.' Whereupon, either dissatisfied
with Aly's hesitating answer, or having already decided in
his mind against him, Abd al Rahman raised his face
toward heaven, and taking Othman by the hand, prayed
thus aloud :—' O Lord, do Thou hearken now and bear me
witness. Verily the burden that is around my neck, the
same do I place round the neck of Othman.' So saying,
he saluted him as Caliph, and the people followed his
example.

It was the first day of the new year, the 24th of the
Hegira. After two or three days spent in receiving the

1st Mo-
harram
24 A.H.
7 Nov.,
644. A.D.

His
inaugural
address.

---

[1] To understand the taunts here bandied, it must be remembered that Abu
Sarh was the foster-brother of Othman, and bore a bad repute, as we shall see
farther on ; and that Ammar was son of a bond-maid called Someyya.

homage of the people, Othman ascended the pulpit, and made a brief and modest speech. 'The first attempt,' he said, ' was always difficult, for he was unused to speak in public. It would be his duty in the future to address them, and the Lord would teach him how.'

Aly's party discontented.   Though Aly, like the rest, took the oath of allegiance, yet his partizans were much displeased, and he himself upbraided Abd al Rahman bitterly with the desire to keep the supreme power out of the Prophet's house and brotherhood. 'Beware,' said Abd al Rahman, with prophetic voice,—' take heed lest, speaking thus, thou makest not a way against thyself, whereof thou shalt repent hereafter.' And so Aly passed out with the words of Joseph on his lips; 'Surely patience becometh me. The Lord is my helper against that which ye devise [1].' Shortly after, Talha returned. Othman acquainted him with what had happened, and as his vote would have ruled the majority, declared that if he dissented, he was prepared even then to resign the Caliphate. But on learning that all the people had agreed, Talha also swore allegiance.

The choice disastrous for Islam.   The choice of Abd al Rahman laid the seeds of disaster. It led to dissensions which for years bathed the Moslem world in blood, threatened the existence of the faith, and to this day divide believers in hopeless and embittered schism. But Abd al Rahman could hardly have anticipated the wanton, weak, and wavering policy of Othman, which slowly but surely brought these results about. There is no reason to think that, in discharging his functions as Umpire, he acted otherwise than loyally and for the best [2].

[1] *Sura* xii. 219.

[2] He discharged the invidious task as a loyal and unselfish patriot. Night and day engaged in canvassing the sentiments of the leading chiefs, he did his best to compose the antagonistic claims of the Electors. The immediate cause of his nominating Othman is not easy to find. Abbasside traditions assume it to have been the conscientious scruples of Aly in hesitating to swear that he would follow strictly the precedents of Abu Bekr and of Omar. The Coran and the precedent of Mahomet he would implicitly obey, but the precedent of the first Caliphs only so far as he agreed with them. In the tenor of the traditions relating how Abd al Rahman first questioned Aly and then Othman, and in their replies, I hardly find sufficient ground for this assumption ; and it looks very much of a piece with the Abbasside fabrications of later days.

An embarrassing incident followed the accession of Othman. Some one told Obeidallah, son of the deceased Murder of
Caliph, that Abu Lulu had been seen shortly before in Hormuzan
private converse with Hormuzan, the Persian prince, and and affair
with a Christian slave belonging to Sad ; and that when son.
surprised, the three separated, dropping a poniard such as
that with which the assassin had wounded Omar. Rashly
assuming a conspiracy, the infuriated son rushed with
drawn sword to avenge his father's death, and slew both
the prince and the slave. Sad, incensed at the loss of his
slave, seized Obeidallah, still reeking with his victims'
blood, and carried him, as the murderer of a believer (for
Hormuzan had professed the Moslem faith), before the
Caliph. A council was called. There was not a tittle of
evidence, or presumption even, of the supposed conspiracy. Aly conceived that, according to the law, Obeidallah must be put to death, as having slain a believer
without due cause. Others were shocked at the proposal :—
' But yesterday,' they said, ' the Commander of the Faithful lost his life, and to-day thou wilt put his son to death ! '
Moved by the appeal, Othman assumed the responsibility
of naming a money compensation in lieu of blood, and this
he paid himself. Some feeling was excited, and people
said that the Caliph was already departing from the strict
letter of the law. The poet, Ibn Lebid, satirised both the
murderer, and the Caliph who had let him off, in stinging
verse. But he was silenced ; the matter dropped, and
there is no reason to think that the judgment was generally
disapproved.

One of Othman's first acts was to increase the stipends Othman
of the chief men all round, by the addition to each of one increases
hundred dirhems. The act, no doubt, was popular, but it stipends.
gave promise of extravagance in the new administration.

CHAPTER XXVIII.

CALIPHATE OF OTHMAN.—GENERAL REVIEW.

24–35 A.H.   645–656 A.D.

Causes of Othman's unpopularity.

THE reign of Othman lasted twelve years. It is usual to say that the first six were popular, and the last six the reverse ; in other words, that during his later years the tide turned, and, discontent ripening into sedition, the storm burst with gathered fury upon the aged Caliph. This is true to some extent ; but in reality the causes of unpopularity were busily at work from the very first. They were twofold, as has been already noticed; first, antagonism between the Arab nation at large and the Coreish ; and, second, jealousy among the Coreish themselves,—namely, between the house of Hashim and that of Omeyya, to which Othman and Muavia belonged.

1. Antagonism between Arab tribes and Coreish.

The Arab soldiery, flushed with the glory and fruits of victory, were spread all over the empire. In Syria, they were held in check by the powerful hand of Muavia, strengthened by the large body of influential citizens from Mecca and Medina settled there. But in other lands, conscious of their power, the Arab tribes were rapidly getting the bit between their teeth. Their arrogant and factious spirit had its focus in Kufa and in Bussorah ; in both these cities, indeed, it had already under Omar shown itself; for even he had not been able effectually to curb their insolence. The Arabs were impatient of control, partly because the success of Islam was due to their arms; partly because in the brotherhood of the faith, all believers, specially those of Arab blood, stood on equal ground. The power of the Caliph, indeed, as successor to the Prophet, was absolute, uncontrolled by any constitutional authority whatever. But even he, yielding to popular sentiment, not only took counsel on critical occasions with the leading men around him, but, as a rule, held himself bound by the same, and enjoined the like on his lieutenants. And so it was that in the concessions which he made to the clamour of the citizens of Bussorah and Kufa, Omar had already set a baneful lesson to his Successor, and given to those constituencies a foretaste of power which they were not slow to take advantage of. Thus the turbulent spirit grew from day to day,—a spirit of opposition to authority, and impatience of Coreishite rule.

The second cause, less threatening to Islam at large, was more insidious, and fraught with greater danger to the Caliphate, and to the person of Othman himself. Had the Coreish rallied loyally around the throne, they might have nipped the Arab faction in the bud. But the weakness of Othman, and the partiality with which he favoured his own people, stirred the jealousy of the house of Hashim, which began now to vaunt the claims of Aly and the Prophet's family, and to depreciate the Omeyyad branch to which the Caliph belonged. That branch, unfortunately for the Omeyyads, had been the tardiest to recognise the mission of the Prophet; and those on whom Othman lavished his favours had been amongst the most inveterate. Every expression uttered by Mahomet during that period of bitter enmity, was now raked up and used to blacken their names, and cast discredit on a government which promoted them to power and honour. Thus the Coreish were divided; rivalry paralysed their influence, and Othman lost the support which would otherwise have enabled him to crush the machinations of the Arab malcontents. Still worse, Aly and his party lent themselves to the disloyal policy of the Bedouin faction which was fast sapping the foundations of the Caliphate, and which, as Aly should have foreseen, would in the end, if he succeeded to the throne, recoil against himself.

2. Jealousy between houses of Hashim and Omeyya.

It was not, however, till later on that these influences,

A.H. 24– though early at work, assumed dangerous prominence.
  35.
         This was in great measure due to the military operations
Factious which, busily pursued in all directions throughout the twelve
spirit
diverted by years of Othman's caliphate, served to divert attention from
military   domestic trouble. Expeditions, as we have seen, had from
service.
          time to time been directed towards the East, and the
          various provinces brought more or less under tributary
Campaigns subjection. Shortly after the death of Omar, a general
in the East.
31 A.H.   rising took place in Persia, and to restore Moslem supremacy,
652 A.D. a series of enterprises were, by command of Othman, set on
          foot. Ibn Aamir, governor of Bussorah, having first re-
          duced the adjoining province of Fars, inaugurated a great
          campaign in the north and east. The land was overrun,
          and the strongholds, after they had been either stormed or
          had surrendered at discretion, were ordinarily left in
          the hands of Native princes on condition of a heavy
          tribute. Nishapur, taken by treachery of one of the Mir-
          zabans, was assessed at a million, and Merve at a million
          and a quarter pieces; and so on with the other States.
          Serukhs surrendered on quarter being given for a hundred
          lives; but in furnishing the list of names, the Mirzaban
          forgot his own, and so was beheaded with the rest of the
          fighting men. A great battle was fought at Khawarezm on
          the Oxus, and the country as far as Balkh and Takharistan
          forced to acknowledge the Caliph's suzerainty. Having
          achieved these splendid victories, in which were taken
          40,000 captives, Ibn Aamir set out for Mecca, on a pil-
          grimage of thanksgiving. The lieutenants whom he left to
          prosecute the campaign, restored authority at the point of
          the sword in the revolted parts of Kerman and Sejestan,
          and brought under obedience the chiefs as far as Herat,
          Kabul, and Ghazni[1]. The control must, however, as yet
          have been but slight and desultory; for long years after, we
          find these outlying provinces continually rising against

---

[1] Idolatry long prevailed throughout these parts. In Sejestan, the general
seized the shrine of an idol made of gold, and the eyes of rubies. The arms
he cut off, and took out the rubies. 'Here,' said he, as he gave them back
to the prince, 'these are thine; this I did only to let thee know that this thing
can neither hurt thee nor can it do thee good.' It may have been a Budd; but
of Buddhism as a religion we hear little or nothing in this direction.

Moslem rule, and again for the time asserting independence. A.H. 24-35. Kerman, however, and the nearer parts were held under a more substantial sway ; forts were erected, watercourses dug, and the land divided among the conquerors ; and so settled rule gradually extended eastward. It was not till 31 A.H. the eighth year of Othman's reign that Yezdegird died. 652 A.D. There are various accounts of his wanderings in the East after the battle of Nehavend, destitute and helpless ; but they all agree in the fact that about this time, taking shelter in a miller's hut, he was there assassinated, and that he was buried with reverence by the Metropolitan of Merve [1]. The knowledge that the line of Nushirvan was at an end, tended no doubt now to the pacification of the East.

Although upon the whole the progress of the Moslems was steadily forward, there were still reverses, and these not seldom of a serious kind. An arduous campaign was carried on during Othman's reign against the hordes of Turks and Khizrs, to the west of the Caspian sea. In the year 32 A.H. these gained so signal an advantage in the mountainous passes of Azerbijan, that in the discomfiture which followed, the Arab leaders and a great body of the veterans were slain. To retrieve the disaster, Othman ordered levies from Syria to reinforce the Kufan army. Bad blood bred between the two; the Syrians refused to serve under a general commanding troops from Kufa ; and an altercation ensued which nearly led to bloodshed. This, adds the historian, was the first symptom of the breach between the Kufans and the men of Syria, which subsequently broke out into prolonged hostility. About the same time, a whole army was lost in deep snow upon the heights of Kerman, only two men escaping to tell the tale. There were also some alarming losses in Turkestan. But Arabia continued to cast forth its swarms of fighting tribes in such vast numbers, and the wild fanaticism of the faith still rolled on so rapidly, that such disasters soon disappeared in the swelling tide of conquest.

Turks and Khizrs, 32 A.H. 653 A.D.

---

[1] We have this in two different traditions. The Bishop summoned the Christians (who would seem to have been at the time a substantial body), and recounting the benefits they had received from the Persian dynasty, made them build a church or shrine over the remains which were buried there.

A.H. 24-
35.

Syria en-
tirely under
Muavia.

Syria had by this time come entirely into the hands of Muavia. On the death of his brother Yezid, Omar gave him the government of Damascus; and as the governors of the other districts passed away, their districts were placed successively under him; till at last, in the early years of Othman, to whom as of the Omeyyad line Muavia was closely related, the entire Province fell to be adminis-

Fighting
with
Greeks,
26 A.H.
647 A.D.

tered by him. Excepting raids of little import, Syria had for some time enjoyed rest, when suddenly in the second year of Othman's caliphate, Muavia was startled by the approach of an army from Asia Minor, which he had not the means to oppose. Help was ordered from the eastern provinces, and 8,000 volunteers soon joined the Syrian army. Thus reinforced, the Arabs repulsed the Byzantine attack. Following up the success, they overran Asia Minor, and passing through Armenia, reached Tabaristan, thus forming a junction with their comrades on the eastern shore of the Caspian. Then turning north, they marched as far as Tiflis, and reached even to the shores of the Black sea. Thereafter hostilities with the Greeks were renewed every summer; and eventually, aided by naval expeditions from the ports of Africa, the Syrian generals pushed forward their conquests in the Levant and Asia Minor, strengthened their border, and enlarged their coasts. A few years before the death of Othman, Muavia, accompanied by Atika, his Bedouin wife, headed one of these expeditions along the coast to the very precincts of Constantinople.

Africa,
25 A.H.
646 A.D.

In Africa, I have already noticed the desperate attack made early in this reign on Alexandria from seaward; the Byzantine forces on that occasion actually regained posses-sion of the city, but were shortly after driven out by Amru; and against the Moslem power in Egypt no further attack was for the present made. Farther to the west, how-ever, the Byzantine arms remained long in force; and along the northern shores of the Mediterranean, strong Arab columns were still actively engaged. Among the chiefs who had joined the Egyptian army was Abu Sarh, already noticed as the foster-brother of Othman. He bore no enviable reputation in Islam. Employed by Mahomet

to record his revelations, he had proved unfaithful to the A.H. 24-35.
trust ; and on the capture of Mecca, was by the Prophet
proscribed from the amnesty, and only at the intercession
of Othman escaped death. An able administrator, he
was appointed by Omar to the government of Upper
Egypt. But some years after, he fell out with Amru, in
whom was vested the supreme control of the province.
Each appealed to Othman, who declared Amru to be
in fault, and deposed him from the revenue and civil con- Amru
trol. Amru objected. 'To be over the army,' he said, 'and superseded by Abu
not over the revenue, was like holding the cow's horns, Sarh,
while another milked her.' He repaired angrily to Othman, 647 A.D.
who, after some words of bitter altercation, transferred the
whole administration into the hands of Abu Sarh. The act
was unfortunate for the Caliph. It threw Amru into the
ranks of the disaffected ; while the bad repute of Abu Sarh,
'the renegade,' as they called him, gave point to the charges
of partiality and nepotism now rife against Othman [1].

Abu Sarh, left thus in sole command, carried his arms Conquest
vigorously along the coast beyond Tripoli and Barca, and 26 A.H.
even threatened Carthage. Gregory, the governor, rein- 647 A.D.
forced by the Emperor, advanced against him with an
army, we are told, of 120,000 men. Othman, warned of
the danger, sent a large contingent to Abu Sarh's
help, with which marched a numerous company of 'Companions.' The field was long and hotly contested ; and
Abu Sarh, to stimulate his troops, promised the hand of
Gregory's daughter, with a large dower, to the warrior who
should slay her father. The enemy was at last discomfited
with great slaughter, and a citizen of Medina gained the
lady for his prize. He carried her off on his camel to
Medina ; and the martial verses which he sang by the
way are still preserved [2]. In this campaign, Othman in-

---

[1] Abu Sarh's name was Abdallah ; he narrowly escaped execution at the
capture of Mecca ; *Life of Mahomet*, p. 425; and party spirit now freely magnified his offence. He was abused as the person alluded to in *Sura* vi. 94 : ' who
is more wicked than he who saith, *I will produce a revolution like unto that
which the Lord hath sent down.*' See Sale *in loco*.

[2] The campaign furnishes plentiful material for the romances of the pseudo-

curred much odium by granting Abu Sarh a fifth of the royal Fifth of booty as personal prize. The rest was sent as usual to Medina ; and here again Othman is blamed for allowing Merwan his cousin to become the purchaser of the same at an inadequate price.

Naval
operations
forbidden
by Omar,
But it is as the first commander of a Moslem fleet that Abu Sarh is chiefly famous, in which capacity he added largely to the conquests of Islam, and also by his jealous pre-eminence contributed anew to the obloquy cast on his master's name. Muavia had long keenly missed the support of a fleet, and in fact had sought permission from Omar to embark his soldiery in ships. 'The isles of the Levant,' he wrote, 'are close to the Syrian shore ; you might almost hear the barking of the dogs and cackling of the hens : give me leave to attack them.' But Omar dreaded the sea, and wrote to consult Amru, who answered thus :—' The sea is a boundless expanse, whereon great ships look tiny specks ; nought but the heavens above and waters beneath ; when calm, the sailor's heart is broken ; when tempestuous, his senses reel. Trust it little, fear it much. Man at sea is an insect on a splinter, now engulfed, now scared to death.' On receipt of this alarming account, Omar forbade Muavia to have anything to do with ships ;—' The Syrian sea, they tell me, is longer and broader than the dry land, and is instant with the Lord, night and day, seeking to swallow it up. How should I trust my people on its accursed bosom ? Remember Ala. Nay, my friend, the safety of my people is dearer to me than all the treasures of Greece.'

but under-
taken by
Othman.
Nothing, therefore, was attempted by sea in the reign of Omar. But on his death, Muavia reiterated the petition, and Othman at last relaxed the ban, on condition that maritime service should be voluntary. The first fleet equipped against Cyprus, in the 28th year of the Hegira, was commanded by Abu Cays as admiral ; it was joined by Abu Sarh with a complement of ships manned by Egyptians, and Arab warriors from Alexandria. Cyprus

Wackidy and later writers. According to some, the maiden leapt from the camel, and being killed escaped thus her unhappy fate.

was taken easily, and a great multitude of captives carried off. The Cypriots agreed to pay the same revenue as they had done to the Emperor; and the Caliph, unable as yet to guarantee their protection, remitted the poll-tax. Of Abu Cays we are told that he headed fifty expeditions by land and by sea, but was killed at last, while engaged in exploring a Grecian sea-port.

Three years after the fall of Cyprus, driven now from the harbours of Africa, and seriously threatened in the Levant, the Byzantines gathered a fleet of some 500 vessels, and defied the Arabs. Abu Sarh was appointed to answer the challenge. He manned every available ship in the ports of Egypt and Africa; and his squadron, though inferior in weight and equipment to the enemy's, was crowded with valiant warriors from the army. The Byzantine fleet came in sight near Alexandria. The wind lulled, and both sides lay for a while at anchor. The night was passed by the Moslems in recitation of the Coran and prayer, while the Greeks kept up the clangour of their bells. In the morning, a fierce engagement took place. The Arab ships grappled with their adversaries, and a hand-to-hand encounter with sword and dagger ensued. The slaughter was great on both sides; but the Greeks, unable to withstand the wild onset of the Saracens, broke and dispersed. The Byzantine commander sailed away to Syracuse, where the people, infuriated at the defeat, despatched him in his bath[1].

This splendid victory notwithstanding, discontent against Othman now for the first time found free and dangerous expression among the leading Companions in the fleet. They murmured thus against the Caliph;—' Othman hath changed the ordinances of his predecessors, he hath made Admiral a man whom the Prophet would have put to death; and such like men also hath he put in chief command at Kufa, Bussorah, and elsewhere.' The clamour reaching the ears of Abu Sarh, he declared that none of the malcontents should fight in his line of battle. Excluded thus, they

---

[1] According to Theophanes, it was Constans II who so perished, but at a later date. See Gibbon, ch. xlviii.

A.H. 24–
35.

Outlook
darkens.

were the more incensed.   Spite of the threats of Abu Sarh,
the inflammatory language spread, and men began to speak
openly and unadvisedly against Othman.

The clouds were louring, and the horizon of the Caliph
darkened all around.

CHAPTER XXIX.

DOMESTIC EVENTS DURING THE LATTER DAYS OF OTHMAN.—HIS GROWING UNPOPULARITY.

30-34 A.H.   651-55 A.D.

KUFA and Bussorah at this period exercised an influence Discontent on the destinies of Islam hardly less potent than that of at Kufa and Bussorah. Medina itself.   The turbulent and factious atmosphere of these cities became rapidly charged with a spirit of disloyalty and rebellion, aggravated by the weak and unwise change of their governors.

Moghira did not long enjoy the command at Kufa.   He Sad reinstated at Kufa, was removed by Othman, who, to fill the vacancy, in obedi- Kufa, ence (some say) to the dying wish of Omar, reinstated Sad 34 A.H. in his former office.   The issue again was unsuccessful.   To 645 A.D. provide for his luxurious living, Sad took an advance from Ibn Masud, chancellor of the treasury, who, by and by, became importunate for repayment.   A heated alterca- tion ensued, and Sad swore angrily at Ibn Masud.   The factious city ranged itself, part with the great warrior, and part with the quondam slave.   The quarrel reached the ears of Othman, who, much displeased, recalled Sad before he had been a year in office.   As successor, the Caliph ap- Superseded pointed Welid ibn Ocba, a brave warrior, but suspected of by Welid ibn Ocba, intemperance, and withal a uterine brother of his own. The choice was all the more unfortunate, because Welid was son of that Ocba who, when taken prisoner at Bedr and about to be put to death, exclaimed in the bitterness of his soul, 'Who will care for my little children?' and was

A.H. 30–
34. answered by the Prophet, 'Hell-fire!'[1]   The words were
not forgotten, and faction was careful now to turn them to
account.   Nevertheless, Welid was popular; and as for
several years he directed successive campaigns in the East
with gallantry and vigour, he managed to divert the restless
spirits from discontent at home.   But in the end, the unruly
populace was too strong for him.   A murder took place,
and sentence of death was executed at the city gate against
the culprits.   Their relatives resented the act of justice,
and watched for ground of accusation against the governor,
whose habits gave them ready opportunity.   Charges of
intemperance were repeatedly dismissed by Othman, for
who is de-
posed for
inebriety.   want of legal proof.   At last his enemies succeeded in
detaching from his hand the signet-ring of office while he
slept from the effects of a debauch, and carried it off in
triumph to Medina.   But still worse, it was established that
Welid had conducted the morning prayers in such a state
that, having come to the proper end of the service, he went
on, without stopping, to commence another.   The scandal
was great; and the majesty of Islam must be vindicated.
Welid was recalled to Medina, scourged according to law,
and deposed.

Abu Musa
deposed at
Bussorah,
29 A.H.
650 A.D.   At Bussorah, too, things were going from bad to worse.
Abu Musa had now been many years governor, when the
restless citizens became impatient of his rule.   He had
been preaching to the pampered soldiery the virtue of
enduring hardness, and going forth on foot to war.   When
the next expedition was ready, they watched to see
whether he would himself set the example.   As his
ample baggage issued forth, winding from the castle on
a long string of mules, they set upon him, crying, 'Give
us of these beasts to ride upon, and walk thou on foot,
a pattern of the hardness thou preachest unto us.'   Then
they repaired to Medina, and complained that he had drained
the land of its wealth, pampered the Coreish, and tyrannised
over the Arab tribes.   Instead of checking their petulance
with promptitude, Othman gave it new life by deposing
Abu Musa, and appointing a certain obscure citizen whom

---

[1] *Life of Mahomet*, p. 235.

they desired, to be their governor. Found unequal to the
post, this man was deposed, and a youthful cousin of the
Caliph, Ibn Aamir, promoted in his room. When tidings
of his nomination reached Bussorah, Abu Musa said: 'Now
ye shall have a tax-gatherer to your hearts' content, rich
in cousins, aunts, and uncles, who will flood you with his
harpies!' And so it turned out; for he soon filled the
local offices and the commands in Persia with creatures of
his own. In other respects, however, he proved an able
ruler; his signal victories in the East have been already
noticed, and in the struggle now close at hand he took
a leading part.

The government of Kufa, vacated by the deposition of
Welid, was conferred by Othman, together with the whole of
Mesopotamia, upon another young and untried kinsman,
Said ibn al Aas. His father was killed fighting against the
Prophet at Bedr; and the boy, thus left an orphan, had
been brought up by Omar, who eventually sent him to the
wars in Syria. Receiving a good account of his breeding
and prowess, Omar summoned him to his court, and gave
him two Arab maidens to wife[1]. This youth, now promoted
to the most critical post in the empire, was not only without experience in the art of governing but, vainly inflated
with the pretensions of the Coreish, made no account of
the powerful Bedouin faction. Accustomed in Syria to
the strong discipline of Muavia, he wrote to Othman, on
reaching Kufa, that licence reigned there, that noble birth
passed for nothing, and that the Bedouins were altogether
out of hand. His first address as governor was a blustering
harangue, in which he glibly talked of crushing the sedition and arrogance of the men of Kufa with a rod of iron.
Countenanced in his overbearing course by the Caliph, he
fomented discontent by invidious advancement of the
Coreishite nobility, and by treating with contumely the
great body of the citizens. 'One Coreishite succeedeth
another as our governor,' they said;—' the last no better than

---

[1] He was nephew to the Khalid who opened so ingloriously the Syrian campaign. Not satisfied with the pair of wives, he had a numerous harem, and left
twenty sons and as many daughters.

A.H. 30-
34.
the first. It is but out of the frying-pan into the fire.' The
under-current of faction daily gained strength and volume.
But the vigorous campaigns of Said in Northern Persia, for
he was an active soldier, served for a time to occupy men's
minds, and to stay the open exhibition of a rebellious
spirit.

Recension
of Coran,
30 A.H.
651 A.D.
Meanwhile other causes were at work—some apparently
insignificant in themselves, but turned adroitly to account
by the enemies of Othman. First was the recension of the
Coran. The Moslem armies were spread over such vast areas
and they, as well as the converted peoples, were so widely
separated one from another, that differences arose in the recitation of the sacred text, as it had been settled in the previous
reign. Bussorah followed the reading of Abu Musa; Kufa
was guided by the authority of Ibn Masud; and the text
of Hims differed from that in use even at Damascus. Hodzeifa, during his long campaign in Persia and Azerbijan,
having witnessed the variations in different provinces,
returned to Kufa gravely impressed with the urgent need
of revision. Ibn Masud was highly incensed with the
slight thus put upon the authority of his text. But Hodzeifa, supported by the governor, urged Othman to restore
the unity of the divine word, 'before that believers begin
to differ in their scripture, even as the Jews and Christians.' The Caliph, advised by the leading Companions
at Medina, called for copies of the manuscripts in use
throughout the empire. He then appointed a syndicate of
experts from amongst the Coreish, to collate these with the
sacred originals still in the keeping of Haphsa. Under
their supervision the variations were reconciled, and an
authoritative exemplar written out, of which duplicates
were deposited at Mecca, Medina, Kufa and Damascus.
Copies were multiplied over the empire; former manuscripts called in and committed to the flames: and the
standard text brought into exclusive use. The action of
Othman was received at the moment, as it deserved,
with general consent, excepting at Kufa. There Ibn
Masud, who prided himself on his faultless recitation
of the oracle, pure as it fell from the Prophet's lips, was

much displeased ; and the charge of sacrilege in having A.H. 30–
34.
burned copies of the divine Word, was readily seized on
by the factious citizens. By and by the cry was spread
abroad ; and, taken up with avidity by the enemies of
Othman, we find it ages afterwards still eagerly urged
by the partisans of the Abbasside dynasty as an unpardonable offence against the ungodly Caliph. The accusation thus trumped up was really without foundation.
Indeed, it was scouted by Aly himself. When, several
years after, as Caliph, he found the citizens of Kufa still
blaming his ill-starred predecessor for the act ;—'Silence!'
he cried ; 'Othman acted with the advice of the leading
men amongst us ; and had I been ruler at the time, I
should myself have done the same[1].'

A great body of the nobility from Mecca and Medina *Many*
about this time transferred their residence to Kufa and *Coreish*
migrate
Bussorah. These had no right to share in the endowments *to Irac.*
of Irac, the special privileges of which, in virtue of conquest, were reserved for the original settlers. They were
allowed, however, now to do so on condition that they
surrendered their properties in the Hejaz. The concession
afforded fresh ground for discontent at the extravagant
pretensions of the Coreish.

The story of Abu Dzarr is singularly illustrative of the *Abu Dzarr*
times, and his treatment formed one of the grounds of com- *Ghifary.*
plaint against the Caliph. He was an early convert to
the faith ; and is said even to have anticipated Mahomet
in some of the observances of Islam. An ascetic in habit, he
inveighed against the riches and indulgences of the day
as altogether alien from the faith, and as evils which,
rushing in like a flood, were now demoralising the people.
Gorgeous palaces, crowds of slaves, horses and camels,
flocks and herds, costly garments, sumptuous fare, and
splendid equipage, were the fashion, not only in Syria and

---

[1] On this recension, see Excursus on the 'Sources for the Biography of
Mahomet,' in the *Life of Mahomet*. The manner in which the Abbasside fac-
tion perverted the facts and turned the charge to malignant purpose against the
Omeyyad house, is well illustrated in the *Apology of Al Kindy*, pp. 25 *et seq.*
The charge against Hajjaj is equally groundless. *Ibid.* p. xi.

Irac, but even now within the Holy cities[1]. The protest of Abu Dzarr was the natural recoil of a strict and fervid believer from the graceless and licentious luxury of the day: but it was seized by the discontented classes as a weapon against the government. Visiting Syria, the ascetic, whose spirit was stirred at the pomps and vanities around him, preached repentance. 'This gold and silver of yours,' he cried, ' shall one day be heated red-hot in the fire of hell ; and therewith shall ye be seared in your foreheads, sides, and backs, ye ungodly spendthrifts[2]! Wherefore, spend now the same in alms, leaving yourselves enough but for your daily bread ; else woe be unto you in that day !' Crowds flocked round him at Damascus, some trembling under his rebuke ; others rejoicing at the contempt poured on the rich and noble; while the people at large were dazzled by the vision of sharing in the treasures of the classes thus denounced. Uneasy at the disturbing effect of these diatribes, Muavia resolved to test the spirit of the preacher. He sent him a purse of 1,000 pieces, and in the morning, affecting to have made a mistake, demanded its return ; but during the night Abu Dzarr had distributed the whole in charity. On this, Muavia, convinced of his sincerity, and apprehensive of the spread of his socialistic doctrines, despatched the preacher to Medina, telling Othman that he was an honest but misguided enthusiast. Before the Caliph, Abu Dzarr persisted in fearlessly denouncing the great and wealthy, and urged that they should be forced to disgorge their riches. Othman con-

---

[1] Masudy dwells on this as one of the causes of demoralisation and disloyalty now setting in so rapidly, and he gives some remarkable instances. *Zobeir* had 1,000 slaves, male and female, and 1,000 horses. At all the great cities he had palaces, and the one at Bussorah was still to be seen in the fourth century. His landed estate in Irac was rated at 1,000 golden pieces a day. *Abd al Rahman* had 1,000 camels, 10,000 sheep, and left property valued at four hundred thousand dinars. *Zeid* left gold and silver in great ingots, and had land valued at 10,000 dinars. The Coreishite nobles built themselves grand palaces in Mecca and Medina and their environs. Othman himself had a splendid palace at Medina, with marble pillars, walls of costly stucco, grand gates and gardens ; he also amassed vast treasures.

[2] *Sura* ix. 36 ; originally applied to Christian priests and monks. *Life of Mahomet*, p. 470.

descended to reason with him. 'When once men have fulfilled their obligations,' he asked, 'what power remaineth
with me to compel any further sacrifice?' and he turned to
Kab, a learned Jewish convert, to confirm what he had
said. 'Out upon thee, son of a Jew! What have I to do
with thee?' cried Abu Dzarr, smiting Kab violently on
the stomach. Argument being thus of no further use,
Othman banished the preacher to Rabadza in the desert,
where two years after he died in penury. Finding the end
approach, the hermit desired his daughter to slay a kid,
and have it ready for a party of travellers who, he said,
would shortly pass that way to Mecca; then, making her
turn his face toward the Kaaba, he quietly breathed his
last. Soon after, the expected party came up, and amongst
them Ibn Masud from Kufa, who, weeping over the departed saint, bewailed his fate, and buried him on the
spot, which became one of holy memory. The death of
Ibn Masud himself, a few days after, added to the pathos
of the incident. The plaintive tale was soon in everyone's mouth; and the banishment of the famous preacher
of righteousness was made much of by the enemies of the
Caliph. The necessity for it was forgotten, but the obloquy
remained[1].

When himself minded to assume the office of censor and
rebuke the ungodliness of the day, the unfortunate Caliph
fared no better. The laxity of Syria had reached even to
the sacred precincts of the Hejaz; and Othman, on attempting to check the games and other practices held

---

[1] Attempts are made by Abbasside tradition to show that Abu Dzarr was
driven into opposition by the tyranny of Muavia's rule, and by divers ungodly
practices permitted by Othman at Medina. But Ibn al Athir justly doubts
this, and distinctly says that his preaching tended to excite the poor against
the rich. Abu Dzarr's doctrines were based on the equality of believers; and
the danger lay in their popularity with the socialists who decried the pretensions
of the Coreish. Before Muavia, he reasoned thus: ' *Riches*, ye say, *belong unto
the Lord* ; and thereby ye frustrate the people's right therein; for the Lord hath
given them to His people.' ' Out upon thee!' replied Muavia; 'what is this
but a quibble of words? Are we not all of us the Lord's people, and the riches
belong unto the same?' Tradition dwells on the want and wretchedness of
Abu Dzarr's life at Rabadza, to add point to Othman's unkind treatment. His
own tribe are said to have resented his ill-treatment by joining in the rebellion.

A.H. 30-
34.
to be inconsistent with the profession of Islam, incurred resentment, especially from the gay youth whose amusements he thwarted. Gambling and wagering, indeed, were put down with the approval of the stricter classes of society; but there were not wanting many who, displeased with the Caliph's interference, joined in the cry of his detractors.

Court of
the Kaaba,
enlarged,
26 A.H.
647 A.D.
The enlargement of the grand square of the Kaaba, commenced by Omar, was carried on by Othman while he visited Mecca on pilgrimage. And here, too, the ill-fated Caliph met with opposition. The owners of the demolished houses refused to accept the compensation offered, and raised a great outcry. The Caliph put them into prison, for, said he, ' My predecessor did the same, and ye made no outcry against him.' But what the firm arm of Omar could do, and none stir hand or foot against him, was a different thing for the weak and unpopular Othman to attempt. He was more successful

andMosque
of Medina,
32 A.H.
653 A.D.
with the Mosque at Medina, originally built by Mahomet, and hallowed by the mortal remains of the Prophet and his two successors. This was now enlarged and beautified. The supports, at first the trunks of date-trees, were removed, and the roof made to rest on pillars of hewn stone. The walls, too, were built up with masonry, richly carved and inlaid with rare and precious stones. It was a pious work, and none objected.

Changes in
pilgrim
ceremonial,
32 A.H.
653 A.D.
Yet another cause of murmuring arose from certain changes made by Othman in the ceremonial of the annual pilgrimage, which, though in themselves trivial and unmeaning, excited strong disapprobation at the Caliph's court. He pitched tents for shelter during the few days spent for sacrifice at Mina, a thing never done before; and, to the prayers heretofore recited there and on Mount Arafat, he added new ones, with two more series of prostrations. The ritual, as established by the Prophet himself, had been scrupulously followed by his two successors, and a superstitious reverence attached even to its minutest detail. When expostulated with on the unhallowed innovation, Othman gave no reasonable answer, but simply said

it was his will to do so. Disregard of the sacred example of the Founder of the faith offended many, and raised a cry among the Companions unfavourable to Othman.

Again, beyond the immediate circle of his kinsfolk, Othman made no personal friends. Narrow, selfish, indiscreet and obstinate,—more and more so, indeed, with advancing years,—he alienated those who would otherwise have stood loyally by him, and made many enemies, who pursued him with relentless hatred. Mohammed, son of Abu Bekr, for example, and Abu Hodzeifa, were among those embittered against him at the naval victory of Alexandria. And yet no very special cause can be assigned for their enmity. The first is said to have been actuated by 'passion and ambition.' The other, nearly related to Othman, and as an orphan kindly brought up by him, was now offended at being passed over for office and command. Both joined the rebellion which shortly broke out in Egypt, and were amongst the most dangerous of the Caliph's enemies. Nor was it otherwise with the people at large. A factious spirit set in against the unfortunate monarch. The leaven fermented all around ; and every man who had a grievance, real or supposed, hastened to swell the hostile cry.

To crown the Caliph's ill-fortune, in the 7th year, he lost the signet-ring of silver which, engraven for the Prophet, had been worn and used officially both by him and his successors. It was a favourite and meritorious occupation of Othman to deepen the old wells, and to sink new ones, in the neighbourhood of Medina. He was thus engaged when directing the labourers with his pointed finger, the ring slipped and fell into the well. Every effort was made to recover the priceless relic. The well was emptied, the mud cleared out, and a great reward offered; but no trace of the ring appeared. Othman grieved over the loss. The omen weighed heavily on his mind ; and it was some time before he consented to supply the lost signet by another of like fashion.

Besides the two daughters of the Prophet, both of whom died before their father, Othman had other wives. Three still survived when, in the 5th year of his Caliphate, being then above seventy years of age, he took Naila to wife. Of her previous history we know little more than that once a Christian, she had embraced Islam. She bore him a daughter; and through all his trials clung faithfully by her aged lord, to the bitter end. The days were coming when he needed such a helper by his side.

CHAPTER XXX.

Dangerous Faction at Kūfa.—Growing Disaffection.

33–34 A.H.   654–55 A.D.

Towards the close of Othman's reign, the hidden ferment, Seditious elements at work, which (Syria perhaps excepted) had long been everywhere at work, began to make its appearance on the surface. The Arab tribes at large were displeased at the pretensions of the Coreish. The Coreish themselves were divided and ill at ease, the greater part being jealous of the Omeyyad house and of the Caliph's favourites. And temptation to revolt was fostered by the weakness and vacillation of Othman himself.

Ibn Aamir had been now three years governor of Busso- Ibn Sauda rah, when Ibn Saba (or, as he is commonly called, Ibn Sauda), preaches sedition in a Jew from the south of Arabia, appeared there, and pro- Egypt, fessed the desire to embrace Islam. It soon appeared that he 32 A.H. 653 A.D. was steeped in disaffection towards the existing government —a firebrand of sedition; as such he was expelled successively from Bussorah, Kufa, and Syria, but not before he had given a dangerous impulse to the already discontented classes there. At last, he found a safe retreat in Egypt, where he became the setter forth of strange and startling doctrines. Mahomet was to come again, even as the Messiah was. Meanwhile, Aly was his legate[1]. Othman

---

[1] What led Ibn Sauda to entertain transcendental ideas of Aly does not appear; and indeed the notices of an 'Alyite sect' at this period, sound somewhat anticipatory and unreal.

Q

was a usurper, and his governors a set of godless tyrants. Impiety and wrong were rampant everywhere; truth and justice could be restored no otherwise than by the overthrow of this wicked dynasty. Such was the preaching which gained daily ground in Egypt; by busy correspondence it was spread all over the empire, and startled the minds of men already foreboding evil from the sensible heavings of a slumbering volcano.

Emeute
at Kufa,
33 A.H.
654 A.D
　　The outbreak of turbulence was for the moment repressed at Bussorah by Ibn Aamir; but at Kufa, Said had neither power nor tact to quell the factious elements around. At the first public service he had offended even his own party by ostentatiously washing the pulpit steps before ascending a spot pretended to have been made unclean by his drunken predecessor. He was foolish enough not only to foster the arrogant assumptions of the Coreish, but to contemn the claims of the Arab soldiery, to whose swords they owed the conquest of the lands around. He called the beautiful vale of Chaldæa *the Garden of the Coreish*—'as if forsooth,' cried the offended Arabs, 'without *our* strong arm and lances, they ever could have won it.' Disaffection, stimulated by the demagogue Ashtar and a knot of factious citizens, culminated at last in an outbreak. As the governor and a company of the people, according to custom, sat in free and equal converse, the topic turned on the bravery of Talha, who had shielded the Prophet in the day of battle. 'Ah!' exclaimed Said, '*he* is a warrior, if ye choose, a real gem amongst your Bedouin counterfeits. A few more like him, and we should dwell at ease.' The assembly was still nettled at this speech, when a youth incautiously gave expression to the wish, how pleasant it would be if the governor possessed a certain property which lay invitingly by the river bank near Kufa. 'What!' shouted the company, 'out of *our* good lands!' And with a torrent of abuse, they leaped upon the lad and his father, and went near to killing both.

Ringleaders
exiled to
Syria.
　　To awe the malcontents, emboldened by this outrage, Ashtar, with ten of the ringleaders, was sent in exile to Syria, where it was hoped that the powerful rule of Muavia and

loyal example of the Syrians might inspire them with better
feelings. Muavia quartered the exiles in a church; and
morning and evening, as he passed by, rated them on their
folly in setting up the crude claims of the Bedouins against
the indefeasible rights of the Coreish. Subdued by several
weeks of such treatment, they were sent on to Hims, where
the governor subjected them for a month to like indignities.
Whenever he rode forth, he showered invectives on them as
traitors working to undermine the empire. Their spirit at
last was broken, and they were released; but, ashamed to
return to Kufa, they remained in Syria, excepting Ashtar,
who made his way secretly to Medina.

A.H 33-
34.

Months passed, and things did not mend at Kufa. Most
of the leading men, whose influence could have kept the
populace in check, were away on military command in
Persia; and the malcontents, in treasonable correspondence
with the Egyptian faction, gained head daily. In an
unlucky moment, Said planned a visit to Medina, there
to lay his troubles before the Caliph. No sooner had
he gone than the conspirators came to the front, and recalled the exiles from Syria. Ashtar, too, was soon upon
the scene. Taking his stand at the door of the Mosque, he
stirred up the people against Said. 'He had himself
just left that despot,' he said, 'at Medina, plotting their
ruin, counselling the Caliph to cut down their stipends,
even the women's; and calling the broad fields which they
had conquered *The Garden of the Coreish.*' The deputy
of Said, with the better class of the inhabitants, sought
in vain to still the rising storm. He enjoined patience.
'Patience!' cried the warrior Cacaa, in scorn; 'ye might
as well roll back the great river when in flood, as quell the
people's uproar till they have the thing they want.' Yezid,
brother of one of the exiles, then raised a standard, and
called upon the enemies of the tyrant, who was then on his
way back, to bar his entry into Kufa. So they marched
out as far as Cadesia, and sent forward to tell Said that
'they did not need him any more.' Little anticipating
such reception, Said remonstrated with them. 'It had
sufficed,' he said, 'to have sent a delegate with your com-

Said ex-
pelled from
Kufa,
34 A.H.
655 A.D.,

plaint to the Caliph; but now ye come forth a thousand strong against a single man!' They were deaf to his expostulations. His servant, endeavouring to push on, was slain by Ashtar; and Said himself fled back to Medina, where he found Othman terrified by tidings of the outbreak, and prepared to yield whatever the insurgents might

and Abu
Musa appointed.
demand. At their desire he appointed Abu Musa, late governor of Bussorah, in place of Said. To welcome him the officers in command of garrisons came from all quarters into Kufa; and Abu Musa received them in the crowded mosque. He first exacted from the inhabitants a pledge of loyalty to the Caliph, and then installed himself by leading the prayers of the great assembly.

Othman's
fatal
mistake.
If, instead of thus giving way, Othman had inflicted on the ringleaders of Kufa condign punishment, he might haply have weathered the storm. It is true that thus he would in all likelihood have precipitated rebellion, not only in that turbulent city, but in Bussorah and Egypt also. Yet, sooner or later, that was unavoidable; and in the struggle he would now have had a strong support. For here the contention was between the Coreish with all the nobility of Islam on the one hand, and the Arab tribes and city rabble on the other; and in this question the great leaders would to a man have rallied round the throne. By his pitiable weakness in yielding to the insurgents, Othman not only courted contempt, but lost the opportunity of placing the great controversy about to convulse the Moslem world upon its proper issue. It fell, instead, to the level of a quarrel obscured by personal interests, and embittered by charges of tyranny and nepotism against himself. The crisis was now inevitable. Men saw that Othman lacked the wisdom and strength to meet it, and each looked to his own concern. Seditious letters circulated freely everywhere; and the claims even began to be canvassed of candidates to succeed Othman, who, it was foreseen, could not long hold the reins of empire in his feeble grasp.

Aly expostulates with
Othman,
Thus, even at Medina, sedition spread, and from thence messages reached the provinces far and near that the sword would soon be needed at home, rather than in foreign parts.

So general was the contagion that besides his immediate kindred, but two or three men are named, as still faithful to the throne. Moved by the leading citizens, Aly repaired to Othman and said :—'The people bid me expostulate with thee. Yet what can I say to thee, who art the son-in-law of the Prophet, as thou wast his bosom friend? The way lieth plain before thee ; but thine eyes are blinded that thou canst not see. Blood once shed, will not cease to flow until the Judgment day. Right blotted out, treason will rage like foaming waves of the sea.' Othman complained, and not without reason, of the unfriendly attitude of Aly himself. 'For my own part,' he said, 'I have done my best ; and as for the men ye blame me for, did not Omar himself appoint Moghira to Kufa ; and if Ibn Amiar be my kinsman, is he the worse for that ?' 'No,' replied Aly ; 'but Omar kept his lieutenants in order, and when they did wrong he punished them ; whereas thou treatest them softly, because they are thy kinsmen.' 'And Muavia, too,' continued the Caliph ;—' it was Omar who appointed him to Syria.' 'Yes,' answered Aly ; 'yet I swear that even Omar's slaves did not stand so much in awe of him, as did Muavia. And now he doth whatever he pleaseth, saying, *It is Othman.* And thou, knowing it all, leavest him alone !' So saying, Aly turned and went his way.

As Aly's message professed to come from the people, who ap- Othman went straightway to the pulpit and addressed the peals to the people. assemblage met for prayer. He reproached them for intemperate speech and subserviency to evil leaders, whose object it was to blacken his name, exaggerate his faults, and hide his virtues. 'Ye blame me,' he said, 'for things ye bore cheerfully from Omar. He trampled on you, beat you with his whip, and abused you. And ye took it patiently from him, both in what ye liked and what ye disliked. I have been gentle with you ; bended my back unto you ; withheld my tongue from reviling, and my hand from smiting. And now ye rise up against me !' Then, after dwelling on the prosperity of his reign at home and abroad, and the many benefits accruing therefrom, he ended—'wherefore, refrain, I intreat of you, from abuse of me and of my governors, lest

A.H. 33–34.

ye kindle the flames of sedition and revolt throughout the empire.' The appeal was marred by his cousin Merwan, who at its close exclaimed, 'If ye will oppose the Caliph, we shall soon bring it to the issue of the sword.' 'Be silent!' cried Othman; 'leave me with my fellows alone. Did I not tell thee not to speak ?' Othman then descended from the pulpit. The harangue had no effect. The discontent spread, and the gatherings against the Caliph multiplied[1].

Close of Othman's 11th year.

Thus ended the 11th year of Othman's reign. Near its close was held a memorable council, of which account will be given in the chapter following. The Caliph performed the pilgrimage as usual. He had done so every year ; this was to be his last.

[1] Merwan is always represented by Abbasside tradition as the evil genius of Othman. The *rôle* he played in this character is no doubt exaggerated.

CHAPTER XXXI.

THE OUTLOOK DARKENS.

34–35 A.H.   655 A.D.

THE unhappy Caliph was now hurried on, by the rapid course of events, helplessly to his end.   Abd al Rahman, who, no doubt, felt himself responsible from the share he took in the nomination of Othman, was about this time removed by death.   But even he had been dissatisfied ; and one of the first open denunciations of Othman's unscrupulous disregard of law,—small it might be, but significant,—is attributed to him.   A high-bred camel, part of the tithes of a Bedouin tribe, was presented by the Caliph, as a rarity, to one of his kinsfolk.   Abd al Rahman, scandalised at the misappropriation of what belonged to charity, laid hands upon the animal, slaughtered it, and divided the flesh among the poor.   The personal reverence attaching heretofore to the ' Successor of the Prophet of the Lord,' gave place to slight and disregard.   In the streets, Othman was greeted with cries that he should depose Ibn Aamir and the godless Abu Sarh, and put away Merwan, his chief adviser and confidant.   He had the countenance of none excepting his immediate kinsmen, and reliance upon them only aggravated the hostile clamour. Othman treated with contumely.

The conspirators had hitherto burrowed under ground.   Now their machinations coming to light, rumours of impending treason began to float abroad.   The better affected classes throughout the empire felt uneasy ;   alarm crept over all Othman sends delegates to test feeling in provinces.

A H. 34–
35.

hearts.   Letters were continually received at Medina, asking what these ominous sounds meant, and what catastrophe was now at hand.   The chief men of Medina kept coming to the Caliph's court for tidings ; but, notwithstanding sullen mutterings of approaching storm, the surface yet was still.   At last, by their advice, Othman despatched a trusty follower to each of the great centres, Damascus, Kufa, Bussorah, and Fostat, to watch and report whether suspicious symptoms anywhere appeared. Three returned saying that they discovered nothing unusual in the aspect of affairs.   The fourth, Ammar, was looked for in vain; for he had been gained over by the Egyptian faction.   Thereupon Othman despatched a royal edict to all the provinces as follows :—At the coming Pilgrimage the governors from abroad would, according to custom, present themselves at court; whoever had cause against them, should then come forward and substantiate the same, when wrong would be redressed ; else it behoved them to withdraw the baseless calumnies that now were troubling men's minds.   Proclamation was made accordingly.   The plaintive appeal was understood ; and people in many places when they heard it wept, and invoked mercy on their Caliph.

Conference of governors at Medina, 34 A.H. 655 A.D.   The governors repaired to Medina at the time appointed, but no malcontent came forward to make complaint. Questioned by Othman, his lieutenants knew not of any grievance, real and substantial.   To the outward eye, everything was calm ; and even the royal messengers had returned without finding anything amiss.   But all knew of the dangerous sore in the body politic, and of its spreading rapidly.   The wretched Caliph invoked their pity and their counsel.   But they could offer nothing of which he might lay hold.   One advised that the conspirators should be arrested and the ringleaders put to death ; another that the stipends of all disloyal men should be forfeited ; a third that the unquiet spirits amongst the people should be diverted by some fresh campaign ; others that the governors should amend their ways.   Othman was bewildered ; one thing only he declared,—to measures of severity he never

would assent; the single remedy he could approve was
despatch of fresh armies to fight in foreign parts.

Nothing was settled to avert the crisis, and the governors departed as they came. When Muavia made ready to leave, he entreated Othman to retire with him to Syria, where a loyal people would rally round him. But he answered: 'Even to save my life I will not quit the land wherein the Prophet sojourned, nor the city wherein his sacred body resteth.' 'Then let me send an army to stand by thee.' 'Nay, that I will not,' responded Othman firmly; 'I never will put force on those who dwell around the Prophet's home, or quarter bands of armed men upon them.' 'In that case,' replied Muavia, 'I see nought but destruction awaiting thee.' 'Then the Lord be my defence,' exclaimed the aged Caliph, 'and that sufficeth for me[1].' 'Fare thee well!' said Muavia, as he departed, to see his face no more.

Leaving the city by the road for Syria, Muavia passed a group of the Coreish, amongst whom were Aly and Zobeir. He stayed for a moment to drop a warning word into their ears. They were drifting back, he said, into the anarchy of 'the days of Ignorance' before Islam. The Lord was a strong Avenger of the weak and injured ones. 'To you' —and these were his last words—'to you I commit this helpless aged man. Help him, and it will be the better for you. Fare ye well.' So saying he passed on his way. The company remained some time in silence. At last Aly spoke: 'It will be best done as he hath said.' 'By the Lord!' added Zobeir, 'there never lay a burden heavier on thy breast, nor yet on ours, than this burden of Othman's just now.'

[1] Quoting from *Sura* xxxix. 39.

CHAPTER XXXII.

THE PLOT RIPENS.—CONSPIRATORS ATTACK MEDINA.—
DEATH OF OTHMAN.

35 A.H. 656 A.D.

Plot to
surprise
Medina.
End of
34 A.H.,
Summer,
655 A.D.

THE plot now rapidly came to a head. A plan of action had been already formed. While the lieutenants of the Caliph were absent from their posts on the occasion just described, the conspirators were to issue from Kufa, Bussorah, and Fostat, and converge upon Medina in combined and menacing force. There, in answer to the Caliph's challenge, they would present an endless roll of complaints, and cry loudly for redress, reform, and change of governors. Denied by Othman, they would demand his abdication, and, in last resort, enforce it by the sword. But as to a successor they were not agreed. Kufa was for Zobeir; Bussorah for Talha; Egypt's favourite was Aly.

Conspira-
tors set out
for Medina,
ix. 35 A.H.,
April,
656 A.D.

The scheme miscarried. But some months later, in the middle of the following year, it was revived and secret preparations made for giving it effect. Under pretext of visiting Mecca for the Lesser Pilgrimage[1], the concerted movement at last took place, two or three months before the annual pilgrimage. Abu Sarh, Governor of Egypt, at once despatched a message to apprise Othman. In reply he was ordered to pursue the rebels; he did so, but too late; they had already marched beyond his reach. On turning back, he found Egypt in the hands of a traitor, and

---

[1] *Life of Mahomet*, p. xii. It may be performed any time of year.

fleeing for his life, took refuge across the border, in A.H. 35.
Palestine. Among the insurgent leaders of Egypt was
Mohammed, son of Abu Bekr.

Startled by intelligence that the insurgents were in full Insurgents
march on Medina, Othman ascended the pulpit and $\frac{\text{encamp}}{\text{near}}$
admitted the real object of attack. 'It is against myself,' he $\frac{\text{Medina ;}}{\text{first retire ;}}$
said; 'by and by they will look back with a longing eye on my
reign, and wish that each day had been a year, because of
the bloodshed, anarchy and ungodliness, that will flood the
land.' The rebels soon appeared, and pitched three separate
camps, from Kufa, Bussorah, and Egypt, in the neighbourhood
of the city. The people put on their armour, a thing
unheard of since the days of the Apostasy, and prepared for
resistance. The insurgents, foiled thus far, sent deputies to
the widows of Mahomet, and chief men of the city. 'We
come,' they said, 'to visit the Prophet's home and resting-
place, and to ask that certain of the governors be deposed.
Give us leave to enter.' But leave was not granted. Then
they despatched each a deputation to their respective candidates. Aly stormed at the messengers, and called them
rebels accursed of the Prophet; and the others met with no
better reception at the hands of Talha and Zobeir. Unable
to gain the citizens, without whose consent their object was
out of reach, the rebel leaders declared themselves satisfied
with the Caliph's promise of reform, and so retired. They
made as if each company were taking the road home, but
with the concerted plan of returning shortly, when they might
find the city less prepared. The citizens, relieved of the immediate danger, cast aside their armour, and for some days
things went on as before, Othman leading the prayers. Sud- but return
denly, the three bands reappeared. A party headed by $\frac{\text{with}}{\text{document}}$
Aly went forth to ask the reason. The strangers pointed $\frac{\text{bearing}}{\text{Caliph's}}$
to a document attested by the Caliph's seal; this, they said, seal.
had been found by the Egyptian company upon Othman's
servant, whom they caught hastening on the road to Fostat;
and it contained orders for the insurgents to be imprisoned,
tortured, or put to death. Aly, suspecting collusion,
asked how the discovery had become so promptly known
to the other companies marching in different directions, as

A.H. 35. to bring them all back at once together? 'Speak of it as ye will,' they said, 'here is the writing, and here the Caliph's seal.' Aly repaired to Othman, who denied knowledge of the document; but, with the view of clearing up the matter, con-

Angry altercation with Caliph.

sented to receive the rebel leaders. Introduced by Aly, they made no obeisance, but with defiant attitude recounted their pretended grievances. They had retired with the promise of redress, they said; but, instead of redress, here was the Caliph's own servant whom they had caught hastening to Egypt with the treacherous document now produced. Othman swore solemnly that he knew nothing of it. 'Then say who it was that wrote and sealed this order.' 'I know not,' said the aged Caliph. 'But it was passed off as thine; thy servant carried it; see, here is thy seal, and yet forsooth thou wast not privy to it!' Again Othman affirmed that it was even so[1]. 'Whether thou speakest truth,' they cried in accents loud and rude, 'or art a liar, either way, thou art unworthy of the Caliphate. We dare not leave the sceptre in the hands of one who, either knave or fool, is too weak to govern those about him. Resign, for the Lord hath deposed thee!' Othman made answer: —'The garment wherewith the Lord hath girded me I will in no wise put off the same; but any evil ye complain of, that I am ready to put away from me.' It was all too late, they cried; he had often made, and as often broken, the promise to amend; they could no longer trust him; now they would fight until he abdicated, or else was slain. 'Death,' said Othman, gathering himself up, with the firmness and

---

[1] The facts regarding this document are obscure. It certainly was sealed with the Caliph's signet; but who affixed it, and how obtained, cannot be told. Nobody alleges Othman's complicity. Most traditions attribute the act to Merwan, the Caliph's unpopular cousin, who, throughout the narrative, receives constant abuse as the author of Othman's troubles; but these are all tinged with Abbasside hatred. Aly's accusation against the insurgents is unanswerable. There must have been a preconcerted scheme between the three camps; and there is strong presumption of something unfair as regards the document itself. It is, of course, possible that Merwan may have taken upon himself the issue and despatch of the rescript; and, indeed, there were not wanting grounds for his venturing on such a course. The insurgents may also have got scent of the document, before they started ostensibly with the purpose of returning home. But these are mere surmises.

dignity that marked his last days—'death I prefer; as for fighting, I have said it already, my people shall not fight; had that been my desire, I had summoned legions to my side.' The altercation becoming loud and violent, Aly arose and departed to his home. The conspirators also retired to their fellows; but they had now secured what they desired, a footing in the city. They joined in the ranks of worshippers at the daily prayers in the Mosque, cast dust in the face of Othman as he stood up to speak, and thrust aside his loyal helpers. The fatal crisis was hurrying on.

On the Friday following, when the prayers were over, Othman ascended the pulpit. He first appealed to the better sense of the citizens, who, although cowed by the rebels, condemned their lawless attitude. Then turning to the conspirators, he continued, 'Ye are aware that the men of Medina hold you accursed at the mouth of the Prophet, for that ye have risen up against his Caliph and Vicegerent. Wherefore wipe out now your evil deeds by repentance, and by good deeds make atonement for the same.' One and another of the citizens arose earnestly confirming the Caliph's words and pleading his cause; but they were silenced and violently set down. A tumult arose. The men of Medina were driven from the Mosque by showers of stones. One of these struck Othman, who fell from the pulpit, and was carried to his house adjoining in a swoon. He soon recovered, and for some days was still able to preside at the daily prayers. At last the insolence and violence of the insurgents forced him to keep to his house, and a virtual blockade ensued. But a body-guard of armed retainers, supported by loyal citizens, succeeded for a time in keeping the entrance safe.

From the first day of the tumult, Aly, Zobeir, and Talha (the three named by the rebels as candidates for the Caliphate) each sent a son to join the loyal and gallant band planted at the palace door. But they did little more; and, in fact, throughout the painful episode, kept themselves altogether in the background. After the uproar and Othman's swoon, they came along with others to inquire how he fared. No sooner did they enter, than Merwan and other kinsmen attending the Caliph, cried out against Aly as the prime author of the disaster, which would recoil, they said (and said truly), upon his own head. Thereupon Aly arose in wrath, and, with the rest, retired home. It was, in truth, a cruel and dastardly desertion, and in the end bore bitter fruit for one and all. Alarm at the defiance of constituted authority, and loyalty to the throne, equally demanded a bold and uncompromising front. The truth was outspoken by one of the Companions at the time. 'Ye Coreish,' he said, 'there hath been till now a strong and fenced door betwixt you and the Arab tribes; wherefore is it that ye now break down the same?'

Othman besieged. Parley with Aly, Zobeir, and Talha. So soon as the conspirators had shown their true colours, Othman despatched urgent calls to Syria and Bussorah for help. Muavia, who had long foreseen the dire necessity, was ready with a strong force, which, as well as a similar column from Bussorah, hurried to their master's rescue. But the march was long, and the difficulty was for Othman to hold out till they should appear. The insurgents had possession of the Mosque and of the approaches to the palace; and, in the height of insolence, their leader now took the Caliph's place at prayer. There were no troops at Medina, and Othman was dependent on the little force that barely sufficed to guard the palace entrance. It was composed besides train-band slaves, of some eighteen near kinsmen, and other citizens, with the sons of Aly, Zobeir, and Talha. Apprehending, from the growing ferocity of the attack, that the end might not be far off, Othman sent to tell Aly, Zobeir, and Talha that he wished once more to see them. They came and stood without the palace, but within reach of hearing. The Caliph, from the flat roof of his house, bade them sit down; and so for the moment friends and foes sat down all together. 'Fellow citizens!' cried Othman with loud voice, 'I have prayed to the Lord for you, that when I am taken, He may set the Caliphate aright.' Then he spoke of his previous life, and how the Lord had made choice of him to be Successor of His Prophet, and Commander of the Faithful. 'And now,' said he, 'ye have risen up to slay the Lord's elect. Have a care, ye men!' (and here he addressed the besiegers); 'the taking of life is lawful but for three things, apostasy, murder, and adultery. Taking my life without such cause, ye but suspend the sword over your own necks. Sedition and bloodshed shall not depart for ever from your midst.' Thus far they gave him audience, and then cried out that there was yet a fourth just cause of death, the quenching of truth by wrong-doing, and of right by violence; and for his ungodliness and tyranny he must abdicate or be slain. For a moment Othman was silent. Then calmly rising, he bade the citizens go back; and himself, with but faint hope of relief, turned to re-enter his dreary home.

The blockade had lasted several weeks, when a mounted messenger arrived with tidings that succour was on its way. This, coming to the insurgents' knowledge, caused them to redouble their efforts. Closing every approach, they allowed neither outlet nor ingress to a single soul. Water hardly obtainable even by stealth at night, the little garrison suffered the extremities of thirst. On the appeal of Othman, Aly expostulated with the besiegers;—'they were treating the Caliph,' he told them, 'more cruelly than they would prisoners on the field of battle. Even infidels did not deny water to a thirsty enemy.' They were deaf to his entreaty. Omm Habiba, touched with pity, sought with Aly's aid to carry water on her mule through the rebel ranks; but neither sex nor rank, nor having been the Prophet's wife, availed to prevent her being roughly handled. They cut her bridle with their swords so that she was near falling to the ground, and drove her rudely back. The better part of the inhabitants were shocked at the violence and inhumanity of the rebels; but none had the courage to oppose them. Sick at heart, most kept to their houses; while others, alarmed, and seeking to avoid the cruel spectacle, quitted Medina. It is hard to believe that, even in the defenceless state of the city, Aly, Zobeir, and Talha, the great heroes of Islam, could not, if they had wished, have raised effective opposition to the lawless work of the heartless regicides. We must hold them culpable, if not of

[marginal note:] Blockade pressed. Suffering from thirst.

A.H. 35. collusion with the insurgents, at least of cold-blooded
indifference to their Caliph's fate[1].

Annual
pilgrimage,
xii. 35 A.H.,
June,
656 A.D.

The solemnities of yearly pilgrimage were now at hand,
and Othman, still mindful of his obligation as head of Islam
to provide for their due observance, once more ascended
the palace roof. From thence he called for the son of
Abbas, one of the faithful party guarding the entrance, and
bade him assume the leadership of the band of pilgrims
who should now proceed to Mecca;—a duty which, much
against his will, as taking him from the defence, he undertook. Ayesha joined the party. She is accused of having
formerly stirred up the people against Othman. Now, at
any rate, the impulsive lady shook herself free from the
insurgents, and also, in order to detach her brother Mohammed from their company, besought him to accompany her
to Mecca. But he refused.

The Palace
stormed,
18 Dzul
Hijj,
June 17.

The approach of succour at last quickening the rebels to
extremities, they resolved on a final and murderous attack.
Violent onset was made from all quarters, and the forlorn
band of defenders, unable longer to hold their ground,
retired within the palace gate, which they closed and
barred, covering their retreat with a discharge of archery,
by which one of the rebels was killed. Infuriated at their
comrade's death, the insurgents rushed at the gate, battered
it with stones, and finding it too strong, sat down to burn

---

[1] The talk among the courtiers of Mamun, as reflected in the *Apology of Al
Kindy*, was that Aly, even at a much earlier period, contemplated the putting
of Othman to death (*Apology*, p. 73). There seems no proof or even presumption
of this; but anyhow, one cannot but feel indignant at the attitude of Aly, who
would do so much, and no more; who sent his son to join the Caliph's guard
at the palace gate, and was scandalised at his being denied water to drink; and
yet would not so much as raise a finger to save his life.

We have also traditions in which Othman is represented as reproaching
Talha for encouraging the rebels in a more strict enforcement of the blockade;
but, whatever his demerits in deserting the Caliph, this seems incredible. The
ordinary account is that Talha and Zobeir, on hearing of the rebel excesses, kept
to their houses; others, again, say that they both quitted Medina.

Omm Habiba, as daughter of Abu Sofian, naturally sympathised with Othman.
A citizen of Kufa, who had accompanied the insurgents, was so indignant at
their treatment of one of 'the Mothers of the Faithful,' that he went off to his
home, and there gave vent to his feelings in verses expressive of his horror at
the scenes enacting at Medina.

it. Meanwhile others, swarming in crowds from the roof of an adjoining building, gained easier access, and, rushing along the corridor, attacked the guard still congregated within the palace gate. One was slain, Merwan was left half dead, and the rest were overpowered. Othman had retired alone into an inner chamber of the women's apartments; and there awaiting his fate, read from the Coran spread open on his knees. Three ruffians sent to fulfil the bloody work, rushed in upon him thus engaged. Awed by his calm demeanour and plaintive appeal, each returned as he went. 'It would be murder,' they said, 'to lay hands upon him thus.' Mohammed, son of Abu Bekr, in his hate and rage, had no such scruples. He ran in, seized him by the beard, and cried, 'The Lord abase thee, thou old dotard!' 'Let my beard go,' said Othman, calmly; 'I am no dotard, but the Caliph, whom they call Othman.' Then, in answer to a further torrent of abuse, the aged man went on,—'Son of my brother! Thy Father would not have served me so. The Lord help me! To Him I flee for refuge from thee.' The appeal touched even the unworthy son of Abu Bekr, and he too retired. The insurgent leaders, now impatient, crowded in, smote the Caliph with their swords, and trampled on the Coran which he had been reading. He yet had strength enough to gather up the leaves, and press them to his bosom, while the blood flowed forth upon the sacred text[1]. Thus attacked, the faithful Naila cast herself upon her wounded lord, and as she shielded him with her arm, a sword-cut severed several of her fingers, which fell upon the ground. The band of slaves

and Othman slain.

---

[1] The blood, we are told, flowed down to the words: 'If they rebel, surely they are schismatics; thy Lord will swiftly avenge you.' (*Sura* ii. v. 138.) The appropriateness of the text, however, may of itself have suggested the story.

When the insurgents first rushed in, he was reading the passage in *Sura* iii. 174, which refers to Medina being attacked at the battle of Ohod. The disaffected citizens are there represented as taunting Mahomet and his followers in these words: '*Verily, the men (of Mecca) have gathered forces against you; wherefore, be afraid of the same.* But it only increased their faith, and they said: *The Lord sufficeth for us; He is the best Protector.*' This was a favourite text of Othman's, and he may perhaps have turned to it for comfort now that vain was the help of man.

A.H. 35. attempted his defence. One of them slew the leader, but was immediately himself cut down. Further effort was in vain. The insurgents plunged their weapons into the Caliph's body, and he fell lifeless to the ground. The infuriated mob now had their way. A scene of riot followed. They stabbed the corpse, leaped savagely on it, and were proceeding to cut off the head, when the women screamed, beating their breasts and faces, and the savage crew desisted. The palace was gutted; and even Naila, all wounded and bloody, was stripped of her veil. Just then the cry was raised, 'To the Treasury!' and suddenly all departed.

His burial. As soon as they had left, the palace gate was barred, and thus for three days and nights the three dead bodies lay in silence within. Then some chief men of the Coreish obtained leave of Aly to bury the Caliph's body. In the dusk of evening, the funeral procession wended its way to the burying-ground outside the city. Death had not softened the rebels' hearts, and they pelted the bier with stones. Not in the graveyard, but in a field adjoining, the body, with hurried service, was committed to the dust. In after years the field was added by Merwan to the main burying-ground—a spot consecrated by the remains of the early heroes of the Prophet's wars. And there the Omeyyads long buried their dead around the grave of their murdered kinsman.

Character. Thus, at the age of eighty-two, died Othman, after a reign of twelve years. The misfortunes amidst which he sank bring out so sharply the failings of his character that further delineation is hardly needed. Narrow, irresolute, and weak, he had yet a kindly nature which might have made him, in less troublous times, a favourite of the people. Such, indeed, for a season he was at the beginning of his Caliphate. But afterwards he fell on evil days. The struggle between the Coreish and the rest of the Arabs was hurrying on the nation to an internecine war. The only possible safety was for the class still dominant to have opposed a strong and united front. By his vacillation, selfishness, and nepotism, Othman broke up into embittered

factions the aristocracy of Islam, and threw the last chance A.H. 35.
away.

The columns hastening from the north for Othman's Columns
relief, hearing on their way the tragic end, returned to their return to
the north.
respective homes.

CHAPTER XXXIII.

ELECTION OF ALY.

35-36 A.H.   656 A.D.

Revulsion of feeling. ON the Caliph's death, his kinsfolk, and such as had helped in his defence, retired from the scene. The city was horror-struck. They had hardly anticipated the tragic end. Many who had favoured or even joined the rebels, started back now the deed was done. The relatives of the murdered Caliph fled to Mecca, with vows of vengeance. A citizen of Medina, wrapping carefully the severed fingers of Naila in the blood-stained shirt of Othman, meet symbols of revenge, carried them off to Damascus and laid them at Muavia's feet.

Aly elected Caliph, 24 xii. 35 June 23, 656. For several days anarchy reigned in Medina. The regicides had mastery of the city. The Egyptians were foremost amongst these in the first days of terror; and prayer was conducted in the mosque by their leader. Of the inhabitants few ventured out. At last, on the fifth day, the rebels insisted that, before they quitted Medina, the citizens should elect a Caliph, and restore the empire to its normal state. Shrinking, no doubt, from the task which Othman's successor would have to face, Aly held back, and offered to swear allegiance to either Talha or Zobeir. But in the end, pressed by the threats of the regicides and entreaties of his friends, he yielded; and so, six days after the fatal tragedy, he took the oath to rule 'according to the Book of the Lord,' and was saluted Caliph. Zobeir and Talha were themselves the first to acknowledge him. They asserted afterwards that they swore unwillingly, through fear of the A.H. 35–36. conspirators. The mass of the people followed. There were exceptions; but Aly was lenient, and would not press the adherents of the late Caliph to swear allegiance. The insurgents, having themselves done homage, departed to tell the tale at Kufa, Bussorah, and Fostat.

No bed of roses was strewn for Aly. Whether at home or abroad, work rough and anxious was before him. To the standing contention between the Bedouins and Coreish was now added the cry of vengeance on the regicides. Red-handed treason had loosened the bonds of society, and constituted authority was set at nought. Bands of Bedouins, scenting plunder from afar, hung about the city. Encouraged by the servile population now broken loose, they refused to depart[1]. Aly was pressed to vindicate the majesty of law, and punish the men who had stained their hands with the blood of Othman. Even Talha and Zobeir, awakening too late to the portentous nature of the crime enacted, with little check from them and before their very eyes, urged this. 'My brothers,' replied Aly, 'I am not indifferent to what ye say, but helpless. The wild Bedouins and rampant slaves will have their way. What is this but an outburst of paganism long suppressed;—a return, for the moment, to the days of Ignorance, a work of Satan? Just now they are beyond our power. Wait; and the Lord will guide us.' This waiting, hesitating mood, was the bane of Aly's life. He was over fifty years of age, and, though vigorous in his earlier years, had become corpulent and inactive now. He loved ease; and while sometimes obstinate and

Declines to punish regicides.

---

[1] A servile population, captives of war, had been pouring for years into Medina as into other centres. They were employed as domestics, warders, body-guards, or followed trades, paying profits to their masters. On the outbreak they broke away into defiant attitude. This would occur the more readily at Medina, as they formed the guards of the Treasury and mansions of the great men; and, being the only trained force there, felt their power. We find them similarly taking part in the outbreaks at Bussorah and elsewhere. Like the Janissaries or Memluks of later days, they were a petulant brood. Immediately on homage being done to Aly, they lampooned him in minatory verses, to which Aly (not to be outdone in the poetry even of slaves) replied in extempore couplets. Proclamation was made that slaves not returning to their masters would be treated as outlaws; but it had no effect.

A.H. 35–36. self-willed, his ordinary maxim was that things left to themselves would mend.

Coreish alarmed.

The Coreish were anxious and alarmed. The revolt, ostensibly against Othman's ungodly rule, was taking now far wider range. The Bedouins were impatient of Coreishite control ; and that which had happened to the Omeyyad family, now forced to fly Medina, might any moment happen to themselves. Yet Aly, though he denounced the work of the regicides as high treason, took no steps to punish it, but temporised. Prompt and vigorous pursuit would no doubt have been joined in, heart and soul, by all the leaders and better classes of Islam. He chose rather to let the vessel drift, as it shortly did, into the vortex of rebellion.

Aly would depose Muavia in Syria,

The confirmation, or supersession, of the provincial governors was another pressing matter ; and here Aly, turning a deaf ear to his friends, proved wilful and precipitate. When the son of Abbas returned from the pilgrimage at Mecca, he found Moghira wisely urging Aly to retain the governors generally in their posts, at least till the empire at large had recognised his succession to the throne. But Aly refused. The son of Abbas now pressed the same view : 'At any rate,' he said, 'retain Muavia ; it was Omar, not Othman, who placed him there; and all Syria followeth after him.' The advice, coming from so near a kinsman, deserved consideration. But Aly, with family hatred against the Omeyyad line, answered sharply, 'Nay ; I will not confirm him even for a single day.' 'If thou depose him,' reasoned his friend, 'the Syrians will question thine election : and, worse, accusing thee of the blood of Othman, rise up as one man against thee. Confirm him in the government of Syria, and they care not who is Caliph. When thou art firmly seated, depose him if thou wilt. It will be easy then.' 'Never,' answered Aly ; 'he shall have nought but the sword from me.' 'Thou art brave,' Ibn Abbas replied, 'but innocent of the craft of war ; and hath not the Prophet himself said, *What is war but a game of deception ?*' 'That is true,' responded Aly, 'but I will have none of Muavia.' 'Then,' said Ibn Abbas, 'thou hadst better depart to thy property at Yenbo, and close

the gates of thy stronghold there behind thee ; for everywhere the Bedouins are hounding along; and if thou
makest others thine enemies, these will surely find thee
out, and lay the blood of Othman at thy door.' 'Come,'
said Aly, trying another line, 'thou shalt go forth thyself to
Syria. See, now, I have appointed thee.' 'That,' replied
Ibn Abbas, 'can never be. Muavia would surely behead
me or cast me into prison because of Othman's death, and
my being kin to thee. Hearken, and make terms with him
ere it be too late.' But Aly turned a deaf ear.

Acting on this wayward impulse, Aly sent men of his   *and ap-*
own to replace existing governors throughout the empire. *point new governors*
In most places these met with but a sorry reception. At   *throughout the Empire,*
Bussorah, indeed, Ibn Aamir, unwilling to provoke hos-   *i. 36 A.H.,*
tilities, retired to Mecca, and his successor, Othman ibn   *July, 656.*
Honeif, entered unopposed ; but the faction which clung to
the memory of the late Caliph was as strong there as that
which favoured Aly, while a third party waited the out-turn
of events at Medina. In Egypt it was much the same. Cays,
appointed to the command, was a wise and able ruler ; but
he only succeeded in crossing the frontier by feigning attachment to the cause of Othman ; while a strong and aggressive
faction in the country, swore that they would not submit until
the regicides were brought to justice. In Yemen, the new
governor obtained possession, but only after his predecessor
had carried off to Mecca all the treasure. The two officers
nominated to Kufa and Syria met with so rough a reception, that they were glad to escape with their lives back to
Medina.

Dispirited by these events, Aly took counsel with Talha   *Sends*
and Zobeir. The sedition he had apprehended was already   *letters to Muavia and*
kindled, and would spread like wild-fire, catching whatever   *Abu Musa.*
might come in its way. 'Then,' replied they, 'let us depart,
that we may do thee service in the field.' 'Wait,' answered
Aly ; 'the cautery must be the last resort.' So he resolved,
in the first instance, to address letters to Muavia, and also
to Abu Musa at Kufa, demanding their allegiance. Abu
Musa replied in loyal terms, but withal, bade the Caliph
beware of the disaffection which in Kufa was rife around

A.H. 35–
36.

Emblems
of ven-
geance
hung up at
Damascus.

Muavia
sends
defiant
answer,
ii. 36 A.H.
Aug.,
656 A.D.

him.   With Syria, communication was utterly cut off;
weeks elapsed, and there was no reply. In truth, a strange
scene the while was being enacted there.

Muavia had no sooner received the emblems of Othman's
murder—the gory shirt and Naila's mangled fingers—than
he hung them on the pulpit of the Damascus mosque.
There suspended, they remained a spectacle maddening
the Syrians to bloody revenge. Still, he took no immediate
action. Biding his time, he waited to see what the new
Caliph might do. Had Aly been wise, he would have
used the angry Syrians to take vengeance on the conspirators, and in so doing crush as well the rising rebellion
of the Arab tribes. In this work they would have been
his strongest help; for Syria never suffered from the
Bedouin turbulence which kept Irac and Egypt in continual
turmoil. It had been the early and favourite field of the
Coreish, who, settling there more largely than elsewhere,
found their influence, in consequence, better recognised.
Moreover, they inhabited the Syrian cities in common with
the Christian population, which had surrendered, for the
most part, on favourable terms. Society was thus throughout all classes orderly and loyal; whereas Bussorah and
Kufa were filled with restless headstrong Arab tribes which
held the conquered lands to be their own private patrimony.
Law prevailed in Syria; in Irac and Egypt, petulance and
pride of arms. Syria was, moreover, attached to the Omeyyad stock, and so remained faithful to the end.

The Syrians had not long to wait the outcome of Aly's
plans. His abortive attempt to supersede Muavia, and
refusal to arraign the regicides, gave colour to the charge
of collusion with them; and having the bloody shirt ever
before their eyes, the Syrians soon raised the cry against
the Caliph. The majesty of outraged law must be vindicated; and if the assassins were not pursued to justice,
who but Aly was responsible? Damascus was in this
excited temper when Aly's letter reached Muavia. At
the first, no answer was vouchsafed. The envoy kept in
waiting witnessed day by day the gathering storm. At last
Muavia sent a despatch,—stranger than ever had been seen

before. The cover was superscribed with this address— *From Muavia to Aly*, and bore the seal of state. There was no other word, all was blank within. The despatch was carried by Cabisa, a Bedouin chief, and with him the Caliph's envoy was given permission to depart. Arriving at Medina three months after Othman's death, Cabisa presented the letter to Aly, who broke the seal impatiently. ' What meaneth this ? ' he cried, starting at the blank despatch ;— ' let the enigma be explained.' Cabisa first inquired whether his life was safe. ' Safe,' answered Aly ; ' the person of ambassador is sacred. Speak on.' ' Know then,' proceeded Muavia's envoy, ' that but now I left behind me, weeping under the blood-stained shirt of Othman, sixty thousand warriors, bent on revenging the Caliph's death—and re-venging it on thee !' ' What !' exclaimed Aly, aghast, ' *On me !* Seest thou not that I am powerless to pursue the murderers ? O Lord ! I take Thee to witness that I am guiltless of Othman's blood. Begone ! See, thy life is safe.' As the envoy withdrew, the petulant slaves and rabble shouted after him, 'Slay the dog; slay the envoy of Syrian dogs !' He turned, and, apostrophising the Coreish, cried at the pitch of his voice, ' Children of Modhar ! Children of Cays! The horse and the bow! Four thousand picked warriors close at hand. See to your camels and your steeds !'

Medina was roused and startled by the envoy's cry. The *Aly* time was come when Aly could no longer put his decision *proclaims* off. Hasan, his elder son, ever poor in spirit, counselled wait- *against* ing ; but Aly saw too plainly the hour for action to be now *Muavia.* or never. He gave vent to his troubled soul in martial lines, which, soon in everyone's mouth, told the people his resolve to make the sword the arbiter betwixt Muavia and himself. An expedition against Syria was proclaimed ; captains were appointed to command the various companies of the ex-pected levies, and banners presented to them by Aly; but he was careful to name no one who had taken part in the attack on Othman. Orders were also sent to Kufa, Bus-sorah, and Egypt, to raise troops for the war. This done, Aly mounted the pulpit and harangued the citizens. If they failed to fight now, he told them, the power would pass away from them, never more to be regained. 'Fight, then, against the cursed schismatics, who would destroy the unity of Islam and rend in twain the body of the Faithful. Haply the Lord will set that right which the nations are setting wrong.' But the people did not respond to the appeal, and the ranks were slow of filling.

Talha and
Zobeir
depart to
Mecca.
Talha and Zobeir, when they saw affairs thus drifting, again asked leave to quit Medina; and so they now set out for Mecca, on pretext of performing the Lesser Pilgrimage.

CHAPTER XXXIV.

Rebellion at Bussorah.

36 A. H.   656 A. D.

BUT, before crossing arms with Muavia, heavy work Ayesha retires to Mecca,
was in store for Aly.

Returning from Mecca, Ayesha was met on her way to
Medina by the tidings of Othman's death and Aly's accession
to the Caliphate. 'Carry me back,' cried the incensed and
impetuous lady; 'carry me back to Mecca. They have
murdered the Caliph. I will avenge his blood.'

In the early period of Othman's troubles, Ayesha, like and there stirs up sedition.
others, had contributed her share towards fomenting public
discontent. But she was no party to the cruel attack of
the conspirators; and had, in fact, sought to detach her
brother from them by inviting him to accompany her to
Mecca. Vain and factious, she had never forgiven the
unhandsome conduct of Aly on the occasion when her
virtue had been doubted by the Prophet[1]; and now she
would gladly have seen Zobeir succeed instead of him. In
place, therefore, of continuing her journey home, she turned
and went straightway back again to Mecca. There the
disaffected gathered round her, while from her veiled retreat
she plotted the revenge of Othman's blood, and with
shrill voice harangued her audience on the enormous crime
that had desecrated the Prophet's home and resting-place.

Thus when Zobeir and Talha reached Mecca, they found

---

[1] *Life of Mahomet,* p. 311 *et seq.*

A.H. 36.
Zobeir and
Talha with
Ayesha
march on
Bussorah,
iv. 36 A.H.
Oct.,
656 A.D. sedition already well advanced. The numerous adherents of the Omeyyad house, who had fled thither on the Caliph's death, or still were resident at Mecca, and the factious and servile mass at large listened eagerly to their tale. 'They had left the men of Medina,' said Talha and Zobeir, 'plunged in perplexity. Right had been confounded so with wrong that people knew not which way to turn. It was for Mecca now to lead, and punish the traitors who had slain their Caliph.' The standard of rebellion thus was raised, and many flocked around it. Bussorah was to be the first object of attack, a city favouring the claims of Talha ; while Ibn Aamir, the late governor and friend of Othman, had still an influential following there. The treasure he had brought away, as well as that carried off by Ala from Yemen, was now expended in equipping the force, and providing it with carriage. Ayesha, spurning the restraints of sex, prepared to join the campaign and stir up the men of Bussorah, as she had stirred up those of Mecca. Haphsa was with difficulty restrained by her brother Abdallah, son of Omar (who had just fled from Medina, and held aloof from either side), from following her Sister-widow. At length, some four months after Othman's death, the rebel army set out 3,000 strong, of whom 1,000 were men of Mecca and Medina. Ayesha travelled in her litter on a camel, destined to give its name to the first engagement in the civil war. The other Widows of Mahomet residing at Mecca accompanied her a little way, and then returned. As they parted, the company gave vent to their feelings, and wept bitterly at the louring outlook;—'there was no such weeping, before or after, as then; so that day was called *The Day of Tears.*'

Ambition
mingled
with cry for
revenge. Questions began to arise whether Talha or Zobeir would in event of victory be the Caliph ; but Ayesha, staying the strife, as premature, desired that Abdallah son of Zobeir should lead the prayers ; and it was given out that the choice of the future Caliph would be left, as heretofore, to the men of Medina. Said, ex-governor of Kufa, distrusting the motives of the leaders, turned aside at the last moment, and with his company went back to Mecca. As the caval-

cade swept by him, shouting that they were on their way
to destroy the murderers of Othman, Said cried out,
'Whither away? the objects of your vengeance are on the
camels' humps' (meaning Talha and Zobeir) 'before your
eyes. Slay these, and return to your homes!' It is not
improbable that with both these, ambition was mistaken
for desire of just revenge. In the whirl of passion, party-
cry too often takes the place of reason ; and we need not
doubt that both leaders and followers had wrought themselves into the belief that punishment of the high treason
enacted at Medina was their real object.

    Notwithstanding all this parade of justice, the conscience *Ayesha's*
of Ayesha was ill at ease. As they journeyed through the *qualm of*
desert, her camel-driver beguiled the tedium of the night *conscience.*
by calling out the names of the hills and valleys through
which they passed. Approaching a Bedouin settlement,
the dogs began to howl;—'*The Valley of Hawab!*' cried the
guide, noting their progress. Ayesha started and screamed.
Something dreadful which Mahomet had spoken about the
barking of the dogs of Hawab, flashed across her memory.
'Carry me back,' she cried ; and, making her camel kneel,
she hastily alighted from her litter. 'Alas and alas!' she
continued, 'for I heard the Prophet say, reproaching us, as
he sat surrounded by his wives one day: "*O that I knew
which amongst you it is at whom the dogs of Hawab will
bark!*" It is me! It is me! the wretched woman of
Hawab. I will not take another step on this ill-omened
expedition.' They sought to persuade her that the guide
had mistaken the name ; but she refused to stir, and the
army halted for a whole day. In despair, they bethought
them of a stratagem. The following night, they raised the
cry that Aly was upon them. The greater terror prevailing, Ayesha hastened to her camel, and resumed the
march.

    The alarm, feigned for the purpose, was not altogether *Aly fails*
groundless. When rumours of the defection first reached *to intercept*
Medina, Aly refused to move against the malcontents so *the rebels.*
long as no overt act of rebellion threatened the unity of
Islam. But shortly after, news arrived of the design on

Bussorah. At the first, Aly was disposed to congratulate himself that the conspirators had not made Kufa, with its greater Bedouin population, their object. The son of Abbas, however, pointed out that Bussorah was really the more dangerous, because fewer of the leading chiefs were there, able to curb the people and repress rebellion. Aly admitted this; and, now thoroughly alarmed, gave orders that the column destined for Syria should march instead to Nejd, hoping thereby to intercept the rebels on their way to Bussorah. But the people still hung back. At last a column of 900 men was got together, at the head of which Aly himself marched hastily in pursuit of the insurgents; but on striking the Mecca road he found that they had already passed. Not being equipped for further advance, he halted there. Messengers were sent to Kufa, Egypt, and elsewhere, demanding reinforcements; and for these the Caliph waited before he ventured forward.

To return to Ayesha. The insurgent army, having resumed its march, reached Bussorah, and encamped close by. Messages were exchanged, and Ibn Honeif, the governor, aware that the cry of vengeance on the regicides really covered designs against his master Aly, called an assembly, to try the temper of the people. Finding from the uproar that the strangers had a strong party in the city, he put on his armour, and, followed by the larger portion of the citizens, went forth to meet the enemy, who, on their side, were joined from the town by all the malcontents. A parley ensued. Talha, the favourite at Bussorah, Zobeir, and even Ayesha with shrill voice, all three declaimed against the murderers of Othman, and demanded justice. The other side were equally loud in their protestations against Ayesha and her attack upon their city. It was a shame, they said, and a slight on the memory of the Prophet, for her to forego the sanctity of the Veil, and the proprieties of 'Mother of the Faithful.' Aly had been duly elected, and saluted Caliph; and now Talha and Zobeir were treacherously violating the allegiance which they had been the first to swear. These, again, both protested that the oath had been forced upon them. On this

point the controversy turned; and from words they fell to A.H. 36.
blows. Night interposed; but fighting was resumed the Reference
following day, and with so serious a loss to the loyalists to Medina
on question
that a truce was called, and agreement come to, on the of compul-
understanding that the facts should be ascertained from sion.
Medina. If force had really been put upon Zobeir and
Talha to take the oath, then Ibn Honeif would retire and
leave the city in their hands. An envoy accredited by
either side was accordingly deputed to Medina. He arrived there while Aly was absent in his camp, and forthwith
proclaimed his mission before the assembled city. The
people at first were silent. At last, one declared that both
Talha and Zobeir had done homage under compulsion,
whereupon a great tumult arose; and the envoy, having
seen and heard enough to prove diversity of view, took
his leave.

When tidings of these things reached Aly, who was with Bussorah
his army in Nejd, he addressed a letter to Ibn Honeif, his seized by
Talha and
governor. 'There was no compulsion,' he wrote, 'on either Zobeir,
Talha or Zobeir; neither of these my adversaries was con- 24 iv.
36 A.H.
strained otherwise than by the will of the majority. By the 19 Oct.,
656 A.D.
Lord! if their object be to make me abdicate, they are with-
out excuse; if it be any other thing, I am ready to consider
it.' So when the envoy returned from Medina, and upon his
report the insurgents called on Ibn Honeif to evacuate the
city according to agreement, he produced the Caliph's letter,
and refused. But the rebels had already obtained a footing
within the city. Arming themselves, they repaired to the
mosque for evening service, and, the night being dark and
stormy, were not perceived until they had overpowered the
bodyguard, entered the adjoining palace, and made Ibn
Honeif a prisoner. On the following day, a severe conflict
raged throughout the city, which ended in the discomfiture
of Aly's party, and so the government passed into the hands
of Talha and Zobeir. True to their ostensible object, these
now made proclamation that every citizen who had engaged in the attack on Othman should be brought forth
and executed. The order was carried rigorously out, and
great numbers were put to death. The life of Ibn Honeif

A.H. 36. was spared. Set at liberty, his head and beard were shaven,
and his eyelashes and moustaches clipped ; and in this
sorry plight the ousted governor made the best of his
way to Aly.

Ayesha
seeks rein-
forcements.
The insurgents communicated tidings of their success to
Syria. And Ayesha wrote letters to Kufa, Medina, and
Yemen, dissuading the people from their allegiance to Aly,
and stirring them up to avenge the death of Othman.

Meanwhile the citizens of Bussorah swore allegiance to
Talha and Zobeir conjointly. To avoid appearance of
rivalry, prayers were conducted alternately by a son of
each. Little active sympathy was evoked by the Usurpers.
Talha proclaimed an expedition against Aly. But no one
responded to the call, and his spirits fell. Thus some
weeks passed uneasily, till the city was aroused by the
announcement that Aly with an army was in full march
upon it.

CHAPTER XXXV.

BATTLE OF THE CAMEL.

36 A. H. 656 A. D.

FINDING that the insurgent troops, with Ayesha, Zobeir, and Talha, had already passed, Aly, as we have seen, halted for a while on the road to Bussorah, with the view of strengthening his army; for, although joined on his march by certain loyal tribes, he still felt too weak for immediate action. To Kufa he addressed a special summons, inhabited as it was by many veterans on whose loyalty he might reasonably depend; and he added force to the call by promising that Kufa should be his seat of government. 'See,' he wrote, ' have not I chosen your city before all other cities for my own? Unto you do I look for succour, if haply peace and unity again prevail as it behoveth among brethren in the faith.' But the summons was at the first unheeded. The overgrown city was made up of many factions; and from some of these the message of Ayesha, demanding revenge for Othman's blood, had already found response. Abu Musa, its governor, was unequal to the emergency. Loyal to the memory of the murdered Caliph, he yet sought to allay the ferment by a neutral course, and urged the citizens to join neither party, but remain at home. A second deputation meeting with no better success, Aly bethought him of sending his elder son Hasan, in company with Ammar, the former Governor of Kufa, to urge his cause. The appeal of Hasan, grandson of the Prophet, had at last the desired effect. The chord of loyalty in the fickle city's heart was

S

A.H. 36. touched ; a tumult arose, and Abu Musa, unable to maintain his weak neutrality, was deposed. The Arab tribes
rallied, and for the moment heartily, around the loyalists.
Soon 10,000 men, partly by land, partly by river, set out
to join the Caliph, who, advancing slowly, awaited their
arrival. Thus reinforced, Aly was able to take the field
effectively, and march on the rebellious city.

Aly's nego-   Bussorah itself was not wholly hostile, and numbers of
tiations
with Talha the citizens went forth, to join the camp of Aly. The in-
and Zobeir. surgent army, which still nearly equalled that of the Caliph,
now marched forth, with Talha and Zobeir at their head,
and Ayesha herself seated in a well-fenced litter. But
Aly's thoughts were for peace if possible. He was a man
of compromise ; and here he was ready, in the interests of
Islam, magnanimously to forget the insult offered him.
Apart, indeed, from personal jealousies, there was no dis-
agreement sufficient to bar the hope of reconciliation.
The cry of Talha and Zobeir was for vengeance against
the murderers of Othman ; and against these, Aly as yet
did not deny that justice should be dealt. But he was
obliged to temporise. He had in his army great numbers
of the very men who had risen against Othman ; and he
felt that to inflict punishment on them, as his adversaries
required, would for the present be impossible. Holding
these views, he halted, still some little way from Bussorah,
and sent forward Cacaa (who with other leaders of renown
had joined him from Kufa) to expostulate with Talha and
Zobeir. 'Ye have slain 600 men of Bussorah,' said Cacaa
to them, 'for the blood of Othman ; and lo! to avenge
their blood, 6000 more have started up. Where is this
internecine war to stop? It is peace and repose that
Islam needeth. Give that, and again the majesty of law
shall be set up, and the guilty brought to justice.' As he
spoke, the truth flashed on the minds of Zobeir and Talha,
and even of Ayesha ; and they returned word that if these
really were the sentiments of Aly, they were ready to
submit. After several days spent in such negotiations, Aly,
glad at the prospect of a bloodless compromise, advanced.

But, as we have seen, Aly's army, recruited at random

from the Bedouin settlements, comprised a great number A.H. 36.
of notorious regicides. Afraid of bringing these into con- Tactics
tact with the heated army of his opponents, still breathing of the
out fire and slaughter against them, Aly gave command regicides.
that none who had shared in the attack on Othman should
for the present accompany him in his advance. These in
their turn, with Ashtar at their head, became alarmed.
Talha's troops, sworn to their destruction, were double
their number; if peace were patched up, no hope remained.
Reasoning thus, they held a secret conclave, and came to
the conclusion that their only safety lay in precipitating
hostilities, and thus forcing Aly's hand to crush their enemies. Accordingly they remained behind, but with the
resolve that at the right moment they would advance and
throw themselves upon the enemy.

The army of Bussorah, numbering some 20,000 men, Negotia-
remained encamped on the outskirts of the city. Aly's tions for a
force, advancing unopposed, halted within sight; and mise.
negotiations for peace went on, evidently substantial and
sincere. Aly himself approached on horseback, and Talha
with Zobeir rode forth to confer with him. ' Wherefore
have ye risen against me,' said Aly; ' did ye not swear
homage to me?' ' Yea,' replied Talha, ' but with the sword
over our necks; and now our demand is that justice be
executed against the murderers of Othman.' Aly replied
that he no less than they held the regicides to be guilty;
he even cursed them in no measured terms, but added that
for their punishment they must bide their time. Zobeir on
his side was softened by certain words of the Prophet
towards him which Aly recalled to his mind, and bound
himself by an oath that he would not fight. Then they all
retired. Both armies, understanding that negotiations were
in progress, went to rest that night in security such as they
had not felt for many weeks.

The spell was rudely broken. Towards morning, a sudden Regicides
shock changed the scene. The regicides, during the night, precipitate
carried their design into execution. Led by them, squad- hostilities.
rons of Bedouin lances bore down, while yet dark, upon the
Bussorah tents. In a moment all was confusion. Each

camp believed that it had been attacked by the other; and the dawn found both armies drawn up, as the conspirators desired, in mortal combat against each other. In vain Aly endeavoured to hold back his men. The sense of treachery embittered the conflict. It was a strange engagement,—the first on which Moslems had crossed swords with Moslems. It resembled a battle of the old Arab times, only that for tribal rivalry were now substituted other passions. Clans were broken up, and it became in some measure a contest between the two rival cities; ' The Beni Rabia of Kufa fought against the Beni Rabia of Bussorah, the Beni Modhar of the one against the Beni Modhar of the other;' and so on, with the various tribes, and even with families, one part of each arrayed against the other. The Kufa ranks were urged on by the regicides, who felt that, unless Aly conquered, they were all doomed men. The fierceness and obstinacy of the battle can be only thus accounted for. One of the combatants tells us that 'when the opposing sides came together breast to breast, with a furious shock, the noise was like that of washermen at the riverside[1].' The attitude of the leaders was in marked contrast with the bitter struggle of the ranks. Zobeir, half-hearted since his interview with Aly, left the battle-field according to promise, and was killed in an adjoining valley. Talha, disabled by an arrow in the leg,

Zobeir and Talha killed.
was carried into Bussorah, where he died. Bereft of their leaders, the insurgent troops gave way. They were falling back upon the city, when they passed by the camel of Ayesha. Attacked fiercely all around, she from within her litter kept crying with fruitless energy, 'Slay the murderers of Othman.' The word ran through the retiring ranks, that 'the Mother of the Faithful was in peril,' and they gallantly stayed their flight to rescue her. Long and cruelly the conflict raged round the fated camel. One after another, brave warriors rushed to seize the standard; one after another they were cut down. Of the Coreish, seventy perished by the bridle. At last, Aly, perceiving that the camel was the rallying-point of the enemy, sent one of his

---

[1] The metaphor will be appreciated by the Eastern traveller.

A.H. 36.

captains to hamstring, and thus disable it. With a loud cry
the animal fell to the ground. The struggle ceased and the
insurgents retired into the city. The litter, bristling with
arrows like a hedgehog, was taken down, and, by desire of
Aly, placed in a retired spot, where Ayesha's brother,
Mohammed, pitched a tent for her. As he drew aside the
curtain, she screamed at the unknown intrusion ;—'Are
thine own people, then,' he said, 'become strange unto
thee?' 'It is my brother!' she exclaimed, and suffered
herself to be led into the tent. The brave but wayward
lady had escaped without a wound.

Losses in the battle.

The carnage in the ill-starred *Battle of the Camel* (for so
it came to be called) was very great. The field was covered
with 10,000 bodies in equal proportion on either side ; and
this, notwithstanding that the victory was not followed up.
For Aly had given orders that no fugitive should be pursued, nor any wounded soldier slain, nor plunder seized,
nor the privacy of any house invaded. A great trench was
dug, and into it the dead were lowered, friends and foes
alike. Aly, encamped for three days without the city,
himself performed the funeral service. It was a new experience to bury the dead slain in battle not against the
infidel, but believer fighting against believer. Instead of
cursing the memory of his enemies (too soon the fashion in
these civil wars), Aly spoke hopefully of the future state of
such as had entered the field, on whichever side, with an
honest heart. When they brought him the sword of Zobeir,
he cursed the man who took his life ; and, calling to mind
the feats displayed by the brave arm that wielded it in the
early battles of Islam, exclaimed : 'Many a time hath this
sword driven care and sorrow from the Prophet's brow.' The
Moslems might well mourn the memory both of Talha and
Zobeir, remembering how on the field of Ohod the former
had saved the life of Mahomet at the peril of his own ; and
how often the latter had carried confusion into the ranks of
the idolaters of Mecca. Their fall, and that of many of the
Companions, was a loss to the empire itself, because
seriously weakening the Coreish in the struggle yet to be
fought out betwixt them and the Arab tribes. In fact, this

A.H. 36. victory of Aly was virtually the victory of the regicides,
——— supported by the factious citizens of Kufa. Thenceforward
Aly was wholly dependent upon these. If, instead, he had
effected a compromise with Talha and Zobeir, his position
would have been incomparably stronger.

Aly's mag- The bearing of Aly was generous towards his fallen foe.
nanimity Having entered the city, he divided the contents of the
towards
the enemy. treasury amongst the troops which had fought on his side,
promising them a still larger reward 'when the Lord should
have delivered Syria into his hands.' But otherwise he
treated friends and foes alike, and buried in oblivion ani-
mosities of the past. Merwan and the adherents of the
house of Omeyya fled to their homes, or found refuge in
Syria. All that remained in the city swore fealty to Aly.
The only class dissatisfied was that of the slaves and rabble,
who murmured at having no share in the treasure, nor any
chance of plunder. These, gathering into marauding bands,
occasioned much disquietude to the Caliph, and hastened
his departure from the city, with the view of checking the
mischief they were bent on.

Ayesha Ayesha was treated by Aly with the reverence due to one
retires to who bore the title of 'the Prophet's Spouse in this life
Medina.
and also in the life to come.' She was now five-and-forty
years of age, but had lost little of the fire and vivacity of
youth. After the battle, the Caliph visited her tent, and
expressed his satisfaction at finding her unhurt; adding
mildly, but half reproachfully: 'The Lord pardon thee for
what hath passed, and have mercy upon thee.' 'And upon
thee also!' was the pert and ready answer. The best house
in Bussorah was given up to her; and there she was waited
on by her own adherents. Not long after, she left with a
retinue of forty handmaids, attended by her brother. Aly
himself accompanied her a short distance on foot; and a large
party went as far as the first stage, to bid her farewell. Proceeding to Mecca, she performed the Lesser Pilgrimage; and
then retiring to Medina, no more attempted to interfere with
the affairs of state. Her nephew Abdallah, son of Zobeir [1],

---

[1] His mother Asma, Ayesha's sister, is famous because on the occasion of
Mahomet's flight from the cave she tore her girdle to tie up his wallet, and was
hence called 'She of the two shreds.'—*Life of Mahomet*, p. 145.

retired with her. He became famous in the subsequent A.H. 36. history of the Caliphate ; but that was not till Ayesha had passed away. She spent the remainder of her days at Medina. There crowds of pilgrims visiting the Prophet's tomb (her own apartment) gazed wonderingly at the once beautiful and favourite wife of Mahomet ; while she, garrulous in old age, became the fertile source of tradition and the narrator of incidents in the Prophet's life beginning with her earliest childhood. She died in the 58th year of the Hegira, aged sixty-six, having passed forty-seven years in widowhood[1].

Aly did not stay long in Bussorah. Having appointed Bussorah. his cousin, Abdallah, son of Abbas, governor of the city, with Ziad, the able administrator, to aid him in charge of the treasury, he set out for Kufa.

[1] Tradition abounds in anecdotes about Ayesha. Aly's army taunted her as ' the *unnatural* Mother of the Faithful.' The soldiers on her side, in reply, extemporised a couplet, extolling her as 'the noblest and best of Mothers.' When they told this to her, she was much affected, and exclaimed, ' Would that I had died twenty years before this ! ' Aly, also, when he heard it, said, ' Would that I too had died twenty years ago ! '

Ayesha, always ready in repartee, was not very particular in her language. Asim approaching her litter on the field, she cursed him for the liberty he had taken. ' It was but a little something red and white,' he said, impudently, ' that I caught a glimpse of.' ' The Lord uncover thy nakedness,' she cried angrily ; ' cut off thy hands, and make thy wife a widow ! ' All which (they say) came to pass. A saucy passage is related between her and the aged Ammar, who said, as she was leaving, ' Praise be to the Lord that we shall hear no more that vile tongue of thine ! '

When starting for Mecca, with Aly and a company around her, she said, ' Let us not entertain hard thoughts one against the other ; for verily, as regardeth Aly and myself, there happened not anything between us' (alluding to her misadventure in the Prophet's lifetime, *Life of Mahomet*, p. 311) ' but that which is wont to happen between a wife and her husband's family ; and verily Aly was one of the best of them that entertained suspicions against me.' Aly replied : ' She speaketh the truth ; there was nought, beyond what she saith, between her and me.' And then he went on to quote Mahomet's own words regarding Ayesha, that ' she was not only his wife in this world, but would be equally so in the world to come.'

CHAPTER XXXVI.

ALY TRANSFERS HIS SEAT OF GOVERNMENT TO KUFA. AFFAIRS IN EGYPT.

36 A.H. 656-7 A.D.

Medina abandoned as capital of Islam. As Aly rode forth from Medina in pursuit of the insurgent army, a citizen seized his bridle ;—' Stay !' he cried earnestly ;—' if thou goest forth from hence, the government will depart from this city never more to return.' He was pushed aside, as one having lost his wits ; but his words were long remembered, and the prophecy was true. Medina was to be the seat of empire no more.

Aly's entry into Kufa, vii. 36 A.H. Jan., 657 A.D. In the 36th year of the Hegira, seven months after the death of Othman, Aly entered Kufa. The first four months had been spent at Medina ; the other three in the campaign of 'the Camel,' and a short stay at Bussorah. No Caliph had as yet visited Kufa. It was now to be the seat of Aly's government. The inhabitants were flattered by the honour thus put upon them. The city had certain advantages ; for in it were many leading men, able, and some of them willing, to support the Caliph. Moreover, Aly might calculate on the jealousy of Irac towards Syria, in the approaching struggle with Muavia. But these advantages were all more than counterbalanced by the factious humour of the populace. It was the focus of Bedouin democracy ; and the spirit of the Bedouins was yet untamed. What had they gained, the men of Kufa asked, by the insurrection against Othman ? The cry of vengeance on the regicides was for the moment

silenced ; but things were drifting back into the old A.H. 36.
Coreishite groove.   The charge was, in fact, the same as the
sons of the desert were making all around.   ' Aly hath set up Factious
his cousins, the sons of Abbas, everywhere — in Medina, spirit there.
Mecca, Yemen, and now again at Bussorah, while he himself
will rule at Kufa.   Of what avail that we made away
with Othman, and have shed our own blood, fighting against
Zobeir and Talha ?'   So spoke the arch-conspirator Ashtar
among his friends at Bussorah ; and Aly, fearful of such
teaching, took him in his train t Kufa, where, among the
excitable populace, there was even greater danger.   Another
uneasy symptom was that the servile dregs, and baser
sort of Bussorah, breaking loose from all control, went
forth in a body and took possession of Sejestan on the
Persian frontier.   They killed the leader sent by Aly to
suppress the rising, and were not put down till Ibn Abbas
himself attacked them with a force from Bussorah.

It was in the West, however, that the sky loured most. Struggle
It was but a shorn and truncated Caliphate which Aly in prospect with Syria.
enjoyed, so long as his authority was scorned in Syria.   A
mortal combat with Muavia loomed in that direction.   But,
before resuming the Syrian thread, we must first turn to
Egypt.

That heavy charge was committed to Cays, son of the Cays,
citizen nearly elected Caliph at the Prophet's death.   Of governor of Egypt,
approved ability and judgment, and a loyal follower of Aly, ii. 36 A. H.
he declined to take soldiers with him to Egypt, saying that Aug., 650 A. D.
the Caliph had more need of them than he, and preferring
instead the support of seven ' Companions,' who accompanied him.   On his approach, the rebel governor fled to
Syria, where he lost his life.   Cays was well received by the
Egyptians, who swore allegiance to him on behalf of Aly.
But a strong faction sheltered in a neighbouring district,
loudly demanded satisfaction for the death of Othman.
Cays wisely left these alone for the present, waiving even
the demand for tithe.   In other respects he held Egypt
with firm grasp.

In prospect of an early attack by Aly, Muavia became
uneasy at the Egyptian border being commanded by so

able a ruler as Cays, whom he made every effort to detach
from Aly. Upbraiding him with having joined a party
still imbued with the blood of Othman, he called upon Cays
to repent, and promised that, if he joined in avenging the
crime, he should be confirmed in the government of Egypt,
and his kinsmen promoted to such office as he might desire.
Cays, unwilling to precipitate hostilities, fenced his answer
with well-balanced words. Of Aly's complicity in the foul
deed there was as yet, he said, no evidence ; he would
wait. Meanwhile he had no intention of making attack on
Syria. Again pressed by Muavia, Cays frankly declared
that he was, and would remain, a staunch supporter of the
Caliph. Thereupon Muavia sought craftily to stir up
jealousy between Aly and his lieutenant. He gave out
that Cays was temporising, and spoke of his leniency
towards the Egyptian malcontents as proving that he
was one at heart with them. The report, assiduously
spread, reached, as intended, the court of Aly, where it
was taken up by those who either doubted the fidelity

of Cays or envied his prosperity. To test his obedience,
Aly ordered an advance against the malcontents ; and the
remonstrance of Cays against the step as premature, was
taken as proof of his complicity. He was deposed, and
the regicide Mohammed, son of Abu Bekr, appointed in his
room. Cays retired in anger to Medina, where, as on
neutral ground, adherents of either side were unmolested ;
but finding no peace there from the taunts of Merwan and
others, he at last resolved to cast himself on Aly's clemency ; and Aly, on the calumnies being cleared away, took
him back at once into his confidence, and thenceforward kept
him as his chief adviser. Muavia upbraided Merwan with
having driven Cays from Medina ;—' If thou hadst aided
Aly with a hundred thousand men, it had been a lesser
evil than is the gain to him of such a counsellor.'

On his own side, however, Muavia had a powerful and
astute adviser in Amru, the conqueror of Egypt. During
the attack on Othman, Amru had retired from Medina with
his two sons to Palestine. The tidings of the tragedy,
aggravated by his own unkindly treatment of the Caliph,

affected him keenly. 'It is I,' he said, 'who, by deserting
the aged man in time of trouble, am responsible for his
death.' From his retirement he watched the struggle at
Bussorah ; and when Aly proved victorious, repaired at
once to Damascus, and presented himself before Muavia.
In consequence of his unfriendly attitude towards Othman,
Muavia at first received him coldly. In the end, however,
the past was condoned and friendship restored. Thenceforward Amru was the trusted counsellor of Muavia.

This coalition, and the false step of Aly in recalling Cays
from Egypt, materially strengthened Muavia's hands. The
success of Aly at Bussorah had also this advantage for
Muavia, that it removed Talha and Zobeir, his only other
competitors, from the field. The position of Aly, again,
as one of concession to the Arab faction, was fraught with
peril. While refusing ostensibly to identify himself with
the murderers of Othman, it was virtually their cause that
he had fought; and therefore equally the cause of the
Arab tribes against the Coreish and aristocracy of Islam.
And Aly might have foreseen that the socialistic element
in this unnatural compromise must, sooner or later, in-
evitably come into collision with the interests of the
Caliphate.

The authority of Muavia rested on a firmer basis ; his
attitude was bolder, his position more consistent. He had
from the first resisted the levelling demands of the faction
hostile to Othman. He was, therefore, now justified in
pursuing these to justice, while, at the same time, in so doing
he asserted the supremacy of the Coreish. The influence
of the 'Companions' had always been paramount in Syria ;
while the Arab element there was itself largely recruited from
the aristocratic tribes of the south ;—the result being that
the Bedouins were by Muavia held thoroughly in check.
The cry for vengeance, inflamed by the gory emblems still
hanging from the pulpit, was taken up by high and low ;
while the temporising attitude of Aly was in every man's
mouth proof of complicity with the regicides. And though
many may have dreaded Aly's vengeance in the event
of his success, the general feeling throughout Syria

A.H. 36.

was a burning desire to avenge the murder of his ill-fated predecessor.

Aly and Muavia in personal antagonism.

Still, whatever the motives at work elsewhere, the contest, as between Aly and Muavia, was now virtually for the crown ; and many looked to 'the grey mule of Syria' as having the better chance. A possible solution lay, no doubt, in the erection of Syria into an independent kingdom side by side with that of Irac and Persia. But the disintegration of the Caliphate was an idea which had as yet hardly entered into the minds of the Faithful. The unity of Islam, as established by the precedent of the quarter of a century, was still, and long continued to be, the ruling sentiment of the nation.

CHAPTER XXXVII.

BATTLE OF SIFFIN.

36–37 A. H. 657 A. D.

AFTER Aly had established himself at Kufa, there followed a short interval of rest. The lieutenants and commanders, from far and near, flocked to the new capital to
do homage to the Caliph. Towards one of these, a Bedouin
chief, Muavia was known to entertain friendly sentiments.
Him, therefore, Aly deputed to Damascus with a letter,
wherein, after making mention of his election to the Caliphate, and the discomfiture of the enemy at Bussorah, he
called on Muavia to follow the example of the empire, and
take the oath of allegiance. As on a former occasion, the
envoy was kept long in waiting. At last he was dismissed
with an oral promise that submission would be tendered if
punishment were meted out to the regicides, but on no
other condition. With this reply the envoy further reported
that Othman's blood-stained garment still hung upon the
pulpit of the Mosque, and that a multitude of Syrian warriors had sworn 'that they would use no water to wash
themselves withal, neither sleep in their beds, till they had
slain the murderers of the aged Caliph, and those that
sheltered them.'

Seeing Muavia thus hopelessly alienated, Aly, resolved
no longer to delay, proclaimed an expedition against Syria.
At first the people were slack in answering the call. But
after a time he succeeded in gathering together an imposing
force of 50,000 men. His plan was to march through

Upper Mesopotamia, and so invade Syria from the north.
A detachment was sent as an advance-guard along the

Aly invades
Northern
Syria,
xi. 36 A.H.
April,
657 A.D.
western bank of the Euphrates, but meeting with opposition
there, was forced to cross back again into Mesopotamia.
Aly himself, with the main body, marched up the Tigris ;
then turning short of Mosul to the west, crossed the
desert of Mesopotamia, and, outstripping his advanced
column, reached the Euphrates in its upper course at
Ricca. An unfriendly population lined the banks ; and it
was not without sanguinary threats that Ashtar forced
them to construct a bridge. The army crossed near Ricca ;
and then marching some little distance along the right bank,
in the direction of Aleppo, they met the Syrian outposts [1].

On learning Aly's approach, Muavia lost no time in
marshalling his forces, which greatly outnumbered the
enemy, and, having no desert to cross, were soon to the
front. Amru was in command, with his two sons as lieutenants. Aly, desirous of averting bloodshed, had given
orders that, as soon as his troops came upon the enemy, they
should halt, and, confining themselves to the defensive, avoid
precipitating hostilities before opportunity was given for
friendly overture. The vanguards spent the first few days in
skirmishing. Ashtar challenged the Syrian officer to single
combat ; but he was told that, having imbrued his hands
in the blood of the late Caliph, he could not claim the
privileges of honourable warfare. When the main armies
came in sight of each other, Aly found Muavia so encamped
as to cut him off from the river, and reduce his army to
straits for water. He therefore brought on an engagement,
in which Muavia was forced to change his ground, and
occupy the fated field of Siffin [2]. Some days of inaction

---

[1] When the people refused to throw a bridge of boats over the river at Ricca,
a detachment moved farther up, intending to cross by the standing bridge at
Membaj ; but meanwhile Ashtar threatening the inhabitants with the sword,
forced them to construct a bridge at Ricca. Ricca (Nicephorinm) is at the junction of the Belik with the Euphrates, near where the river having approached
Aleppo trends thereafter eastward. The outposts met at Sur al Rum, now in
ruins, a little to the west of Ricca. It lies near Thapsacus of the ancients, on
the line of Cyrus' march.

[2] Siffin lay to the west of Ricca, half-way to Balis (one of Chesney's steamer

followed ; after which Aly sent three chiefs to demand A.H. 36–
37. that, for the good of the commonwealth, Muavia should tender his allegiance. A scene ensued of fruitless re- crimination. Muavia demanded that the murderers of Othman should be brought to justice ; while the demand was stigmatised as a mere cat's-paw covering ambitious designs upon the Caliphate. This was resented as a base calumny by Muavia. ' Begone, ye lying scoundrels ! ' he cried ; ' the sword shall decide between us.' So saying, he drove them from his presence. Finding all attempt at compromise vain, Aly marshalled his army into eight separate columns, each under a Bedouin chieftain of note. As many separate columns were similarly formed on the Syrian side. Every day one of these columns, taking the Desultory
fighting,
xii. 36 A.H.
May,
657 A.D. field in turn, was drawn up against a column of the other army. Desultory fighting in this singular way was kept up throughout the month, there being sometimes as many as two engagements in a day. But the con- test was hardly yet in earnest. On either side they feared to bring on a common battle, ' lest the Moslems should be destroyed, root and branch, in the internecine struggle.'

The new year opened on combatants, wearied by such Truce
during first
month of
37 A.H.
June,
657 A.D. indecisive strife, and inclined to thoughts of peace, and so a truce was called, to last throughout the month. The interval was spent in deputations, but they proved as fruitless as those which had gone before. Aly, under the influence of the heated Bedouins around him, was hardly disposed even now to blame the attack on Othman. When pressed by the Syrian delegates, he avoided a direct reply. ' I will not say,' was the evasive answer, ' that he was wrongly attacked, nor will I say that the attack was justified.' ' Then,' Fruitless
negotia-
tions. answered the Syrians, ' we shall fight against thee, and against every one else who refuseth to say that Othman was not wrongfully put to death;' and with these words took their final leave. On his side, Muavia declared to the messengers of Aly that nothing short of the punishment of

stations), and about 100 miles from the coast ; south-east of Aleppo, and north- east of Hims.

A.H. 36-
87. the regicides would induce him to quit the field. 'What?'
exclaimed some one; 'wouldest thou put Ammar to
death?' 'And why not?' answered Muavia; 'wherefore
should the Son of the bondwoman not suffer for having
slain the Freedman of Othman[1]?' 'Impossible,' they cried;
'where will ye stop? It were easier to bale out the floods
of the Euphrates.'

Renewal of
hostilities,
ii. 37 A.H.
July, 657.
So passed the month; and Aly, seeing things still unchanged, commenced hostilities afresh. He caused proclamation to be made along Muavia's front, summoning
the Syrians to allegiance. But it only made them rally
more closely round Muavia; and a company, girding themselves with their turbans in token of the vow, swore that they
would defend him to the death. The warfare thus resumed,
daily becoming severer and more embittered, Aly at last
made up his mind to bring on a general and decisive
battle. Thus, ten days after the renewal of hostilities, both
armies, drawn out in entire array, fought till the shades of

Battle of
Siffin,
11, 12, ii.
37 A.H.
29, 30 July.
evening fell, and neither had then got the better. The
following morning, the combat was renewed with greater
vigour. Aly posted himself in the centre with the flower of
his troops from Medina; the wings were formed one of warriors from Bussorah, the other of those from Kufa. Muavia
had a pavilion pitched upon the field; and there, surrounded by five lines of his sworn body-guard, watched the
day. Amru, with a great weight of horse, bore down upon
the Kufa wing, which gave way; and Aly was exposed to
imminent peril, both from thick showers of arrows and
from close encounter. Reproaching the men of Kufa for
their cowardice, the Caliph fought bravely, his unwieldy
figure notwithstanding, sword in hand, and manfully withstood the charge. Ashtar, at the head of three hundred
Ghazies[2], led forward the other wing, which fell with fury

[1] Othman's freedman was slain at Medina in the final onslaught of the conspirators. The life of Ammar, son of the bondwoman Sommeya, was forfeit for
this lesser crime, much more for the assassination of the Caliph. Such was
Muavia's argument.

[2] *Readers* or *Reciters* of the Coran, those, namely, who, having it by heart,
were able to repeat it from beginning to end. They were the most fanatical
part of the Moslem forces, answering to the Ghazies of our day.

on Muavia's 'turbaned' body-guard. Four of its five A.H. 36-
ranks were cut to pieces, and Muavia bethinking himself 37.
of flight had already called for his horse, when a martial
couplet flashed on his mind, and he held his ground. Amru
stood by him,—' Courage to-day,' he cried, ' to-morrow victory.' The fifth rank repelled the danger, and both sides
again fought on equal terms. Feats of desperate bravery
were displayed by both armies, and heavy was the carnage.
On Aly's side fell Hashim, the hero of Cadesiya. Of even
greater moment was the death of Ammar, now over ninety
years, and one of the leading regicides. As he saw Hashim
fall, he exclaimed, ' Paradise ! how close thou art beneath
the arrow's barb and falchion's flash ! O Hashim ! even
now I see heaven opened, and black-eyed maidens bridally
attired, clasping thee in their embrace ! ' So, singing, and
refreshing himself with his favourite draught of milk and
water, the aged warrior, fired with the ardour of youth,
rushed into the enemy's ranks, and met the envied fate.
Mahomet had once been heard to say to him :—' By a godless and rebellious race, O Ammar, thou shalt one day be
slain ; ' in other words, that Ammar would be killed fighting on the side of right. Thus his death, as it were, condemned the ranks against whom he fought, and spread
dismay in Muavia's host. But Amru answered readily :
' And who is it that hath killed Ammar, but Aly and the
" rebellious race" that brought him hither ? ' The clever
repartee ran through the Syrian host, and did much to
efface the evil omen.

The fighting this day was in real earnest ; darkness failed Battle still
to separate the combatants ; and, like Cadesiya, that night rages on
third day,
was called a second 'Night of Clangour.' The morning 13 Safar,
broke on the two armies still in conflict. With emptied 31 July.
quivers they fought hand to hand. Ashtar, the regicide,
resolved on victory at whatever cost, continued to push the
attack with unflinching bravery and persistence. Muavia,
disheartened, began to speak of a judicial combat with a
champion on either side. 'Then go forth thyself, and
challenge Aly,' said Amru. ' Not so,' answered Muavia, 'I
will not do that, for Aly ever slayeth his man, and then

T

thou shouldest succeed me.' Amru, indeed, well knew that
this was not Muavia's line, who himself, like his antagonist, was now of an unwieldy mien. It was no time for
continuing grim pleasantry like this; and so Amru bethought him of a stratagem. 'Raise aloft the leaves of
the Coran,' he cried; 'if any refuse to abide thereby, it
will sow discord amongst them; if they accept the hallowed symbol it will be a reprieve from cruel slaughter.'
Muavia caught at the words. And so forthwith they fixed
the sacred scrolls on the points of their lances, and raising
them aloft, called out along the line of battle: 'The law of
the Lord! The law of the Lord! Let that decide betwixt

Hostilities
suspended
for arbitra-
tion by
Coran. us!' No sooner heard, than the men of Kufa leaped forward, re-echoing the cry: 'The law of the Lord, that shall
decide between us!' As all were shouting thus with one
accord, Aly stepped forth and expostulated with them:
'It is the device,' he cried, 'of evil men; afraid of defeat,
they seek their end by guile, and cloak rebellion under
love of the Word.' It was all in vain. To every argument
they answered (and the Ghazies loudest of all): 'We are
called to the Book, and we cannot decline it.' At last, in
open mutiny, they threatened the unfortunate Caliph, that,
unless he agreed, they would desert him, drive him over
to the enemy, or serve him as they had served Othman.
Seeing opposition futile, Aly said: 'Stay wild and treasonable words. Obey and fight. But if ye will rebel, do as
ye list.' 'We will not fight,' they cried; 'recall Ashtar
from the field.' Ashtar, thus summoned, at the first refused. 'We are gaining a great victory,' he said, 'I will
not come;' and he turned to fight again. But the tumult
increased, and Aly sent a second time to say: 'Of what
avail is victory when treason rageth? Wouldst thou have
the Caliph murdered, or delivered over to the enemy?'
Ashtar unwillingly returned, and a fierce altercation ensued
between him and the angry soldiery. 'Ye were fighting,'
he said, 'but yesterday for the Lord, and the choicest
among you lost their lives. What is it but that ye now
acknowledge yourselves in the wrong, and the Martyrs
therefore gone to hell?' 'Nay,' they answered; 'yester-

day we fought for the Lord; and to-day, for the same Lord we stay the fight.' On this, Ashtar upbraided them as 'traitors, cowards, hypocrites, and villains.' In return, they reviled him, and struck his charger with their whips. Aly interposed. The tumult was stayed. And Ashath, chief of the Beni Kinda, was sent to ask Muavia ' what his meaning in raising the Coran aloft might be.' ' It is this,' he sent answer back, ' that we should return, both you and we, to the will of the Lord, as set forth in the Book. Each side shall name an Umpire, and their verdict shall be binding.' Aly's army shouted assent. The unfortunate Caliph was forced to the still deeper humiliation of appointing as his arbiter one who had deserted him. The soldiery cried out for Abu Musa, the temporising governor of Kufa who had been deposed for want of active loyalty. 'This man,' answered Aly, 'did but lately leave us and flee; and not till after several months I pardoned him. Neither hath he now been fighting with us. Here is a worthy representative, the son of Abbas, the Prophet's uncle; choose him as your Umpire.' 'As well name thyself,' they answered rudely. 'Then take Ashtar.' 'What!' said the Bedouin chiefs in the same rough imperious strain, 'the man that hath set the world on fire! None for us but Abu Musa.' It was a bitter choice for Aly, but he had no alternative. The Syrian arbiter was Amru, for whose deep and crafty ways the other was no match. He presented himself in the Caliph's camp, and the agreement was put in writing. As dictated from Aly's side, it ran thus: '*In the name of the* *Lord Most Merciful!* This is what hath been agreed upon between the Commander of the Faithful, and ——' 'Stay!' cried Amru (like the Coreish to the Prophet at Hodeibia[1]); 'Aly is *your* Commander, but he is not ours.' Again the helpless Caliph had to give way, and the names of the contracting parties were written down simply as between ' Aly and Muavia.' The document bound them ' to follow the judgment of the Coran ; and, where the Coran was silent, the acknowledged precedents of Islam.' To the Umpires, the guarantee of both Aly and Muavia was given of safety for

---

[1] *Life of Mahomet*, p. 372.

themselves and for their families; and the promise of the
people that their judgment should be followed. On their
part, the Umpires swore to judge righteously and reconcile
the Faithful. The decision was to be delivered after six
months, or later if the Umpires saw cause for delay, and at
some neutral spot midway between Kufa and Damascus.
Meanwhile hostilities should be suspended. The writing,
having been duly executed and signed, was numerously
witnessed by leading chiefs on either side. Ashtar alone
refused :—'Never should I acknowledge this to be mine
own right hand,' he said, 'if it did but touch a deed like
this.'

Aly and
Muavia
retire.
And so the armies buried their dead, and quitted the
memorable but undecisive battle-field. Aly retired to Kufa;
and Muavia, his point for the present gained, to Damascus.
As Aly entered Kufa, he heard wailing on every side. A
chief man, whom he bade to pacify the mourners, answered:
' O Caliph, it is not as if but two or three had been slain; of
this clan alone hard by, an hundred and fourscore lie buried
at Siffin. There is not a house but the women are weeping
in it for their dead.'

Discord at
Kufa.
The slaughter, indeed, had been great on both sides.
And what gave point to Aly's loss was that the truce was
but a hollow thing, with no hope in it of lasting peace or
satisfaction. The Arab faction, to whose insolent demands
he had yielded, was more estranged than ever. When the
men of Kufa murmured at the compromise, Aly could but
reply that the mutinous soldiery had extorted the agreement from him; and that having pledged his faith, he could
not now withdraw. He had thrown in his lot with traitors
and regicides, and was now reaping the bitter fruit. Muavia
alone had gained.

CHAPTER XXXVIII.

THE KHAREJITES, OR THEOCRATIC FACTION, REBEL AGAINST ALY.

37 A.H. 657 A.D.

THE quick sagacity of Amru had never been turned to better account than when he proposed that the Coran should be the arbiter between the contending parties. To be judged by the Book of the Lord had been the cry of the democrats from the beginning. The sacred text gave countenance neither to the extravagant pretensions of the Coreish, nor to their rule of favouritism and tyranny. Its precepts were based on the Brotherhood of the faithful; and the Prophet himself had enjoined the absolute equality of all. No sooner, therefore, was the Coran proclaimed than, as Amru anticipated, the Arab chiefs, caught in the snare, took up the cry, and pledged themselves thereto.

Arab faction caught by appeal to Koran.

Reflection soon tarnished the prospect. They had forgotten how narrow was the issue which the Umpires had to decide. The Bedouins and democrats were fighting not for one Caliph or the other, but against the pretensions of the Coreish at large. It was this that nerved them to the sanguinary conflict. 'If the Syrians conquer,' cried one of their chiefs, 'ye are undone. Again ye will be ground down by tyrants like unto the minions of Othman. They will seize upon the conquests of Islam, as if, forsooth, they were theirs by inheritance, instead of won by our swords. We

Dissatisfied.

shall lose our grasp both of this world and the next.' Such
were the alleged evils for which they had slain Othman, and
from which they had been fighting for deliverance. By the
appointment of an Umpire, what had they gained? It was
a *Theocracy* they had been dreaming of, and now they were
drifting back into the abuses of the past. The Umpires
would decide simply as between Muavia and Aly; and,
whatever the verdict, despotism would be riveted more
firmly than ever upon them. What they really wanted
had been lost sight of: nor was there any longer a prospect of its being won.

Draw off Angrily arguing thus, a body of 12,000 men fell out from
into hostile Aly's army on their homeward march, but kept side by side
camp near with the rest, at some little distance off. Loud and violent
Kufa; in their speech, they beat about their neighbours in rude
Bedouin fashion with their whips, and accused one another
of having abandoned the cause of Islam into the hands of
godless arbitrators; while others repented at having betrayed the Caliph on the field of battle, and thus separated themselves from the body of the Faithful. In this
frame of mind they avoided Kufa, but encamped in its
vicinity at the village of Harora. They chose for themselves a temporary leader. Their resolve however, was, that
when they gained ascendency, they would no longer have
any Prince or Caliph at all, nor any oath of allegiance but
to *the Lord alone*; and vest the administration of affairs in
a Council of State. Such theocratic dreams were not confined to these schismatics, but had widely leavened that
factious and fanatic city, Kufa.

Aly, aware of the danger, sent his cousin, Ibn Abbas, to
reason with the seceding body, but to no effect. He then
proceeded to their camp himself, and gained over their
but per- leader by the promise of the government of Ispahan. He
suaded by urged that, so far from being responsible for 'the godless
Aly, compromise,' as they called the truce, he had been driven to
it against his better judgment by their own wayward and
persistent obstinacy; that the Umpires were bound by its
terms to deliver their decision in accordance with the Sacred
text, which the Theocrats equally with himself held to be

the final guide ; and if the Umpires' deliverance should
after all be in disregard of right, he would without hesitation reject the same, and again go forth to fight with them
against their enemies.

For the present they were pacified by these assurances ; retire to
and so, breaking up their camp, they returned to their their
homes, there to await the decision of the Umpires.

CHAPTER XXXIX.

DECISION OF THE UMPIRES.

37 A.H.   658 A.D.

THE interval passed uneasily.   Muavia ruled in Syria;
Aly, over the rest of the Moslem world.   Neither, for the
moment, interfered with the other.   The empire was in
suspense.

Within the time appointed, Amru appeared at Duma,
half way across the desert and, shortly after, Abu Musa;
each followed, as agreed upon, by a retinue of 400 horse.
Thither also flocked multitudes from Irac and Syria, from
Mecca also and from Medina.   With intense interest they
watched the strange proceeding, which was to decide the
future of Islam.   The leading chiefs, too, of the Coreish
were there; some with the distant hope that the choice
might haply fall on one of them.

The Umpires met in a pavilion pitched for the occasion;
and there a private conference was held between the two
alone.   The account preserved is brief and uncertain.   Abu
Musa, pressed by his astute colleague, admitted that the
assassination of Othman was a wicked and unjustifiable
act.   'Then why,' rejoined Amru, 'wilt thou not take
Muavia, the avenger of the Caliph's blood, for his successor?'   'If it were a mere question of blood-feud or
kinsmanship,' said Abu Musa, 'then Othman's sons would
have the nearer claim.   But succession to the throne must
be determined by the chief Companions' vote.'   Amru then

proposed his own son. 'A just and good man,' replied Abu
Musa, 'but one whom thou hast already made to take sides
in the civil war ; and, above all things, we must beware of
kindling mutiny again amongst the Arab tribes.'   A
similar objection shut out Abdallah son of Zobeir ; and
Omar's son was put aside as not having qualities fitted for
command.   'Then,' asked Amru, when all possible candidates had been named and negatived, 'what may be
the judgment thou wouldest give?'   'My judgment,'
answered Abu Musa, 'would be to depose both Aly and
Muavia, and then leave the people free to choose as Caliph
whom they will.'   'Thy judgment is also mine,' said Amru
promptly ; 'let us go forth.'

The people, in breathless expectation, crowded round the and
pavilion as the Umpires issued from it.   'Let them know,' judgment,
said Amru to his fellow, 'that we are agreed.'   Abu Musa
advanced, and with voice loud and clear, said : 'We are
agreed upon a decision such as, we trust, will reconcile the
people, and reunite the empire.'   'He speaketh true,' said
Amru : 'step forth, O Abu Musa, and pronounce thy judgment.'   Then spoke Abu Musa : 'Ye people! we have
considered the matter well.   We see no other course for
peace and concord, but to depose Aly and Muavia, both
one and other.   After that, ye shall yourselves choose a fit
man in their room.   This is my judgment.'   He stepped deposing
aside, and Amru advancing said : 'Ye have heard the Aly.
sentence of Abu Musa.   He hath deposed his fellow ; and
I too depose him.   But as for my chief, Muavia, him do I
confirm.   He is the heir of Othman, the avenger of his
blood, and the best entitled as Caliph to succeed.'

The assembly was thunderstruck.   Even the Syrians had The people
never dreamed of Muavia achieving such a triumph; nor staggered.
had it entered the minds of those on Aly's side, that their
Umpire could be overreached thus shamefully.   'What
could I do?' cried Abu Musa, assailed on every hand ; 'he
agreed with me, then swerved aside.'   'No fault of thine,'
said the son of Abbas : 'the fault of those who put thee in
the place.'   Overwhelmed with reproaches, Abu Musa
escaped to Mecca, where he thenceforward lived in

obscurity.   In the heat of indignation, the commander of the Kufa bodyguard seized Amru, and was roughly handling him, when the people interposed to set him free. Amru returned forthwith to Damascus, where by acclamation Muavia was saluted Caliph.

How the startling intelligence affected Aly, may be judged by the fact that to the prescribed daily service he now added a petition cursing by name, Muavia, Amru, and their chief adherents.   Muavia was nothing loth to follow his example.   And so the world was edified by the spectacle of rival Commanders of the Faithful uttering commination one against the other, in the public prayers[1].

---

[1] The imprecation used by Aly was as follows : 'O Lord, I beseech Thee, let Muavia be accursed, and Amru,' and so on with the chief leaders by name. 'Let them be accursed all!'   Muavia's imprecation, in the same way, included Aly, his sons Hasan and Hosein, and Ashtar.

CHAPTER XL.

THE KHAREJITES, OR THEOCRATIC SEPARATISTS, DEFEATED AT NEHRWAN.

37 A.H. 658 A.D.

ALY was not content with heaping on his rival maledic- Aly's design against Syria. He resolved on immediate renewal of hostilities. There was, however, other work before him in first dealing with an enemy nearer home.

Ever since they had broken up their camp at Harora, the Kharejites, instead of settling down in sentiments of loyalty and peace, had been gaining in aggressive force and turbulence. There should be no oath of fealty, was the theocratic cry, but to the Lord alone, the Mighty and the Glorious. To swear allegiance to either Aly or Muavia was in derogation of that great name. 'Both sides,' they said, 'are coursing along, neck and neck, in the race of apostasy: the Syrians run after Muavia right or wrong, and ye swear for Aly through black and white. It is nought but blasphemy.' So they drew up their creed in one short sentence: *No rule but that of the Lord alone ;* and this they insolently flung in Aly's teeth[1]. In vain the Caliph argued, as before, that Arbitration had been forced upon him by themselves. 'True,' they readily replied ;

Hostile attitude of theocratic faction,
ix. 37 A.H.
Jan., 658.

---

[1] *La hukm illa lillahi.* The creed of the Separatists was that, Believers being absolutely equal, there should be no Caliph, nor oath of allegiance sworn to any man, the government being in the hands of a Council elected by the people.

A.H. 87.
Aly's for-
bearance.

'but we have repented of that lapse; and thou must repent of it too, or else we shall fight against thee; and if so be we are slain, we shall gladly meet our Lord.' Aly yet hoped to win them over. He bore with their seditious talk; and made his intention known of treating them forbearingly. 'They should have free access to the mosques for prayer. If they joined his army, they would share the booty like the rest. So long as they refrained from any overt act, he would use no force of arms against them.'

Kharejites
march on
Nehrwan,
x. 37 A.H.
March,
658 A.D.

Instead of pacifying the fanatics, this moderation but emboldened them. At last, when the Umpires' judgment was delivered, they denounced it as amply justifying their secession, and resolved at once to raise the divine standard. They looked for heavenly interposition; but even if they perished, it was a righteous cause which must triumph in the end; and they themselves, protesting against a wicked world, would surely be inheritors of the world to come. Accordingly, about a month after the Arbitration, they began, in concert with the brethren who sympathised with them at Bussorah, to leave their homes by stealth. The band from Bussorah, 500 strong, was pursued by the governor, but effecting their escape, joined the party which in greater force had issued forth from Kufa. Secular power, and the pomp of this life, were abhorrent from the covenanting creed; and it was only after many had declined the dangerous pre-eminence, and then simply as a temporary expedient, that a chief was prevailed on to accept command. The design was to occupy Medain, and there, under a Council of Representatives, establish theocratic rule as a model to the ungodly cities all around. But the governor had timely warning, and repulsed the attempt. They passed on, and in small bodies crossing the Tigris farther up, assembled at Nehrwan 4000 strong.

Aly orders
levy for
Syrian
campaign,

Aly did not at first recognise the serious bearing of the movement. The number was comparatively small; and he hoped that, immediately they saw their former comrades in arms marching against the graceless Syrians, they would not hesitate again to join his standard. So he mounted the pulpit and harangued the men of Kufa. He denounced

the Umpires as having cast the Book of the Lord, equally
with the Prophet's precedent, behind their backs. Both were
apostates, rejected of the Lord, of His Prophet also, and of all
good men ;—' Wherefore,' said he, ' we must fight our battle
over again at the point where, on the eve of victory, we were
forced to leave it off. Prepare to march for Syria, and be
ready in your camp without the city, by the second day of
the coming week.' Then he indited a despatch to the and sum-
fanatics at Nehrwan. It was couched in terms similar, and ${}^{\text{mons Kha-}}_{\text{rejites, who}}$
ended thus : ' Now, therefore, return forthwith and join the refuse to
army. I am marching against the common enemy, yours ${}^{\text{join him.}}$
and ours. We have come back to the time when at Siffin
ye fought by my side ; now follow me again.' In reply
they sent an insulting message :—' If Aly would acknowledge
his apostasy and repent thereof, then they would see
whether anything could be arranged between them ; otherwise they cast him off as an ungodly heretic.' The stiff-
necked Theocrats were thereupon, for the present, left to
their own devices, and the business of raising levies for
Syria proceeded with. But little enthusiasm was anywhere
displayed. Of 60,000 fighting men on the stipendiary roll
at Bussorah, 3000 were with difficulty got together. At Aly sets
Kufa, after vain appeal, a conscription was ordered through ${}^{\text{out for}}_{\text{Syria ;}}$
the heads of clans ; and thus at length an army of 65,000
was brought into the field.

With this imposing force, Aly had already commenced but is
his march on Syria, when tidings reached him that the ${}^{\text{diverted by}}_{\text{Kharejite}}$
fanatic host was committing outrage throughout the country excesses,
in the very outskirts of the camp[1]. A messenger sent to
make inquiry, met the common fate. Tidings becoming
more and more alarming, the army demanded to be led
against them ; ' for how,' said they, ' can we leave such
outlaws at large behind us, with homes exposed to their
unlicensed cruelty?' Aly, himself convinced of this,
changed his course, crossed the Tigris, and marched

---

[1] These outrages were to the last degree barbarous and cold-blooded.
Travellers, men and women, refusing to confess the theocratic tenets were
put to death ; a woman great with child ripped up with the sword, and so
forth.

A.H. 37. against the fanatics.   When now near Nehrwan, he sent
a messenger to demand surrender of all such as had been
guilty of outrage and murder. 'Give up these to justice,'
he said, ' and ye shall be left alone, until the Lord grant us
victory in Syria, and then haply He shall have turned your
hearts again toward us.' They replied that 'they were all
equally responsible for what had passed, and that the blood
of the ungodly heretics they had slain was shed lawfully.'
A parley ensued, in which the Caliph expostulated with
the misguided fanatics, and offered quarter to all who
who are   should come over to his army, or retire peaceably to their
dispersed   homes.   Some obeyed the call and came over ; 500 went
and slain.
off to a neighbouring Persian town, and many more dispersed to their homes.   Eighteen hundred remained upon
the field, martyrs to the theocratic creed.   With the wild
battle-cry, *To Paradise !* they rushed upon the lances of the
Caliph's force, and to a man were slain.   Aly's loss was
trifling.

The Kha-   It had been better for the peace of Islam if not one of the
rejites a   4000 had escaped.   The snake was scotched, not killed.
chronic
thorn in   The fanatic spirit was strangely catching ; and the theo-
the empire.   cratic cause continued to be canvassed vigorously and
unceasingly, though in secret, both at Bussorah and Kufa.
However hopeless their object, the fanatics were nerved, if
not by expectation of divine aid, at the least by sure hope
of the martyr's crown.   In the following year, bands of
insurgent fanatics once and again appeared unexpectedly
in the field, denouncing Aly, and proclaiming that the
Kingdom of the Lord was at hand.   One after another they
were cut to pieces, or put to flight with ease.   But such
continual risings could not but endamage the name and
power of Aly, who now reaped the fruit of his weak compromise with the enemies of Othman, and neglect to bring
them to justice.   Fanatics in their extravagant doctrine,
these men were too sincere to combine with any purely
political sect, and hence they seldom came near to leaving
any permanent mark of their creed behind them.   But
both in the present and in succeeding reigns, we find them
every now and then gathering up their strength dangerously

to assail the empire, and as often beaten back.   Ever and
anon, for ages, these *Kharejites* (as the name implies) ' went
forth[1] ' on their desperate errand, a thorn in the side of the
Caliphate, and a terror to the well-disposed.

---

[1] *Kharejite,* ' one who goes forth,' that is to say, against the government,
demanding, as Covenanter, a reform.

CHAPTER XLI.

REVOLT OF EGYPT.

38 A.H.   658 A.D.

Aly gives
up Syrian
campaign.
End of
37 A.H.
April,
658 A.D.

HAVING dispersed the fanatics at Nehrwan, and re-crossed the Tigris, Aly turned his face again towards Syria.   But the troops urged that, before so long a campaign, their armour needed refitting.   'Let us return for a little to our homes,' they said, 'to furbish up our swords and lances, and replenish our empty quivers.'   Aly consenting, they marched back and encamped in the vicinity of Kufa.   The soldiers dropped off in small parties thither ; and in a short time the camp was left almost empty.   Aly, finding that none returned, became impatient, and himself entering Kufa, again harangued the people on the obligation to go forth with him and make war on Syria. But exhortation and reproach fell equally on listless ears. There was no response.   Aly lost heart.   The Syrian expe-dition fell through ; and no attempt was made to resume it.

Position
of Aly and
Muavia.

Thus closed the 37th year of the Hegira.   The situation was unchanged.   Muavia, with now a colourable title to the Caliphate, remained in undisturbed possession of Syria, strong in the loyalty and affections of his subjects ; while Aly, mortified by an indifferent and alienated people, was now to experience a severer trial in the loss of Egypt.

Egypt in
revolt.

We have seen that a powerful faction in that dependency sided with those demanding satisfaction for the blood of Othman ; and that Cays having been recalled for not suppressing the dissentients, Mohammed son of Abu Bekr

had been appointed in his room. Casting aside the wise A.H. 38.
policy of his predecessor, Mohammed demanded of the
recusants at once to submit, or to be gone from Egypt.
They refused, but, masking their hostile designs, watched
the issue of the struggle at Siffin. When on its conclusion
Muavia was still left master of Syria, they gained heart and
began to assume the offensive. Though repeatedly defeated,
the slumbering elements of revolt were everywhere aroused,
and Muavia, seeing his opportunity, commissioned Amru to
regain the province of which he had been the first conqueror.

Aly saw too late the mistake which he had made. He Amru conquers
would have reappointed Cays ; but Cays declined again to Egypt for
take the post. The only other fitted for the emergency Muavia,
was Ashtar, the regicide, whom he sent off in haste to ii. 38 A.H. July,
Egypt. But on the way he met with an untimely death, 658 A.D.
having been poisoned (at the instigation, it is said, of
Muavia) by a chief on the Egyptian border with whom he
rested. There was joy at the death of the arch-regicide
throughout Syria, where he was greatly feared. Aly was
equally cast down by the untoward event. His only
resource was now to bid Mohammed hold on, and do
what he could to retrieve his position. But the faction
which favoured Muavia gained ground daily ; and when
Amru, at the head of a few thousand men, crossed the
border, he was joined by an overwhelming body of insurgents. Mohammed, after a vain attempt to fight, was
slain, and his body ignominiously burned in an ass's
skin[1]. Thus Egypt was lost to Aly; and Amru, as
lieutenant of the rival Caliph, again became its governor.

The loss of Egypt was the harder for Aly to bear, as Aly's mor-
immediately due to his own mistake in removing Cays ; tification at loss of
and even now it might have been retrieved if the men of Egypt.
Kufa had not been heartless in his cause. Over and again
he implored them to hasten to the defence of Mohammed.

---

[1] Amru had offered Mohammed quarter. But he was caught in his flight by
a chief so incensed against the regicides that he slew him in cold blood, and
having put his body in an ass's skin, cast it into the flames. Ayesha was inconsolable at her brother's fate, and, though her politics were all against Aly, she
now cursed Muavia and Amru in her daily prayers, and thenceforward ate no
roasted meat or pleasant food until her death.

A.H. 38. With difficulty two thousand men were got together, but after
so long delay that they had hardly marched before news
of the defeat made it necessary to return.   Aly thereupon
ascended the pulpit, and upbraided the people for their
spiritless and disloyal attitude.   For fifty days he had been
urging them to go forth, to avenge their fallen brethren,
and help those still struggling in the field.   Like a restive,
wayward camel, casting its burden, they had held back.
'And now,' he said, in grief and bitterness of spirit, 'the son
of Abu Bekr is fallen a martyr, and Egypt hath departed
from us.'

CHAPTER XLII.

REMAINDER OF ALY'S REIGN.

38–40 A.H.   658–60 A.D.

NO gleam of fortune lighted up the remaining days of <aside>Remainder of Aly's reign.</aside> Aly's reign. What with fanatics at home, and the rival Caliphate abroad, his life was one continual struggle. And, moreover, the daily exhibition of indifference and disloyalty in Kufa, the city of his choice, was a mortification hard to bear.

The loss of Egypt, and cruel death of Mohammed, preyed <aside>Rising at Bussorah suppressed, 38 A.H. 658 A.D.</aside> upon his mind. He withdrew into strictest privacy. His cousin, Ibn Abbas, governor of Bussorah, fearful lest he should resign, or do something rash and unadvised, set out to visit and comfort him. Muavia seized the opportunity for stirring up the disaffected elements at Bussorah. Among the various clans, he was sure of finding many who, equally with himself, sought to avenge the blood of Othman ; few were zealously attached to the cause of Aly ; the remainder were mostly of the theocratic faction, now quite as hostile to Aly as to Muavia. The Syrian emissary, carrying a letter to the citizens of Bussorah, was so well received, that Ziad, who held temporary charge, was forced to retire with the treasure and pulpit of state into the stronghold of a loyal clan, from whence he wrote for help to Kufa. Aly at once despatched a chief of influence with the local tribes, who were by his persuasion induced to rally round Ziad. After severe fighting in the

A.H. 38–
40.
———

city, the rebels were at last defeated, and driven for refuge to a neighbouring castle. There surrounded, the castle was set on fire, and the Syrian envoy, with seventy followers, perished in the flames. The victory was decisive for the time; but the insurrection had brought to light the alarming spread of disaffection, and showed how precarious was Aly's grasp upon the Bedouin races of factious Bussorah.

Kharejite risings.

The spirit of disturbance and unrest was not confined to Egypt and to Bussorah. In a single year, we read of some half-dozen occasions on which considerable bands of *Kharejites* were impelled by their theocratic creed to raise the standard of rebellion. One after another they met the common fate of slaughter and dispersion. But though crushed, the frequent repetition of such desperate enterprises, the fruit of a wild and reckless fanaticism, had a disturbing effect. The most serious of these risings was that led by Khirrît; and it is the more remarkable, because this chief had fought bravely with his tribe by Aly's side in the battles both of the Camel and at Siffin. He was driven, like many others, by strong conviction to rebel. Boldly approaching the throne, he told Aly that since he had referred a divine issue to human arbitration, he could obey him now no more, neither stand up behind him in the Mosque at prayer; but henceforth was sworn to be his enemy. Aly, with his usual patience, said that he would argue out the matter with him, and arranged a meeting for the purpose. But the night before, Khirrît stole away from the city with his following. 'Gone,' said Aly, 'to the devil; lost, like the doomed Thamudites!' They were pursued, but effected their escape to Ahwaz. There they raised the Persians, Kurds, and Christian mountaineers, by the specious and inflammatory cry that payment of taxes to an ungodly Caliph was but to support his cause, and as such intolerable. With a band of rebel Arabs, they kindled revolt throughout Fars, and put the governor to flight. A force from Bussorah drove them to the shores of the Indian Ocean. But luring the people by delusive promises, they still gained head; and it was not till after

Rebellion
of Khirrît
in S. Persia,
38 A.H.
658 A.D.

a bloody battle, in which Khirrît lost his life, that the A.H. 38-
supremacy of the Caliphate was re-established in Southern 40.
Persia. The Mussulman prisoners in this campaign were Khirrît defeated
set at liberty on swearing fresh allegiance; but 500 Chris- and slain.
tians were marched away to be sold into captivity. The
women and children, as they were torn from their protectors, wailed with loud and bitter cry. The hearts of
many were softened. Mascala, one of the captains, touched
by the scene, took upon himself the cost of ransoming the
Christian captives, and set them free. Aly, hearing of it,
demanded from him immediate payment at a thousand
pieces for each captive; and Mascala, unable to pay down
so great a sum, fled and joined Muavia.

The defeat of the Kharejites did not at once restore Ziad
peace to Persia; for Fars and Kerman threw off their governor of Fars,
allegiance, and expelled their governors. To quell the 39 A.H.
spreading insurrection, Aly employed Ziad from Bussorah, 659 A.D.
a man, as we have seen, of conspicuous administrative
ability. He carried with him a great court and retinue;
but it was mainly by setting one rebellious prince against
another, and by well-appointed promises and favours, that
he succeeded in restoring peace; and by his success earned
the government of Fars. He fixed his court at Istakhr
(Persepolis), and his administration there became so famous
as to recall to Persian memories the happy age of Nushirwan.

Though successful thus in Persia, Aly was subject to Syrian
trouble and molestation nearer home. Muavia, relieved expeditions against
now from apprehension on the side of Egypt, began to Irac,
annoy his rival by frequent raids on Arabia and the cities 38, 39 A.H.
beyond the Syrian desert. The object was various—now 659 A.D.
to ravage a province or surprise a citadel, now to exact the
tithe from Bedouin tribes, or secure allegiance to himself.
Such inroads, though not always successful, inspired a sense
of insecurity; and worse, betrayed the lukewarmness of the
people in the cause of Aly. These would stir neither hand
nor foot to repel the Syrians invading villages close even at
their doors. To show his displeasure at their listlessness and
disobedience, Aly went forth himself into the field almost
unattended. On this, the men of Kufa, partly from shame,

40.

Muavia
visits
Mosul.

Raid of
Bosor on
Arabia,
40 A.H.
660 A.D.

Infant
children
of Aly's
cousin
slain.

partly lured by promise of increased stipends, marched to
the defence of their frontier. In the year 39 A.H. there
were nearly a dozen inroads of the kind. Though eventually repelled, it was not always without loss in prisoners,
plunder, and prestige. On one occasion Aly's commander,
with a flying column, pursued the raiders back into the
heart of Syria as far as Baalbek; and thence, turning
northward, escaped by Ricca again into Irac. On the
other hand, Muavia, to show his contempt for the power of
Aly, made an incursion right across Mesopotamia, and for
some days remained encamped on the banks of the Tigris.
After leisurely inspecting Mosul, which he had never seen
before, he made his way back to Damascus unmolested.

The 40th year of the Hegira opened with a new grief for
Aly. When the time of pilgrimage came round, Muavia
sent Bosor, a brave but cruel captain of his host, with 3000
men, into Arabia, to secure for him the allegiance of the
Holy places. As he drew nigh to Medina, the governor fled,
and Bosor entered unopposed. Proceeding to the Mosque,
he mounted the sacred steps of the Prophet's pulpit, and,
recalling Othman to mind, addressed the people thus : ' O
citizens of Medina! The Aged Man! Where is the grey-
haired aged man whom, but as yesterday, and on this very
spot, I swore allegiance to? Verily, but for my promise
to Muavia, who bade me stay the sword, I had not left here
a single soul alive!' Then he threatened the leading citizens
with death if they refused to acknowledge Muavia as their
Caliph ; and so, fearing for their lives, all took the oath of
allegiance to the Omeyyad ruler. Passing on to Mecca,
the same scene was enacted by the imperious envoy there,
and with the same result[1]. Then he marched south to
Yemen, where he committed great atrocities upon the
adherents of Aly. The governor, a son of Abbas, escaped
to his cousin at Kufa. But two of his little children, falling
into the tyrant's hands, were put to death in cold blood,
with their Bedouin attendant, who in vain protested against

[1] On Bosor's approach, Abu Musa fled from Mecca for his life. The unfortunate man had been living there ever since the Arbitration, equally obnoxious to
both sides.

the cruel act. An army of 4000 men was despatched in haste from Kufa, but too late to stop these outrages ; and Bosor made good his escape to Syria. The wretched Peninsula fared no better at the hands of the relieving army. Many of the inhabitants of Najran were put to death because they had belonged to Othman's party. The men of Mecca were forced to recall the oath they had just taken, and again do homage to Aly. Similarly, the citizens of Medina swore allegiance to Hasan, son of Aly, at the point of the sword ; but no sooner were the troops gone, than the leader of the opposite faction resumed his functions. The cruel death of his cousin's infant children preyed on Aly more, perhaps, than all his other troubles ; and he cursed Bosor in the daily service with a new and bitter imprecation. The disconsolate mother poured forth her sorrow in plaintive verse, some touching couplets of which are still preserved [1].

Yet another grief was in store for Aly. He had pro- moted his cousins, the sons of Abbas, to great dignity, giving the command of Yemen to one, of Mecca to another, of Medina to a third ; while Abdallah, the eldest, held the government of Bussorah, the second city in the empire. Complaints having reached the court of irregularities at Bussorah, Aly called upon his cousin to render an account. Scorning the demand, Abdallah threw up the office, and, carrying his treasures with him, retired to Mecca. Aly was much mortified at this unfriendly act ; and still more so by the desertion of his brother Ackil to Muavia.

These troubles, crowding rapidly one upon another, at last broke Aly's spirit. He had no longer heart to carry on hostilities with Syria. If he might secure the Eastern provinces in peaceful subjection to himself, it was all he could hope for now. Accordingly, after a lengthened correspondence, an armistice was concluded between Aly and

---

[1] For example :

> Ah ! who hath seen my two little ones—
> Darlings hidden, like pearls within their shell?

As grandchildren of Abbas, their fate naturally occupies a conspicuous place in Abbasside tradition. Aly cursed Bosor, praying that he might lose his senses, and in answer to the prayer he became, we are told, a hopeless, drivelling idiot.

Muavia, by which they agreed to lay aside their arms, re-spect the territory of each other, and maintain in time to come a friendly attitude.

The double
Caliphate.
It is possible that the double Caliphate thus recognised, in two separate and independent empires, by the respective Rulers of the East and West, might have been prolonged in-definitely, or even been handed down in perpetuity, had not the tragical event occurred to be narrated in the following chapter.

CHAPTER XLIII.

ASSASSINATION OF ALY.

40 A.H. 661 A.D.

THE theocratic Separatists were sorely troubled at the Conspiracy to assassinate Aly, Muavia, and Amru, 40 A.H. 661 A.D. prospects of Islam. It was not that raids and robbery, dissension and strife, had been the order of the day; for to them bloodshed was more tolerable than apostasy. To the Kharejite, the cessation of war brought no peace of mind. A settled government was the ruin of his hopes. Aly having come to terms with Muavia, there was no longer room to expect that the ungodly kingdoms of the earth would be overthrown, and the reign of righteousness restored. Thus the theocratic party brooded over the blood that had been shed in vain at Nehrwan and on other battle-fields, and for the present abandoned hope. Many took refuge from the godless tyranny in the sacred precincts of the Hejaz, where they might lament freely over the miserable fate of Islam. As three of these thus mourned together, a gleam of hope shot across their path;—
'Let us each kill one of the tyrants; Islam will yet be free, and the reign of the Lord appear.' And so, as in the case of Othman, but under another guise and urged by bolder hopes, the three conspired against the State. The fatal resolve once taken, details were speedily arranged. Aly and Muavia both must fall; and Amru also, not only as the impious Arbitrator, but also as the likeliest successor to the throne left vacant by the other two. Each was to dispose of his fellow, as he presided at the morning service, on the same

A.H. 40. Friday when, being the Fast, the Grand mosques of Kufa,
―――― Damascus, and Fostat would be thronged with worshippers.
They dipped their swords in powerful poison, and separated,
swearing that they would either fulfil the task or perish in
Amru the attempt. Amru escaped. He was sick that day, and
escapes. the captain of his guard, presiding at prayers, died in his
Muavia stead. Muavia was not so fortunate. The blow fell upon
wounded; him, and was near to being fatal. His physician declared
recovers. his life could be saved only by the cautery, or by a potent
draught that would deprive him of the hope of further
progeny. He shrank from the cautery, and chose the
draught. The remedy was effectual, and he survived.

Aly   At Kufa things turned out differently. The conspirator
wounded Ibn Muljam was able on the spot to gain two desperate
in the
Mosque at accomplices from the Beni Taym. That tribe, deeply im-
Kufa. bued with the fanaticism of the day, suffered severely in
the massacre of Nehrwan, and ever since had nursed
resentment against the Caliph. Ibn Muljam loved a maid
of the Beni Taym, who having on that fatal day lost father,
brother, and other relatives, was roused thereby to a savage
ardour. 'Bring me,' said the damsel to her lover, 'the
head of Aly as my dower; if thou escapest alive, thou
shalt have me as thy guerdon here; if thou perish, thou
shalt enjoy better than me above.' So she introduced him
to two accomplices, who, burning with the same spirit of
revenge as Ibn Muljam, were to lie in wait on either side of
the door leading into the crowded mosque. At the time
appointed, the Caliph entered the assembly calling aloud as
usual, *To prayers, ye people! To prayers!* Immediately he
was assailed on either hand. The sword of one conspirator
fell upon the lintel; but Ibn Muljam wounded the Caliph
severely on the head and side. He was seized. Of his
accomplices one was cut to pieces, the other in the tumult
fled. Aly was carried into the palace with strength enough
to question the assassin who was brought before him. Ibn
Muljam declared boldly that the deed had been forty days
in contemplation, during all which time it had been his
prayer 'that the Wickedest of mankind might meet his
fate.' 'Then,' replied Aly, 'that must have been thyself.'

So saying, he turned to his son, Hasan, and bade him keep A.H. 40.
the assassin in close custody : ' If I die, his life is forfeit ;
but see thou mutilate him not, for that is forbidden by the
Prophet.' During the day Omm Kolthum went into the
assassin's cell and cursed him, adding, what no doubt she
would have fain believed, 'My father shall yet live.' 'Then,
Lady,' replied the fanatic, ' whence these tears? Listen.
That sword I bought for a thousand pieces, and a thousand
more it cost to poison it. None may escape its wound.'

It soon became evident that the wound indeed was Death of
mortal. They asked the Caliph whether, if he died, it was Aly, 17 ix.
40 A.H.
his will that his son should succeed to the throne. Still 25 Jan.,
true to the elective principle, Aly answered : ' I do not 661 A.D.
command it, neither do I forbid. See ye to it.' Then he
called Hasan and Hosein to his bedside, and counselled
them to be steadfast in piety and resignation, and kind to
their younger brother, the son of his Hanifite wife. After
that he wrote his testament, and continuing to repeat the
name of the Lord, so breathed his last. When they had
performed the funeral obsequies, Hasan arraigned the
assassin before him. Nothing daunted, Ibn Muljam said : Ibn Mul-
' I made a covenant with the Lord before the Holy House jam put to
death.
at Mecca, that I would slay both Aly and Muavia. Now,
if thou wilt, I shall go forth and kill the other, or perish in
the attempt. If I succeed, I will return and swear allegiance
unto thee.' ' Nay,' said Hasan, ' not before thou hast
tasted of the fire.' He was put to death, and the body, tied
up in a sack, was committed to the flames.

Aly died sixty years of age. His troubled and contested Aly's
reign had lasted but four years and nine months. In his wives and
children.
youth, he was one of the most distinguished heroes in the
early wars of Islam. But after the Prophet's death he
took no part in any of the military expeditions. In his
later years he became heavy and obese, and his bald and
portly figure was a subject of ridicule to his enemies. For
a time he was content with a single wife, the Prophet's
daughter Fatima, by whom he had three sons[1] and two

---

[1] One of these died in infancy.

A.H. 40. daughters, the progenitors of the Syed race,—the nobility
of Islam. After she died, he took many women into his
harem, both free and servile; by whom he had, in all,
eleven sons and fifteen daughters. Aly was a tender-
hearted father. In his later years, a little girl was born
to him, with whose prattle he would beguile his troubles;
he had her always on his knee, and doted on her with a
special love[1].

Aly's forbear-ance and magnani-mity.

In the character of Aly there are many things to com-
mend. Mild and beneficent, he treated Bussorah, when
prostrate at his feet, with a generous forbearance. Towards
theocratic fanatics, who wearied his patience by incessant
intrigue and insensate rebellion, he showed no vindictive-
ness. Excepting Muavia, the man of all others whom he
ought not to have estranged, he carried the policy of con-
ciliating his enemies to a dangerous extreme. In compromise,
indeed, and in procrastination, lay the failure of his
Caliphate. With greater vigour, spirit, and determination,
he might have averted the schism which for a time
threatened the existence of Islam, and which has since
never ceased to weaken it.

Wise but inactive.

Aly was wise in counsel, and many an adage and sapient
proverb has been attributed to him. But, like Solomon,
his wisdom was for other than himself. His career must
be characterised a failure. On the election of Abu Bekr,
influenced by Fàtima, who claimed and was denied a share
in her father's property, he retired for a time into private
life. Thereafter we find him taking part in the counsels of
Abu Bekr and his successors, and even performing the
functions of chief judge. But he never asserted the leading
position, which, as cousin and son-in-law of the Prophet,
might have been expected of him; nor is there aught to
show that this was due to other cause than an easy and
inactive temperament. One indelible blot rests on the
escutcheon of Aly, his flagrant breach of duty towards his

Desertion of Othman a blot upon his name.

[1] The mother of this little girl belonged to the Beni Kilab. The child
lisped, and pronouncing *l* like *sh*, was unable to say *Kilab*; when asked to what
tribe she belonged, she would imitate the bark of a dog (kilab or kalb meaning
' a dog '), to the great delight of Aly and his courtiers.

sovereign ruler. He had sworn allegiance to Othman, and   A.H. 40.
by him he was bound to have stood in the last extremity.   ——
Instead, he held ignobly aloof, while the Caliph fell a victim
to red-handed treason. Nor can the plea avail that he was
himself under pressure. Had there been a loyal will to
help, there would have been a ready way. In point of fact,
his attitude gave colour to the charge even of collusion[1].
And herein Aly must be held accountable not only for a
grave dereliction of duty, but for a fatal error, which shook
the stability of the Caliphate itself, as he was himself not
long in finding to his cost.

Tradition, strange to say, is silent, and opinion uncertain,   Burial
as to where the body of Aly lies. Some believe that he   place un-
was buried in the Great mosque at Kufa, others in the   known.
palace. Certainly, his tomb was never, in early times, the
object of any care or veneration. The same indifference
attached then to his memory throughout the realm of
Islam, as had attached to his person during life, and it was
not till a generation had passed away that any sentiment
of special reverence or regard for the husband of the
Prophet's daughter, and father of his only surviving progeny,
began to show itself.

There is no trace whatever at this period, of the extra-   Divine
vagant claims of later days. On the contrary, even at Kufa,   Imamate a
the capital that should have been proud of its Caliph, there   later
prevailed at this time towards him and his family an utter   growth.
want of enthusiasm and loyalty, amounting at times to
disaffection. The fiction of divine *Imamship* was a reaction
from the coming tragedy at Kerbala, and cruel fate of the
Prophet's progeny, which, fostered by Alyite and Abbasside
faction, soon became a powerful lever skilfully and un-
scrupulously used to overthrow the Omeyyad dynasty.

[1] See above, p. 240, and note.

CHAPTER XLIV.

Hasan succeeds Aly.—Abdicates in favour of Muavia.

40–41 A.H. 661 A.D.

Hasan succeeds his father, 40 A.H. 661 A.D.

WHEN they had committed Aly, we know not where, to his last home, Kufa did homage, as it were by common consent, to Hasan, his eldest son. But Hasan was a poor-spirited creature, more intent on varying the charms of his ever-changing harem than on the business of public life, and altogether unworthy his descent as grandson of the Prophet[1].

But is attacked by Muavia, and mobbed by his own troops.

It was now Muavia's opportunity for asserting his title to the whole Moslem empire. Already, in accordance with Amru's verdict at the Arbitration, he was recognised as Caliph throughout Syria and Egypt. Resenting the succession of Hasan, Muavia at once gathered a powerful army and marched against Kufa. No sooner was this intelligence received, than the citizens, indignant at the prospect of falling under the rule of Syria, rallied beneath the new Caliph's standard, and an army, 40,000 strong, was ready

---

[1] His vagrant passion gained him the nickname of *The Divorcer*, for only by continual divorce could he harmonise his craving for new nuptials with the requirements of the law, which limits freeborn wives to four. He is said to have exercised the power of divorce, as a matter of simple caprice, seventy (others say ninety) times. The leading men complained to Aly that his son was continually marrying their daughters, and as often divorcing them. Aly said the remedy lay in their own hands; they should refuse to give him their daughters to wife. These divorced wives were irrespective of slave-girls, for whom there is no limit.

to repel the attack. But Hasan had no stomach for the
war. Sending forward his vanguard of 12,000 men, under
the brave and faithful Cays, to meet the enemy, he followed
himself irresolutely ; and, with the bulk of his army, rested
at Medain amidst the luxurious gardens of the old Persian
court. While thus ignobly holding back, the report gained
currency at Medain that Cays had been defeated and slain.
An *émeute* ensued. The troops rose mutinously upon the
Caliph. They rushed into his sumptuous pavilion, and
plundered the royal tents even to the carpets. A project
was set on foot to seize his person, and, by delivering him
up to Muavia, thus make favourable terms. The faint-
hearted Caliph, alarmed at the outbreak, took refuge in the
Palace of Chosroes, a more congenial residence than the
martial camp ; and, trusting no longer to his fickle and
disloyal people, sent letters of submission to Muavia. He
agreed to abdicate and retire to Medina, on condition that
he should retain the contents of the treasury, five million
pieces ; should receive the revenues of a Persian district ;
and the imprecation against his father be dropped from the
public prayers. Muavia granted the first two requests ; as
for the third, he consented that no prayer reviling Aly
should be recited within hearing of the Son. The truce was
ratified accordingly.

Thus, after a brief and inglorious reign of five or six
months, Hasan, with his household and belongings, quitted
Kufa for Arabia. The people wept at his departure. But
Hasan left them without regret. They were a race, he said,
in whom no trust could be reposed, and who had set
purpose neither for evil nor for good.

Cays, whose ability and prowess were worthy of a better
cause, remained for some while longer in the field. At
length, having obtained terms for all who had been fighting
on the side of Aly, and there being no longer any master
now to fight for, he laid down his arms and did homage to
Muavia.

Thus, at last, Muavia was able to make triumphal entry
into Kufa. Having there received the homage of the
Eastern provinces, he returned to Syria sole and undisputed

A.H. 40-
41.
___

Continued
impreca-
tion against
Aly.

Hasan
poisoned
by his
wife.

Caliph of Islam.   Damascus thenceforth was the capital of
the empire.

The imprecations against the memory of Aly, his house,
and his adherents, still formed part of the public service;
and so, indeed, they continued throughout the Omeyyad
Caliphate.

The short-lived Caliph retired to Medina, where, with
ample means to gratify his ruling passion, he passed his
time in ease and quietness, giving no further anxiety to
Muavia.   He survived eight years, and met his death by
poison at the hand of one of his wives.   It was a not
unnatural end for ' Hasan the Divorcer.'   Alyite tradition,
indeed, would have us believe that the lady was bribed to
commit the crime, and thus exalts the libertine to the
dignity of 'Martyr.'   But Muavia had no object in
ridding himself of the harmless creature ; and the jealousies
of Hasan's ever-changing harem afford a sufficient and a
likelier reason.   Of his brother Hosein there will be more to
tell.

CHAPTER XLV.

MUAVIA.

40–60 A.H.   661–80 A.D.

FROM the death of Othman 35 A.H., Muavia was _{Muavia's} independent ruler of the West; and from the abdication _{reign, 40–60 A.H.} of Hasan till his death, that is, for nearly twenty years, he _{661– 680 A.D.} was undisputed Caliph of all Islam. During this long reign there was prosperity and peace as a rule at home, disturbed only by intermittent outbursts of Kharejite zealots, and by factions still ardent for the house of Aly. Both were easily suppressed, though not without bloodshed, by the strong arm of the Caliph and his able lieutenants. Abroad his rule was equally successful, and extended the boundaries of Islam in all directions.

Amru held the government of Egypt during the rest of _{Amru.} his life, which, indeed, had been one of the most eventful in _{His death. 43 A.H.} this history. No man influenced more than he the fortunes of the Caliphate. Brave in the field, astute in counsel, coarse and unscrupulous in word and deed, it was mainly to Amru that Muavia owed his ascendency over Aly, and the eventual establishment of the Omeyyad dynasty. The conqueror of Egypt, and for four years its governor under Omar, he continued in the same post a like period under Othman, who by his recall made him in an evil hour his enemy. Finally reappointed by Muavia on the defeat of Mohammed, he was still at his death the governor of Egypt. He died 73 years of age, penitent, we are told, for his misdeeds.

x

The career of Moghira, though less brilliant, was not less singular.   A native of Tayif, he had been deputed by the

Prophet, in company with Abu Sofian, to hew down the tutelar idol of that city[1].   He was ill-favoured, having lost an eye on the field of Wacusa.   Clever and designing, he survived the disgrace at Bussorah, which nearly cost him life as well as honour, and rose again to influence.   Finally, appointed by Muavia to that most difficult post, the government of the no longer regal Kufa, he held under strict control the turbulent and restless city, still the frequent scene of theocratic outburst, and of those dangerous conspiracies in favour of the house of Aly which began soon to disturb the Omeyyad dynasty.

But perhaps the greatest service which Moghira rendered to Muavia, was that he succeeded in reconciling Ziad to his sovereign.   The history of this man is also one of the most remarkable of the time.   He was the reputed son of Abu Sofian, who chanced to meet his mother, a vagrant bondwoman, before his conversion at Tayif. By the faithful discharge of important trusts Ziad overcame the disadvantage of servile birth, rose to important office, and eventually was appointed by Aly to the government of Bussorah and Istakhr.   Powerful, wise, and eloquent, he was by far the ablest statesman of the day.   Devoted to the cause of Aly, he was bitterly opposed to the pretensions of Muavia, even after the abdication of Hasan.   Called by Muavia to render an account of his stewardship in Persia, he refused to do so or to appear at' court, even when threatened if he continued to absent himself, with the life of his sons in Bussorah.   A thorn in his side, he caused continual alarm to Muavia. At last, in the year 42, Moghira, who had not forgotten the occasion on which he owed his life to the partial evidence of Ziad [2], repaired to Istakhr, and persuaded him to tender his submission.   Under a safe-conduct he appeared before the Caliph at Damascus, and as a royal gift, together with his arrear of revenue, presented a million pieces.   He

---

[1] *Life of Mahomet*, p. 467.   [2] Above, p. 185.

was dismissed with honour, and provided with a residence A.H. 40-60. at Kufa.

A year or two afterwards a curious episode in his life Ziad disturbed the equanimity of the Moslem world. As Ziad acknowledged as grew daily in royal favour, Muavia was seized with the brother by desire to remove the stain upon his descent, and thus Muavia, 45 A.H. prove him not the supposititious, but the real and legiti- 665 A.D. mate, son of Abu Sofian, his own father. A commission appointed for the purpose held this established ; upon which Muavia publicly acknowledged Ziad to be his brother. The announcement raised a scandal throughout Islam, first as contravening the law of legitimacy, and still more as making Omm Habiba, also the child of Abu Sofian and one of the ' Mothers of the faithful,' to be the sister of what, the decision notwithstanding, was held to be an adulterous issue. Not only so, but Muavia's own kinsfolk, the house of Omeyya, were displeased at the affront thus put upon the purity of their blood. The feeling, however, soon passed away, as it was seen that a pillar of strength had been gained for the Omeyyad dynasty[1]. Shortly after, Ziad Appointed governor of was made governor of Bussorah in addition to his Persian Bussorah, command. His strong hand fell heavily on the restless population of that turbulent city, now patrolled incessantly by an armed police of a thousand men. None might venture abroad at night on pain of death ; and so ruthless was the order, that an unlucky Arab, wandering unawares into the precincts, was executed for the involuntary offence. The supremacy of law, an experience new to Bussorah, repressed rebellion, and effectually enforced order, where strife and faction had heretofore prevailed.

---

[1] When Ziad proposed to go on pilgrimage to Mecca, his brother (who, offended at his tergiversation in the case for adultery against Moghira, had never spoken to him since) sent a message to dissuade him : ' Thou wilt meet Omm Habiba,' he said, ' if thou goest on pilgrimage. Now, if she receive thee as her brother, that will be regarded as a slight upon the Prophet ; if otherwise, it will be a slight upon thyself.' So Ziad gave up the design. Again, Ziad, wishing to extract an acknowledgment of his birth from Ayesha, addressed her a letter in which he subscribed himself, *Ziad son of Abu Sofian* ; to which she replied, without committing herself, ' To my dear son Ziad.' Abbasside writers name him without any patronymic, ' Ziad, *son of his father.*' He is also called after his *mother,* ' Ziad ibn Sommeyya.'

On Moghira's death, he was elevated to the governor-ship of Kufa also, and his habit was to spend half the year there and half at Bussorah. A reign of terror now began. At his first address in the mosque of Kufa, stones were cast at him. To discover the offenders, all present were put to the oath, and some fifty men who refused to swear had their hands cut off. The Alyite faction which

His severe adminis-tration, and splendid court.
reviled Othman abounded in both cities, and strong measures were no doubt needful to repress conspiracy; but cruelty and bloodshed went far beyond the bounds of need. Tales abound of parties refusing to curse the memory of Aly,— one especially, headed by the grandson of the famous Hatim—being ruthlessly beheaded; and the tyranny thus inaugurated by Ziad casts a dark stain upon his memory.

From Istakhr, Ziad brought with him the pride of an Oriental court. Abroad he was followed by a crowd of silver-sticks and lictors, and at his gate 500 soldiers mounted guard. He was the most powerful lieutenant the Caliphate yet had seen. The entire East was subject to him. From the Oxus and the Indus to the Persian Gulf his sway was absolute [1]. His sons held important commands in Khorasan and the frontier. One of these carried with him 50,000 citizens of Kufa, whom by a wise policy he planted in Khorasan with their wives and families. Ziad did not long enjoy the splendid position he had thus achieved. Not satisfied with the East, he coveted also

His death, 53 A.H. 673 A.D.
charge of the Hejaz with its holy cities. The inhabitants in terror prayed to the Lord that he might not have it; and so (says our annalist) his hand was smitten with a malignant boil, of which he died.

Progress in the East.
Great progress was made by Muavia in extending his rule eastward. The conquered peoples and their chiefs, impatient of the tribute and restraints of Islam, were con-tinually casting off their allegiance; but the yoke was yearly becoming more secure. Herat having rebelled was stormed A. H. 41; and two years later Kabul also was

---

[1] He divided the East into four commands, Merve Nisabur, Merve Rudh, Herat, and Badghis.

besieged for several months, and taken after the walls had A.H. 40–60. been breached by catapults. Similar operations are noticed against Ghazni, Balkh, Candahar and other strongholds. In the year 54, one of Ziad's sons, crossing the Oxus and mountain range on camels, took Bokhara ; and two years later a son of Othman beat back the Turkish hordes and gained possession of Samarcand and Tirmidz. The territories in the far north and east continued long on a precarious tenure ; but in the south all the country up to the banks of the Indus was gradually being consolidated under Mahometan rule or suzerainty.

The experience of Africa along its northern shore did Africa. not materially differ from that of the East, for the Berbers were ever and anon rebelling after they had tendered their submission. Indeed, the struggle was harder here, for the Roman settlements enabled the native population to offer a stubborner resistance. And yet, in the end, the overthrow was not less complete, so that the bright seats of civilization and of the Christian faith were soon known only by the ruins of their temples, aqueducts, and civic buildings. Ocba, appointed by Amru A.H. 41, waged war Ocba founds Cairowan, against the Berbers, and for several years the littoral was ravaged as far as Barca and Waddan. In the year 50, 50 A.H. 670 A.D. strengthened by Muavia with a body of 10,000 Arabs, he founded the settlement of Cairowan, to the south of Tunis, and strongly fortified it against the Berbers. Ever since it has been regarded as a sacred centre. Tradition tells us of the miraculous flight of wild beasts and reptiles with their young from its site at the conqueror's prayer; and that the Berbers, convinced by the prodigy, accepted Islam at once and settled on the spot. But a few years later Ocba was surprised by a joint Roman and Berber army, and driven Is defeated and slain. back on Barca, where he miserably perished with his whole army.

On the side of Armenia and Greece, hostilities, suspended Hostilities with Greece. during the contest with Aly, were resumed by Muavia at its close, and we read of a serious defeat sustained by the Greeks, A.H. 42. The Moslem army wintered in Armenia, and the campaign was prosecuted both by land and sea. In

A.H. 40–
60.

A.H. 50 a formidable expedition was directed against Constantinople. The army suffered severely from want of provisions and sickness; and Muavia sent his pleasure-loving son Yezid, much against his will, to join the army

Attack on
Constantinople.

with large reinforcements. The force landed near Constantinople, the safety of which is ascribed by some to the use of Greek fire, discovered about the time. There was much fighting, and the Moslem loss was heavy. But misfortunes notwithstanding, efforts against the city were not abandoned. We read of almost yearly expeditions, and in A.H. 53, an island near Constantinople was seized and held by a Moslem garrison for seven years; but the position was abandoned by Yezid on his father's death. —

Death of
Abu Ayub
and other
Companions; also
of Ayesha
and widows
of Mahomet.

In the Grecian campaign a famous Companion, Abu Ayub was killed under the walls of Constantinople, where his tomb was tended and visited by pilgrims for ages. It was the same who entertained the Prophet in his house for the first half-year after his arrival at Medina[1]. Early memories are also recalled by the death of Arcam, whose abode,—thence called ' the house of Islam'—was the resort of Mahomet and his followers when he first began his teaching at Mecca. About the same time also we read of the death of Ayesha, nearly 70 years of age, and of four other of the ' Mothers of the faithful,' also thus advanced in years[2].

A son of
Khalid
poisoned.

A blot rests on the name of Muavia for compassing the death of Abdul Rahman, son of the great Khalid. The splendour of his father's memory, and his own success in the campaign against the Greeks, invested him with such distinction throughout Syria, as to arouse the fears and jealousy of Muavia, who employed (it is said) a Christian agent to poison him. It is rare to find an imputation of the kind against Muavia, who though backward in checking the cruelty of his lieutenants, was himself on the whole mild and just in his administration.

Project of
carrying
Mahomet's
pulpit to
Damascus.

In the 50th year of the Hegira, Muavia entertained the project of removing the pulpit and staff of the Prophet

---

[1] *Life of Mahomet*, p. 68.
[2] Safia, Joweiria, Omm Salma, and Omm Habiba.

from Medina to Damascus, now the capital of Islam. But the impious project was, by divine interposition, checked. For, 'on its being touched, the pulpit trembled fearfully, and the sun was darkened, so that the very stars shone forth, and men were terrified at the prodigies.' The fond tradition is significant of the superstitious regard in which everything connected with the Prophet's person was now held. Muavia was dissuaded from his design by the consideration urged upon him, that where the Prophet had placed his pulpit and his staff, there they should remain. And so they were left as relics in the Great Mosque hard by the last home of Mahomet.

CHAPTER XLVI.

Yezid appointed Heir Apparent.—Hereditary Nomination becomes a Precedent.

56 A.H.   676 A.D.

Precedents for nomination or election of Caliph. THE election of a Caliph on each succession had been followed by serious peril to the peace of Islam. The choice was supposed to be a privilege vested in the inhabitants of Medina, ' Citizens,' as well as ' Refugees ;' but the practice had been various, and the rule had been oftener broken than observed. The Prophet himself nominated no one. Abu Bekr we may say was chosen by acclamation[1]. He again, on his death-bed, named Omar as successor ; and Omar, establishing yet another precedent, placed the choice in the hands of Electors. It is true that on both these last occasions the succession was ratified by the homage of Medina ; but that was little more than formal recognition of appointment already made. At the fourth succession, the election of Aly, though carried out under compulsion of the regicides, resembled somewhat the popular election of the first Caliph. Then followed the rebellion of Talha and Zobeir, based on the allegation that homage had been extorted from them. After that ensued the struggle between Muavia and Aly, which ended in the so-called Arbitration of Duma, and the double Caliphate. On the death of Aly, who declined to nominate a successor, his son Hasan was elected, not, as

---

[1] Mahomet, as we have seen, appointed him on his death-bed to lead the prayers; but he made no express nomination.

heretofore, by the people of Medina, but by the citizens of
Kufa. And, finally, we have the first example of abdica-
tion, when Hasan resigned his rights into the hands of
Muavia, and left him sole Caliph of Islam.

Whatever the right of Medina originally may have been, Initiative
circumstances had now materially altered the means of no longer
possible at
exercising it. Abandoned as the seat of government, Medina Medina.
had practically lost the privilege of choosing a successor to
the throne, or even of confirming the nomination made by
others. Succession, as in the case of Hasan, followed necessarily, and at once, upon the death of the reigning Caliph,
and Medina had no choice but to acquiesce in what had
already taken place elsewhere. The elective function was
thus, from the course of events, transferred to the inhabitants of the seat of government, wheresoever that
might be.

Again, the troubles which followed the election of Aly Danger
might recur at any moment. Zobeir and Talha raised the at each
succession.
standard of revolt on the plea of compulsion ; while between
Aly and Muavia there followed a long and doubtful contest. These internecine struggles had imperilled the fortunes of Islam. Not only had the ranks of the Faithful
been seriously thinned, but, from without, enemies might
have taken dangerous advantage of the strife ; as indeed
would have been the case had Muavia not made a truce
with the Byzantine Court while civil war impended. But if
a similar opportunity again offered, the foes of Islam might
not be so forbearing, and a fatal wound might be inflicted
on an empire torn by intestine conflict.

Influenced by such considerations, and also no doubt by Muavia's
the desire of maintaining the Caliphate in his own line, design to
nominate
Muavia entertained the project of declaring his son, Yezid, his son.
to be Heir-Apparent. By securing thus an oath of fealty
throughout the Moslem world, he would anticipate and
prevent the peril of a contested election. Ziad was favourable to the scheme, but enjoined deliberation, and a cautious
canvass throughout the provinces. He also counselled
Yezid, who was devoted to the chase and careless of public
affairs, to amend his ways in preparation for the throne,

A.H. 56. and show before the people a character more fitted for the
high dignity in prospect. Moghira likewise was favourable
to the project. But it was not till both these counsellors
had passed away that Muavia found himself in a position
to proceed with the design.

Yezid de-
clared
Heir-
Apparent,
56 A.H.
676 A.D.

So soon as Muavia felt secure of adequate support, and
especially that Medina would not resent the invasion of
her elective privilege[1], deputations from all the provinces
and chief cities presented themselves at Damascus. These,
received in state, affected to press the nomination; and
accordingly, without further ceremony, the oath of allegiance was taken by all present to Yezid as the next
successor. Syria and Irac having without demur tendered
homage, Muavia set out for Mecca with a retinue of 1000
horse, ostensibly to perform the Lesser Pilgrimage, but in
reality to obtain the assent of the two holy cities to the
succession of Yezid. The leading dissentients at Medina
were Hosein son of Aly, Abd al Rahman son of Abu Bekr,
and the two Abdallahs sons of Omar and Zobeir. Muavia
on entering the city received them roughly, and so, to avoid
further mortification, these left at once for Mecca. The
remainder of the citizens consented to the nomination of
Yezid, and took the oath accordingly. Continuing his
journey to Mecca, the Caliph carried himself blandly towards the people for the first few days, which were occupied
with the rites of the Lesser Pilgrimage. But as his time
of departure drew nigh, he stood up to address them on his
errand, and though his speech was gilded with assurances
that the rights and privileges of the city would be respected,
there was at the first no response. Then arose Abdallah

Mecca and
Medina
forced to
swear
allegiance.

---

[1] When Merwan, governor of the city, placed the matter before the men of
Medina, he was at first violently opposed. Amongst others, Abd al Rahman,
son of Abu Bekr, said, 'This thing is naught but fraud and deception. In
place of election, the right to which vesteth in this city, ye will now make the
succession like unto that of the Greeks and Romans—where one Heraclius
succeedeth another Heraclius.' On this, Muavia quoted from the Coran: 'Say
not unto your parents, *Fie on you!* neither reproach them' (*Sura* xvii. 24);
signifying, it may be, that the very practice of nomination, now opposed, had
been introduced by Abu Bekr himself in appointing Omar. Abdallah, son of
Omar, is said to have been gained over by the gift of ten thousand golden
pieces.

son of Zobeir, and declared that the recognition of an A.H. 56.
Heir-Apparent would run counter to all the precedents of
Islam. On this the Caliph urged the risks to which
Islam was ever and anon exposed from a contested succession. Others then spoke thus :—'We consent,' they
said, 'to any one of these three things. *First*, do as
the Prophet did, and leave the election to the citizens of
Medina. Or, *secondly*, do as Abu Bekr did, and nominate
a successor from amongst the Coreish[1]. Or, *thirdly*, like
Omar, appoint Electors who shall, from amongst themselves,
choose a candidate to succeed thee. Only, like them, thou
must exclude thine own sons and thy father's sons.' 'As
for the first course,' replied Muavia, 'there is none now left
like unto Abu Bekr, that the people might choose him.
And for the rest, verily I fear the contention and bloodshed
that would follow if the succession be not fixed aforehand.'
Then finding his arguments of no effect, he called out the
bodyguard, and at the point of the sword caused the
city to take the oath.

The example of Syria, Irac, and the holy cities was Muavia's
followed throughout the empire without reserve. And ever action be-
after the precedent more or less prevailed. The fiction of received
an elective right vested in the whole body of the Faithful, precedent
though still observed more or less in form, ceased now to of Islam.
have reality, and the oath of allegiance was without hesitation
enforced by the sword against recusants. The reigning
Caliph thus proclaimed as his successor the fittest of
his sons, the one born of the noblest mother, or otherwise most favoured, or (in default of issue) the best
qualified amongst his kinsmen. To him, as Heir-Apparent,
an anticipatory oath of fealty was taken, first at the seat
of government and then throughout the empire, and the
succession as a rule followed the choice. Sometimes a
double nomination was made, anticipating at once thus two
successions : but such attempt to forestall the distant future

---

[1] That the Caliph must be of the Coreishite stock was axiomatic, excepting
with the Kharejites, who denounced all privilege. The stricter Kharejites held
that there should be no Caliph, but only a Council of State. If there were a
Caliph, they were indifferent as to what stock he came from.

too often provoked, instead of preventing, civil war. The practice thus begun by the Omeyyads was followed equally by the Abbassides; and proved a precedent even for later times.

Yezid and his mother. Muavia had other sons, but Yezid's mother, Meisun, was of noble birth, and as such her son took precedence [1]. The story of this lady has special attraction for the early Arab writers. Amid the courtly luxuries of Damascus, she pined for the freedom of the desert, and gave vent to her longing in verse of which the following may be taken as a specimen.

The tent fanned by desert breeze is dearer far to me than these lofty towers.

I should ride more joyously on the young camel than on the richly caparisoned steed.

The wild blast over the sandy plain is sweeter far to me than flourish of royal trumpets.

A crust in the shade of the Bedouin tent hath better relish than these courtly viands.

The noble Arab of my tribe is more comely in my sight than the obese and bearded men around me.

O that I were once again in my desert home! I would not exchange it for these gorgeous halls.

The lady's verses, coming to Muavia's ears, displeased him. Like Aly, he had become from luxurious living obese and portly, and felt the taunt of his wife as if aimed at himself. So he dismissed Meisun with Yezid to the tents of her tribe, the Beni Kelb, where in boyhood he acquired his Bedouin taste for the chase and a roving life.

---

[1] By Mahometan law, the son of the bond-woman is equally legitimate with the son of the free. But the Arab sentiment of noble birth prevailed; and it still prevails, as we daily see in such petty principalities as Afghanistan.

CHAPTER XLVII.

Death of Muavia.—Yezid succeeds.—Hosein and Zobeir.—Tragedy at Kerbala.—Death of Hosein.

61 A.H. 680 A.D.

After a long and prosperous reign, Muavia came to Death of Muavia, vii. 61, April, 680. die, some 75 years of age. As he felt the end approach, he brought forth a casket, carefully kept, with parings of the Prophet's nails. O these, ground fine, he bade them sprinkle the powder in his eyes and mouth when dead, and bury him, for a winding-sheet, in a garment given to him by Mahomet. Fortune had favoured his rule. Since the abdication of Hasan, there had been peace throughout the empire. Wise, courageous[1], and forbearing, he held the dangerous elements around him in check; consolidated and extended the already vast area of Islam; and nursed commerce and the arts of peace, so that they greatly flourished in his time. But he looked to the future with anxiety.

The nomination of Yezid as successor was sure to meet Dying caution to Yezid. with opposition when he was gone. From his death-bed,

---

[1] His courage, however, was moral rather than physical. Both he and Aly, as already stated, had become obese (at Kufa, Aly went by the nickname of 'the pot-bellied'), and in their later years there was little occasion for active bodily exertion. Still, even as late as Siffin, we have seen that Aly fought with his early gallantry; while Muavia shrank from a personal encounter. Aly was, without doubt, the braver of the two in physical courage; but Muavia, beyond comparison, the abler and bolder ruler.

A.H. 61. therefore, he sent a message to Yezid, who was absent at
——   his hunting-place, warning him of the rocks that lay ahead.
          There were three, he said, whom he must beware of. The
          two Abdallahs, sons of Omar and Zobeir, and Hosein, son
          of Aly. The first, a pious devotee, would easily be put
          aside. ' As for Hosein,' he continued, ' the restless men
          of Irac will give him no peace till he attempt the empire ;
          when thou hast gotten the victory, deal gently with him,
          for truly the blood of the Prophet runneth in his veins. It
          is Abdallah son of Zobeir that I fear the most for thee.
          Fierce as the lion, crafty as the fox, destroy him root and
          branch.'

Hosein and   The first care of Yezid on assuming the Caliphate was to
Abdallah
ibn Zobeir require those who had before refused to swear allegiance
escape to at Medina, now to take the oath. Two of these, the sons
Mecca.
           of Omar and Abbas [1], at once complied with the command.
           But the son of Zobeir and Hosein, feigning time for
           consideration, escaped to Mecca.

Ibn Zobeir   Since its capture by Mahomet, no enemy had dared to
dissembles.
           go up against the Holy city ; and there, inviolate as the
           doves that fluttered around the Temple, conspirators abusing
           the asylum, were wont to plot against the empire. As
           Muavia had foreseen, the ambitious son of Zobeir aimed
           at the Caliphate ; but so long as Hosein remained he
           dissembled, professing to bow to the superior claims of the
           Prophet's grandson.

Citizens of   At Kufa, the house of Aly was still after a fashion
Kufa invite
Hosein   popular. Hasan, it is true, found little support, during
thither.   his short-lived Caliphate there ; but the fond and fickle
           populace now turned eagerly to his brother. Promises
           of support poured in upon him, if he would but appear at
           Kufa, and there claim his regal rights. His friends at Mecca
           besought that he would not trust to the slippery missives
           of that factious city. But the son of Zobeir, to be rid of
           his rival, fostered the design ; and Hosein, yielding to his
           advice, in an evil hour was tempted to accept the call. His
           cousin, Muslim, was sent before to prepare the way for his

----

[1] Uncle of the Prophet, and progenitor of the Abbasside dynasty.

approach[1]. The plot becoming known at court, Yezid de- A.H. 61.
puted Obeidallah son of Ziad, from Bussorah (whose rule Muslim
there was as stern as had been his father's), to take command sent in advance, is put
at Kufa. On his arrival, search was made, and Muslim to death
discovered lurking under protection of Hani, a friend to the at Kufa.
house of Aly. The populace, suddenly siding with the pretender, rose on Obeidallah, and besieging him in his castle,
went near to turning the tables against him. The
ebullition, however, soon subsided. Obeidallah regained
the lead, and Muslim with his protector was put to death.

Meanwhile, toward the close of the year A.H. 60, on Hosein sets
the first day of Pilgrimage, Hosein, heedless of the re- out for Kufa,
monstrances of faithful friends, started from Mecca with 8 xii. 60 A.H.
his whole family and a little band of devoted followers. 10 Sept., 680 A.D.
He had already passed the desert, advancing upon Kufa,
when tidings reached him of the fate of Muslim. He was
staggered, for it might well have seemed a mad attempt to
venture, with the ladies of the household, into the fickle
city. It was yet possible to retrace his steps. But
Muslim's brethren were clamorous that he should avenge
his blood; and there was still the forlorn hope that those
who had drawn Hosein by their specious promises would
rally round his person so soon as he appeared. But each
succeeding messenger was fraught with darker tidings.
Farazdac, the poet, passed that way from Kufa; all that
he could say to his princely friend was,—*The heart of
the city is with thee; but its sword against thee.* The
Bedouins, ever ready for a fray, had been swelling the
little band into a considerable force; but now, seeing the
cause to be hopeless, they drew off; and so Hosein, already
two or three weeks' journey on his way, was left with nothing
but his original following of some 30 horse and 40 foot[2]. A
chieftain by the way besought him to divert his course to-

---

[1] Muslim was cousin of Aly and grandson of Abu Talib, Mahomet's uncle.
The actors in this melancholy chapter have become household names,—words
either of love or intensest hate,—in the mouths of Moslems, especially of the
Shiyites.

[2] The number varies; but none places it higher than 40 horse and 100 foot.
Seventy heads were brought into Kufa, probably those of all the combatants.
The rest were, no doubt, camp-followers, &c.

A.H. 61.
——
Met by
Horr near
Kufa,
1st Mohar-
ram,
61 A.H.
1 Oct.,
680 A.D.

wards the hills of Aja and Selma, 'Where,' said he, 'in ten days' time, 20,000 lances of the Beni Tay will rally round thee.' 'How can I,' replied Hosein, 'surrounded as thou seest by women and children, turn aside with them unto the desert? I must needs go forward.' And so forward he went to his sad fate. They had not proceeded far when they were met by a troop of Kufan horse under an Arab chief named Horr, who courteously but firmly refused to let him pass. 'My orders,' he said, 'are to bring thee to the governor; but if thou will not go, then turn to the right hand, or turn to the left, as thou choosest, only the way back again to Mecca, that thou mayest not take.' So the little band, leaving Kufa on the right, marched to the left, skirting the desert for a day or two along the western branch of the Euphrates. In so doing, Hosein had apparently no immediate object beyond avoiding attack from Kufa. Horr kept close by, and courteous communications still passed between them.

Stopped by
Amr at
Kerbala.

But it was dangerous leaving the Pretender to hover about the city already excited by the affair of Muslim. So Obeidallah sent Amr son of Sad with 4000 horse and a second summons[1]. Thus arrested, Hosein pitched his camp on the field of Kerbala on the river bank, five-and-twenty miles above Kufa. At repeated interviews, Hosein disclaimed hostilities, which indeed with his slender following, and no prospect now of a rising in the city, were out of thought. He would submit, but only thus, he said:— 'Suffer me to return to the place from whence I came; if not, then lead me to Yezid, the Caliph, at Damascus, and place my hand in his, that I may speak with him face to face; or, if thou wilt do neither of these things, then send me far away to the wars, where I shall fight, the Caliph's faithful soldier, against the enemies of Islam.' But Obeidallah insisted upon unconditional submission; and, to

---

[1] His father Sad was the hero of Cadesiya. The story goes that Obeidallah offered Amr the government of Rei on condition of bringing in Hosein dead or alive. Amr wavered between duty to the grandson of the Prophet and the bribe. He yielded, and for mammon sold his soul. But all this, *cum grano*; for tradition is now rising to fever heat.

effect this without resort to arms, he ordered Amr to cut off A.H. 61.
access to the river, hoping that thirst might thus force sur- Shamir
render.   But Hosein, who feared the cruel tyrant worse sent to
than death, stood firm to his conditions.   He even prevailed to Kufa,
on Amr to urge that he might be sent direct to the Caliph's 8th Mohar-
court.   Well had it been for the Omeyyad house, if the
prayer had been agreed to.   But impatient of delay, Obeidallah sent instead a heartless creature called Shamir
(name never uttered by Moslem lips without a shudder)
to say that Amr must dally no longer with Hosein, but,
dead or alive, bring him in to Kufa ; should Amr hesitate,
Shamir was to supersede him in command[1].   Thus forced,
Amr forthwith surrounded closely the little camp.   Hosein
resolved to fight the battle to the bitter end.   The scene
that followed is still fresh in the believers' eye ; and as
often as the fatal day comes round, the 10th of the first
month, it is commemorated with the wildest grief and
frenzy.   Encircled with harrowing detail, it never fails to
rouse horror and indignation to the utmost pitch.   The
fond believer forgets that Hosein, leader of the band,
having broken his allegiance, and yielded himself to a
treasonable, though impotent, design upon the throne, was
committing an offence that endangered society, and demanded swift suppression.   He can see nought but the cruel
and ruthless hand that slew with few exceptions all in whose
veins flowed their Prophet's sacred blood.   And, in truth,
the simple story needs no adventitious colouring to touch
the heart.

[1] Shamir ibn Dzu al Joshan is a name never pronounced by the pious Moslem
but with ejaculatory curse.   Obeidallah (so the story goes) was at first inclined
to concede the prayer of Hosein, as urged by Amr, for a safe-conduct to the
Caliph at Damascus, when Shamir stepped forward, and said that Obeidallah,
for the credit of his name, must insist on the Pretender's surrender at discretion.
So he obtained from Obeidallah a letter to Amr, threatening that if he failed to
bring Hosein in, Shamir should take the command, and also obtain the government of Rei in his stead.   The name is variously pronounced as Shamir, Shomar,
or Shimr.

The whole of the sad tale becomes at this point so intensified, and so overlaid
with Alyite fiction, that it is impossible to believe a hundredth part of what the
heated imagination of the Shiyites has invented.   The names are all ranged,
either on one side or on the other (especially with the Shiyas), as models of
piety, or as demons of apostasy.

A.H. 61.

Hosein's
prepara-
tions for
defence,
9th Mohar-
ram.

Hosein obtained a day's respite to send his kinsmen and family away. But one and all refused to leave him. The tents were then rudely staked together, and barricades of wood and reeds set round, a poor defence against the unequal foe. During the night, Zeinab overheard her brother's servant furbishing his sword and singing the while snatches of martial verse on the impending combat. Her heart sank at the thought; drawing her mantle around her, she stole in the dark to her brother's tent, and flinging herself upon him in wild grief, beat her breast and face, and fell into a swoon. Hosein poured water on her temples; but it was little that he could do to comfort her. Aly, Hosein's little son, lay sick of a fever, but there was no drop of water to slake his parched lips. The women and children passed the night in wailing and in terror.

Attacked
and with
all his
company
slain,
10th Mo-
harram,
61 A.H.
10 Oct.,
680 A.D.

On the morning of the fatal 10th, Hosein drew out his little band for battle. There was a parley; and again he offered to retire, or be led to the presence of the Caliph. Finding all in vain, he alighted from his camel; and, surrounded by his kinsmen, who stood firm for his defence, resolved to sell life dear. At length, one shot an arrow from the Kufan side, and, amid the cries of the women and little ones, the unequal fight began. Arrows flew thick, and did their deadly work. Casim, the nephew of Hosein, ten years of age, bethrothed to his daughter Fatima, was early struck, and died in his uncle's arms. One after another the sons and brothers, nephews and cousins of Hosein, fell before the shafts of the enemy. Some took shelter behind the camp. The reeds were set on fire, and the flames spreading to the tents added new horror to the scene. For long none dared attack Hosein, and it was hoped he might even yet surrender. At last, driven by thirst, he sought the river bank. The enemy closed up, and he was cut off from his people. The 'cursed' Shamir led the attack. Hosein, struck by an arrow, fell to the ground, and the cavalry trampled on his corpse.

Their
heads
taken to
the gover-
nor.

Not one of the band escaped. Fighting bravely, they left of the enemy more than their own number dead upon the field. Two sons of Hosein perished early in the day;

and at its close there lay amongst the dead six of his
brothers, sons of Aly; two sons of his brother Hasan; and
six others, descendants of Abu Talib, Aly's father. The
camp was plundered; but no indignity was offered to the
survivors, mostly women and children, who were carried,
together with the ghastly load of seventy trunkless heads,
to Obeidallah's palace. A thrill of horror ran through the
crowd, when the gory head of the Prophet's grandson was
cast at Obeidallah's feet. Hard hearts were melted. As
the governor turned the head roughly over with his staff
(though we must be slow to accept the tales of heartless
insult multiplied by Shiya hate), an aged voice was heard
to cry: 'Gently! It is the Prophet's grandson. By the
Lord! I have seen these very lips kissed by the blessed
mouth of Mahomet.'

The sister of Hosein, his two little sons Aly Asghar and Hosein's family sent to Medina.
Amr, and two daughters, sole survivors of the family, were
treated by Obeidallah with respect, and sent along with
the head of the Pretender to Yezid at Damascus. Whether
sincerely, or to escape the execrations already heaped upon
the actors in the tragedy, the Caliph disowned responsibility
for the death of Hosein, and reproached Obeidallah for the
deed. The ladies and children were honourably received
into the royal household, and sent eventually, with every
comfort and consideration, to their Medina home. This
destination, meant in kindness by Yezid, turned out badly
for the Omeyyad house. At Medina, their return caused
a wild outburst of grief and lamentation. Everything
around intensified the catastrophe. The deserted dwellings Reaction in favour of the house of Aly.
inhabited heretofore by the family and kinsmen of the
Prophet, the widowed ladies, the orphaned little ones,—
all added pathos to the cruel tale. That tale, heard yearly
by groups of weeping pilgrims at the lips of the women
and children who survived to tell it—and coloured, as oft
repeated, with fresh and growing horrors—spread over the
empire. The tragic scene was repeated in every household,
and bred pity for the lineage of Aly. It soon was seen that
the zeal of Obeidallah to suppress the rebellion of Hosein
had overshot the mark. The claim of Aly's line to rule,

A. H. 61. heretofore unknown, or treated only with indifference, struck
deep now into the heart of multitudes; and a cloud of
indignation began to gather, which ere long burst upon
the dynasty which had caused the sacrilegious massacre.
The tragedy of Kerbala decided not only the fate of the
Caliphate, but of Mahometan kingdoms long after the
The Mo-   Caliphate had waned and disappeared.   Who that has
harram.
seen the wild and passionate grief with which, at each
recurring anniversary, the Moslems of every land spend
the live-long night, beating their breasts and vociferating
unweariedly the frantic cry—*Hasan   Hosein!   Hasan
Hosein!*—in wailing cadence, can fail to recognise the
fatal weapon, sharp and double-edged, which the Omeyyad
dynasty allowed thus to fall into the hands of their
enemies[1]?

[1] In this outburst the name of Hasan is added to that of Hosein, not only
because the Shiyas hold him to have been entitled to the Caliphate (though he
resigned it), but because he, too, is regarded as a martyr poisoned by his wife,
at the instigation, they say, of Muavia, but, as we have seen, without any
sufficient presumption.

The tragedy is yearly represented as a religious ceremony, especially by the
Shiyites, in the 'Passion Play,' throughout which are interwoven, in a super-
natural romance, the lives of the early worthies of Islam, ending with the
pathetic tale of the Martyr company of Kerbala; while Abu Bekr, Omar, and
Othman are execrated as usurpers, and the whole Omeyyad crew, Obeidallah,
Hajjaj, &c., are held up to malediction.

CHAPTER XLVIII.

REMAINDER OF YEZID'S REIGN.—REBELLION OF ZOBEIR.

61–64 A.H.   680 A.D.

YEZID soon felt the evil which the tragedy of Kerbala *Danger from the Alyite reaction.* had inflicted on the Omeyyad throne, and the rebound caused thereby in favour of the house of Aly. Kufa, with proverbial inconsistency, was now eager to espouse the cause of a dynasty which, over and again, it had cast aside. The Kharejite heresy, in ever varying form, gained new impetus, especially at Bussorah. Its adherents, repenting of their desertion of Aly after the battle of Siffin, and grieving at the fate of his family, entered into a covenant of revenge, and of never-ceasing hostility against the government. But it was from a different quarter that peril first assailed the Caliphate. It arose, as Muavia had foreshadowed, from Abdallah Ibn Zobeir.

He it was, who, to be rid of Hosein, had encouraged that *Ibn Zobeir affects the Caliphate, 61 A.H. 680 A.D.* unfortunate Prince in his desperate venture. No sooner did the sad story reach Arabia than Ibn Zobeir arose and harangued the citizens of Mecca with fierce invective against the ruling power. Veiling his ambitious design, he began by assuming the modest and pious title of *Protector of the Holy house*. But he soon went beyond this, and before the end of the year commenced to canvass, though at first secretly, as claimant of the throne. On this reaching the ears of Yezid, he swore that the rebel should yet be

A.H. 61–
64.

brought to Damascus, bound by the neck. Repenting of the oath, though wishing formally to fulfil it and yet leave Ibn Zobeir a way of escape, he sent a deputation to Mecca with a silver chain, and a silken dress of honour to conceal the same, and invited him so robed to come to court; but Ibn Zobeir scorned the offer and imprisoned the embassy.

Medina
rebels,
62 A.H.
682 A.D.

Meanwhile, Medina was in a ferment. The crafty Pretender, still feigning friendship with Yezid, advised him to send a milder governor there, as likely to conciliate the people. Accordingly, Yezid deputed in his place a young and inexperienced relative, who in an evil hour despatched a company of leading citizens to Damascus, hoping that they might there be won over by the gifts and promises of the Caliph. They returned munificently rewarded. But, accustomed as they had been to the frugal and pious habits of the Prophet's home, they were shocked at the profane behaviour and indulgent excesses of the Syrians; and brought back such an account of the luxury and ungodliness of the Court,—wine and music, singing men and singing women, cockfighting and hounds,—that the Caliph was at once denounced, and a rival sworn to in his room. The young governor was fain to fly; the Omeyyad party, 1000 strong, were put in durance, and only allowed to leave the city

Is attacked
and sacked.
End of
63 A.H.
682 A.D.

after swearing that they would not assist the enemy. To chastise the rebellious citizens, and thereafter proceed against Ibn Zobeir, the Caliph despatched a column which, in a bloody battle, defeated the troops sent out from Medina; and the unfortunate city was for three days given up to the license and rapine of the Syrian army. After forcing the citizens, at the point of the sword, again to swear allegiance to Yezid, the force continued its march on Mecca.

Siege of
Mecca,
i. 64 A.H.
Sept.,
683 A.D.

Ibn Zobeir had nothing effectual to oppose. He was indeed supported by the malcontent fugitives from Medina, and by the Kharejites who from all quarters flocked to the defence of the Holy house. People hardly believed that even the most sacrilegious tyrant would have the hardihood to attack the sacred places. 'Good heavens!' they cried,

looking upwards, 'will ye fall down upon us[1]!' And in like A.H. 61–
64.
security Ibn Zobeir was probably the less careful to prepare
for his enemys' advance.   It was early in the year 64,
that, when going forth to oppose the Syrian army, he was
driven back with loss.   For two months the city was City bom-
besieged and shot cast into it by the Syrians from the barded and
Kaaba
heights around.   The Kaaba caught fire and was burned destroyed,
to the ground[2].   And so the siege went on till the third iii. 1.
64 A.H.
month, when tidings came of the death of Yezid, and Nov.,
683 A.D.
thereupon hostilities ceased.   So poor at the moment were
the prospects of the Omeyyads under the weak son who
succeeded Yezid, that the Syrian general offered to swear
allegiance to Ibn Zobeir if he would but accompany him to
Syria, where alone he had any chance of successful candi-
dature.   But the 'Protector of the Holy house' would not
leave his chosen spot.   Here he remained to rebuild the
sacred Shrine.   Though himself a warrior, and the son of one
of the most renowned heroes in the Prophet's train, he went
out no more into battle, but from his quiet retreat maintained, as rival Caliph, an acknowledged rule, as we shall
see, in the troubled years that follow, over a large portion
of the Moslem empire.

Yezid died in his hunting castle 40 years of age, after a Death of
reign of three-and-a-half years.   He is described as a dis- Yezid,
iii. 64 A.H.
sipated monarch, and though the patron of learning and Nov. 683.
himself no mean poet, he is only remembered for the tragic
scene of Kerbala, and the sacrilegious attack upon Mecca, and
hence his name is branded by the faithful with infamy.

No progress was made in this reign to extend Islam ; on Islam
the contrary, as we have seen, there were serious disasters in stationary
in his
the north of Africa. reign.

[1] The exclamation is attributed to Abdal Melik, who with his father Merwan
was sent as a deputation by Yezid to Ibn Zobeir, and by him detained in
durance ; 'and yet,' adds the annalist, 'this same Abdal Melik, when Caliph,
himself sent Hajjaj to besiege the Holy city, cast shot at the Kaaba, and
slay Ibn Zobeir.'

[2] Some say that the conflagration originated in the fires kindled around the
Kaaba by Ibn Zobeir's own followers.   But the weight of authority is the other
way.   Bokhary tells us that Ibn Zobeir did not attempt to extinguish the conflagration kindled by the naphtha of the engines, but rather used the sight
of the ruined Temple to stir up the indignation of his followers.

CHAPTER XLIX.

MUAVIA II, MERWAN, AND ABD AL MELIK, CALIPHS.—
REBELLION OF IBN ZOBEIR AND MUKHTAR;
AZRACKITES AND KHAREJITES.

64–73 A.H.   683–92 A.D.

Short
and feeble
reign of
Muavia II,
iii. 64 A.H.
Nov.,
683 A.D.
YEZID'S early death was a misfortune to the Omeyyad
rule. He was succeeded by his son Muavia II, a weak and
sickly youth, who survived but three months. Anticipating
his decease, he told the people from the pulpit that, like
Abu Bekr, he would have appointed a successor, but there
was none he saw of Omar's stamp ; that like Omar he would
have nominated electors, but neither so did he see any men
fit for such a task ; and accordingly that he left them to
choose a successor for themselves. The short and feeble
reign served but to relax the sinews of the empire.

Ibn
Zobeir's
power
extends,
vii. 64 A.H.
March,
684 A.D.
On his death, the Omeyyad counsels were divided, and
various aspirants to the throne appeared. Ibn Zobeir, now
the acknowledged Caliph at Mecca and Medina, succeeded
during the next few months in being recognized ruler also
over Egypt, and greater part of Syria. Obeidallah with
difficulty escaped from Bussorah, which as well as Kufa
went also over to Ibn Zobeir. Persia was in the hands
of Kharejites. Syria, and only part even of that, remained
under the government of Damascus.

Merwan
elected
Caliph.
Had Ibn Zobeir left his sanctuary for Syria, there is little
doubt but that he would have succeeded, and the Caliphate
might then have been established in his family. Even at

Damascus, there was a numerous party in his favour, and A.H. 64–
most of the strongholds in Syria and Mesopotamia sided   73.
with him. But the Syrian army, now returning from Arabia,
was staunch to the Omeyyad interest. Dhahhak, governor
of Damascus, temporized. The young Caliph had left no
child, but there was a brother, a younger son of Yezid, named
Khalid. The family favoured him : but the chief men of the
court felt that a stronger hand was needed, and they put
forward Merwan. An Omeyyad, he came from another
branch, but had rendered devoted service to Othman and
to the dynasty at large[1]. After much dissension, he was Opposed
saluted Caliph, on condition that Khalid should succeed on by Ibn
reaching man's estate. Dhahhak now showed his colours, party.
and retired with the adherents of Ibn Zobeir to Merj Rahit,
a battle-ground in the vicinity. Merwan led out his army
against him, and pitched at Jabia. The Arabs were divided.
A strong antagonism was growing up between the two
Bedouin branches, Cays and Modhar, drawn respectively
from the south and from the north of the peninsula. The
former or Yemenite clans, especially the Beni Kelb, from
which the Caliphs had taken wives, were devoted to the
Omeyyad house ; the Beni Cays and southern tribes were
equally prejudiced against it, and joined Dhahhak on the

[1] The subjoined tree will show the relationship and descent of the Omeyyad
family.

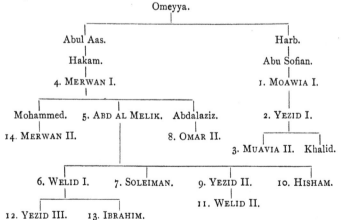

A.H. 64–
73.

Battle of
Merj Rahit.

side of Ibn Zobeir. Several months passed thus; at last towards the close of the year, Merwan attacked his enemy, and after some weeks of fighting, completely discomfited him, Dhahhak being left dead upon the field. Thereupon all Syria returned to its allegiance. Egypt also was regained; and an army under Musab, brother of Ibn Zobeir, seeking to recover Syria, was put to flight.

End of
64 A.H.
Merwan's
death,
ix. 65 A.H.,
April, 685.

In the midst of his success, Merwan came to an ignoble and untimely end. Fearing the stability of his throne, he set aside the arrangement by which Khalid, brother of the late Caliph, should succeed him, in favour of his own son Abd al Melik, whom he proclaimed Heir Apparent. Then either with the view of reconciling Khalid's mother, that is, the widow of Yezid, or of weakening her son's claim, he took her himself to wife. Further, he made light of her son, and treated him with indignity. The proud Bedouin dame was offended, and took a signal revenge. As the Caliph slept by her side, she smothered him with a pillow, so that he was found dead in his bed. Born at the beginning of the era, he was now over threescore years of age, and had gained an unenviable notoriety as an unscrupulous agent of the faction of Othman, though his demerits have no doubt been magnified by the opposite party. His reign lasted

Succeeded
by Abd al
Melik.

barely a year. He was succeeded by Abd al Melik, whose authority was at once recognized throughout Syria and Egypt.

Hostilities
in the East
between
Arabs of
the South
and North,
64–65 A.H.

It may be useful for a moment to notice events transpiring in the East which illustrate the intense jealousy that reigned between the two divisions just named of the Arab race, often with serious injury to the State. About this time, it broke out in Persia into fierce internecine warfare. For a whole year, Ibn Khazim, who was Ibn Zobeir's governor in Khorasan, fought on the part of the Modhar (or southern) branch against the Beni Bekr (or northern), and in a victory gained

Ibn Khazim and
Horeish.

at Herat slew 8000 of his foes. His son having been killed by a party of the Temim tribe commanded by Horeish, fighting was kept up for two years, when that chief challenged his adversary to settle their differences by single combat. In a heated combat, Horeish struck Ibn Khazim

a blow which brought the plume of his helmet down upon
his face; but the other cut through his stirrup so that he
was powerless to follow up the advantage. Both retired,
and Horeish marched off with his followers towards Merve.
Ibn Khazim pursued him; but on meeting, they generously
laid aside their enmity and Horeish restored the plume of
his adversary to its place. 'Thy touch, this day,' said Ibn
Khazim courteously, 'is lighter than thy touch of yesterday.' 'Heaven forgive me!' replied Horeish, 'for had my
stirrup stood, by the Lord! thy head had gone.'

In the following year, Ibn Khazim, still seeking to avenge
his son's blood, stormed a fortress in which some eighty of
the Beni Kelb had taken refuge. Marvellous tales are
related of the feats and prowess of the little band; but their
end was to be starved to death. Their chivalry has been
handed down in verses by Horeish, which are still preserved.
Such are the scenes over which, both in prose and verse, the Arab
Arab loves to dwell: and too much prominence may per- sympathy
chance have been given to them by our annalists. But the combats.
tribal jealousies and bloody engagements long prevailing
amongst the Arab battalions in Khorasan and Eastern Persia,
serve no doubt to explain why for many years there was so
little progress made in the settlement of that territory, and
in the extension of the frontier to the North and East.

On the restoration of peace in Syria, Merwan had des- Compli-
patched an army under Obeidallah to reoccupy Mesopotamia Mesopo-
from Mosul downwards, and thereafter advance on Kufa. tamia and
A second, intended to recover Medina, was routed on its Arabia.
way by the troops of Ibn Zobeir, whose supremacy continued
to be recognized throughout Arabia, Irac, and the East.
His brave brother Musab continued governor of Bussorah,
though exposed there to serious jeopardy from the
Kharejites. These at the first rallied round Ibn Zobeir in Kharejites
defence of Mecca against the army of Yezid. But when he fall out
laid claim to the Caliphate, they demanded that he should Zobeir.
join with them not only in condemning the 'murderers' of
Hosein, but also in denouncing Othman as a tyrant justly
put to death. This he could not do, without compromising
his whole career; for, in company with his father Zobeir, he

A.H. 64–
78.

had waged war with Aly for the avowed purpose of avenging the blood of that unfortunate Caliph. The theocrats, incensed at his refusal, now turned against Ibn Zobeir, whose brother Musab had hard work in opposing them. Over and over again they got possession of Bussorah, and when driven out they retired to Ahwaz and spread themselves over Persia. There committing continual ravages under one name or another (for they split up into many sects), they were with difficulty held in check by Mohallab, a brave general who had already distinguished himself in Khorasan, and was now summoned for this task by Musab.

Mukhtar at Kufa. His previous history.

Meanwhile an adventurer of a very different type, named Mukhtar, came on the scene at Kufa. He was son of the Abu Obeid slain in the battle of the Bridge. Designing and unprincipled, Mukhtar was ever ready to take the side most for his own advantage. He was one of those who pursued Hasan when, as Caliph, he fled from Kufa to Medain ; and, on the other hand, he took part with Muslim, when deputed by Hosein to Kufa. On the last occasion, he was seized by Obeidallah, then governor of the city, who struck him a blow that lost him an eye. Escaping to Arabia, he swore that he would revenge the injury on the tyrant by cutting his body into a thousand pieces. After that, he aided Ibn Zobeir in opposing the Syrian attack on the Holy city; but distrusted by him, he departed and set up on his own

Returns to Kufa, end of 64 A.H. 683 A.D.

account. Towards the close of the year 64, returning to Kufa, now under one of Ibn Zobeir's lieutenants, he gained a name by joining in the cry of vengeance raised by the Alyite party of the city, against all who had been concerned in the attack upon Hosein. But, suspected by the governor of sinister designs, he was seized and cast into prison.

Kharejite rising at Kufa to revenge death of Hosein, 64 A.H.

For, about this time, a wild fanaticism had seized the Kharejites of Kufa, to revenge the death of Hosein. Ever since the tragedy at Kerbala, indeed, a party there had more or less conspired together to slay all those who had joined the enemies of their Prophet's grandson. The feeling

The Penitents.

now became intense. Early in the year 65, numbers of 'the Penitents', as they called themselves, visited the tomb of Hosein at Kerbala, and gathering there 'in a throng thicker than the throng that gathers around the Kaaba,' raised A.H. 64–73. a bitter cry, and spent the night in loud wail of self-reproach for having deserted in his extremity the son of Fatima and Aly. Then they set out to attack the godless Routed at Syrians. Met near Kirkesia by the Caliph's troops, they Kirkesia, iv. 65 A.H. fought with desperate bravery, but were utterly defeated, Nov. 684. their leaders slain, and the remnant driven back to Kufa[1].

Mukhtar from his prison sent to the defeated 'Penitents' Mukhtar gains possession of Kufa as agent of the Hanefite, iii. 66 A.H. Oct., 685 A.D. a fulsome panegyric with hopes of future victory. Having obtained his liberty, he set up as the professed delegate of Mohammed the Hanefite son of Aly, commissioned by him to execute vengeance on the enemies of his father's house. By dint of specious assertions and forged letters, and a certain countenance from Mohammed himself then at Medina, he gained over Ibraham ibn al Ashtar[2], and other influential men of Kufa. By their aid he expelled the governor of Ibn Zobeir, gained possession of the city, and succeeded in extending his sway over Irac, and even over parts of Persia and Arabia.

The first great effort which he made was directed against Mukhtar sends army against Obeidallah, 66 A.H. 686 A.D. his old enemy Obeidallah, who during the past year had been endeavouring to reduce the power of Ibn Zobeir in Mesopotamia, and now threatened Mosul. For this end he despatched Ibn al Ashtar with an army; but no sooner Uproar in Kufa. had it left Kufa, than the citizens, many of whom had no sympathy with the Alyite movement, and were indeed themselves amongst the 'murderers' of Hosein, rose in rebellion against Mukhtar. He hastily recalled Ibn al Ashtar for his defence. A terrible conflict ensued in the streets of Kufa, tribe against tribe, Yemen against Cays, faction against faction,—till the cry on one side 'Down with the murderers of Hosein!' and on the other 'Down with the murderers of Othman!' resounded throughout the city.

---

[1] The wild fanaticism of these people is illustrated by the war-cry of one who thus exhorted his fellows : ' Whoso desireth the life after which there is no death, the journey after which there is no weariness, the joy after which there is no grief, let him draw nigh unto his Lord in this battle, and breathe out his soul in Paradise.'

[2] Son of the Ashtar who bore so prominent a part on Aly's side in the battle of Siffin.

A.H. 64–
78.
___
Massacre
of all con-
cerned in
attack on
Hosein.
End of
66 A.H.
At last, after some 800 had been slain, Mukhtar's party gained the victory. An amnesty was called ; but from it all who had taken part against Hosein were shut out. These including, besides Shamir, Amr and other leading actors in the tragedy, no fewer than 284 citizens of lesser note, were ruthlessly put to death. And so Mukhtar at once achieved the ostensible object of his mission, and avenged himself by horrid cruelties upon his enemies[1]. The heads of Amr and of his son, slain after he had given them quarter, were sent to the Hanefite, with this message,—'I have destroyed every man within my reach concerned in the attack upon Hosein, thy martyred father ; and I will yet slay the remainder, if the Lord will.' Only a few escaped to Bussorah.

Ibn al Ash-
tar defeats
Obeidallah,
who is
slain,
i. 67 A.H.
Aug.,
686 A.D.
While the emeute and slaughter were going on, Obeidallah had taken Mosul, and was advancing on Irac. Mukhtar, now that he was rid of his foes at home, hurried off the army once again under Ibn al Ashtar to meet his arch-enemy. He himself accompanied it a short way, when a scene, worthy of the unprincipled pretender, was enacted to stir the fanatic zeal of the troops. A party of his followers drew near with a worn-out chair borne upon a mule. 'The chair of Aly!' cried Mukhtar; '*A messenger from heaven*[2] sent to slay thousands upon thousands of the wicked ones ; even as the ark brought victory unto the children of Israel!' 'Nay!' cried the pious Ibn al Ashtar, as the crowds with uplifted arms shouted around the chair,—'Call it rather the golden Calf which led the Israelites astray.' The wretched scandal thus countenanced by Mukhtar tended to lower him in the eyes of all the thinking citizens. Meanwhile, with an immense force, Obeidallah was advancing from Mosul, and the Kufan army hurried on to anticipate him before he should invade

---

[1] 'Some they stoned, some they stabbed, and some they shot with arrows like as they had shot at Hosein.' Of one, Mukhtar had the four limbs cut off, and the wretched creature so left to die ; another, half dead, they burned in the fire. The feeling ran so high as to override the ties of nature ; thus the citizen who had brought in from Kerbala the head of Hosein was hunted down till at last he was pointed out by the fanatic piety of his own wife and slain.

[2] Quoting the Coran, *Sura* lxxvii. 1.

Irac. The two armies met on the banks of the Zab. A.H. 64-
73.
But there was treachery in the Syrian camp. The Beni
Cays had not forgotten the field of Merj Rahit, and they
carried the left wing in a body over to the enemy. Beaten
at first by the other wing, Ibn al Ashtar recovered his position ; and in a furious charge, nerved by the cry of ' vengeance on the tyrant Obeidallah and the murderers of
Hosein !' routed the Syrian force, of which the most that
escaped the sword perished in the swift waters of the Zab.
The head of Obeidallah was carried to Kufa, and cast before Obeidal-
lah's head
sent to
Kufa.
Mukhtar on the same spot where, six years before, as
governor of Kufa he had so roughly handled the gory head
of the Prophet's grandson[1]. Thus early was the tragedy of
Kerbala avenged in the blood of its chief actor, and of
almost all who had taken part in the same.

The victory of Ibn al Ashtar made Mukhtar for the Mukhtar
falls out
with
Zobeir.
moment undisputed master of Mesopotamia. His fortune,
however, built up as it was on a sand-bed of false pretences,
was but of short duration. He tried to hold with Ibn
Zobeir ; but Ibn Zobeir had no faith in him ; and to test
his profession of loyalty summoned him to Mecca. Thereupon Mukhtar assumed a hostile attitude, and sent a force
to succour the Hanefite son of Aly, whose life Ibn Zobeir
had threatened unless he would do him homage[2]. He also
despatched an army to Medina with the ostensible object
of defending it from Syrian attack ; but Ibn Zobeir,
divining his ambitious designs, sent a force in the same
direction which cut it to pieces.

Musab, brother of Ibn Zobeir, was still governor of Musab
defeats
Mukhtar,
67 A.H.
686 A.D.
Bussorah. The Kufáns who had escaped thither from
the tyranny of Mukhtar, now besought Musab to rid them
of their adversary. Nothing loth, he summoned the brave
Mohallab from Fars, where he was still fighting against
the Kharejites ; and thus, some little time after the battle
of the Zab, Musab, supported by him, set out for Kufa

---

[1] The feeling of abhorrence towards Obeidallah may be gathered from the
tradition that a viper issued from his head and kept crawling from his mouth
into his nose, and so backwards and forwards.

[2] Eventually the Hanefite tendered allegiance to Abd al Melik, and we hear
little more of him.

A.H. 84–
73.
with a fully equipped army. He was met on the way by the troops of Mukhtar, which he totally discomfited. Mukhtar then rallied his adherents in Kufa, and himself at their head encountered the enemy just outside the walls ; but he was driven back, and with some 8000 followers forced to take refuge in the fort. For several months they held out, but with little sympathy from the citizens at large. At last, driven by hunger and thirst, Mukhtar called on the garrison to go forth with him and fight either for victory or a hero's death. He was followed but by nineteen, and with

Mukhtar slain, ix. 67 A.H. March, 687 A.D.
them met his fate. The rest surrendered at discretion. There was much discussion as to whether these should be spared, or at least those of Arab blood amongst them, who numbered 700[1]. But the army was incensed, and the citizens of Kufa had no favour for them ; and so Musab gave command, and the whole seven or eight thousand were beheaded. It was a deed of enormous ferocity, and brought Musab into well-merited disfavour with his brother, Ibn Zobeir. The hand of the Pretender was nailed to the wall of the Mosque, where it remained till taken down by Hajjaj ; and the cruelties were crowned by putting to death one of the widows of Mukhtar, who refused to speak otherwise than well of her husband's memory[2]. Thus ended the short-lived triumph of this unprincipled adventurer but a year and a half from his seizure of the city.

67–69 A.H. 687–8 A.D. Outbreak of Kharejites.
During the next two years there was little change in the relations subsisting between the several provinces. The Kharejites kept the East in constant alarm. They scoured the country, made cruel attacks on the unoffending people[3], took Rei, besieged Ispahan for months, overran Ahwaz and Kerman, and even threatened Kufa. Mohallab, the only general able to cope with these savage

---

[1] It is instructive to observe the distinctive value at this period placed on the life of Arabs, when it was calmly proposed to set the Arab prisoners free and slay the ' clients ' of foreign blood.

[2] Elegies by different poets mark the horror entertained of this atrocious act.

[3] These theocratic fanatics seem throughout to have had a strange fascination for the most savage cruelties, regarding them apparently as service to God, if only perpetrated against those held by them as heretics. They even cut up women big with child.

fanatics, had been unwisely withdrawn from the field for the government of Mosul. Musab now again sent him against the Kharejite bands ; and after eight months of unceasing warfare he succeeded in dispersing them for the time. The temporary quiet which, apart from these Kharejite out-rages, at this period prevailed throughout the empire is signalized by the singular spectacle chronicled by tradition, that whereas the Meccan solemnities were always headed by the Sovereign himself or by his lieutenant, there were in the year 68, four leaders who without any breach of harmony presided at the Pilgrimage each over his own adherents, namely Ibn Zobeir, the Hanefite son of Aly, the Kharejite Najda who held the south of Arabia, and the deputy of Abd al Melik himself.

A.H. 64-73.

Pilgrimage xii. 68 A.H. June, 688 A.D.

Abd al Melik had for some time been contemplating operations against Ibn Zobeir, and had in fact started on more than one occasion for a campaign to commence in the north of Syria, and sweep down upon Irac and Arabia ; but a severe famine paralyzed his efforts for a time. At last, in the beginning of the year 70, he attacked Kirkesia, but was recalled by a danger which threatened his throne, and led to an act which has left an indelible stigma on his name. At the time of Merwan's accession, it will be remembered that the minor son of Yezid was to have the next claim. A similar expectation was held out, either then or after-wards, to Amr ibn Said, cousin of the Caliph and governor of Damascus.   Both expectations were defeated by the nomination and subsequent succession of Abd al Melik, and the injury rankled in the mind of Amr.   Accordingly, on the Caliph's camp nearing Aleppo, Amr left it secretly by night, re-entered Damascus, and set up for himself as Caliph. Abd al Melik thereupon hurried back, and after some inconclusive engagements offered an amnesty, on which the fighting ceased, and a deed of pardon was given to Amr. A few days after, the Caliph, who had resolved on his death, summoned him to his presence. He went against the advice of his friends, clad in armour below his dress, and with a large following, which, however, were shut out at the palace gates. Accosting him in friendly accents, Abd al

Rebellion of Amr ibn Said, 70 A.H. 689 A.D.

Melik bade him sit down by him, and after indifferent conversation, signified that he wished to fulfil an oath he made
on first hearing of Amr's rebellion, namely that he would
bind him hand and foot; but that having fulfilled his oath
he would afterwards unloose him.   Amr submitted, but no
sooner was he bound than the Caliph smote him violently,
and having bid his brother Abdalaziz to put him to death,
went forth to the evening prayers.   Returning shortly, he
was startled to find his victim still alive; and, taunting his
brother, who said he had not the heart to take the life of
Amr, with cowardice, himself stabbed him to death, and
then cast his head with a heavy largess to the crowd without.   Amr's following was put to flight; his sons and
adherents, with difficulty spared, were banished, and
peace restored.   The Caliph then sent to the widow for
the deed of amnesty; — 'It is in the grave with my
husband,' she replied, 'that he may arraign thee before
his Lord thereby.'   Abd al Melik was not otherwise a
cruel or hard-hearted man; but this act of refined and
ruthless treachery created a wide-spread impression against
him at the moment[1].

Caliph's
campaign
against
Musab,
A.H. 71.
A.D. 690.

Secure in Syria, Abd al Melik renewed his design
against Ibn Zobeir and Musab.   There was a strong party in
the Caliph's favour at Bussorah; but an endeavour through
an emissary to stir them into active loyalty having failed,
the Caliph resolved himself to head a force for Mesopotamia and Irac.   The Greeks, taking advantage of the
divisions in the Moslem empire, pressed heavily at this
time on the Syrian frontier; and Abd al Melik, to be free
for his enterprise, had to make a truce with them at
the weekly tribute of 1000 golden pieces.   It was the
year 71 before Abd al Melik again broke ground.   Having
sown disaffection widely in Kufa and Bussorah by missives
promising pardon and rewards, he laid seige to Kirkesia,
where Ibn Zobeir's governor shortly accepted the offer of

---

[1] For example, it alarmed the Hanefinite son of Aly, and prevented his coming
in for a time.   The Caliph is represented as rather boasting of it at Kufa:
'Beware,' he said, 'for I have the bonds by me which I cast around the neck of
Amr ibn Said.'

amnesty, and with his son joined the Caliph's army. A.H. 64–73.
Musab, now thoroughly alarmed, sought the help of
Mohallab, but that general was hotly engaged with the
Kharejites, who were close upon the walls of Bussorah.
So he had to meet the Caliph on the Syrian frontier
with only Ibn al Ashtar, who, though tempted with the
promise of Irac, stood fast by Musab. When the two
armies met, it was soon seen that the Caliph's missives
had taken effect, and that treachery was rife in Musab's
camp. Ibn al Ashtar fell battling bravely; and Musab, Who is slain in battle.
deserted by his troops, and refusing quarter, was slain
fighting, with his son by his side, a hero to the last.
His head, with the nose cut off, was sent round by Abd
al Melik to Kufa, Egypt and Damascus. It was then
to have been shewn over the cities of Syria, when the
Caliph's wife, with better feeling, had it washed and buried.
Musab died aged 36. He was handsome and brave ; but
his memory is stained by the butchery perpetrated by his
command at the death of Mukhtar.

On Musab's death, the Kufan army swore allegiance to Caliph re-gains Kufa and Irac.
Abd al Melik, as did also the Arab tribes of the Syrian
desert. Advancing on Kufa, he encamped by the city
forty days. There, one of the citizens made him a great
feast at the ancient palace of Khawarnac[1], open to all.
Abd al Melik was delighted :—' If it would only last ! ' he
said,—' but as the poet sang ' (and he quoted some verses),
' *all is transitory here.*' Then he was taken over the palace,
and being told of the ancient princes of Hira who lived
there, extemporized a couplet (for he was himself a poet),
signifying that the world passes away, and but repeats
itself[2]. The Caliph was fortunate now in obtaining the
adhesion of Mohallab, whom he confirmed in his commission against the Kharejites ; and having arranged for the

---

[1] For the Palace of Khawarnac see *Life of Mahomet*, 1st edition, vol. I.
p. clxxi.

[2] Be not vexed with care, for thou too shalt pass away :
   Therefore enjoy thyself, O man! whilst thou can ;
   For that which was, shall not be again when it hath passed ;
   And that which shall be, only as what hath already been.

A.H. 64–
73.
administration of Kufa, Bussorah and the various Eastern posts, returned to Damascus.

Ibn Zobeir
at Mecca.
Abdallah ibn Zobeir in his retirement still held to his claim of the Caliphate. Virtual ruler for several years of the greater part of the empire, he had remained singularly inactive at Mecca. His chief domestic work had been the restoration of the Holy house destroyed A. H. 64. Having removed the debris, he came upon remains of the ancient limits of the Ishmaelite structure, and enlarged the walls accordingly[1]. Fire, we are told, flashed from the sacred rock, when Ibn Zobeir had the temerity to strike the foundation with his pickaxe, and the same terror overawed the people as sixty years before when, in the youth of the Prophet the, Kaaba was dismantled and rebuilt. If instead of remaining inactive at home, and contenting himself with the issue of orders from the Holy city, he had gone forth to head his armies, it seems not improbable that the Caliphate thus usurped might have been established in his line. But the defeat of his brother came upon him as an unlooked-for and fatal blow. He mounted the pulpit and harangued the people on the treachery of the men of Irac, and his readiness to die in defence of the Kaaba. But trusting perhaps to the immunity of the Sanctuary, he took no further steps.

Hajjaj
attacks
Mecca,
v. 72 A.H.
Oct.,
691 A.D.
If such were his thoughts, they were in vain; for after Irac had been reduced, Abd al Melik resolved on putting an end to the pretensions of his rival. He therefore sent a column of horse and foot under Hajjaj, an able officer now coming to the front. Marching from Kufa, Hajjaj reached Tayif in the vicinity of Mecca, without opposition, and forwarded letters of pardon to Ibn Zobeir, if only he would submit. But Ibn Zobeir declined the offer, and marched out with his followers to Arafat (the Mount of pilgrimage), on the road to Tayif. There he was met by

---

[1] A tradition is quoted from Ayesha of Mahomet having told her that he would himself have restored the Kaaba to its ancient wider dimensions, but that the people having been so recently reclaimed from idolatry, he feared the effect upon them of appearing to tamper with the sacred edifice. Hajjaj subsequently took the temple down and rebuilt it on its former lines.

Hajjaj and driven back on Mecca. Hajjaj then sought and obtained from the Caliph leave to besiege the Holy city. Men remembered how shocked the same Abd al Melik had been when eight years before Mecca was stormed by order of Yezid, and said that the Caliph had gone back in his religion. But this was hardly fair to him ; for so long as Ibn Zobeir was rival Caliph in that otherwise secure sanctuary, the empire could not be free from the danger of revolt. It was close upon the month of Pilgrimage when Hajjaj, strengthened by reinforcements from Medina, invested the city and mounted catapults on the surrounding heights. As the engines opened with their shot, the heavens thundered (so tradition goes), and twelve of the Syrian army were struck by lightning; but next day the storm returned, and the impartial thunderbolts fell upon the men of Mecca, an incident from which Hajjaj drew happy augury. During the days of pilgrimage, the bombardment was at the intercession of Omar's son held over, and the solemnities proper to the season were partially performed. The siege was shortly turned into a strict blockade, and in a few months the inhabitants, suffering the extremities of want, began to desert in great numbers to the enemy. Even two of his own sons did so, at Ibn Zobeir's advice ; but a third preferred to stay and share his father's fate. The siege had now lasted seven months, when Ibn Zobeir lost heart. He was tempted to give in ; but he would first consult his mother, Asma daughter of Abu Bekr, now 100 years of age. The scene is touching. With the ancient spirit of the Arab matron, she exhorted her son, if still conscious of the right, to die as a hero should. ' That,' said he, as he stooped to kiss her forehead, ' is what I thought myself; but I wished to strengthen my thought by thine.' And so, putting on his armour, he rushed into the thickest, and fell in the unequal fight. The heads of Ibn Zobeir and two of his leaders were exhibited at Medina, and thence sent on to Damascus. Hajjaj, giving thus early proof of his hard and cruel nature, had the Pretender's body impaled on the outskirts of the Holy city. Abd al Melik blamed him for his inhumanity, and bade him give the body up to

Asma, by whose loving hands it was washed and committed to the grave.

Ibn Zobeir and his mother Asma. Thus ended the rule of Ibn Zobeir, a man of noble but inactive spirit, who for nine years held the title, and much also of the real power, of Caliph. He died aged 72.

His mother, Asma, is the same who, at the Hegira, seventy-three years before, tore off her girdle to bind withal the Prophet's wallet to his camel as he took his flight from the cave of Mount Thaur, and thus earned the historic name of 'The Woman of the shreds[1].' It is one of the last links that connect the Prophet with the chequered days on which we now have entered. What a world of events had transpired within the lifetime of this lady!

Ibn Khazim faithful to Ibn Zobeir. The only one of Ibn Zobeir's governors who remained faithful to his memory was Ibn Khazim, who was still fighting with rival clans in Khorasan. Abd al Melik offered if he swore allegiance to confirm him in Khorasan; but he indignantly rejected the offer. He would have slain the envoy, he said, had he not been of his own Caysite blood. But he made him swallow the Caliph's letter. Thereupon Abd al Melik sent him the head of Ibn Zobeir, in order to assure him of his end. Ibn Khazim embalmed the relic, and sent it back to the Pretender's family. He was shortly after slain in battle by one whose brother he had put to death in his intertribal warfare.

[1] *Life of Mahomet*, p. 145.

CHAPTER L.

REMAINDER OF ABD AL MELIK'S REIGN.—HAJJAJ;
MOHALLAB; REVOLT OF ABD AL RAHMAN.

73–86 A.H.   692–705 A.D.

ON the death of Ibn Zobeir, who for thirteen years had held *Abd al Melik* his ground as rival of successive Caliphs, the Omeyyad *universally* rule was anew recognised, without dispute, over the whole *recognized.* Moslem realm, and Abd al Melik named as Caliph in *73 A.H. 692 A.D.* the prayers of every mosque from East to farthest West. He was able now to turn his arms again towards the North, where the Moslems obtained material victories over the Greek forces in Asia Minor and also in Armenia; so that apprehension in that direction was for the present at an end.

But throughout the remainder of this reign the leading *Hajjaj* figure was unquestionably Hajjaj, whose cruelties have *governor in Arabia.* stamped him as the worst tyrant of the age. For some time after the sack of Mecca he remained governor of Arabia. Having removed the unhallowed vestiges of the sacrilegious siege from the precincts of the Kaaba, which was by him restored to its anterior dimensions, he visited Medina. There he denounced in no measured terms the city in which Othman had been murdered, and even branded certain of the citizens, known as hostile to the Omeyyad line, with the mark used for a subject race.

In the following year, a branch of the Kharejites called *Azrackite rebels in* Azrackite[1], assumed threatening attitude on the Persian *Irac,*

*74 A.H.
693 A.D.*

[1] So called from a leader of the name of Azrack, who flourished some fifteen or twenty years before.

frontier, and the governor of Irac deputed Mohallab from
Khorasan again to fight against them, and also sent heavy
contingents from Bussorah and Kufa to help him. But on
the governor dying shortly after, the troops from both
cities began to desert Mohallab and, despite remonstrance,
return to their homes. The Caliph now saw that none but
a strong hand could curb the license of the men of Irac,
and so Hajjaj was appointed governor. He forthwith set
out from Medina with a small mounted escort, and crossing
the desert by forced marches arrived in the early dawn unknown at Kufa. He entered the Mosque as men were
assembling for early prayer, and mounting the pulpit sat
down, with face concealed behind the folds of his red turban.
'To prayers! To prayers! he cried aloud, and still sat
muffled. Some thinking him a Kharejite adventurer, took
up stones to cast at him. But they dropped them in terror
as, uncovering his stern features, they recognized that it
was Hajjaj. In verses full of threat and fury, he upbraided
the city for its treachery; 'Beware,' he said, 'for verily it
is as if I saw many a head before me all gory in its blood!'
Then he commanded the Caliph's rescript to be read aloud.
It opened with the greeting of *Peace*; but there was no
response. 'Stop!' said Hajjaj in anger, to the reader;
'is it come to this, that ye respond not to the greeting
of the Caliph? I will teach you soon to mend your ways.'
The affrighted company at once joined in the loyal response,
—'Peace and blessing on the Caliph!' The letter read,
Hajjaj resumed his threatening tone,—'If ye reform not
forthwith, there will soon be widows and orphans enough
amongst you. Unless ye depart within three days for
Mohallab's army, I swear that I will slay every man of
you I find behind.' And he was as good as his word.
The citizens streamed day and night across the bridge;
but some who failed to hasten their departure, an aged man
amongst them, were barbarously put to death. At Bussorah,
the same scene, with even increased severity, was enacted.
It was emphatically now the reign of terror[1].

Hajjaj appointed to Irac, 75 A.H. 695 A.D.

His severe adminis- tration.

---

[1] Ibn al Athir notices the growing barbarity of public executions. With the
early Caliphs, the culprit's turban was simply removed and the head bared

With the view of encouraging Mohallab in his harassing campaign, Hajjaj with a column from Bussorah encamped in his vicinity. There his troops mutinied for an increase of pay, such as had been given them by Musab; and at one time Hajjaj, refusing it, and left almost alone, was in peril of his life. In the end, order was restored, and an amnesty proclaimed. Not many were put to death, but amongst them was the son of Anis, once body-servant of the Prophet, and now an aged citizen of Bussorah[1]. Not content with executing his son, Hajjaj confiscated the possessions of the father, and on his expostulating covered him with invective. Stung by his reproaches, Anis appealed to the Caliph, who upbraided his lieutenant in terms of gross indecency such as few but Arabs know to give, and ordered him on pain of personal chastisement to withdraw his words, and treat Anis with the honour due to one who had in person served the Prophet. Hajjaj, much disconcerted, made the best amend he could. Anis accepted the apology, but added what should have touched the despot more even than the Caliph's reprimand ;—' Had a Nazarene, with all his infidelity, seen one who had served the Son of Mary but for a single day, truly he had done him honour, as thou hast not done to me, who served the Prophet of the Lord for full ten years.' It is the last link that connects the pages of tradition with the person of the Prophet.

Though Hajjaj escaped the danger that now had threatened him, his viceroyalty was during the next two or three years seriously disturbed by Kharejites of various shades. Some were dissatisfied with a government that seemed to trample on the sanctions of Islam, and would return to the days of Omar, under a Caliph to be chosen, —some still holding to the Coreish, and others not,— by the voice of the people at large. The Theocrats,

[margin notes:] A.H. 73–86.

Hajjaj in jeopardy.

Harsh treatment of Anis, the Prophet's servant.

Kharejite insurrection.

Shebib. 76–77 A.H. 695–6 A.D.

---

just as the falchion was to strike it off. Musab had the hair and beard shaved off; and the victim exposed thus to public derision, was decapitated. Now he was pinioned and often suspended by wedges to the wall, and so struggling, with his hands torn by the nails or hooks, his head was struck off.

[1] *Life of Mahomet*, pp. 210–392.

on the other hand, would none of any Caliph,—their cry, as of old, was *No Rule but the Lord's alone*, and a Council for the same. But all were nerved to action by the tyranny of Hajjaj, and by the countenance accorded him by the Caliph. The most dangerous was the latter class. These had no worldly views. As a matter of conscience, they fought with equal bravery whatever the chances of success, goaded by a wild fanaticism. Their leader Shebib, with his few hundreds, put to flight the thousands of Hajjaj. By rapid counter-marches, he outmanœuvred his enemy, and with desperate bravery over and again discomfited the columns which, for two years, were continually sent against him. He repeatedly stormed the walls of Kufa, and on one occasion effecting an entrance, made havoc in the city, and slew many of the worshippers assembled in the Mosque. Abusing the Kufans, in his despatches to the Caliph, for their cowardice, Hajjaj was reinforced by a contingent of Syrian troops. With their aid he succeeded at last in dispersing the followers of Shebib, who was drowned by his horse stumbling on a bridge of boats over the river at Ahwaz[1].

Mohallab's campaign against Azrackites, 76–78 A.H. 695–7 A.D.   Mohallab was still engaged in Persia with Kharejites of the Azrack sect. Driven out of Fars, they fell back on Kerman, and for a year and a half eluded or defied the Caliph's forces. Their chronic rebellion might have lasted longer, had they not fallen out among themselves, and broken up into parties that were soon effectively dispersed. Thus the Azrackites, having kept Irac and Persia more or less in turmoil for a period of twenty years, were at last put an end to. In recognition of his success, Hajjaj received Mohallab with great honour at Bussorah, and invested him (for as Viceroy he made all appointments in the East) with the government of Khorasan. From Merve, Mohallab crossed the Oxus, and with his sons

---

[1] There is a story that his body was sent to Hajjaj, who had his heart taken out. It was hard as a stone, rebounding when cast on the floor; and within was found a drop of coagulated blood, such as that from which the Coran tells us man was evolved. *Sura* xxii. 5, xcvi. 2; *Ibn Khallican* i. 617. His mother was a Greek captive girl.

warred for two years against the Turcomans in that direction, which, notwithstanding previous campaigns, waged
with various success, were yet but partially brought under
Moslem influence. He died 82 A.H.; and was at first
succeeded by his sons. His services to Islam in the long
and obstinate struggle with the Kharejites were great;
and the name he left behind singularly fair and unsullied.

Hajjaj was yet to be exposed to another danger: the
Great king beyond Sejestan, named Ratbil, when attacked
drew the Moslem forces into difficult passes of Afghanistan, from which they were allowed to retire only on the
payment of a humiliating ransom. To avenge the affront,
a great army was raised, and equipped at the cost of a heavy
war cess on Bussorah and Kufa. The command was unwisely placed in the hands of Abd al Rahman, the ambitious
grandson of Ashath, who marched against Ratbil, 80 A.H.,
put him to flight and ravaged his land. Mindful, however,
of the recent misfortune, Ibn al Ashath (for so he is commonly called) would have held his hand for a time till
the country settled down; but Hajjaj, upbraiding him
with faintheartedness, peremptorily bade him to war on;
and when expostulated with, threatened supersession. The
army, equally with their commander, resented the action
of the tyrant,—' Enemy, (as they named him) of God and
man;' and, declaring war against both him and his master,
swore allegiance to Ibn al Ashath, who making favourable
terms with Ratbil, forthwith marched on Irac. The Caliph,
in alarm, sent reinforcements, which Hajjaj pushed on to
the frontier. But Ibn al Ashath beat them back at Toster,
and crossing the Tigris, advanced on Bussorah, from which
Hajjaj was forced to fly. The rebel entering the city
was received with open arms, and at once done homage to
as Caliph [1].

---

[1] The reason assigned for this sudden acceptance of the Pretender is singular,
and is illustrative of the progress of Islam in Irac. Hajjaj, finding that the Jewish
and Christian cultivators, to escape the *Jizia* or capitation-tax, embraced Islam
and flocked in crowds to the cities, so that the revenues were from this cause
seriously depressed, ordered his governors to send all such back to their villages
and farms, and to take the tax from them as before. There was, in consequence,
great lamentation among these village refugees, who went about crying,

A.H. 73–
86.
———
Campaign
against
Ibn al
Ashath,
82 A.H.
Early in the following year, Hajjaj, having entrenched himself outside the city, gained a victory over Ibn al Ashath, who thereupon fell back on Kufa, where he was received with the same readiness as he had been at Bussorah. The latter city being now at his mercy, Hajjaj took a signal revenge by treacherously slaying (so we are told) 11,000 of the inhabitants after promising them quarter. Meanwhile crowds of the discontented citizens of Bussorah streamed forth to Ibn al Ashath, who was able once more to meet Hajjaj, half-way between the two cities, with 100,000 men. The Caliph was now so alarmed that he offered terms to the rebels by the hand of his son and brother. Hajjaj was to be superseded, and suitable provision made for Ibn al Ashath. Hajjaj remonstrated with the Caliph, reminding him of Othman's fate, but he was firm. Ibn al Ashath was inclined to accept the offer; but his army rejected it with scorn, and prepared for battle. Several

months were spent in skirmishing and single combats; and it was not till the middle of 83 A.H., that a great battle was fought. The leader of the Ghazies,—the Coran-readers of the day, and mainstay of the rebels, falling early in the fight, his followers fled in dismay, and the army, thus disheartened, was totally discomfited. Ibn al Ashath retired hastily to Bussorah, and was there joined by many followers, who, though an amnesty was proclaimed, covenanted to fight with him to the death. Pursued by Hajjaj, he was again beaten in a heavy engagement on the Persian border, and

thence effected his escape to Kerman. Eventually he took refuge with Ratbil, who a year or two afterwards, under pressure, put him to death, and sent his head to Hajjaj.

In his flight Ibn al Ashath had been followed to the East by some 60,000 of his defeated troops,—who either hating Hajjaj, or too deeply compromised in rebellion, refused the amnesty. These, failing to induce Ibn al Ashath to leave his protector and again try the fortune

---

O Mahomet! O Mahomet! and knew not whither to go. The population were deeply touched at their lamentations, especially the ' Coran Readers ;' and this was one of the reasons, we are told, which led to the sudden acquiescence of the city in the revolt against Hajjaj and the Caliph.

of war, set out on their own behalf, and took possession
of Herat. Yezid, son of Mohallab, governor at Merve,
ordered them to evacuate the place and move elsewhere ;
but choosing rather to fight, they were by him defeated
and dispersed. Many were taken prisoners, and those
of note sent to Hajjaj, who, both now and after the recent
engagements in Irac, shed the blood of his captives with
unsparing hand and heartless cruelty. He was on this
occasion vexed with Yezid for having pardoned some
leading men, because, as he suspected, they were of Yemen
blood, while he himself was partial to the Caysite clan ;
and this is assigned as the reason for his shortly after super- Superseded
seding him and his brothers by the famous Coteiba.   by Coteiba.

In this year the military station of Wasit was founded, Wasit
so called, as midway between Kufa and Bussorah. The founded,
main object was, no doubt, to have an independent canton- 83 A.H.
ment holding in check both restless cities. The immediate 702 A.D.
cause, however, was impatience of the Kufans at the license
of the Syrian soldiers quartered in the city,—an evil precedent attributed to Hajjaj. Conveniently situated in the
well-watered plain betwixt the Tigris and Euphrates,
Wasit became the chief military centre of the empire, and
so continued as long as the Caliphate itself.

While these events were passing in the East, Abd al Melik Hostilities
was able, after the fall of Ibn Zobeir, to throw aside the with Greece,
humiliating treaty concluded with the Emperor ; and from 73–84 A.H.
the year 73, his generals, some of them his own sons, 692–703 A.D.
prosecuted with vigour, but not always with success, yearly
campaigns in Asia Minor, Armenia, and the coast of Africa.
Up to the year 76, the relations between the two Courts were
friendly ; but then a singular incident broke the peace. The
Caliph, according to Moslem habit, headed a letter to the
Emperor with mention of the Prophet, and the verse—*Say,
He is God alone* ; whereupon the Emperor threatened that if
such affront were repeated, he would strike coins with words
respecting Mahomet grievous to his followers. Heretofore
the Byzantine mint had, in conjunction with the old Persian
coinage, supplied the currency in common use throughout
the empire. The Emperor's hostile threat caused Abd al

A.H. 73–86.
——
Mint of Damascus.

Melik now to establish a royal mint at Damascus, and coin silver dirhems and golden dinars with a Moslem legend[1]. The amity of the two courts thus rudely broken, war was prosecuted vigorously. Its fortune varied. In 79 A.H., Antioch was seized by the Greeks for a time; and under Justinian severe reverses were inflicted on the Moslems. On the other hand, the latter took many strongholds in Asia Minor, and penetrated as far as Erzerum. The people on the border-lands of Syria and Armenia suffered greatly in this chronic warfare; and in 84 A.H., so many churches were set on fire that the year was called 'The year of burning.'

Reverses in Africa, 62–69 A.H.
681–688 A.D.

With even greater energy, but more chequered fortune, the Moslem forces were engaged in Africa. Ocba pushed his armies from Cairowan to the verge of the Atlantic. At Tangier he heard from Count Julian a tempting account of the prize that lay across the strait; but the attempt on the Spanish coast was not to be just yet. The Berbers were treated as an inferior race; and Koseila, one of their chiefs, who had embraced Islam, was embittered by being put to some menial office. Carrying his countrymen with him, and joining the Greeks, this rebel advanced with an overwhelming force against Ocba, who was slain, and his whole army destroyed. Koseila thereupon reoccupied Cairowan, but entered into an agreement to respect the Moslem families (now his co-religionists) settled there.

---

[1] Weil, guided by discovery of Moslem coins prior to this reign, relates this incident somewhat differently from our Arab authorities. It is no doubt true that we find silver coins struck by Omar in the old Persian mints with short sentences as 'Praise be to the Lord,' &c.: and this went on, more or less, throughout the reign of Muavia, who struck golden coins with the design of a sword. No doubt, also, local governors coined Moslem money before this reign. But notwithstanding, the Greek and old Persian currencies held their ground throughout the empire until now. It was not till this reign, as we are distinctly told by Arabian writers, that the Mussulman coinage became trustworthy either in weight or touch. The mintage of Hajjaj was held the purest even by Abbasside Caliphs; but the pietists objected to its use, because it had as its legend a verse of the Coran, which might fall into the hands of the infidel or of Moslems ritually unclean. For the defect of a single grain, each of the 100 workmen now employed in the mint received 100 stripes; making thus, as we are told, '10,000 stripes for a single grain.' Ibn al Athir's chapter on this subject contains some curious details on the new coinage, vol. iv. p. 337.

Most of the Arabs then retired to Egypt, and it was
not till 69 A.H. that anything farther was attempted.
In that year, Abd al Melik sent an army under Zoheir,
one of Ocba's old commanders. In a great battle, in
which Koseila was slain, he beat the Greeks and
Berbers; but these, reinforced by sea from Sicily, again
advancing, took Zoheir unawares, and cut his entire force
to pieces.

Such repeated calamities were sorely felt at Damascus; Conquests
but some years elapsed before steps could be taken to re- in West
store the prestige of the Moslem arms. At last, in 74 A.H., Africa.
an army 'greater than ever before had entered the land of 74 A.H.
Africa,' was despatched under command of Hassan. From 693 A.D.
Cairowan they marched to Carthage, and put to flight
the Greeks and Berbers massed in great numbers for its
defence. Then they stormed the city,—the inhabitants
escaping as best they could by sea to Sicily and Spain,—
took much booty, and prisoners without number; and
having destroyed many of the Roman buildings, and
ravaged the country far and near, returned to Cairowan. But good fortune had not yet dawned on African
adventure. A 'Priestess' wielding a mysterious influence
had succeeded Koseila: and she, inspiring the Berbers
with new courage, inflicted a signal defeat on Hassan,
who was driven back on Barca, and there for five years
forced to remain inactive[1]. Then, reinforced by the Caliph,
he overthrew the Priestess, who was slain in the fight.
Thereupon, her sons, with 12,000 of their army, joined
the Moslem force, which then reoccupied Cairowan. Islam
now spread rapidly amongst the natives. Hassan remained
in command till 89 A.H., when he was superseded by Musa,
of whom we shall hear more anon.

The progress of the Moslem power during this Cali- Musa, Ibn
phate in the far East and beyond the Oxus, was paralyzed career in
for a time by the continued jealousies and discord of the Khorasan.
Arab tribes that formed its garrison. The story of Musa,
son of Ibn Khazim, illustrates both this feeling and the

[1] He fortified the place, and 'The Castles of Hassan,' says Ibn Athir, 'are
known by his name to the present day.'

relation in which the independent or protected states beyond
the frontier stood towards the Moslem Court. Ibn Khazim,
it will be remembered, having put many of the Beni Tamim
to death, was deserted by his followers, and retiring to Nisa-
pur, sent his son Musa to save his property at Merve, and
place it in some stronghold across the Oxus. This he did
with a following of one or two hundred mounted men.
The Prince of Bokhara, and other chiefs whom he approached, refused to take him up; but Tarkhun, king of
Samarcand, received him into friendship. One of his followers having killed a Turcoman, he was obliged to fly to
Tirmidz, where, treated kindly by the chief, he took advantage of a feast to oust his friend and seize his fortress.
Established there, the soldiers who had served under his
father resorted to him, and refugees also from Kabul and
Herat flocked thither, to the number of some 8000. With
this aid, he beat back not only the Turcomans, but the
Moslem columns sent from Merve to dislodge him. Thus
prospering, his followers pressed him to recross the river,
and take possession of Khorasan. But he was content
with the country beyond the Oxus, and with expelling
therefrom the provincial governors, or Residents, sent from
Merve. Mohallab, and after him his sons, thought best to
leave him alone; and so for fifteen years Musab was undisputed ruler of this great tract. At last, one of Mohallab's
sons, thinking to please Hajjaj, sent an army against him,

Defeated
and slain,
85 A.H.
which was joined by 15,000 of Tarkhun's Turks; and by
which, after a long siege, Musa was defeated and slain,
85 A.H. But so inveterate were the tribal leanings of
Hajjaj—who, as we have lately seen, was vexed at Yezid
having spared some of Ibn al Ashath's followers because
they were of Yemen blood—that he was little pleased with
tidings of the death of Musa. 'I bade Yezid,' he said,
'slay the Yemenite, and he replied that he had given him
quarter; and now his brother hastens to tell me of the
death of this noble Caysite, Musa, son of Ibn Khazim, as
if that would rejoice my heart!' So strong was the
clannish jealousy and party spirit of the Arab race.

Abd al Aziz, brother of the Caliph, who had long been

governor of Egypt, held the next title to the throne, A.H. 73–
having been nominated thereto by his father Merwan. 86.
Abd al Melik now sought to set his claim aside in favour Welid
of his own son Welid, and was supported in his desire by Heir
Hajjaj. But Abd al Aziz would not surrender his right; Apparent.
nor would he agree to the nomination of Welid even to suc- 85 A.H
ceed himself; 'for,' said he, 'do not I see in mine own son 704 A.D.
what thou seest in thine? Besides, we know not which of
us may die the first ; leave it therefore thus alone.' And he
did so. Next year Abd al Aziz died ; and Welid was then
done homage to, as next in succession, throughout the
empire. The only opposition was at Medina, where a
recusant, affirming the old doctrine of popular election,
demurred even under threat of the sword, to the declaration of an Heir Apparent. Abd al Melik, however, contented himself with inflicting stripes upon the malcontent.

In the following year Abd al Melik died, 60 years of age, Abd al
having reigned 21 years, during the first portion of which Melik dies.
his title was disputed by Ibn Zobeir. From his death-bed 705 A.D.
he enjoined on his sons mildness and concord, and bade
them make much of Hajjaj ; 'for,' said the dying Caliph,
'it is he that hath made our name to be named in every
pulpit throughout Islam, and subdued our enemies under
us.' He was buried at the Jabia Gate of Damascus.

Of Abd al Melik the Arabian historian says :—He was His
the first Caliph that resorted to treacherous execution, as in character.
the case of Amr ibn Said ; the first to conduct the exchequer in Arabic instead of Persian ; the first to prohibit
men talking in the Caliph's presence ; the first to play the
miser ; the first to declare, as on the death of Ibn Zobeir,
'Let no one enjoin equity and the fear of God upon me,
or I will strike his head from off his shoulders.' But if
such things were really spoken of him, we must attribute it
in great part to the prejudice of Abbasside writers, and to
the odium naturally attaching to the siege of the Holy
city and the destruction of the Kaaba. Apart from the
case of Amr ibn Said, we are told of nothing in his
personal administration inconsistent with a wise, mild,
and just administration ; although, by the support accorded

A a

to Hajjaj, he must undoubtedly be held responsible, at second hand, for the cruelty and injustice of his lieutenant. The charge of penuriousness, too, appears equally unfounded ; for at least in one respect he was lavish. Himself a composer of no mean merit, he encouraged poets by a princely liberality. Many stories are told of literary contests held before him by such poets as Jerir, Farazdac, Kotheir, and Akhtar the Christian, and of the largesses conferred on such occasions. Of niggardliness in any branch of the administration, no instance has been given.

And successful reign.

Upon the whole, the verdict on Abd al Melik must be in his favour. His life was a stormy one. As a boy he witnessed the tumultuous scenes at Medina ending in the outrage on Othman's life,—scenes, as we know from his addresses to the inhabitants of that city, which made a lasting impression on him. He was early employed in the affairs of Mecca, and accompanied his father thither in the negotiations held with Ibn Zobeir. During the first half of his reign, the throne was often in jeopardy, and a coalition of his adversaries would probably have overthrown it. Yet, with but one exception, we never hear of his being betrayed into acts of bitterness and retaliation : on the contrary, he repeatedly, before resorting to extremities, made offers of pardon and reconciliation. In the end, having triumphed over all his enemies, he left to his sons a splendid inheritance, and with it the ample and ready means for extending the same on every side[1].

---

[1] He had fifteen sons by eight wives, besides slave-girls. Four of his sons, as we shall see, succeeded to the throne.

CHAPTER LI.

CALIPHATE OF WELID.—CONQUESTS IN CENTRAL ASIA,
SIND, ASIA MINOR, AFRICA, SPAIN.—DEATH OF
HAJJAJ.

86–96 A.H. 605–15 A.D.

HAVING performed the funeral service over his father's Welid,
grave, Welid returned to the Mosque, and ascending the $\frac{\text{86 A.H.}}{\text{705 A.D.}}$
pulpit, delivered an address lámenting the loss of his father
and blessing his memory.

Welid, reposing the same trust as his father in Hajjaj, Omar
maintained him in the Viceroyalty of the East. But beautifies
Arabia he made over to his cousin, the pious Omar, son of cities.
Abd al Aziz, under whom, for several years, Mecca and
Medina enjoyed a mild and beneficent administration.
Aided by a council of learned citizens, his government
of Medina was popular. He beautified and enlarged the
Mosque by embracing in its court the apartments of the
Prophet's wives, and others originally built around it.
Artificers were furnished by Syria ; and the Emperor, in-
formed of the pious undertaking, sent a gift of gold, forty
camel-loads of mosaics, and 100 Byzantine masons[1]. Under
Welid's instructions, Omar also had the roads and passes

---

[1] The Emperor presented 100,000 mithcals of gold. It reads somewhat
oddly immediately after :—' In the same year, Maslama, the Caliph's brother,
warred against the Greeks, took three fortresses, one being the *Fort of Constantine,* and slew of the mongrel Arabs 1000, carrying off at the same time heavy
spoil.' But we are also told that in the year 90 A.H. (708 A.D.) the Moslem
admiral was taken prisoner, and as a matter of grace restored to the Caliph.

A.H. 86–
96.
on the pilgrim routes made easy, wells dug about the desert stations, and fountains to play at Mecca and Medina[1]. It was all for Omar a labour of love; and so well did he carry out these useful and ornamental works, that the Caliph, on pilgrimage some time after to the Holy cities, expressed his delight and thankfulness at all he saw.

Severity of
Hajjaj.
The attractions of Omar's beneficent rule drew away from the heavy hand of Hajjaj great numbers of the men of Irac, who took refuge from his tyranny in Mecca and Medina. This irritated Hajjaj all the more, and Omar felt bound to inform the Caliph of his increasing severity. Hajjaj, on the other hand, complained bitterly of the shelter given to his malcontent subjects in the Holy cities; and Welid, yielding to Hajjaj, recalled Omar. In his room two governors were appointed to Mecca and Medina; these ruthlessly expelled the immigrants, and threatened with death any citizen who dared to give them shelter. Ibn Jobeir, one of these refugees, had been paymaster of Ibn al Ashath's army, whom, after an affecting interview with his family, Hajjaj executed with heartless cruelty. This was about a couple of years before his own death, and remorse for it affected his mind. At night he would awake with the vision of his victim clutching the bedclothes and crying out, *O Enemy of the Lord, for what hast thou slain me?* whereupon the tyrant would keep calling aloud, *What have I to do with thee, thou son of Jobeir!*

Yezid ibn
Mohallab
escapes
from him
to Solei-
man,
90 A.H.
His treatment of the sons of Mohallab, Yezid and his brethren, was equally cruel and vindictive. Against these, it will be remembered, Hajjaj had a grudge on account of their Yemenite leanings. They were now imprisoned on the convenient charge against retiring governors, of embezzlement. Having to set out on a campaign against the

---

[1] There was need of some such supply at Mecca, for the multitude of pilgrims was now so great that in a dry season the water was altogether short. In fact, one year the want was so pressing that Omar bade the people join him in prayer; and shortly after rain fell in such torrents that the city was inundated. The pious traits of Omar are a popular subject with the traditionists.

The governor succeeding Omar was profane enough to praise Welid at the expense of Abraham,—the former having brought sweet water into Mecca, whereas Abraham only gave them the brackish well of Zemzem.

Kurds, he took them with his camp, under a Syrian guard. A.H. 86-96.
Yezid was subjected to torture, which he bore with fortitude ; but on one occasion the instrument of torture pierced
his leg, and he cried out. His sister, one of Hajjaj's wives,
alarmed at the cry, screamed, whereupon the tyrant divorced
her on the spot. The prisoners were fortunate enough to
effect their escape ; and Hajjaj, thinking they had fled to
Khorasan, warned Coteiba of the danger. But they had
taken horse in the opposite direction, and found refuge
with Soleiman, the Caliph's brother. Hajjaj was instant
with the Caliph that Yezid should be delivered up ; whereupon Soleiman sent him, and his own son with him, to
Damascus, both in chains, with a letter supplicating mercy.
Welid, touched at the sight, let them depart in peace, and
forbade Hajjaj to interfere. Yezid continued to live with
the Heir Apparent as his intimate, and, as we shall see
hereafter, favourite courtier [1].

During the remainder of his life we do not hear much of Death of
Hajjaj, and it was well for him that he died before Welid, Hajjaj, 95 A.H.
for he had given mortal offence to Soleiman, whose right of 713 A.D.
succession Welid desired to set aside in favour of his own
son, and in the design was encouraged by Hajjaj. But the
wrath of Soleiman, escaping the father, fell, as we shall see,
with terrible severity on his family and adherents. Hajjaj
stands out in the annals of Islam as the incarnation of
cruelty. But the Caliphate owed much to him. For
twenty years the absolute ruler of the East in times of
trouble and danger, with anarchy abroad, perversity and
fickleness at home, rebellion and wild fanaticism at his
doors, Hajjaj, by his bravery and resolution, maintained
the strength and restored the prosperity of the empire in
Irac, Arabia, and Khorasan. Severity was no doubt often
justified in quelling the turbulent elements around ; but
nothing can excuse the enormous bloodshed and inhumanity which have handed down his name as that of
one of the cruellest tyrants the world has ever seen [2].

---

[1] Soleiman was so much attached to Yezid that whenever he received a
special rarity, or beautiful slave-girls, he sent them to his friend.

[2] Tradition puts the number of lives sacrificed by Hajjaj (apart from carnage

A.H. 86–
96.

Wars of
Coteiba in
Khorasan,
86–96 A.H.
705–714
A.D.

87 A.H.

An indirect advantage has by some been attributed to the tyranny of Hajjaj, in that his reign of terror drove many from their homes to swell the armies in the field, and so help forward the conquests for which the Caliphate of Welid is famous. A brief outline of these will now be given, beginning with the campaign of Coteiba in Central Asia. That great warrior advanced every summer into the provinces beyond the Oxus, retiring as autumn advanced to winter in Merve. Up to this time the Moslem campaigns appear to have been of the nature of *razzias,* or raids, bringing the subdued lands into the category of allied, protected, or tributary, rather than of conquered and subject states. The proceedings were now of a more permanent nature. Coteiba's first advance was against Balkh, Takharistan, and Ferghana. At Balkh, among the captives, was the wife of Barmek a physician, who was taken as a slave-girl into the harem of Abdallah, Coteiba's brother. Soon after, peace being made, the lady, as a matter of grace, was restored to her husband; but the result of the short union with Abdallah was a son, acknowledged by him, and known in after days as Khalid the Barmecide[1]. The next campaign was against Peikund, a trading emporium of Bohkara, beyond the Oxus. The Turcomans of Soghd and other hordes swarmed in such multitudes around Coteiba for the defence of this rich city, as to cut off his communications. For two months Hajjaj received no tidings, and had prayers offered up for him in the mosques throughout the East. At last the city fell. The fighting men were put to the sword, their families

on the field of battle) at 120,000,—mere guess-work of course. He was fond of making copies of the Coran with his own hand, and as a work of merit making distribution of the same; but he was bitterly opposed to Ibn Masud's text,—declaring that he would behead any one who followed it. Many savage sayings are attributed to him. The odium attaching to his name has no doubt magnified his demerits, which, however, with every allowance for exaggeration, were pre-eminently bad.

[1] Weil thinks the story was invented to give the Barmecide family a status they would not otherwise have had as mere natives of Balkh. There is, however, nothing unlikely in the incident. It was altogether in accord with law and habit, only in this case the lady was given back,—an act which, even with the dishonour, must be regarded as merciful in a Moslem conqueror.

taken captive, and vast stores of gold and silver vessels and A.H. 86–
other precious things, 'spoil such as never before seen in ^{96.}
Khorasan,' became the conqueror's prize. In 88 A.H. another 88 A.H.
advance was made on Bokhara, and many places of note
were taken. A heavy battle was fought with a vast host
from Soghd and the surrounding districts, commanded by
'a nephew of the Emperor of China,' who after a determined resistance was put to flight. Next year Coteiba 89 A.H.
again advanced through Soghd and Kish, and was met by
Werdan, king of Bokhara. For two days he fought
against Coteiba, when he took to flight ; but the city
resisted every attempt to storm it. Hajjaj upbraided
Coteiba with the failure, and bade him renew the attack
after instructions based on a plan furnished to him of the
defences. This he did with a strong force, which mainly Bokhara
through the bravery of the Beni Temim (for the Beni Azd taken,
at first gave way before the fierce onset of the Turks[1]), 90 A.H.
routed the enemy. Bokhara was taken, and the surrounding province completely subdued.

On the approach of winter, as the Moslem troops were Rising in
being withdrawn for the season, Nezak, minister of the Tokhari-
Prince of Tokharistan, formed a conspiracy with the sur- 91 A.H.
rounding powers to cast off the foreign yoke which too
evidently was now settling down heavily upon them. To
prevent his sovereign, who opposed the design, from interfering, and yet give an appearance of respect, he placed
links of gold upon him ; then expelled the Moslem Resident[2], and proceeded to enlist the potentates and levy aid all
around for defence, from Balkh as far as Kabul[3]. Beyond
posting a column under his brother, to guard the frontier,
Coteiba could do nothing till the following year, when,
largely reinforced from Persia, he again broke ground.

---

[1] The Moslem women from the camp rushed out screaming and, beating the
horses of the retreating column on their heads, thus forced them back upon the
enemy. So even in these advanced and exposed campaigns we see that the
Moslems carried their women and families with them.

[2] The *Amil* or ' Agent' of Coteiba :—the Representative or Resident of the
Caliph or of his Viceroy, to enforce Moslem supremacy in this transitional period.

[3] The countries named as furnishing help and joining in the rising, are—
Asbahbâdh, Badhân, Merve-rudh, Talicân, Faryâb, and Juzajän.

Carrying all before him, he found Nezak strongly posted
in Khulm, at the entrance of a pass guarded by a fort.
Bribing a deserter, he was shown a route to turn the pass,
and so fell upon the rear of the enemy, who effected escape
across the valley of Ferghana. Here Nezak was again
taken in a defile guarded on one hand by Coteiba and on
the other by his brother. Thus hemmed in for months, he
suffered the extremity of want. But the season again
forcing a return to winter quarters, Coteiba, unwilling to
leave Nezak still abroad, beguiled him into his camp with
promise of safe-conduct. Reporting the capture to Hajjaj,
he asked for leave to put him to death. After a long
delay permission came ; and so, with 700 of his followers [1],
Nezak was slain and his head sent to Hajjaj. The Prince
of Tokharistan was now released, and with his retinue
sent to Damascus, where he was kept till Welid's decease.
The perfidy of Coteiba towards Nezak was so gross, that
the Moslem public, though not unused to guile in war, was
scandalized, and upbraided him for it. Another painful,
but less inexcusable, incident occurred about the same
time. On Nezak's defeat, the king of Juzajân, a member
of the coalition, sought terms of peace, which being granted,
Coteiba invited him to his camp, sending one Habib as a
hostage, and taking hostages in return. The king died
while in Coteiba's camp ; and his subjects, suspecting foul
play, put Habib to death ; whereupon Coteiba retaliated
by slaying the native hostages to a man. Having pushed
his conquests still further into Soghdiana [2], Coteiba returned
92 A.H. by Bokhara to Merve. Next year he proceeded to Sejestan against Ratbil, but was set free by the conclusion of
peace with that potentate.

In 93 A.H. Coteiba again crossed the Oxus, and marched

---

[1] Some traditions say 12,000 ; but these reports must be taken *cum grano*.
The popular voice ran strongly against Coteiba's treachery, and would be
inclined to exaggerate.

[2] The King of Shoman had expelled the Moslem Resident, thinking his fortress impregnable. It was stormed by catapults, which must have been very
effective, as the missives entered the king's chamber. Kish and Nusaf were
overrun; Faryâb offering opposition, was ravaged and set on fire, so that it was
called 'the burned land.' The males were all put to death, and the women
taken captive.

on Khowarizm, the Shah having offered him 10,000 cattle if
he would deliver him from a rebellious brother.   The
rebels were routed, and 4000 prisoners put to death.   The
rebellious brother and his followers were made over to the
Shah, who slew them and conferred their property on
Coteiba.   He was now recalled by the news that Samarcand had thrown off the Moslem yoke.   Making a rapid
descent upon it, Coteiba thus in a speech addressed his
troops:—'The wretched Soghdians are verily fallen into
our hands; they have broken their treaty with us, as ye
have heard; and truly the Lord will deliver Khowarizm and
Soghd into our hands, even as He delivered the Beni
Coreitza and Nadhir into the hands of the Prophet[1].'   The
city held out long, and engines had to be brought up to
batter the walls.   Fearing an assault, the king sued for
terms.   Coteiba agreed to retire on a heavy tribute and
quota of horsemen; but first he must enter, build a mosque,
and inaugurate religious service there; after that he would
evacuate the place.   He entered.   The fire-temples were
destroyed and the images burned, but the city was not
given up[2].   Coteiba's repeated perfidy was much spoken
against; and some Syrian is said to have prophesied, but
too truly, that the Caliphate would yet pay the penalty,
and Damascus be ravaged by these wild Turcomans.
Meantime the conqueror's hand fell heavily on Samarcand.
Moslem families brought from Khorasan in great numbers
were settled there; the natives were all disarmed, and
none dared walk abroad at night on pain of death.

During the next two or three years, aided by large contingents of horse from the tribes he had subdued (the
favourite policy in the East of using subject peoples to rivet
their own chain[3]), Coteiba pushed his conquests forward,
taking Khojend, Shush, and other cities of Ferghana, till

---

[1] Two Jewish tribes destroyed at Medina, *Life of Mahomet*, pp. 292, 329.

[2] One of the idols was held so sacred that anyone who touched it would
immediately die.   Coteiba seized a torch, and with a loud Takbir set it on fire;
the golden nails in it weighed 50,000 mithcals.   A granddaughter of Yezdegird, taken captive here, was sent to Damascus, and taken into the royal
harem.   Welid had a daughter by her.

[3] In 95 A.H. 20,000 native levies are said to have followed Coteiba from
Bokhara, Kish, Nusaf, and Khowarazm.

A.H. 86–
96.

he reached Kashgar and the confines of China. A curious tale is told of an interview with 'the King of China,'—probably a border Mandarin,—who, to release Coteiba from an oath that he would take possession of the land, sent him a load of Chinese soil to trample on, a bag of Chinese coin by way of tribute, and four royal youths on whom to imprint his seal. Coteiba had now reached the limit of his conquests. While on this campaign he received tidings of the Caliph's death : suddenly the scene is changed, and his future all overcast.

Campaign
of Ibn
Casim on
the Indus,
89–96 A.H.
714–717
A.D.

Like Coteiba in Central Asia, Mohammed ibn Casim, cousin of Hajjaj and governor of Mekran, was the first great conqueror on the Indian border. With a well-appointed army of 6000 men, he advanced on Sind and laid siege to its capital, Deibul. A catapult named *the Bride*, worked by 500 men, laid waste the city, and a stone shot from it overthrew the pinnacle of the famous temple of Budd, from which flaunted its great red flag. The omen struck terror into the enemy; the king fled, and Ibn Casim, leaving a garrison in the city, pursued him across the Indus, where, surrounded by his elephants, he was slain in a severe engagement. His wife and maidens, rather than suffer dishonour, set fire to their palace, and were consumed with all their treasure. Then the conquerer took Brahminabad by storm[1], and having made terms with Rôr, crossed the Biyas and invested Multan, which after a prolonged siege, the water having failed, surrendered at discretion. The fighting men were put to the sword, and their families, with the crowd of attendants on the shrine of Budd, made captive. Multan was then a centre of pilgrimage, people coming from all quarters to worship the idol. It was 'the Gateway of India and the House of gold.' The spoil was incredible, and double the whole cost of the expedition, which was estimated by Hajjaj at 60,000,000 pieces. While Ibn Casim rested here, enjoying the fruits of his splendid conquests, tidings of Welid's decease arrested his farther progress eastward. He was recalled to Irac, where, with certain

Multan
taken.

[1] Two parasangs from the later Mansûra 'the Victorious.' Spoken of as in the hilly country of Belochistan.

other adherents of Hajjaj, he was put to the torture and
died.

With our historian we may here anticipate a little the
Moslem rule in India. Habib, one of Mohallab's family
(on which now shone the sun of courtly favour) governor
of Sind, fixed his court at Rôr, and allowed the princes displaced by Ibn Casim to return, as protected, to their several
states. The devout Omar II summoned them to embrace
Islam, on which they received Arabian names. In the
days of Hisham, Joneid pushed the Moslem bounds still
further east. But the prestige of Islam again waned for a
time. Most of the princes relapsed into heathenism, and
to hold them in check, the fortified camp Mahfuza (the
Protected) was founded, from which expeditions, both naval
and military, were sent forth. Things, however, says Ibn
al Athir, 'remained in India on a weak and feeble footing
until the blessed accession of the Abbassides.'

It should be noted here that in India there was an altogether new departure in the treatment of the subject races.
Idolatry was tolerated. Temples were left standing, and
their worship not disallowed. By divine letter, Jews and
Christians might continue to profess their faith under
Moslem rule ; and even Parsees were, by a strained interpretation, brought within the exemption[1], as followers of
the 'Book' of Zoroaster. But idolaters were to be pursued to the bitter end, and utterly rooted out. Such, the
plain teaching of the Coran, had been the habitual policy
hitherto ;—the policy still, as we have seen, pursued in Central Asia. But in India a new leaf was turned. As Weil
remarks,—' It no longer was a Holy War,—with the view,
that is to say, of the conversion of the heathen. That
object was now dropped. Side by side with Allah, idols
might be worshipped, if only tribute were duly paid.' And
so, even under Mahometan rule, India remained largely a
pagan land.

Throughout this reign Moslem armies, commanded generally by leaders of the royal blood, made yearly inroads
into Armenia and Asia Minor, which the Greeks, from re-

[1] *Life of Mahomet,* p. 469.

A.H. 86–
96.
verses nearer home, were little able to withstand. In the year 89 a campaign against the Turks on the Caspian was undertaken with notable success. But all other conquests of this reign fade before that of Spain. It is a conquest which, though demanding a separate chapter for itself, we must be content to treat in briefest outline.

Campaign
of Musa
in Western
Africa,
89 A.H.
708 A.D.
Musa was, in 59 A.H., appointed governor of the Mediterranean coast to the west of Egypt, by Abd al Aziz, brother of the Caliph and governor of Egypt, of which 'Africa [1]' was a dependency. His predecessor had already retrieved the disasters that successively befel the Moslem army at Cairowan : and Musa having consolidated his power in the older districts, now, with the aid of his two sons, pushed the Moslem conquests to the farthest west. In successive engagements at Sus and Tlemsen, he completely overthrew the Berbers, took incredible multitudes prisoners[2], and at last brought the native population, even to the bounds of Morocco, under his authority. Opposition ended, 'Readers of the Coran' were appointed to instruct the people in the faith[3]. Naval expeditions were also set on foot, and successful descents made on Majorca and Sardinia[4]. Having established his freedman Taric at Tangier, as lieutenant over the newly conquered districts in the west, Musa returned to his head-quarters at Cairowan.

Musa's
designs on
Spain,
90 A.H.
709 A.D.
The kingdom of Spain was at this period ruled by Roderic, a usurper, to whom Count Julian, ruler of the coast lying over against Tangier, was bitterly opposed[5].

[1] 'Africa' was the name for the Moslem conquests stretching westward from Egypt to the Atlantic.
[2] The Fifth of the captives, the share of the State, amounted to 60,000 ;—the entire number being thus 300,000—the greatest, our historian adds, ever known. But the traditions regarding Musa are liable to a touch of romance.
[3] A few years further on we are told that by 100 A.H. 'the whole of the Berbers were converted to Islam.'
[4] A long account is given of the capture of its harbour, 92 A.H. ; of the recovery of treasure cast into the sea, and secreted in the roof of the great church ; and of the riches of the spoil. Other descents are mentioned 135 and 323 A.H., and finally in 400, when, however, the Moslem fleet of 120 ships was discomfited ; after which no attempts were made on the island.
[5] The daughters of the Spanish nobles, we are told, used to be sent to Court to be educated ; and Roderic had taken advantage of this to dishonour Julian's daughter, which was the cause of this bitterness.

Ceuta, on the African side, was part of Julian's domain. It A.H. 86–
occurred to him that with the help of the invaders from the 96.
East, he might now drive the usurper from the throne. He 90 A.H.
therefore entered into friendly relations with Musa, and at an
interview explained the ease with which the narrow strait
might be crossed; and Musa, nothing loth, was lured by the
inviting prospect of a campaign in Spain. The Caliph,
fearing the sea, at the first hesitated ; but when it was
explained how close was the opposite shore, he gave consent. Next year, by way of trial, Musa sent a few hundred Descent
men in four ships under command of Tarif, who made an x 91 A.H.
easy descent on the near coast at a place that still bears his July,
name, and returned with a spoil so rich that the army 710 A.D.
longed to repeat the attack upon a larger scale. Musa,
thus emboldened, placed a force of 7000 men, chiefly
Berbers and freedmen, with some Arabs, at the disposal of
Taric, who, crossing the straits, took possession of the fortress called after him, Gibraltar[1]. From thence he ravaged and of
the adjacent country of Algezira[2], when Roderic, receiving vii. 92 A.H.
tidings of the descent, hastened to repel the invader. Taric, April,
apprized of this through Julian and his followers, appealed 711 A.D.
for additional troops to Musa, who sent him 5000 Arabs.
Thus reinforced, Taric was able now, with 12,000 men, to
hold his ground against the great army of Roderic. They
met on the banks of the Guadalete, to the north of Medina
Sidonia. For a week the issue was uncertain. But there
was treachery in the Spanish camp. The numerous party
opposed to Roderic, buoyed with the hope that the Arabs,
satiated with spoil, would soon recross the sea, and leave
the throne to its proper claimant, fought feebly, and at last
gave way. The Spanish force was routed, and Roderic in
his flight drowned. But the spoil had not the effect ex- His
pected. Instead of retiring, the Arabs, flushed with victory, victories.
stormed Ecija ; and, daily swelled by fresh contingents ix. 92 A.H.
scenting from afar a rich reward, spread themselves over
the land. Malaga and Granada were captured and the
province overrun. The people everywhere fled to the
hills and fortresses, vainly fancied impregnable ; and all the

---

[1] Jebel-Taric, the hill of Taric. [2] Arabic for *peninsula.*

A.H. 86–
96.
quicker, at the fearful report spread by the conquerors that they fed on human flesh. Leaving Cordova besieged by one of his generals, Taric, guided still by Julian, hastened to Toledo, the capital, which to his astonishment he found
Toledo
taken.
deserted by all but Jews. These, delivered from Christian thraldom, now threw in their lot with the invaders (how different from the days of Mahomet!), and were placed in charge of cities which the conquerors found themselves too few to occupy. The inhabitants had all fled in terror, some as far even as Galicia. But it was by no means the policy of the Arabs to make the land a desert. And so the people were gradually tempted back by promise of security, toleration for their religion if only preached unostentatiously, and the establishment of Christian courts. In a city beyond the hills, carried there perhaps for safety, a relic beyond all
Table of
Solomon,
93 A.H.
value fell into Taric's hands, the famous *Table of Solomon*, set with pearls and rubies and all manner of precious stones, and having 360 feet. With this priceless jewel, Taric returned to Toledo, having within the short space of two years reduced the greater part of Spain, and put every enemy to flight that dared to meet him in the field.

Descent
of Musa,
ix. 93 A.H.
June,
712 A.D.
The splendid exploits of his lieutenant made Musa envious. To rival his success, he set out himself with a large force and many warriors of note, and landed in Spain, 93 A.H. Guided in a course which Julian promised him would eclipse the glory of Taric, he struck out a new line of victory, stormed Sidonia, Carmona, and the ancient capital Seville. Merida was laid seige to, and the walls battered by engines. It resisted many months, and the garrison fought with desperate bravery. A spot, our
Merida,
94 A.H.
historian tells us, was still in his day called the 'Martyrs' bastion,' where a column of Moslems was cut to pieces by a party issuing from a hole beneath the wall. At last it fell, and Musa, on the way to Toledo, met Taric at Talavera. He received him angrily, struck him on the head with his whip, and demanded an account of the booty. Friendly relations restored, the famous table was given up to Musa[1].

---

[1] One of the feet was wanting, supplied by a golden substitute. More of this in note below.

The generals then separated, Taric for Saragossa, and A.H. 86-96. Musa for Salamanca and Astorga. Saragossa held out Saragossa. long, and it was not till Musa had rejoined his lieutenant there that by their united efforts it was stormed. Musa then continued his victorious progress to the extreme north-east of Spain, and occupying Tarragona and Barcelona, reached as far even as to Gerona, on the border of France. There, tradition says, he was confronted by an image with the words engraved '*Sons of Ismail, hitherto and no further—Return!*' and so he turned back[1]. Taric, taking a more southerly course, overran the entire coast, reducing Tortosan on the Ebro, Valencia, and other leading cities on his way.

The tidings of Musa's ill-treatment of Taric had mean-Musa while reached the Caliph, who, displeased therewith, and recalled, not unlikely jealous of his independent attitude, sent a 95 A.H. messenger to recall the viceroy to Damascus. The sum-713 A.D. mons met him on a new campaign to the West. Bidding the messenger fall into his train, Musa continued his progress of victory and devastation, till entering Galicia, he came in sight of the blue waves of the northern sea[2]. A second messenger followed him to Lugo, with a sterner and immediate mandate. He was turned out of the camp by the imperious conqueror; who now, however, felt that the summons could no longer be disobeyed. Carrying Taric therefore with him, he turned his face southward: and so marching through the scenes of their unparalleled achievement, the two conquerors made their way back to the straits of Gibraltar. Before quitting Spain, Musa placed his son Abd al Aziz at the head of the government. Two other sons were also put in command, the one at

---

[1] The tradition is curiously proleptic, and shows how fable often enters our annals. The words given are : ' Sons of Ismael ! here is your limit. Go back ! And if ye ask why, I tell you, that otherwise ye shall return to discord among yourselves, so that ye shall slay and behead one another.'

[2] 'Carrying the messenger with him he passed on to new parts, slaying and taking captive, pulling down churches and breaking up their bells, till he reached the high lands overlooking the green ocean. When the second messenger came in the city of Lugo, he seized the reins of his mule and marched him out of the camp,' &c.

A.H. 86–
96.

Cairowan, the other over Western Africa. Perhaps no family at the moment ever enjoyed a wider fame or power more uncontrolled.

Musa's fall, 96 A.H. 114 A.D.

The marvellous achievements of Musa—with but few parallels in history,—were sufficient to have disturbed the equilibrium of any mind. But this will hardly excuse the indiscretion which led the recalled conqueror to make his return through Africa a royal and triumphal progress, and thus justify the suspicions which had no doubt already marked him out at Court as a subject of danger. He carried with him countless store of rare and precious things, laden on endless lines of wagons and camels. A multitude of virgins of noble birth with their attendant maidens, and a vast crowd of Gothic captives in their strange attire, following in his train, attracted the gaze of the astonished people as he passed along[1]. At Cairo he stayed some time, and distributed rich marks of favour among his friends, specially the family of his patron Abd al Aziz, the late governor of Egypt, to whom he owed his rise. The progress was thus so slow that he did not reach Damascus till after the death of Welid. The new Caliph, Soleiman, received him coldly, deposed him from all his commands, cast him into prison, and laid such heavy demands upon him, that he was reduced to poverty, and when released, forced to

Musa's son murdered, 97 A.H. 715 A.D.

beg from his friends the means of living. To add to his misfortune, his son Abd al Aziz, whom he had left to succeed him in Spain, was assassinated, as is supposed, by secret orders from Damascus; and the heartless Soleiman sent his head to the father with an insulting message :—'a grievous error on the Caliph's part,' justly adds the Arabian annalist. Taric also must have retired into private life, for we hear no more of him. The fall of both resembles that of Khalid,—an ungrateful end for the three great conquerors of their age[2].

---

[1] 'Thirty thousand virgins with their attendant maidens': but the whole story of Musa is cast in an extravagant style.

[2] Another, but more romantic, and less likely, narrative is as follows:—

Musa reached Damascus while Welid was yet alive (which, if we look only to the dates, is not improbable). He vaunted himself at court, in depreciation of Taric, as the conqueror of Spain; and among the spoils belonging to him-

The era of Welid was glorious both at home and abroad.
There is no other reign, not excepting even that of Omar,
in which Islam so spread abroad and was consolidated.
We may safely accept the judgment of the impartial
Weil, who tells us that, 'although Mussulman historians,
because of his supporting Hajjaj, call Welid a tyrant, he
is in our eyes the greatest, and in every respect the most
powerful and illustrious, ruler amongst all the Commanders
of the Faithful.' From the borders of China and the
banks of the Indus to the Atlantic, his word was law. In
his reign culture and the arts began to flourish. He enlarged
and beautified the Mosques of Medina and Jerusalem, and
founded one at Damascus, which still exists. He established
schools and hospitals, and made provision for the aged,
blind, and lame. He frequently visited the markets; and
so encouraged manufacture and design, that people began
to take an interest in their advancement. Roads, with wells
at convenient stations, were made throughout the kingdom,
and the comfort of travellers, notably of pilgrims to the
Holy places, specially cared for. More perhaps than
any other Caliph, he knew how to hold the balance
between the Arabian tribal rivalries, and ruled at large
with a powerful hand. If Hajjaj be an exception, Welid,

self and as such presented to the Caliph, was 'Solomon's table.' Taric upon
this claimed that the prize was his, which Musa denied. 'Ask him then,' said
Taric, 'what has become of the lost foot' (see former note). Musa could not
tell; whereupon Taric (who had kept it by him for just such an occasion) produced the wanting piece. And so Welid was satisfied that Musa had really
treated Taric badly.

A curious account is also given of the death of Abd al Aziz, Musa's son.
Himself an excellent man, he fell under the influence of Roderic's widow, who
persuaded him to adopt the courtly habits of the country. His followers being
slow to make courtly obeisance (as resembling prostration at prayer), she had
a low threshold made, through which all had to stoop as they approached the
throne. She also made him wear Roderic's jewelled crown. His followers on
this conspired to slay him as a renegade 97 A.H. Others hold that Soleiman,
probably fearing that Abd al Aziz might assume regal and independent power,
sent orders for his death at the time his father came to grief at court, and that
his enemies fell upon him as he was praying in his chamber with the Coran
before him. 'When the head was sent to his father with the Caliph's cruel
question, "Dost thou recognize it?" he exclaimed,—"Welcome to thy
martyrdom, my son; for truly they did slay thee in thy piety and uprightness."
And it was counted as one of Soleiman's chief misdeeds.'

at the least, held him in better check than did his predecessor. Looking at it from first to last, we shall not
find in the annals of the whole Caliphate a more glorious
reign than that of Welid.

Welid mild
and con-
descending.

As a proof of his mildness and consideration, it is told
of him that when in 91 A.H., on pilgrimage, he visited
Medina and made large presents to the people, the court
of the Mosque was cleared of worshippers, that he might
in company with Omar inspect at leisure the improvements
he had made. One old man alone would neither rise
up nor salute the Caliph. Omar tried hard to divert
the attention of his cousin from the uncourtly worshipper ;
but Welid saw, and at once recognized him. 'How art
thou, Said?' said the Caliph. Without the slightest movement or salutation, the aged man replied :—'Very well,
I am thankful to say, and how doth the Commander of
the Faithful?'—'The last of his race!' said Welid, in admiration of the fast vanishing homeliness and simplicity
which others might have rebuked as uncourtly rudeness.

Death of
Welid,
vi. 96 A.H.
Feb.,
715 A.D.

It has been already noticed that Welid wished to dis-
place his brother Soleiman from being Heir Apparent in
favour of his own son. He died before the change could
be accomplished : but the effect was, not the less, to create
an intense feeling of resentment in the mind of Soleiman,
especially towards Coteiba and the adherents of Hajjaj,
both of whom had encouraged Welid in his design.

Welid was forty-five at his death, and he had reigned
nearly ten years.

CHAPTER LII.

SOLEIMAN.

96–99 A.H.   715–17 A.D.

SOLEIMAN succeeded at once to the throne. It went Soleiman, 96 A.H. 715 A.D.
as a saying at Damascus that Welid's turn was for art;
Soleiman's for the harem and good living; Omar's (the
next to follow) for devotion. The fashion of the Court
changed accordingly. With the first, the talk was of culture; with the second, of slave-girls, marriage, and divorce;
with the third, of austerity, and recitation of the Coran
over night. The prowess of the empire waned under
Soleiman. He was called, indeed, the Key of blessing,—
but only because he nominated Omar for his successor.

He weakened the administration of Spain by conniving Declension in Spain and the East.
at,—if indeed he did not actually order,—the murder of
Abd al Aziz, the able follower of his father Musa; the Christians, profiting by the neglect that followed, rose upon their
conquerors in Asturias, and the mountainous region in the
north. Ibn Casim, the successful invader of India, recalled
as a follower of the hated Hajjaj, came to an evil end.
And under one of the sons of Mohallab (now the favoured
house) that succeeded, the progress of Islam in the far
East slackened, and its prestige declined.

With Coteiba, the death of Welid caused the utmost Rebellion and end of Coteiba.
consternation. Appointed by Hajjaj, he well knew the
bitterness of Soleiman towards all his adherents, and the
danger in which they stood from the enmity of Yezid,
the favourite of the day. In an evil hour, he set up for

himself, and called on the army to join him against the
government. But miscounting his influence, he fatally
overshot the mark. The troops did not respond. The
Yemen faction was hostile, and rallied under an opposing
banner. Fighting thus with but a scanty following, he
was slain, and his head, with those of eleven of his brethren,
sent a welcome offering to the Caliph. And so the conqueror of Bokhara, Samarcand and Kashgar came to an
untimely and dishonoured end. It was said of him by a
Turk, *Coteiba at the world's end was more terrible to us,
than Yezid at our very door.* He had been one of the
greatest heroes of Islam, were not his name stained by
treachery and bloodshed, and his career cut short by a
heedless rebellion.

Yezid, the Caliph's minion, was at first appointed to
Irac, but unwilling to incur unpopularity in collecting the
severe assessments of Hajjaj, which barely sufficed for the
now lavish expenditure at Damascus, he obtained the
nomination of a financial officer to undertake the ungrateful
task. Finding, however, the exchequer thus closed against
his own extravagance, he prevailed on the Caliph, by the
vain boast that his conquests would cast Coteiba's into

the shade, to give him Khorasan. Arriving at Merve
nearly a year after the outbreak of Coteiba, he felt bound
to make good his boast; and casting aside his luxuries,
took the lead of the army, now 100,000 strong, of whom
some 60,000 were Arabs. His efforts were directed to the
tract lying on the south-eastern recess of the Caspian Sea.
There Jorjan and Tabaristan had, as we have seen, been
overrun by Said ibn al Aas so long ago as the reign of
Othman. But though tributary in name, the native rulers,
conscious of their strength, were ever withholding payment of their dues, and no one dared to set foot within
that inaccessible and rebellious region. This region
formed a barrier to communication between Irac and
Merve, and a southern circuit had therefore to be made
by troops and travellers for Central Asia. It was therefore an important object to reduce the intervening space.
Starting from Merve, Yezid first attacked Jorjan; and

its defenders were driven back into their defiles, where after suffering much hardship they came to terms. Here Yezid gave first proof that he might vie with Coteiba in cruelty as well as conquest; for although all who had made terms were spared, the country was ravaged, innumerable captives taken, and multitudes slain in cold blood[1]. Leaving 4000 men in Jorjan, he marched south-west to Tabaristan, where the prince, notwithstanding help from Gilan and Deilem, was discomfited and driven into the hills. Thither the Moslems following were drawn within dangerous defiles, whence severely punished, they were pursued again into the plain. This reverse encouraged the men of Jorjan, breaking their treaty, to fall upon the garrison, and slay them to a man. Alarmed at his rear being thus cut off from Merve, Yezid made peace with Tabaristan; and, turning back to Jorjan, swore a great oath (similar to that of Khalid) that he would not stay his sword till he had eaten bread of corn ground by the blood of his enemies. The city, strongly planted on an eminence, held out for seven months, and then fell into the hands of the inhuman conqueror, who butchering thousands of his victims in an adjoining valley, turned the stream upon a mill that overlooked the ghastly scene, and so fulfilled his oath. He also lined the approaches to the city on the right hand and on the left, for miles, with impaled bodies[2]. Yezid returning to Merve, reported his success to the Caliph, and with a vain-glorious boast magnified the booty into an enormous sum, such as would have yielded four million pieces for the Fifth[3].

To counterbalance the victories in Central Asia, Soleiman had the mortification of finding the vast preparations made to storm Constantinople useless. Shortly before his death, Welid had fitted out a fleet to attack the Byzantine capital by sea, while columns from Armenia and Asia Minor co-

Marginal notes:
A.H. 96–99.

Yezid's campaign in Jorjan and Tabaristan, 98 A.H. 716 A.D.

His cruelty in Joran.

Unsuccessful attack on Constantinople, 96–98 A.H. 714–716 A.D.

---

[1] Tradition places the number at 14,000, which seems hardly credible.

[2] Tradition varies as to the numbers from 12,000 to 40,000; but here again the statement seems incredible.

[3] Another tradition says six millions. His secretary warned him of the danger of making so extravagant an estimate, a danger which, as we shall see, came true.

A.H. 96–
99.
operated by land.   Everything appeared to favour the project.   Rebellion at home had paralysed the Greek power,
while the disloyalty of Leo the Isaurian, who joined hands
with Maslama son of Abd al Melik, the Moslem leader,
afforded the best prospect of success.   Unexpectedly,
Leo himself was raised to the throne, and threw the
98 A.H. unnatural alliance over.   The Moslem troops on both sides
of the Bosphorus were defeated, and suffered such hardship from hunger, frost, and pestilence, that after lying
before Constantinople for a year, the fleet was forced to
retire, and the invasion came to a disastrous and inglorious
end.

Death of
Soleiman,
ii. 99 A.H.
Sept.,
717 A.D.
Soleiman died early in 99 A.H., at Dabic, in the north,
whither he had gone to watch the Byzantine struggle.
A son, nominated his successor, died before him.   On his
death-bed the Caliph wished to appoint another son, a
minor; but was persuaded instead, to name Omar, son
of his father's brother Abd al Aziz so long the governor
of Egypt, and after him his brother Yezid to succeed.
For the nomination of Omar, the memory of Soleiman
is blessed, though he himself receives but little other
praise.   The following incident illustrates his heartless
cruelty, and how the manners of his court did but follow
suit.   On pilgrimage to Mecca, he halted at Medina, where
a convoy of 400 Greek captives were brought into his
camp.   Doomed to death, they were ranged before the royal
assembly for the courtiers and poets in the Caliph's train,
by way of sport, to try their hands upon.   One after
another, these brought their swords down upon the neck
of a wretched captive, and at each ringing stroke, the
head of a victim rolled off.   The turn came to Farazdac,
the poet, who was handed a sword the worse for wear.
Once and again the blow failed of its effect, whereat the
Caliph and those around him jeered.   Upbraided thus
for his awkwardness, Farazdac cast the sword away, and
extemporized some couplets which turned the laugh aside [1].

---

[1] The poetry is indubitable evidence of the cruel tale being founded on
fact.   The point of it lies in this, that a somewhat corresponding failure had
once been experienced by a chief of the Beni Abs.   These were the maternal

Soleiman was not only cruel but dissolute and jealous;
and as such was used to guard his harem by a watch of
eunuchs. Handsome in mien and feature, it is related of
him that at Dabic, arrayed in a green robe and turban,
he looked at himself in the mirror, and said, ' Am I not
the kingly youth?'   A slave-girl stood admiring by;
'What thinkest thou?' he said to her.   ' I was thinking,'
she sang in plaintive verse, ' that thou art the best of joys,
if thou wouldest but remain; yet for mankind there is no
continuing here. No blemish can I see in thee that is
in other men, excepting only that thou, like them, must
pass away.' And he died within the week,—having reigned
two years and a half.

relatives of the Caliph, and it was they who, joining their master, exposed
Faıazdac to the ridicule of the company; and so he adroitly turned the
laugh against them in his stinging verses, which ridiculed the failure of their
own chief.

The first captive brought up, a Patrician, was assigned as a mark of honour
to a great-grandson of Aly, to behead. The poet Jarir was also honoured with
a captive of rank. It is almost incredible that such heartless despite should
have been shown towards human life. But so we read, and that without any
comment or expression of surprise. How low the morale of the court under
Soleiman!

CHAPTER LIII.

OMAR II.

99–101 A.H. 717–20 A.D.

IF Soleiman differed from Welid, Omar differed incomparably more, not only from both, but also from all other Caliphs both before and after him. An unaffected piety, tinged albeit with bigotry, led to uprightness, moderation, and simplicity of life, and to a rule that was eminently just and peaceful. On assuming the Caliphate, the royal grooms brought before him the prancing steeds of the court stables to choose from; but he preferred his own modest equipage. He bade his wife surrender to the treasury the costly jewels given by her father Abd al Melik, else he could no longer live with her; and she obeyed. On Omar's death, her brother succeeding to the throne, offered to restore them, but she, mindful of her husband's wish, declined. Calling his other wives and slave-girls to him, he told them, that as now he had to bear the weight of empire, they must no longer expect from him the same attention and benevolence as before; but it was open to them to leave: they wept, and all declared that they would not be parted from him. In his first oration he invited only those to join his company who would help in doing that which was just and right. Poets, orators, and such like, soon found that his court was no place for them, while it was thronged by the pious, and by

devout divines. His scruples led him sometimes into acts A.H. 99-
of questionable expediency. The demesnes at Fadak, 101.
reserved by the Prophet for public charity[1], but some Pious and
time back wrongfully appropriated by Merwan for the bigoted, but just.
expenses of the court, were now restored to their original
use ; and this, with other resumptions of the kind, created
ill-feeling in the royal house. His devotion to Islam prejudiced him against the employment of Jews and Christians: and in a rescript addressed to his lieutenants he
bade them exalt the true faith, abase all others, and
appoint none but Moslems to offices of trust,—quoting
verses of the Coran in support of his command[2]. He was
also hard and unpitiful in exacting from those of other
creeds the severest burdens it was lawfully to impose.
But whatever the bigotry or even fanaticism of his rule,
and however much he may have sought to proselytize by
favouring his own religion, his justice in administering
the law according to the dictates of Islam, was surpassed
by none. When he was appealed to by the Christians of
Damascus to give them back the Church of St. John,
turned by Welid into the city Mosque,—though unable to
concede their request, he restored to them other churches,
which under the capitulation should have been theirs,
in compensation.

Hitherto in the public prayers on Friday throughout Discon-
the empire, a petition cursing Aly had been in use. tinues im-precation
The imprecation was now withdrawn. A sense of duty on Aly.
no doubt led to this action, justified, as he thought, by
a passage in the Coran, which enjoins justice and kindness towards relatives[3]. When a schoolboy at Medina,
the practice was denounced to him by a holy man, whose
teaching he adopted, and never departed from. Omar
had urged his father to discontinue it when governor
of Egypt, who replied that the cessation, however otherwise right and proper, would damage the Omeyyady reign,
and favour transfer of the Caliphate to the house of Aly.
The imprecation was resumed after Omar's death. But

---

[1] *Life of Mahomet,* pp. 516–548.   [2] Coran iii. 118 ; v. 58.
[3] Coran xvi. 90.

A.H. 99-
101.
its temporary abolition did no doubt stimulate the movement then taking shape against the Omeyyad dynasty.

Kharejite
rising in
Irac,
100 A.H.
In the second year of his reign there was a theocratic
rising in Irac that did not differ from others of its kind,
excepting that from the leniency of Omar it gained a
dangerous head, requiring in the end 10,000 men to put
it down. His conduct was certainly here characterised
by weakness. Though up in arms against him, he forbade
them to be attacked until they had first shed blood. He
sent for their leaders, to argue their grievances and traitorous tenets out with them. He heard their scruples
patiently and answered them, but without effect. What
troubled him most was their plea that, though he might
himself be orthodox and saintly, yet the godless Yezid
would succeed him. Omar could only answer that with
succession to the throne he could not interfere, as it had
been so provided by the same authority from which his
own title was derived. The theocratic faction was stimulated by Omar's concessions to their prejudices; and
equally so were the Omeyyad family troubled at his
attitude, as dangerous to their dynasty[1].

Efforts at
conversion
in Africa
and Spain.
There is not much to record of adventure, military or
administrative, in the reign of Omar. His first concern
was to bring safely back what remained of the armament
so bootlessly launched by his predecessors against Constantinople. Large supplies of food and carriage were, for
this end, sent to Maslama, and the withdrawal was successfully carried out. Elsewhere the efforts of Omar were
mainly marked by endeavours to convert the people to
Islam. Among the Berbers these were most successful.
But in Spain the task was not so easy; and therefore, to
reduce the influence of the Christians, their lands were
divided amongst the conquerors. A royal mosque was
also founded in this reign at Saragossa. To promote
conversion in the East, Omar addressed a rescript to the
kings of Sind, inviting them to embrace Islam, with the

---

[1] It is even asserted that they set one to poison his drink, and that of this he
died. But this is not consistent with other traditions, and looks like a fabrica-
tion of the Abbasside enemies of the Omeyyad line.

promise of thereby enjoying all the privileges and im-
munities of the Arab race. This they did, and obtained
Arabian names, but again, in the reign of Hisham, apo-
statized.

The most marked event, however, in the reign of Omar,
was the arraignment of Yezid, son of Mohallab. Even
Soleiman is said to have become dissatisfied with his favourite ; and Omar, regarding him now as a tyrant, summoned
him to give an account of his stewardship in Khorasan.
Yezid no sooner set foot in Irac than he was put in chains,
and so conducted to Damascus. Omar held him to the
letter of his reported victories and prize in Central Asia.
In vain Yezid protested that the report was made to
magnify the achievement in the people's eyes, and that
he had never thought of being called to account for the
exact amount which he had named. Omar would none
of the excuse ; Yezid must produce a reckoning of the
whole, and make good what was due. Finally, he was
banished in coarse prison dress to an island in the Red
Sea.   But warned of his dangerous aims even in that
isolated place, the Caliph removed him to Aleppo, where
he was kept in strict confinement. His son, whom he had
left to take his place at Merve, came to intercede for him,
but in vain ; and dying shortly after, Omar performed the
funeral service over him, saying that he was a better man
than his father. Yezid had fancied Omar to be but a sanctimonious hypocrite; he now found him terribly in earnest ;
but he had reason to fear his successor even more. On
hearing that Omar had sickened, he bribed the guard, and
effected his escape to Bussorah, where he raised a dangerous rebellion, as we shall in the sequel see.

The policy pursued in Khorasan and Central Asia after
the recall of Yezid is another evidence that the Caliph was
more intent on the spread of the faith than on temporal
aggrandisement.   There were loud cries of harshness and
exaction from the professed converts of Khorasan. Omar
sent for a deputation of these to represent their grievances,
and finding their complaint well-founded, deposed Jarrah
the Viceroy, and insisted that all who said the creed and

joined in the religious services should be exempt from burdens, and placed on the same footing as themselves. To consolidate his rule, he stayed the sword against outlying countries, and called in the garrisons and columns that had been settled in those heathen parts. In all the provinces retained, the people finding now the comfort and advantages of conversion, began to flock in multitudes to the faith. At first they were tested by their willingness to be circumcised; but Omar hearing of it, forbade a test nowhere enjoined in the Coran; 'for Mahomet,' said he, ' was sent to call men to the faith, not to circumcise them.' The burdens on unbelievers were imposed, as elsewhere, to the utmost, but justice towards them must be observed. No churches, synagogues, or fire-temples were to be destroyed: but the erection of new ones was forbidden. The policy of Omar was thus to fill Khorasan and the adjoining districts with a population of contented believers; to consolidate the faith and cast the sword aside. And in this policy, so far as his short and transient reign allowed, he was successful.

Death of a pious son.
A son of seventeen died before him. Some touching passages are related of his conversation with this youth, who was like-minded with his father in high religious aspiration. He urged his father to enforce reform and bring back society to the primitive practice of what was right. Omar replied that he had done what he could by gentle means, but if Moslem rule were to be regenerated as his son desired, it must be accomplished by force; and 'there is no good,' said he, 'in that reform which can only be enforced by the sword.'

Attractive character.
Though devoid of stirring events, there is much that is attractive and instructive in the reign of Omar. It is a relief, amidst bloodshed, intrigue, and treachery, to find a Caliph devoted to what he believed the highest good both for himself and for his people. The saint might be morbid, over-scrupulous, and bigoted; but there are few, if any, throughout this history, whose life leaves a more pleasing impression on the reader's mind than that of Omar.

It was the middle of 101 A.H., after a reign of nearly two years and a half, that Omar sickened. In a few weeks he died, and was buried at Dair Saman, near Hims. He was succeeded by his cousin Yezid, son of Abd al Melik, according to his brother Soleiman's last will.

A.H. 99–101.

Death of Omar II, Reyab, 101 A.H. Jan., 720 A D.

CHAPTER LIV.

YEZID II.

101–105 A.H.   720–24 A.D.

Yezid II,
101 A.H.
720 A.D.

THE Kharejite outbreak in Irac had hardly been quelled when a more serious rising threatened Yezid II,—the rebellion of his namesake Yezid, son of Mohallab. The accession of the new Ruler revived the tribal jealousies. His wife was niece to Hajjaj ; and so throwing over the Yemen faction, Yezid II took up the cause of the family and adherents of Hajjaj, all of whom, as we have seen, had been sorely pursued by Soleiman. The favourite of Soleiman, Yezid had, unfortunately as it now turned out for himself, carried out the orders of his patron with great severity, and had confiscated to a vast amount the wealth which the present Caliph's wife in-

Rebellion
of Yezid,
son of
Mohallab.

herited from her father. Yezid had turned a deaf ear to her cry ; and so her husband, the present Caliph, had threatened that if he ever came to power, he would cut him into a thousand pieces. This was the reason why Yezid, when he heard of Omar's last sickness, and knew that his enemy must succeed, escaped from prison, and fled to Bussorah. There he rallied numerous friends around him, for with all his failings Yezid was free and openhanded, and having attacked the palace, slew the governor, seized the treasury, and by profuse largess raised a threatening force. The Caliph, now alarmed, sent to offer a free pardon ; but Yezid had too deeply compromised himself,

and must fight to the bitter end.　The rebellion gained
so great a head, that Yezid was able to send governors
to Fars, Kerman, and other centres in the East.　At
Bussorah all the adherents of Hajjaj that fell into his hands
were slain, but the chief men of the city, even such as
favoured Yezid, fearing to compromise themselves with
the Court, made their escape to Kufa.　Yezid himself
settled down inactive at Bussorah, till tidings of an army
80,000 strong advancing from Syria under command of
Maslama, the Caliph's brother, forced him to take the field.
His brothers urged him to leave Irac and occupy Khorasan,
or the strongholds in the nearer mountains, where the
discontented would flock to him, and thus weary out the
Syrian force ; but he declined to be ' like the bird that
flies from hill top to hill top,' and so moving forward he
occupied Wasit.　Maslama advanced on Kufa, where there
was a strong party in favour of Yezid ; and having deposed
the governor, with difficulty suppressed a rising.　Then
crossing the Euphrates, he took ground on the left bank
of the river.　Yezid, leaving one of his brothers with a
strong reserve at Wasit, marched against his enemy.
A week passed in skirmishing and single combats.　Then
Yezid attacked the Caliph's army by night, but they were
on the alert and the onset failed.　Next day there was a
great battle.　Yezid harangued his army, denouncing the
Omeyyads as a godless race, against whom it were a more
sacred duty to war than against the Turks, and thus bring
back the pure observances of their holy faith,—words
that must have sounded strange from the lips of the
unprincipled worldling.　On the other side, to nerve his
men by making retreat impossible, Maslama set fire to
the bridge behind them.　The rebel army, unable to **His defeat**
sustain the Syrian onset, fell back ; and Yezid, hearing **and death.**
that his favourite brother was killed, rushed upon the
enemy's ranks, crying that life after that was no longer
worth living, and was slain.　On this, his brothers, unable
to hold their position at Wasit, retired, after beheading
all the prisoners in their hands ; and, with wives and
children, took ship by the gulf to a fortress in Kerman,

hoping that its governor, who owed his post to Yezid,
would give his family and kindred shelter. But they
were mistaken ; the brothers were put to death, and the
women and children sold into slavery[1]. Equally cruel
with the fate of the prisoners at Wasit was that of
those at Kufa, where 300 were by the Caliph's orders
slain. In companies of twenty and thirty, they were
brought out, some of them naked, and decapitated in cold
blood. Thus the Caliph slaked his wrath against the
faction hostile to Hajjaj. And so perished the house
of Mohallab, none of whose descendants were meet representatives of that great man. The butcheries and
contempt of human life we now so often read of, are a
painful feature of the day. The cruel scene, however, is
but a fit ending to the career of the man who drove the
corn-mill of Jorjan with his victims' blood.

Rising in
Khorasan,
102–104
A.H.
The services of Maslama in this dangerous rebellion, and
in the campaign against the Greeks, were rewarded by the
government of Irac and Khorasan. As his lieutenant at
Merve, Maslama appointed his son-in-law Said, a weak man,
called in derision *Khozeina*, from affecting in his dress the
attire of a Persian lady. The choice was far from fortunate.
There was a general rising of the hordes in Khojend and
Ferghana, which became dangerous owing to inactivity
on the Moslem side. The tributary Soghdians, threatened
by these, sought protection from Merve ; but help being
slow of coming, they meanwhile made overtures to the
Turks, and between the two suffered grievously. When
Moslem forces did arrive, the Soghdians returned at first
to their allegiance. Information, however, reached the
Moslem general of the murder of an Arab,—for numbers
of Arabians and Persians had begun to settle in the
land,—and he sent for the culprit, and slew him in his
tent. The Soghdians retaliated by putting to death the
Mussulman prisoners in their hands, 150 in number ;
whereon the general fell upon the Soghdian residents,

---

[1] A cruel and apparently unlawful act in the case of women professing the
faith of Islam.

who having been meanwhile disarmed, had only staves A.H. 101- 105. wherewith to defend themselves. The whole, 3000 in number, fell by the sword[1]. Fighting went on more or less throughout the reign in these outlying provinces, but with no very marked results.

Maslama being unequal to the difficult task of collecting Irac, Asia Minor, and Armenia, 102–104 A.H. the revenue in Irac, the government was given to Omar Ibn Hobeira, an ambitious scion of the Fezara tribe, in reward for his military service. He had distinguished himself in the campaign against the Kharejites, and more recently on the northern border of Mesopotamia. In Asia Minor, the Moslem possessions were quiet. But towards the North-east several heavy, and not always fortunate, operations were carried on against the Khizr, Kiphjak, and other hordes inhabiting the mountain region between the Black and Caspian seas. The first army sent thither 104 A.H. suffered a bad defeat, losing their camp, and being driven out of the country. A second force retrieved the disaster, and occupied Balanja and other important cities; but incautiously pressing their advance too far, were overtaken by winter, and were surrounded and cut off by Turcoman hordes. The Caliph promised fresh support, but dying shortly after, left the task to his successor.

In Africa things went from bad to worse. The Caliph ap- Africa. pointed one who had been a favourite secretary of Hajjaj as governor ; and he, practising the harsh tactics he had learned of his master, against the converted Berbers, roused an insurrection which ended in his death, and relaxed the bonds of discipline and attachment to the Court.

Spain, as a dependency of Africa, was in an even less Spain.

---

[1] Another tradition says 7000, which, even with any conventional margin, seems incredible. The Soghdian merchants were allowed to retire before the massacre. A romantic story is told of the fort of Bahli, occupied by a clan of the Soghdians who remained loyal. One of the Turcoman generals wished to marry a lady in the fort ; on her refusal they besieged the place. A Moslem column came on the scene just as they were on the point of surrendering from thirst. The Turks were attacked and routed. They fled out of sight, and the Mussulmans meanwhile bore away every man, woman, and child to a place of safety. The Turks returning, found the fortress empty, not a soul to be seen, and declared that it was the genii who had done the miracle.

A.H. 101–
105.
___
satisfactory relation to the Caliphate. Its authority being
mediate and intermittent, the governing hand, strong
elsewhere, was for this great conquest changeful and
often weak, while the leaders, though valiant in the field,
were in the civil branch intent chiefly on their own aggrandisement. In the year 100 A. H., the Moslem troops,
attracted by the weakness of France, which was at the
moment torn by internal discord, and by the hatred of
the native race to their new masters from the north,
made an inroad into the southern provinces. Ravaging
the land as far as Nismes, they returned to Spain laden
with booty. Tempted by this success, two or three years
after they again crossed the Pyrenees, stormed Narbonne
and garrisoned its fortress as their permanent head-quarters.
Advancing, they laid siege to Toulouse, but were forced to
raise it on the approach of the enemy, by whom they were
put disastrously to flight. The scattered fragments rallied
under the banner of the famous Abd al Rahman[1], and
found a safe retreat in Narbonne. But the reverse, bruited
far and wide, emboldened the Northern Spaniards, who had
already in Asturias thrown off the yoke, to fresh efforts
against the Moslems, on whom about this time they inflicted
a serious defeat. The mountainous region was a source of
strength to them; and there the seeds of a new power were
being sown, which in the fulness of time brought Moslem
rule to an end in Spain[2].

*Inroad into France.
100 A .H.
718 A·D.*

*Pyrenees crossed again,
103 A.H.*

Alyite and Abbasside canvass.
In a reign so weak and so unpopular, it is no wonder
that intrigue on the part of the Alyites, and now also on
that of the descendants of Abbas (of whose designs mention
is now for the first time made), gained ground throughout
the East. A deputation from Irac canvassing the cause, in
the harmless garb of merchants, was arrested in Khorasan
and taken before 'Khozeina.' But he, listening to their
feigned story, and accepting the guarantee of their friends,
allowed them to go. And so the cause insidiously grew.

Last of the Companions.
Year by year, tradition has up to this time been chro-

[1] Or, as he is called by European writers, Abderame.
[2] The Moslems lost Narbonne, and were finally driven out of France in
759 A. D. See M. Reinaud's *Invasions des Sarrazins,* Paris, 1836.

nicling the death of aged men who having been in the society A.H. 101–105. of Mahomet, are dignified as his *Companions*. Such notices, by the lapse of time, now come to a natural close. In 89 A.H. the last two of these who lived in Syria died, one aged 100, the other, a 'Companion who had seen the two Kiblas [1].' Others survived in Irac for a year or two later. But the last of all who had seen and known the Prophet, died at Mecca in the year 101 [2]. 'Companions' enjoyed a high distinction in Moslem society. They would have done so under any circumstances, as having seen and conversed with Mahomet himself. But a fresh value as time went on began to attach to their words. The Coran, Collectors at first the sole guide in all concerns, social, legal, and of tradition. spiritual, was gradually found inadequate for the novel wants of an ever-expanding Moslem world. The word and wont (*sunnat*) of the Prophet was thus called in to supplement it. Collectors of tradition, accordingly, sprang up everywhere, who sought out 'Companions' from the ends of the earth, and spent their lives in taking down their remembrance of incidents connected with the life of Mahomet. Nothing, however trivial, came amiss; for every word and every act might form a precedent hereafter in social or legal obligation. The profession thus came to be one of high repute, and hundreds of thousands of traditions have been handed down of every shade of credibility, upon which to a great extent the law and custom of Islam has been built, and which incidentally also have given us a clear and authentic view of the Prophet's life itself.

Early in his reign Yezid was persuaded to nominate as Hisham successor his brother Hisham, and after him his own son nominated successor. Welid, then but eleven years of age. Homage was done

---

[1] That is, remembered when Mahomet prayed with his face towards Jerusalem as his Kibla, before he changed towards Mecca. See *Life of Mahomet*, p. 198.

[2] His name is Amir Abul Tufeil. Others are mentioned as dying in this year who were born in Mahomet's lifetime; but they had not seen him. One of these died in 98 A.H. over 100 years old. He had gone as a boy to Medina to make confession of his faith to Mahomet, but arrived just after his death, and so never saw him alive; another is mentioned as surviving till 109 A.H., who must have been over 100.

A.H. 101–
105.

Yezid's
passion
for a slave
girl.

to both accordingly throughout the empire. A few years later he repented that he had not given the succession immediately to his son ; but did not venture on a change.

Yezid had even a greater passion for the harem than any of his predecessors, but it was more fixed and constant. We are told of a slave-girl Habîba and a songstress Sallâma. His attachment to the former was so great that he did not many days survive her death. He had retired with her for a season to a garden retreat in Palestine, and there, casting playfully a grape-stone into her mouth, it choked her, and she died upon the spot. For three days he clung weeping to her relics. At last he was persuaded to let her be buried. The funeral service was performed by his brother Maslama, who feared that if the Caliph were seen by the people, they would be scandalized at the extravagance of his grief. He never recovered composure or self-control, and died within a week. The cry of Sallâma, who was tending his last moments, was the first intimation of the fact to his family and attendants [1].

Death of
Yezid II
vii. 105A.H.
Jan.,
724 A.D.

Yezid II died at the age of forty, having reigned a little over four years ;—an inglorious reign, which failed to stay, if it did not actually hasten, the decadence of the Omeyyad house. He was succeeded by his brother Hisham, another son of Abd al Melik.

---

[1] The romantic tale of Habîba throws a strange light on the royal harem, and the conditions of its domestic life. Some years before his accession, when on pilgrimage to Mecca, Yezid purchased her for 4000 pieces of gold ; but his brother Soleiman, then Caliph, was displeased at the purchase ; and so he returned her to the merchant, who then sold her to an Egyptian. When Yezid succeeded to the throne, his wife, a grand-daughter of Othman, said one day to him,—'Is there yet any one thing in the world, my love, left thee to desire ? ' 'Yes,' he answered, 'and it is Habîba.' 'So she sent to Egypt and bought the object of his heart's desire. Then having adorned her as a bride, she seated her on a couch in an inner chamber behind a curtain, and called her husband ; and as they talked, again she asked " Is there aught yet in the world left for thee to long after ? " " Yea, and thou knowest it all thyself." So she drew the curtain aside, and saying, " Yes, I know it ; there sits Habîba waiting for thee," she arose and left them together. And Yezid loved his wife all the more for it.'

CHAPTER LV.

CALIPHATE OF HISHAM.—CONTINUED DECADENCE OF OMEYYAD DYNASTY.

105–125 A.H.   724–43 A.D.

HISHAM now entered peaceably on a long reign. Exemplary as a true believer, he banished, like Omar II, from his Court all things inconsistent with the profession of Islam, and his mild and generally upright administration might have restored prosperity to the empire, had not the evil genius of his predecessors still cast its blight upon the throne. There was much besides to cause depression. His lieutenants were not always happily chosen, and they so played upon his two defects of character, avarice and suspicion, as sometimes to betray him into unguarded and cruel action, as well as cause him to miss the friendship and popularity which a well-timed liberality would have secured. Military enterprise was nowhere successful in his reign, and indeed repeatedly suffered severe disaster. From the first, Hisham threw himself into the arms of the Yemen party, and thus alienated from his rule the opposing faction.

Hisham, 105 A.H. 724 A.D.

From early times, anterior even to the birth of Mahomet, there existed a rivalry between the two chief stocks of the Coreish, the descendants namely of Hashim and of Omeyya[1].

---

[1] See *Life of Mahomet*, pp. xxii. and 570. This table will explain the relation between the two branches, the Hashimite and the Omeyyad :—

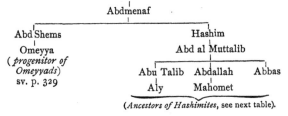

(*Ancestors of Hashimites*, see next table).

A.H. 105–
125.

Antago-
nism be-
tween the
houses of
Hashim
and
Omeyya.

The Prophet, sprung from the former, suffered bitter opposition, both in field and forum, from the Omeyyads, till the conquest of Mecca converted the whole body of the Coreish, and welded friend and foe equally within the bonds of Islam. In the first enthusiasm of the faith, all distinctions of the kind vanished. But they gradually came to life again, and burst out fiercer than ever on the murder of Othman, and in the struggle between Muavia and Aly; while the Kharejites, who were continually rising in rebellion, recognized neither the one house nor the other but demanded a purely theocratic rule. Things calmed down in the lengthened reign of Muavia. But the tragic end of Hosein and his family at Kerbala, caused a strong reaction towards the house of Aly; and so there arose the party called Shie-ites (or Sectaries), advocating the divine right of succession in that line, and in it alone;—a doctrine which began to be busily but secretly circulated by a widely scattered and disloyal body[1].

Claim of
Moham-
med de-
scendant of
Abbas.

But now another and more dangerous aspirant came upon the scene. This was Mohammed, great-grandson of Abbas, the Prophet's uncle. No pretensions had been heretofore advanced by this branch of the Hashimite stock. The idea of their right to the sovereignty was of recent growth, and it was not till the present reign that it took definite shape in supersession of the house of Aly. The Abbasside advocates, to conciliate the Shie-ite interest, spread the report that the son of Hosein (the 'Hanefite' pretender) had on his death-bed bequeathed his right to Mohammed. Whether this be so or no, the plea of both parties was based in common on the immeasurable superiority of the branch from which the Prophet sprang, over the Omeyyad. These latter were moreover incessantly maligned by Alyites and Hashimites alike, as sprung from the enemies of Mahomet, as persecutors of his descendants,—a wicked and dissolute race of tyrants, neglectful of the sanctions of Islam, given to wine and hounds, music and singing, and revelry, in short to every

---

[1] Shia (Sheea) means 'sect'; and so the sect or branch holding these views are called 'Shie-ites.'

kind of profanity ;—charges, indeed, for which the dynasty A.H. 105-125.
had too often given good ground.

Deputations from Mohammed, who lived in a retreat to Abbasside canvass.
the south of Palestine, frequently visited Khorasan, in the
garb of merchants. They plotted in secret, and though
often discovered and put to a cruel death, persevered in
their canvass and nursed the cause. Such emissaries
burrowed busily in the purlieus of all the great towns
throughout the East, and the Abbassides began to gain
in name and popularity throughout Irac and Persia, as well
as Khorasan[1].

One of Hisham's first acts was to supersede Omar Ibn Khalid governor of Kufa, 105 A.H.
Hobeira in the government of Irac, to which he nominated
Khalid, a favourite courtier of Yemenite descent. Ibn
Hobeira met the too common fate in those days of fallen
rulers, being cast into prison and tortured for arrears of
revenue. He escaped, but was pursued and murdered.
The Caliph caused the murderer to be put to death ; but
contented himself with an expression of displeasure towards Khalid, who had apparently instigated the deed.
Khalid gave his brother Asad the command in Khorasan,
and himself continued for fifteen years in the government
of Irac. Towards the end of that period there were several

---

[1] The relation of the Shie-ite, or Alyite family, to that of the Abbassides, as
descended respectively from Abbas and Abu Talib, uncles of the Prophet, will
appear from this tree :—

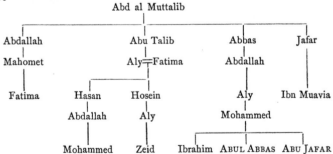

Abul Abbas (Saffah) and Abu Jafar were the first two Abbasside Caliphs.
Aly, Mohammed's father, having given offence to the Caliph Abd al Melik by
marrying a wife divorced by him, and being on that account ill-treated at court,
had retired to Homeima, a village on the borders of Arabia, where the alleged
transfer of the Hanefite's rights is said to have taken place.

A.H. 105–
125.

Kharejite
outbreaks
in Irac,
118–119
A.H.
Kharejite outbreaks. One of these, led by a sorcerer, though followed by only a few disciples, is remarkable for the strange doctrines, such as the divinity of Aly, held by them, as well as for their barbarous end. They were burnt to death at the stake with faggots steeped in naphtha. Another of a more serious character was raised by a man from Wasit, who declaimed against the use of wine, and denounced Khalid as 'the son of a Christian' (his mother having been of that faith), 'who let mosques go to ruin, while he builded churches and synagogues, gave office to magicians, and favoured marriage between Moslems and unbelievers.' The cause was popular. Great numbers rallied under his black standard and fought with determined bravery. Twice they routed considerable columns sent against them, and it was only by an army drawn at once from Syria, Kufa, and Mosul, that they were at last dispersed and their leader slain. Several other equally fanatical insurrections had to be put down by military force. The leader of one of these, after committing many outrages, was brought in wounded, with a body of his followers. Khalid, astonished by his doctrine and knowledge of the Coran, sought to spare him : but the Caliph resented his repeated intercession ; and so with his whole company the rebel was committed to the flames, all the while reciting passages from the Coran. He died with this verse on his lips : ' Say, the fire of hell is fiercer in its heat, if they but knew it[1].' Such was the wild fervour of these fanatics.

Apart from such insurrections, which in themselves caused some anxiety, Khalid, after many years of faithful service, at last lost the favour of his master, who either suspected embezzlement, or was jealous, perhaps not without cause, of disloyal attachment to the house of Hashim[2]. He therefore appointed Yusuf, governor of Yemen, to succeed him. Without warning, Yusuf ap-

---

[1] *Sura* ix. 82.

[2] He possibly was so in reality, though not openly. When accused of partiality towards the house of Aly, and of lending them money, he answered how could that be, when every day he cursed Aly in the public prayers ; but that the people said was merely to curry favour.

peared at Kufa to Khalid's dismay, carrying with him A.H. 105–
125.
the Caliph's command to realize with all due severity the
last farthing of arrears, from 'the son of the Nazarene'
and his lieutenants. Yusuf was nothing loth to execute
his commission ; for he sorely hated Khalid as the per-
secutor of his clansman, the son of Hobeira. It was now
the turn of the officers of Khalid to be cruelly treated,
and on himself a demand was made altogether beyond his
power to liquidate. He was tortured (meet reward for the
cruel treatment of his predecessor) and cast into prison.
After a year and a half, the Caliph ordered his release,
and allowed him, against the reclamations of Yusuf, to join
the army then fighting against the Greeks. But in the
next reign, as we shall see, he was again pursued by the
relentless hate of Yusuf.

The supersession of Khalid was highly unpopular, espe- Yusuf ap-
cially with the Yemenite clan in Irac. His successor, pointed to
succeed
besides being of Modhar blood, had already distinguished him.
himself, by a tyrannous administration in South Arabia.
He is praised, indeed, for restoring the prestige of Islam,
and humiliating the Jewish and Christian faiths. But
though devout and given to long prayers, soft in speech,
and a master in poetry, Yusuf was of a cruel and even Canvass
savage nature[1]. In the course of his enquiries, he dis- of Zeid,
grandson
covered that Khalid had made over large sums of money of Hosein.
to Zeid, a grandson of Hosein, suspected of pretensions
to the throne. The Caliph summoned him to his presence,
and, dissatisfied with his attitude, sent him for further

---

[1] For example, he was capricious about his garments, and chastised the
tailor if they were not fitting to his taste. He would draw his nail across
the stuff, and if it stuck anywhere, have the weaver beaten, or even his hand cut
off. His secretary one day, slack at work, complained of tooth-ache as the
cause ; the barber removed the suffering tooth, and the next one also as a
punishment. One of the tales passes belief. Preparing for a journey, he
asked one of his slave-girls whether she wished to follow ; on her answering in the affirmative, he abused her as thinking of nothing but love, and had
her beheaded : a second, preferring to stay with her child, shared the same
fate. A third replied in terror that she knew not what to say, as either way
she must give offence, and for presuming thus to argue, she too was beheaded.
The currency of such tales, even if not actually founded on fact, shows what a
tyrant they had to deal with, and also throws a lurid light on the habits and
morals of the day.

A.H. 105– inquiry to Yusuf. Zeid, however, managed to retire into
125. privacy, and canvassed the Arab tribes in Irac, living now
with one and now with another, and ingratiating himself
especially by frequent matrimonial alliances with maidens
of the Yemen line[1]. He soon accepted homage as the
rightful Caliph from thousands in Kufa and its vicinity,
with the pledge to fight under his banner. This went on
for months. At last his followers urged him, 'now that the
full time had come for the downfall of the Omeyyad house,'
no longer to delay. It is significant of the yet undefined
relation of the two branches of the Hashimite stock,—the
descendants of Aly and those of Abbas,—that Daud, one
of the latter, sought to dissuade him from a step so premature. He bid him not to trust in his twenty, or even
forty thousand[2]; 'for think,' he said, 'how many of the
80,000 fickle Kufans pledged to fight for Hosein, stood by
him in the hour of need?' The advice was good, but
unheeded. In one respect the theocratic zealots were
dissatisfied with Zeid; for, like Zobeir, he declined to say
that Abu Bekr and Omar were usurpers of the Caliphate.
Apart, however, from any such scruples, the light-hearted
and pleasure-loving Kufans were hardly prepared for a
serious rising. They were ready enough to covenant, but
His rebel- lacked the covenanting spirit. At last Zeid fixed the day.
lion at
Kufa, Secret information reached Yusuf, who, from his palace in
122 A.H. the vicinity at Hira, gave command for the citizens to be
740 A.D. gathered, both for safety and lest perchance they too might
rise, into the court of the Great mosque. During the night
the Shie-ite banner paraded the city, with the old battle-cry,
Ya Mansur! In the early morning, Zeid issued forth,

---

[1] The names of two are given. A charming lady, but of mature years, came
to do homage as an ardent Shie-ite; and Zeid, her age notwithstanding, asked
her to be his bride. Excusing herself on her being no longer young, she suggested that her daughter, fairer and more elegant than she, would be more
suitable. Zeid laughed, and was well pleased to accept the daughter in the
mother's stead.

[2] The numbers are variously given at from 15,000 to 40,000. These all took
an oath 'to set up the Book and the testimony and godly discipline, to follow
the descendants of the Prophet, and to fight against the enemies of the same
both in secret and in public.' Whereupon the covenanter placed his hand within
Zeid's, and the obligation and homage were complete.

expecting to find a multitude ready to salute him. There
were but 218. Nevertheless, he made his progress through
the streets, driving the police and soldiery before him,
from quarter to quarter, but with little other result. He
was watched by Yusuf and the chief men of Kufa from
afar. 'Where are my men,' he cried, 'the 40,000 men that
pledged their troth to me?' but none responded to the
martial call. A follower answered, more sanguine than the
rest, 'They are shut up within the Mosque; let us march
and set them free.' Arrived there, they waved their banners high over the gates, and shouted, 'Come from shame
to glory; come forth for this world and also for the
next; of neither have ye now any part nor lot!' But the
answer was only a shower of stones. Darkness coming
on, Zeid retired to the great storehouse of the city, where
with his little company he passed the night. Next morning he was attacked by a Syrian column, which he bravely
met, and killing seventy drove them back from place to place.
So passed the day; but as night set in, an arrow struck Defeated
him on the temple. He was carried to the house of a and slain.
follower, where, so soon as the arrow was drawn, he died.
They buried him secretly; but Yusuf discovering the place,
sent the head to Hisham, and had the body, with those of
the other leaders, hung up in a public place. The head
was stuck for a time on one of the gates of Damascus, and
then sent to be similarly exhibited at Medina. The body
remained exposed at Kufa till Welid II, on his accession,
had it taken down and burned.

This emeute, though apparently unimportant in itself, Abbasside
proved the turning-point in the destiny of the house of Aly. way cleared
thereby.
Although Yahya, the son of Zeid, escaped, to the Caliph's
great mortification, the Shie-ite cause had hopelessly
collapsed. Up to this time, the aspiration of the Abbassides, as descendants of the Prophet's uncle, had paled before
that of the Alyites, in whose veins ran the blood of the
Prophet himself. The Hashimite interest in the impending canvass now centred in the Abbassides alone, and they
were able to enter upon it with invigorated hope and redoubled effort. The Omeyyads could have done their

A.H. 105-
125.
antagonists no better service than thus rid them of such dangerous rivals in the struggle for the throne[1].

Various
campaigns
in Kho-
rasan.
Throughout the twenty years of this reign, the Moslem arms suffered many reverses beyond the Oxus, where things at the last remained pretty much as at the first.

Asad,
brother of
Khalid,
105-109.
Asad had been early appointed by his brother Khalid as lieutenant there. But he was a tyrant, and having inflicted chastisement on certain leading men, who had incurred his displeasure, was recalled. During this period, the Khacan with his hordes kept the country in chronic disquiet; and there was at least one serious defeat, the Moslem host being surrounded for many days, and with difficulty effecting its escape. An emeute also, causing some anxiety, broke out between the Yemen and Modhar tribes, which ended, not without bloodshed, in favour of the latter.

Ashras,
109-111
A.H.
Ashras, the new governor, threw the entire country of Bokhara and Soghd into rebellion by his breach of faith in first promising remission of capitation-tax for all who embraced Islam, and again reimposing it. The rebels were supported by the Khacan, and the Moslems suffered

Joneid
succeeds.
greatly at his hands[2]. In 111 A.H., to better matters, Joneid was transferred from Sind[3]; but though an able warrior, he was less fortunate even than his predecessor. On his way to join the army at Bokhara, he narrowly

---

[1] It is true that there was extant another branch descended from Aly, the progeny namely of Hasan, brother of Hosein; but like Hasan himself, who resigned the Caliphate into the hands of Muavia, they had but little ambition. An amusing, but not very edifying, account is preserved of a disputation held before Khalid (who is supposed to have had Shie-ite leanings) between Zeid as descendant of *Hosein*, and the head of the house of *Hasan*, who both, in gross Arab style, fell to abusing each other's mothers. But the descendants of Hasan never seem as yet to have taken any practical step as aspirants to the throne.

[2] For example, Kamanja, 'one of the greatest cities in Khorasan, and full of Mussulmans,' was beseiged by the Khacan for fifty-eight days with innumerable hordes drawn from Ferghana, Nasaf, and the country all around Bokhara. A chief having been killed by an arrow from the battlements, the Turks slew the Mussulman prisoners, 100 in number, and cast their heads over the wall into the citadel, on which the Moslems in revenge slew 200 hostages in their hands. At last, driven to extremities for water, the siege was raised on condition that the Moslem should retire.

[3] Joneid owed his promotion (easy way of earning a command) to offering the wife of Hisham a rare and costly piece of Indian jewelry, which Hisham admired so much that Joneid presented another like it to him.

escaped capture by the Khacan. In the following year,
marching on Takharistan, he received an alarming message
from Saurat, governor of Samarcand, that the Khacan had
surrounded the city, which, being from its great circuit
beyond his power to defend, he must at all hazards, if not
quickly relieved, go out and fight the enemy. Joneid resolved on marching to his relief, but the forces under his
command were scattered in all directions, and he had but an
inadequate column, with which, against the reclamation of
his officers, he at once set out. When about half way, he
was surrounded by the hordes of the Khacan, and the
battle raged with terrible slaughter. Prodigies of valour,
as of old, held the enemy at bay. One who had just
returned from pilgrimage to Mecca, where he besought his
mother to pray that he might be blessed with martyrdom,
and had with the same object lavished charity, obtained
now the longed-for prize. Another, while the fight was
hot, returned to prepare his wife for his being brought in
all gory from the battle : rending her garments, she exclaimed in agony, ' Ah why, leaving thine earthly love,
wilt thou seek the embrace of the Houris in Paradise ? '
Heedless of her cry, he hastened back to the field, and met
the fate he coveted. Joneid was in despair ; he called his
cavalry to dismount, and they fought fiercely hand to hand
with the barbarians. Eighteen leaders bearing the great
banner fell one after another, and the dead were strewed
over the field in hundreds. At last he retired to a defile,
threw up entrenchments, and called a council of war.
' Either thou must perish,' they said, ' or Saurat.'. So he Joneid
sacrifices
Saurat and
garrison of
Samar-
cand.
sent to Saurat, ordering him to march out of Samarcand,
and so draw off the enemy. Saurat remonstrated against the
mad attempt ; but on Joneid angrily threatening to supersede him by one who was his bitter enemy, he issued forth
with 12,000 men. After a long march, when close to
Joneid, the Khacan turned upon him, and a fierce encounter ensued. The day was hot, and the Turks set fire to
the dry jungle behind. Saurat resolved on a dash through
the enemy's host, so to reach Joneid's camp now close
at hand. The Khacan giving way, drew him into the

midst of the burning grass, hidden by the clouds of dust raised by his horse. There, part enveloped in the flames, and part slain by the sword, ten or eleven thousand perished. The remnant escaped to a supposed friendly chieftain, who betrayed them to the Khacan. They were all but seventeen cruelly massacred; and in the end, but three out of the 12,000 got safely away. Having thus sacrificed Saurat, Joneid seized the opportunity to emerge from his retreat, but coming on the flaming jungle he again retired; and then the Khacan came down upon him. In this strait, he proclaimed that if the slaves of his camp would fight with him, they should have their liberty; and they did fight with such prodigious bravery, that Joneid was able to force his way to Samarcand. He had not, however, been long there when tidings came that the Khacan now threatened Bokhara. So leaving a garrison behind, he fought his way back, carrying with him the families of the annihilated force, who were sent safely on to Merve. The Caliph was deeply affected by the loss of Saurat and his army; and reinforced Joneid with five-and-twenty thousand troops from Irac [1].

Joneid forces his way to Samarcand, ix. 112 A.H.

With the help of these reinforcements and the able generals with whom he surrounded himself, Joneid succeeded during the next two or three years in restoring order beyond the Oxus [2]. But he had no sooner done so than (such was the caprice of the rulers of the day) he was ignominiously deposed for no other reason than that he had married a daughter of the rebel Zeid, son of Mohallab; and Asim, an enemy of his, was appointed in his place. Joneid at the moment lay sick of a fatal illness; but Hisham was so enraged at the alliance he had formed, that, aware of his condition, he bade Asim, if breath still remained, to put the dying man to torture. Death happily

Trans-oxiana, 113–115 A.H.

Fall of Joneid, 116 A.H.

---

[1] The campaign of Joneid is told with much fervour by the historians: prodigies were seen in the sky at the battle of the defile, a pavilion in the heavens, smell of musk on the field of the slain, &c. Joneid, in reporting his defeat to Hisham, laid the blame on Saurat for not staying, as he had ordered him, by the stream which lay between them: but it would seem unjustly.

[2] Above all others Joneid knew how to select his men, and his generals are described as masters of war each in his own department.

released Joneid from the hands of the new governor; who A.H. 105–125.
vented his spleen, according to the wont of the day, on
those who had held office under his unfortunate predecessor. As one result of this harsh treatment, a leader Rebellion
named Harith raised the standard of revolt, with the of Harith.
Kharejite cry, 'To the law and to the testimony and the
will of the people.' He possessed himself of Balkh and all
the surrounding country. Then followed by 60,000 Arabs,
chiefly of Azd and Temim descent, he unwisely advanced
on Merve, where deserted by many of his followers, he
suffered defeat and loss, and with the remnant was forced
to recross the Oxus. Notwithstanding, several thousand
Arabs still followed his banner, and the provinces in Cen-
tralA sia, owing to the inaction of Asim, remained long
in a state of revolt.

After a year of misgovernment and mishap, Asim was Asad re-
deposed, and Asad again appointed to Khorasan[1]. His appointed.
117 A.H.
hand was soon felt in the reduction of the country, and the
defeat of Harith and other rebellious leaders. The followers
of Harith came to a grievous end. A party of his relatives
and their dependants were by Asad's troops captured in
a fort, and sold, noble-born Arabs with the rest, as slaves
to the highest bidder in the bazaar of Balkh. In another
fortress, 450 dying of thirst had to surrender at discretion.
The chiefest of these, fifty in number, were beheaded. The
rest were, by Asad's order, divided into three lots, of
which one was slain, a second had hands and legs both
cut off, while the third their hands only. Such was the
barbarity of Asad. Harith himself effected his escape;
and (a thing hitherto unheard of in Islam) joined himself
to the pagan Turk.

Balkh, which must have suffered badly throughout the Balkh
insurrection, was now rebuilt and beautified by Barmek made
capital of
(father of the Barmecides) and a cantonment laid out in Central
its vicinity[2]. An exchequer, with offices of civil and mili- Asia,
118 A.H.
tary administration, was established at this new capital of 736 A.D.

---

[1] The appointment of Viceroy was in the gift of his brother Khalid, governor
of Irac. Khorasan seems sometimes to have been thus immediately under
Irac, at others administered direct from Damascus.

[2] The troops had previously been cantoned at Barucan, two parasangs off.

A.H. 105–
125.

the provinces in Central Asia, which thus settled down into comparative order. Asad now set on foot a campaign into Khottal, which the Khacan hearing of, marched, with Harith in his train, upon Balkh. He had surprised Asad's advanced column, taking the camp with much spoil and all the women, when Asad came up just in time to save the force from being cut to pieces, and a parley ensued. The Khacan, interpreted through one of Harith's followers, charged Asad with the lust of conquest in seeking to wrest from him Khottal, which had been his people's for generations past: 'Rest satisfied,' he said, 'with what is beyond the river to the south, for that alone is yours.' The conference ended without result; and Asad, not prepared for battle, retired to winter at Balkh, and the Khacan to Takharistan.

Asad beats Khacan and Harith, 119 A.H.

In the following spring Asad went forth again with a strong army, completely routed the Khacan, and rescued from captivity all the Moslem prisoners, male and female. The enemy fled to Takharistan, from whence the Khacan, supported by Harith, was about to attack Samarcand, when he was waylaid and killed by one of his chiefs with whom he had a quarrel. The joy at Damascus was unbounded. Hisham refused to believe the good tidings till confirmed by a second messenger; and then he prostrated himself in thanksgiving before the Lord.

Death of Asad. Nasr pacifies Transoxiana, 120 A.H.

In the following year Asad died, fortunately just before the fall of his brother Khalid, or he would have shared in the evils that befell him[1]. Nasr, who succeeded, was a wise and able ruler. He carried his arms into Ferghana. The task was now comparatively easy; for since the fall of the Khacan, the Turcoman hordes had broken up into parties, which offered no effective resistance. By the promulgation of a general amnesty, the Soghdians were brought back to their allegiance. And so after having been so long harassed by rapine and war, the provinces in Central Asia at last enjoyed repose.

In Sind and Western India there is little to record of

---

[1] The immediate cause of his death was indulgence in pears, brought as a rare present from Herat,—the first apparently which the Moslems had seen.

progress during the present reign. Joneid, the governor, afterwards transferred to Merve, made some successful raids in the East; but he injured the Moslem name by warring against Jeishaba, an Indian prince, who, notwithstanding his profession of the faith, was made prisoner in a sea-fight and put to death. His brother set out for Kufa to lodge complaint against this unjust attack, when he too was caught on the way in the tyrant's toils and put to death. The result of such treatment was that under his successor, a general revolt was made against a rule hateful to the Indians; and so it became necessary to found in the tract bordering on the Indus, two strongly fortified garrisons, *Mahfuzah* and *Mansurah*[1]. By these the surrounding country was long held in check, and forward movement from them made into the rich provinces of the Deccan.

A.H. 105– 125.

Sind and India, 107 A.H. 725 A.D.

Against the Greeks there was as usual a yearly campaign. The Byzantine empire being at this time weakened by opposition to the iconoclastic energy of Leo, the Moslems were, upon the whole, more successful here than elsewhere. But fortune was varied by severe reverses; and on one occasion a whole column of 1000 men was cut to pieces. Battâl, a famous general, took captive a Greek prince, who was sent to Jerusalem, and there, an unwonted sight, allowed to walk abroad[2]. After a famous career, in which Battâl struck such terror throughout Asia Minor that mothers used to frighten their crying children by his name, he lost his life in a serious defeat.

Asia Minor.

Battâl, a famous general, killed, 123 A.H.

In Armenia, the conquests already achieved were retained with difficulty and not without some terrible disasters. Peace had been restored and the country to the shore of the Caspian made tributary, when war again

Armenia and Caspian border.

---

[1] That is, the Protected and the Victorious.

[2] The Greek prince is named Constantine, afterwards emperor; but, as the Byzantine authors say nothing, it must have been some less notable person.

Of Battâl marvellous stories are told. Falling sick on a journey, he was carried insensible into a convent, and tended by a nun. A neighbouring Patrician, angry at her attention to a Mussulman, was set upon by Battâl, who singly put his whole retinue to flight, slew the Patrician, cast his head into the convent, and carried the whole body of nuns to the army. He married the nun who had tended him, and she was known long after as 'the mother of Battâl's children.'

A.H. 105–
125.
___

Jarrah and
his army
slain,
112 A.H.

Maslama.

broke out, and Jarrah, the commander (who had been removed from Khorasan), was overtaken by hordes of Turcomans, and with his whole army destroyed. A new levy was forthwith despatched, and swelled by Ghazies on its way. The calamity was thereby retrieved ; after repeated engagements, the Khizrs were driven back, and the family of Jarrah and other Moslem ladies recovered. Maslama, now sent by his brother to take the command, ravaged the country north as far as Derbend, when he too was surrounded by the Turcomans, and in the ignominious flight lost his life. The Mesopotamian border was by this defeat so seriously threatened, that Merwan[1], who was with the discomfited army, hastened in person to inform his cousin Hisham of the disaster. A great army of 120,000 men was gathered from every quarter, with which Merwan, now appointed to the command, beat back the enemy, and recovered the country as far as the Caspian Sea. The chief of the Turcomans now submitted to the terms imposed by Merwan. These among other things included the tribute of 1000

Merwan's
victories,
118–122
A.H.

head of cattle, 500 slaves, and 500 ' black-haired ' girls, the first of the fair Circassian maidens that were in the future so plentifully to grace the harems of the East. In 118 and again in 122 A.H., Merwan carried the Moslem arms against the hordes to the south of the Caspian as far as Tabaristan, thus effecting a junction with Khorasan. But beyond successful raids and siege of towns, with the slaughter of the men and slavery of the women that fell into the conqueror's hands, little further is to tell.

Reverses
in Africa,
116–124
A.H.

More serious were the disasters in Africa and Spain, where the Moslem arms not only suffered frequent defeat, but, worse than all, the bond of subjection to Damascus became daily weaker. In the year 116 there was a general rising of the Berbers along the coast of Africa, caused partly by the reimposition of taxes on the Moslem converts, as though they had been heathen, and partly by the outbreak of new Kharejite factions[2]. The loyalist armies

[1] Grandson of Merwan I, and nephew of Abd al Melik; afterwards Merwan II, and last of the Omeyyads.
[2] A new branch arose, called from its founder Soffarides. These and the other

were again and again beaten with great loss, and victory in A.H. 105–
the end hardly won.   A famous battle, known as 'the Field ^{125.}
of idols,' was fought a few miles from Cairowan, 117 A.H.,
against 300,000 Berbers ; the issue, long doubtful, was at
last gained by the Arabs, urged forward by the 'Readers,'
the cries of the women and fear of the fate that might
await them[1].   The western provinces of Africa continued
all in uproar till 124 A.H., when the governor of Egypt was
sent to stem the insurrection, and peace was at last restored.
During this period the navy was not inactive.   In the year
111 A.H. a descent was made on Sicily, and great spoil
brought back ; but three years after, the fleet was wrecked ;
and the admiral, for exposing it to the winter storms, cast
into prison and publicly beaten in the streets of Cairowan.
In 117 Sardinia was ravaged ; and in 122, Sicily was again
invaded, and Syracuse laid under tribute.   A project set on
foot for reducing the whole island was dropped, owing to
the troubled state of Africa.

Spain, as a dependency of Africa, was closely affected Spain.
by the insurrection there, and by the constant change of
governors.   Its rule was also distracted by the disloyalty of
the Berber population, which streamed across the strait,
and vastly outnumbered the Arabs, who, as elsewhere, were
divided among themselves by their chronic tribal enmity.
Elements of trouble thus rife all round produced the
natural result of disorder and revolt.

Anbasa, appointed to the government early in this reign, Campaign
occupied himself at first in restoring order within the in France,
Peninsula.   Afterwards he crossed the Pyrenees, with the 725 A.D.
view of restoring the shattered prestige of the Moslem
arms in France.   Carcassone was stormed ; Nismes fell
into his hands ; the south of France was overrun ; the
churches and convents despoiled.   Shortly after, he was

---

sects that swarmed along the coast recognized the claim neither of the Hashimites
nor of any other to the Caliphate, but were pure theocrats, or it may be socialists.

[1] ' 180,000 were counted on the battle-field ; there was no such battle since
the days of Bedr as the battle of the Place of idols.'   Another engagement was
named ' the battle of the Nobles, from the vast number of Arab chiefs slain in
it.'   It would be unprofitable to follow these campaigns farther in their wearisome and often fabulous detail.

A.H. 105–
125.

Abd al
Rahman,
113 A.H.

Over-
thrown by
Charles
Martel,
ix. 114 A.H.
Oct.,
732 A.D.

killed ; and the restless state of Spain prevented further action for the time. Some six years after, Abd al Rahman, again appointed to command, renewed offensive operations, and chastised Abu Nesa, an Arab chief, who had rebelled and joined Count Eudo[1]. In the following year he marched from Spain with an enormous force, and overran the land as far as Poitiers. It was then that Charles Martel, in answer to the bitter cry of Eudo for help, hurried south to stem the sweeping Moslem wave. Between Tours and Poitiers the armies met ; the field was hotly contested, but at last the invaders were driven back and fled in confusion, leaving Abd al Rahman dead on the field. Next morning, the conqueror, ready to renew the conquest, found not a single soldier within sight ; all had disappeared[2]. The fate of France, perhaps of Christendom, hung on the issue of that day. And in God's good providence Christendom was saved.

Further
campaign
in France,
116–119
A.H.
734–737
A.D.

Misrule in
Spain.

Two years later, Ocba, son of Hajjaj, returned to the charge, and effecting a junction with a body of Frank nobles hostile to Eudo, again invaded France. Arles, Avignon, and other places were surrendered into his hands, Valencia and Lyons besieged, Burgundy and Dauphiné ravaged as far as the Rhone. But Charles Martel, freed now from the Saxon war, again came to the rescue, reconquered Avignon, and drove the Arabs back as far as Narbonne. Hostages were then taken from the disloyal chiefs of Southern France, not again to make common cause with the enemy. Ocba died soon after, in the midst of Spanish anarchy. One general after another usurped command. The Berbers sought to be independent of the Arabs, and the Arabs were split up amongst themselves. Order was not restored till after the death of Hisham. Meanwhile the Christians in the mountainous regions of the North, profiting by the misrule elsewhere, maintained their independence[3].

[1] Abu Nesa is changed by European writers to Munuza.

[2] Ramzan 114, or Oct. 732. The victory is ascribed to the Franks finding their way to the enemy's camp, when the invaders, fearing the loss of their spoil, hurried back to save it.

[3] As regards the invasion of France, the Arabian authorities are very brief. I have borrowed largely from Weil and Reinaud.

Such was the long and chequered reign of Hisham,— A.H. 105–125. with all his demerits, if we except occasional outbreaks of cruel tyranny,—one of the most exemplary of the Caliphs Hisham's either before or after. It was not his fault that the empire, just reign. already undermined, continued sinking. Abbasside emissaries on the one hand, and Kharejite theocrats on the other, labouring in the dark, left no stone unturned to overthrow the dynasty, casting the blackest and often undeserved obloquy upon it. His virtues failed to arrest the downward progress. The archives of state were during his time kept with a scrupulous care unequalled in any other reign. There was no extravagance, and he left the imperial treasury full. Indeed, it was unwillingness to scatter largesses, and parsimony degenerating often into a mean and miserly habit, that injured his popularity and impaired his influence[1]. As an instance of his justice, he refused to let a Christian be punished for having chastised a Moslem servant, and chided his son for urging it. Scandalized at the Dissolute dissolute character of his nephew Welid, the heir-apparent, character of Welid, who even on the pilgrimage to Mecca indulged in wine and heir-hounds,—abomination to the true believer[2],—he had some apparent. thoughts of superseding him by his own son, till he found that he was little better. Welid was not only intemperate in his life, but impatient of control, and insolent in his attitude towards his uncle; and so leaving the Court betook himself to a country retreat in Palestine. Hisham removed from him his evil advisers, and imprisoned his secretary, after inflicting stripes upon him. Welid, resenting the indignity, addressed the Caliph a satire breathing hatred and contempt. He remained in his retreat during the rest of the reign.

[1] As a specimen of his meanness, a man is said once to have brought as an offering two rare and beautiful birds, expecting a present in return. 'What shall I give thee?' said the Caliph. 'Whatever thou pleasest,' he replied. 'Then take one of the birds for thine own.' He chose the most beautiful. 'So thou art leaving me the worst of the two,' said the Caliph; 'I will keep them both.' And he ordered him the shabby gift of a few silver pieces.

[2] This was nine years before Hisham's death. The wild youth had even thought of pitching a pavilion hard by the Kaaba wherein to have a carousal with his boon companions; but was dissuaded from the mad design. The tale is almost incredible, and may have been invented or coloured by Abbasside historians, always ready to blacken this dynasty. But no doubt he was bad enough.

Hisham
refrained
from re-
viling Aly.

When Hisham was on pilgrimage, the year after his accession, he refrained in the public services from the customary imprecation on the name of Aly. He was urged by one of Othman's descendants to resume it;—'This is the holy place,' he said, 'and it becomes the Commander of the Faithful to rescue the memory of the murdered Caliph in the same.' Hisham, displeased at his words, replied,—'I come not here to revile any one, nor to curse; but to perform the rites of pilgrimage.' On another occasion having unadvisedly reviled a courtier, he was much

Occasional
acts of
cruelty.

distressed, and humbly made apology. Although thus in general disposition mild and upright, the reader will remember instances in which he was severe and cruel, not to say unjust, towards lieutenants who had fallen under his displeasure. One heretic he caused to be put to death for denying that the Coran was uncreate. Another, who rejected the doctrine of inspiration, was by his command impaled after his limbs had first been cut asunder. There is the less doubt about such accounts, for though handed down by the unfriendly pen of Abbasside writers, they would not be regarded by them as discreditable to the Omeyyad race, but rather as meritorious acts of faith.

Death of
Hisham,
iv. 125 A.H.
Feb., 743
A.D.

Damascus was much exposed to epidemic plague, and to avoid contagion the Caliphs with their families were in the habit of seeking the purer air of the desert. Such favourite retreat was Rusafa, a city adorned with Roman buildings near to Kinnisrin. There Hisham spent much of his time; and there he died of quinsey in the 20th year of his reign, aged 56.

CHAPTER LVI

WELID II, AND YEZID III.

A.H. 125–126. A.D. 743–744.

THESE two brief reigns contributed nothing but disaster to the Omeyyad cause and to the empire at large.

The tidings of his uncle's death were received by Welid with indecent delight.   Notorious profligacy and incapacity notwithstanding, he succeeded without opposition to the throne.   He made haste to send and seize the property of the late Caliph's relatives and favourites and to treat them with every indignity.   Hisham's son Soleiman was beaten, shaven, exiled, and cast into prison.   The well-filled treasury was quickly emptied by largesses to his courtiers and increased pay to the soldiery.   Such free hand, and a generous provision for the blind and infirm, gained for Welid a certain degree of popularity.   But his intemperate and dissolute life caused great scandal throughout the nation.   Besides such conventional profanities as wine, music, and hounds, his debauched habits alienated from him the regard of all the better classes.   He was accused of tampering with the virtue of his predecessor's harem, and even darker vices were bruited abroad.   To make matters worse, he appointed two sons of tender age his successors, and such as refused the oath of allegiance were imprisoned The discontent rose to such a pitch, that even the Omeyyads plotted against him and encouraged Yezid, another grandson of Abd al Melik, to seek his downfall.

Khalid, the former governor of Kufa, having escaped the

A.H. 125-
126.

Khalid
tortured to
death by
Yusuf.

Yezid, son
of Welid,
rebels
against
him,
vi. 126 A.H.
April, 744
A.D.

tyranny of Yusuf, was now living at Damascus. Loyal to
the throne, he refused to join the conspirators: and fearing
that the Caliph might be waylaid on an intended pilgrimage
to Mecca, dissuaded him from attempting the journey.
The Caliph, angry because Khalid did not tell him more of
the suspected intrigues abroad, and also declined to do
homage to his sons, had him beaten and cast into prison;
and he farther revived against him the demand for arrears
of revenue which Hisham had allowed to drop. Yusuf, still
bent on the ruin of Khalid, now saw his opportunity,
and visiting Damascus with large gifts for the Court,
'bought' his victim from Welid at the price of that
demand, amounting to fifty million of pieces. The
unfortunate Khalid was then carried back to Kufa, where
he expired under the barbarous treatment of Yusuf, and
was buried with indignity[1].

The treatment of Khalid kindled the indignation of the
Yemen stock from which he sprang. Verses taunting these
with cowardice in suffering their kinsman to be thus
trampled under foot, were freely circulated, and roused
an intense excitement against the Caliph. His cousin
Yezid had by this time gained a large following. Abbas
his brother, and also Merwan, commanding in Armenia,
both endeavoured to dissuade him from his traitorous
design, which they foresaw must hasten the downfall of
their dynasty. But he persisted; and now supported
by the Yemenite malcontents, who flocked around and
saluted him as Caliph, he raised the standard of rebellion,
and marched upon Damascus. The Court and chief
officers were mostly away in the country, to avoid the
pestilential air of the capital, and so Yezid easily possessed
himself of the treasury. Then with its contents bribing
the soldiery, he despatched a body of troops against Welid.
The wretched Caliph, enjoying a retreat in the south of
Syria, having at the moment but a small following for his

---

[1] According to some traditions, he had his legs broken, and the rack drawn
over his chest, under which he died. His mother was a captive Greek who
never embraced Islam. Khalid built a church or convent for her, which made
him unpopular with strict believers.

defence, took refuge in a neighbouring fortress. Abbas,
brother of the conspirator, was on his way to support
Welid, when he was taken by the rebels and forced to join
their standard. Welid at first sought to parley with his
enemies, who would not listen, but covered him with
reproaches for his ungodly life. He then issued forth
and fought bravely, but was forced by overpowering
numbers back into the fort. There he took the Coran
into his hands and began to read its pages, saying—' It
is in this day, as it was in the day of Othman,' and so was
slain. His head was carried to Yezid, and by him paraded
in the streets of Damascus. He had reigned but little
more than a year.

Yezid III now ascended his illgotten throne. From the
first he had serious difficulties to contend with. Owing his
victory to the Yemenites, the Modhar tribes were naturally
his enemies, and moreover, the murdered Caliph came of
their stock on the mother's side. Though not a profane
person, like his predecessor, he was obnoxious to the
Orthodox, because he denied the doctrine of predestination.
The people at large, accustomed to the sacredness of the
Caliph's person, were shocked at the murder of Welid ;
while the army murmured at the withdrawal of the increase
lately granted, which the failing treasury rendered it impossible to continue. The inhabitants of Hims, stirred
by the wailing of the women of Welid's harem domiciled
there, plundered the house of Yezid's brother Abbas, and
outraged the sanctity of his harem. Gaining over the
troops, they then set out, with the cry of revenge for the
blood of Welid, to attack Damascus. Yezid on this despatched two strong columns under his brother Masrur, and
Soleiman son of Hashim who had escaped from confinement and joined the new Caliph. These met the insurgents
a few miles from the capital, and after a severe engagement, put them to flight; upon which the oath of allegiance
to Yezid was taken both at Hims and Damascus. Soon
after a still more serious rising took place in Palestine,
which it required an army of 80,000 to put down, as well
as promise of office and largess to the rebel leaders. Such

A.H. 125–
126.

were the weakness and confusion into which the body politic had fallen.

Troubles at Kufa.

In Irac things were not much better. Kufa was glad to be rid of the tyrant Yusuf, who fled for his life to Syria. Arrested there in woman's disguise, he was cast with contumely into prison. His successor was hated as a godless man sharing the Caliph's heretical opinions. Yezid was therefore obliged to remove him and send in his place Ibn Omar, son of the pious Caliph, saying that the Kufans would surely reverence him for his father's sake. But troubles continued to break out, and uproar between the discordant tribes in Syria and Irac.

Khorasan: Abbasside canvass.

While authority was thus relaxed at home, the outlying provinces had it much their own way. Khorasan especially was in a state of unrest, and strange apprehensions were abroad of coming change. Mohammed, the Abbasside pretender, had died the year before, aged 73[1]; and now his son Ibrahim, who succeeded him as ' Imam,' sent a deputation, with tidings of the Pretender's death, to his adherents, who formed a strong and increasing body at Merve. These kissed the testament in which Ibrahim was named successor, and forwarded to him large offerings, which they had gathered for his house. But as yet the canvass was concealed from public view.

Nasr holds on there.

Nasr still held the viceroyalty there. Welid, in his wild caprice, had directed Yusuf to summon him to Court with a rich assortment of gold and silver vessels, falcons, palfreys, games, and every kind of musical instrument, and with a following of maidens also. Nasr obeyed, but, foreseeing storms, journeyed slowly; and so, before he reached Irac, getting tidings of Yezid's rebellion, he returned to Merve. The new governor of Kufa sought to supersede him by a creature of his own; but Nasr would not give way, and so succeeded in holding on. To lighten his treasury, a dangerous temptation for the rebels all around him, he distributed the vast store of precious things and slave-girls, gathered for Welid, among his own family and retainers, as well as in payment of the troops. The old feud of Modhar

---

[1] See table at p. 391. His father Aly died seven years before.

and Yemen was, however, continually breaking out afresh. A.H. 125–
The Yemenites were at this time headed by one called 126.
(from his birth-place) Kirmany, and riots and fighting prevailed between the two clans.　Nasr, who belonged to the
Modharite faction, was hard pressed by the other.　Things
were composed for a time ; but Nasr had dark days before
him.

　It was at this juncture that Harith, who had gone over Harith
to the Khacan, and fought under the Turcoman banner $\frac{\text{returns to}}{\text{his con-}}$
against his fellows, returned.　At the instance of Nasr, freres.
who, surrounded by enemies, feared his hostility and that
of the Turks, he was pardoned by the Caliph and allowed,
after having for twelve years fought on the enemy's side, to
come back and resume his position among his brethren ;
a singular instance of condonation for an apostate's crime.
We shall hear more of him hereafter[1].

　Yezid was at last to be threatened by an enemy far more Merwan
formidable than any that had hitherto appeared.　This was $\frac{\text{attacks}}{\text{Yezid III.}}$
Merwan, grandson of Merwan I, and conqueror of the
Caucasus, who had vainly sought to dissuade him from
his treason against Welid.　Merwan's son, on returning from the summer campaign in Asia Minor, found
Mesopotamia in confusion, took possession of Harran, and
wrote to his father urging him to hasten and avenge the
blood of Welid.　Merwan set out from Armenia, and from
Harran despatched an army thence against Damascus.
Yezid in alarm meanwhile sent to offer terms ;—he Com-
would continue Merwan as Viceroy of all the provinces $\frac{\text{promise}}{\text{between}}$
which his father and he had held, including Mesopo- them.
tamia, Armenia, Mosul and Adzerbijan.　Merwan accepted
the offer, and did allegiance to Yezid.

　Towards the close of the year, Yezid fell sick, and in Death of
anticipation of decease was persuaded by his heretic friends $\frac{\text{Yezid III,}}{\text{xii.126A.H.}}$
to appoint his brother Ibrahim, also an adherent of the Oct. 744
Free-will doctrine, as his successor.　Shortly after he died A.D.

---

[1] I remember no other instance of a Moslem joining the ranks of a pagan
enemy.　On returning, Harith expressed his penitence, saying that during these
twelve years he never had a moment's peace till he was received back into the
bosom of Islam.

at Damascus, aged forty-six, having reigned but six months. His mother was the grand-daughter of Yezdegird, brought as a captive maid from Khorasan[1].

---

[1] Her great-grandmother was a daughter of the Caysar, married to the Chosroes, and also descended from a daughter of one of the Khacans, so that she had thus the blood of all three potentates in her veins. Yezid used therefore to sing:—

> I am son of Chosroes; my father was Merwan:
> Caysar was my ancestor, and so was the Khacan.

CHAPTER LVII.

IBRAHIM AND MERWAN II, LAST OF THE OMEYYADS.

126–130 A.H.   744–48 A.D.

IBRAHIM can hardly be said to have succeeded his ^{Ibrahim's} brother Yezid. He assumed indeed the government at ^{partial succession,} Damascus, and held it for three or four months. He ^{126 A.H.} was addressed by some as Caliph, by others only as ^{744 A.D.} Ameer. No general homage was done to him. It seems to have been felt that he had no proper hold on the Caliphate, as events, in point of fact, did soon determine.

For Merwan, immediately on receiving tidings of Yezid's ^{Merwan} decease, started from Harran, his residence in Mesopotamia, ^{advances on Damas-} with a heavy force for Syria. At Kinnisrin, the Modharite ^{cus.} party gave up two brothers of the late Caliph who were in command there, and joined his standard. Strengthened by their adherence, he advanced on Hims, which refusing to acknowledge Ibrahim, had been invested by his troops. Raising the siege, and with an army now of 80,000 men, he continued his march upon the capital. A force had already started from thence to stay his approach. It was commanded by Soleiman son of Hisham, and composed chiefly of the Yemenite and other adherents of the late Caliph, numbered 120,000 men. Merwan's ranks, however, were full of veterans used to the field. They met in a valley between Baalbec and Damascus. Merwan demanded of his enemy the release of two sons of Welid, now in confinement at Damascus, promising that if this were done, he would spare all those concerned in their father's

death. It was refused, and the armies joined battle. They
fought all day, but Merwan, used to warlike tactics, in
the evening sent a column by a circuit, which taking his
enemy in the rear put them to a disastrous flight; 17,000
were left on the field and as many more taken prisoners.
Damascus thus left defenceless, Ibrahim and Soleiman made
their escape from thence, but not before they had plundered the treasury and put the two sons of Welid to death,
also Yusuf, the late tyrant of Kufa. They had no sooner
fled than the adherents of Welid rose upon the relatives of
the fallen ruler with slaughter and riot, and having exhumed
the body of Yezid III, impaled it at the Jabia gate of the
city. Merwan, on coming up, had the bodies of Welid's
sons honourably buried, as also that of Yusuf. And, there
being now none with a better claim, he was saluted Caliph,
and thereafter returned to his palace at Harran. Ibrahim,
who survived only a year or two, was admitted to amnesty;
and so also was Soleiman, who to outward appearance was
reconciled, and in token thereof gave his sister in marriage
to the son of Merwan.

His success notwithstanding, embers of disaffection were
ever bursting into flame around Merwan. The support
accorded him by the Modhar clan, and the sanguinary
defeat inflicted by them, rankled in the breast of the Yemen
tribes. Kharejite adventurers sprang up in every quarter
of the empire; and the Hashimite conspiracy spread with
alarming rapidity, especially in the East. Disaffection
brooded over the empire. Merwan, with all his strength
and warlike prowess, was ever endeavouring to stem the
rising wave. His reign was one continual struggle, which,
spite of all his difficulties, would without doubt have put
rebellion down, had the Syrian forces held a united and
faithful front; but that, tribal jealousies prevailing, they
failed to do, and the result was fatal to Omeyyad rule.

Merwan had not returned to Harran three months, when
Hims, incited by the Yemenite faction, broke out into
rebellion. It was reduced, but not without great slaughter.
The city walls were demolished and 500 bodies of the
rebels hung around it. At the same time, the Yemen tribes

settled in and about Damascus attacked that city; they A.H. 126–130.
were discomfited by a detachment from Hims, and their
villages in the beautiful vale of the Barada burned to the
ground. Shortly after a serious insurrection breaking out
in Palestine, threatened Tiberias; the rebel leader, one of
Merwan's own generals in the Caucasus, was taken prisoner
with three sons. The arms and legs of all four were cut
off, and their bodies impaled at the gates of Damascus.
Tadmor also rose against the Caliph, but was reduced and its
walls demolished. And now that Syria was quieted Merwan
retired to his palace at Rusafa. His two sons were declared
Heirs-apparent, and, to conciliate the other branches of the
Omeyyad family, married to daughters of Hisham. But
he had not rested long when troubles afresh broke out.

It is a sign of the restlessness of Moslem feeling at this Rebellion of Ibn Muavia,
time, that besides the claims of the representatives of Muavia,
Abbas the uncle, and of Aly the cousin and son-in-law of descendant of Jafar,
Mahomet, a pretender from another branch of which we 126 A.H.
hear nothing before, now appeared at Kufa, in the person 744 A.D.
of Ibn Muavia, great-grandson of Jafar, brother of Aly,
who was killed in the battle of Muta[1]. This man was
honoured on account of his birth by the governor Ibn
Omar, who even provided for his support, but kept a
watchful eye upon him. His pretensions to the throne
were warmly espoused by the citizens. When after the
accession of Merwan, Ibn Muavia stepped forth to claim
his pretended right, crowds followed after him, so that
the plain from Kufa to Hira was white with them. But Expelled from Kufa,
immediately a force was directed against him, his brave 127 A.H.
supporters, after the fashion of the fickle city, fell away. 745 A.D.
And so, after some desultory fighting, he was allowed,
with the adherents still clinging to him, to depart across
the Tigris to Medain. There he succeeded in establishing
a footing. Many flocked to his standard, including crowds
of the servile class from Kufa. With their aid he gained
possession of Holwan and the hill country east of the Tigris.
In the next two years, supported by the Kharejites, he played

---

[1] *Life of Mahomet,* pp. 409, 410. Jafar was the son of Abd al Muttalib:
see table supra, p. 391. He was killed two years before Mahomet's death.

A.H. 126–130.

Success in Persia, 128 A.H. 746 A.D. Defeated by Ibn Hobeira, 129 A.H. 747 A.D.
a marvellous rôle in Persia, establishing his court at Istakhr, and acknowledged in Ispahan, Rei, Cumis, and other chief cities in the East. In 129, however, the Kharejites having been subdued, the followers of the pretender were dispersed by the Syrian columns, and he himself forced to fly to the far East[1]. By this time Abu Muslim (of whom we shall hear more shortly) had established himself in the Hashimite interest at Merve; and Ibn Muavia, learning that he was fighting for the house of Hashim, repaired to the governor of Herat and urged his claims as a scion of the same. 'Give us thy pedigree,' said the governor, 'that we may know who thou art.' 'The son of Muavia, who was the son of Abdallah, who was the son of Jafar.' But *Muavia*, as the reader will understand, was a name of evil omen to a Hashimite; and so the answer ran, —'Abdallah we know, and Jafar we know; but as for *Muavia*, it is a name we know not of.' 'My grandfather,' explained the fugitive, 'was at the court of Muavia when my father was born, and the Caliph bade him call the infant by his name, and for that received the gift of 100,000 dirhems.'—'An evil name, verily, for a small price,'

was the reply; 'we recognize thee not.' On the matter being reported to him, Abu Muslim bade them release the rest of the party: but Ibn Muavia was too dangerous a fugitive as a descendant of Abu Talib, to be spared, and so, by command of the Abbasside viceroy, he was smothered under a mattress, and buried at Herat, where, says the historian, his tomb has become a place of pilgrimage. Abu Muslim had cause to rue the cruel deed.

No sooner had Ibn Muavia quitted Kufa, than a serious rebellion broke out in Irac under a Kharejite leader named Dhahhak. To suppress this, Merwan gathered a force at Kirkesia to be led by Yezid ibn Hobeira[2]. But as it was assembling, 10,000 of the number, Yemenites from Syria, conspired against the Caliph, and persuaded the ungrateful Soleiman, by the prospect of the throne, to put himself at

[1] His following must still have been great, as 40,000 are said to have been taken prisoners, but released by Ibn Hobeira.

[2] Yezid was son of Omar ibn Hobeira, murdered by Khalid (p. 391); but like his father he is ordinarily called simply Ibn Hobeira.

their head. Crowds of disloyalists flocked to his banner at A.H. 126–130.
Kinnesrin, and Merwan had to recall Ibn Hobeira from
pursuit of Dhahhak to oppose the army, now swelled to
70,000, led by this new and formidable rival. After a
heavy battle, Soleiman was completely defeated, losing his
sons and 30,000 men ; for Merwan would allow no quarter
nor prisoners to be taken. Soleiman fled to Hims ; and on Defeated;
his followers being again beaten, escaped to Dhahhak. joins Dhahhak.
Merwan was still held back from attacking the Kharejites
by Hims, which, having thrown off its allegiance, had to be Hims
besieged. Though surrounded by eighty catapults, which besieged
threw shot day and night over the walls, it held out for ten
months, but at last capitulated.

Meanwhile Irac was in a state of dangerous rebellion. Rebellion
After the expulsion of Ibn Muavia, the never-ending feud of Dhah-
of Yemen and Modhar broke out with redoubled violence hak,
at Kufa,—the latter clan siding naturally with Merwan's 127 A.H.
governor, the former with his ousted predecessor, the Son 745 A.D.
of Omar, who took possession of Hira ; and thus for
four months a civil war was kept up between Kufa
and its suburb. Dhahhak, who with a large body of
Kharejites and Soffarides had taken advantage of the
troubled times to ravage Mesopotamia, now hearing
of this state of things, seized the opportunity for attacking Kufa ; and, although both sides joined to resist him,
they were beaten and the invaders took possession of
the city. Ibn Omar fled to Wasit, but after three months
he gave in and joined Dhahhak, in whose ranks he found
Soleiman also. Dhahhak had now been above a year and
a half master of the greater part of Irac when, thus reinforced, he was invited by the men of Mosul to take possession of their city, which he did. Merwan, still at Hims,
sent his son Abdallah with a column of 8000, to hold him
in check ; but he had no sooner, with this view, thrown
himself into Nisibin, than Dhahhak besieged him there
with an army of 100,000. Hims having surrendered, it was Beaten by
now high time for Merwan himself to take the field ; and Merwan II.
this he did with all the force at his disposal. The two End of
armies met near Mardin : the battle raged all day and 128 A.H.
746 A.D.

E e

A.H. 126-
130.
___

well on into the night, when search being made on the field, the body of Dhahhak, who with 6000 sworn followers dismounted to fight to the death, was found pierced through with twenty wounds. Next day, battle renewed, the leader of the Kharejites, by a wild onset on the imperial centre, placed Merwan in such peril, that he fled for several miles, but returning found that the wings holding firm, the enemy had been completely routed[1]. Having sent the rebel's head all round Mesopotamia, Merwan pursued the

who retakes
Mosul,
129 A.H.
747 A.D.

Kharejites, who still held together 40,000 strong, to Mosul, and after several months' fighting drove them across the Tigris and dispersed them in the East. Soleiman escaped, but only to meet his end at the hands of the coming dynasty[2]. Irac was still in the hands of the rebels; and it was not till the middle of 129 A.H., that Ibn Hobeira, after more fighting, expelled them from Kufa and Bussorah.

Various
Kharejite
risings.

Though order was thus at last restored to the nearer parts of the empire, the Kharejites had entire possession of Azerbijan, from which they drove out the imperial troops. Throughout Arabia also they more or less prevailed, and Abu Hamza their leader was so powerful that at one time he had possession of both the Holy cities; and the Caliph was obliged to send a large force to restore order there. Though Abu Hamza appeared at the Pilgrimage with 700 followers against the Omeyyads, clad in black and with black banners the emblem of the Abbassides, yet as a Kharejite he was equally opposed to the Hashimite pretender; for neither the Omeyyad nor yet for the Abbasside race did he profess any partiality or respect, but rather for the memory of Abu Bekr and Omar. It will thus appear that these Puritan covenanters, all over the empire, if not in the

___

[1] We are told that after this engagement, *battle in line* was given up, and fighting carried on by battalions (karâdis).

[2] We may here follow Soleiman to his end. He escaped with his family and retainers to Sind, and eventually presented himself, as an enemy of the Omeyyads, before the Hashimite Caliph, who at the first received him graciously. One of his courtiers seeing this recited verses warning the Caliph against appearances, and the danger of sparing any Omeyyad. Thereupon he retired, and shortly after gave orders for Soleiman, like the rest of his race, to be put to death.

ascendancy, were yet powerful enough, even where baffled, A.H. 126–130. to confuse and often paralyze the government.

In the West, as elsewhere, the administration was weak and unsettled. The governors throughout Africa had to Africa. keep up a continual contest against the Berbers and the Kharejites. In Spain, the Kharejite element was weak, and Spain the Hashimite unknown ; but in all other respects, Syria gradually slipping repeated itself in the Peninsula. The Arabs flocking thither from in vast multitudes were taught to forget their native land, Eastern control. or rather to reproduce it in the West. Spain became to them a second home. The landscape of the Peninsula, to the Bedouin imagination, conjured up the lands of Syria and of Palestine, and the Bedouins seemed to nestle again in the scenes of their childhood. ' Thus,' we read, that ' the Arabs spread themselves over the land ; the men of Damascus settled in Albera because of its likeness to their native vale, and called it Damascus ;' and so on with those who had come from Tadmor, Hims, Kinnesrin and other cities of the East[1]. But with the similitude of the old country, arose also its wretched feuds. Yemen fought against Modhar, and Modhar against Yemen. The contest was maintained even more fiercely than against the infidel, till at last they agreed to appoint a neutral chief of the Coreish. But even this failed, and for some months, there being no Ameer, anarchy was rife. Then they settled to have an Ameer one year from the Modhar, and the next from the Yemen tribe. But at the end of the first term the Modharite ruler refused to resign. And so things went on in the distracted land, till, as we shall see, Spain slipped entirely from the grasp of the eastern Caliphate.

At various periods, the Greeks made inroads upon Growing the border lands of Asia Minor and Syria, which Mer- difficulties. wan, with trouble on his hands at home, had no means

---

[1] Other places are mentioned, thus :—' The men of Hims settled in Ishbelia, and called it Hims ; of Kinnesrin, in Jian, and called it Kinnesrin ; of Jordan, in Berea, and called it Jordan ; of Palestine, in Shadzuna, and called it Palestine ; of Egypt, in Todmir, and called it Egypt, from its similitude to the same ;' and so on.

A.H. 126-
130.

of opposing.   He had also, for the same reason, to turn a
deaf ear to Nasr's cry for help from Khorasan,—where
events, as will be shown in the next chapter, were rapidly
hastening the downfall of his dynasty.

Merwan
retires to
Harran,
130 A. H.
748 A.D.

On the restoration of order in Mesopotamia and Irac,
Merwan returned to Harran, his residence in the desert, and
there remained in dangerous and inopportune repose, till
he was called away by the fatal campaign of the Zab.

CHAPTER LVIII.

REMAINDER OF MERWAN'S REIGN.—ABBASSIDE RISING
IN THE EAST UNDER ABU MUSLIM AND CAHTABA.
—RECOGNITION OF ABBASSIDE CALIPH.—BATTLE
OF ZAB.—DEFEAT AND DEATH OF MERWAN.

130–132 A.H.   748–50 A.D.

THE progress of events in the East has been kept for Growth of separate treatment. The same causes were there at work influence as elsewhere,—Kharejite risings and tribal jealousies. But in the East. there were besides special elements of weakness. The authority of the Court was felt less in Khorasan than elsewhere, and in fact was fast disappearing altogether. Hashimite treason, long secretly hatching its disloyal brood, was now coming to an open head: and powerful clubs in support of the same were appearing fearlessly everywhere. The body politic was falling to pieces; and the specious claim of the Prophet's house as against the ungodly Omeyyads, paved an easy way for the great change now looming in the future.

The position of Nasr, Viceroy in Khorasan, had become Nasr, the in the last degree critical. Kirmany, as already said, had viceroy, drawn to his standard the Yemenite faction, that namely by tribal hostile to Nasr. Put in prison as a dangerous agitator, and other difficulties, he effected his escape, and kept up an armed opposition. 126–8 A.H. To increase the disorder, Harith, for whom Nasr had 743–5 A.D. obtained amnesty from the Court, turned against him; and, confederate as he had been of the pagan Turk, assumed now a high religious profession, and raising the black

A.H. 130–132.

flag, demanded a reform of government in accordance with 'the Book of the Lord.' After many fruitless negotiations, Nasr offered to help him if he would again depart and fight beyond the Oxus, but he preferred to remain and battle, now on the side of Kirmany, and now against him. In one of these engagements he was killed: but Kirmany maintained his ground against Nasr, and even seizing Merve, plundered the treasury. It was still the endless quarrel of Modhar and Yemen pitted one against the other, with no decisive result other than that Khorasan was left with hardly even the form of government.

Abu Muslim agent of the Hashimites.

Just then, towards the end of 129 A.H., the great black standard of the Abbassides was unfurled in Khorasan, by Abu Muslim. The origin of this famous man, who, though still young, was already the hero of the new dynasty, is obscure. Amidst much that is discordant, we may assume that he was born a slave. In the year 125 (743 A.D.) Mohammed, head of the Abbasside house, with a party of his adherents, visited Mecca ; and anticipating his decease (he died the same year) bade his followers in that event to take his son Ibrahim as his successor. At the same time he purchased Abu Muslim, then not twenty years of age, as a likely agent for the service of the house. Abu Muslim fulfilling thus the office of confidential agent, was kept going to and fro between Khorasan and Homeima (the village in South Palestine where the family lived), to promote the cause, and to report its progress. At last, in 129 A.H., he gave so promising an account of the zeal of his adherents, of the impotence of Omeyyad rule in Khorasan, and of the distractions there, that he received from Ibrahim command to delay no longer, but raise at once the banner of the new dynasty. In the month of Ramzan accordingly, Abu Muslim proceeding to the far East, sent forth his emissaries in all directions with instructions when and how the rising was to take place. Before the month was over, contingents had begun to pour in from every quarter. In one night there arrived no fewer than sixty from as many different places. The Omeyyad garrisons were expelled from Herat and other cities in the far East. Elsewhere, Abu Muslim's

Raises black standard in the East. ix. 129 A.H. May, 747 A.D.

agents sought to win over the Modhar, by abuse of the A.H. 130- Yemen tribes; and the Yemen by abuse of the Modhar. ^{132.} Even Nasr and Kirmany were tampered with; and Nasr, fearing that Kirmany might go over, had him made away with. Then Abu Muslim, joined by the sons of that chief[1], drove Nasr out of Merve and took possession of the citadel. But this success at last united the Syrians of either party against the Hashimite rebellion; and if the Caliph had only been able to strengthen Nasr's hands, the event must have been very different. The unfortunate Viceroy appealed to Merwan in bitter terms that he was left without support; and quoting verses to the effect that beneath was a volcano ready at any moment to burst forth, he added the fateful words—*Is the house of Omeyya awake, or is it slumbering still?* On receiving this despairing cry, Merwan ordered Ibn Hobeira to hasten reinforcements to the East; but with disaffection around him in the West, it was little that general could do for Nasr. About the same time, the Caliph intercepted a letter from Ibrahim to Abu Muslim, upbraiding him for not making more rapid progress in Khorasan, and warning him against the hostility of the Arabs and Syrians towards the rising cause. Startled and alarmed at his rival's machinations, Merwan bade the governor of Belcaa arrest Ibrahim. He was accordingly seized in his house at Homeima, and sent to Harran, where shortly after he died, but whether by a violent death, or a natural one, is uncertain[2]. On the arrest, his brothers Abul Abbas, and Abu Jafar, with the rest of the family, fled to Kufa, where they remained for the present in concealment.

Meanwhile Abu Muslim was making steady progress in the East. His open unassuming habits, with neither bodyguard nor courtly ceremony, attached men to him. He

Marginal notes: Takes Merve. Nasr appeals for help. Arrest and death of Ibrahim. Abu Muslim's able administration.

---

[1] The two sons of Kirmany were, however, found by Abu Muslim, probably from their Syrian associations, to be inconvenient allies; and were, with their attendants, treacherously put to death. Abu Muslim made no scruple of assassinating by any underhand means those whom he found in his way.

[2] Some say he died of the plague; others that he was poisoned in a draught of milk; others that Merwan caused his prison house to fall upon him. The presumption is against a violent death.

A.H. 130–
132.

committed the ordinary administration to a council of twelve, chosen from the earliest adherents of the cause. He was also wise enough to make his watch-word simply the *House of Hashim*, without declaring by name the master for whom he fought. There were still many who held by the line of Abu Talib, and wished to see one of his descendants rather than of Abbas, succeed ; the cry, therefore, embraced all these branches, including that of Aly. At one time Abu Muslim opened friendly communications with Nasr, who, seeing no hope of help from Syria, had thoughts to throw in his lot with him ; but fearing treachery, he at last

Nasr flees
south, is
defeated by
Cahtaba,
end of
130 A. H.

resolved on flight, and so, with the troops still faithful to the Omeyyad cause, hastened south to Serakhs, and thence to Nisabur. There pursued by Cahtaba, Abu Muslim's famous general, he suffered a defeat in which he lost his son. Thence he fled to Jorjan, where was a strong force of friendly Syrians. But fortune had deserted the Caliph's cause, and Cahtaba again achieved a signal victory, slaying thousands of his enemy[1]. Nasr, again appealing bitterly

Death of
Nasr,
iii.131 A.H.
Nov., 748
A.D.

but in vain for help, continued his flight westward to Rei. There he fell sick, and was carried on towards Hamadan, but he died upon the way. He was eighty-five years old, and his long and distinguished services as viceroy of Khorasan deserved a better fate.

Cahtaba
advances
on Kufa,
131 A. H.
749 A.D.

Cahtaba now advanced rapidly westward. Entering Rei, he restored order there, while his son, Ibn Cahtaba, with other generals, reduced the country all around,—the adherents of the Omeyyads, as well as the Kharejites, whose rebellion had recently been quelled, flying terrified before them Ibn Cahtaba then laid siege to Nehavend. The Caliph's army from Kerman (now released by Ibn Muavia's defeat and flight) 100,000 strong, advancing to its relief, was intercepted by Cahtaba, who with 20,000 men, after a fierce battle, entirely routed his enemy, and took his camp, itself a little city filled with all the luxuries of the East. After a three months' siege, Nehavend fell, and then Cahtaba, fetching a circuit to avoid Ibn Hobeira, the Syrian general at Jalola, made direct for Kufa, where, with expect-

---

[1] The numbers slain are variously put at from 10,000 to 30,000.

ations raised by the tidings of recent success, the Hashimite A.H. 130-
party looked impatiently for his appearance. It was now 132.
the beginning of the year 132, when Cahtaba crossed the Defeats Ibn
Euphrates, some thirty or forty miles above Kufa; but Hobeira,
Ibn Hobeira was before him, and the two armies met some- who falls back on
where in the vicinity of Kerbala. In this encounter the Wasit, 8th i.
Syrians were worsted, but the Hashimites too suffered a loss, 132 A.H.
for Cahtaba fell upon the field. His son, Ibn Cahtaba, took
command, and, following up his father's success, forced
Ibn Hobeira, abandoning his camp and all its stores, to
retire on Wasit. Kufa thus uncovered, the Hashimite Takes
force advanced, and after slight opposition,—for the Syrian Kufa; Abul
troops deserted hastily the Omeyyad leader,—took posses- Abbas
sion of the city; and shortly after Abul Abbas with his emerges from
family and relatives emerged from their hiding-place. In hiding,
anticipation of the new order of things (reserved for another 10th i. 132 A.H.
chapter), Abu Salma, who had been one of the busy agents 29 Aug.,
of the Hashimites in Khorasan, was recognized provision- 749 A.D.
ally as 'Wazeer of the house of Mahomet,' and Mohammed,
son of Khalid (former governor of Kufa), as ' Ameer.'

  Meanwhile, stirring events were passing in Upper Meso- Abu Aun
potamia. Cahtaba, in his victorious progress westward, had defeats Merwan's
detached Abu Aun, an able general, from Nehavend to son on
press forwards to Mesopotamia. Reaching Shahrzor, east Little Zab, 20 xii.
of the Little Zab, towards the end of 131 A.H., he there 131 A.H.
defeated with great slaughter the troops of Abdallah, Aug., 749 A.D.
Merwan's son, and occupied the region east of Mosul.
Merwan himself, since his campaign against the Kharejites, Merwan II
had remained inactive at Harran. He was now roused, by at last takes the
seeing the enemy at his very door, to take the field in field.
person, which earlier done, the issue might have been very
different, but now with rebellion, defeat, and disaffection
around, the ground was sinking under foot. Crossing the
Tigris, he advanced upon the Greater Zab with an army of
120,000, sufficiently strong in numbers to meet his enemy,
but made up in great measure of lukewarm Yemen tribes
and Kharejites. Meanwhile, Ibn Hobeira having retired
on Wasit, Abul Abbas, the rival Caliph, was able from
Kufa heavily to reinforce Abu Aun. To give the army

A.H. 130–132. also an imperial bearing, he sent his uncle Abdallah as commander-in-chief: and to him accordingly Abu Aun resigned the state-pavilion, mark of supreme command.

Battle of the Zab, 11th vi. 132 A.H. 25 Jan., 750 A.D. Abdallah found Merwan encamped with his great host on the right bank of the Zab, and Abu Aun with only 20,000 on the left. A party of the latter crossed, but after a skirmish retired. Next day, Merwan, against advice, threw a bridge across the river, and advanced to fight. His son at the first beat back a column of the enemy; and Abu Aun, lest the report should dishearten the army, resolved at once to bring on a general action. The historians tell us that Merwan did nothing that day to prosper; but the real truth is that the Syrians had lost both loyalty and heart. Abu Aun made his men dismount on the first attack, and plant their lances in the ground; while Abdallah incited them, as the heroes of Khorasan, to revenge the death of his nephew Ibrahim; he shouted, *Ya Mohammed! Ya Mansur!* and the battle-cry was taken up by all around. Merwan, on his side, called aloud to the Arab tribes, one after another by name, to advance, but none responded to the call. Then in an evil moment, expecting thereby to raise their zeal, he made known that he had treasure in the camp and would reward the brave; on which, some of the soldiers turned aside, hoping at once to secure the prize. To prevent this, Merwan detached his son; and as he turned back with guard and standard to protect the camp, the Defeat and flight of Merwan II. army took it for flight; and with the cry of *Defeat! Defeat!* broke and gave way. Merwan, to stay the flight, cut the bridge adrift; and more were drowned in the Zab than perished by the sword[1]. This battle, which foretold the fate of the Omeyyad Caliphate, took place in the year 132 A.H., or 750 A.D. Abdallah remained for a week on the field, and reported his victory to Abul Abbas, who,

---

[1] A grandson of Abd al Melik being seen struggling in the waves, Abdallah, the new Caliph's brother, is said to have cried, 'Let him alone,' quoting from the Coran the passage on the destruction of the Egyptians: 'Verily, when We divided the sea and saved you alive, but drowned the host of Pharaoh therein, while ye looked on.' *Sura* ii. 47.

overjoyed at the tidings, ordered 500 golden pieces, and A.H. 130–132. promise of increased pay, to be given to every combatant.

Merwan fled. At Mosul, his followers cried out, 'It is Flight of the Caliph, let him cross.' 'A lie,' they answered from Merwan. the other bank, 'the Caliph doth not fly;' and so they showered abuse upon the fallen monarch, and glorified the triumphant 'House of the Prophet.' Merwan then made the best of his way to Harran, where he spent some weeks in the vain endeavour to raise another army. But Abdallah was on his track, and so he hurried on to Hims, and thence, receiving no support, to Damascus. But neither could he safely make any stay there, and so desiring the governor, his son-in-law, to hold on, and raise another army, he fled to Palestine, where he found refuge with an Arab chief.

Meanwhile, under orders from Kufa, Abdallah had ad-Damascus vanced from the Zab to Mosul, where they streamed forth to taken by Abdallah, meet him with open arms, clad in the black colours of the brother of Abul new dynasty. At Harran, the governor, Merwan's nephew, Abbas. came out in similar attire to make his submission; and there Abdallah avenged the death of Ibrahim, his nephew, by the unmeaning demonstration of demolishing the house which had formed his prison[1]. Passing onward to Syria, he received the adhesion of all the chief places by the way. At Damascus reinforcements joined him from Kufa under his brother Salih, raising the force to 80,000. The city closed its gates against him, but after a short resistance was stormed, and the governor slain. Thereupon the black standard of the Abbassides was unfurled in triumph on the citadel, the 5th Ramzan, 132 A.H., eight months from the 18th April, entry into Kufa, and three from the battle of the Zab. 750 A.D. After a short stay, Abdallah passed on to Palestine in pursuit of Merwan, but found that he had fled to Egypt. Here, under orders from the new Caliph, he despatched his Merwan II brother Salih and Abu Aun with a force to follow up the pursued in Egypt, fugitive. At Said he found that, to stay pursuit, Merwan's xi.132 A.H. followers had burned all supplies of grass and fodder in June, 750 A.D.

---

[1] This action is in favour of the impression that Ibrahim did not die a violent death.

A.H. 130-
132.
———
Slain,
26 xii.
132 A.H.
5 Aug.,
750 A.D.

the neighbourhood.   Passing on to Fostat, Abu Aun was detached with a column, which took prisoners a troop of cavalry still attached to the fallen Caliph.   Some they put to death ; the rest were faithless enough to purchase their lives by disclosing their master's hiding-place.   He had taken refuge in a church at Busîr, where surprised by a small party he was overpowered and slain, just as the year expired.

Head sent
to Abul
Abbas.

The head was sent to the commander Salih, who had the tongue cut out and thrown contemptuously to a cat. Thus disfigured it was despatched to Kufa.   On seeing it, Abul Abbas bowed low in adoration.   Then raising his head towards heaven, he praised the Lord who had given him the victory and his revenge over an ungodly race. He recited also a verse indicative of the fire that still burned within:—'Had they quaffed my blood, it had not quenched their thirst; so neither is my wrath slaked by theirs.' True to the sentiment, he named himself (as we shall see) *Saffâh*, the Blood-thirsty, and by that title he has ever since been known.

His sons
and daugh-
ters.

Two of Merwan's sons fled to Abyssinia, where, attacked by the natives, one was killed ; the other escaped, and lived in concealment in Palestine, from whence he was sent many years after to the court of Mehdy.   The ladies of Merwan's family had been placed for safety in a church, from whence they were dragged to the presence of Salih[1]. Before him the elder daughter pleaded for mercy.   She was answered with reproaches for the cruel treatment by her people of the house of Hashim:—'How,' said the Caliph's uncle, ' can I spare any of this wicked race ?' Again she pleaded for grace and mercy:—'Nay,' he replied, ' but if thou wilt, thou mayest marry my son and save thyself.'   ' What heart have I now for that ?' she answered ; 'but send us back to Harran again.'   And when they returned there, and saw the old home and palace of Merwan, they lifted up their voices and wept.

His cha-
racter.

Merwan was over three-score years at his death, and

---

[1] The servant is said to have had instructions to put them to death if Merwan lost his life.

had reigned for nearly six. His mother was a Kurdish
slave-girl, and from her he inherited a handsome countenance, with blue eyes and a ruddy complexion. He was
called the *Ass of Mesopotamia*, not in derision, but in virtue
of his great power of physical endurance. He was one
of the bravest and best of his house, and deserved a better
fate[1].

So perished the Omeyyad dynasty, and on its ruins rose End of
the house of Hashim.   Omeyyad
                                                         dynasty.

[1] He was also called Al Jadi, from professing the heretical views of Jad, a
theologian who held the doctrine of Freewill, and denied that the Coran was
eternal and uncreate. But this may have been one of the calumnies heaped by
the Abbasside courtiers on the house of Omeyya. His mother was the Omm
Walad of Ibrahim al Ashtar, taken over by his father the day her master was
slain.

CHAPTER LIX.

THE ABBASSIDE DYNASTY.

132–656 A.H.   750–1258 A.D.

IN passing from the Omeyyad to the Abbasside Caliphate we reach in many respects a fresh departure which justifies a pause and some words in explanation of the change.

New features in the Abbasside Caliphate.

The first new feature is, that while the Omeyyad Caliphate, from first to last, was co-ordinate with the limits of Islam, this is no longer true of the Abbasside. The

The Caliphate no longer co-ordinate with Islam.

authority of the new dynasty was never acknowledged in Spain; and throughout Africa, excepting Egypt, it was but intermittent and for the most part nominal; while in the East, as time rolled on, independent dynasties arose. Islam thus broke up into many fragments, not necessarily in any way dependent on the Caliphate, each with its own separate history. But with all this, the Abbasside was the only dynasty that truly represented the proper Caliphate. Monarchs reigning in Cordova could only be recognized as 'Caliphs' in so far as every supreme ruler of Islam holds in his hand the spiritual as well as the secular authority, and may thus in some sense claim to be the Caliph or *Successor* of the Prophet. But the Abbassides alone had any colour of pretension to the name and dignity by virtue of legitimate succession[1].

Remainder of this work.

It being, then, the author's sole object to trace the Caliphate, properly so called, to its close, the rest of this work

---

[1] The Spanish dynasty, though sprung from the line of Omeyyad Caliphs, did not at first venture to assume the title. Abd al Rahman (Abderame, 300–349 A.H.) was the first who did so.

will be restricted to a narrative of the dynasty of the A.H. 132–
Abbassides as they rose first to the crest of glory, and then 656.
sank gradually under the sway of Sultans and Grand Vizi- Restricted
ers till they ended a mere phantom, vanishing into the to Abbas-
shadowy pageantry of attendants on the Mameluke kings phate.
of Egypt. Events outside the Caliphate will only so far
be noticed as they bear upon the individual history of the
dynasty. Thus alone will it be possible to keep the remainder of this book within reasonable dimensions.

Another marked feature in the era on which we enter is Arab
the change which comes over the Arabs and the attitude nation
of the new dynasty towards them. To their hardy life martial
and martial fire were mainly due the spread of Islam and vigour.
material prosperity of the Caliphate. But the nation had
by this time lost much of its early hardihood and vigour.
Enriched with the spoil of conquered peoples, the tempta-
tions to pride and luxury had gradually sapped their warlike virtue, and so they either settled down with well-filled
harems, living sumptuously at their ease ; or, if they still
preferred the field, yielded there to petulance and insubordination, preferring, too often, the interests of person, family,
and tribe, to the interests of Islam. The fervour of religious
enthusiasm had in great measure passed away, and self-
aggrandisement had taken the place of passion for national
glory and extension of the Faith. The Saracen was no
longer the conqueror of the world.

Added to this, the Abbassides on their accession lost Cast off by
confidence in their own people ; indeed, they had already Abbas-
done so for several years before. They were brought to sides,
the throne, and supported there, by levies from Persia
and Khorasan ; while of the Omeyyads, the Syrians were
the last support, and the Arab tribes, whether Modhar or
Yemen, were ranged upon their side. Ibrahim felt this so
strongly, that in the letter intercepted by Merwan, in which
he chided Abu Muslim for his delay in crushing Nasr and
Kirmany, he added angrily,—' See that there be not one
left in Khorasan whose tongue is the tongue of the Arabian,
but he be slain !' It was among the Arabs of Syria and
Mesopotamia that dangerous revolt repeatedly took place

who throw
themselves
into hands
of Turks
and Per-
sians.

against the new dynasty, and so they continued to be looked askance upon.   Before long the Caliphs drew their body-guard entirely from the Turks about the Oxus ; and that barbarous race, scenting from afar the delights of the south, were not slow to follow.   Before long these began to overshadow the noble Arab chieftains; and so we soon find the imperial forces officered almost entirely by Turcomans, freedmen or slaves, of strange descent and uncouth name. In the end the Caliphs became the helpless tools of their protectors : and the Arabs, where not already denationalized by city life, retired to roam at will in their desert wilds.

With the rise of Persian influence, the roughness of Arab life was softened ; and there opened an era of culture, toleration, and scientific research.   The practice of oral tradition was also giving place to recorded statement and historical narrative,—a change hastened by the scholarly tendencies introduced from the East.

Persian
influences.

To the same source may be attributed the ever increasing laxity at Court of manners and morality ; and also those transcendental views that now sprang up, of the divine Imamat or spiritual leadership of some member of the house of Aly ; as well as the rapid growth of free thought.

These things will be developed as we go on.   But I have thought it well to draw attention at this point to the important changes wrought by the closer connection of the Caliphate with Persia and Khorasan, caused by the accession of the Abbassides.

CHAPTER LX.

ABUL ABBAS, SAFFAH.

132–136 A. H.   749–54 A.D.

A BRIEF review may here be necessary, to recall the circumstances attending the establishment of the new Caliphate at Kufa.

In a previous chapter we have seen that while Merwan still tarried at Harran, Ibn Hobeira was defeated in the vicinity of Kufa by the army of Cahtaba, and obliged to fall back on Wasit. Abu Salma, heretofore a busy leader and agent of the Hashimite cause in Khorasan, now encamped at Kufa, meeting with little opposition, took possession of the city in the beginning of the year 132, and for a time carried on the government under the title of ' Wazeer of the house of Mahomet.'   On the arrest of Ibrahim, two or three years before, his two brothers, and all their relatives of the house of Hashim, fled from Homeima to Kufa, where they had remained ever since in concealment ; they were now taken charge of by Abu Salma, but for several weeks were still kept by him in the strictest privacy. When urged to declare the advent of the new dynasty, he said that it would be premature and dangerous so long as Ibn Hobeira maintained his stand at Wasit. Some suspected him of favouring that branch of Hashimite stock which had descended from Aly, but of these none had the ambition or the courage to come forward. However that may be, the Abbasside party were impatient at the delay, and learning that Ibrahim had declared his younger brother Abul Abbas (son of a noble mother, while his brother Abu Jafar was son of a slave-

F f

Marginal notes:

Abul Abbas, Saffah, 132 A. H. 749 A. D.

Abbasside family brought into Kufa, ii. 132 A. H. Oct., 749 A. D.

A.H. 132-
136.
girl) his successor, they brought him out openly; and finding the people with them, proceeded on a public demonstration. It was about three months after the occupation of Kufa by the Hashimite troops that, apparently with the consent of Abu Salma, they mounted Abul Abbas upon a piebald horse, entered the palace, and thence proceeded

Abul
Abbas done
homage to,
12 iii.
132 A.H.
20 Oct.,
749 A.D.
to the Great Mosque. There Abul Abbas ascended the pulpit and made his first address. He magnified the virtues and claims of the descendants of the Prophet, denounced the usurpation and crimes of the Omeyyads and their Syrian followers, praised the Kufans for their fidelity to his family, which he promised to reward by an increase of their stipends; and ended by declaring it his mission to root out all opposition, for, said he, 'I am the Great Revenger, and my name *Saffâh*, the Shedder of Blood[1].' His uncle Daud followed with still fiercer words. He styled Merwan 'the enemy of the Lord, and Caliph of the Devil,' and affirmed that the only real successors of the Prophet were two—Aly his son-in-law, who had stood in that very pulpit, and now another standing in the same, even Abul Abbas—the true Commander of the Faithful. 'Delay not then,' he said, 'to take the oath of fealty. The dominion is ours, and with us it will remain, till the day when we shall render it up to Jesus Son of Mary.' Having thus delivered themselves, they both descended from the pulpit, and entered the castle, whither the people flocked till it was dark, doing homage to the new Caliph. Abul Abbas then returned to the encampment of Abu Salma, where for some months he occupied the same abode[2].

Caliph
retires to
Hashimiya.
By and by Abul Abbas became alienated from Abu Salma, whether from any well-grounded suspicion against him, Alyite, or otherwise, cannot be said. But, whatever

---

[1] His usual name, Saffah, was given on account of his many bloody executions, which of course were yet in the future. It is not unlikely that the name may have been imported into his first harangue by anticipation; but I give the speech as I find it. Abul Abbas was suffering from an attack of fever, which made him cut short his address.

[2] The 'same apartment,' we are told, separated by a simple curtain between the two. This does not look as if suspicion existed, at any rate at this time, against Abu Salma, of Alyite tendencies or other disloyalty.

the cause, now quitting his house at Kufa, the new Caliph A.H. 132–136.
repaired to Anbar, in the neighbourhood of which he laid
the foundation of a courtly residence, and called it after his
family *Hashimiya.* From thence he despatched his uncles
and other relatives, among whom were several men of sufficient ability, with commands in various directions to replace the officers of the fallen dynasty. Acting under his
direction, these soon earned for Abul Abbas a solid claim
to the sanguinary title he aspired after.

His earliest care was to sweep from the face of the earth Omeyyad house pursued to death.
the entire Omeyyad race. Such wholesale butcheries cast
into the shade anything the previous dynasty had ever been
accused of. The cruellest of them was that perpetrated by
the Caliph's uncle in Palestine. An amnesty was offered
to the numerous branches of the family congregated there ;
and to confirm it they were invited, some ninety in number,
to a feast. Suddenly a bard arose reciting in verse the evil
deeds of the Omeyyads, and on signal given, the attendants
fell on the unsuspecting guests, and put them all to death. Wholesale butchery in Palestine, 133 A.H. 751 A.D.
A carpet was drawn across the ghastly spectacle, and the
tyrant resumed his feast over the still quivering limbs of
the dying. All in whose veins ran the blood of Omeyyad
princes were relentlessly pursued, and only such as were
of tender years[1], or successfully effected flight, escaped.
At Bussorah, the like scene was soon after enacted; the
miserable victims were slain and their remains cast into the
streets to be devoured of dogs. Those that escaped wandered about in terror, seeking vainly in disguise some
place of secrecy. One such, a descendant of Abu Sofian,
finding his life a burden, cast himself at the feet of an uncle
of the Caliph, who, touched with pity, obtained a rescript
not only sparing him, but granting a general amnesty to
such as still survived. Nevertheless in the following year,
we find another less merciful uncle of Saffah initiating a
fresh slaughter of those that had taken shelter in the holy
cities of Mecca and Medina.

Nor did it suffice that they should vent their rage on the Desecration of dead.
living, the fear of whose machinations might possibly be

[1] The phrase used by the historian is 'sucklings.'

pleaded in feeble excuse. The tombs of the Caliphs were
unearthed. Of the great Muavia there was nothing that
remained but dust; and of the other Caliphs little more,
excepting only Hisham, whose frame was found in singular
preservation. This they scourged with whips, hung up for
a while, and then burned, scattering the ashes to the winds.
Such outrage raised indignation throughout Syria and
Mesopotamia. Omeyyad households also were treated with
indignity by the creatures of the new dynasty. One of their
minions, caught in the act of carrying off as slaves the
harem of the distinguished warrior Maslama, was slain by
the governor of Kinnesrin, which forthwith rose in rebellion.
Rebellion All Syria, with Damascus at its head, followed suit. The
in Syria
and Meso- Caliph's uncle Abdallah, at that moment quelling a rising
potamia. in the Hauran, came to terms with the insurgents, and
hastened to the north, where he was met by a defiant
force of 40,000 men. After much fighting and various
fortune, he defeated his enemy and restored order. A
still more dangerous revolt threatened Hashimite rule in
Mesopotamia, where an army of 60,000 Syrians in the
field laid siege to Harran. To meet the emergency, Abul
Abbas detached a column under command of his brother
Abu Jafar, from the army then besieging Ibn Hobeira in
Wasit. This force advancing to the northern coasts of the
Euphrates, dispersed the insurgents, but with some difficulty, for Someisat was not recovered till after a siege of
seven months. Bussorah also resisted all the attempts of
the Hashimite general, supported by a column from Khorasan. That unfortunate city was also distracted within
itself, apart altogether from the Abbasside attack; for the
Modharite party, having gotten the ascendancy after severe
fighting, overthrew the opposite faction; and the city,—
suffering thus whichever party conquered,—was for three
days given up to pillage and outrage. The Omeyyad
leaders, however, kept possession of it until Wasit fell.

These risings, if guided by an able leader with united
interest and common design, might have changed the order
of events, and raised the fallen dynasty, which still had
Syria for its support. It failed mainly from the fatal step

of Ibn Hobeira, who, as we have seen, instead of hastening A.H. 132-136.

north at his call to the support of Merwan, fell back on

Wasit, and there shut himself up with the flower of the Ibn Hobeira

Omeyyad troops. He was afraid, we are told, of Merwan, capitulates

because he had not obeyed the order to detach troops for at Wasit.

the support of Nasr in Khorasan ; but whatever the cause,

it proved fatal to his master; for defeat in Syria was

beyond comparison more to be dreaded than the loss of

Wasit, important as it was. The siege of that cantonment

was pressed vigorously by Ibn Cahtaba. The powerful

garrison made no way against it, partly owing to the

depressing influences of a failing cause, and partly to

the tribal jealousies that still paralyzed the Syrian sol-

diery. Thus things went on for eleven months, during

which the Omeyyad cause was being lost in Syria. At

last, the Caliph, recalling his brother Abu Jafar from

the north, sent him to take the command at Wasit ; and

the tidings of Merwan's death having meanwhile reached

Ibn Hobeira, he thereupon offered to capitulate[1]. A full

amnesty concluded by Abu Jafar, was ratified by the

Caliph under solemn oath ; and Abu Jafar, who received

Ibn Hobeira graciously, was intent upon respecting it.

But the Caliph, having consulted Abu Muslim then at Treacher-

Merve, and received his counsel to get Ibn Hobeira 'as a ously put to

death with

stumbling-stone out of his way,' persistently urged his followers.

death. At last Abul Abbas sent two creatures of his own

to do the deed, if Abu Jafar should still decline. Abu Jafar

gave way ; and summoning two-and-twenty of the leading

Modhar chiefs to an interview, had them bound two and

two, by a party concealed in an adjoining apartment, and,

spite of their appeal to the Caliph's solemn oath, beheaded.

Ibn Hobeira and his son were at the same time.slain by

the two emissaries of the Caliph, who repaired to his house

under pretence of taking over the treasure. The historian

adds pathos to the cruel tale of perfidy; for he tells us

[1] When he heard of Merwan's defeat and death, he is said to have written to
Mohammed ibn Abdallah, a grandson of Hasan son of Aly, offering to support
his claim to the throne, but waiting long for a reply, and the Caliph's emissaries
beginning to tamper with the Yemenite party in his army, he capitulated ; of
this Ibn Abdallah we shall hear more in the next reign.

A.H. 132-136.

that Ibn Hobeira, suspecting no treachery, had at the moment, on his knee, a little son, whom they snatched from his embrace as he fell on his knees imploring mercy[1].

Bloodshed in Mosul.

Notwithstanding that the Hashimite banner everywhere prevailed, outrage still survived in many parts of the empire. A terrible calamity overtook Mosul. The people refusing obedience to the new governor as a low-born stranger, expelled him from their city. On this, the Caliph sent his brother Yahya, who proved himself worthy of his relationship to the 'Shedder of blood.' The townsmen were persuaded to gather in the court of the mosque, under promise of full security, but the gates were no sooner closed upon them, than they were massacred to a man[2]. The city, deprived thus of its protectors, was given up for three days to sack and outrage. Besides the regular soldiery, there were with the troops 4000 negroes who shamelessly violated the women, till one of these, bolder than the rest, appealed to Yahya, the reins of whose horse she seized, and asked whether followers of the Prophet were now abandoned to the embrace of slaves. To appease the outcry, the entire body of the negroes was put to the sword. The Caliph removed his brother for his cruelty, but nevertheless put him over another province.

Fighting elsewhere.

Elsewhere troubles prevailed to the end of the reign. The viceroy of Sind and India refused to recognise Hashimite rule; after heavy fighting, he was beaten, and died of thirst in his flight through the desert. Bussorah being at last reduced by a force of veterans from Khorasan, the adherents of the old dynasty fled to Oman, where they were joined by a vast host of Kharejites. They were in the end defeated by the imperial troops, and incredible numbers slain or burned to death. In Khorasan there were similar outbreaks with even greater slaughter. The

---

[1] The Caliph's oath of amnesty was couched in the most stringent and solemn terms, and condign punishment from ' the Searcher of hearts ' was invoked on him who might violate its conditions. The historian adds (but hardly by way of justification) that Ibn Hobeira once addressed Abu Jafar as ' O man ' or by some such term; but immediately apologised for it as a slip of the tongue.

[2] The numbers are given at 10,000, but probably with the usual exaggeration of the slaughter made in the reign of Saffâh.

rebels of Bokhara, Soghd, and Ferghana, were aided by A.H. 132– 'the king of China,' but put to flight by Ziad, governor of 136. Samarcand, with terrible carnage[1].

We have seen that the Caliph on his accession, after Abu Salma living for some time in closest intimacy with Abu Salma, treacher- one of the leading supporters of the Hashimite cause in ously put Khorasan and their 'Vizier' at Kufa, became alienated to death. from him, and departed from his residence to Anbar. It is said that Abu Salma had a favour for the house of Aly, which stirred the Caliph's jealousy. Whether this be so or no, Abul Abbas cherished enmity against him in his heart, and wrote to Abu Muslim at Merve for his advice, which came to put him to death. The Caliph was dissuaded from ordering the execution, by an uncle who dwelt on the danger of revenge by Abu Salma's influential followers from Khorasan, and suggested that Abu Muslim should be asked to send an assassin for the purpose. This was done. Abul Abbas then ordered a crier to go forth and proclaim Abu Salma as 'the man whom the Caliph delighteth to honour.' So he was called and arrayed in a robe of honour, and entertained by the Caliph till night was far advanced. As he wended his way home alone, he was waylaid and as- sassinated. Report was diligently spread that the Kharejites had done the deed; but all well knew where the motive lay[2].

Shortly after, Abu Jafar was deputed to Merve, with the Abu Mus- view of feeling the pulse and attitude of Abu Muslim Khorasan. himself; and there conceived towards him a bitter ani- mosity. As viceroy of Khorasan, Abu Muslim exercised an

---

[1] 50,000 slain beyond the Oxus, and 20,000 taken prisoners. In Oman, 900 Kharejites were killed in battle, and ninety burned alive. Then the troops attacked the town, which was built of wood, and pouring naphtha on the houses, set them thus ablaze; then rushing sword in hand on the terrified inhabitants, they slew 10,000,—' all counted and the heads sent to Bussorah.' One may hope that these butcheries are vastly exaggerated; but they point to the lament- able disregard for human life that now prevailed.

[2] This is the most received report. Another is that the Caliph, fearing that Abu Muslim shared the Alyite tendencies of which Abu Salma was suspected, sent Abu Jafar to sound Abu Muslim; and that the latter, to prove his loyalty, despatched an assassin who committed the deed as above narrated.

Abu Muslim at the same time sent agents to put to death all the governors who had been appointed by Abu Salma while he ruled in Fars.

A.H. 132–
136.

unlimited, and, as Abu Jafar thought, a dangerous supremacy. Thus for an imprudent word, and on slight and arbitrary suspicion, he put to death Ibn Kethir, one of the earliest and most valuable advocates of the Hashimite mission in Khorasan[1]. This was done openly before Abu Jafar, who as we shall see never forgot the crime, and on his return to Irac told his brother that he was no longer

Attempt to assassinate him,

135 A.H.

Caliph unless he got rid of this wilful autocrat. The Caliph took it to heart, but bade his brother for the present keep the matter secret. A year or two later, Ziad the governor of Samarcand, which had recently been strongly fortified, set up for himself, and Abu Muslim went to fight him. On the way he discovered that an emissary of the Caliph (who is accused of having himself instigated the rebellion in order to weaken the too powerful Viceroy) was in his camp in league with Ziad, and that he had instructions to compass his death. The plot thus coming to light miscarried. Ziad was deposed and put to death by his own subjects; and the would-be assassin was beheaded.

Abu Muslim's pilgrimage with Abu Jafar,

136 A.H.

In the following year, Abu Muslim, undeterred by the machinations at Court, asked permission to visit the Caliph at Anbar, and thence proceed on pilgrimage to Mecca. Leave was granted, but his following limited to 1000 men. He started with 8000, but left 7000 at Rei. The Caliph received him with every mark of honour, and gave permission to proceed to Mecca; but informed him that his brother Abu Jafar would probably be appointed to preside at the pilgrimage, a dignity Abu Muslim apparently expected for himself. Meanwhile Abu Jafar, who now resided at the Court, and both hated and feared the Viceroy, persuaded his brother to order his execution; he was to be cut down from behind as he was conversing with the Caliph. But the Caliph changed his mind. Dreading the revenge of the Khorasan troops, should he put their favourite to death, he withdrew the order. The pilgrimage

---

[1] Abu Muslim was jealous of this man's influence: and had conceived a hatred for him, because when Ibrahim first selected Abu Muslim as the Hashimite plenipotentiary in Khorasan, Ibn Kethir had sought to dissuade him on account of his extreme youth. Abu Muslim never forgave him, and now took advantage of the incautious speech to put him to death.

accordingly was undertaken by Abu Jafar and Abu Muslim A.H. 132-136.
both together.   But though the former led the ceremonial,
he was outshone by the splendour of Abu Muslim's equipage
and his princely liberality.   The pilgrimage completed,
tidings of the Caliph's death reached the returning caravan.
Abu Jafar had Abu Muslim now entirely in his power, but he
was obliged, as will be explained in the following chapter,
to veil his hatred for a time.

Abul Abbas died of small-pox in his palace at Anbar, a Abul
few days after the pilgrimage at Mecca was ended.   His Abbas dies on 13 xii.
age is given at from twenty-eight to thirty-five years.   He 136 A.H. 9 June,
left a daughter[1], afterwards married to her cousin the 754 A.D.
Caliph Mehdy.   Abul Abbas was vain of his appearance,
and little is said by the annalists of his death, beyond a
description of the varied wardrobe which he left behind.   It
is also related of him, that as he stood looking at himself
in a mirror, he exclaimed,—' I do not say, as Soleiman,
Behold the kingly youth; but I say, *Lord, give me long
life and health to enjoy the same.'*   As he spake, he heard a
slave say to his fellow hard by, regarding some mutual
concern,—' The term between us two months and five days.'
He took it as an evil augury ; and so he sickened, and death
overtook him as the term expired.

Thus closed the sanguinary reign of Abul Abbas, which Palace of
lasted a little less than five years, during the last two of Hashimiya, and public
which he resided in the palace now completed at Anbar. works.
Of public undertakings, the only thing we are told is that
he had towers constructed for protection of the pilgrims
at convenient distances all the way from Kufa to Mecca,
and also mile-stones.   Khalid the son of Barmek (the
' Barmecide'), of whom mention has been already made,
accompanied Cahtaba from Balkh, and being a man of
singular ability was promoted by the Caliph to be chief
of the Exchequer, and with the rest of the family attained
a high position at Court.   In the last year of his reign Abu
Abbas nominated his nephew Isa, to be heir-apparent after

---

[1] Only a daughter, we are told. A son indeed is mentioned as accompanying
Isa in the expedition against the Alyites, 145 A.H.; but as he is not spoken of
elsewhere, he was probably of ignoble birth.

A.H. 182–
136.
_____
Isa nomin-
ated heir-
apparent
after Abu
Jafar.
Saffâh the
Blood-
thirsty. his brother Abu Jafar. The patent, inscribed upon a silken sheet, and sealed with the signets of the Caliph and of the chief heads of the royal family, was placed in custody of Isa himself, now governor of Kufa.

The name by which Abul Abbas is most commonly known is Saffâh, the Blood-thirsty, and he is well so called; for as such he is distinguished beyond all others in a dynasty that had small respect for human life. He intensified his cruelty and guilt, if that were possible, by treachery in face of solemn oaths, and also by ingratitude, for amongst his victims were those who had spent their lives in helping him to the throne. That the attempt should have been made to extenuate his crimes is strange; and is thus referred to by the impartial Weil, in whose judgment I concur;—

'We can but marvel,' he says, 'that many Europeans have sought to defend this Caliph who was worse than any Omeyyad,—as if he did not deserve the name of Blood-shedder, which indeed he himself assumed. He may not with his own hands have strangled victims; but not the less was it by his express mandate that the Omeyyads in Syria, and Soleiman in his very presence, were perfidiously slain. At his command must Abu Muslim hire the assassin of Abu Salma, to whom the Abbassides owed so much. It was at his repeated requisition that Abu Jafar, in treacherous disregard of solemn oaths, slew Ibn Hobeira and his fellows; and it certainly is not due to his innocence that the fate of Abu Salma did not during his own reign overtake Abu Muslim also. Abul Abbas was not merely a barbarous tyrant; he was a perjured and ungrateful traitor.'

Such is the not overdrawn character of the first of the Abbassides, Abul Abbas, Saffâh, the 'Blood-shedder.'

CHAPTER LXI.

ABU JAFAR, MANSUR.

136–158 A.H. 754–75 A.D.

AT the death of Abul Abbas, Abu Jafar, as we have seen, Abu Jafa Dzul Hijj, 136 A.H.
was on pilgrimage at Mecca. His cousin, Isa, whom the
late Caliph had nominated as second in succession, caused June, 754 A.D.
Abu Jafar to be at once proclaimed at Kufa, and the oath
of allegiance was taken accordingly. On receiving tidings
of his brother's death, Abu Jafar returned immediately to
Kufa, and inaugurated his succession by leading prayers in
the Great Mosque with the usual address; and then went
on to the palace at Anbar. He assumed the name of
Mansûr, the Victorious.

Abu Muslim, as already said, was also on pilgrimage with Rebellion of Abdallah, the Caliph's uncle.
him. Abu Jafar, directly on hearing of his brother's death
while on the homeward route, sent for him and told him
that he feared the attitude of his uncle Abdallah. Abu
Muslim bade him set his mind at ease, promising in the
event of Abdallah's rebellion to proceed at once against
him. There was ground for the alarm. Abdallah was
in command of a powerful force on the border of Asia
Minor. He now asserted that the late Caliph had promised
him the succession, in reward for his campaign against
Merwan; and so, persuading the army to do homage to
him as Caliph, he set siege to Harran. Abu Jafar was the
more anxious for the services of Abu Muslim, as there
were in the rebel army 17,000 men of Khorasan devoted
to their old leader. On Abu Muslim's approach, Abdallah

A.H. 186-
158.
_____
Defeated
by Abu
Muslim,
ii. 137 A.H.
Nov.,
754 A.D.
raised the siege, and marched north to Nisibin, where he entrenched himself in a strong position; but on his way, fearing the Khorasanies, he cruelly put the whole of them to the sword [1]. To decoy him from his stronghold, Abu Muslim made as if he would march for Syria; on which the rebel army, mostly Syrians, alarmed for their families, insisted on following the same course; whereupon Abu Muslim returning occupied the deserted vantage-ground. Fighting went on for five months with various success, till in the end, through Abu Muslim's able tactics, the Syrian army was totally discomfited. Abdallah fled, but was eventually placed under charge of his brother Soleiman, governor of Bussorah.

The thankless Caliph, instead of rewarding a man who had founded, and now had saved, his throne, was bent on the death of one for whom, having served his purpose, he had no farther need, and whom he both feared and hated. While yet on the field of battle, the great warrior divined the temper of his master, who, much to his mortification, sent a courier to take count of the spoil; and bethought him of retiring to Khorasan. This, in fact, was what the Caliph dreaded; and so with many fair words that he wished to keep him near his person, he offered him the .government of Syria and Egypt. Abu Muslim replied that there was ever danger in a powerful subject being near the Court; at a distance he would be the Caliph's devoted servant; but otherwise he would have no alternative but to break allegiance. An angry correspondence ensued, and Abu Muslim began his march to Khorasan. At Holwan, he received a peremptory mandate to repair to Medain, where the Caliph waited for him. Distracted by various counsel,—friends, once faithful but now won over to deceive, advised him to obey; and so, trusting to fair promises, he proceeded to the Court. As he drew near, Abu Ayub, the Vizier, fearing the warrior and his followers

---

[1] The enormous butchery of 17,000 soldiers is narrated without comment. Cruelty and treachery seem innate in the whole family. On two occasions in this march, Abdallah sent chiefs whom he was afraid of, to his creatures elsewhere, with letters which they unsuspectingly carried containing orders for their assassination. One of them had occasion to open his missive, and so escaped.

if he came in wrath, bribed one to meet and assure him of the Caliph's favour and good will. Abu Muslim's apprehensions thus disarmed, he entered the palace, and was graciously welcomed; kissing the Caliph's hand, he was bidden to rest awhile and refresh himself with a bath. The following day, again summoned to the Court, the Caliph at first addressed him softly thus ;—'Tell me of the two daggers that Abdallah had.' 'Here,' said he, 'is one of them,' and he handed it to the Caliph, who put it under his pillow. Then with some warmth,—'And the girl of his whom thou tookest?' 'Not so,' replied Abu Muslim ; 'but I feared for her, and so carrying her to a tent left her in safe custody.' On this, with growing warmth Abu Jafar brought charge upon charge against the ill-fated man,— Why had he slighted him on the pilgrimage? set out for Khorasan against his orders? made himself out, though a mere slave, as if of Abbasside descent, and sought the hand of the Caliph's aunt? and worst of all, why had he slain Ibn Kathir, long before him the early and faithful supporter of the dynasty[1]? As he waxed fiercer at every charge, Abu Muslim could but urge his life-long service to the throne, kiss the Caliph's hand, and plead for pardon. But in vain. Abu Jafar clapped his hands, and at the signal five armed men stepped from behind the curtain, and as the victim screamed for mercy, cut him in pieces, while the Caliph cursed. To calm the crowd without, it was told them that 'the Caliph was in conclave with his Ameer'; and believing it to be so, Isa, the heir-apparent, entered and asked where Abu Muslim was. 'He was here but now,' answered the Caliph. 'Ah,' replied Isa, 'I knew that he was loyal and would obey thy call.' 'Fool that thou art!' cried Abu Jafar ;—'thou hadst not in all the world a worse enemy than he; look there!' he said, as the carpet was raised revealing the mangled corpse. Isa horrified retired. Shortly after Abu

---

[1] See above, p. 440. The charge of making himself out of Abbasside descent was true enough. When in the zenith of his glory, there were not wanting creatures who, to cover his servile origin, invented a story of Abbasside descent ; a fatal adulation that only added fuel to the Caliph's jealousy.

Ishac, one of Abu Muslim's staff, was summoned; 'What
hast thou now to say about thy master,' asked the Caliph,
'and his intended move to Khorasan?' Terrified, he
glanced first to the right and then to the left, as if fearing
lest Abu Muslim might be near to overhear. 'No need for
fear!' exclaimed the Caliph; and the covering was again
removed. 'Thanks be to the Lord!' cried Abu Ishac, as he
bowed low and long in worship; and, gazing at the corpse
exclaimed,—'Thanks for my deliverance from thee, O
tyrant!' Then turning to the Caliph,—'I swear, not a
day passed that I felt my life my own for fear of him,
nor came into his presence but prepared for death.' So
saying, he drew aside his robe and disclosed a winding-
sheet beneath. Moved with pity, the Caliph spared him
the fate awaiting an adherent of his fallen chief.

Character
of Abu
Muslim.
Having received the congratulations of his courtiers, who
wished him joy that now at last he was the real king, Abu
Jafar went forth and harangued the multitudes brought together by the startling news:—'It was,' he said, 'a lesson
to be laid to heart; the man began well, but ended ill,
and now by pride and rebellion had forfeited his life.' The
scene is one the annalists dwell much upon; and rightly so.
For Abu Muslim is without doubt the leading figure of
the age. Hardly thirty-five years old, he had by his rare
wisdom, zeal, and generalship, changed the whole outlook of
Islam, and raised the house of Abbas upon the ruins of the
house of Omeyya. He deserved his fate, no doubt,—for the
blood of multitudes was on his head, but not at the hand
of Abu Jafar, who owed his all to him. It was jealousy of
Abu Muslim's influence that had fed the Caliph's hatred.
The estimate of Isa was the truer; for there is nothing in
the acts or attitude of Abu Muslim to show that he was
other than a loyal supporter of the dynasty which owed its
existence to himself [1].

---

[1] 600,000, we are told, 'met their death at his hands in cold blood, besides
those slain in battle:'—a wild estimate, no doubt, but significant of his contempt of life. Apart from this, his character was popular, and gave him the
supreme command of men. Hospitable and generous, he held in Khorasan a
court of great magnificence. Simple in respect of his harem, he was yet strangely

The story of Abu Nasr, whom Abu Muslim had left in charge of his camp at Holwan, is also worth recording. Abu Jafar, desirous to have this able officer in his power, sent him a summons, as if from Abu Muslim, to come at once to him at Court with all his goods, and sealed it with his master's seal. But Abu Muslim had warned his friends not to hold any letter from him genuine unless it bore but half his seal. Detecting the deception thus, Abu Nasr fled to Hamadan. To calm suspicion, the Caliph then sent a patent appointing him governor of Shahrzor; but at the same time also a letter to the governor of Hamadan to take his life as he passed. The former first arrived, and so starting at once, Abu Nasr escaped the intended fate. At last, seeing no security anywhere, he sought the Caliph's presence, and confessing that he had advised his master to seek refuge in Khorasan, threw himself on his Sovereign's mercy, and promised faithful service. Abu Jafar let him go; and his clemency, as we shall see, had its reward.

A.H. 136–158.

Story of Abu Nasr.

It was not for another year or two that peace was restored either in Mesopotamia or Persia. In the latter, serious rising threatened the empire under a singular leader, Sinbad the Magian, who stepped forth as the avenger of Abu Muslim, and with a large following gained possession of the country from Rei to Nisabur [1]. A similar rebellion followed in Mesopotamia, where the imperial forces were repeatedly defeated. In the following year, however, victory crowned the army of the Caliph, and peace was restored both there and in Persia.

Peace restored in Persia and Mesopotamia, 138 A.H. 756 A.D.

The Caliph, relieved thus of all the dangers that had threatened him, might now have left his uncle Abdallah alone at Bussorah; but hearing that he had, mistrusting his nephew, retired for safety into hiding, he sent to his uncles, Soleiman and Aly, to bring him to court. Relying

Caliph imprisons his uncle Abdallah. End of 139 A.H. 757 A.D.

jealous. The mule that brought his bride was slain and the saddle burnt, that none might ride again upon it.

[1] Whether the Magian counted Abu Muslim one of his followers, is not quite clear. There must apparently have been something more than mere regard for his memory. The rising was serious, as multitudes of women were carried off, and in the end 60,000 of his followers (so we are told) were killed, besides captives. He was two and a half months in the field.

A.H. 186–
158.
on his solemn promise of a full pardon, they brought him, and presented themselves before the Caliph. He received them graciously, and engaged them in conversation, while Abdallah, who remained without, was carried off a prisoner to the castle. After a little while he bade them go and rejoin Abdallah. Thus overreached, they returned to expostulate, but were denied admittance. Their followers, enraged at the perfidy, would have offered resistance, but were disarmed, several put to death, and the rest sent to Khorasan, where they met the same fate. The wonder is that in so faithless, treacherous, and cruel a monarch any confidence anywhere was left. The reason no doubt is that such shameless breach of faith was only practised when personal or dynastic danger threatened. Apart from this, as a whole, the administration of Abu Jafar was wise and just.

Fighting in Asia Minor, 138–9 A.H.
During 138 A.H. Constantine waged war with the Syrian army, and took Malatia, destroying its fortifications. The following year it was retaken, repaired, and heavily garrisoned. The campaign is remarkable for the presence of two princesses, cousins of the Caliph, who joined the army in fulfilment of a vow taken some years before, that if Merwan fell they would serve in the holy war against the infidels. The Caliph now entered on an exchange of prisoners with the Emperor, and a truce of seven years was agreed to; for events at home began to occupy every resource at his disposal.

Pilgrimage, 140 A.H. 758 A.D.
In 140 A.H. the Caliph performed the yearly pilgrimage, visited Jerusalem, and made a progress through Syria and Mesopotamia. On his return a strange rising placed him in imminent personal danger.

Rising of Rawendies at Hashimiya, 141 A.H.
A Persian sect, called Rawendies (from the name of their town), holding such doctrines as the immanence of divinity and transmigration of souls, visited Hashimiya. The commandant of the Body-guard, they held, was inhabited by the soul of Adam; another courtier by that of Gabriel, and so on; and the Caliph, the adumbration of Deity itself. Surrounding the palace, they shouted, 'It is the house of our Lord, he that giveth us food to eat and water to drink.' The Caliph had 200 of their leaders imprisoned, which so enraged the rest that they

stormed the prison and rioted all round. Abu Jafar ventured forth without an escort to quell the uproar; but the
wild sectaries, no longer regarding him divine, made an
onset, and had it not been for Abu Nasr (already mentioned), and an Omeyyad adherent,—who thus secured
grace—both throwing themselves between the rioters and
the Caliph's person, it would have gone hard with him.
Troops fortunately came up at the moment, and the Rawendies, on whom the people shut the city gates, fled in
confusion[1].

Soon after, the governor of Khorasan rebelled, and Abu
Jafar sent Ibn Khozeima, a general of note, to put the outbreak down, and with him his son, Mehdy, now about twenty
years of age. On their approach, the rebel was attacked by
his own people, who, mounting him backward on an ass, sent
him thus to the Caliph. Both he and his followers were
treated with horrid cruelty, and tortured till they gave
up all they possessed. The hands and feet of the rebel
governor were cut off, he was then beheaded, and his son
sent in banishment to an island in the Red Sea.

The Moslem arms were now directed against Tabaristan,
the ruling Ispahend of which had cast off subordination to
Islam. The campaign was prosperous. In the following
year, however, the prince again rebelled, and in his impregnable fortress defied attack. But a pretended deserter having ingratiated himself and gained his confidence, opened
the gates to the Moslem force. The fortress taken thus,
the fighting men were put to the sword, and their families
made captive. Mehdy chose two of the maidens for himself, and the Ispahend's daughter was taken by his uncle[2].
The army then turned towards Deilem; but here the
insurrection was so serious, that a fresh levy was ordered
from Irac and Mosul, which was kept in the field all the
following year. Meanwhile, Mehdy returned to court;

---

[1] The Caliph could not find a horse to mount, till he picked up one on his
way. Stables were now attached to the palace, for there had been none
before.

[2] Such slave-girls are only mentioned in connection with issue borne to their
masters, otherwise they were taken as the conquerors might fancy into their
harems as a matter of course, and without any special notice.

A.H. 186–
158.
———
Mehdy
returns,
144 A.H.
761 A.D.

and being now twenty-three years of age, married Rita, the only child of his uncle, the late Caliph. He then returned to Khorasan, where he remained for some time longer. The Caliph went this year, as he did several other times, on pilgrimage.

Moham-
med and
Ibrahim,
descend-
ants of
Hasan,
rebel,
144 A.H.

A new danger now threatened the dynasty. It was from the house of Hasan son of Aly. The head of this family was Hasan's grandson Abdallah, whose two sons Moham-med and Ibrahim had for some time held ambitious designs[1]. Abu Jafar entertained suspicions against them ever since his first pilgrimage, when they failed to present themselves. As usual, he proceeded by stratagem. A creature of his, by feigned communications from Khorasan, where there ever was a strong faction for any scion of the house of Aly, gained the father's confidence, and succeeded in so implica-ting him that with all the family he was cast into prison. The two sons, however, escaped to Aden and Sind, and returning secretly to Irac,—now at Medina, now among the Bedouin tribes,—were hunted everywhere by the Caliph's emissaries. On his pilgrimage in the present year, Abu Jafar demanded of the father and relatives, who were still in prison, that they should deliver up the two sons now in hiding. On failing, they were carried off to Kufa, and treated with shocking barbarity. The son of Ibrahim, a fine youth, was told by the cruel Abu Jafar that he would die a death worse than any he had ever heard of; and the tyrant was as good as his word, for he was built up alive into the prison wall[2]. Of the rest, some were slain and some poisoned; but few were spared. The head of one was sent round Khorasan as that of Mohammed the elder brother, in the hope of disheartening the party there.

Rising at
Medina and
Bussorah,
145 A.H.
762 A.D.

These atrocities, followed by stringent measures for the discovery of Mohammed, then in hiding at Medina, preci-pitated his rebellion there, while his brother Ibrahim can-vassed for him at Bussorah. At Medina, the city rose, the governor was cast into prison, and the administration was proclaimed in the name of Mohammed; around whom

---

[1] See table, p. 391. Mohammed is the one with whom Ibn Hobeira tried to communicate when besieged in Wasit. Supra, p. 437.

[2] I give the story as I find it, though hardly credible.

rallied the great body of the citizens, though many held
back from fear of the Caliph. On tidings reaching the
Court[1], Abu Jafar was much concerned, for although Alyite disturbances had hitherto been mainly on the side of
Hosein's descendants, the claims of the house of Hasan
(Aly's elder son) were, to say the least, not inferior.
He at once addressed to Mohammed a despatch, in which, Corres-
after various threats, he offered pardon and ample main- pondence between
tenance to the whole family. The rebel sent an indignant Caliph and Moham-
answer; it was rather for him, he said, to offer pardon to med.
Abu Jafar, who had usurped the rights of the progeny
of Aly by the Prophet's daughter, in virtue alone of
whom the Hashimite cause had any ground whatever to
stand upon. And, even so, what trust could be placed on
the word of one who had so flagrantly broken it already
with Ibn Hobeira, Abu Muslim, and his own uncle? The
Caliph replied in a despatch of weary length, in which,
dwelling on the inferiority of woman, he scorned the claim
of Fatima and of female descent in general, and extolled
the Abbassides as the male, and therefore ruling, line of
the Prophet's house[2].

Nothing gained by argument, Abu Jafar had recourse Isa discom-fits Mo-
to the sword. He was the more alarmed as it had become hammed at
a popular cry at Kufa, that 'Khorasan was with the Medina, 145 A.H.
Abbassides, Irac with the Alyites, and the Syrians infidels 762 A.D.
who would readily follow any rebel.' In fact, however,
the emissaries of Mohammed found no support in Syria,
where, after so much suffering, the people were glad to
be at rest; and his chief following was at Mecca, Medina,
and Bussorah. Against Medina, the present centre of
rebellion, the Caliph now sent his nephew Isa, with a
Syrian army. And it is characteristic of his treacherous
instincts, that he told a familiar he would be equally

---

[1] 'The messenger was nine days on the road, and received from the Caliph 9000 dirhems, i. e. 1000 for each day.

[2] A very lengthy and curious document it is, elaborately reviewing the history of the house: e. g. Fatima's not inheriting the property of her father, Aly not succeeding till after three other Caliphs, the insignificant part taken by Aly's family in the *rôle* of Islam, &c. It is very unlike a document written under the circumstances, and probably a bit of servile pleading to please the Abbassides.

A.H. 136-
158.

pleased whichever fell, *Mohammed* or *Isa*, whom he was now scheming to supplant, as heir-apparent, in favour of his own son Mehdy. Apart from the prevailing sentiment of sacrilege in fighting against a descendant of Mahomet, Isa had no very difficult task. Mohammed, following the example of his namesake the Prophet, set to digging a trench about the city: but on the approach of Isa, the inhabitants fled in crowds, and Mohammed was left with

14 ix.
145 A.H.

but a small body of faithful followers. Rejecting an amnesty, he girded on him the Prophet's sword, Dzulficar[1], and went forth to fight, but fell pierced by an arrow. His head, sent to the Caliph, was paraded about Kufa and other cities. At Medina, the bodies of the slain were hung up along the Syrian road for three days, when they were cast into the Jewish burying-ground; but at the intercession of his sister, that of Mohammed was buried in the ancient grave-yard of Backie. Medina suffered severely

Rising of
slaves.

in consequence of the rebellion. The Syrian troops were so overbearing that the slaves rose *en masse*; the governor had to fly; and it was only the fear that Abu Jafar would utterly destroy the city, that led the insurgents to call him back. The hands of the leaders were cut off, and peace at last restored. To mark his displeasure, the Caliph stopped the supplies on which the city depended by sea, and the embargo was not removed till the accession of his son[2].

Ibrahim
continues
the rebellion at
Bussorah.

A still graver danger threatened from Bussorah. There, Ibrahim, after canvassing in secret, had already raised the standard of rebellion in his brother's name. Ever inclined to insurrection, Bussorah now with ardour embraced the cause; and numbers of the learned,—amongst them the great doctor Malik ibn Anas[3],—gave in their adhesion to the same. The imperial troops were defeated, the palace stormed, and the treasure distributed amongst Ibrahim's supporters. Fars, Ahwaz, and Wasit were occupied by the rebels, and other places where the cause was rife. On receiving tidings of his brother's death, Ibrahim set up on his

---

[1] *Life of Mahomet*, p. 238.
[2] Supplied from Egypt since the reign of Omar, supra, p. 171.
[3] One of the four great heads of Moslem jurisprudence.

own account, and started for Kufa, where he had expectations A.H. 136–158.
of a general rising. Though here and elsewhere there were
100,000 on his roll, he was followed now but by 10,000. Kufa rises.
Nevertheless the crisis was sufficiently grave to alarm the
Caliph. He was at the moment laying out the new capital
of Bagdad ; but on receiving tidings of Ibrahim's advance,
he hastily retired to Kufa, where the populace were ready to
break out and join the descendant of 'their own Caliph
Aly.' The troops were all away in Persia, Africa, and
Arabia, and but a small garrison left at head quarters.
News kept coming in of defection all around, while at
Kufa ' 100,000 of the Kufa rabble were ready to rush against
the Caliph with their swords.' In the utmost distress Abu Jafar
Abu Jafar swore that if he got over the crisis, he would alarmed.
never leave the capital with less than 30,000 men. For
seven weeks he kept curtained in his closet, sleeping on his
carpet of prayer, and never once changing dress but for the
black robes at public prayer. Two damsels were sent as
a gift to him : 'They will feel slighted,' his attendant
said, 'if thou wilt not go in unto them.' ' That I will not,'
he answered, 'it is no day for women this : I will not go in
unto any maiden, until I see at my feet the head of Ibrahim,
—or mine be cast at his.' At last the tide turned. Mehdy
sent troops from Rei which put down the rising in Fars
and Ahwaz, while Isa hastened from Medina to anticipate
Ibrahim's attack on Kufa. The two armies encountered Ibrahim
each other sixteen leagues from that city. The vanguard defeated
of Isa's army at first beaten back, carried part of the main 24 xi.
body with it, and for the moment, the Alyite banner 145 A. H.
seemed in the ascendant ; but shortly after, Ibrahim was
shot by an arrow, and his army fled. Thus after holding
the empire for three months in terror, the Alyite rebellion
came to a close.

At the first tidings of Isa's army giving way, the heart Abu Jafar's
of Abu Jafar failed, and he was on the point of flying to joy at the
intelli-
his son at Rei. Correspondingly his joy was unbounded gence.
when the head of Ibrahim was cast at his feet. It was
' like the delight,' he said (quoting from the poet), ' of the
thirsty wayfarer coming on a living stream.' But, before

A.H. 136–
158.
the world, he veiled his joy ; and as in public he took the
gory head of the rebel in his hands, he wept and spake well
of him. His indignation fell terribly upon the city which
had supported the claims of the pretender. Not only were
houses confiscated and demolished, but, what was a more
lasting calamity, the date-groves around Medina were all
cut down.

Bagdad
founded,
145 A. H.
762 A. H.
When this cloud had passed away, Abu Jafar returned
to the site of his new capital, whose foundations had been
laid in the previous year. It was the danger he was
exposed to from the onset of the Rawendies that first
convinced him of the need of a more secure residence for
his court. Hashimiya was also too near the fickle and
restless Kufa, the disloyal factions of which and of Bussorah
might sap the faithfulness of his guards. Searching as far
as Mosul for a likely spot, he found one on the right bank
of the Tigris, some fifteen miles above Medain, mentioned
in the wars of Mothanna as ' old Baghdad[1].' A monastery
was near, and the Patriarch and monks spake well of the
climate, water, and surroundings. Here, accordingly, Abu
Jafar resolved to found the new capital of Islam. The
lines of the city wall and chief places were dug[2], vast stores
of material collected, bricks burned, and artificers summoned
from all parts of the empire. The first brick was laid by
the Caliph's own hand with these words,—' In the name of
the Lord ! praise belongeth unto Him and the earth is His :
He causeth such of His servants as He pleaseth to inherit
the same. Success attend the pious ! Now, with the
blessing of the Lord, build on !' The walls were but a few
feet high when news of Ibrahim's rebellion made the Caliph
hasten back to Kufa ; and the intendant left in charge,
fearing lest the mass of stores should fall into the enemy's
hands, set them on fire, much to his master's disappoint-
146 A. H.
763 A. D.
ment. No sooner was Ibrahim discomfited, than Abu
Jafar returned to the work. Khalid the Barmecide, now

---

[1] P. 95.

[2] As a perpetual evidence of the city lines, burnt cotton rags mingled with
sand were buried in the foundations ; a mode familiar in the East, as the rain
causes the cotton ash indelibly to stain the soil all round.

put in charge, remonstrated against the demolition of Medain,—with its ancient memories of Seleucia and Ctesiphon,—to provide material for the new capital. 'The great Iwan of the Chosroes,' he urged, 'is one of the wonders of the world; and there, too, Aly had his place of prayer.' 'Ah!' replied the unconvinced Caliph, 'it is naught but thine old love for the Persians!' The noble arch, however, hard as iron, withstood the pick-axe. 'Now,' said Khalid, 'I advised thee against it; but as thou hast begun, go on, lest men should upbraid thee, saying that the Caliph began but could not pull down that which another had built up!' But it was of no use; and there still stands the grand monument in majesty, while all around is now a bare and sandy plain. For the portals, Kufa, Wasit, and even Damascus, were robbed of their iron gates. The walls were built in a circle so that none of the courtiers might be far from the palace, which with the great mosque lay in the centre; while the bazaars were thrust outside. The cost of the whole was four million of dirhems[1].

Lying on the west bank of the Tigris, with deep canals in rear, and ready access to the Persian Gulf,—as well as to Arabia, Syria, Armenia and the East,—Bagdad, besides holding Kufa, Wasit, and Bussorah, in immediate check, was admirably situated as the heart of the empire. The eastern shore, more open to attack, was provided with accommodation for a large force, which was thus further cut off from the heated influence of Kufa and Bussorah. Separate cantonments were here planted for the Yemen and for the Modhar clans, as also for the Khorasan levies. While there was safety in the diverse interests of the three, it was to the Khorasan levies that Abu Jafar mainly looked for his own protection; and also as a countervailing power to lower the pretensions of the Arab soldiery, who still

Bagdad as a military position.

---

[1] The iron gates from Wasit were cast by Hajjaj, and of Kufa by Khalid ibn Abdallah. The Greek ambassador having been taken round the city, said: 'It is beautiful; but thine enemies are with thee in the market-places.' Whereupon the Caliph had all the bazaars removed outside towards Kerakh, saying that they invited attack for plunder, and also a lodgement for spies. The initial cost was about £200,000. An overseer (ustad) got every day a kirat of silver, and the common labourer two pence (hubbas).

lorded it over the nations as the flower and chivalry of Islam ; and in this unwise design the Abbassides (as already noticed) too soon and too well succeeded. A few years later, a palace was built also on the eastern bank for Mehdy, called Rusâfa, and there on his return from Khorasan, he welcomed and fêted his friends and kinsmen.

It was hardly in the mind of Abu Jafar that his new capital should become the grand and populous emporium which it speedily did. Rather he founded it purely for his Court as a strong military position, and enjoined it on his son not to permit the growth of any suburbs, especially on the left bank. The same policy led him to establish on the upper reaches of the Euphrates a strong citadel, Rafica, opposite Ricca, which should hold the country on either side of the river under control. He is said to have attributed (and with reason) the sudden fall of Merwan to his having had no such stronghold to fly to after his defeat on the Zab, and hence to have spent the more pains in this direction. The defences of Kufa and Bussorah were also strengthened[1].

Mehdy
appointed
heir-appa-
rent,
147 A.H.
764 A.D.
In the eleventh year of his reign, Abu Jafar resolved on a project long in his mind of making his son Mehdy, now twenty-five years of age, heir-apparent in place of Isa. On the latter refusing, Abu Jafar was much displeased, degraded him from the seat of honour on his right, and treated him with contumely. Failing in his endeavours, he told Isa that he knew it was for his son Musa he was desirous of the succession ; on which some of the courtiers set upon Musa as if to strangle him ; and Isa, alarmed at his cries, thereupon consented that Mehdy should precede him as heir-apparent[2].

[1] Both cities were assessed with a poll-tax to defray the expense, for which purpose Abu Jafar resorted to a characteristic device. He first distributed a largess of five dirhems to all comers ; then taking the numbers of the recipients, he assessed each at forty dirhems. A squib was in everyone's mouth :—

Mark, my friends, the Caliph's bounty,
He gives us five, and then takes forty.

[2] The Caliph is even said to have given Isa a poisonous drink, from which, however, retiring for a while to his government at Kufa, he recovered. Another story is that the Caliph got Khalid the Barmecide to suborn witnesses

But Abu Jafar hated Isa the more, and contrived a plot, A.H. 136–158.
—more cruel and cunning than can well be conceived,—to
be rid at once of him and of his uncle Abdallah, who still Caliph's double plot against Isa and Abdallah.
lingered on in prison. He made Abdallah over to Isa,
with the private command to put him to death, while
he himself was away on pilgrimage to Mecca. On the 147 A.H. 764 A.D.
journey, he wrote asking whether the order had been
carried out, and was assured that it had. But Isa here
told an untruth; he had not put his uncle to death. On
the advice of his secretary, who suspected treachery, he
had only put him away in hiding. And so it turned out.
For on the Caliph's return, the friends of Abdallah were
set up to beg for his pardon. This the Caliph granted, and
Isa was bidden to make Abdallah over to them. 'Didst
thou not bid me put him to death?' said Isa; 'and I have
done as thou biddedst me.' 'Thou liest,' replied the Caliph;
and he made Isa over to Abdallah's brethren to wreak their
vengeance on. But as they were carrying him off, Isa
upbraided the Caliph; 'Thou commandedst me to put him
to death, that thou mightest be rid both of him and of me;
but here he is alive;' and forthwith Abdallah was brought
out, to the mortification of the Caliph. It was, however, of
little avail; for Abdallah was cast into a cellar with a damp
and deadly saline floor, and so at last expiated his rebellion
by a virtually violent death. Isa in disgrace was deposed
from the government of Kufa, which he had for thirteen
years ably administered.

Turning now to the dependencies of the empire, we note Spain.
that Spain was during this reign finally detached from the
eastern Caliphate. Even under the former dynasty it had
got much out of hand. In a long intestine struggle, the
Modhar had at last triumphed over the Yemen faction,
and set up Yusuf as ruler. A son of the Omeyyads was
now to take the throne. This was Abd al Rahman, grand- Abd al Rahman escaping from Syria,
son of Hisham. He escaped the massacre of his house in
Palestine, and we have a touching story of his flight and

who swore that Isa had resigned his right. Such traitorous traditions, right or
wrong, show what a wretched character for deception Abu Jafar bore, to let
them get abroad.

wanderings. Hiding in a village by the Euphrates, his little boy rushed to him with the terrified cry, ' The black flags ! the black flags coming ! ' Abd al Rahman got off with a cousin of thirteen, and swam the river; the lad, unable to stem the tide, turned back on the cry of an amnesty, but was put to death by the cruel soldiers. Hiding in the forest by day, and journeying stealthily by night, Abd al Rahman at last reached Africa, where he was joined by his sister, and a faithful servant Bedr with the family jewels. He narrowly escaped the governor of Africa, father of Yusuf, and succeeded in sending Bedr across the sea to tell the Omeyyad adherents of his arrival. These sent a ship for him, and he landed in Spain early in 138 A. H. With the help of the Yemenites, who rallied enthusiastically round him, he entered in triumph the palace of Cordova. The whole Peninsula was against the Abbassides. As Syrians they favoured the Omeyyads. The Kharejites, a numerous faction, who would have preferred an Alyite to the Abbasside branch of the Hashimite house, made no opposition. And so the nation, weary of discord, after several ineffectual risings, fell under the unquestioned sway of Abd al Rahman. The Caliph of Bagdad, indeed, once and again sought to gain a footing by his emissaries. Failing in his endeavours, he sent an embassy to King Pepin, which, after remaining several years at the Gallic court, came back with a deputation from the Franks. These eventually returned to Europe laden with rich Oriental gifts. Nothing, however, came of the negotiation, excepting, perhaps, that apprehension of attack from the Christian monarch may have forestalled any hostile intention of Abd al Rahman against the Caliph of Bagdad. The Abbasside suffered the Omeyyad to remain in peace ; and so Spain henceforward falls altogether out of our view.

lands in Spain, iii. 138 A.H. Aug., 755 A.D.

148–157 A.H. 765– 774 A.D.

Africa. Africa, though for a time, unlike Spain, independent neither in name nor in fact, was for the greater part of this reign almost equally out of hand. Both Berbers and Arabs, leaning towards the Kharejite heresy, disowned the Abbasside succession. Over and again, generals were sent to fight against them, but with little success. Among

these was Aghlab, father of the founder of the dynasty of A.H. 136-158.
that name; he was killed near Tunis, where his grave was
honoured as a martyr's. Cairowan was repeatedly taken
and retaken. Rebellion ruled until, near the close of his 155 A.H.
reign, the Caliph, now relieved of his other adversaries, was
able to send a great army which for the time restored
Abbasside authority over the whole province.

There were troubles also at different times elsewhere, Armenia,
but not such as seriously to threaten the empire. In 145 A. H.
Armenia, the Khizr hordes issuing from their passes, made
great havoc, and carried away multitudes of men and women
prisoners. An army sent to punish them was cut to pieces;
Tiflis was taken, and Armenia remained long in revolt.
In the East, a serious rebellion was led by the ruler of Rising at Herat, 150 A.H.
Herat, Ustad Sis, who set up as a prophet, and, followed
by an immense army, possessed himself of great part of
Khorasan and Sejestan. Beating the imperial troops, he
carried everything before him, till he was overcome by the
tactics of Ibn Khozeima, who made great slaughter in the
field, and put 14,000 prisoners to the sword[1]. The rebel
fled; but afterwards gave himself up, and with the remainder of his followers was spared. Kheizran, daughter
of this chief, was taken by the Caliph's son Mehdy into his
harem, and became the mother of Hady and Harun.

Another rising took place, about the middle of the reign,
in the country round about Mosul. It caused the greater and Mosul,
alarm, because a strong Alyite feeling prevailed in Hama- 148 A.H.
dan, from whence the revolt was led. The rebels, supported
by the Kurds, spread over Persia and reached as far as
Sind. They were eventually put down; but Abu Jafar
was so incensed against Mosul, that he thought of utterly
demolishing it; and was only dissuaded by the advice of
the great doctor, Abu Hanifa, who declared the project
opposed to the law of Islam[2].

The riots in Mosul led to Khalid the Barmecide being

---

[1] The numbers are no doubt exaggerated. The rebel's army is put at 300,000,
of whom 70,000 fell in the battle, besides the prisoners slain.

[2] The opinion is not embodied in very edifying language. It is to the effect
that a woman who has gone astray is not on that ground open to outrage;
neither was Mosul. Abu Hanifa died two years later.

A.H. 136–
158.

Khalid the
Barmecide
governor of
Mosul.

promoted to the command of that city, with which is connected a curious episode. For some cause, the Caliph
demanded of him three millions, to be made good in three
days (so the tale runs), on pain of his life. His son Yahya
begged all round of his friends, but on the third day there
was still short a tenth of the sum, when fortunately the
alarming news from Mosul led to the choice of Khalid
for the post. The Caliph started with him at once, as
if for Ricca on a pilgrimage to Jerusalem; then turning
suddenly north, he arrived at Mosul unexpected, and so
taking the governor unawares, deposed him and installed
Khalid in his room. Khalid's administration, severe, but
tempered with kindness, was much appreciated, and he remained there till the Caliph's death. His son, Yahya, at
the same time was appointed to Azerbijan. At Rei there
was born to Yahya a son named Fadhl, simultaneously with
Mehdy's son Harun, whose mother suckled both; and so
Harun and Fadhl were reckoned foster-brothers[1].

Abu Jafar's
son at
Mosul.

A romantic tale of the early life of Abu Jafar while
a refugee at Mosul, illustrates at once his character and
the manners of the age. While in concealment in the city
he married an Arab maiden. Leaving her with child,
he gave her a document which he bade her present at
court whenever the family should come to power. In due
time, the lady's son, Jafar by name, went to Bagdad, and
became secretary to Abu Ayub, the Vizier. In that capacity
he served the Caliph as a scribe, who took a liking for
him, found out his history, and saw the note he had left
with his mother. Accordingly he despatched the youth to
Mosul, bidding him bring his mother to Bagdad. But Abu
Ayub, who was now jealous of the favourite, sent men to
assassinate him on the road. Days passed, and getting no

Vizier put
to death for
his murder,
153–4 A. H.

tidings, the Caliph set on foot a search for Jafar. The facts
transpired; and the crime brought home to the Vizier, he
was not only put to the death he deserved, but the same

---

[1] The demand from a faithful servant of three millions on pain of death,
seems almost incredible; but it is chronicled without any expression of surprise,
nor is any imputation of embezzlement mentioned. It is curious that Ibn Athir
repeats the incident 158 A.H., just before the Caliph's death; but no doubt the
earlier date is the right one.

fate was meted out to his brother and nephews, who were A.H. 136-158.
also executed with barbarous cruelty[1].

The last few years of the Caliph's reign were free from Asia Minor. 158 A.H.
anxiety, domestic or foreign. In a raid on Laodicæa, 6000
women and children were taken captive. Shortly after the
Emperor asked for peace, and submitted to the payment
of a yearly tribute.

Towards the close of 158 A.H., Abu Jafar, who had Illness and pilgrimage of Caliph, 158 A.H.
already gone several times on pilgrimage, prepared to assist
at the annual ceremonial. On the road to Kufa, he fell
sick, and rested in a castle by the way with his son Mehdy,
to whom, apprehending that his end was near, he gave
much wholesome advice on the obligations that would
devolve upon him. He warned him against allowing Bagdad to spread on the eastern bank; bade him return to
their owners various properties he had unjustly confiscated;
' it will make thee liked,' he said, ' and will strengthen thy
hands: and see,' he added, ' that thou make much of the
men of Khorasan, for they verily have expended their lives
and means on our behalf.' After several days thus passed,
he bade his son a sorrowful farewell, and proceeded onwards.
As he journeyed, the illness increased, and he said to his
servants :—' Haste thee with thy master, who now fleeth
from his sins, unto the sacred territory of his Lord!' While His death. End of 158 A.H. Oct., 775 A.D.
yet three miles from Mecca he died in his camp, and was
buried in the holy city[2]. He reigned nearly twenty-two
years, and was aged about sixty-five. He had issue by
three wives : and also by three slave-girls, of whom one
was a Kurd, and one a Greek.

If we could forget his perfidy in compassing the death Character of Abu Jafar, Mansur.
of such as he feared and hated, our estimate of Abu Jafar
would be very different. As a Moslem, his life was religious
and exemplary. Nothing profane or unseemly was ever
seen at his court. He was diligent in the business of the
state, to which he devoted the first part of every day : the

---

[1] Their hands and feet were cut off while still alive. It is possible, but not
so stated, that they also may have been implicated in the crime.

[2] One hundred graves were dug : but he was buried in another, that no
enemy might know and desecrate the spot.

afternoon he spent with his family: and again, after evening prayer, he heard the despatches of the day and took counsel with his ministers, retiring late to rest and rising with the dayspring for morning prayer. The army was fitted throughout with improved weapons and armour ; and the minister employed in this department relates, that so hard was he worked by the Caliph, that though he began with not a white hair in his head, in nine months he had not a black one left. His hand was light, yet firm, upon his governors, and the administration consequently good. But he was parsimonious, and hoarded his revenues to such an extent that, as he told Mehdy, he had amassed treasure sufficient for ten years' expenditure. With all his good qualities, nevertheless, the verdict must be against Abu Jafar as a treacherous and cruel man. His victims, it is true, did not approach in numbers those of Saffâh the Bloody; but he was not less unscrupulous in taking life wherever personal interests were concerned, and even exceeded him, though on comparatively rare occasions, in refinement of perfidy, and heartless cruelty.

Influence of Persia; political, social, and literary.

During this reign the East began to exercise a marked effect on the manners and habits of the people. Persian costume became the fashion and, with the tall Zoroastrian hat[1], the dress at court. Scholars from the East held high and influential place. Magians came over in large numbers to the faith, and brought with them the learning and philosophy at once of India and of Persia. The Arabs lost their preeminence not only in the army and at court, but in society at large. Hitherto the dominant caste, looking down with contempt on nations every way their superiors in science, art, and culture, they were now fast sinking to a lower level. As already observed, tradition, no longer oral, began to be embodied by the great doctors of the law in elaborate systems of jurisprudence adapted to the expanding range of Islam and the necessities of an advancing civilization[2].

---

[1] Calansua.

[2] Two of the four great founders of the recognised systems of law, Abu Hanifa and Malik ibn Anas, flourished in this reign. Neither was much esteemed at court ; the former, as we have seen, supported the claims of Ibrahim at Bussorah ; and the latter declined to be judge of Bagdad, to which office

Literature, history, medicine, and especially astronomy (for A.H. 136–
Abu Jafar was given to astrology) began to be studied; and 158.
the foundations were thus laid for the development of intellectual life in subsequent reigns; all of which is mainly
due to the encouragement given to the people of Khorasan
and Persia, and in some degree also to the more liberal
intercourse that grew up with the Grecian empire in the
present reign.

the Caliph desired to put him at its foundation, and so Abu Hanifa accepted
the humbler charge of looking after the bricks and labour.   The popular tradition is that he ended his life in prison for his refusal to be Cazee.

CHAPTER LXII.

MEHDY, SON OF MANSUR.

158–169 A.H.   775–785 A.D.

THE ten years' reign of Mehdy, who immediately succeeded his father Abu Jafar, is mainly noticeable as a
mean between the rough and rigorous rule of the first
Abbassides, and the palmy days which followed,—a kind
of preparation, as it were.   Mehdy was by nature mild
and generous.   He inaugurated his accession by opening
the prison doors to all but the worst and most dangerous
class of felons.   The treasure accumulated by his father gave
ample means for profuse liberality.   He enlarged and
beautified the mosques of the Holy cities, and of the
capital towns elsewhere[1].   The pilgrim caravanserais, provided now with fountains and establishments, were made
commodious and secure.   The postal service, accelerated
on mules and camels, was greatly developed.   Imperial
agents[2], located at the provincial centres, kept the court
informed of the progress of public affairs, which throughout
the empire were administered, upon the whole, with justice
and moderation.   Cities were put in good defence; and
especially Rusâfa, the eastern suburb of Bagdad.   The
capital became already an emporium of trade with all parts
of the world.   Music, poetry, literature, and philosophy
refined the age; while the example of the court both as

[1] Ibn Athir tells us that 630 A.H. he saw in the court of the mosque of
Mosul a slab with an inscription ascribing its extension to Mehdy.
[2] 'Ameens.'

to wine and the fair sex tended to laxity of manners. Princely progresses were repeatedly made by Mehdy with his court to Jerusalem and the holy cities, and the cortege was supplied with ice from the mountains, all the way to Mecca. There he clothed the poor and distributed among the citizens largesses of almost fabulous amount. The coverings of the Kaaba sent yearly by the Caliphs had hitherto been draped one over the other; and, being of rich brocade, had latterly become so weighty as to endanger the edifice. They were now removed, and their place supplied by the single covering sent every year by Mehdy—a precedent followed by succeeding Caliphs. Five hundred *Ansars*, or Citizens of Medina, followed the Caliph, as an imperial guard to Bagdad, where lands were assigned for their support;—a wise measure, which if maintained might have checked the insolent and dangerous pretensions of the Turkish soldiery; but the practice must have been given up, for we hear no more of these Medina men.

Guard of Medina men.

But there was another side to the reign of Mehdy, marked occasionally by outbursts of hideous cruelty [1]. Early in his reign a dangerous rebellion was raised by one Yusuf in Khorasan. He was taken prisoner, carried with his comrades, face backwards, on a camel, and thus brought into Rusâfa. There the Caliph had the rebel's hands and feet cut off, and then with all his fellows decapitated. The case of the Vizier Yacub is also illustrative of his mode of life. He had been arraigned as an adherent of the house of Aly, and as such imprisoned by Abu Jafar. Released by Mehdy, he became his favourite, the boon companion of nightly revels, and a minister of unbounded power throughout the empire. His prosperity at last raised enemies, who poisoned the ear of the Caliph against him, as still devoted to the Alyite faction. To test his loyalty, Mehdy had recourse to stratagem. Invited to spend the

Cruel treatment of a rebel. 16o A.H.

and of his Vizier,

---

[1] Weil extenuates such barbarities by the prevailing contempt of life amongst Mahometans of the day, and the consequent necessity for adding pains and penalties to simple death; also by the statute of the Coran for punishing robbers with the loss of limb. But the extenuation is altogether inadequate.

evening in a beautiful garden, Yacub found the Caliph seated in the company of a slave-girl of surpassing charms. The minister was overpowered by the enchanting scene. 'Ah!' said the Caliph, 'it is indeed a paradise of delights; and I will give all to thee, and this damsel with it, if thou wilt rid me of that Alyite,'—naming one he had doomed to death. Yacub embraced the offer with transport, and became at once the happy master of the fairy scene. The Alyite was summoned to his fate; but he pleaded his case so warmly that Yacub was softened, and bade him fly the place. The maiden, curtained close by, heard it all, and let the Caliph know. And so, when Yacub assured his master that he had carried out his wish, the truth came to light, and Yacub was cast into a pitch-dark prison, where

and of a minister's son. he remained so long that he lost his sight[1]. Another minister, who had faithfully attended Mehdy throughout the campaigns in Khorasan, incurred the resentment of a courtier named Rabie, who finding no other ground, accused his rival's son of being a Manichæan heretic. The Caliph called the son, and examining him on the Coran found him ignorant of its contents, and thereupon judging the imputation proved, had him beheaded. The father was deposed, and Rabie succeeded to his office.

Persecution of Manichæans. Hatred of the *Zendics,* or Manichæan heretics, indeed, and their cruel persecution, is one of the chief traits of Mehdy's life, and of his son Hady's short reign. During the stay of Mehdy in Khorasan, he had imbibed an intense abhorrence of their tenets, which not only contravened Islam, but loosened the bonds of social and domestic morals. Suspicion whispered into the Caliph's ready ear, led often without trial to a fatal end. Thus a blind poet, ninety years of age, was arraigned by enemies, smarting under his satires, on charge of heresy, and notwithstanding his poems being free of the taint, put to death. At Aleppo, on his

---

[1] Yacub relates that after he had remained in utter darkness, he knew not how many years, he was summoned to the presence, and desired to make obeisance to the Caliph, who asked, 'Knowest thou who I am?' 'Surely it is Mehdy,' he replied. 'Ah,' said the Caliph, 'he has long ago been dead.' 'Then Hady.' 'He too is dead.' 'Then Harun.' 'That I am,' answered the Caliph, who thereupon granted his request of permission to retire to Mecca.

way to Syria, Mehdy had a gathering of Manichæans, A.H. 158-
hunted out from all that neighbourhood. They were all 169.
beheaded, and their bodies cut in pieces.   Thereafter he Inquisi-
established a department of state with a minister whose tion, 167 A.H.
duty it was to put down the heresy,—a kind of inquisition ;
and accordingly we read in the following year of ' a great
multitude ' being apprehended as heretics and put to
death.

Another strange but ephemeral heresy gave trouble Mocanna
beyond the Oxus.   It was led by a fanatic, who, from claims divine
masking his ill-favoured countenance, was called *Mocanna,* honours in Central
the Veiled one.   He taught the immanence of the Deity in Asia,
Adam, in Abu Muslim, and lastly in himself.   Vast multi- 158–161 A.H.
tudes of Turks, as well as Moslems, followed and worshipped
him as god.   For four years, in Bokhara and surrounding
provinces, they beat back column after column of the
Moslem troops.   At last fortune turned against the
impostor, who, deserted by the rest, found refuge with
but 2000 of his followers in a fort.   Then reduced to
straits, he set fire to the place, and calling on his women
and all who would ascend with him to heaven to follow his
example, cast himself with them into the flames, and
perished.   The report of this scene gave fresh impulse to
the sect, and though practised secretly, it was long before
it died out in the East.

War was waged with Greece throughout the greater part War in
of the reign.   Inroads into Asia Minor as far as Ancyra, Asia Minor,
led to reprisals by Michael[1], who ravaged the Syrian border 159–162
and inflicted a serious defeat on the Moslem arms.   To A.H. 775–778
avenge the injury, Mehdy marshalled an army of 100,000 A.D.
men and with it crossed the Euphrates to Aleppo. Thence Campaign
he sent forward in command his son Harun, though hardly of Harun to the
twenty years of age, accompanied by Khalid the Barmecide, Bosphorus, 156 A.H.
as guardian ; and, supported by able generals, he made a
victorious march along the coast as far as the Bosphorus.

---

[1] Lachanodrakon.   It is illustrative of the Caliph's arbitrary rule that on one
of the generals retiring before Michael's superior force (164 A.H.) he was on
the point of punishing him by death : but on the intercession of his friends cast
him instead into prison.

A.H. 158-169. There the regent, Queen Irene, was obliged, on payment of heavy ransom, to conclude a peace, and moreover, to provide for the safe return to the frontier of Harun, who had got entangled in defiles. The spoil was immense, and the number slain incredible[1]. It is interesting to note that in the early part of this reign, a descent from Africa to restore

Spain, 161-3 A.H. Spain to the Caliphate ended in disaster; and that, on the other hand, the Ruler of Spain[2] had in preparation an expedition against the Abbassides in Syria, but was hindered therefrom by troubles at home.

India, 160 A.H. There were expeditions in other quarters, but none requiring notice, excepting perhaps that to India, which stormed the city of Barbad, and burned the image of Budd, with a company of its worshippers. But the end was disastrous: the army lost 1000 men by a 'mouth disease,' and the fleet was wrecked by a storm on the Persian shore.

Mehdy marries Kheizran, 159 A.H. Shortly after his accession, Mehdy gave her freedom to Kheizran, mother of his sons Hady and Harun, whose influence over him even in affairs of state was great, and married her. The unfortunate Isa, whom Abu Jafar had forced to postpone his claim to Mehdy, was now compelled altogether to relinquish his title to the throne, which he had now held for three-and-twenty years; and

Hady heir-apparent, 160 A.H. and Harun, 166 A.H. Musa, surnamed *Hady* (the Guide), was proclaimed heir-apparent. With Harun, the younger son, his father was so pleased after the expedition to the Bosphorus, that he placed him in charge of all the Western provinces with Azerbijan, though still quite a youth; and two years later proclaimed him, under the title of *Rashîd* (the Upright[3]), second in succession. But Harun was so much the favourite of his mother, and was also so preferred by his father, that Mehdy went a step farther, and a year or two after called on Hady to waive his claim of precedence in his favour. Hady, at the time prosecuting a campaign in Jorjan, naturally resisted the demand, and

[1] 54,000 Greeks slain; 5000 taken prisoners, of whom 2090 were 'executed in cold blood'; 20,000 cattle driven off, and 100,000 slain.
[2] He is called simply the Omeyyad 'Ruler' (Sahib) of Spain.
[3] Or 'rightly directed.' Pronounced Hârûn ar Rashîd.

treated contumeliously a second messenger, summoning him A.H. 158–
to Bagdad. Mehdy thereupon, accompanied by Harun, set 169.
out with an army to reduce his contumacious son, but Mehdy's
died on the way, from eating a poisoned pear intended by death, 22 i.
one of his slave-girls for a favoured rival[1]. He was buried July,
on the spot, aged forty-three, in the beginning of the year 785 A.D.
169, Harun performing the service over the bier.

Little more need be said of the character of Mehdy. Character
His administration was upon the whole such as to of Mehdy.
promote the welfare of the nation, and usher in the
brilliant era that followed ; but his life was stained by
many acts of tyranny and cruelty, nor was it altogether
even in private such as a rigid Mahometan would
approve. Naturally soft and amiable, he maintained his Attach-
attachment to Kheizran, the princess of Herat, who it ment to
will be remembered was taken as a slave-girl into his and a
youthful harem, unabated to the end. It is also told of favourite
him that he so doated on a young daughter Yacuta (the daughter.
Ruby), that he could not let her out of his sight even
when in public. He had her dressed in male attire, and
as such she rode by his side. He was disconsolate when
she died a year before him ; but in the end was comforted
by the condolence of his friends.

[1] Another account is that out hunting his horse rushed after the hounds and
game into a ruin, and that, struck by the lintel, he was killed. But this is hardly
consistent with the mystery that plainly surrounded his death, of which the army
accompanying him only knew on their return to Bagdad.

CHAPTER LXIII.

HADY AND HARUN AL RASHID.

169–193 A. H.　785–809 A. D.

Hady,
169 A.H.
785 A.D.

HARUN wisely recognized the succession of his brother, and at once despatched to him in Jorjan the imperial seal and sceptre. The army that had accompanied his father was dismissed to Bagdad, where they broke out into mutiny, stormed the Vizier's house, and demanded largess. Kheizran summoned the Vizier, and Yahya son of Khalid the Barmecide; but the latter, knowing Hady's jealousy of his mother, took upon him, without waiting on her, to satisfy the troops by a two years' grant. The Vizier, who obeyed her call, nearly forfeited his life for doing so; but by the offer of large gifts regained the Caliph's favour.

Alyite
rising at
Medina.

In the short reign of Hady few events occur of interest outside the capital. There was a Kharejite rising in Mesopotamia, and also an Alyite in Mecca and Medina. Strange to say, this last arose from the intemperance of some members of the saintly house of Aly, who for drinking wine were paraded with halters about their necks in the streets of the Holy cities. The family thereupon broke out into rebellion, and some hard fighting was needed before peace could be restored. Among those who escaped was Idris, great-grandson of Aly. Aided by postal relays, he made his escape through Egypt to Tangier, where he was welcomed by the Berbers, and laid the foundation of the Idrisite dynasty. The postmaster of Egypt was beheaded for having connived at his flight [1].

Idris
escapes to
Africa.

[1] Some authorities lay this at the door of Harun, and Weil charges it against that Caliph as one of his cruel acts.

Resembling his father in most things, in one he differed, A.H. 169–
for he would not allow Kheizran to have any hand in the
affairs of state. Accustomed as that lady had been to Hady
crowds of suitors seeking influence with her husband, when inter-
she attempted the like with her son, he bade her mind her ference of
own concerns, withdrew her escort, and forbade the courtiers Kheizran.
to wait upon her [1]. The proud woman smarted under the
insult, and watched the opportunity for revenge.

In his treatment of the Manichæans, Hady followed too His cruel
closely at once the counsel and example of his father. treatment
Strange to say, there were amongst these heretics several of heretics.
of Hashimite descent, whom Mehdy, who had sworn never
to take the life of any of his own house, left to his son with
the fatal injunction to put them to death. How this pesti-
lent heresy found adherents amongst the faithful of Arabia
and Irac, is difficult to understand, and one may hope that
of many sins laid to their charge, they were falsely accused [2].
Shortly before his death Mehdy declared that he would
destroy the whole brood of Zendics, root and branch; and
he is said to have ordered a thousand palm-stakes to be
erected, on which as many heretics should be impaled,—a
report, the existence of which shows at any rate the prevailing belief in the intensity of his hatred towards the sect.

Following his father also in another respect, Hady formed Hady en-
the project of setting his brother aside, and proclaiming his deavours
young son heir-apparent. He was supported by all the sede
court, excepting Yahya the Barmecide, who succeeded once Harun.
and again in dissuading him from so precipitate and unwise
a step. Harun, now treated with indignity, retired into private life. At last, after much vacillation, the Caliph, at the
instigation of the creatures around him, who were forward
to take the oath, proclaimed his son successor, and cast
Yahya into prison. Hady was just then at his country
seat near Mosul; and there he fell sick and died. His end

[1] He is even said to have attempted to poison her, but the imputation is
doubtful. Weil thinks it was fabricated to justify the Queen Mother's unnatural
conduct towards Hady.

[2] Thus the daughter of one of these condemned Hashimites is said to have
confessed that she was with child by her own father, and when carried before
the Caliph, died of fright.

A.H. 169-
193.
_____

His death

is obscure. The ordinary version is that when he sickened, his mother induced certain of his slave-girls to smother him. We are told further that she had despatches in readiness for the various governors to recognize the succession of Harun, which would imply complicity of some kind in the death of Hady. We hear little more of her ; and she herself died shortly after.

Harun
succeeds,
170 A.H.
786 A.D.

Instance of
capricious
cruelty.

On his brother's death, Harun, now nearly twenty-five years of age, hastened to the spot, performed the funeral obsequies, and was saluted Caliph without opposition. Hady's young son was easily persuaded to drop his claim ; but a circumstance connected therewith showed thus early that Harun, though called *Rashíd*, was as prone to vindictive cruelty, when moved to hate or jealousy, as any of his predecessors. When some time before Harun was about to cross the Tigris, the courtier in charge of Hady's son called out from the other side of the bridge to ' stay until the heir-apparent had passed over'; and Harun answered,—' The Ameer's humble servant !' The incident rankled in his breast, and on his accession he had the unlucky courtier put to death. On the same day his son Mamun was born, and Amin some little time later ;—the latter, as son of Zobeida, grand-daughter of Mansur, taking precedence over the former, whose mother was an eastern slave-girl. As Harun crossed the bridge re-entering Bagdad, he bade divers to search in the river for the ' Mountain,' a famous ring worth 100,000 golden pieces, given to him by his father. On Hady's demanding this ring, he had flung it into the Tigris ; and now as he pointed out the spot, it was discovered by the divers, to his great delight.

Recovers
his ring in
the Tigris.

The Bar-
mecides.

Yahya the Barmecide, whom Hady had imprisoned and threatened with death, was now brought to court, and installed as Vizier. His two sons, Fadhl and Jafar, also exercised unbounded power ;—the former, foster-brother of the Caliph, and a statesman of unrivalled ability[1]; the latter, the favourite of Harun and boon companion of his privacy. These were the three leading men of the Barmecide

[1] See above, p. 460. The two mothers suckled each other's babes. The relation of foster-mother is much esteemed in the East.

house, the fall of which, seventeen years later, has left A.H. 169-
193.
an indelible stigma on the Caliph's name.

Harun is noted for his careful observance of the ritual of Harun's
religious
life.
Islam: daily he performed one hundred prostrations, and
distributed 1000 dirhems in alms. In the very first year
of his reign he performed the pilgrimage to Mecca, and
repeated it afterwards in some nine different years. On
every occasion he scattered munificent largesses amongst
the people, and carried in his train crowds of indigent
pilgrims. He was surrounded also by a magnificent court, Magnifi-
cent court.
both when on pilgrimage and on other journeys, and by a
host of learned men, doctors of the law, poets and philosophers; and it is in part these princely progresses that
have shed so great a lustre on this reign.

Harun was perhaps the ablest ruler of the Abbasside Wise, and,
on the
whole, just.
race. He is likened to Abu Jafar, but without his par-
simony. If we except some flagrant instances of tyrannous
cruelty, his government was wise and just; as without
doubt, it was grand and prosperous. Bold and active in
his habits, he followed up his early campaign against the
Greeks, by repeatedly himself again appearing in the field.
Eight or nine years after his accession, he forsook Bagdad Dislikes
Bagdad,
and retires
to Ricca.
and set up his court at Ricca, in the north of Syria.
This he did ostensibly to hold disloyal Syria in check, in
spite (as he said) of his loving Bagdad better than any
other place in the whole world. But it seems likelier that
he had contracted an aversion towards Bagdad, for he never
again resided there, and seldom even visited it.

In the second year of this reign, a serious rising under a Rising at
Mosul,
171 A.H.
Kharejite leader stirred the whole province of Mosul into
insurrection. Abu Horeira, the governor of Mesopotamia,
was discomfited by the rebel, who gained possession of the
city. Fresh troops were despatched, and in the end peace
was restored. But the Caliph was so displeased with the
failure of Abu Horeira, that he was in consequence brought
to Bagdad, and there put to death.

The security of the Syrian frontier was the early care of Asia
Minor.
Harun, both on the side of Armenia, threatened by the
Khizr hordes, and of Asia Minor, by the Greeks. One of

A.H. 169-
193.

Created
separate
govern-
ment,
170 A.H.

Naval
operations,
175 A.H.

Harun
takes the
field,
181 A.H.

Irene
tributary,
186 A.H.

Insulting
letter of
Nice-
phorus,
187 A.H.
803 A.D.

Harun's
reply.

his first acts was to create a new change towards the west, under a Turkish general[1], with Tarsus strongly fortified its headquarters. War was waged almost every year with the Greeks, and Harun over and again either joined his forces, or watched their progress on the frontier, for which his residence at Ricca gave him easy opportunity. The Moslems also began to be successful at sea; Crete and Cyprus were attacked and the Greek admiral taken prisoner[2]. In the raids on the frontier, a multitude of captives and vast booty were secured. But fortune varied; there were serious reverses, and on one occasion, severe loss and suffering from cold in the passes. In 181 A.H., Harun headed a large force in person, and Constantinople being distracted at home, great victories were achieved as far as Ephesus and Ancyra. Prisoners were thereafter exchanged ; 4000 Moslems were recovered amid great rejoicings ; and Irene, on payment of tribute, obtained a four years' truce. An advance was subsequently made by Casim, the Caliph's third son; but withdrawn on the Greeks sending in several hundred prisoners. Soon after, Nicephorus having succeeded to the throne, sent this insulting epistle to the Caliph :—'From Nicephorus, king of the Greeks, to Harun, king of the Arabs. Irene hath parted with the castle, and contented herself with the pawn. She hath paid thee moneys, the double of which thou shouldest have paid to her. It was but a woman's weakness. Wherefore, return what thou hast taken, or the sword shall decide.' Harun reading the letter fell into a rage, and calling for pen and ink wrote on the back of the letter :—'From Harun, Commander of the Faithful, to Nicephorus, dog of the Greeks. I have read thy letter, son of an unbelieving mother. The answer is for thine eye to see, not for thine ear to hear.' And Harun was as good as his word; at once he started and ravaged the land as far as Heraclea, before the Emperor, hampered by rebels, had stirred a step; and

---

[1] The first notice of a Turkish chief placed in a military command. We shall soon find them coming to the front in all departments, and especially at the head of the Moslem armies.

[2] This from Greek authorities, who state that on refusing to embrace Islam, Harun had him beheaded. Moslem writers do not mention him.

so an ignominious peace, and renewed tribute, were the end
of that foolish boasting. Over and again when Harun was
engaged elsewhere, Nicephorus broke his treaty, and as
often was beaten. At last, near the close of his reign, the
Caliph marched again with 135,000 men, took possession of
Heraclea, and besides tribute, reduced Nicephorus to the contempt of a personal impost on himself and on each member
of the imperial house. Cyprus was anew overrun ; 17,000
prisoners carried off to Syria; and for the ransom of its
Bishop alone, 2000 golden pieces had to be paid. But in
the following year the Greeks once more advanced, and
inflicted severe loss on the enemy both at Marash and
Tarsus, which Harun, having trouble elsewhere on his
hands, was not in a position to retrieve. The end of it all,—
the bitter end of all such wars,—was to inflame religious
hate. The Caliph caused all churches in the border-lands
to be cast down, and the obnoxious distinctions of dress
and equipage to be enforced with the utmost rigour upon
the Christian population.

Africa continued farther and farther to drift from Abbasside control. After various fortune of victory and
defeat, Harthama, an able general, was despatched with
a large force, who succeeded in beating down opposition ; but a short experience convinced him that hostile
interests throughout the land were so inveterate as to leave
little hope of eventual success ; and, anxious now for the
more attractive field of the East, he resigned. Thereafter
the Aghlabite dynasty, though at first nominally subordinate to Bagdad, became eventually independent at
Cairowan ; as already was the Idrisite at Tangier in the
farther West.

In 176 A.H., the ancient Syrian jealousies between the two
Arab stocks broke out into open feud, and kept Damascus
for two years in continual ferment; a state of things, however,
which gave the Caliph little concern, as it simply weakened
the power of the disloyal Syrians. Ten years afterwards
they began again to fight against each other ; but this
time Harun interfered to compose their differences. Somewhat later Mosul was the scene of a rebellion, which lasted

A.H. 169– two years, until Harun himself took possession of the city,
193.   razed its walls, and was again with difficulty dissuaded
Kharejite from destroying it altogether. A still more alarming out-
rising in break occurred at Nisibin under a Kharejite leader, who,
Armenia
and   after ravaging Armenia and Azerbijan, descended on
Holwan, Mesopotamia, and crossing the Tigris to Holwan, held the
177 A.H.
whole province in terror. In the end he was defeated and
slain. This campaign is notable for the beautiful elegy of
Leila on the death of her brother, the rebel,—to avenge
which she had ridden forth disguised in armour, but retired
in maidenly confusion on being recognized by the general
of the Caliph's army. Harun was so alarmed at the near
approach of this danger, that to commemorate the victory,
he performed in thanksgiving both the Lesser and the
Greater pilgrimage, visiting on foot the various holy
stations.

Treacher- Passing over various outbreaks on the outskirts of the
ous dealing
with the empire, there is one in the north which deserves notice
Hasanite as illustrating the faithlessness of the Caliph. Yahya, a
prince of
Deilem,   descendant of the Prophet's grandson Hasan, gained pos-
176 A.H. session of Deilem, and grew so mightily in power as to
extend his kingdom on the borders of the Caspian, and
attract to his brilliant court followers from all parts of the
world. Harun, jealous at once of his influence and of his
distinguished birth, sent Fadhl the Barmecide, then governor of Persia and Jorjan, with a great army to oppose him.
Yahya was drawn into an apparently friendly communication with Fadhl, and agreed that he should submit to the
Caliph a proposal for presenting himself at Bagdad under a
covenant of honourable treatment, the bond to be witnessed
not only by doctors of the law but by representatives of
the Hashimite house. Harun, overjoyed at the prospect of
being rid of his rival, confirmed the covenant, and in due
course received him with much distinction and princely
gifts ; but shortly after he allowed his jealousy to override
his conscience. The chief Cazee was obsequious enough
to discover a flaw in the document ; but an equally
distinguished doctor declared that the covenant made with
a power backed by an army in the field was indefeasible.

Harun, nevertheless, supported by the former, cast Yahya A.H. 169-
into prison; and having called for the solemnly attested $\underline{193.}$
document, tore it into shreds.

While yet but five years old, Harun's son by Zobeida, pre- Amin heir-
ferred in virtue of his noble birth, was nominated heir- apparent,
apparent, under the title of Amin. Some years later, his 175 A.H.
other son, Abdallah, several months older, was declared the
next successor, both being now twelve years of age. The
latter, surnamed Mamun [1], was placed under the guardian- and
ship of Jafar the Barmecide, and at an early age given Mamun,
charge of Khorasan and all the countries from Hamadan 182 A.H.
to farthest East. On a brilliant pilgrimage to Mecca, the Harun's
Caliph presented each of these sons with the munificent gift arrange-
of a million golden pieces, and caused two documents, pilgrim-
witnessed by the chief ministers of state, to be hung up age,
with solemn ceremony in the Kaaba, inscribed, one in favour 802 A.D.
of Amin, the other of Mamun. He also gave Mesopotamia
and the Greek frontier in charge of Casim, the youngest son,
who might, but only at the discretion of Mamun, succeed
to its eventual sovereignty. Further still, some years later, 189 A.H.
when on a journey to the East, he willed (a singular condition) that the army, with all its treasure and munitions of
war, should fall to the lot of Mamun; and he caused oaths
of allegiance to the three sons to be renewed both at
Bagdad and throughout the empire in accordance with
these arrangements. People marvelled that so wise a ruler
should so soon forget the lessons of the past, and from such
strange provisions foreboded evil in the future. It is not
often that our annalists indulge in reflections such as these;
but here we have the proverb applied by them to Harun,
'Self-conceit makes a man both blind and deaf.'

We now come to the startling narrative of the fall of the Fall of the
Barmecides. The course of this distinguished family has cides.
been already traced, from its rise in Balkh, through successive
generations to the highest posts of honour and influence in
the state. Yahya, son of Khalid, now advanced in years,
had resigned office into the hands of his sons Fadhl and

---

[1] One in whom faith is placed, 'the Trusted': Amin signifying 'the Faithful'; grand epithets, if they had only been true.

Jafar. The former, possessed of boundless authority, and regarded by the people with love and esteem, was virtual ruler of the empire. The latter, more given to indulgence, was the constant companion of Harun's hours of pleasure and amusement; yet even he must have inherited the ability of the house, having had charge of the youthful Mamun with the whole government of the East, and though only thirty-seven years of age having held the Vizierate for seventeen years. Poets were never weary of extolling the Barmecides, nor historians of narrating their virtues, munificence and power. Suddenly Jafar was put to death, and the family disappears from the scene. The cause assigned was this :—

Story of
Jafar's
disgrace,
Jafar, as said above, was the boon companion of the Caliph, who loved to have his sister Abbasa also with him at times of recreation and carousal. But Moslem etiquette forbade their common presence ; and, to allow of this, Harun had the marriage ceremony performed between them, on the understanding that it was purely nominal. But the ban was too weak for Abbasa. A child given secret birth to was sent by her to Mecca ; while a maid, quarrelling with her mistress, made known the scandal. Harun when on pilgrimage ascertained that the tale was

and death,
187 A.H.
but too true. On his return to Ricca, shortly after, he sent a eunuch to slay Jafar, whose body was despatched to Bagdad, and there, divided in two, impaled on either side of the bridge. It continued so for three years, when Harun, happening to pass through Bagdad from the East, gave command for the miserable remains to be taken down and

and fall of
whole Bar-
mecide
family.
burned. On the death of Jafar, his father and brother were both cast into prison at Ricca, and orders passed all over the empire to confiscate the property of any member of the family, wherever found. Both Yahya, an aged and now heart-broken man, and Fadhl, yet young but paralyzed from the shock, died in confinement shortly before Harun himself. Men grieved at their death ; poets sang the praises of Fadhl, and annalists fill their pages with tales of his princely generosity, and laud his memory as of one of the most distinguished of mankind. The

grandeur, power, and popularity of the house, as well as A.H. 169– the services it had rendered to the dynasty, both in the 193. conduct of the empire and upbringing of the minor princes, intensified the tragedy and the scandal before the public; and although other causes have been assigned, the fact of Jafar's violent end leaves little doubt upon the general accuracy of the outline given above.   Harun himself kept a mysterious silence.   Once questioned by his beautiful and accomplished sister Oleiya, he is said to have stayed her with these words ;—'Life of my soul! if but my innermost garment knew of it, I would tear it into shreds[1].'

The painful episode was followed by the murder of Ibrahim, a faithful friend of Jafar, who mourned over his loss, and in private spoke bitterly of his miserable end. *Another murder.* The Caliph hearing of this, invited him to a convivial bout alone, and having plied him with wine, pretended to mourn the loss of Jafar, whom, he said, he would now willingly part with half his kingdom to have back again.   Ibrahim thus deceived, began in his cups to unbosom himself to the apparently repentant monarch, in praise of Jafar and grief at his death.   Whereupon Harun cast him out, cursing him as a traitor, and shortly after had him put to death.

We turn with relief to notice what was passing on the outskirts of the empire.   The East was fast becoming firmly consolidated under the strong Turkish interest at court.   There was, indeed, a serious rebellion under a *Persia and Khorasan, 180 A.H.*

---

[1] Weil has gone very fully into the question, and leaves little room to doubt the outline as a whole.   The story is one eminently fitted to excite the Oriental imagination.   Thus Ibn Khallican, in his gossiping way, tells us that Abbasa, conceiving an uncontrollable passion for her husband, persuaded his mother (who used to send a slave-girl every Friday as her son's companion for the night) to make use of her for once instead.   She was sent accordingly in disguise, and Jafar, under the influence of wine (nabidh), discovered the deception but too late, and then was overcome by terror at the possible results.   It may be a tale, but even so, it points to the popular belief, and the notices both in prose and verse are entirely in accord therewith.   Some authorities pass the matter by in silence, or attribute it to other causes,—as, escape of an Alyite offender by Jafar's connivance ; his princely palace exciting Harun's jealousy ; Yahya's entering the presence without authority ; Alyite tendency of the family, &c. ; but all are inadequate for the execution of Jafar and downfall of the family.

Abbasa and her child are also said to have been made away with, but this is doubtful.

A.H. 169-
193.
___ Kharejite leader, who ravaged Persia and the outlying
provinces as far as Herat, but it was at last put down
by the governor, Aly ibn Isa. Some years after, the
Caliph, hearing unfavourable reports of his lieutenant's

Harun
visits Rei,
189 A.H.
tyranny, marched with Mamun to Rei. There, to answer
the charges against him, he summoned Aly, who by
splendid gifts to the Caliph and to the court rendered
his position again secure. Harun stayed four months
at Rei, which he loved, as his birth-place, and there
receiving duty in person from the native chiefs to the
North,—who still retained something of their ancient
power under the suzeranity of the Caliphate,—he settled
the affairs of Tabaristan, Deilem and other provinces in
that direction. He then returned by Bagdad to his
court at Ricca.

Rebellion
of Rafi in
Samar-
cand,
190 A.H.
Some little time later a serious rebellion arose in the
East out of a strange origin. A wealthy lady in Samarcand, whose husband had been long absent in Bagdad,
bethought herself of another, and being told that it was
the easiest way of dissolving the knot, abjured Islam and
then married her suitor, one Rafi. The first husband complained to the Caliph, who, scandalized at the affront on
the Moslem faith, not only ordered that Rafi should divorce
the lady, but be paraded on an ass and cast into prison.
Thence he effected his escape, and after wandering about
the country, returned to Samarcand, slew the governor, and
raised the standard of rebellion. Aly ibn Isa, alarmed lest
Rafi should steal a march on Merve, quitted Balkh, and set
out thither ; thereupon Rafi rapidly gained possession of
all the country beyond the Oxus. Meanwhile reports again
reached the Caliph of the tyranny and rapacity of Aly, and
so, with the double view of superseding him, and subduing

Harthama
supersedes
governor,
192 A.H.
the rebellion, he sent Harthama, now returned from his
African command, with a large force, and secret orders to
assume the government. Arrived at Merve, Harthama at
first received Aly graciously, but shortly after, showing his
patent of command, confiscated the vast wealth of the
tyrant, and despatched it on 1500 camels to the avaricious
Caliph. Aly himself, seated on a bare-backed camel, was

sent in disgrace to Ricca,—the common fate of rulers of A.H. 169-
the day.   193.

Harthama lost no time in attacking Rafi, and having Har-
beaten him in the field besieged him in Samarcand; but it thama's
campaign
was several years before the rebellion was quelled. Meanwhile against
the Kharejites, taking advantage of the disturbances beyond 192-5 A.H.
the Oxus, rose on the south of the river, and threatened
the eastern provinces of Persia. Things looked so serious
that Harun resolved himself on a progress thither, and
towards the end of 192 A.H. set out from his residence at
Ricca for the purpose. Leaving Casim there to control Harun
himself
Syria and the West, he journeyed to Bagdad, in charge takes the
of which he placed Amin. He would also have left field,
192 A.H.
Mamun behind; but Mamun, dreading lest his father, 808 A.D.
who had already sickened, should die by the way, in which
event Amin might, with the help of his royal mother,
depose him from the government of the East,—asked
permission to join his father on the march, which after
some demur Harun granted. Travelling slowly over the
mountain range into Persia, Harun one day called his
physician aside, and, alone under the shelter of a tree,
unfolding a silken kerchief that girded his loins, disclosed
the fatal disease he laboured under. 'But have a care,' he
said, 'that thou keep it secret; for my sons' (and he named
them all and their guardians) 'are watching the hour of my
decease, as thou mayest see by the shuffling steed they will
now mount me on, adding thus to mine infirmity.' There
is something touching in these plaintive words of the great
monarch, now alone in the world, and bereft of the support
even of those who were bound to rally round him in his
hour of weakness. Early in the following year he reached Sickens on
the way,
Jorjan, where, becoming worse, he sent on Mamun with a ii. 193 A.H.
portion of the army to Merve; and himself, journeying End of
808 A.D.
slowly, reached Tus, where, despairing of life, he had his
grave dug close by his dwelling-place. The brother of
Rafi was brought in a prisoner when Harun was near his
end; 'If I had no more breath left,' he said, 'but to say a
single word, it should be *Slay him*'; and so the dismembered
wretch was slain before the dying monarch. Shortly after,

A.H. 169–
198.

Dies, vi.
193 A.H.
March,
809 A.D.

he breathed his last, and one of his younger sons prayed over the bier. He was forty-seven years of age, and had reigned three-and-twenty. When nineteen, he married Zobeida of royal birth, who survived him over thirty years. He had seven wives, but only four were alive at his death. Besides Amin, the son of Zobeida, there were ten sons and fourteen daughters, all the progeny of slave-girls.

Embassy
to Harun
from
Charles the
Great.

Though not mentioned by native chroniclers, Harun received an embassy from Charles the Great, two Christians and a Jew, who sought that facilities might be afforded to the West for pilgrimage to the Holy Land, and also for the fostering of trade. They returned with splendid gifts, elephants, rare ornaments, and a water-clock; but the effort was followed by no material result. An embassy was also sent by Harun to the Chinese emperor, no doubt to establish friendly relations with his rulers on the trans-Oxus border ; but neither is this mentioned by the native annalists[1].

Splendid
reign.

Harun and his son Mamun, stand out in history as the greatest Abbasside monarchs. Harun might indeed have been ranked along with some of the best of the Omeyyad dynasty, had it not been for the dark spots of treacherous cruelty that track his whole career[2]. Splendid in his courtly surroundings and princely in his liberality, he gathered his treasures,—leaving 900 millions in his vault,—by oppressive and often unscrupulous means. His administration, with these exceptions, was just and prosperous. Accustomed from youth to martial life, he frequently joined his troops in the field ; and his many victories, especially over the Greeks, have shed lustre on his reign. No Caliph, either before or after, displayed such energy and activity in his various progresses whether for pilgrimage, for administration, or for war. But what has chiefly made his Caliphate illustrious, is that it ushered in the era of letters. His court was the centre to which, from all

[1] The Chinese writers call the Caliph *Galun*.

[2] Weil is excessively severe on Harun,—a singular exception to his usual calm and impartial judgment. He makes him out the greatest tyrant of his race, though he really was not so bad as many others both before and after. It is the Barmecide tragedy that has given him so unenviable a pre-eminence in Eastern story.

parts, flocked the wise and the learned, and at which
rhetoric, poetry, history and law, as well as science,
medicine, music, and the arts, met with a genial and
princely patronage,—all which bore ample fruit in the
succeeding reigns[1].

The witchery of Oriental romance has cast an adventitious glow around the life of Harun al Rashid ; but even
when that has faded away before the prosaic realities of
history, enough remains to excite wonder and admiration
at the splendour of this monarch's Caliphate.

---

[1] Savants of every branch were entertained with princely liberality ; but poets were the recipients of his special bounty. For example, Merwan having presented a sonnet in his praise, he forthwith gave him a purse of 5000 golden pieces, a robe of honour, ten Greek slave-girls, and one of his own steeds to ride on.

CHAPTER LXIV.

Amin at Bagdad : Mamun at Merve.

193–98 A.H.   808–13 A.D.

Breach
between
Amin and
Mamun,
193 A.H.
808 A.D. IN his unwise division of the kingdom, Harun left a fatal legacy that was not long in bearing bitter fruit. Amin, as occupying Bagdad, the seat of empire, had the advantage of Mamun. In anticipation of his father's end, he had deputed an agent to the camp at Tus with letters to be kept hid until the event. Immediately on his death, they were produced. In one, Mamun, then at Merve, was bidden to have oaths of allegiance sworn to them both, in accordance with their father's will. But a second, in direct contravention of that will, ordered the army with all its munitions of war, to return at once to Bagdad. On hearing of it, Mamun sent messengers to expostulate against this violent breach of conditions to which all had taken solemn oath ; but the troops were already well on their way, hurrying too gladly homewards to heed the appeal. On their return to Bagdad, Amin signalized his accession by distributing a year's pay to the army, which he had thus against his father's covenant stolen away from Mamun.

The relations between the brothers were thus from the first strained. Mamun, guided by an able adviser, Fadhl ibn Sahl, temporized. This man, as a recent Persian convert and *protégé* of the Barmecides, was well fitted to secure a stable and popular rule throughout the East for Mamun, who was now its rightful sovereign. Under his guidance all classes were conciliated, both the Arabs settled tribally in great numbers in and around Merve, and also the Turkish chiefs and princes, from whom a fourth of their tribute was now forgiven. Mamun's mother was Persian, a fortunate relation that commended him to the affections of the people. 'Son of our sister,' they said, 'he is one of ourselves, and an Abbasside to boot.' As the breach with his brother widened, he assumed the title of Caliph, making Fadhl his Prime Minister, both civil and military, whose rule ran from Hamadan to Thibet, from the Caspian to the Persian Gulf[1]. Meanwhile peace was restored throughout Khorasan. Harthama after a long siege took Samarcand, and Rafi, hearing of Mamun's benign administration, threw himself on his mercy, and was pardoned.

A.H. 193-198.

Mamun Caliph of East, with Ibn Sahl Prime Minister, 196 A.H. 811 A.D.

Amin on the other hand was a weak voluptuary, led at will by those about him. His Vizier was another Fadhl, Ibn Rabia, who having been chief minister with Harun at Tus, was party to what took place there upon his death. In consequence he dreaded the vengeance of Mamun, should he ever come to power, and persuaded Amin to proclaim that his son's name should have precedence of Mamun's in the public prayers. Mamun retaliated by dropping from the weekly service all mention of Amin, and by effectually closing every avenue of communication with Bagdad. At last Amin took the fatal step of declaring his brother altogether deposed from the succession, and his own son heir-apparent. Of a piece with this high-handed act, he sent to the Kaaba for the two documents, solemnly suspended by his father within the sacred walls, and tore them in shreds. Surrounded by eunuchs and women, he passed his time in revelry and dissipation. Songstresses and slave-girls, gathered for their beauty from all parts of the empire and arrayed in splendid jewelry, were the chief society of himself and his boon companions. For his *fêtes* on the Tigris he had five gondolas, in the shapes of lion, elephant, eagle, serpent and horse. Besides the private carousals in which he made no secret of drinking wine, his festivities were of the most sumptuous kind. For

Strained relations between Amin and Mamun.

Amin deposes Mamun, 194-5 A.H. 810 A.D.

His dissipated character.

---

[1] He was called *Dzu Riasatein,* 'Minister of the two departments,' i. e. both civil and military.

one of these he had the banquet-hall decked out with gorgeous carpets, couches and trappings; a hundred songstresses sang in unison before him, then breaking into companies of ten, and with palm-branches in their hands, each group advanced in turn and sang before him. But on this occasion his wayward fancy took the songs as of evil omen, and he had the hall dismantled and destroyed. Such revels, with music, dancing, and wine, were peculiarly obnoxious to Moslem sentiment; and our annalist (who seldom indulges in any such comment) remarks—'We find of him no good thing to say.' Still Amin was a favourite at Bagdad, a city already demoralized by a long course of sensuous living; and he was popular there, partly because of the money which he lavished on the troops and populace, and partly also because, while Mamun was dreaded for his Persian proclivities, Amin represented the Western sentiment that ruled in the capital of Islam.

Amin's
generals
beaten by
Tâhir, who
advances
on Irac,
195 A.H.
811 A.D.

When Amin found that his unjust pretensions were ignored at Merve, he resolved on reducing Mamun by force of arms; but from beginning to end he was unfortunate in his commanders. The first was Aly ibn Isa, hated in the East for his tyranny, and deposed, as we have seen, on that account, with indignity by Harun. He was now despatched with 50,000 men, and met with no opposition till he reached Rei. There lay Tâhir, posted by Mamun with a small force to watch the frontier, who disdaining to wait for reinforcement, gave battle at once. Aly was slain in single combat by a blow from Tâhir's left hand, for he wielded arms equally with both hands; and the Caliph's army fled [1]. This Tâhir, of Persian descent, the wise and brave founder of the Tahiride house, was well chosen for the attack which Mamun now ordered on Bagdad. On his march to Holwan successive armies were sent by Amin against him, but he defeated them all.

[1] He was called 'the Ambidexter,' and had also lost an eye, as we shall see noticed below. The command of Tâhir illustrates the change now rapidly coming over society in the relative position of the Arab tribes towards the conquered nations. He was the great-grandson of a Persian slave belonging to an Arab chief of the Khuzaite clan, and, as his freedman, became a 'client' of the same. The proud Arab, of the dominant caste, had now sunk in the scale, and the descendant of the slave or 'client' risen above him.

Harthama, despatched with heavy reinforcements from A.H. 193-198. Merve, was left in charge of Holwan by Tâhir, who then advanced upon Ahwaz and Sus, and from thence threatened the capital itself.

Fadhl ibn Rabia sought to rouse Amin to a sense of the crisis, but the voluptuous monarch, immersed in pleasure, gave a readier ear to the auspicious presages of the creatures around him, and to the fond omens of his maidens and eunuchs. Chafing under repeated defeat, he confiscated the estate of Mamun, including the million of pieces given him by his father. Some even advised to put Mamun's two sons left at Bagdad to death, but he had still the virtue to frown at the proposal. Meanwhile a new danger threatened in Syria. A pretender, claiming to represent in his person descent at once from the house of Aly and of Muavia,—sires that had contended for the Caliphate on the field of Siffin,—gained possession of Damascus and the surrounding country, and made such progress that he might indeed have founded a new dynasty in the West, had not the miserable jealousies, between the Yemên and Modhar tribes, set up a rival against him. Troops were sent to quell the rebellion, but so long as misrule reigned at the capital, nothing effectual could be done; and so for two or three years Syria was the scene of anarchy. One of the commanders of the Caliph's Syrian army was Hosein, the son of Aly ibn Isa slain by Tâhir,—an ill-conditioned man who alienated the Syrian troops by his partiality for the men of Khorasan. This captain suddenly returned with his army to Bagdad. Summoned on his arrival at midnight by Amin, he sent back the insolent reply that being neither jester nor musician, it was not his wont to appear by night, but that he would do so in the morning. His object, however, was to dethrone Amin. By daylight he had raised the malcontents of the city, whose only safety, he told them, lay in anticipating the certain victory of Mamun. Hosein then crossed the river, and dispersing the Caliph's guards, seized both him and his mother[1] and imprisoned

Amin's evil courses.

Rebellion in Syria. End of 195 A.H.

Syrian general deposes Amin, 196 A.H. 812 A.D.

---

[1] Zobeida, who had left Ricca on Abu Jafar's death, was met (193 A. H.) by Amin and his chief men at Anbar, and conducted in state to Bagdad.

A.H. 193-198. them in one of the palaces. He then proclaimed Mamun as Caliph. But at heart Bagdad hated the Khorasanies. Hosein had moreover no money wherewith to gain over either the mob or the soldiery; and the leading men dreaded the advent of Mamun. And so it came to pass that in a few days a counter-force was mustered against but is taken Hosein, who was taken prisoner and brought before Amin, prisoner now reinstated in the Caliphate. The weak monarch not only pardoned Hosein, but gave him a new command to proceed to Holwan against Mamun. But as he crossed the bridge, the people following hooted at him, and he fled. He was pursued by order of the Caliph, overtaken a short and slain. way from the city, and slain. Ibn Rabia, the Vizier, who had assisted Hosein in this singular outbreak, retired from the court and went into close hiding.

Advance of Tahir, 196 A.H. 812 A.D. Meanwhile Tâhir was steadily advancing. Column after column was despatched against him by Amin; but they had little power to stay the tide of conquest. The provinces east of the Tigris had already sent in their adhesion to Tâhir at Ahwaz; and now all Arabia, with the holy cities, came over and swore allegiance to Mamun. The governor of Mecca, a descendant of the house of Aly, denounced in public the iniquity and sacrilege of Amin in destroying the documents suspended in the Kaaba. Proceeding to Merve, he was honourably received by Mamun, always favourable to that house, and sent back with splendid gifts. At last Tâhir crossed the Tigris at Medain, almost within sight of Bagdad, and captured Wasit. Kufa, seeing no alternative, now accepted Mamun; and Mesopotamia from Bussorah to Mosul followed suit. The wretched capital alone remained. Amin sought to bribe his followers to fight, and those of the enemy to desert, by Tâhir and money cast lavishly amongst them. But all in vain. Before Harthama before the close of the year Tâhir, ready to bombard the city, Bagdad, planted his camp before the Anbar gate. Harthama, xii. 196 A.H. similarly approaching from the east, sat down outside the August, quarter on the other bank of the river. 812 A.D.

The sufferings of Bagdad throughout the siege, which lasted for a whole year, were terrible beyond description.

The struggle was prolonged not only by the advantage the
capital had in lying on either bank of the river with all its
means of transport, but also by the canals which intersected Siege and
and protected it.   The prisons were broken, and there was sufferings
of Bagdad,
riot day and night.   Catapults planted all round the walls 197 A.H.
cast shot into the city; while streams of Greek fire directed 812–13
A.D.
from within against the engines of war, caused great loss
of life without.   Hand to hand fighting went on in every
street, and as the citizens threw down stones and missives
on the advancing soldiers, Tâhir had to raze to the
ground whole quarters of the city for his own protection.
The sufferings of the inhabitants thus hemmed in, and cut
off from all supplies of food, were frightful; and the distress
of the women and children heartrending,—described by
the poets of the day as drawing 'tears of blood' from those
who witnessed them.   Palaces costing millions were left in
ashes; and the beautiful city into which the riches of the
world had for fifty years been pouring, became a heap of
ruins.

As one quarter after another fell into the hands of Tâhir, Distress at
the generals of Amin began to drop off into his camp.   In Bagdad.
vain Amin emptied his treasury, and when that failed
melted vessels of gold and silver to gain men for his
defence.   The populace held by him; but most of those
who had anything still to save went over to the invading
force.   Things had gone on thus throughout the year
197 A.H., and the wretched city was now reduced to the City
last extremity of distress and want, when Tâhir, supported stormed
198 A.H.
now by most of Amin's own generals, resolved on the final Sept.,
storm.   In concert with these, and with Harthama, who 813 A.D.
had in Tâhir's view been too long inactive on the eastern
side, the bridges were cut away and the city carried on
every side at the point of the sword.   Amin, finding his
palace untenable, fled with his mother and children into
the strong citadel which Mansur had built for himself on Amin takes
the brink of the river; while the inmates of his harem, refuge in
citadel.
crowds of eunuchs and damsels, fled hither and thither in
terror for their lives.   The citadel was defended by a faithful few, who planted engines at the gates to keep off attack;

A.H. 193–198. and here, under shelter of its battlements, Amin prolonged for two or three days his miserable life.

Evening scene on river bank. His uncle Ibrahim, one of the few nobles that still held by him, tells us that, about this time, to relieve the sultry closeness of an autumn evening, Amin issued from the palace to breathe the fresh air of the river bank, and called for him. ' I went, and as we sat in a balcony overlooking the swift stream, Amin said, " How balmy the river air ; how calm and clear the moon-beams playing on the water[1]! " Then he said, " Have ye here any wine ? " which when they brought we both drank of it ; and after that I sang to him one or two of the songs he liked. When I had done, he called for the chief songstress and bade her sing to him. She began with a well-known ode on a pack of bloodhounds. Starting at the words, he bade her sing something else ; and so she warbled a tearful sonnet on loved ones far away. " Out upon thee ! " he cried : " hast thou nothing else ? " " That song thou used to love," she said, as she began a third about the fate of monarchies. " Begone ! " cried the Caliph, swearing angrily at her, " and let me see thy face no more ! " The startled damsel, as she hasted away in the dim moonlight, stumbled on a priceless crystal goblet set before Amin, and it broke in pieces. " See ! " he cried again ; " all are against me, and the end is near. Hark ! didst thou hear that voice, as if a solemn verse of the Coran, from across the river ? " We listened ; it was but the strained imagination : all was still, and we retired into the citadel.'

Amin's attempted flight. But two courses now were open to Amin ;—either to surrender, or issuing forth by night, make a bold dash for Syria. He chose the latter ; for there were yet horses enough in the royal stables, and faithful men to mount them as his body-guard. But Tâhir, learning the design, threatened the chief men still waiting on Amin, that if they did not force him to surrender, he would visit them with condign punishment. The timid monarch was easily persuaded to exchange the risks of flight for the prospect of ease and

[1] It was the third week of the first month of the year 198 A.H., when the moon would be bright in the evening, as Ibrahim tells us.

pleasure in banishment. But he resolutely refused to resign
himself into the hands of Tâhir, whom as a Persian he stood
in dread of ; it was only Harthama, who promised to be his
friend, that he would surrender to.   Tâhir objected, for this
would have implied that Harthama and not Tâhir was the
conqueror of Bagdad.   At last it was arranged that while
Amin gave himself up to Harthama, the sceptre, signet,
and royal robes should be given to Tâhir; and so Harthama prepared at once to convey the fallen monarch to
his camp across the river. Tâhir, however, fearing collusion
in reference to the compromise, posted men all round the
citadel ; and Harthama hearing of it bade Amin wait till
he could protect him on the following day.   But the unfortunate monarch could remain no longer in his lonely palace.
Deserted by his followers, he had not even water to quench
his thirst ; and he resolved to leave at once.   So embracing
his two sons, and wiping the fast-falling tears away with his
cloak, he rode down to the river bank, where Harthama
waited in a skiff to carry him across.   As he embarked,
Harthama kissing his hands embraced him, and quickly
bade them to put off ; but they had hardly left the shore,
when Tâhir's people attacked the boat with stones and
arrows. It sank; Harthama was barely saved, the boatmen His death,
seizing him by the hair of his head. Amin casting off his $\frac{24}{198}$ i. A. H.
clothes, swam to the shore. Naked and shivering with   Sept.,
fright, he was carried to a house, where the following night   813 A.D.
he was slain by a party of Persian soldiers. His head,
after being exposed by Tâhir on the battlements, was sent,
together with the emblems of royalty, to Mamun.

The troops and people of Bagdad repented now that they An inglo-
had not fought more bravely for Amin ; but that, says our rious reign.
annalist, was because of the treasure he used to lavish on
them.   Indeed there was little more that could be said
to favour him. His troubled and inglorious reign lasted
four years and eight months.

CHAPTER LXV.

MAMUN.

198–218 A.H.   813–33 A.D.

Mamun persuaded by Fadhl to stay at Merve, 198 A.H. 813 A.D.

MAMUN had no affinity to the debauchee. We nowhere read of any revelries like his brother's, nor indulgences at variance with the teaching of Islam. On the contrary, his life was commendable, and his reign, if we except certain flagrant cruelties, not only illustrious, but just. Singularly susceptible to influences about him, and loving the East as much as he disliked the West, Mamun now made the fatal mistake of holding on at Merve, where he fell blindly under the mastery of Fadhl his Vizier, and embraced the dogmas of the Alyite persuasion,—dogmas not only hateful at the capital, but dangerous to the stability of his throne. Hence trouble in prospect for Bagdad, and for the empire at large.

Tahir supplanted by Hasan, brother of Fadhl.

Not long after Bagdad had been taken, the local troops and populace rose upon Tâhir for the murder of their favourite Caliph, and the banishment of Zobeida with his two sons to Mosul ; but after a few days, pacified by gifts, they returned to order. Tâhir continued at the head of affairs, till Mamun, at the instance of Fadhl, sent his brother Hasan ibn Sahl as viceroy to supersede him ;—a doubly unfortunate step, alienating Tâhir, and arousing antagonism throughout the older provinces, which feared the flood-tide of Persian interest. First, Nasr, an Arab chieftain,

Rebellion of Nasr in AsiaMinor.

faithful to the memory of Amin, took up arms to avenge

his fall, and, followed by a host of Arabs, seized on the A.H. 198–
218.
country between Aleppo and Someisat. Tâhir, sent to op-
pose him, but sick at the course events were taking, entered
without heart on the contest, and, after some unsuccessful
battles, retired. Thus Nasr for many years dominated the
border-lands of Asia Minor, while Tâhir, in charge of Syria
and Mesopotamia, remained spiritless and inactive at
Ricca.

In the following year a more dangerous rebellion was Rebellion
headed by Abu Saraya, a notable adventurer, who, beginning of Abu
Saraya at
as a brigand, soon raised a great following, and having Kufa and
Bussorah,
gained possession of Kufa, there set up as ruler a descen- 199 A.H.
dant of Aly. The fickle city, ready at any moment to rise 814 A.D.
in favour of the house of Aly and, like others, displeased
at the Caliph falling under Persian influence, went entirely
over to Abu Saraya, who gained possession of Bussorah
and great part of Irac, beating back army after army, sent
against him from Bagdad. He even coined money in the
name of his *protégé*, and sent envoys of the Alyite stock
throughout Arabia and elsewhere. At last, Bagdad itself
was threatened, and the Viceroy in alarm sent for Harthama,
who, vexed like Tâhir with the state of affairs, had retired
into seclusion. Harthama soon changed the scene, drove
Abu Saraya back into Kufa, and besieged him there. The
Kufans, tired of the Pretender and his marauding followers,
gave them no further countenance, and so Abu Saraya
effected his escape with 800 horse. Pursued over the Defeated by
Harthama
Tigris, he was taken prisoner before Hasan the viceroy, and slain,
who sent his head to Mamun, and had the body impaled 200 A.H.
815 A.D.
over the bridge at Bagdad. His career was thus, after
ten months, cut short ; but it was some time before Bussorah
and Arabia settled down. The Alyite governors of Abu
Saraya committed great atrocities in various quarters,—
to such an extent indeed that one earned the name of ' the
Butcher,' and another of 'the Burner.' At Mecca, the Dzul Hijj,
upstart envoy attempted to head the pilgrimage, and the 199 A.H.
ceremonies ended in great disorder. The golden linings
of the Kaaba and its treasury were plundered, and the
brocaded covering torn down and divided amongst the

A.H. 198–
218.

insurgents[1]. A rival Caliph was even set up, who continued to rule there for a time, but eventually submitted himself to Mamun and was pardoned.

Hartha-
ma's jour-
ney to
Merve,
200 A.H.

Harthama having subdued this rebellion returned to Nehrwan without visiting the viceroy. There he received orders from the Caliph to take up the government of Syria and Arabia. But he resolved first to go direct to Merve, and there warn Mamun of the critical state of things, which his Vizier was hiding from him, and that the West would speedily slip from his grasp, unless he made an early return to Bagdad. But Fadhl, anticipating Harthama's errand, poisoned his master's mind against him. It was near the end of the year before he reached Merve, which he entered with martial music, fearing lest the Vizier should con-

Received
angrily by
Mamun,
xi. 200 A.H.
June,
816 A.D.

ceal his errand. Apprised thus of his arrival, the offended Caliph summoned him at once to his presence, and covered him with reproaches for not more speedily and effectively suppressing the rebellion of Abu Saraya. As the loyal general opened his lips to make explanation and deliver his warning, the body-guard rushed upon him, fiercely buffeted him on face and body, and hurried him off to prison, where he shortly died of his injuries, or, (as popularly

His death.

believed) was put to death by Fadhl. So perished, the victim of cruel ingratitude, this great captain who had fought for the empire from Africa to Khorasan, and to whom in great part Mamun owed success over his faithless brother.

Rising at
Bagdad,
200 A.H.

The fate of Harthama, a favourite in the West, caused fresh excitement in Bagdad. The troops rose against Hasan, and abused him as the tool of his brother

Hasan flies
to Wasit.
Beginning
of 201 A.H.

Fadhl,—'the Magian and son of a Magian.' After three days' fighting, Hasan driven from the city, took refuge in Medain, and eventually retired to Wasit. Continual encounters ensued for many months, but without material result. Meanwhile confusion prevailed at Bagdad; and the unfortunate city was for a time at the mercy of bands of robbers, which committed all kinds of plunder and excess.

---

[1] Al Kindy, the contemporary Christian apologist, tells us that Othman's exemplar of the Coran, deposited in the Kaaba, was burned in the conflagration which he says took place at this time. *Apology*, S. P. C. K., p. 75.

But the better class of citizens at last banded themselves A.H. 198–
together, and outnumbering the rabble, held them in check;   218.
while two chief men, respected for their wisdom and probity,
were placed at the head of affairs. Mansur, son of the
Caliph Mehdy, was offered the throne. He declined, but
agreed to conduct the government in the name of Mamun.
Towards the close of the year, weary of the struggle, the
leaders at Bagdad came to terms with Hasan, the viceroy, Peace re-
who published an amnesty, promising six months' pay to the $\frac{\text{stored to}}{\text{Bagdad,}}$
troops, and the people their allowances according to the x. 201 A.H.
stipendiary roll. Things were settling down on this footing,
when the capital was again thrown into confusion, by an
act of inconceivable infatuation on the part of Mamun.

This was no less than the adoption by the Caliph of Aly, Mamun
surnamed *Ridha* ('the well pleasing[1]'), a descendant of $\frac{\text{proclaims}}{\text{Aly Ridha}}$
Aly, who was summoned to Merve and, though twenty-two heir-
years older than the Caliph himself, proclaimed heir-ap- $\frac{\text{apparent,}}{\text{ix. 201 A.H.}}$
parent. The Vizier, no doubt, persuaded his subservient 817 A.D.
master that this was the likeliest means of putting an end
to the Alyite insurrection in the West. At an earlier
period, a coalition between the houses of Aly and Abbas
might possibly have been successful. It was now an idle
dream; and at the present moment, when the two factions
were arrayed against each other in strife implacable, the
act was one of suicidal folly. Thus the edict went forth
throughout the empire that allegiance was to be sworn
to Aly Ridha as next in succession to the throne; and the
more publicly to mark the new departure, the national dress
was changed from Abbasside black to Shie-ite green.
Towards the end of the year, Hasan received from his Bagdad
brother command to carry out this order, which fell like revolts.
a thunder-bolt upon the capital. The Shie-ites were feared
and hated there, and the Abbassides at Court felt the blow
as aimed at the very existence of their dynasty. All rose
in rebellion, ready to depose Mamun and choose another
Caliph. Mansur no longer opposed the measure; and so
on the last Friday of the year, instead of prayer for Mamun

---

[1] That is, 'the one chosen as such from amongst the Prophet's descendants.'
Ibn Athir.

as reigning sovereign, Ibrahim, brother of Mansur, was
saluted Caliph ; and shortly after the oath of fealty taken

Ibrahim
proclaimed
Caliph, 1 i.
202 A H.
July,
817 A.D.
in his name. It is the same Ibrahim whom we have already
met in the moonlight scene by the Tigris. He was the
son of Mehdy by an African slave-girl ; proficient in
music, song, and poetry, he altogether lacked strength
for the difficult position which he now assumed, and which
with difficulty he held for two years.

Bagdad and
Irac in
rebellion,
202-3 A.H.
Hasan, Mamun's viceroy, was obliged on this again to
retire to Wasit, and fighting was renewed between the
imperial troops and those of the usurper. Hasan, thinking
to gain over Kufa with its Shie-ite proclivities, appointed
as its governor a brother of Aly Ridha ; and it is significant of the caprice of that fickle city, and the hopeless-
ness of the new coalition, that, while ready to receive him
as a purely Alyite leader, they would hear nothing of him
as the Persian representative of Mamun ; and so fighting
went on there as elsewhere. While the West was in this
state of turmoil, a fresh and startling change took place
at Merve.

Mamun's
eyes
opened,
202 A.H.
817–18A.H.
Mamun's eyes at last were opened. The first to tell
him the truth, strange to say, was Aly Ridha himself.
Things had gone on from bad to worse since his adoption
the year before. He ventured now to warn the Caliph that
his Vizier was hiding from him the truth ; that the people
of Irac held him to be either half-witted or bewitched ; and
that between Ibrahim and the Alyites the empire was slipping from his hands ;—Hasan, the Vizier's brother, was
hurrying the West to ruin, and Tâhir, who might have
righted the vessel in the storm, was thrust neglected into
Syria. A body of leading men, guaranteed against the
resentment of the Vizier, confirmed the facts, and advised
Mamun's return at once to Bagdad, as the only safety for
the empire. This, they added, was the loyal errand of
Harthama, had his master but listened to him two years

Sets out for
Bagdad,
viii. 202
A.H. Feb.,
818 A.D.
before. Mamun, now convinced that the insurrection was
due to his own subservience to Fadhl and his Shie-ite
teaching, gave orders for his Court to march towards the
capital. Arrived at Sarrakhs, Fadhl, who had vented his

displeasure against the informers, was found murdered in A.H. 198–
218.
his bath. A reward was offered for the assassins; but
these asserted that they had done what they did by com- Murder of
mand of the Caliph. They were executed nevertheless, Fadhl,
and their heads sent to Hasan with a letter of condolence March,
ix. 202 A.H.
on the death of his brother, and the promise that he should
succeed to the vacant office. Mamun further showed his
attachment to Hasan by contracting a marriage with his
daughter Burân, a child then of ten years of age; but the
bridal ceremony did not take place for another eight years.
About the same time, he gave one of his own daughters in
marriage to Aly Ridha, who was now fifty-four years of
age, and a second to Aly Ridha's son, thus to all outward
appearance cementing his alliance with him. A brother
of Aly Ridha was also nominated to the high office of
presiding at the annual pilgrimage.

Shortly after this another unexpected event took place. Death of
Aly Ridha
In his progress westward, Mamun rested in the autumn ii. 203 A.H.
for a while at Tus. There Aly died suddenly of a surfeit August,
818 A.D.
of grapes, and Mamun buried him by the side of his father.
The world was startled by this death, following so rapidly
on that of Fadhl; and the report went forth that the grapes
had been poisoned by Mamun. Our annalist (it may be
for decency's sake) says he does not believe it; and, indeed,
the favour shown to the deceased, and the marriages just
mentioned, make against the dark impeachment. On the
other hand, Aly and Fadhl were the two insuperable
obstacles in Mamun's way, and by their disappearance the
Gordian knot was solved. And so, while in a letter to
Hasan he lamented the death of Aly, the Caliph at the same
time wrote to the citizens of Bagdad saying that as Aly
against whose succession they had been so bitter was gone,
nothing was now left against returning to their loyalty.
Though this advance met with but an unceremonious answer,
the cause of Mamun began to be canvassed there with some
success. Meanwhile, Ibrahim, by his weak and harsh administration, was alienating even the few friends remaining. His troops made no head against the Caliph's; and
Medain, where he had been holding his court, fell into

A.H. 198–218. their hands. During the winter months, things went from bad to worse with him; and as the captains of Mamun closed in upon the capital, the chief men, one after another, went over to them. At last, about the end of the year, these gained possession of the city. Ibrahim escaped into hiding, after an ignoble reign of close on two years. For eight years he was lost sight of, but was at last apprehended by the police, walking abroad at an untimely hour of the night in female disguise. He offered his costly ring as a bribe, but that only revealed his birth; and he was carried an object of ridicule in woman's attire to the court of the Caliph. 'Bravo!' cried Mamun; 'is it thou, Ibrahim?' He appealed for mercy; and it was granted, for it was the time of the bridal ceremony with Buran, and she made intercession for him. Ibrahim celebrated the royal clemency in a poem which is much admired. On its being recited before him, Mamun was greatly pleased, and exclaimed in the words of Joseph to his brethren:—'There shall be no reproach on you this day; the Lord, most merciful, pardon you!'

Flight of Ibrahim, xii.203 A.H. May, 819 A.D.

While the capital was being recalled to its allegiance, Mamun advanced slowly, halting as he journeyed to secure complete restoration of order before his entry. At Jorjan he remained a month, and a week at Nehrwan, whither the members of the royal house, captains, and chiefs of State came out to bid him welcome, and Tahir also, by invitation, from Ricca. So advancing, he entered Bagdad early in 204 A.H. The edict still held for green, and so the people at the first dressed accordingly. Mamun, however, having invited his court to make known their requests, the first preferred by Tahir was that black might be reverted to. The Caliph graciously acceded, and bestowed dresses of honour in that colour upon his courtiers. Indeed, the advent of Mamun, after the long rebellion, was conspicuous for the absence of a single retaliatory measure. Fadhl ibn Rabia, in hiding ever since Mehdy's death, and Isa, Vizier of Ibrahim, who had both thrown all their influence into the opposite cause, were now re-admitted to favour. The whole attitude of Mamun was, on this occasion, generous and forgiving.

Mamun enters Bagdad, ii. 204 A.H. August, 819 A.D.

Tahir was appointed governor of Bagdad, and his son

Abdallah, equally distinguished, left to succeed him at Ricca. A.H. 198–
But whether suspicious of Tahir's ambitious aims, or (as is   218.
also said) his presence reminding him of his brother's Tahir
sad death, Mamun now conceived an aversion from him. viceroy
Tahir, aware of it, prevailed on the Vizier to propose him 204–5 A.H.
for the viceroyalty of the East, where a strong hand was
needed. Why, if suspicious of his fidelity, Mamun consented
to appoint him to so great a charge, is not clear. We are
told that a confidential eunuch accompanied him with secret
orders to administer poison if ever he should swerve from
his loyalty. After ruling successfully for two years, Tahir,
as had been feared, showed signs of insubordination. At
the weekly service, he dropped the Caliph's name from its
place in the accustomed prayer, substituting for it some
vague petition for guidance. The Master of the post (an
office everywhere charged with the duty) immediately
reported the alarming incident to the court ; and the next
day's despatch, awaited with anxiety by Mamun, brought
the expected tidings of Tahir being found dead in his bed. His death,
The circumstances of his viceroyalty are singular and 207 A.H.
obscure, and his opportune decease justifies the suspicion 822 A.D.
of foul dealing. Still more singular, the name of Tahir
remained so great, that, imputation of disloyalty notwithstanding, the Viceroyalty of the East was continued in his
family. Tahir is famous not only as a soldier and a ruler, Tahir's
but also as a generous patron of learning and poetry. A character.
letter addressed to his son on being appointed to Mesopotamia, in which are embodied instructions on all the duties
of life, social and political, is justly regarded as a model,
not only of perfect writing, but of culture and precept.
As such, the Caliph so greatly admired it, that he had
copies multiplied and spread all over the empire. Tahir,
we have seen, was called from his dexterity in the field, ' he
of the two right hands,' and he had but one eye, so that a
hostile poet said of him :—' O thou Ambidexter, thou hast
an eye too little and a hand too much,' signifying that he
was a brigand who should lose a hand [1]. His eldest son,

---

[1] The penalty in the Coran for robbery. His letter is given at length by Ibn
Athir,—occupying eleven pages of the printed edition.

A H. 198– 218.

Tahiride family hold government of Khorasan.

Abdallah, being engaged in the West, Mamun appointed his brother Talha to succeed. At the same time he sent his Vizier to see to the establishment of a loyal and efficient administration. The Vizier so deputed crossed the Oxus and waged a successful campaign in Central Asia. On leaving, he received from Talha a purse of three million pieces, and his secretary 500,000; such was the lavish fashion of the day.

End of Nasr's rebellion, 210 A.H.

Nasr, up to this time, was still in rebellion on the Western frontier. Tahir, when in Syria, had of purpose carried on operations languidly against him. But Abdallah, on succeeding his father, attacked him more vigorously, and drove him into an impregnable fortress on the borders of Asia Minor, from whence, after a five years' siege, he was induced to submit himself to the Caliph; and his return to Bagdad as a loyal subject was celebrated with great rejoicings. A party, however, of malcontents, who had been in hiding with Ibrahim ever since his deposition, now sought to create a diversion against Mamun by sundering the bridge of boats as the procession carrying Nasr approached.

Cruel treatment of rebels.

Headed by Ibn Ayesha, a relative of the royal house, they were seized and treated with singular cruelty by Mamun, who had the leader exposed in the palace court under a burning sun for three days, then scourged, and with several of his comrades put to death. His body was impaled in public, the first instance of one of royal blood being so treated. The Caliph may have had reason for the execution of these conspirators; but it was rare for him to resort to such inhuman practices. Ibrahim himself was also arrested about this time, but, as we have seen, freely pardoned.

Mamun's marriage to Buran, ix. 210 A.H. Jan., 826 A.D.

In the same year Buran, now eighteen years of age, was married to Mamun. Her father Hasan celebrated the occasion with a magnificence truly Oriental, at his country residence near to Wasit. Thither flocked the court and its surroundings in great splendour; Zobeida too, and the grandmother of the bride, who on the marriage-night showered a heap of pearls upon the bridegroom: these, gathered up by his command to the number of 1000, were

bestowed upon Buran. Invited to ask for any special favours, she obtained grace for Ibrahim, and leave for Zobeida
to go on pilgrimage. The bridal chamber was lighted with
candles of costly ambergris, and Zobeida arrayed the bride
in a robe of priceless pearls. Mamun spent a fortnight in
this brilliant company, and Hasan, to mark his gratitude
for the royal favour, spent fabulous sums in presents to all
around [1]. Balls of musk were cast amongst the crowd who
rushed about to catch them. In each was the name of an
estate, slave-girl, steed, or other prize, which fell to the lot
of him who caught it. Dresses of honour were conferred
on all, and so this festival, unparalleled in its magnificence,
came to an end. To make amends for all that he had spent,
the Caliph placed the revenues of certain provinces at Hasan's disposal for a year ;—such were the vast fortunes that
fell in these days to the lot of men in power. Buran survived her husband over fifty years.

Egypt had been long the scene of chronic revolt, aggra- Insurrec-
vated by the inroad of Spanish refugees, who joined the _{tion in} Egypt,
insurgents, and for several years held Alexandria. Abdallah, 200–210
to whose charge it belonged, while engaged with Nasr in _{A.H.}
the north, was unable to turn his arms in that direction.
He now attacked the rebels and suppressed the insur- put down,
rection. The Spaniards took ship for Crete, which thus 212 A.H.
fell into the hands of the Moslems. About this time also
Sicily fell under the Aghlabite arms, which farther ravaged
Lower Italy, and as a maritime power dominated the shores
of the Mediterranean all around. But with these western
lands the Caliphate now had small concern.

Abdallah having reduced Egypt was now employed Babek,
against the brigand Babek. This famous freebooter arose _{201 A.H.} _{816 A.D.}
in the beginning of the century, and was for twenty years
the terror of the northern provinces of the Caliphate. He
professed strange doctrines, as transmigration, incestuous
marriage [2], and other tenets of the Eastern mystics. He
was followed by multitudes, and held the difficult country

---

[1] Tradition speaks of sums amounting to a million sterling.

[2] Hence called from a Persian term Khurramies, or Voluptuaries. He is
mentioned by Al Kindy as the scourge of the empire. *Apology*, p. 46.

A.H. 198–
218.

Babek
unsuccess-
fully at-
tacked,
214 A.H.

towards Azerbijan. One after another he routed the imperial forces, which sometimes were cut entirely to pieces in
the mountain passes through which they sought to pursue
the enemy. Abdallah now sent to the attack, had hardly
the opportunity of crossing arms with him; for an outbreak occurring just then at Nisabur, he was called away to
Khorasan, where he remained as viceroy. The Moslem
army being also now engaged with Greece, Babek was left
for a time alone.

AsiaMinor,
i. 215 A.H.
March,
830 A.D.

What made Mamun, in the later years of his reign, take
the field in person, which he had never done before, is
nowhere explained; nor why a new war was now waged
with the Greeks. The reason may have been that they had
made common cause with Babek on the confines of Armenia.

Further
campaigns
there,
216–17
A.H.

However that may be, early in the year 215 A.H. Mamun
set out from Tarsus, and from thence led a successful
campaign against the Emperor Theophilus. On the way
he received Mohammed, son of Aly Ridha, gave him in
marriage the daughter to whom he had been affianced
thirteen years before, and accorded them leave to settle at
Medina. There followed in the two succeeding years a
second and a third invasion of Asia Minor, and likewise
an expedition to Egypt, which was again disturbed;—all
three campaigns commanded in person by Mamun.

Mamun
com-
mences
foundation
of Tyana
citadel.

At the close of his life Mamun was still in the vicinity
of Tarsus, returning from his last campaign against the
Greeks. To hold them the better in check, he had begun
the foundations of a grand military settlement at Tyana,
70 miles north of Tarsus. The plan was laid out by Mamun
himself. The walls, three leagues in circumference, were
pierced by four gates, each to be guarded by a strong
fortress. Artificers were gathered from all quarters of the
empire; and the Caliph, on returning, left his son Abbas
to carry on the work. This martial ardour, emulating even
that of Harun, and coming, as it did, at the close of an
otherwise pacific life, is a remarkable trait in the changeful
character of Mamun.

Mamun
visits
Damascus.

On these expeditions he repeatedly visited Damascus,
and gave princely donations to the chief families residing

there, and also to the Syrian poets who sang his praises, A.H. 198– for he was bountiful even to extravagance. But he had no love for the people of Syria ; and, when asked to regard them with the favour wherewith he regarded the Persians, he was not slow in recounting their misdeeds and disloyalty towards his dynasty. At the Great Mosque of Damascus he was shown a rescript from the Prophet and his seal, which he pressed to his eyes in reverence, and shed tears upon.

In point of fact, Mamun never shook off the preju- dices acquired in Persia, nor with them his Alyite procli- vities. In the later years of his reign there was from these evolved a remarkable (though by no means rare) com- bination of free-thought and intolerance. In some matters indeed the liberality of Mamun was singularly wide. Thus a few years previously, he abolished the ban imposed by his predecessors on the favourable mention of Muavia or any of the Omeyyad ‘ Companions ’ ; and even to Christians liberty of discussion on the comparative claims of the Gospel and Islam was allowed [1]. But the Persian predilec- tions which he all the time entertained, inclined him at last zealously to canvass the doctrines of the free-thinking Mo- tazelites. He surrounded himself at the same time with theologians and divines of all the schools, and had discus- sions in his presence on such abstract doctrines as man’s relation to the Deity, and the nature of the Godhead itself. In the end he avowed his conversion to certain tenets opposed to the Orthodox faith. Amongst these he held Freedom of the Will in place of Predestination ; and that the Coran, though inspired, was ‘ created,’ in place of the hitherto undisputed tenet that it is ‘ uncreate and eternal.’ He also declared his belief that, after the Prophet, Aly was the chiefest of mankind ; on which dogma is also built up the divine Imamate, or spiritual leadership vested from time to time in some member of the house of Aly.   Hence also it began to be taught that, apart from the Coran and tra- dition, there might be other infallible sources of divine guidance. The Coran itself was explained allegorically,

A.H. 198–218.

Mamun's Persian proclivities. 211 A.H. 826 A.D.

Heterodox views on Coran, Freewill, &c., 212 A.H.

---

[1] E. g. the *Apology of Kindy* could only have been possible under a Motaze- lite court like Mamun’s.

A.H. 198–
218.

and difficulties besetting the Orthodox, such as offended reason or cramped the growth of society, were thus easily evaded [1]. With advancing years the conviction of Mamun in respect of the Coran being an emanation in time, led to the unfortunate resolve to impose this view by pains and penalties, on his subjects [2]. When on his last campaign in Asia Minor, he sent a mandate to the governor of Bagdad to summon the leading doctors, and having tested them on that vital doctrine to report their answers to him. At this inquisition, held repeatedly, most quailed under the process and confessed. Others stood firm, among whom was Ahmed ibn Hanbal (founder of the Hanbalite school), who was ordered in chains to the Caliph's camp. We are told of threats, even of death, against two others; and twenty more who refused to confess were sent under escort to await at Tarsus the return of the Caliph from the wars; but on the way tidings were received of his death. Such cruel intolerance dims the lustre of Mamun's later years [3].

Enforces his views with intolerance and cruelty, 218 A.H. 833 A.D.

Development of science and literature.

For his reign was without question a glorious one, ushering in, as it did, the palmy days of literature, science, and philosophy. He was himself addicted to poetry, and once struck a poet with amazement who, on reciting an original piece of a hundred stanzas, found the Caliph readily ' capping ' every verse as he went along. At his court were munificently entertained men of science and letters, poets, physicians and philosophers. Besides philologists and

---

[1] It was easy thus to justify, for example, the use of wine and temporary marriage (Muta). The latter, by which a conjugal contract can be entered into for a limited period, is still a tenet of the Shiyas; but is justly reprobated by the Orthodox. As regards wine, though we nowhere hear of Mamun's being given to its indulgence, it certainly was handed round in golden beakers at his marriage with Buran ; and other occasions are mentioned by Weil.

[2] One of his arguments was this syllogism; God created all things ; the Coran is a thing : therefore the Coran is created. Also such passages as (*Suras* xxi. v. 2 and xli. v. 2) ' We have *made* or ordained for thee the Coran in the Arabic tongue,' &c. ' Yes,' replied the witness, ' it may have been " made " or ordained, but not created.'

[3] Curiously enough, in a later passage under the reign of the orthodox Motawakkel, Ibn al Athir traces the Motazelite doctrines by tradition to Labid the Jew, who bewitched Mahomet, taught that the Old Testament was created, and spread the Zendic creed. It is more likely to have been an off-shoot of the Buddhist and Zoroastrian teaching of India and Central Asia.

grammarians, it was the age also of the collectors of tradition, such as the great Bokhari, and of historians, as Wackidi [1],
to whom we owe the most trustworthy biography of the
Prophet; and of doctors of the law, as Shafie and Ibn
Hanbal [2]. Moreover Jews and Christians were welcome to
the Court not only for their own learning, but as versed both
in the Arabic tongue and in the language and literature of
Greece. The monasteries of Syria, Asia Minor, and the
Levant, were ransacked for manuscripts of the Greek philosophers, historians, and geometricians. These, with vast
labour and erudition, were translated into Arabic; and thus
the learning of the West was made accessible to the Moslem world. Nor were their efforts confined to the repro-
duction of ancient works; in some directions they extended
also to original research. An observatory, reared on the
plain of Tadmor, furnished materials for the successful
study of astronomy and geometry. In other walks of
literature, we have books of travel and history, and, above
all, of medicine; while much attention was paid to the less
practical, but more popular, branches of astrology and
alchemy. It was through the labours of these learned men
that the nations of Europe, then shrouded in the darkness
of the Middle Ages, became again acquainted with their
own proper but forgotten patrimony of Grecian science and
philosophy.

Mamun was upon the whole undoubtedly a ruler at once
just and mild. Repeated change in views and sentiment,
both political and religious, was due partly to Persian
training and affinity, partly to a yielding nature which

Mamun's reign bril-liant and just;

---

[1] Mohammed Ibn Omar died 207 A. H.: and his Secretary, who wrote from
his master the famous biography, was one of those had up before the Inquisition on the question of the Coran.

[2] Founders of two out of the four great schools of law. The other two were
Abu Hanifa (d. 150) and Malik (d. 178), the former followed by the Turks,
the latter by the Africans. The Shafieite school prevails in the East, and the
Hanbalite in Arabia. There is no material divergence in doctrine between the
four,—mainly matters of ritual. For example, the Hanifites are taught to say
Amen softly, and forbidden in adoration to raise the hands to the ears; also to
pray with the legs apart, or to fold their hands across the breast. Our Indian
fellow-subjects are much exercised on these trivial points. See judgment of
the Privy Council, reported in *The Times*, February 23, 1891.

A.H. 198–
218. made him unduly subject, as in the case of Fadhl, to personal influence. He cannot be acquitted of acts of capricious violence, some of which are just as cruel as those which stain the memory of his predecessors. One instance of singular inhumanity I should not omit. Abu Dulaf, a brave and noble Arab, was chief of the principality of Ha-madan, where his family held a high repute. Having taken the side of Amin, he was unwilling after his fall to bow before Mamun, and so retired to his Persian home. A blind poet composed a beautiful but extravagant panegyric laud-ing him as the first of Arabs, which so irritated Mamun, as if aimed in depreciation of himself, that he had him cruelly put to death. Abu Dulaf shortly after surrendered, and his honourable reception is extolled as an act of grace on the Caliph's part, which cannot, however, affect our judgment of his heartless criminality towards the blind poet[1]. For the rest, even leaving out of account the dark imputations as to the death of Fadhl and Aly Ridha, we have still the cruel treatment of Ibn Ayesha, as well as the fate of Harthama and Tahir, to both of whom he owed so much; and lastly his bitter intolerance towards victims of the barbarous Inquisition. But considering the length of his reign, and his magnanimous attitude towards the rebels of Bagdad, the balance must incline to the verdict of leniency and moderation in a Caliphate which, taken as a whole, is one of the most brilliant in the history of Islam.

certain ca-
price and
cruelty not-
withstand-
ing.

Death of
Mamun,
vii. 218 A.H.
August,
833 A.D.

Mamun was eight-and-forty years of age, when death

[1] According to a grand-nephew of the Caliph, who tells the story, the verse which offended Mamun was to the effect that 'every Arab entering the lists of glory, must borrow his nobility from Abu Dulaf,' which Mamun thought to be a slight upon himself. The blind poet excused the obnoxious verse by saying that of course he regarded the Caliph as altogether beyond the range of com-parison. Mamun then said he would execute him not for that verse, but for another verse, in which he ascribed divine attributes to a mortal, whereupon his tongue was cut out and the poet died a miserable death. The narrator is a son of Motawakkel, who reversed the policy of Mamun. Weil holds it to be a well-grounded 'historical fact'; but it is not given in the annals of the day; and one would be glad to question it as, at the least, greatly exaggerated.

I should also mention that under the year 200 A.H., i.e. while Mamun was yet in Merve, I find the entry: 'Mamun in this year slew Yahya, because he called out to him—"O thou Caliph of the Unbelievers."' There is no further explanation given.

overtook him near Tarsus, in his third campaign against the Greeks.   It was a hot autumn day, and he sat with his brother Abu Ishac on the bank of a mountain stream, in the clear cool flood of which they laved their feet. 'Come,' said he to the companion who tells the story, 'come see how refreshing to the limbs are these limpid waves.   All that we want is but a dish of dates to make the moment perfect!' Just then a mule was heard approaching with a burden of that very fruit.   Two baskets full of the choicest dates, fresh gathered from the tree, were brought.   They partook plentifully of them, with draughts also of the delicious icy water.   As they arose, all three were struck with a burning fever.   It was Mamun's last illness.   The fever gained rapidly; and finding his end to be near, he had a rescript drawn up for all the provinces, proclaiming his brother Abu Ishac successor, under the title of Motassim [1].   Then he gave minute instructions as to his own funeral and grave, directing that none should weep or mourn threat.   Calling his brother, he specially enjoined upon him, along with other admonitions for a religious life and just administration, to enforce the right teaching which he held as to the Coran and other doctrines of Islam, and to hasten back to Irac.   So passed Mamun away, and was buried at Tarsus, having reigned twenty years, besides the five preceding, during which he held at Merve the government of the East.

[1] 'He who maketh his refuge in the Almighty.'

CHAPTER LXVI.

MOTASSIM AND WATHIC.

218–232 A.H.   833–47 A.D.

Motassim
218 A.H.
233 A.D.

THE troops, at the first, refused to do homage to Motassim, preferring rather, in their growing insolence, to elect Abbas, son of the late Caliph ; but he, summoned from Tyana, at once swore allegiance, and the army followed. Tyana was abandoned, the rising walls demolished, and whatever could not be carried off committed to the flames. Motassim then returned to Bagdad.

Intolerant
supporter
of Mamun's
heterodoxy.

Motassim followed his brother, or surpassed him rather, in the two weak points of his rule, intolerance, to wit, and preference for the Turkish soldier. Freedom of discussion, indeed, to an extent never dreamed of till the days of Mamun, still prevailed, excepting in respect of the new dogmas of the court. Science and philosophy flourished under such distinguished professors as Al Kindy, 'the philosopher of the Arabs,' whose works, both original and borrowed from the Greeks, have won a European reputation. But from the Motazelite creed no divergence was tolerated ; to it every Moslem must conform. Two dogmas were especially dear to the Caliph, namely, that the Coran was not eternal, and that by the disembodied eye in the future life, the Deity could not be seen. The severest pains and penalties, even to the death, awaited those who dared to differ. Bagdad was much disquieted by the intolerant rigour of the Caliph and his heated doctors ; the famous

Ibn Hanbal was again arrested, and being firm in the faith, A.H. 218-
232.
was pitilessly scourged, and cast scarred and senseless into
prison.

But a still greater trouble threatened the city in the Increasing
ribaldry of
Turkish
soldiery at
Bagdad.
swarms of Turkish soldiery that in daily-increasing num-
bers were planted in and around it. Thousands of *Memluks*[1]
were yearly imported from the East. Some formed the
body-guard, the remainder swelled the army; and such as
displayed military talent and presence, gaining the Caliph's
favour, rose rapidly to chief command. Thus were the
Arab soldiery, captains as well as rank and file, rapidly
displaced; and retiring to their deserts, instead of as heretofore pillars of the Caliphate, became a chronic element
of disturbance and revolt. The evils of this system,—cul-
minating hereafter in the Mameluke dynasty, the curse of
Egypt,—were for the present confined to the capital and its
outlying cantonments. The Turkish horse, galloping in
unbridled license wildly about the streets, kept the women
and children in constant jeopardy; and affrays and
murders were the consequence. Riding through the city,
a Sheikh began to accost Motassim in the simple Arab
style,—'O Abu Ishac!' The escort set upon him as an
ungainly intruder, but the Caliph stayed them, and listened
to his words :—'A horde of foreigners,' he said, 'have been
planted in our midst, and from their insolence and rapine
there is no escape.' Motassim never again rode abroad
in Bagdad. This incident led to the founding of Samira, Leads to
the found-
ing of
Samira.
with its palaces and imperial barracks, some sixty miles
higher up the Tigris. Thither the Caliph retired the
Turkish troops, and Samira thenceforth was made the seat
of his court. Bagdad was relieved, but the Caliph fell
more than ever under the hand of these foreign levies[2].

The Moslem arms being engaged in many quarters, soon

---

[1] The past participle of *malak*, 'to own'; signifying purchased slaves, chiefly
from Turkestan.

[2] Samira, properly *Sarr-man-raa*, 'whoever saw it rejoiced,' or *Delight of
the Eyes,* from the beauty of its situation; or as was wittily said, ' *whoever saw
it* with the Turks settled there, *rejoiced* at Bagdad being well rid of them.'
Harun had begun to build it when he first left Bagdad. But when he passed on to
Ricca and settled there, the place fell into ruins till Motassim began to rebuild it.

A.H. 218–
232.

Peace with
Emperor,
218 A.H.
833 A D.

Inroad of
Zatt insur-
gents,
219-20
A.H.

after his accession, Motassim made peace with the Greeks and arranged an exchange of prisoners[1]. Among the troubles that threatened, there was first the strange tribe named Zatts, supposed to have been immigrants from the Indian border, who ravaged Lower Mesopotamia. They were put to flight by Ojeif, an Arab general, who brought several thousands of them by boat to Bagdad, whence they were exiled to Asia Minor, and there attacked and dispersed by the Greeks[2]. An Alyite pretender also occasioned some anxiety in Khorasan, but was suppressed by Abdallah ibn Tahir, now nearly independent ruler there.

Babek's de-
feat and
escape,
218 A.H.

Taken
captive,
222 A.H.
837 A.D.

The rebel who continued to cause the most anxiety at Bagdad was the famous Babek, who long held sway in Azerbijan, and had there the countenance of Armenia and Greece. He now sent his columns south, and the terror spread as far even as Hamadan. Vast multitudes in Northern Persia adopted his faith and flocked to his standard. They were attacked with great slaughter, and pursued into Grecian territory. Against the freebooter himself, who retired into inaccessible haunts towards the Caspian, the Caliph sent Afshin, one of his ablest Turkish generals, with a large and well-ordered force. But it was not before two years of hard fighting beyond Ardebil, and not without acts of treachery (too common with these Turkish leaders), that, one after another, the strongholds of Babek were taken ; he himself effected his escape into Armenia, where he was captured and made over to Afshin by an Armenian prince, with whom he had taken refuge. Thousands of Moslem captives, women and children, were recovered and restored to their families. Afshin seized the vast treasures which had been amassed by Babek during all these years, and from them richly rewarded his officers. He then set out for Samira, carrying the famous freebooter and his brother in his train. The long career of this brigand prince, who had been now for twenty years the lord of Azerbijan, and whose endless

---

[1] An embassy to Bagdad is mentioned by the Byzantine writers, headed by John the Grammarian ; but it is not noticed by Arab annalists.

[2] Their history is obscure. They may have been a Buddhist sect ; but why they should have come across Persia from the East, and fallen upon Mesopotamia at this time, does not appear.

roll of outrages and of Moslem generals beaten and armies A.H. 218–
destroyed, had for a whole generation struck terror into the 232.
people's mind[1], made the march a royal ovation for Afshin.
As he drew near to Samira, the Caliph sent him every day
a fresh dress of honour with splendid gifts ; and as the
cortege approached, went forth in state with his son and the
royal household, to bring him in with every mark of honour.
Babek was kept under guard, and thither Motassim himself and cruelly
with his chief Cazee, went in disguise to gaze upon 'the executed.
Shaitan of Khorasan,' as they called him ; who was then
paraded over the city. Brought back to the palace, the
Caliph, surrounded by his men of war, commanded Babek's
own executioner to fall upon him, sever his limbs, and then
plunge the knife into his still quivering trunk. The head
was sent round the cities of Khorasan, and the body impaled
near the palace. Babek's brother was reserved to be treated
in like manner as a sight for the city of Bagdad, and his
body there hung up by the river bank.

The Emperor Theophilus, taking advantage of the Mos- War with
lem arms being engaged against Babek, with whom the the Emperor,
Greeks are said to have made common cause, had mean- v. 223 A.H.
while been ravaging the south of Asia Minor, and carrying March,
838 A.D.
fire and sword even into the heart of Syrian territory. The
bitter cry of a captive Hashimite lady, *Shame on Motassim!*
reached the Caliph's ear. *Ready!* he exclaimed, starting
up as if he heard her voice ; and commenced forthwith
preparations for war on the grandest scale. It was the
spring of 233 A. H. when he marched for Syria. Passing on
to Tarsus, he there marshalled his army in three divisions,
led mainly by Turkish captains, and advanced against the
Emperor. 'Which is the virgin fortress of the Greeks?' he
asked, resolved to mark his vengeance by a feat surpassing
all before. 'It was Amoria,' they said,—the famous Amorium, more than half way across the peninsula ;—and so

---

[1] Babek is said to have defeated six famous generals in these twenty years,
slain 255,000 men, taken 3300 men, and 7600 women prisoners. Comparing
this with the ravages of Mahomet's army, Al Kindy asks the Mahometan advocate, ' Tell me, now, wherein the difference lieth between thy Prophet and Babek
Khurramy, whose insurrection hath caused such grief to our lord the Commander
of the Faithful, and disaster to mankind at large.' *Apology,* p. 46.

A.H. 218–
232.

Siege of
Amorium.

thither the columns were ordered to converge.   Theophilus, defeated in a pitched battle, left the city to its fate.   After fifty-five days of siege, a renegade led the engines to a defenceless point, and the walls were about to be stormed when a general, named Vendu, issued from the city, and offered to surrender, if terms were given.   He was graciously received, and the garrison, relying on the parley, held their hand. But the faithless Caliph meanwhile signalled a fresh attack, and Vendu, riding by his side, saw in consternation when too late that he was overreached.   The city, thus easily captured, was treated with the last severities of war.   Multitudes took refuge in the cathedral, which was set on fire, and all perished in the flames.   The chief families were set aside for heavy ransom, with all the goods worth carrying away ; and the rest were put up to the highest bidder.

Burned and
destroyed.

All that remained was committed to the flames, and Amorium left a desolation.   There was shortly after an exchange of prisoners, and the relations with the emperor became for a time of a pacific character.

Conspiracy
against
Caliph.

The happiness of Motassim was, however, damped by an attempt which nearly brought his reign to an untimely end. Ojeif, the Arab chief, who had distinguished himself in the Zatt campaign, and now commanded the centre against the Emperor, was roused to jealousy by the favours lavished on the Turkish generals, and by their insolent bearing towards himself and his fellows.   Goaded thus, he conspired against Motassim ; and persuaded Abbas to aspire to the throne which at the first he had renounced.   The plot, joined by other Arab leaders, and even by some of the Turks, was delayed till Amorium should fall, and then the distribution of the spoil was to be the signal for slaying the Caliph and his two Turkish favourites, Afshin and Ashnas.   An attempt to plunder the spoil and in the confusion accomplish the traitorous design, was crushed by Motassim, who boldly rushed upon the plunderers sword in hand, and dispersed them.   The plot came prematurely to light by the talk of some drunken confederates.   The Caliph disbelieved the existence of so wide-spread a conspiracy, till Abbas himself, plied with wine, confessed to him the whole. He was made over to Afshin, who, withholding water to drink, thus starved him to death, and Ojeif met the same fate. For another, carried into Syria, a well was dug, into which he was cast, and the pit filled in upon him while yet alive. And thus, with signal pains and penalties, the chief conspirators were all destroyed. The conspiracy had moreover the disastrous effect of throwing the Caliph altogether into the hands of his Turkish captains, and of gradually ousting the alienated Arab leaders from all chief commands. Among the Turks themselves there was but little love or loyalty to lose; envy and hatred, greed and lust of power, made the East but the theatre of intrigue, treachery and violence, in which there was respect neither for life nor right. And they who suffered most were the Caliphs themselves, who, as long as the court remained at Samira, became the miserable puppets of their Turkish generals or the helpless victims of military outrage.

Afshin himself was soon to fall. Maziar, the native prince of Tabaristan, withholding tribute, ravaged the south-east coast of the Caspian, and rebelled against Abdallah ibn Tahir, now the acknowledged chief of Khorasan. Afshin hated Abdallah because he had exposed his appropriation of Babek's spoil, and he also coveted his government. He therefore secretly encouraged Maziar, in the hope that he might himself be sent with a force to suppress the rising, and so supplant Abdallah. But Abdallah was able without help to defeat Maziar, who, taken captive, was sent to Samira; and there, confronted with Afshin, accused him of abetting the rebellion.

Misdeeds of misappropriation were also charged against Afshin. The attitude of the Caliph now changed towards him. In alarm he attempted to escape to the Caspian shores, but failing, was arrested and cast into prison. A court was constituted of the chief Cazee, the Vizier, and other Courtiers. But, strange to say, the charge was neither for treachery nor embezzlement. He was arraigned for holding Magian doctrines, and for covert hostility to Islam. Princes from Soghd were summoned as witnesses. Two

A.H. 218–
232.

men in rags, with scarred backs, were brought forward. 'Knowest thou these?' asked the Vizier, who conducted the trial. 'Yes,' answered Afshin: 'the intendants of a mosque in Soghd. They built the same on the site of a temple which they razed to the ground, after casting out the idol from the shrine. Now the treaty ran that all were free to follow each his own religion; and so, as breakers of the treaty, I caused them to be scourged.' 'And this golden and jewelled book of thine, wherein is blasphemy against the Most High?' 'It is a book,' he replied, 'inherited of my father, wherein is the wisdom of the Easterns—good morals and also heresy; the first I used, the last I left alone.' Other imputations Afshin contended were worthless, as based on Magian evidence. At last Maziar deposed that Afshin's brother had written a letter couched in opprobrious terms against the whole Moslem race and their religion, and urging return to the old Magian faith. 'For what my brother wrote,' Afshin said, 'I am not responsible; but doubtless it was written for expediency's sake, and to advance the conquests of the Caliph by artifice, even as Abdallah doth, in the regions beyond.' The chief Cazee, doubting the evidence, came to no conviction on the charge of heresy, but sent Afshin back handcuffed to his prison, where, not long after,

Afshin's
death,
226 A.H.

partaking of a dish of fruit sent by the Caliph, he died. His body was hung up to public derision and then burned. Strange rumours spread abroad of idols, jewelled figures, and Magian books found in his house: but the excited Moslem mind was ready to accept any tales regarding the Magians of the day. Maziar was scourged so cruelly that he sank under the infliction [1]. The trial of Afshin throws interesting light upon the Caliph and his court, as well as showing the hold which Magian doctrines and worship still retained, and the toleration accorded them in the far East.

Motassim died not long after, having reigned nearly nine years. With an arbitrary, but on the whole a kindly dispo-

[1] He acknowledged he was not circumcised, and stated personal reasons for omission of the rite. The jewelled book was no doubt Magian; or possibly Buddhist.

sition, he did nothing to stay the decline of the Caliphate. A.H. 218–232.
Of the Turkish captains on whom he leaned, in his later
days, he bitterly complained[1]. Had he looked to able
Arab chiefs for support, it was yet possible to have restored
vigour to the body politic. But he went over entirely to
the Turks, and courted the influx of barbarian races, whose
fatal yoke his successors could not throw off. As proof of
his kindness we are told that the beast of a poor husband-
man having fallen into a quagmire, he helped him up with
its burden again. On this, contrasted with the destruction of Amorium, Gibbon has the reflection:—'To a point
of honour, Motassim had sacrificed a flourishing city, 200,000
lives, and the property of millions. The same Caliph descended from his horse, and dirtied his robe to relieve the
distress of a decrepid old man, who with his laden ass had
tumbled into a ditch. On which of these actions did he
reflect with the most pleasure, when he was summoned by
the angel of death?'

Motassim was succeeded by his son Wâthic, who, though
born of a Greek slave-girl, inherited his father's Persian
proclivities, and indeed with even greater intolerance. He
was weak and arbitrary in his administration. The story
of the Barmecides having been related to him, and how
Rashid had recovered vast sums from their estates, he exclaimed, 'What a fine example my grandfather hath set for
me.' He immediately proceeded to arraign his ministers
and their secretaries, and having beaten one and threatened
others, despoiled them of vast sums, from 100,000 to 1,000,000
dinars each. What a vivid conception does not this give us
of the corruption of the minions at court, and the caprice
of their master !

During this reign there were risings, more or less,
throughout the empire ; in the parts about Mosul from the
Kharejites ; and in Persia from a rebellion of the Kurds ;
but the worst disturbances were in Syria and Arabia.

Side notes: A.H. 218–232. Motassim's death, iii. 227 A.H. Jan., 842 A.D. and character. — Wathic succeeds, 227 A.H. — His rapacity. — Disturbances.

---

[1] In his last days, comparing Mamun's able officers with his own, he said to
one of his courtiers:—'See what Afshin hath come to. Ashnas, a poor creature; Itach and Wassif, nothing in them.' Yet these were the men on whom
he leaned.

Just before the decease of Motassim, a serious insurrection broke out in Palestine. A lady having been ill-treated

by a soldier who sought to force her door, the husband went against the government, and set up as a leader of the Omeyyad line. Known as *Mobarca*, from his face being always veiled, he roused the whole country west of the Jordan. The general sent by the Caliph was still engaged with this impostor, when a still more dangerous outbreak at Damascus called him thither. A battle was fought outside the city, and after over a thousand had been slain, order was at last restored. The force then returned to Palestine, where harvest having thinned the insurgent ranks, an easy victory was gained, but at great cost of life to the rebels, of whom some 20,000 were slain. Mobarca was carried off a prisoner to Samira.

A year or two afterwards Arabia fell into a troubled state. The Beni Soleim and other Bedouin tribes, with now no career to divert their marauding tendencies, attacked the Holy cities, plundering the markets and committing havoc everywhere. They were defeated by Bogha, a Turkish general, who to strike terror imprisoned 1500 of them at Medina. While he was called away by fresh disturbances on the Syrian border, this great body of prisoners attempting to break away, were surrounded by the inhabitants, and slain by their negro slaves to a man. Order restored in the north, Bogha returned, and waged a long and not always successful campaign against insurgent tribes in the centre and south of the Peninsula.

But the danger that chiefly threatened Wathic was nearer home ; and arose, in short, from the rigour with which he enforced his heterodox views. The men of Bagdad, greatly irritated, set on foot a plot against the hated government. It was headed amongst others by a Moslem saint, named Ahmed, whose unmeasured denunciation of the intolerant Caliph gathered around him a great following. The day was already fixed for a threatening demonstration with flags and drums, when two of the conspirators fell to drinking, and issued forth a night too soon. The plot thus prematurely disclosed, Ahmed was sent to Samira, where the Caliph

arraigned him before a court, not, however, on the charge of
a treasonable rising, but of heresy. 'What sayest thou of
the Coran?' asked the Caliph. 'That it is the word of
God,' replied Ahmed with heavenly ardour, for he coveted
martyrdom, and had anointed his body for the burial.
'Nay, but is it not create?' rejoined the angry Caliph.
'It is the word of God,' repeated Ahmed, calmly. 'And
what about the beatific vision?' continued the Caliph.
'This that the Prophet hath told us, *Ye shall see your Lord
at the Day of Judgment, even as ye see the full moon.*'
'That he said but in a figure,' answered Wathic; and he
began to argue the point. 'Dost thou command me
then?' asked Ahmed. 'Yea, verily.' 'Then I may not
swerve from the clear teaching of the Prophet.' 'Ye have
heard him yourselves,' said Wathic to the assembled court;
'what think ye?' The Cazee of the Western Quarter
cried, 'By thy sacred Majesty! Verily his blood is lawful!'
'O satisfy our thirst therewith!' exclaimed the rest,—all,
excepting Ibn Daud, the chief Cazee, who said,—'Give space
to repent; haply, he is crazed.' 'Nay, nay,' shouted the
Caliph; 'leave me alone, while thus in his blood I expiate
my sins.' And calling for Samsat (the famous sword of
Madikerib[1]), he gave him a mortal blow upon the neck.
Thereupon, the rest plunged their swords into him, and
he fell a mangled corpse. The body was hung at Samira
by that of Babek, and the head, sent to Bagdad under a
guard, was set up with this inscription,—*The head of
Ahmed, the Heathen and accursed Polytheist.*

Towards the close of his reign there was an exchange
of prisoners between the Caliph and the Emperor. The
two camps were formed on either side of a river beyond
Tarsus. There were over 5000 Moslems, men and women,
to be freed; but even here the bigotry of Wathic prevailed,
for with an intolerance almost inconceivable, none were
received in ransom but such as confessed the two favourite
dogmas of the court.

In the year following, Wathic was seized with an insuffer-

Side notes:
A.H. 218–232.

Martyrdom of Ahmed.

Exchange of Greek prisoners, 231 A.H. 846 A.D.

Death of Wathic, 232 A.H. 847 A.D.

---

[1] Supra, p. 37. This sword, of which he was despoiled in the war of the apostasy, is famous in Arab song, as of marvellous temper, and extreme antiquity.

able thirst, the result of dissipated living. The remedy prescribed was exposure in an oven, which overheated caused his death. The only credit given to his short reign of six years was for generosity and benefactions, missed especially by the poor of Mecca and Medina. It would take, however, some more substantial praise than this to set against the bigotry and cruel tyranny of which examples have been given above.

CHAPTER LXVII.

MOTAWAKKIL.

232–247 A.H.   847–861 A.D.

'WITH Motassim,' writes Gibbon, 'the eighth of the Mota-
Abbassides, the glory of his family and nation expired.' wakkil,
232 A.H.
The glory of the *nation*—the Arabian—had already paled 847 A.D.
before the rise of their Turkish rivals ; the glory of the
family was fast setting under the outrage and violence of
the same barbarians, whom they had summoned from the
East to ' the City of Peace.'   The royal house were apt
scholars, as well as abject slaves.   In the school of tyranny
and extortion, perfidy and bloodshed, they quickly became
their masters' equals.   And so the Caliphate hurried on to
its decline and fall, with only here and there an impotent
struggle to arrest the downward course.

On the death of Wathic, the courtiers would have done His cruelty
homage to his son, but being yet a boy, the royal turban, and rapacity.
robes and sceptre were all too great for his small frame; and
so they chose instead Motawakkil, Wathic's brother [1].   The
new Caliph was not long in showing a cruel and vindictive turn.   A couple of months had hardly passed, before
the late Vizier, who under his brother's reign had treated
him with contumely, was cast into prison, and his property
throughout the empire confiscated.   For months he was

---

[1] Caliphs are no longer known by their proper names, but by their royal
title, signifying some attribute of faith or trust in the Almighty; as here, ' He
that putteth his trust (in the Lord).'   And so with all the future names.

A.H. 232– subjected to the refined torture of being kept awake while
247. he would have slept.   At last he was left alone and slept
a day and night.   Thus strengthened for the trial, he was
put into a barbarous press (instrument of torture invented
by the Vizier himself) so narrow that the sufferer was with
difficulty forced within it, and lined with spikes which
made shift impossible.   Thus in agony he lay for days, and
died.   This as a specimen must suffice.   Various other
officers of State were victims of his cruel rapacity ; and
specially the commander-in-chief, who too had been
wanting in respect, and would have shared like fate with
the Vizier, had he not purchased pardon by the fine of
eleven million pieces.

Fall of   Another dark picture casts a lurid light upon the court
Itakh, and Caliph's life.   Itakh, a general of renown in the Amu-
234 A.H. rian war, and in the campaign against Babek, a favourite
also of the preceding Caliph, was now commandant of the
body-guard, and boon companion of Motawakkil.   In a
brawl over their cups one night, Itakh, steeped in wine, so
far forgot himself as to fall upon the Caliph and threaten
his life.   Next morning, coming to himself, he begged that
the affront might be forgotten, and was apparently forgiven.
Advised to proceed to Mecca, he was placed over the
pilgrim escort with a robe of honour, and given command
of all the towns through which the pilgrims were to pass.
His treach- It was but an artifice to put him off his guard.   As he
erous returned through Bagdad, the governor went forth to meet
death, him with a royal robe and gifts, and, on pretence of
235 A.H. presenting him to a Hashimite assembly, closed the door
upon his escort as he entered.   'Had it been elsewhere
than Bagdad,' cried the victim, 'he had not dared thus ' ;
for Bagdad hated the Turks, and Itakh's friends were all at
Samira, the Caliph's court.   Cast into prison, he lingered
for some months, weighted with heavy chains, and at last,
being denied water to drink, died of thirst.   His secretary
and sons were also kept in durance till the Caliph's death.

    Motawakkil's reign was marked by the return to ortho-
doxy.   The heresies of Mamun were abjured ; and the
Motazelite professors had now their turn to suffer persecu-

tion. The eternity of the Coran was reasserted; and even to discuss the question of its creation proscribed throughout the empire. The body of Ahmed, the confessor, was brought back with due solemnity to Bagdad and there, the head rejoined, prepared for burial; while innumerable crowds pressed round, if they might but touch the saintly relics. Among others who suffered for the now discarded faith, was the noble and learned Ibn Abu Daud, who had held the office of chief Cazee under the three preceding reigns. He was deposed and cast into confinement with his family, and their wealth and lands confiscated. One of the sons purchased freedom by the incredible sum of sixteen million golden pieces: but the father died a few years after still a prisoner.

A.H. 232–247.

Motawakkil returns to orthodoxy; persecutes Free-thinkers, 237 A.H. 851 A.D.

Equally violent was the reaction against the descendants of Aly, on whom such favour had of late been lavished. Motawakkil hated them, and their teaching also. In company with his boon companions he treated the memory of Aly the Prophet's son-in-law with indecent contumely. A bare-headed buffoon, with a pillow stuffed in front, dared dance before the Caliph, while they sang around, *Behold the pot-bellied bald one, the Caliph of Islam*[1]. And Motawakkil, enjoying the scene, joined in laughter with the rest. Such ribald and profane contempt of that which was most dear and sacred to the Moslem heart, alienated his followers at large and met reproaches from his own son[2]. So far indeed did Motawakkil carry his hostility that he had the tomb of Hosein razed to the ground, ploughed over and sown with corn; and he even threatened with imprisonment any pilgrims who ventured to visit the shrine of Kerbala. On the other hand, he honoured the first three Caliphs and even the Omeyyad dynasty, and we read of one beaten to death for speaking opprobriously of Abu Bekr, Omar and Ayesha. He was thus a thorough Syrian, and loved the Arab race.

and Aly-ites.

With the return to orthodoxy, the sumptuary laws

---

[1] See above, p. 299.

[2] The profane buffoonery must have produced profound sensation; for the annalist adds, 'This was one of the causes which justified Muntassir in taking his father's life.' But that no doubt is an after-thought.

A.H. 232–
247.

Severe
enactments
against
Jews and
Christians,
235–39
A.H.

against Jews and Christians, long fallen into desuetude under the tolerant reigns preceding, were now reimposed with the utmost stringency, and with new marks of degradation. Coloured stripes must be sewn upon their garments and those of their slaves, with restrictions as to flowing girdles; their women to wear yellow veils abroad; riding confined to mules and asses, with wooden stirrups and knobs upon their saddles; the figure of Satan must be on the door-posts of their houses, on which moreover was imposed a special tax; tombs must be level with the ground; they were debarred from offices of state; their children forbidden to be taught in Moslem schools or by Moslem masters; churches recently built to be demolished; and no cross paraded at their festivals, or erected in any street. To such extent did intolerance march hand in hand with orthodoxy[1].

Division of
empire,
235 A.H.

Early in his reign Motawakkil divided the provinces among his sons, giving the western to Mustain the eldest, and the eastern to Mutazz. But gradually the latter became his favourite. He was placed in possession of the mint and treasuries; and his name was stamped upon the coinage, indicating him thus as successor to the throne.

Rise of
Saffarides.

With such a ruler, and so demoralized a court, we need not wonder that the bonds of order were everywhere relaxed. Abroad, as at home, rebellion more or less prevailed. In Sejestan the Saffaride, adventurers began to supplant the Taharide family. Azerbijan rebelled, and was with difficulty reduced. Lower Egypt was attacked by a Byzantine fleet which for some time held Alexandria; and Upper Egypt by pagan tribes, which withheld the tribute due from the gold mines, and spread terror over the land. To check these ravages, troops were sent to the southern districts, which (as in our own day) were supplied with provisions by sea from the Suakin coast. The insurrection was quelled, but not without much blood-

Outbreak
in Upper
Egypt,
241 A.H.

[1] A Christian apothecary who embraced Islam, but after several years returned to his ancestral faith, refusing to recant was put to death, and burned (242 A.H.). This, however, would be held by Moslems to be in accordance with their law.

shed. The leader, Aly Baba, admitted to terms, was
carried to Samira, where he was received with special
honour by the Caliph, and put in charge of the pilgrim
road between Egypt and Mecca. His tribe still held to
their fetish faith, and Aly Baba shocked the men of
Samira by carrying with him an idol of stone, the object
of his daily worship. The heathen was tolerated and
honoured with an important trust, while Christian captives,
refusing Islam, were put to death.

In Armenia, which in the war with Babek had been on
friendly terms with the Moslem court, the overbearing conduct of a Moslem general, who treacherously sent some of
the patricians to Samira, led to a serious outbreak, in which
the hated officer was slain and his troops cut to pieces or
scattered in the hills to perish in the cold. A heavy
campaign under Bogha 'the elder,' took a signal revenge,
30,000 were slain and great numbers sold into slavery.
Bogha then advanced to Tiflis, where a prince of the
Omeyyad line had established himself as independent
ruler. The city, built of wood, was destroyed by streams
of naphtha, and 50,000 perished in the flames. He then
advanced to the shores of the Caspian and the Black sea.
Certain Armenian princes were sent from thence to the
Caliph's court, who, refusing to accept Islam, fell martyrs
to their faith [1].

On the side of Asia Minor, the border was the scene of
raids first by the Moslem troops and then by their enemies.
The Greeks carried off so many prisoners, that thousands
are said to have been put to death by the Empress
Theodora, and only those spared who embraced the Christian faith. Some 900 men and women alone were left for
ransom [2]. In the next few years, the Greeks again
advanced towards Syria and laid siege to Sameisat; and
then the Moslems, aided by the Paulician enemies of the

A.H. 232–247.

Bogha's success in Armenia, 237-8 A.H.

AsiaMinor, 241 A.H.

---

[1] This, told by the Byzantine writers, is not mentioned by our annalist; see
Weil, ii. 362.
[2] The number put to death by the empress is given at 12,000. Bar Hebraeus
speaks of 20,000 prisoners of whom 8000 were given up, and 12,000 put to
death. We must hope that in such statements there is vast exaggeration.

A.H. 232-247.

Emperor, made reprisals, carried off immense booty in herds and flocks, and took the town of Lulu. It was restored in return for a thousand captives, but beyond this, and large moneys paid in ransom, no permanent gain accrued on either side. At home, the northern tracts of Syria were in a disturbed condition. Hims expelled its governor, and continued in rebellion for a length of time. Troops from Damascus and Ramleh at last restored order, and many captives were sent to Samira. But it was the Christians that here as elsewhere suffered most. Having made common cause with the rebels, they were expelled the city, their churches demolished, and one that adjoined the Great mosque taken within its bounds.

Rebellion at Hims, 240-1 A.H.

Caliph tries Damascus for his court, 244 A.H.

After holding his court for twelve years at Samira, the Caliph transferred it to Damascus. His predilections were always with the West; and at the capital of the Omeyyads, while regaining the friendship of the Syrians, he would be free from the tyranny of the Turkish soldiery. But after a residence of two months, he found the climate too severe and returned to Samira[1]. In that neighbourhood he spent his later years, and lavished untold sums in founding a new residence called Jafariya on the river bank. There he built the *Pearl*, a beautiful palace, and the *Hall of Delight*, surrounded with parks, and streams, and gardens, and crowded with every means of enjoyment, music, song, and gay divertisement. Vast treasures thrown away, for on his death the fairy scene soon became a deserted ruin.

Founds Jafariya.

Capricious cruelties.

To supply the means for such extravagance, recourse was had to all kinds of extortion. The offices of state were given to such as bid the highest for them. The case of Najah, chief of the exchequer, is a sample of what prevailed. He made a demand on two officers for arrears of revenue at four million pieces. Obeidallah the Turk whose help, as Motawakkil's Vizier, the debtors sought, bade them give him a note acknowledging two millions. At the same

[1] He went, we are told, in the months of Safar and Rabi I., i. e. May to July, and began to build offices for the various departments of State, but was driven away by boisterous weather, cold and snow;—a strange experience there for the middle of summer.

time he persuaded Najah to tell the Caliph that he had
made the demand in error when under the influence of
wine and now withdrew it altogether. Thereafter the
Vizier went to his master, and showed the note of hand
admitting half the claim. Delighted to get even so much,
the Caliph was equally enraged at the apparent deceit and
malversation of Najah, who was accordingly made over to
the two debtors to punish as they willed. These subjected
him to torture under which he expired, and confiscated
the entire property of the family, which just equalled the
debt they had to pay[1]. Intemperate hatred of the house
of Aly was kept up to the end. The famous grammarian
Ibn Sikkit, tutor in the house of Tahir, and employed in
the same capacity by Motawakkil himself, happening to
enter while the young princes were present, the Caliph
asked him, ' Which dost thou prefer, Ibn Sikkit ?—these my
two sons, or Hasan and Hosein ? ' Making no pretence of
preferring the latter, Motawakkil bade his Turkish guard
trample on his body, and he was carried out dying to his
home.

The Caliph, gradually estranged from his eldest son
Muntassir, had already, as we have seen, conferred on
Mutazz the second, marks of superior favour. His preference became year by year more marked, and Muntassir
was not only subjected to indignities whenever he appeared
at court, but the Caliph, when unable to preside at the
public prayer, sent his brother in pomp to take his place.
Things became worse and worse ; and one night after a
carousal, Motawakkil, overpowered with wine, abused
Muntassir so grossly that he could bear it no longer and
resolved on putting an end to his father's life. This could
the easier be done, as Motawakkil had alienated Wassif
and other Turkish leaders, confiscated their estates, and
made them over to new favourites of his own. So during
the night, when he had well drunk and gone to sleep, and
the gates had been closed by the guards already gained
over by Muntassir, Bogha ' the less,' surnamed ' the Wine-

---

[1] The torture applied to Najah is too gross to be repeated. Ibn Khallican,
iii. 61.

A.H. 232–
247.

bibber,' Musa (acting for his father Bogha the elder, who was in command at Someisat) and other conspirators of barbarous name, rushed in upon the senseless monarch and despatched him with their swords. By his side, a favourite Turk who never left him was also slain. The report was spread that Motawakkil had been assassinated by this favourite, whom for the crime they had put to death,—a tale which of course found little credence anywhere.

Orthodox but cruel, bigoted, and dissipated.

Praise given by the annalists to this reign of fifteen years for the Caliph's return to orthodoxy and generous patronage of poets and men of learning, makes but sorry amends for a life of cruel tyranny, bigotry, and self-indulgence.

CHAPTER LXVIII.

MUNTASSIR AND THREE FOLLOWING CALIPHS.

247–256 A.H.   861–870 A.D.

AIDED by the Turkish faction, Muntassir succeeded Muntassir, 247 A.H 861 A.D. without much diffiulty to the throne. His pious title,— *He that triumpheth in the Lord,*—did not avail to prolong his reign above half a year, or save him from the pangs of a parricide. Notwithstanding his crime, he is lauded because, unlike his father, he loved the house of Aly, and removed the ban on pilgrimage to the tombs of Hasan and Hosein. The Turkish party, fearing the revenge of his brothers for having connived at the murder of their father, prevailed on Muntassir to disentail them from the succession, and in their place appoint his son as heir apparent. The Vizier, jealous also of Wassif, persuaded Muntassir to send him on a campaign against the Greeks. Early in the following year the Caliph died, but His death, 248 A.H. 862 A D. whether a natural death, or poisoned, is uncertain[1].

On Muntassir's death, the Turkish chiefs held a conclave Mustain elected by Turks. to select his successor; they would none of Mutazz, nor his brothers, for the reason just stated; so they elected in his stead another grandson of Motassim, and saluted him under

---

[1] He is the first of the Abbassides whose tomb is known; it was made by his mother, a Greek slave-girl. The earlier Caliphs desired their tombs to be kept secret, for fear of desecration.

A.H. 247–256.
——
Disorder at Bagdad and Samira.

the title of Mustain[1]. Suddenly the Arabs and western troops from Bagdad, displeased at the choice, attacked the courtly assembly, broke loose the prison, and plundered the treasury and armoury. They were attacked by the Turkish and Berber soldiery, and after a round fight, in which many fell, succumbed. Bagdad had yet to learn that the Caliphate no longer depended on Arabian choice, but had passed into other hands. Mohammed, grandson of Tahir, governor of Bagdad, persuaded the city to submit, and the succession was thereafter peaceably acknowledged throughout the land. Mutazz, and Moayyad his brother, threatened by the troops, resigned their title to succeed, and were then, by way of protection, kept in durance. On a second outbreak in their favour, the Turks would have put them both to death, but the Vizier interposed and saved their lives, for which his property was seized by the Turkish soldiery, and he banished to Crete. The new Vizier, Atamish, held the entire patronage of office at his pleasure, and so his fellows as a rule were presented to provincial governments and commands. The empire, in fact, both at home and abroad, had passed into the hands of Turcomans.

Disasters in Asia Minor and Armenia, 249 A.H. 863 A.D.

In the following year, the Moslem campaign against the Christians was singularly unfortunate. Two whole corps in Armenia and Asia Minor, some 3000 strong, with their leaders, were cut to pieces. The tidings drove Bagdad wild. The ancient cry for a holy war rang through the streets. It was the godless Turks that had brought disaster on the faith, murdered their Caliphs, and set others at their

---

[1] This table will explain the relationship :—

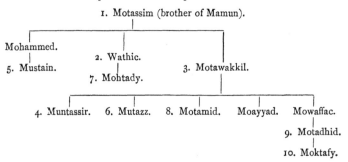

1. Motassim (brother of Mamun).

Mohammed.
5. Mustain.

2. Wathic.
7. Mohtady.

3. Motawakkil.

4. Muntassir.   6. Mutazz.   8. Motamid.   Moayyad.   Mowaffac.
9. Motadhid.
10. Moktafy.

pleasure up. With such cries the city rose in uproar; the gaols were broken and the bridges burned. But Bagdad could no longer dictate to its rulers, it could only riot. The crusading spirit was, however, strong enough to draw large levies from the provinces around, who flocked as free lances to fight against the infidel. But the Turks cared for none of these things, nor did the Caliph. They were far otherwise engaged. The leaders had fallen out among themselves. There was riot and plundering and breaking of the gaols again at Samira. After this was put down, Bogha and Wassif conspired against Atamish the Vizier, who was accused of squandering the revenue on the Caliph's mother and retainers. Attacked in the palace, he attempted in vain to fly, or secure protection from the Caliph; and after being surrounded for two days was seized and put to death. One Vizier succeeded another at the caprice of the tyrant courtiers of Samira, who kept Mustain at their mercy by having his brother Mutazz as rival in reserve.

Meanwhile, things were not prospering elsewhere. Kufa threw itself into the arms of Yahya, a descendant of the Prophet, who beat back the imperial troops; but at last fell in battle. His head was exposed at Samira, and then sent to Bagdad for a similar purpose. But so vast were the crowds that thronged the spot, and so intense their excitement as they cried,—' What would the Prophet say to this outrage on his own flesh and blood!'—that the head had to be removed, placed in a box, and guarded in the armoury. In the East, the Tahiride dynasty, still nominally dependent on the Caliphate, and hitherto a real support, was falling rapidly into decay before its Saffaride enemies on the side of Sejestan, and the Alyite aspirants on that of Tabaristan[1]. The latter, now founding a Shie-ite dynasty that survived for half a century, advanced upon Irac, and an army had to be sent for the protection of that frontier. To the south, another Alyite pretender, with a following of freebooters, ravaged Arabia, plundered the Kaaba, exacted heavy ransom from

[1] There is mention of two elephants sent to Bagdad with some idols by the Tahiride prince, taken at Kabul, where idolatry seems still to have prevailed, or perhaps some development of Buddhism.

the Holy cities, slew over a thousand pilgrims, and after keeping the peninsula throughout the year (251) in terror and distress, retired at its close to Jedda. In Mosul and Palestine, in Hims and Ispahan, in fact, in every quarter, we see anarchy and rebellion rife.

Mustain retires to Bagdad.
Beginning of 251 A.H.
865 A.D.
For Mustain himself the end was now at hand; and for Bagdad the horrors of another siege. Bogha 'the less' and Wassif, the two chief Turkish leaders, fell out with Baghir, another Turk, about an estate received in reward for Motawakkil's murder. The quarrel, as usual, bred riot and danger to the Caliph, who, hearing that Baghir's party sought his life, proceeded in concert with the other two to seize and imprison Baghir, and eventually put him to death. Thereupon the Turkish troops in Samira rose in anger and rebellion; and the wretched Caliph, to escape his tyrants and the impending danger, descended by boat, with Bogha, Wassif, and others, to Bagdad. The Turks sent after him a party of their captains, entreating him to return to Samira. He reproached them for ingratitude:—'Did ye not ask of me and I gave you houses for your families,—2000 boys and 4000 girls, and wives to boot, with portions for them all?' They fell at his feet for pardon, and he gave it. 'Wilt thou not then,' they said, 'return with us to Samira?' But this the Caliph would not, and hard words followed between the two sides, in the heat of which one of the Turkish speakers

Turks elect Mutazz Caliph, march on Bagdad,
received a blow. The insult rankled in their minds, and on returning to Samira, the troops rose *en masse*, and bringing forth Mutazz from his confinement, saluted him as Caliph. Within a few weeks, his brother Abu Ahmed, with 50,000 Turks and Khorasanies, and 2000 Berbers, bore down upon Bagdad, which meanwhile had been preparing as best it could for defence by entrenchments, stores of naphtha, and

and besiege the city throughout the year 251 A.H.
865 A.D.
engines planted at the gates. It is a harrowing chapter which details the horrors of the year,—the siege and sallies, —while the country all around was embroiled and suffered with its capital. Victory was now on this side, now on that. Persia and the provinces were mostly in the interest of Mustain; but all were so disorganized that no real help arrived; and supplies and tribute sent were mostly inter-

cepted on the way.   In truth, the Arabs, Mustain's chief A.H. 247-256.
support, could not stand against the Turkish hordes.   A
column sent from Ricca for the defence of Bagdad having
been ignominiously defeated, the governor exclaimed,—
' *What use of Arabs now without the Prophet and angelic
aid ?* '   The taunt had truth.   It was no longer for the faith
they fought, the faith that had nerved them in bygone days
to victory.   It would be unprofitable to follow the weary
accounts given us month by month of fighting in and around
the capital.   The Turks began gradually to gain ground,
and the chiefs around Mustain to desert the failing cause.
The citizens at last suspected their Tahiride governor, End of
hitherto the Caliph's loyal supporter, of leaning towards 251 A.H.
the rebels ; and he, driven to extremities by plots and
treachery all around, induced Mustain by alternate threats
and promises to abdicate in favour of Mutazz.   He Mustain
was to live at Medina with a sufficient income ; Bogha abdicates.
and Wassif, who had faithfully stood by him, were to have of 252 A.H.
important governments; the treasure was to be divided 866 A.D.
between the garrison of Bagdad and the Turks, the latter
with a double share.   The conditions signed, the governor
received the ministers and courtiers of Mustain, and having
assured them that he had done what he had for the best
and to stop farther bloodshed, sent them to Samira to
do homage to the new Caliph, who ratified the terms, and
took possession of Bagdad in the early days of 252.   He also
sent to Mustain his mother and family from Samira, but not
until they had been stripped of everything they possessed.

Mutazz, thus placed upon the throne, proved but too apt Mutazz
a pupil of his Turkish masters.   He was surrounded by succeeds.
parties each jealous of the other.   At Samira, the Turks
were at daggers drawn with the ' Westerns [1] '; while the
Arabs and Persians at Bagdad who had supported Mustain,
regarded both with equal hatred.   Mutazz was thus hemmed
in by a horde of hungry harpies, ready for plot or treachery
whether against each other or against himself :—a poor
justification, however, for the perfidy and bloodshed which
he, not less than they, pursued.

[1] So called, as Berbers and other African races from the West.

A.H. 247–
256.

Mutazz
causes
Mustain
to be as-
sassinated,

He began with the deposed Caliph. The conditions solemnly guaranteed were cast to the winds. Instead of finding a refuge at Medina, Mustain was kept at Wasit. Thence he was treacherously despatched, together with his wife, by Ahmed ibn Tulun, to the house of an assassin, who put them both to death. Carrying Mustain's head to the Caliph, 'Here,' cried the executioner, 'behold thy cousin's head!' 'Lay it aside,' answered the heartless Mutazz, who was playing at chess,—'till I have finished the game.' And then, having satisfied himself that it was really Mustain's head, he commanded 500 pieces to be given to the assassin

and one of
his own
brothers.

as his reward [1]. Muayyad, his own brother, being the heir-apparent, was also cruelly put to death. The Turkish soldiery, in a brawl with the Westerns, had taken the brother's part, and the jealous Caliph forthwith cast him, and also his other brother, Abu Ahmed, who had bravely led the troops in the late struggle on his side, into prison. There the Turks attempted Muayyad's release, and Mutazz, the more alarmed, resolved on his death. He was smothered in a downy robe (or, as others say, frozen in a bed of ice); and the body was then exposed before the court and Cazees, as if, being without mark of violence, he had died a natural death:—a transparent subterfuge.

Riots in
Bagdad,
252 A.H.

Bogha and Wassif, instead of their promised posts, were cut off altogether from the civil list; orders were also issued for their assassination; but, at the intercession of a princess at court related to them, their lives were spared. They returned with their families to Samira; and Bogha, in the strange vicissitudes of the day, became soon after the prime favourite of the Caliph. Riot succeeded riot, both at Samira and Bagdad. The revenues were squandered at the profligate court, and little left wherewith to pay the troops. The city guards at the capital surrounded the palace at Bagdad, clamorous for their pay. The governor wrote to Mutazz for an advance; but he, prompted by the Turks, replied that 'if the guards were needed for himself, he might himself pay them; if for the Caliph, he cared not for them.'

---

[1] So according to Ibn Athir. Other authorities are not so clear as to the connivance of Ahmed, founder of the Tulunide dynasty. Weil, ii. p. 398.

Thereupon the tumult was renewed; the mob refused to let A.H. 247–256. the Caliph be named in the mosque, and so there were no prayers observed that Friday. Before the insurrection was put down, the governor had to burn one of the bridges, and set fire to an adjoining bazaar, in order to keep the rebels off. Nor were the outbreaks at Samira less outrageous. and Samira. The Turks fell out with the Westerns, and fought till it was arranged that they should have each a representative in the chief offices of State. Next year all joined together, Turks, Palace stormed, 253 A.H. Africans, and Persians, to storm the palace for their pay. Wassif and Bogha, now the Caliph's chief advisers, sought to appease them. 'Here, take this,' the former cried, as he cast a handful of sand to them,—'it's all we have.' The other promised to represent their case to the Caliph, and while he went, the savage soldiery fell on Wassif, and Wassif and Bogha murdered, 254 A.H. having cut him to pieces, stuck his head upon a chimney. To the offices of the deceased succeeded Bogha, who for the moment ruled supreme. But his time, too, shortly came. He sought the following year to induce Mutazz to transfer his court to Bagdad, where he would be more independent of the foreigners. His jealous rivals represented this as treachery; and Bogha fled but only to be seized and slain. His head was exhibited both at Samira and at Bagdad, where the Westerns vented their hate by burning it to ashes.

Babkial succeeded Bogha. He was invested with the Ahmed ibn Tulun appointed to Egypt. government of Egypt, which, like other Turks promoted at the court, he administered through a deputy; and for the post he appointed as his representative Ahmed ibn Tulun, the one concerned in the death of Mustain, and founder of the Tulunide dynasty. Ahmed's story is typical of the times, both in respect of the sudden rise of slaves to office, and the tendency of local governors to become independent of the central power. His father, a Mameluk, captured in Ferghana, was presented to Mamun, and brought up among the Turkish slaves at court to the military profession. Ahmed, bred thus in the school of Samira, was favoured by the Caliph as excelling both in the art of war and in letters and the arts of peace. Mustain promoted him to a post of honour, and gave him a young slave to wife, who became mother of the Tulunide princes. Babkial now sent him as his deputy to Egypt, where gradually growing in power, he at last threw aside the yoke of the decrepid Caliphate, and became the independent ruler.

Foreign policy not successful. The policy of Mutazz was as crooked abroad as it was at home. The Tahiride dynasty in its decay was sorely pressed by Yacub the Saffaride [1] of Sejestan, who had designs of annexing Kerman, and to validate his claim sought the grant of its government from the court of Bagdad. Aly, the governor of Fars, who also aimed at independence, made the like request. Mutazz conferred the title at once on the one and on the other, hoping by the contest that must ensue to weaken both. The Saffaride in the end prevailed. Nowhere did the arms of Mutazz meet success. Mosul, with the surrounding country, was seized by Mosawwir, a Kharejite, who held it in rebellion for many years. In Asia Minor the Moslem forces were beaten by the Greeks, one of the generals being made prisoner. And even from the adjacent provinces immediately around Bagdad the revenue was withheld.

Military riot for arrears of pay. Little more need be said of Mutazz. A dwindling revenue precipitated the end. Their pay withheld, Salih, son of Wassif, on behalf of the army, seized the personal secretaries of Mutazz and of his brother, and the ministers of departments, demanding from them the money embezzled or concealed. There being no answer but an empty treasury, they were put in irons. The Caliph besought the insurgents to release his private secretary, but they were deaf to his entreaty. The accounts of the unfortunate ministers were seized, but neither thus nor otherwise could anything be extracted from them. Returning to the Caliph, they agreed that if he would advance but 50,000 pieces, they would for the present be content. Mutazz, in this extremity, sent to his mother Cabîha, a sobriquet given her by Motawakkil for her beauty [2]. Her arts and influence had gained for her vast treasures, hoarded by her in secret places.

---

[1] So called, the founder having been a brazier (saffâr) by trade.

[2] Cabih, 'horrid,' 'bad'; as we should say by contraries, 'the little wretch.'

Appealed to now, the heartless creature, clinging to her ill- A.H. 247–
gotten lucre, replied that she had nothing by her. Salih _{256.}
and Musa son of Bogha, now driven to extremities, re-
solved, in concert with Babkial, to depose Mutazz, and
carried out the design with brutal inhumanity. Followed Mutazz
by a clamorous troop, they seated themselves at the palace put to
gate, and called for the Caliph to come out. He had taken death.
physic, he sent to say as an excuse; and not suspecting
treachery, called them in. Entering, they beat him with
clubs and kicked him; then dragging him by his torn robes
outside, they left him seated there in the scorching heat of
the midsummer sun. Taken thence, he was shut up in a
room alone without food or water; and so after three days
the wretched Caliph died, at the early age of twenty-four.

The choice of the Turks now fell on Mohtady, son of Mohtady
Wathic by a Grecian slave-girl. Retired and unassuming, succeeds,
they regarded him as one likely to serve their ends. But June,
they mistook the man. Firm and virtuous as compared 869 A.D.
with those before him, he held to his own purpose. Earlier,
and supported by the Arabs, he might have restored life
to the Caliphate. But, both as regards number and discipline, foreigners had now the upper hand. Mohtady
came too late. 'The wide world,' says our annalist, 'was
all upside down.' At first he declined the offer, thinking it
unjust to Mutazz. But the deposed Caliph, brought before
him, resigned into his hands the burden he could no longer
bear; and so all Samira did homage. But Bagdad rose in
tumult, and demanded that Abu Ahmed, the late Caliph's
younger brother and the people's favourite, should succeed.
Money from Samira—the panacea of the day—pacified
the people; riot thus stayed, the oath was taken. The
court soon saw a transformation, unwonted for many a
day;—singing girls and musicians expelled; menageries
slaughtered, and hounds turned adrift; justice done daily
in open court; wine and games proscribed; and a frugal
household. The new Caliph, in fact, had set the pious
Omar son of Abd al Aziz before him as his exemplar.

On Mutazz's fall, Salih son of Wassif, lost no time in Salih's
stripping of their wealth such of the courtiers as had tion.

fattened under the recent Caliphate. The secretaries were imprisoned, and forced by the lash to disgorge. Two died under the infliction. Cabiha had fled to a vault outside Samira with her treasure. She was traced, and confessed to having at Bagdad over a million pieces of gold. It was all seized, and with it a store of emeralds, pearls, and rubies of untold size and beauty; while she herself was banished to Mecca. As she left, Salih upbraided her for having with all these treasures grudged a paltry fifty thousand to save her son; and she in return cursed him in vilest terms,—a painful picture of courtly Samira. The tyranny of Salih, and fate of the officers tortured, affected Mohtady deeply. Referring to Cabiha,—'I have no mother[1],' he said, 'on whose slave-girls and retainers to spend hundreds of thousands; I have no need but for myself and my brethren, and that but little.'

A few months after, there occurred another riot at Bagdad. The Persian governors, especially those recently appointed of the Tahiride family, were attended by escorts from the East, whose names not being entered on the civil list, they were paid from a separate fund, and adjustment made from the treasury of Merve. Soleiman, head of that house, hard pressed by his enemies and obliged to fly from Khorasan, was now nominated governor of Bagdad; and his predecessor having carried off the eastern fund, he was driven to pay his escort from that belonging to the native garrison. These resented the misappropriation and, joined by the citizens, rose against the eastern troops, who retaliated in robbery and outrage. The danger was increased by a Persian general who had accompanied Soleiman with a great following of soldiers and freebooters; and these now spreading themselves over Mesopotamia, drew thousands by the cry of plunder to the unfortunate city. After much fighting, they were forced to leave, and taking their way back by Nehrwan, ravaged the country as they went. Thus from every side, foreign levies, attracted like vultures

---

[1] On Wathic's death, Mustain had taken her to wife, and on his assassination, she was confined by Mutazz in Bagdad, where she died. Such was the wretched life of these Abbasside princesses.

to their prey,—whether Turks and Khorasanies, Persians, A.H. 247-256.
Negroes, or Berbers,—all brought misery and outrage on
the wretched ' City of Peace.'

Musa, son of Bogha, had been under the previous reign Musa's
sent to war against the Alyite dynasty set up in Deilem, attack on
which had assumed a threatening attitude.   On the troops 255 A.H.
conspiring against Mutazz, Cabiha had urged Musa to
return and save her son ; but soon after news of his death
reached the camp, and so Musa remained with the army
for the defence of Rei.   Then followed tidings of the
excesses and extortion of Salih ; and Musa's captains,
lusting for a share in the spoil, forced him, against Mohtady's command, to return with them to Samira.   There
he went straight to the Caliph, who was seated on the
bench dispensing justice, and after altercation, carried him
off on one of the attendant's horses, when the usual scene of
riot and plunder followed.   Reasoned with by Mohtady on
the scandalous affront thus offered to his Sovereign's person,
Musa and his followers returned to their loyalty, on assurance given that the crimes of Salih would be reckoned
with and justice done.

Salih, now deserted by his friends, fled into hiding. Salih pur-
Thence, by an unknown hand, he sent the Caliph a letter, sued,
offering submission to trial and restitution.   Mohtady being Dec.,
in favour of this, the Turks assumed that he knew his 869 A.D.
hiding-place, and was conniving with him.   They resolved
on his dethronement ; but Mohtady bravely met them
sword in hand, ready to thrust through the first that should
approach.   He protested that he knew nothing of Salih's retreat, and promised public inquisition on the morrow after
prayers.   Meanwhile, the people learning the traitorous
proceedings of the Turks, were so touched by the peril in
which a sovereign whom they had learned to respect and
love was in, that they scattered throughout the streets and
lanes of Bagdad sheets, on which was inscribed a call for
prayer and intercession with the Lord to save their pious
Caliph and confound the designs of the rebel Turks.   A
band of the foreign troops, touched by the appeal,
rallied round Mohtady, who promised his best to reform

A.H. 247–
256.
____
and mur-
dered, ii.
256 A.H.
Jan.,
870 A.D.

the government, provide for payment of all dues, bring
Salih to justice, and Musa also to account. Search for Salih
still contined without success and danger to the Caliph,
when fortunately he was discovered, pursued by the mob,
and delivered over to Musa's retainers, who slew him and
exposed his head, with the proclamation (strange sentiment
for the Turks), ' Such is the fate of him that slayeth his
master.'

Mohtady
again in
difficulties.

Things went on thus for several months, when the cry
arose again for arrears of pay from the Turkish garrison
of Bagdad. The Caliph told them that the treasury
was empty, as Musa's brothers—sons of the elder
Bogha, the party now in opposition to Mohtady—had
embezzled the revenues. These fled to Musa, who, with
Babkial, was now engaged at Mosul with Mosawwir's insurrection. Driven to desperation, Mohtady himself stooped
to perfidy. He sent, or suffered a Turkish party to send,
promise of safe conduct to the brothers ; and when they
came not only exacted great sums of revenue from them,
but caused one to be slain and cast into a well. Then he
wrote to Musa to make over the army to Babkial and return to Samira ; while at the same time he wrote to Babkial
to compass the death of Musa. But Babkial, on whose
loyalty and friendship Mohtady had counted, went over to

Defeated
by insur-
gents.

the side of Musa. Having shown him the letter, they
resolved to return at once to Samira, and there bide their
time for putting an end to the Caliph's life. On their
arrival, however, Mohtady, anticipating their design, seized
Babkial, and resolved bravely to fight for the right, or perish
in the attempt. Six thousand soldiers rallied round him,
mostly Arabs and Westerns ; but amongst them were also
one thousand of the late Salih's Turks. The rebels came on,
double the number, to the attack of Mohtady ; whereupon
he gave the order to slay Babkial, and cast his head into
the rebel ranks. But the day was gone. The faithless
Turks deserted to the other side, and the rest lost heart.
In vain Mohtady shouted, ' Here is the Commander of the
Faithful ; haste to the rescue of the Caliphate ! ' There
was no response. Passing the prison, he threw open its

gates, hoping that the inmates would help him ; but this too
was in vain. And so he fled for refuge to the commander
of his body-guard's house. Thence, seated on a mule, he
was carried to the palace of a Turkish general, and pressure
put on him to abdicate. He refused, and prepared for the
end. Then, to give the appearance of justice to their work,
the conspirators produced a paper in which Mohtady had
guaranteed Musa and the rest that he would not use
treachery towards them, which if he did they were released
from their oath of fealty. Having thus, to their satisfaction, justified the sentence, they fell tumultuously upon
him, with blows and kicks, and removed him into confinement, where, a few days after, he died. Witnesses deposed
that there were no marks of violence on his body, which
was buried with his predecessors. He was aged thirty-
eight, and had reigned less than a year. The annalists
laud his justice and his piety ; and had he not yielded at
last and met perfidy with the like, we might have placed
Mohtady among the most excellent of his race.

Mohammed, one of Bogha's sons, was found dead on
the field. Over his grave, after the rude fashion of the
Turcomans, a thousand swords were shivered.

A.H. 247–
256.

Put to
death, vii.
256 A.H.
June,
870 A.D.

A Turkish
funeral.

CHAPTER LXIX.

MOTAMID, AND MOWAFFAC HIS BROTHER.

256-279 A.H. 870-892 A.D.

Transient
return of
prosperity. AT this point, we come unexpectedly on a brighter view
of the Caliphate, with a fair promise, maintained to the end
of the century, of returning vigour and prosperity. The
brave example of Mohtady, however sad its ending, and a
succession of able rulers, contributed, no doubt, to this result. But the main cause was the return of the court to
Bagdad, where, supported by native feeling, it could better
avoid the outrage, curb the influence of the Turkish soldiery,
and bring the Western element to check the Eastern. At
any rate, during the next three reigns, there was no repetition of the shameful attacks upon the person of the Caliph,
which had made the court of Samira a byword among the
nations.

Motamid,
256 A.H.
870 A.D. On Mohtady's deposition, the leading courtiers brought
out from his confinement at Samira the eldest surviving
son of Motawakkil, and saluted him as Caliph under the
title of Motamid. Musa ibn Bogha, engaged with the
Kharejites at Ahwaz, hastened back to court and did
obeisance. Indeed, Musa, turning a new leaf, henceforth
proved himself a brave and loyal servant, and some time
after was appointed by the Caliph guardian of his son, to
whom as heir-apparent the Western half of the empire was
entrusted. Motamid himself proved but a poor and help-

less monarch. But his brother, Mowaffac, already mentioned under the name of Abu Ahmed, was the real ruler and
stay of the empire. On the Zenj rebellion bringing danger
near to Bagdad, Motamid in alarm summoned him from his
government at Mecca. Thenceforward he held the reins,
and continued to do so till his death near the close of
Motamid's life.

The Zenj insurrection, just noticed, spread terror and
outrage for fifteen years all around. The leader, a Persian,
gave himself out as a descendant of Aly. At the first, as
such he set up certain spiritual assumptions ; but soon he
so plainly showed his real colours as an outlaw, that he was
called *Khabîth,* that is, the Reprobate. After canvassing in
Arabia with little success, he raised at Bussorah the standard of rebellion, proclaimed liberty to the captive, and endless spoil and rapine to all that should follow his standard.
A text inscribed on his banner was perverted to mean the
knell of slavery [1]. Little wonder that slaves, taught by him
to insult their masters, flocked in thousands to Khabith,
and Bedouins also in their lust of plunder. Zenj means
' Ethiopian,'—the slavish dregs of Africa,—and hence the
name of the insurrection. It was in 255 A.H., that they
first took the field in force, and in the next two years
spread themselves across the whole delta of the Euphrates,
and the banks of the Karoon as far as Ahwaz. Over and
over again they beat back the imperial troops, and by their
fleets dominated both rivers. Emboldened by this success,
they attacked Bussorah, took it by storm, and for three
days subjected the citizens to every kind of outrage.
Quarter was at last announced, and the multitude, drawn
together by the treacherous proclamation, mercilessly massacred. The Great mosque was destroyed, and the city set
on fire. The Caliph at last, alarmed by their near approach
to the capital, summoned Mowaffac to take the field. He

Marginal notes:
A.H. 256–279.

His brother
Mowaffac
the real
Ruler.

Zenj in-
surrection,
255 A.H.
869 A.D.

---

[1] A curious perversion of *Sura* ix. v. 113 :—'The Lord hath purchased from
Believers their souls (or their own selves) and their substance by the promise of
Paradise' ; meant by the Prophet as an incitement to fight in the ways of the
Lord, but here travestied as teaching that the persons of all believers, having been
thus purchased, are thereby redeemed and no longer subject to slavery.

carried on the war vigorously against them, but at first with only partial success,—being obliged to suspend operations from time to time from pressing dangers elsewhere. A similar fortune attended Musa and other generals. Year after year, even under defeat, great bodies of the Zenj invaded Irac, Khuzistan, and Bahrein, whether as marauding hordes, or in regular line, striking terror into the helpless villagers, who fled to Bagdad for refuge. Ahwaz was sacked, and Wasit captured as a centre for their devastating operations. Thus for ten years the miserable land was kept in suffering

263 A.H.
878 A.D.
and alarm. At last Mowaffac, relieved from external foes, concentrated his forces under his own immediate command, and that of his son Motadhid. The tide now turned against the servile swarm. They were gradually driven out of Khuzestan and cooped up in the lower Delta; but there they continued to hold a secure position, guarded by strong fortresses and the deep canals surrounding them. The contest, which still dragged its length for five years more, is told with wearisome detail. Even after the enemy was driven from their other strongholds, the chief fortress still resisted for three whole years the regular approaches of a siege, intermitted for a season in consequence of

Defeat and
death of
the Zenj
leader,
270 A.H.
883 A.D.
Mowaffac being wounded. Finding the cause hopeless, the rebels began to go over in great numbers to Mowaffac, who received them kindly, and even offered the arch-offender pardon, which he insolently rejected. At last the citadel fell, and multitudes of women delivered from captivity were returned to their homes. Khabith, overtaken in his flight, was slain, and as his head was held up before the assembled force, they fell prostrate, giving thanks to heaven for being at last delivered from the cursed Reprobate[1].

The outlying provinces of the East have now in our his-

---

[1] The inordinate length of the story and tendency to magnify show what a deep wound this savage and inveterate enemy inflicted on the country surrounding Bagdad. In 267 A.H., 5000 women released from one of the fortresses were sent to Wasit to be distributed to their homes; shortly after we are told that 20,000 captives belonging to the Kufa villages were taken from another citadel. Mowaffac's force is given at 50,000, and we are told that the Zenj were six times that number. With all allowance for the mass of slaves that flocked to the Reprobate, such numbers are clearly fabulous.

tory but a secondary interest. The traditional dominance
of the court at Bagdad still imparted weight, if nothing
more, to any title derived therefrom ; and the Caliph was
everywhere prayed for in the public services, excepting in
the case of open enmity. The Tahirides, beaten by the
Saffarides, now retire from the scene, and are hereafter mentioned only as resident in Bagdad, and holding chief muni-
cipal office there. The Alyite dynasty still retained the
districts south-east of the Caspian ; but a new enemy now
arose against them in the Samanide house,—a noble family,
which held ancient office in Khorasan, and now aspired to
independence. These distant movements, however, and
the career of Khujistany, an adventurer who from 261 to
268 A.H., rose to great power in the East, affected the
Caliphate little. But Yacub, the Saffaride, was a cause of
danger. Not content with the outlying provinces his family
had secured in the East, his ambition turned westward,
and coveting Fars, he asked the Caliph for it. Motamid,
offended at the demand, assembled the pilgrims returning
eastward, and proclaimed in their ears that he had deposed
Yacub from Khorasan. Yacub hastened to retaliate by an
advance not only on the western provinces of Persia, but on
Bagdad itself. Rejecting concessions which the Caliph,
now alarmed, was ready to make, he crossed the Tigris
below the capital, passed Wasit, and was already close
to Bagdad when he was met by Mowaffac, routed with
great slaughter, the loss of his camp, 10,000 mules, and vast
spoil, and driven back into his Persian provinces. The
last of the Tahiride rulers who, beaten by Yacub, had been
kept by him as a prisoner, escaped on his defeat, and welcomed at Bagdad was there installed as governor. It is
curious to note that the Zenj-ite Reprobate, while yet in the
field, offered to join Yacub after his defeat, in a fresh attack
on Bagdad. The offer met this scornful reply :—' Say,
O ye believers ! I worship not that which ye worship ;
neither do ye worship that which I worship [1].' Some years
passed, and a friendly message was again sent by the Caliph
to Yacub, who still held the western parts of Persia. The

[1] *Sura* cix.

A.H. 256–
279.
    grand old warrior lay on his death-bed, the sword by his side, and a crust with onions as a relish for his frugal meal.

Yacub's
death.
    Starting up in his couch, he replied to the envoy,—' Speak thus to thy master. I am sick unto death. If I die, I am quit of thee, and thou of me ; if I live, there is nought betwixt us but this sword, that I may take my revenge of thee ; or beaten, retire content (pointing to the crust) with this simple fare.' He died. Amr, his son, succeeding, dropped the father's hate, submitted himself to the Caliph, and was confirmed, with every honour, in the East to the

Saffaride
dynasty,
271–4 A.H.
    farthest bounds of Khorasan and Sind. Some years after things changed again ; for Mowaffac, now relieved of domestic as well as external pressure, and seeking to restore the Tahiride dynasty, had the Saffarides denounced from Moslem pulpits, and meeting Amr in the field, drove him from all his western possessions back to Sejestan. Towards the close of the reign we find Amr again in favour, and acknowledged as before. But in the end he fell, as we shall see, before the various antagonists who now sprang up in the East and fought for its supremacy.

Tulunide
rule in
Egypt,
254–70
A.H.
868–73 A.D.
    We now turn to Egypt, where Ahmed ibn Tulun, appointed as we have seen governor of Fostat in 254 A. H., had gradually assumed independent power over the whole country. A wise and able ruler, the land flourished under his government as it had never done before. The revenues, instead of passing to Bagdad, were expended in public works at home ; buildings, canals and charities were the object of his care, and a Mosque bearing his name is still the ornament of Cairo ; learning was promoted, while a magnificent court and powerful army maintained the dignity of Egypt without unduly increasing the financial pressure. Ahmed had for a while to fight at home against Alyite and other pretenders, whom he subdued ; and then with like success against Ibrahim the Aghlabite ruler of Cairowan, who, after signal conquests in Sicily, had turned his aspira-

262 A.H.
    tions eastwards. Then Mowaffac, jealous of the Tulunide's independent attitude, sent Musa, with the view of again reducing him to subjection. The Egyptian with his large resources easily repelled the invasion, while Musa's army,

in want and discontent, mutinied at Ricca, and after long months of inaction forced him to retrace his way to Irac.

About this time, the Byzantine court, taking advantage of the Caliph's domestic troubles, was making serious advances in Asia Minor. Tarsus, unfortunate in its governors, allowed the fortress of Lulu to fall into the enemy's hands. Ahmed ibn Tulun had long sought for leave to carry his arms against the Greeks, but Mowaffac had scorned the offer. The Caliph, who regarded him with more favour than his brother, now committed the campaign into his hands. Placing his son Khomaria in charge at home, Ahmed gladly seized the opportunity, passed at once into Syria, which opposed his advance; but easily defeating the governors who came out against him, he took Damascus and Antioch, and advanced upon Tarsus. There he was ill received, and obliged to return to Syria, leaving the Greeks to pursue their victories. But he maintained his hold of Syria, and turning his arms eastward took Harran. While carrying all before him in his further advance on Mosul, he heard that his son Khomaria had left the capital and retired to Barca with all the treasure. There the foolish youth sought to found a new kingdom of his own; but warring westward was beaten back by the Aghlabites on Barca. He was seized by his father's troops, and carried back to Fostat, a miserable spectacle. By command of Ahmed, his son inflicted with his own hand condign punishment on the advisers who had led him astray. He was then beaten with a hundred stripes, after which Ahmed wept as with a father's bowels of compassion he upbraided him for his folly [1].

Meanwhile Lulu, the freed Memluk of Ahmed, had been pursuing the victorious course begun by his master, and extending the Tulunide rule from Syria to Mosul, when an

[1] The scene is told with much pathos. The punishment which Ahmed made his son inflict on his evil counsellors is, however, so barbarous as to destroy the effect altogether; and I have not ventured to translate it into the text. The truant son was commanded to cut off both their hands and their legs, leaving them miserable living trunks. One may hope that these things are exaggerated. But even worse things were in store for wretched Egypt under the Mameluke dynasty.

A.H. 256-
279.

unexpected turn of affairs occurred. Mowaffac being still in mortal combat with the Zenjites, the empire suffered everywhere from the helpless incapacity of his brother Motamid. The ambitious Ahmed here saw his opportunity. The Caliph, chafing at having only the shadow without the power of sovereignty, was to fly to Egypt, where the Tulunide, his faithful vassal, would secure to him the substantial enjoyment of the throne, and victory over his

Motamid
forced to
return,
269 A.H.

domineering brother. But he had not calculated on the vigilance of Mowaffac who, apprised of the plot, caused Motamid to be seized in his flight towards Mosul, and with his chief followers in chains, sent back ignominiously to Samira. Ahmed, thus foiled, vented his chagrin by dropping Mowaffac's name from the public prayers; and Mowaffac retaliated by obliging Motamid to anathematize his protégé in all the mosques that still acknowledged the Caliphate. Equally unsuccessful was Ahmed's attempt to assume the presidency at the Annual pilgrimage; for the officer whom he sent to represent him at Mecca was discomfited by the imperial troops supported by the Persian pilgrims; and here, too, in the Holy house, the Tulunide was denounced at the public service before the assembled multitude. Worse, however, than all, was the defection of Lulu, his general in Syria, who went over to Mowaffac at Wasit, carrying with him his whole force. There he was received with open arms, and aided materially in bringing to a close the Zenj rebellion. But a few years after, Lulu, despoiled by Mowaffac of his vast riches (they were, Lulu asserted, his only fault), returned a beggar to Egypt with but one attendant;—an apt example of the instability of the times, and (our annalist adds) just reward of ingratitude towards the

Death of
Ahmed ibn
Tulun,
xi. 270 A.H.
884 A.D.

master who had freed him. Not long after, Ahmed having ruled sixteen years in Egypt, and a considerable period in Syria also, died, and was succeeded by Khomaria, an unworthy successor to his father's great name. A struggle followed for several years, between him and the Caliphate,

271 A.H.

for the rule in Syria and Mesopotamia, which, after many battles, left the state of things pretty much as before.

Mosul and its surrounding districts, having been long

harassed by Kharejite insurrections, and latterly by the A.H. 256-
encroachment of Egyptian generals, was now for a time   279.
regained by the Caliphate.   But Alyite risings continued The
throughout the whole reign to disturb the empire.   Kufa provinces.
was seized by one of these pretenders, who was defeated
after some heavy fighting.   Kufa, however, had now fallen
from its pre-eminence, and ceased to be an element of much
anxiety.   Medina was attacked by a force headed also by
Alyite rebels, and was again subjected to such outrage, that
for four weeks none ventured for prayer into the Mosque of
Mahomet; and the city remained in terror till these unworthy descendants of the Prophet were driven out.

During the early years of the reign, the Kaiser Basil, Hostilities
taking advantage of the distractions of the Caliphate, made with the
Greeks in
inroads on the Syrian border, and as we have seen seized AsiaMinor.
the fortress Lulu.   In succeeding years, though opposed by
the Paulicians, who sided with the Arabs, the Greeks
obtained other victories, in one of which an Arab general
was taken captive, and carried to the Byzantine court.   In
later years the tide turned, and a series of fields were
won by the Tulunide governor of Tarsus, who in the end,
however, lost his life, shot by a ball from the walls of a
town he was besieging.

Early in 278, Mowaffac, while engaged in a campaign Illness of
towards the North, was seized with elephantiasis, and carried Mowaffac,
278 A.H.
on a litter to Samira.   He had long been the real ruler.   So 891 A.D.
far back as 294 A. H. Motamid had sought to appoint a
Vizier of his own, but fled across the river when Mowaffac
drew near; and so entirely did he succumb as, at his
brother's command, even to send the favourite he had
but just nominated to prison.   When Mowaffac, therefore,
fell sick, he resolved to transmit the substantial authority
he possessed to his own son Motadhid.   This prince was
a favourite at the capital.   On one occasion, claiming the
government of Syria, instead of another to which he had
been appointed, his father was displeased; and having
placed him under arrest, the city was in uproar, fearing
for his safety, till he was released.   Now a similar feeling
was abroad.   As Mowaffac's end drew near, his brother

Motamid was brought over to Bagdad from Medain, his enforced residence, by the Vizier; and the populace, apprehending that the Vizier had gone over to the side of the imbecile Caliph, rose in tumult against him. In point of fact, Motadhid was in some danger; but his friends succeeded in bringing him safely to his father's chamber, by whom, thus upon his death-bed, he was formally invested with the same supreme power which Mowaffac had himself so long held and vigorously used for the maintenance of the empire. Shortly after, he expired at the age of forty-nine.

His death.

Death of
Motamid
and suc-
cession of
Motadhid,
vii. 279 A.H.
Sept,
892 A.D.
Motamid never regained any real power: in fact, he had often, both now and before, to struggle in penury with but a few dinars in his purse. In the year following his brother's death, he was obliged publicly to depose his own son from the succession, and recognize Motadhid as heir-apparent. He did not long survive, having drunk himself to death in a night carousal, at the age of fifty years, of which he had been Caliph, though in little more than name, for twenty-three. And Motadhid his nephew reigned in his stead.

CHAPTER LXX.

MOTADHID AND MUKTAFY.

279–295 A.H.   892–907 A.D.

MOTADHID, already in possession of supreme power, Motadhid
continued as Caliph ably to administer the same. Egypt 279 A.H.
892 A.D.
returned to her allegiance, for Khomaria, tempted by the
honour, gave his daughter in marriage to the Caliph with a
great dower, and promise of a yearly tribute. He was
shortly after murdered in circumstances little creditable to
the morality either of himself or of his court. The country Egypt.
fell into disorder under his young son, who, after a few
months' reign, was also assassinated; and another son,
Harun, who succeeded, suffered things to go from bad to
worse.

Khorasan begins to fade from our view. The rulers, even Khorasan.
in the far East, were still glad to get their title accredited Samanide
chief
from Bagdad. But there was little virtual power beyond beats Amr
Saffaride;
the limits of Irac. The Samanide house rose on the decay sends him
of the Saffaride, whose rule was now confined to Sejestan; to Bagdad,
288 A.H.
and the chief of the latter, Amr ibn Leith, taken prisoner
by the Samanide, was by him sent to Bagdad ; where, after
remaining some time in prison, he was at last, by the tacit
sign of Motadhid on his death-bed, executed. The Alyite 287 A.H.
dynasty, so long dominant in Tabaristan, was also swallowed
up by the Samanide. The immediate authority of the
Caliph reached eastward only as far as Rei ; and even

within that limit, the powerful family of Abu Dulaf[1] had hitherto been more or less independent; it was now, however, reduced by Muktafy the Caliph's son, so that the west of Persia continued still to acknowledge the court of Bag-

Mesopo-
tamia. dad. In Mesopotamia, the Caliph and his son were long engaged in a campaign against the Kharejites, still rampant from Mosul to Amid. In the end that region, which had long been disturbed, partly by rebel Bedouin bands, partly by the rivalry between Egyptian and imperial generals, was for the time restored to order.

Motadhid's
administra-
tion. Motadhid was a brave and energetic ruler. He was so tolerant towards the house of Aly, that when a heavy largess was sent to them by the Alyite prince of Tabaristan, he was not displeased, as his predecessors would have been; but only bade that it should be done openly. Towards the Omeyyad race he was not so just. He went so far as to have them anathematized in the public prayers. He had even a volume of their misdeeds rehearsed from the pulpit, and forbade favourable mention of them in debate at the clubs and religious gatherings. Bagdad was scandalized at this treatment; and in the end the Caliph withdrew his abusive book. Motadhid was also cruel in his punishments, some of which are not surpassed by those of his predecessors. For example, a Zenj rebel, admitted to pardon, but afterwards found tampering with the army, was bound to a stake and, after being scorched with fire, taken down, beheaded, and the body impaled on the great bridge. The Kharejite leader at Mosul, who fell by treachery into his hands, was first paraded about Bagdad clothed in a robe of silk (the wearing of which Kharejites denounced as sinful) and then crucified, crying aloud, ' The rule shall yet be the Lord's alone, let the unbelievers rage never so much ! ' And yet another of these Kharejites was ' skinned alive,' so says our annalist, ' as you would skin a sheep.'

Muktafy,
289 A.H.
902 A.D. After a prosperous reign of nearly ten years, Motadhid died ; and Muktafy his son, by a Turkish slave-girl, suc-

---

[1] The same whose praises, sung by the blind poet, so irritated Mamun. Supra, p. 506.

ceeded to the throne. In command at Ricca, at the time, A.H. 279-
he at once returned to the capital, where he became a 295.
favourite of the people from his generosity, and for abo-
lishing his father's subterranean prisons, the terror of Bagdad. During his reign of nearly seven years the empire was
threatened by various dangers which he bravely met and
overcame. Chief was that from the Carmathians, a race of
fanatics which had sprung up during the late reign, and of
which mention will be made in the following chapter.

In beating back the savage Carmat hordes which spread Egypt re-
over Syria and besieged Damascus, the Caliph received stored to
the Cali-
substantial aid from the Egyptian army, under command phate,
of Mohammed ibn Soleiman. Afterwards this general, 290 A.H.
903 A.D.
seeing the helplessness of the Tulunide government, and the
consequent disorder of his country, not only transferred his
allegiance to the Caliph, but advanced with a powerful army
to reduce Egypt itself, and restore it to the Caliph ; while
with the same object a fleet from Tarsus entered the Nile.
As Mohammed approached Cairo, most of the leading
captains went over to him, and left Harun with diminished
forces. These again fell out among themselves, and Harun, Harun
in the attempt to quell the tumult, was killed by an arrow. killed,
292 A.H
Egypt thus restored to the Caliphate was ravaged by the
invading force, and the grand works of the last twenty years
destroyed. The Tulunide family, with all their property,
were transported to Bagdad, and the dynasty ceased. Notwithstanding his great services, and the vast treasures he
brought with him from Egypt, Mohammed was cast into
prison, and tortured to reveal some part of the spoil he was
suspected of keeping back. The banished captains of the 293 A.H.
old dynasty again returned to Egypt, and set up afresh a
rebel government at Fostat ; but they were beaten, and
Egypt finally restored to its allegiance.

Mosul was again the scene of serious attack. The Kurds Mosul,
came down from their hill retreats in great multitudes on 293-4 A.H.
Nineveh. The government was at the time in the hands
of a chief of the Hamadan family (founder of that house [1]),
who had to draw for reinforcements on Bagdad, and

---

[1] Arabs of the Beni Taghlib clan.

A.H. 279–   with that help pursued the Kurds into Azerbijan, and at
295.   last restored order.   The Samanide ruler of Khorasan was
about the same time attacked by countless hordes of Turcomans, and placed in such danger, that, instead of being
able to render aid against the Kurds, he sent an urgent
appeal for help to Bagdad, which was read out from all the
pulpits there, but with small result.

War with   Throughout these two reigns, hostilities prevailed more or
the Greeks, less with the Greeks, who were not slow to take advantage
285–6 A.H.
of the exigencies of the Caliphate.   In 285 A. H. a Byzantine
fleet was set on fire, and 3000 sailors decapitated [1].   But
there were reverses also.   Tarsus was closely besieged by
the Greeks, and the governor taken prisoner.   Still worse,
Egyptian rebels, to spite the Caliph, induced the Tulunide
governor of Tarsus to burn the Moslem fleet of fifty vessels
at anchor in their port.   In consequence the Greeks were
able to ravage the coasts at pleasure, both by land and sea;
carrying vast numbers away captive.   War was kept up
with various fortune.   Ten golden crosses, each followed by
10,000 men, swept devastation and captivity along the

292 A.H.   Moslem shores; while, on the other hand, a Moslem fleet
under a renegade Greek, and manned by negroes, ravaged
the coast opposite Byzantium.   There followed further fight-
294 A.H.   ing, till in the end peace was made and prisoners on either
side exchanged or ransomed.

Death of   Thus, after a stormy reign of between six and seven years,
Muktafy,
ii. 259 A.H. Muktafy could look round and find the Caliphate more
907 A.D.   secure than since the days of Motassim it had been.   One
of his last acts was, on the death of the Samanide prince,
to recognize the succession of his son in Khorasan, and
forward to him a banner mounted by his own hand.   He
died at the early age of thirty-three, and left the throne to
a minor brother.   But, before proceeding with the melancholy sequel of the Caliphate, some account should be given
of the Ismailians, who arose about this time and materially
influenced the future history of Islam.

---

[1] So our authorities, though one can hardly believe it.

CHAPTER LXXI.

Ismailians, Carmathians, and Fatimides.

EVER since the tragedy of the Kerbala, the Moslem Alyite
fanaticism. world was exposed, as we have seen, to outbursts of fanaticism in favour of the house of Aly. Persian Shie-ism, with its mystic tendencies, stimulated the sentiment, while the decline of the Caliphate, and the disorder prevailing in consequence, offered ready advantage to pretenders. Hence the growing frequency of Alyite risings. The feelings thus abroad were now to assume concrete and permanent form.

The numerous sects and schisms at this time developed, Various
mystic
sects. were all based on the sanctity of the line of Aly, and the survival therein of a divine authority. Some held to twelve of the line; others to seven, that being a number to which singular virtue was ascribed. Schools multiplied all over the land in which the mystic faith was quietly and cautiously taught, embracing such recondite doctrines as the formation of the universe by the Divine Reason, transmigration of souls, immanence of Divinity in the Mehdy[1], and the early expectation of his coming. The novice was initiated in such esoteric doctrines, under oath of secresy, and became henceforward, soul and body, his leader's devotee. The teaching of the Mehdy might supersede the Coran, the tenets of which were allegorically rendered; and the changes both of dogma and ritual were so strange and sweeping

---

[1] That is the 'Guide' or divine leader of the day, being in direct descent from Aly.

·that the Prophet himself would hardly have recognized the
system thus evolved as in any respect his own. The superstition spread with marvellous rapidity over the whole East,
and along the southern shores of the Mediterranean. It
was no doubt held by multitudes in simple faith; but by
designing men it was made a stalking-horse for the overthrow of governments, and the reaching of power thereby.
Still worse, its deluded votaries were led to believe they
were doing God service in scenes of plunder and rapine
more cruel and outrageous even than those of the Zenj.

Ismailians.   In the latter half of the third century, there arose an
enthusiast of this school, who propagated a system de-
signed to weld all religions into a universal faith. It was
to be the seventh and last religion of the world, under
the Seventh in succession from Aly—the divine Mehdy
Mohammed son of Ismail. From his patronymic the faith
is named the *Ismailian.* During the reign of Motadhid,
a leader of this persuasion opened canvass in Irac and
gained a great following both there and in surrounding

Carma-
thians.   lands. His name was Carmat, and after him the sectaries
are called Carmathians. He appeared while the Zenj were
yet in the field, and offered to join the Reprobate with
100,000 swords; but unable to adjust the tenets of a
common faith, they parted. A leader then arose in Irac,
Zakaruya by name; he had two sons, one the 'Sheikh,' the
other from a divine mark on his face the 'Spotted,' who

Their
excesses,
290-1 A.H.
902-3 A.D.   spread rapine and terror over the land. The former was
killed in the attempt to storm Damascus; the latter ravaged
Syria, murdering and pillaging wherever he went, and yet,
strange to say, he was prayed for in the pulpits of the wretched
province as 'the Mehdy that was for to come'; and with
him was a cousin named *Modathir,* 'the Veiled,' an epithet
of Mahomet[1]. The alarm was so great at Bagdad that, as
we have seen, Muktafy sent the Egyptian general, Mohammed, to attack the fanatic host, himself accompanying
the army as far as Ricca. The Carmats were totally beaten,
the 'Spotted' with his cousin and some followers escaping

---

[1] *Sura* lxxiv.

into the desert. Discovered there, they were carried to the Caliph at Ricca, and thence sent to Bagdad, where, paraded on an elephant and camels, they were made a spectacle to the city. Kept in prison till the return of Mohammed with more Carmat captives, they were all beheaded after their legs and arms had been cut off. For the 'Spotted,' a death was reserved of exquisite cruelty. Scourged with a hundred stripes, his hands were cut off, then he was scorched, and when in the agonies of the fire, his head was struck off and raised aloft on a pole, amidst the shouts of the multitude, *Allah Akbar*, Great is the Lord! There were other scenes of the kind, but this may suffice. *Their defeat and terrible punishment.*

One marvels at the tenacity of this noxious heresy. Beaten here it suddenly reappears there, scattering havoc and outrage in its track. Men were everywhere in expectation, and mused in their hearts whether this pretender or that were the coming Mehdy. The leaders too often acted from low and corrupt motives, and were followed by marauding Bedouins who, no longer enlisted in the imperial forces, lusted after rapine and plunder. But apart from unworthy aims of the kind there must have been some spiritual force behind to hold together such vast masses and nerve them for the dangers, as well as for the spoils, of rebellion. *Marvellous tenacity of these enthusiasts.*

And so another year had hardly passed when,—the imperial arms being engaged in Egypt—outrages were renewed with even greater barbarity than before. Zakaruya, who had for years lain hid in a subterranean dwelling, now wrote to his people, that a heavenly messenger had revealed to him the death of his sons, and that the Mehdy was on the point of appearing. They were to go forth to war, and on the day of sacrifice enter Kufa, where thousands would rise and join them[1]. Thereupon Syria, from one end to the other, was subjected to fire and sword, and every kind of license. Urgent appeal was made to Muktafy, who sent his best generals without success against *Renewed outbreak, 292 A.H.*

[1] He quoted as a command from the Mehdy *Sura* xx. 55, where Moses appointed the feast-day for his meeting with Pharaoh.

them. Just then Zakaruya emerged from his hiding. He was received with divine honours by the deluded throng and carried veiled upon their shoulders as the Vicegerent of the Almighty. The Carmats were thereupon filled with such wild enthusiasm that they routed the Caliph's hosts, slaying 1500, and striking terror into the heart of Bagdad. Zakaruya now formed the diabolical design of lying in wait between Bussorah and Kufa for the caravans just then returning from pilgrimage. The first escaped, but the village that connived at their deliverance was utterly destroyed. The second was overtaken, and few lived to tell the tale: even the women were slain excepting those kept for a worse fate. The third was warned to hold on till imperial succour came: but the Carmats choked the wells, arrested help, and fell upon the multitude dying of thirst. Another butchery ensued; the Carmat women carried water round to see if life was left in any yet; and if one gasped for a draught, the *coup de grace* was given [1]. Twenty thousand were left dead on the fatal camping ground; and twenty million pieces plundered, part of the Tulunide treasure carried by way of Mecca with the pilgrim caravan for safety. But the days of the 'cursed Reprobate' (for so, like the Zenj leader, he was now fitly called) were drawing to an end. A Turkish general, Wassif, sent with a great army, after two days' desperate fighting, discomfited the fanatic host and dispersed it with great slaughter. Zakaruya, taken prisoner, died of his wounds before reaching Bagdad, and the populace, eager for a cruel spectacle, had to be satisfied with the sight of his lifeless body. The fragments of his army were pursued into Syria, where, still holding their leader alive, they for long carried on depredations upon Moslems and Christians alike, the pilgrim caravans of the latter to Jerusalem suffering equally.

In the following reign we come upon even more fearful

294 A.H.

Attack on pilgrim caravans.

---

[1] We meet with the same savagery on the part of the women in the battle of Cadesiya, but then against the infidels. What adds point, if that were possible, to the inhumanity on the present occasion, is that the victims were of their own faith, and were returning from performance of the highest function of the Moslem worship.

outbreaks of the savage fanatics who still held the province
of Bahrein.   Early in the fourth century, their chief Solei- Renewed
man was induced to make a diversion in favour of the Fati- outbreak,
mide ruler in Africa (of whom more below); and thereupon 307 A.H.
stormed and sacked Bussorah. A few years after he surprised
that unfortunate city again by night, and for seventeen days Attack on
made it the scene of fire, and blood, and rapine. It was not Bussorah, and pil-
till the approach of troops from Bagdad, that the Carmats grimage
retired laden with spoil and multitudes of captives whom 312-13A.H.
they sold as slaves. The pilgrim caravans were again the
object of savage attack. Successive companies were treated
with brutal cruelty as before ; thousands plundered, slain,
or taken captive. One caravan of 7000 was pursued and
scattered close to Kufa, which was stormed, and for six Kufa.
days subjected to like treatment as Bussorah. Soleiman stormed.
had then the insolence to demand the government of
Ahwaz, and being refused, spread his followers over Mesopotamia and Irac. The divine promise of victory inscribed
on his white banner[1], waving over the fanatics, nerved
them to beat back over and over again the Caliph's armies
led by his best generals, and even to threaten the capital
itself. The affrighted inhabitants fled across the river to
the eastern quarter, and on one occasion to the hills beyond.
Rapine and terror were thus the fate of the unhappy land
for three or four years. At last suffering defeat they withdrew into Arabia ; but only to renew their horrid outrages 317 A.H.
at Mecca. The Holy city was given up to plunder ; and
so little regard shown to the sacred places, that bodies of
the slain were cast into the sacred well Zemzem. The
Kaaba itself was robbed of its precious things, and to
crown the sacrilege despoiled of the Black Stone, which
was carried off to Hejer, and not restored for above twenty
years. The Fatimide prince now interfered to stay the
scandal and ravages of the Carmats, which hitherto had
been of service to him against the Caliphate. Soleiman
returned to Hejer, and we hear little more of him. But the

---

[1] It had this text as its legend ;—WE (the Most High) desire to show Our
favour unto those who are weak in the land, and make them leaders and heirs
(of the kingdom). *Sura* xxviii. 4.

Carmats still survived. Some years afterwards they again attacked the pilgrims, and plundered Kufa. After this they

325 A.H. fell into dissensions; but they must long have retained a strong hold of Syria, for in 360 A. H. we find them joining in a league with the Caliph to oust the Fatimides from that province; and the Fatimides were obliged to appease them by a yearly tribute. Some fifteen or twenty years later they are again mentioned in connection with the struggles that were prolonged for many years in Asia Minor and Egypt; and, strangely enough, it was a Carmat who ruled in Multan when, 396 A. H., it was taken by Mahmud.

Origin of the Fatimide dynasty, 280 A.H.
It will be convenient here to notice another branch of the Ismailites from which sprang the Fatimide dynasty of Egypt. The new transcendental doctrine was widely spread in Southern Arabia, and its votaries so grew in power that their leader gained possession of Yemen and Sanaa. This success induced one Mohammed Alhabîb, who claimed to be the descendant of Ismail, to send an envoy to Africa named Abu Abdallah. There, following up the canvass of previous missionaries, this emissary played a *rôle* of unexampled and romantic success. He found the Berbers so ready for the call, that he drew vast crowds after him, by their help defeated the Aghlab dynasty, and after much fighting gained possession of their capital and kingdom. He preached the impending advent of the Mehdy, and to meet the expectation so raised summoned Obeidallah, son of his deceased master Mohammed. The adventures of this Mehdy in his flight through Egypt, and wanderings as a merchant with a caravan to Tripoli, form quite a romance of themselves. Suspected by the Aghlabites, he was cast into prison, and so remained till released by the victorious Abu Abdallah, who for a time professed to be in doubt

297 A.H. 909 A.D.
whether Obeidallah were the veritable Mehdy or not. At last, however, he placed him on the throne, and himself reaped the not unfrequent fruit of disinterested labours in the founding of a dynasty; for he was assassinated by command of the monarch who owed to him his throne but had now become jealous of his influence. Assuming the title, Commander of the Faithful, Mohammed, in virtue of

his alleged descent from the Prophet's daughter, became the *Fatimide* Caliph of a kingdom which embraced both the dominions heretofore held by the Aghlabite dynasty, and the nearer districts of the Caliphate bordering on the Mediterranean. He made repeated attempts to gain Egypt 306–9 A.H. also, but was repulsed by Munis, Muctadir's commander there. Some fifty years later, however, both Syria and 358 A H Egypt were conquered by his followers, and the founda- 969 A.D. tions laid firm of the Fatimide Anti-caliphate. A literary duel then opened between Fostat and Bagdad on the purity of Obeidallah's descent from Aly and Fatima, on which the claims of the Egyptian dynasty rested. The heated debate was maintained long after its political moment had ceased. Renewed in modern times, the question hangs in the balance still unsolved.

When the Fatimide dynasty had passed away, the Druses, Ismailite faith was banished from Egypt by Saladin, who circa, 400 A.H. was strictly orthodox in his profession. Another branch of 1009 A.D. the superstition, however, still curiously survives,—that namely of the Druses. This strange sect was established, early in the fifth century, by the impious Fatimide Hakim, whom the Druses were encouraged to worship as an incarnation of the Deity. Driven from Egypt by his successor, they retired to the heights of Lebanon, where they still look for the return of their Caliph, the divine Hakim.

About the same time another offset of the faith was Assassins. established by a Persian fanatic, which, under the title of Assassins[1], long held in check the princes of the East, and earned for themselves an unenviable fame in the days of the Crusaders. They retired on the invasion of the Mongols, but still survive a small and now an inoffensive sect in the Lebanon and elsewhere.

---

[1] Curiously enough, they answered in character to the name that arose from quite another derivation, namely, the drug *Hashîsh,* to which they were addicted. They were long the terror of the East for the treacherous use of the dagger, both for the fanatical ends of their sect, and also as hired assassins. The Assassins of Syria have never entirely disappeared. Even at this day they are to be found in the Lebanon. Some representatives of the sect also exist in Persia, and even in Zanzibar; but since the thirteenth century they have become inoffensive. *Enc. Britt.* vol. xvi. p. 594.

CHAPTER LXXII.

MUCTADIR, CAHIR, AND RADHY.

295–329 A. H.   907–940 A. D.

Renewed decadence of the Caliphate.
THE stand made in the last three reigns to stay the downward progress of the Caliphate came now to an end. There remains little of our history to tell, but a weary and ungrateful story of weakness, misfortune, cruelty, and shame. And there being nothing either attractive or instructive to detain us, the remainder will be briefly told.

Muctadir 295 A.H. 907 A.D.
Muktafy, having been several months on his sick bed, intrigue had been for some time busy as to his successor. The choice lay between his minor brother, whom the Caliph himself favoured, and a son of Mutazz. The Vizier, hoping for the more thorough subservience of the minor, carried his appointment. Though but thirteen years of age, this boy assumed the title of Muctadir, ' Mighty by the help of the Lord,' a sad misnomer, for even in manhood he was but a weak voluptuary, in the hands of the women of his court, and of their favourites. His five-and-twenty years' reign is the constant record of Viziers, one rising on the fall, or on the assassination of another. Few weeks elapsed

296 A.H.
before the first Vizier was murdered by conspirators who placed the son of Mutazz upon the throne. But Munis, commander-in-chief, stood by his boyish sovereign; and the pretender, obtaining no support in the city, was with

137 A.H.
his followers slain. Some twenty years later, Muctadir

was again subjected to a like indignity. The leading A.H. 295–
courtiers having conspired against him, he was forced to   329.
abdicate in favour of his brother Cahir ; but, after a scene
of rioting and plunder, and loss of thousands of lives, the
conspirators found that they were not supported by the
troops; and so Muctadir, who had been kept in safety by
Munis, was again placed upon the throne.   The finances,
always straitened, fell after this outbreak into so wretched
a state that, spite of ruthless confiscation and resumption,
nothing was left to pay the city guards with.   A quarrel, 318 A.H.
stimulated by their rival demands, arose between the
cavalry and infantry ; the latter worsted, were most of them
massacred, and the rest driven from the city. Things became
so bad that Munis, thwarted by the Vizier of the day in all
attempts at reform, retired and with his followers took up his
residence at Mosul.   Meanwhile the city fell into fearful dis- 319 A.H.
order ; and abroad, the Greeks as well as Persians beat back
such forces as still held the field.   The people, angry at
the success of the ' Infidels' in Asia Minor, cast it in the
Caliph's teeth that he cared for none of these things, but,
instead of seeking to restore the prestige of Islam, passed
his days and nights with slave-girls and musicians.   Uttering such reproaches, they threw stones at the Imam, as in
the Friday service he named the Caliph in the public prayers.

Muctadir invited Munis to return, who loyally answered Muctadir's
the call.   But the foolish Caliph, as he drew near to Bagdad, death,
was persuaded by his favourites, who dreaded the return of 320 A.H.
Munis, to change his mind, and instead of welcoming him
as his friend, to go forth with his guards against him.   Clad
in the Prophet's mantle, girt about with the sword Dzul
Ficar, and holding the royal sceptre, the wretched Muctadir
issued from his palace, and was slain outside the city gate.
His long reign had brought the Caliphate to the lowest ebb.
External losses were of secondary moment ; though even
so, Africa was lost, and Egypt nearly.   Mosul, under chiefs
of the Hamadan line, had thrown off its dependence, and
the Greeks could make raids at pleasure on the helpless
border.   Yet in the East, there still was kept up a formal
recognition of the Caliphate, even by those who virtually

A.H. 295–
329.

Wretched
degrada-
tion of the
Caliphate.

claimed their independence; and nearer home, the terrible Carmathians had been for the time put down. In Bagdad the Caliph, the mere tool of a depraved and venal court, was at the mercy of foreign guards, which, commanded for the most part by Turkish and other officers of strange descent, were ever and anon breaking out into rebellion. Thus, abject and reduced, twice dethroned, and at the last slain in opposing a loyal officer whom he had called for his support, it is no wonder that the prestige which his immediate predecessors had regained was lost, and that the throne became again the object of contempt at home, and a tempting prize for attack from abroad. The people also were demoralized. Bagdad was no longer the centre of a vigorous population that might defend, and at times even govern, themselves. Contending in wild factions, they could redden the streets with blood, as they fought now over the interpretation of a text, and now, with the Hanbalites, rise in tumult over the remains of the great Tabari, denounce him as a heretic, and refuse his remains the rites of burial. But as for manhood, virtue, and power, these had altogether vanished [1].

Cahir,
320 A.H.
932 A.D.

On the death of Muctadir, the loyal Munis, whose only object in returning had been to restore security to his master, now wished to place his son upon the throne. But afraid that he might revenge his father's death upon them, his followers chose rather in his stead the late Caliph's brother, Cahir, already mentioned as having for a few days held the Caliphate; and he proved a more miserable ruler even than Muctadir. With an outward affectation of piety, he went to every excess of cruelty and extortion. He even tortured the mother of Muctadir and his sons and favourites, to squeeze from them the treasures amassed during the late reign. Many fled from the

---

[1] The verse that caused uproar was simple enough :—' Peradventure the Lord will raise thee up unto a noble place.' The contention of the Hanbalites was that Mahomet was here promised a place near the throne in heaven; while the others held that it referred to the rank of intercessor, and hence the heated strife. As to the historian Tabari, the Hanbalites were angry, because in his history he had not noticed Ibn Hanbal among the great jurists of Islam. Tabari b. 224; d. 310. His friends had to bury him secretly by night.

tyrant's grasp. Conspiracies were rife at court; and to A.H. 295–329.
anticipate the machinations of the treacherous Caliph,
Munis and his friends endeavoured to place him under re- 321 A.H.
straint, and failing in the attempt, resolved to dethrone him.
The plot, however, came to light; and the opposite faction,
having gained over the guards by bribes, imprisoned the
conspirators, and appointed a new generalissimo (Ameer
ul Omra, as he now was called) in Munis' room. The
Caliph caused his wretched nephew, who was to have
succeeded, to be immured alive; and Munis with his Munis beheaded.
partizans were, on the guards rising in his favour, beheaded. Cahir, thus relieved from immediate danger,
broke out into such tyranny, equally against friend and
foe, as to render his rule unbearable. A fresh conspiracy Cahir deposed and blinded,
was set on foot, and the besotted Caliph, overcome at
night by wine, was attacked in his palace. Refusing to 322 A.H. 934 A.D.
abdicate, his eyes were blinded, and he cast into prison.
Eleven years after he was liberated, and might be seen
led about a wretched mendicant in beggar's dress and
wooden sandals;—sad contrast to his high-sounding title,
Câhir billahi, 'Victorious by the grace of God,' and meet
type of the fallen Caliphate.

The seven years' reign of Radhy son of Muctadir, who Radhy, 322 A.H. 934 A.D.
followed, was but a succession of misfortune. Praised for
his piety, he became the mere tool of the Ameer ul Omra
of the day. It would be unprofitable to detail the intrigues of his court, or the treachery by which even the
few provinces still remaining around the capital fell into the
hands of his professed servants. The authority of the
Caliph, indeed, excepting in an uncertain and intermittent
way, extended hardly beyond the precincts of the city.
After one Vizier had been imprisoned by his enemies, and
another had absconded in disgrace, Radhy fell into the
hands of an able but cruel ruler, Ibn Raic, who held so
absolutely the reins of government that his name was
conjoined with the Caliph's in public prayer. To enable
him to combat with the provincial governors, who began
to raise their heads in revolt all around, Ibn Raic called
to his aid Bajkam, a chief from Deilem, with his Turkish

A.H. 295– horde. But after two years the intrigues and machinations
329.
_____　　became intolerable.

Bajkam,　　　　The cruelties perpetrated are hardly credible. One who
Ameer ul
Omra,　　held the office of Vizier had his hand cut off; and
326 A.H.　 still intriguing, his tongue cut out, whereof he died in
prison.　　Becoming jealous of Bajkam, Ibn Raic de-
signed to supplant him ; whereupon Bajkam, hasten-
327 A.H.　 ing from his camp, entered the city in force. Ibn Raic
disappeared into hiding ; and in his room Bajkam rose
to the plenitude of power. Taking the Caliph in his
train, he next year attacked the Hamadanite prince at
Mosul, and gained advantage over him. But in his absence
Ibn Raic, emerging from his hiding at the head of a body
of Carmats,—for these were now drafted into the Caliph's
army,—seized the capital. This obliged Bajkam to hurry
328 A.H.　 back, and leave the Hamadanites independent as before.
Indeed, it was only to them that the Caliphate now owed
the defence of the northern border, which otherwise would
have been at the mercy of Grecian inroad. Ibn Raic,
on the approach of Bajkam, tendered submission, and receiving pardon, was given the government of Syria and
Northern Mesopotamia. But for these he had to contend
with Ibn Toghej, the governor of Egypt and founder of
Ikshidite　the Ikhshidite dynasty. Like others, appointed from
dynasty in
Egypt,　　Bagdad to the charge of Egypt, this officer had set up as
321–50 A.H. independent sovereign, and ruled there, himself and his
successors, for a quarter of a century[1]. After some fighting
Ibn Raic was able to come to terms with the Ikhshidite,
and so retained his command in the north.

Rise of the　　A new enemy had meanwhile appeared in the East,—
Buyides,
322 A.H.　 the Buyide house,—which in a few years was to be
934 A.D.　 supreme in Bagdad. The Buyides were sons of Buyeh, a
prince in the hill country of Deilem, and leader of a
Turkish horde, engaged now on one side, and now on the
other, in the wars between the Samanides and the Alyide
rulers on the Caspian shore. Freed at last from such
service, the sons, tempted like other adventurers of the

---

[1] *Ikhshid* was the title of the princes of Ferghana, one of whom took service
under Motassim, and was grandfather of Ibn Toghej.

day, turned their arms westward, and took possession of A.H. 295–329. Fars. There coming in conflict with the outlying governors of the Caliphate, they passed on to Ispahan and
Shiraz, and even threatened Wasit. Bajkam, alarmed at 327–8 A.H.
their progress, now took the field, and was on the point of
gaining advantage over them, when he had to hurry back
because of the treachery of one of his captains, who in his
absence threatened Bagdad. And so the Buyides were left
for the time, to consolidate their conquests all around.

Regarding Bagdad during this reign, we are chiefly told Fanaticism
of the heated outbursts of fanaticism and intolerance that rife at Bagdad.
still prevailed. The Hanbalites, supported by popular
sentiment, carried things with a high hand. Forcing their
way into private dwellings, they overthrew everything not
in strict conformity with their tenets ; emptied vessels of
wine wherever found, broke in pieces musical instruments,
pried into the details of trade and commerce, and set up in
fact a kind of inquisition. Thus a professor of the Shie-ite
creed, for holding transmigration, was impaled and eventually burned alive. A famous doctor also was badly
handled for affirming some various readings of the Coran,
of no apparent moment in themselves ; and, notwithstanding that he submitted written recantation, had to fly Bagdad lest he should be torn in pieces by the angry mob.

Radhy died at the age of thirty-three. He is commonly Death of
spoken of as the last of the real Caliphs ;—the last, our Radhy, 329 A.H.
Annalist tells us, to deliver orations at the Friday service, 940 A.D.
hold assemblies to discuss with philosophers and divines the
questions of the day, or take counsel on the affairs of state ;
the last to distribute largess among the needy, or interpose
to temper the severity of cruel officers. And yet, with all
this, he was the mere dependant of another. To outward
appearance, indeed,—in the weekly presidency at the great
mosque ; in the formal, though it might be but empty,
sanctioning of successions in the executive ; and in the
semblance of a certain courtly ceremonial,—he might still
be taken for the Caliph. But beyond the shadow there
was little left at home. And abroad, even less. The East
was gone ; Africa and Egypt also, with great part of Syria

A.H. 295–
329.
and Mesopotamia; Mosul independent; Arabia held by Carmats and native chieftains; even Bussorah and Wasit in revolt. What was there but the capital? and there, how little!

Radhy's
poetry.
Radhy was the last of the Caliphs whose poetry has been preserved. The remains, both in sentiment and cadence, are of a high order. 'In them,' Weil writes, 'Radhy gives expression to deep religious feeling, and to his sense of the instability of human greatness, and the transitoriness of all things here below;—sentiments of which the tale of his successor, and indeed his own surroundings, offer so apt an illustration.'

Decay of
Kufa.
Kufa, as we have seen, was no longer a source either of danger or of material support. Gradually decaying ever since the transfer of the court to Bagdad, it had lost the power to disturb by its factious outbreaks the affairs of state, and, in point of fact, is seldom mentioned now.

CHAPTER LXXIII.

MUTTAKY AND MUSTAKFY.

329–334 A. H. 941–946 A. D.

BAJKAM, Ameer ul Omra, was at the time of Radhy's death engaged in a campaign against Barîdy, a Persian chieftain, who had already held the office of Vizier, but, like others, had since set himself up as independent ruler of an adjacent province, and was now even threatening Medain. Of such little moment had the Caliphate become, that Bajkam, on receiving tidings of Radhy's death, con-- tented himself with sending his secretary, who assembled the chief men as well of Alyite as of Abbasside descent, to elect a successor. The choice fell on the deceased Caliph's brother Muttaky, who assumed the office after it had been some days vacant; and whose first act was to send a banner and dress of honour to Bajkam, a needless con- firmation of his rank. Bajkam routed Baridy, but before returning to Wasit, where he now held his court, went out on a hunting party, and met his death at the hands of a band of marauding Kurds. The wretched capital became the scene of renewed anarchy. The Deilem troops fell out with the Turks, and going over to Baridy, enabled him to retake Wasit and enter Bagdad as Ameer ul Omra. Fresh disturbances breaking out, he was obliged after reigning for a few weeks to fly, and was succeeded by Kurtekin, a Deilem chief. His tyranny, however, was so intolerable that Ibn Raic, then governor of Syria, at the Caliph's call,

A.H. 329–
384.

Flies to
Mosul,
330 A.H.

hastened to the capital, and expelling Kurtekin, assumed supreme control. But Baridy had meanwhile repossessed himself of Wasit, and gaining over the Turkish mercenaries again attacked Bagdad, whereupon Ibn Raic persuaded the Caliph to fly with him to Mosul. Muttaky was handsomely welcomed there by the Hamadan princes, who organized a campaign to restore him to the capital. But their ends were purely selfish; and so, regarding Ibn Raic in their way, they assassinated him, and having added his Syrian government to their own, turned their ambition towards Bagdad. And thus it came to pass that before the close of the year, the Hamadanite chief, with the title of Nasir ud Dowla, advanced on Bagdad with the Caliph in his train, and after driving out Baridy, entered it in state.

Hamadan
princes'
short rule
at Bagdad.

Tuzun,
331 A.H.
943 A.D.

But however powerful the Hamadan chiefs were at home amongst their Arab brethren, and splendid their victories over the Greeks, they found it a different thing to rule at Bagdad. Arabs were no longer able to contend with the wild elements that dominated there. The foreign mercenaries, rank and file as well as leaders, had for long years cast off subservience and respect for Arabian chiefs; and even in the field, the Arab soldiery, discountenanced and cast aside, could nowhere hold their own against the well-organized Turkish forces. And so in less than a year, the Hamadan chiefs had to return to Mosul; for a Turkish general called Tuzûn[1], having beaten Baridy at Bussorah, entered Bagdad in triumph, and was saluted Ameer ul Omra. Fresh proceedings against the same enemy obliged Tuzûn to quit the capital; and during his absence a conspiracy broke out which placed the Caliph in danger, and obliged him again to appeal to the Hamadan prince

Muttaky
escapes to
Ricca,
944 A.D.
332 A.H.

for help. Troops sent in response enabled him to escape; he fled to Mosul and thence to Nisibin. Shortly after, peace being restored between Tuzûn and the Hamadan chiefs, Muttaky took up his residence at Ricca,—a wretched fugitive in the city which had so often been the proud court of his illustrious ancestors.

There, under the surveillance of a Hamadan prince,

---

[1] By Weil, *Turun.*

Muttaky, who had now been many months a refugee from
his capital, bethought him of the Ikhshidite, his former
governor of Egypt, and now its ruler. Appealed to, the
Ikhshidite hastened to the Caliph, and offering splendid
presents with humble homage, besought him to return with
him to Egypt, warning him at the same time to beware of
Tuzûn. But neither he nor the Hamadan princes had
other object in offering the Caliph an asylum, than by
possession of his person to gain a title to the contested
province of Syria. And so Muttaky, distrusting both,
threw himself, the warning notwithstanding, into the hands
of Tuzûn, who swore with the most sacred oaths that he
would render true and faithful service. Spite of it all, he
soon after deposed him from the Caliphate, and had his
sight destroyed.

The same day, Tuzûn installed the blinded Caliph's
brother as his successor, with the title of Mustakfy, *For
whom the Lord sufficeth.* The Buyide columns beginning
now to hover about the capital as vultures over their prey,
Tuzûn, with the Caliph in his train, marched out to Wasit
and discomfited them. The tribute due from Mosul being
withheld, and the treasury in straits, Tuzûn, again carrying
the Caliph with him, marched against the Hamadanites;
but friendly relations re-established, he returned. Soon
after, Tuzûn died, and was succeeded by Abu Jafar, one of
his generals. Bagdad now fell into a fearful state of
distress. Supplies stayed by the enemies all around no
longer reached the markets, and people were reduced to
eat dogs and cats and even offal. Plunder and rapine rife,
the mob were driven by starvation to rifle the shops of their
remaining stores. Multitudes fled the city for Bussorah or
elsewhere, dying in great numbers from want and weakness
by the way. Abu Jafar at last, finding himself unable to
control affairs, besought the aid of Nasir ud Dowla from
Mosul; even offering, if he would come, to vacate in his
favour the supreme command. But the Hamadanite arms
were at the moment engaged on one hand with the Russians
in Azerbijan, and on the other with the Ikhshidites in
Syria. Just then the governor of Wasit surrendered that

citadel to the chief of the Buyides, and joining him marched on Bagdad. Terror reigned in the city. Abu Jafar and the Caliph fled into hiding; but relieved of the Turkish garrison, which to escape the approaching conqueror evacuated the city and marched off to Mosul, both reappeared. The Caliph then received, with outward expressions of satisfaction, the secretary whom the Buyide chief sent on

before him to make terms of peace. The Caliph expressed himself ready to receive the conqueror, and confirm his title to all the surrounding districts which he had overrun. Thereupon he entered Bagdad, and under the new title of *Sultan,* Muizz ud Dowla assumed the supreme command. The Caliph tendered,—as how could he else?—an abject submission to the Sultan, whose name, in addition to Mustakfy's, was now stamped upon the coinage, and recited as that of sovereign in the public prayers. It was all in vain. Muizz ud Dowla feared the Caliph as a creature of the Turks, whose return from Mosul he might at any time invite. There may have been cause. At any rate, the Sultan took offence at an entertainment given by the chief lady of the Caliph's harem to the leaders of the Deilemites and Turks still remaining in the city, as if meant to gain

them over to the Caliph's cause. Mustakfy in vain excused himself as unconcerned with the feast. Three weeks followed without warning, when the Sultan, having arranged for the reception of an embassy from the East at the Caliph's palace, seated himself by his side, with his retinue in waiting. Suddenly two Deilemite chiefs rushed forward and offered to shake the Caliph's hand, who gave it, suspecting nothing. Catching hold, and throwing his turban round his neck, they dragged him by it to the Sultan's palace where (common fate now of dethroned Caliphs, for Muttaky and Cahir still survived in darkness), he was deprived of sight. He had been Caliph for little over a year. The city rose in tumult, and the Caliph's palace was plundered till but the bare walls remained. The tyrant had the lady's tongue cut out who had organized the hateful entertainment.

The fallen state of the Caliphate has made it no longer

needful to notice passing events elsewhere, in the shaping
of which the Caliph could have but little or no hand now.
A solitary instance we find in which the authority of Muttaky was invoked in a matter which, spiritual in itself, led
to an important result. In the year 332 A.H., the Greeks
carried their inroads so far as to beleaguer Edessa. The
only hope of saving it was to surrender the precious relic,
called *our Saviour's napkin,* treasured in the Edessa
cathedral; which obtained, the Greeks would then retire.
The lawfulness of its surrender was debated; and at last
referred for decision to the Caliph, who summoned a court
of jurists and doctors of the law. Permission was given,
and the cession of the relic not only saved Edessa, but
purchased liberty to a great multitude of Moslem prisoners.

CHAPTER LXXIV.

THE BUYIDE DYNASTY.—THE CALIPHS MUTIE, TAIE, CADIR, AND CAIM.

334–447 A.H.   946–1055 A.D.

Buyide
dynasty. THE Buyides had every advantage on their side.   Borne along by a brave Deilemite following, trained on the south-east shore of the Caspian in the protracted warfare between the Alyite dynasty and the Saffar and Samanide races, they spread rapidly over the provinces to the east of Bagdad, and at last, as we have seen, entered in triumph the capital itself, distracted as it was by the rivalries of Turkish cap-tains, wild licence of the soldiery, misrule, anarchy, and want.   The only adversary at all likely to oppose was the Hamadan house of Mosul, which without much difficulty could be held in check.   And so the Buyides maintained their hold of Bagdad over one hundred years.   But their rule was weakened by family quarrels, and by the Shie-ite tendencies of the race.   For the Deilem troops as well as their masters had imbibed those doctrines on the Caspian shore from the Alyite rulers whom they served, while the Turkish soldiery, as well as the populace of Bagdad, were devoted to the orthodox faith.   The city was thus con-tinually rent by dissensions ending in outbursts of violence between the two factions, which paved the fall of the Buyides and entry of the Seljuk conquerors.

The material position of the Caliphs throughout the

Buyide reign was at its lowest ebb. Abject dependants, A.H. 334 they were often carried in their master's train while fighting 447. at a distance from the capital. So inclined, moreover, was Position of Muizz ud Dowla, the first Buyide prince, to the Shie-ite Caliphate under it. faith, that he was only prevented from raising to the Caliphate a scion of the house of Aly, by alarm for his own safety and fear of rebellion, not in the capital alone, but all around. For the Caliphate of Bagdad, on its spiritual side, was still recognized throughout the Moslem world wherever the orthodox faith prevailed, excepting always Spain. The Fatimide Caliphs, on the contrary, claimed spiritual supremacy not only in Egypt, but as Shie-ites contested the pulpits of Syria also, and on one occasion even at Bagdad. In the East the spiritual dominance varied, but Persia and Deilem excepted, the balance clearly favoured orthodoxy. The Turcomans were staunch Sunnies. The great Mahmud held always a friendly attitude towards the Caliphs, and his splendid victories in the East were accordingly announced from the pulpits of Bagdad in grateful and glowing terms. The pages of our annalists are now almost entirely occupied with the political events of the day, in the guidance of which the Caliphs had seldom any concern, and which therefore need no mention here. We shall notice only the few occasions on which we hear of their existence.

The new Caliph, son of Muctadir, and called Mutie, *Obedi-* Mutie, *ent to the Lord*, had long aspired to the office ; and between 334-63A.H. him and Mustakfy a bitter enmity existed, which led him 945-73A.D. to retire into hiding. When the Buyides entered Bagdad, he came forth from his retirement, established himself at the new court, and by his sinister influence contributed to his cousin's fall. When this occurred, and he succeeded to the Caliphate, the Sultan made over Mustakfy to him; and it was while under his custody that the wretched man had his eyesight blinded. But neither did Mutie gain much by his subserviency. He was no longer allowed a voice in nominating the Vizier. A mere pittance doled out for his support, the office was shorn of every token of respect and dignity. Shie-ite observances were set up,—as public

A.H. 384–
447.

mourning on the anniversary of Hosein's death, and re-joicing on that of the Prophet's supposed testimony in Aly's favour [1]. On one occasion they went so far as to post on the city mosques sheets inscribed with malediction of the early Caliphs, and even of Ayesha, Mahomet's favourite spouse. The city was exasperated by the insult, and the placards torn down by the infuriated mob. Such outbursts occurred from time to time; and after one of them, the Caliph, who had held office thirty years, and now suffered from paralysis, was forced to abdicate in favour of his son.

Taie,
363–81 A.H.
973–91 A.D.

During the Caliphate of Taie, of whom personally, and of his official life, we hear next to nothing, Syria was torn by contending factions, Fatimide, Turkish, and Carmathian; while the Buyide house was split up into parties which fell to fighting among themselves. After holding the office eighteen years, Taie was deposed and cast into durance, to gain his property, which was coveted by the Buyide ruler.

Cadir,
381–422
A.H.
991–1031
A.D.

In place of the deposed Caliph, his cousin Cadir, grandson of Muctadir, was chosen. Banished from the capital for designs upon the Caliphate, he was now recalled and appointed to the office he had long desired, and which he was destined to hold for more than two score years. It was during his Caliphate that Mahmud of Ghaznie arose, threatening the West; and but for the dissensions that broke out in the family upon his death, the Buyide kingdom, paralyzed by internecine war, would have been swallowed up by hordes of Turcomans. Of Cadir there is hardly anything told, excepting that he succeeded in establishing an orthodox doctor as supreme judge, while the Buyide was content with a Shie-ite *Nackib*, or 'Leader,' to determine cases for

---

[1] Namely, 18th Dzul Hijj. The received tradition is that on that day, coming home from the Farewell pilgrimage, Mahomet gathered his followers at the pool Khum, and addressed them on their various obligations. Referring to Aly, he said,—'Whosoever loveth me, will choose Aly also for his friend. The Lord be with them that support him, and forsake them that oppose him.' Aly had just been appointed to command in Yemen, to the discontent of many, and to stop their murmuring this was said. The word *mowla* signifies both 'friend' and 'master,' and the Shie-ites make the most of it in this latter sense. Aly himself referred to the words when, as Caliph at Kufa, he was contending with Muavia.

that sect. He died eighty-seven years of age, and was A.H. 334-447.
succeeded by his son.

During the first half of Caim's long reign, hardly a day Caim,
passed in the unfortunate capital without tumult and blood- 422–68A.H. 1031–1075
shed between the opposing factions still embittered by A.D.
religious hate. Frequently the city was left without a
ruler; the Buyide, though styled 'King of kings,' being
often obliged to fly for safety from his capital. Meanwhile
the Seljuk house arose; and Toghril Beg, with countless
hordes issuing from the east, overran Syria and Armenia.
At last he cast an eye upon Bagdad. It was at a moment
when the city was in the last throes of violence and fanaticism. The chief officers also were at variance with one Entry of the
another. The Deilemite captain Basisiri accused the Seljuks, 447 A.H.
Vizier of making overtures to the Seljuks; while the Vizier 1055 A.D.
accused Basisiri of seeking to supplant the Caliph by the
Egyptian anti-Caliph. The populace rose against Basisiri,
and the Buyide prince, Melik Rahim, at the Caliph's
entreaty, sent him away in exile. Just then Toghril Beg,
under cover of intended pilgrimage to Mecca, entered Irac
with a heavy force, and assuring the Caliph of pacific views
and all subservience to his authority, begged his leave to
visit the capital. The Turks and Buyides were averse ; but
the Caliph himself was only too glad to give it. On this
the great conqueror's name was recited by the Caliph in
the public prayers; and a few days after, Toghril Beg
himself—having sworn to be true not only to the Caliph,
but also to the Buyide, Melik Rahim—made his entry into
the capital, where he was well received both by chiefs and
people.

CHAPTER LXXV.

BAGDAD UNDER THE SELJUKS.

447–575 A.H.   1055–1180 A.D.

TOGHRIL BEG was in no haste to leave Bagdad, and it was not long before he found, in a riot of the populace against his wild troops, excuse for casting Melik Rahim into prison, and assuming in his own hands the government of the city.   So ended the Buyide rule, a century of decay for the Caliphate, and misfortune for Bagdad.   The Deilemite soldiers were at once disbanded.   Quitting Irac, they rallied round Basisiri, who had joined the Fatimide cause in Syria, and who soon waxed strong enough to rout a column of the Seljuk forces.   Alarmed at the tidings, Toghril, after having rested a year in Bagdad, during which the Caliph in vain besought him to rid the city of his Turkish hordes, set out on a campaign to Nisibin and

Mosul.   Returning victorious, he was met by the Caliph with crowns and dresses of honour, and saluted as ' Emperor of the East and of the West.'   But in the following year, Toghril, being called back by the revolt of his brother to Persia, Basisiri, at the head of his Syrian levies, entered

Bagdad and proclaimed the Caliphate of the Fatimide ruler of Egypt.   The Grand Vizier of Toghril was taken prisoner, and, exposed in an ox-hide to the contempt of the populace, was so hanged.   Even Caim, abjuring his own right, was forced to swear fealty to the rival Caliph.

The emblems of the Abbasside Caliphate, robes and tur- A.H. 447–
ban, ancient jewels, and royal pulpit, were sent to Cairo, 575.
with Caim's formal renunciation of the dignity[1]. But the
hateful usurpation was not to last long. The supporters of
Basisiri fell away as Toghril Beg again approached; and
just a year after his entry the usurper fled, and Caim re-
assumed his office. He continued in honour with the
Seljuk monarch, who sued for the hand of his daughter.
At first refused, the Sultan obtained it in the end, but died 453-5 A.H.
shortly after the marriage feast.

Alp Arslan's reign which followed, not only extended far Death of
and wide the spiritual dominion of Caim, but restored to Caim.
Bagdad a security long unknown, and with it again the arts
of commerce, peace, and learning. But we hear little of
Caim, who throughout his prolonged Caliphate showed
himself but weak and aimless. He died two years after
Alp Arslan, and was followed by his grandson.

Muctady, the new Caliph, was honoured by the Sultan Muctady,
Melik Shah, during whose reign the Caliphate was recog- 468–87A H.
nized throughout the extending range of Seljuk conquest. A.D. 1075–94
Arabia, with the Holy cities, recovered from the Fatimide
grasp, acknowledged now again the spiritual jurisdiction of
the Abbassides. The Sultan gave his daughter in marriage
to the Caliph; and on the birth of a son, dreamed of com-
bining in him at once the Caliph and the Sultan on a
common throne. But the dream was fruitless. The lady,
dissatisfied, retired with her infant to the court of Ispahan.
And the Sultan himself, becoming jealous of the Caliph's
interference in the affairs of state, desired him to refrain,
and retire to Bussorah; but the death of Melik Shah
shortly after, made the command inoperative.

Mustazhir succeeded his father. During his five-and- Mustazhir,
twenty years' incumbency there were stirring times; yet 487–512 A.H.
whether in the history of the fanatical strife at home, or of 1094–1118
the startling Crusade of the Christians in the West, the A.D.
Caliph's name is hardly ever noticed. The Seljuk, whose
rule was weakened by intestine broil, cared little for the

---

[1] The robes, &c., were sent back by Saladin, but the pulpit is said to be still
in Cairo.

A.H. 447–
575.

497 A.H.
1103 A.D.

Capture of
Jerusalem,
15th July,
1099 A.D.

interests of Islam.   Towards the close of the fifth century,
the Christian arms spread all over Syria, and a bootless attempt was even made by Raimond, with a force of 30,000
Crusaders, to fall upon Bagdad by an eastern circuit, and so
inflict a deadly blow upon Islam.   In the year 492 A.H.,
consternation was spread throughout the land by the capture of Jerusalem, and cruel treatment of its inhabitants.
Preachers went about proclaiming the sad story, kindling
revenge, and rousing men to recover from infidel hands the
Mosque of Omar, and scene of the Prophet's heavenly flight.
But whatever the success elsewhere, the mission failed in
the East, which was occupied with its own troubles, and
moreover cared little for the Holy Land, dominated as it
then was by the Fatimide faith.   Crowds of exiles, driven
for refuge to Bagdad, and joined there by the populace, cried
out for war against the Franks.   But neither Sultan nor
Caliph had ears to hear.   For two Fridays the insurgents,
with this cry, stormed the Great Mosque, broke the pulpit
and throne of the Caliph in pieces, and shouted down the
service.   But that was all.   No army went.

Mustar-
shid,
512–29A.H.

Dubeis and
Zenky.

The Seljuks at this time, engaged by intestine war in the
East, left Bagdad much to itself; and we are startled by
finding Mustarshid, son of the preceding Caliph, once more
seeking independence in the field.   Risings in Irac were at
this time rife.   One was led by the famous general Dubeis,
whom the Caliph pursued to Bussorah ; and who thence
joined first the Crusaders, and eventually a rebel brother of
the Sultan.   A year or two after the two made a dash at
the capital ; but Mustarshid, with 12,000 men, anticipated
their movements and put them to flight.   Emboldened by
such success, the Caliph took the field against Zenky, the
terrible foe of the Crusaders, pursued him to Mosul, and besieged him there for three months.   Not long after, Mustarshid persuaded a disloyal scion of the Seljuk family to join
him in a campaign against the Sultan himself.   He attacked
the Sultan's army near Hamadan ; but, deserted by his
troops, was taken prisoner, and pardoned on promising not
to quit his palace any more.   Left in the royal tent, however,
in the Sultan's absence, he was found murdered, as is sup-

527 A.H.
1132 A.D.

posed, by an emissary of the Assassins, who had no love for A.H. 447-
the Caliph. To remove the suspicion from himself, the 575.
Sultan threw the blame on the Caliph's old enemy, Dubeis,
and had him put to death. Both Mustarshid and Dubeis
are praised by their contemporaries as poets of no mean
name[1]; and the Caliph, had he held his hand from the
temptation of arms (for him a dangerous anachronism),
might have built up the Caliphate by the peaceful arts he
was better fitted to employ.

Rashid, following his father's steps, made another un- Rashid,
fortunate attempt at independence. He insulted the Seljuk 529-30A.H.
monarch's envoy; incited the mob to plunder his palace;
and then, supported by Zenky,—now on the Caliph's side,—
set up a rival Sultan and levied war. The Sultan, Masud,
hastened to the rebellious capital, and as the Caliph dare
not venture outside the walls, laid siege to it. Bagdad,
well defended by the river and its canals, long resisted the
attack; but at last the Caliph and Zenky, despairing of
success, escaped to Mosul. The Sultan's power restored, a
council was held, the Caliph deposed, and his uncle, son of
Mustazhir, appointed in his stead. Rashid fled to Ispahan,
where he fell another victim to the Assassin dagger.

The continued disunion and contests of the Seljuk house Muktafy,
afforded the new Caliph, Muktafy, opportunity not only of 530-55A.H.
maintaining his authority in Bagdad, but of extending it
throughout Irac. At the head of an organized force, he
was able to defend the capital from various attack. But he 551 A.H.
was ill-advised enough to support the rebellion of a son of
the Sultan, who thereupon marched against Bagdad and
forced the Caliph to take refuge in the eastern quarter,
where he was only saved by the recall of the Sultan, to quell
a more serious rising in the East. Muktafy was, however, 552 A.H.
again received into favour by the Seljuk, who betrothed
himself to one of his daughters. During this Caliphate, the
Crusade was raging furiously, and in the war Zenky obtained
high distinction as a brave and generous warrior both from
friend and foe. At one time hard pressed, he made urgent
appeal for help to Bagdad, where, yielding to popular

---

[1] Dubeis is mentioned with distinction in the *Mocamat Hareri.*

tumult, the Sultan and the Caliph despatched 20,000 men. But in the breast neither of the Seljuks, nor of the Caliph, nor yet of their Ameers, was enthusiasm ever kindled into farther effort against the Frank Crusade.

Muktafy is praised by our Annalists as virtuous, able and brave. During his Caliphate of five-and-twenty years, he conducted many minor expeditions against enemies in the vicinity, but none deserving any special notice. Of the next two Caliphs there is little else to say than that they continued to occupy a more or less independent position, with a Vizier and courtly surroundings, and supported by a force sufficient for an occasional campaign of but local and ephemeral import. Meanwhile Nurudin and Saladin were pushing their victorious arms not only against the Crusaders but against the Fatimides of Egypt. That dynasty was at last extinguished, having lasted for two centuries and three quarters. Their conqueror, Saladin, though himself an orthodox Moslem, dared not at the first proclaim the Sunnite faith in the midst of a people still devoted to the tenets and practice of the Shie-ite sect. But he soon found himself able to do so; and thus the spiritual supremacy of the Abbassides again prevailed, not only in Syria, but throughout Egypt and all its dependencies.

CHAPTER LXXVI.

THE CALIPH NASIR, HIS SON AND GRANDSON.

575–640 A.H.   1180–1242 A.D.

WE now reach an attempt to restore the Caliphate to its ancient *rôle* among the nations; it was but the flicker of an expiring flame.   Nasir, 'Defender of the Faith,' not only held the capital in strength, but extended his sway into Mesopotamia on the one hand, and into Persia on the other.   Ambitious in his foreign policy, he looked to farther conquest ; selfish and cruel at home, he caused his first two Viziers in fits of jealousy to be put to death.

The grand object of his earlier years was to crush the Seljuk power, and on its ruins build up his own.   For this, he fomented rebellion, and took the part, from time to time, of discontented branches of the Sultan's house.   At last, the Kharizm Shah, Takash, at his instigation attacked the Seljuk forces, and defeated them, leaving Toghril, last of his race, upon the field.   The head of the fallen monarch was despatched to the Caliph to be exposed in front of the palace at Bagdad.   Takash, recognized now as supreme ruler of the East, conferred on the Caliph certain provinces of Persia, heretofore held by the Seljuks.   In token of his loyalty, Nasir sent by the hand of his Vizier to the conqueror a patent of rule and a dress of honour.   But by a stupid want of tact, the Vizier so irritated the churlish Turk, that he attacked the Caliph's troops and routed them.   Thereafter hostile relations, or at best hollow truce, prevailed

A.H. 575- between the two for many years. The Caliph, to be rid of an
640.   obnoxious governor of the Shah's, against whom he dared
——   not levy open war, had him assassinated by an emissary of
          the Ismailites, who having dropped their Alyite tenets, but
          not the dagger, were now in favour at the court of Bagdad.
          The Shah retaliated by having the body of Nasir's Vizier,
          who died on a campaign against him, exhumed, and the
          head stuck up at Kharizm. Irritated at this and other
          hostile acts, the Caliph showed his vexation by treating
          with indignity the pilgrims who came from the East under
          the Kharizm flag. But beyond such poor revenge, he was
          powerless for any open enmity against a Potentate whose
          rule stretched unopposed from the Jaxartes to the Persian
          Gulf.

Kharizm   Mohammed son of Takash, exasperated at these proceed-
Shah's ad- ings, now aimed not simply to crush the temporal rule of
vance on
Bagdad,   the Caliph, but by setting up an anti-Caliph of the house of
612–14A.H. Aly, to paralyze his spiritual power as well. A council
1216–7A.D.
          of learned doctors, assembled at Kharizm, accordingly de-
          posed Nasir as an assassin and enemy of the faith, and
          nominated a descendant of Aly to the Caliphate, who was
          prayed for in public and his name struck on the coinage of
          the eastern empire. Following up this act, Mohammed
          turned his resistless arms upon Bagdad. Nasir in alarm
          sent a distinguished envoy to plead his cause, but he was
          haughtily rejected, with the assurance that the conqueror
          was about to instal the worthier scion of a worthier house
Nasir in- upon his Master's throne. On this, Nasir bethought him
vites
Jenghiz   of an appeal to Jenghiz Khan, the rising Mongol chief, to
Khan.   check Mohammed's progress; and against the pious re-
          clamations of his court, sent an embassy to him;—the
          Defender of the Faith appealing for help to the pagan head
          of a pagan horde! It would have been all too late, for
          Mohammed, the Kharizm Shah, had already taken Eastern
          Irac, and Bagdad lay at his mercy, when, by the opportune
          inclemency of an early winter, he was forced to return to
          Khorasan. The Caliph soon after found his diplomacy
          bearing evil fruit. The steppes of Central Asia were set
          in motion by Jenghiz Khan, and his hordes put to flight

the Kharizm Shah, who died an exile in an island of the
Caspian. But it had been well for the Caliph if he had left
these Mongol hosts alone in their native wilds.

Turning now to the Holy Land, we find that Saladin, over
and again, when hard pressed by the Crusaders, urgently
appealed for help to Nasir who, caring for little beyond
his own aggrandisement, contented himself with sending a
store of naphtha with men to use it against the invaders in
the field. To Aly, one of Saladin's sons, who in the dissensions of the family sought to recover Damascus, he
promised help, but it ended in an idle play upon their
names;—'Aly,' he said, 'on the Prophet's death had no
defender; whilst now the Caliph is (Nasir) the Defender of
Aly[1].'

There is little more to tell of Nasir. Besides his occasional conquests, he held uninterruptedly the Irak Araby
from Tekrit to the Gulf, of which he is described as having
been a severe and oppressive ruler. His long reign of forty-
seven years is chiefly marked by ambitious and unscrupulous
dealings with the Tartar chiefs, and by his unholy invocation of the Mongol hordes, which so soon brought his own
dynasty to an end. But in his day there was comparative
peace at Bagdad; learning flourished; schools and libraries
were patronized; while refuges for the poor, and other
works of public interest, were encouraged.

His son and grandson succeeded Nasir, during the next
eighteen years; but there is little said of them beyond that
they were mild and virtuous. The Crusades still dragged
on their weary course, while the heirs of Saladin were contending bitterly among themselves. The Caliphate, however, concerned itself little with the wars in Syria. It was
kept in frequent alarm by the Tartar inroads. The Mongols
came on one occasion as near as Holwan and Khanikin,
and on another even to Samira, so that the terrified
inhabitants of Bagdad hastened to put their defences in
order. But the danger for the moment passed off, and
there peace still reigned in the city. It was but the lull
before the fatal storm.

Marginal notes:
A.H. 575–640.

617 A.H. Nasir leaves Crusaders alone, 577–89 A H. 1180-93 A.D.

Nasir's Caliphate.

Zahir and Mustansir, the two succeeding Caliphs, 622–40A.H. 1225-1242 A.D.

---

[1] The Vizier of this prince was brother of our annalist, Ibn al Athir.

CHAPTER LXXVII.

MUSTASSIM, THE LAST OF THE CALIPHS.

640–656 A. H. 1242–1258 A. D.

Mustassim last Caliph, 640-56 A.H. 1242-58 A.D.   IN the year 640 A. H. Mustassim became Caliph,—vainly so called as *He that maketh the Lord his refuge;* a weak and miserly creature, in whose improvident hands the Caliphate, even in quieter times, would have fared ill. Between the Chief Secretary an ambitious and unprincipled courtier, and the Vizier, bitter enmity prevailed. The Vizier, strange to say, was a Shie-ite; as such he is of course denounced by orthodox annalists, who even accuse him of seeking relief for his persecuted fellow sectaries by treacherous communication with the Mongols. Others assign him a more patriotic *rôle*; and, indeed, we need not to travel beyond the imbecility of the Caliph, and the demoralization of his now shrunken kingdom, for the causes of impending ruin.

His character.   Of Mustassim himself there is little to relate. As characteristic of his meanness, we are told that he appropriated the state jewels of the Chief of Kerak, who with difficulty obtained their partial restitution by proclaiming the Caliph's dishonesty before the assembled pilgrims at Mecca. His influence was felt, however, somewhat in Egypt. The Abbasside faith now recognized there, the Sultan sought and obtained at Mustassim's hands recognition of his title and the insignia of investiture. The Caliph also repeatedly inter-

posed to mediate between the Ruler of Damascus and the A.H. 640-656.
Sultan of Egypt. It was for his interest to help towards
the establishment of a stable government, such as the
Ayubite, in Syria, which might shield the Caliphate from
its impending fate. But it was all too late.

Meanwhile, as a tiger watching its prey, the Mongol was Holagu's designs on the West,
preparing from afar for the fatal irruption on the fair pro-
vinces of the West. Mustassim had been now thirteen 653 A.H.
1255 A.D.
years on the throne, when Holagu proclaimed a campaign
against the Ismailians, and invited all to join in crushing
the hateful race. The call met with no response from the
Caliph. In the following year, the overthrow of the Ismailian power left the conqueror free for his designs on
the farther West. The state of Bagdad may be surmised
at this time as the theatre of unceasing strife between the
two hostile ministers already named, who accused each the
other of treason. The Secretary went so far as to rise
against the Caliph himself, and, with the mob at his back,
forced him not only to declare him blameless, but to have
his name recited in the public prayers.

Just then, Holagu, who was resting at Hamadan, sent a His advance on Bagdad,
threatening embassy to Bagdad. First, he upbraided Mus-
tassim for having failed to aid in the campaign against the 655 A.H.
1257 A.D.
Ismailians, as the enemies of mankind. Now, therefore, he
bade him to raze the defences of Bagdad; and commanded
that, to learn his will, he must forthwith repair in person
to his court, or else send his Vizier and chief officers for the
purpose;—which done, he was ready to leave Mustassim in
secure possession of what he had. The foolish Caliph in
reply descanted on the multitudes ready to hasten for the
defence of the Vicegerent of the Prophet; and while declining to dismantle the city, sent an envoy with presents
and an otherwise soft reply. An immediate advance was
the sole response of Holagu.

The helpless Caliph, persuaded by his Vizier, had already City seized and sacked,
marshalled an embassy of submission, when the Secretary 656 A.H.
1258 A.D.
and excited populace forced him instead to send a letter of
defiance, reminding the conqueror of the Saffarides' fate, and
that of others who had dared attack the ' City of peace.'

A.H. 640–656. The warning was not without effect upon the superstitious Mongol, whose fears were now excited, and now quelled by his astrologers. At last, satisfied of the safety of the enterprise, he made his Tartar hordes, from every side, converge upon the fated city. There the weakling at one moment wildly sought to gather troops for its defence ; at another sent offers of a yearly tribute to his enemy ; ever and anon he looked for some ready fortune, such as had saved in like case his predecessors, and expected even the hand of Heaven to interpose. In the first month of 656 A.D. the Mongols routed a column which held Anbar, and i. 656 A.H. Jan., 1258 A.D. pursued the few survivors to the western quarter of the city. Shortly after, Holagu himself, marching down the eastern bank, attacked the opposite quarter. In vain the Caliph sent his sons to plead for mercy: in vain he deputed the Vizier to seek for terms. All that could be wrung from the conqueror was safety for the chief inhabitants. Holagu had already stormed part of the city when he sent for the commander-in-chief of the Caliph and his Secre- 4th of second month, 3rd March. tary to arrange for the cessation of hostilities. They went, but, notwithstanding promise of safe-conduct, were put to death, with all their followers. Nothing remained for Mustassim but to go forth himself, which he did, the be- ginning of the second month, followed by his sons and the leading citizens. They were received with outward cour- tesy ; the Caliph and his sons were remanded to a tent ; and the inhabitants warned to quit the city, which would then be given up to plunder. The wretched Caliph, follow- ing in the tyrant's suite, was forced to witness the sacking of his palace, and there point out his hidden treasures, with golden ingots of untold weight. After many days of rapine and conflagration, Holagu put an end to the pil- Last of the Caliphs put to death, 14th ii. 656 A.H. 13th Feb., 1258 A.D. lage, and took the city for his own. Mustassim, now in the Mongol's way, was put to death in the middle of the second month, and with him all the members of the house on whom hands could be laid. And so, suffering a fate similar to that which five centuries before it had inflicted on the Omeyyads, the Abbasside dynasty came to a violent and untimely end.

CHAPTER LXXVIII.

THE SO-CALLED CALIPHATE UNDER THE MEMLUKS OF EGYPT.

659–926 A. H.   1261–1520 A. D.

THE Caliphate, long in hopeless decrepitude, had now Mustansir, disappeared, and there remained no possibility of its revival. the Egyptian Caliph, But a shadow survived in Egypt,—a race of mock-Caliphs, 659 A.H. having the name without the substance ; a mere spectre 1261 A.D. as it were. Shortly after his accession to the throne, Beibars, hearing that a scion of Abbasside descent survived in Syria, conceived the design of setting him up as Caliph, and of receiving at his hands a spiritual blessing and title to the Sultanate. Sought out from his hiding, the Abbasside was brought to Cairo. At his approach, the Sultan with his court went forth in pomp to meet him. Even the Jews and Christians had to follow in the train, bearing the Book of the law, and the Evangel, in their hands. Soon after this, Mustansir Caliph-nominate, robed in gorgeous apparel, girt with the sword of State and mounted on a white steed, was installed in the office, and sworn fealty to by Beibars, his Ameers, and the people ; which function ended, there was read from the pulpit a pompous patent by the Caliph, conferring on Beibars the sovereign title, and impressing upon him the duty of warring for the Faith, and other obligations which Mustansir now devolved upon him.

A.H. 659-
926.
Then, with sound of trumpet and shouts of joy, the royal
procession wended its way through the streets back to the
palace ;—the Caliph following the Sultan on horseback,—
all the rest on foot.

His at-
tempt on
Bagdad.
A few months later, Beibars resolved to reinstate his so-
called Caliph in Bagdad, and accompanied him for this end
to Damascus, with an army. There, however, the Mosul
chiefs, who were to have joined the expedition, warned
Beibars of possible danger to himself from a resuscitated
Caliphate ; and so, withdrawing from the enterprise, the
Sultan suffered his *protégé* to pursue his march with a
diminished following, composed chiefly of Bedouin clans.

Killed in
battle,
660 A.H.
1262 A.D.
The Mongol governor of Bagdad met the attack at Hit,
defeated the Caliph, and left him dead upon the field. So
ended Mustansir, his high title of the *Heavenly Conqueror*
notwithstanding.

Line of
nominal
Caliphs,
661-926
A.H.
1263-1520
A.D.
The following year, Beibars secured another scion of Abbasside descent, and installed him as Caliph, but now on
an altogether different footing,—that, namely, of a priestly
attendant at his court, or as we might say a high ecclesiastic,
to give at each succession his benediction and formal title
to the throne, and also to lead the public prayers. A mere
creature of the court, he was lodged, more or less under
surveillance, in the citadel, and occupied a quite dependent,
and in the main servile, place.

Their posi-
tion and
functions.
The succession of such Egyptian Caliphs was maintained
unbroken in the same line, on the nomination of the Sultan
of the day, throughout the dynasty of the Mamelukes,
which for two centuries and a half forms one of the most
painful episodes of tyranny and bloodshed in the history
of the world. During this long period we hear little of
these Caliphs, excepting so far as it devolved upon them to
enthrone each new Sultan, and validate his title with the
sanction, as it were, of the Moslem Church. The Caliph
also presided at the public prayers, in which his name was
pronounced after that of the reigning monarch. Beyond
this, the notices are sparse and rare, and for the most part
unimportant. Here we read of a Caliph carried in the
Sultan's train to witness his conquests, or perchance with

him be taken captive by the enemy ; anon we hear of another A.H. 659– 926. imprisoned by his sovereign, or it may be deposed and exiled for interfering in the affairs of state, or conspiring against the throne.   But once, we find a Caliph elevated to the Sultanate ; not, however, in virtue of his office, and but for half a year.   Now he is preaching a holy war against the Mongols or Osmanlies, and again employed in the more fitting task of mediating peace, or heading a procession of Moslems, Jews, and Christians, each holding aloft their scriptures, and praying for deliverance from the plague.   In the eighth century of the Hegira, the Caliph, in company with the Sultan, received a deputation bearing precious gifts, from Mohammed son of Toghluk, who prayed for a patent of investiture from him, and for the mission of a Doctor of Abbasside lineage to instruct his Indian subjects in the faith.   But, whether in honour or in neglect, we seldom find the so-called Caliph, throughout these 260 years, other than the tool and servant of the ruler of the day.

But a new power now arose in the East, which was soon Rise of the to crush the Mameluke dynasty, that namely of the Osman- Osmanlies, lies [1].   Like other hordes that overspread the West, these, in the seventh century of the Hegira, issued from the steppes of Central Asia beyond the Caspian.   In the eighth century they achieved the conquest of Asia Minor, and eventually crossing the Bosphorus, planted the crescent on the walls of Byzantium.

After a long struggle on the plains of Syria, the Mameluke who con- arms finally gave place to the Osmanly.   In the year quer the Mame- 922 A.H., on the fateful field of Merj Dabik, the Egyptian lukes, troops suffered defeat, and Kansuweh, the last but one of the 922 A.H. 1516 A.D. Mamelukes, was left on the field.   The remnants fled to Damascus ; but the Caliph Mutawakkil, who had followed in Kansuweh's train, waited on Selim the conqueror at Aleppo, and was by him courteously received.   Tuman-beg, the last of the Egyptian dynasty, vainly endeavoured to resist the advance of his enemy, whose offers of peace were rejected.   On the Egyptian plain of Ridaniah his

[1] So called from Othman (pronounced in the West *Osman*), son of Ertogral, who settled in Asia Minor in the latter half of the seventh century.

A.H. 659–
926.
troops were finally defeated, about the close of the year ;
and on the first days of the following, Selim made his

Selim
enters
Cairo,
i. 923 A.H.
Jan.,
1517 A.D.
triumphal entry into Cairo, with the Caliph in his train.
There Mutawakkil used his influence with the conqueror to
stay the tumult and rapine raging in the city, and to save
the Mameluke chiefs, of whom some thousands fell victims
to Osmanly hate. The Sultan, who had fled across the
Nile, was betrayed by a Bedouin chief, whose protection he
had sought, and put to death.

The Caliph
carried to
Constanti-
nople,
923 A.H.
1517 A.D.
Thus came to an end the dark and hateful Mameluke
rule. Selim rested eight months in Cairo, abandoning himself to a course of dissipation, of which even a Mameluke
might have been ashamed. He then returned to Constantinople, and with other Egyptians carried Mutawakkil
also with him. There at first he was held as Caliph in
high honour and esteem ; but this he gradually forfeited
Im-
prisoned,
926 A.H.
1520 A.D.
by a graceless and unworthy life. Two or three years
later, convicted of the misappropriation of property committed to his trust in Egypt, he was cast into confinement
in the fortress of Saba Kuliat. Selim's successor, Soleiman,
set him at liberty, and allowed him to return to the capital,
Resigns
office into
Sultan's
hands.
where he lived for a time on a miserable pittance. Shortly
after, he resigned his rights into the hands of the Osmanly
monarch, and retired into Egypt. We hear no more of
him but that he joined a rising there 929 A. H., and died in
the year 945. Thus ended the last shadow of the Abbasside Caliphate.

Claim of
Osmanly
Sultans to
the title.
In virtue of Mutawakkil's cession of his title, the Osmanly
Sultans make pretension not only to the sovereignty of
the Moslem world, but to the Caliphate itself,—that is to
the spiritual as well as political power held by the Successors
of the Prophet. Were there no other bar, the Tartar blood
which flows in their veins would make the claim untenable.
Even if their pedigree by some flattering fiction could be
traced up to Coreishite stock, the claim would be but a
fond anachronism. The Caliphate ended with the fall of
Bagdad. The illusory resuscitation by the Mamelukes
was a lifeless show ; the Osmanly Caliphate, a dream.

CHAPTER LXXIX.

REVIEW.

IN gathering up the more important points of this his- The Omeyyad, better than the Abbasside, dynasty. tory, it is to the writer clear that the palmiest days of Islam, after those of Abu Bekr and Omar, are the Omeyyad. Muavia and Welid are not eclipsed by either Harun or Mamun. The tendency of the annals on which we are dependent, written as they were under the influence of Abbasside supremacy, is to exalt that dynasty at the expense of the Omeyyad. Still, with all its adventitious colouring, the Abbasside reign pales before the glory of the Omeyyad, which by its conquests laid broad the foundations of Islam in the East and in the West. Moreover, the wholesale butcheries, cold-blooded murders, and treacherous assassinations, which cast a lurid light on the court of Saffah and his successors, find, as a whole, no counterpart among the Omeyyads. And if we regard the environment of the throne, although some of the Omeyyads were dissolute to the last degree, and sometimes cruel also, I should incline to strike the balance, even as regards morality, in favour altogether of Damascus. The history of the Abbassides can bring nothing to compare with the exemplary lives of Omar II, or Hisham ; and whether from the point of natural law, or of Moslem obligation, the scandal of Bagdad without doubt casts into the shade anything that can be charged against Damascus.

The chief reason for the superiority of the Omeyyads

Arab sup-
port secret
of Omeyyad
greatness.
was the manly, frugal, and hardy habit of the Arab nation on whom they leant. These formed the main staple of their court, their ministers, their generals and associates. Conquest and spoil of war had already heated them, long before their fall, to luxurious living and voluptuous indulgence. But even so, the love of desert life, indigenous in the Arab, was to some extent corrective of the laxity and demoralization creeping over the Moslem world. Under the Abbassides all was changed. Chief commands, both civil and military, fell rapidly into the hands of Turkish and Persian adventurers. The Arabs, too, in rank and file, were as a rule disbanded ; and the imperial forces recruited from the tribes of Central Asia or from the Berbers of the West. And so the Arabs—those that yet maintained their simplicity and vigour uncontaminated by city life—retired to the desert ; ready, instead of as heretofore the prop and pillar of the Caliphate, to follow any outlaw, Zenj or Carmat, appealing to their innate love of rapine, lawlessness, and plunder.

Influence
of Persia.
The influence of Persia affected also the spiritual, intellectual, and philosophical development of the nation. While, on the one hand, it enervated and tended to demoralize the 'City of Peace,' on the other, with the help of Greece, it introduced the era of science, philosophy, and art, which formed the glory of Mamun and his immediate successors, and overshadowed the more substantial, though less lustrous grandeur of the Omeyyad line. Persian influence was also strongly in favour of Shie-ite doctrine and transcendental philosophy. The countries in which Arabs mostly spread and settled, and where consequently Arab sentiment most prevailed, are still those devoted to the Orthodox faith as set forth by the four great doctors of the same. Where there has been inclination to diverge, it has been, not in the direction of Alyite doctrine, but of the Kharejite schism,—that namely which takes its stand on the simplicity of the faith as first delivered by the Prophet. Revivals follow a corresponding course. Amongst the Orthodox, the quickened spirit shows itself in implicit return to the letter of the Coran ; in

Shie-ites
and
Orthodox.

the protest against forms and superstitions inconsistent with the sacred text; in outbursts of zeal to 'fight in the ways of the Lord;' and generally, in a tendency (as amongst the Wahabies) towards the ancient tenets of Kharejite theocracy. Among the Shie-as, on the other hand, the spirit of revival breaks out in a wild and mystical devotion, Soofee or Motazel; and in the profane extravagancies of the divine Imamate or other emanation of the Deity. Persia remains the only important nation devoted to the Shie-a faith. In India, the Emperors, being of Turkish blood, were generally orthodox. They encouraged the immigration of vast crowds of Arabs from their native soil, especially from the Holy cities, who were strictly orthodox; and so throughout Hindustan the Soonnie has always overshadowed the Shie-a faith[1].

Between Turkey and Persia there is a broad distinction in respect of tolerance. The Osmanlies, notwithstanding close contact with enlightened nations, are, in virtue of their orthodoxy, intolerant of the least divergence from the faith; while Persia, following in the wake of the Motazelite Caliphs, is less impatient of other creeds, and more amenable to outer influence[2]. In other respects, too, the ancient sentiment dividing Soonnie and Shie-a is as bitter now as it was in the days when Aly cursed Muavia, and Muavia cursed Aly, in the daily public service. The hopeless schism has tended to slacken the progress of Islam, and abate its aggressive force. Thus recently, when a deadly blow was aimed at the head of the Moslem empire on this side the Bosphorus, the sectarians of Persia, through hate and jealousy of the Soonnie creed, declined to rally round the banner of the Crescent; and, indeed, so far as any help or sympathy from Shiyas went, Islam might have been blotted

Bitter feeling between the two.

[1] *Soonnies* are those who hold by the *Sunnat*, or precedent, established by the practice of Mahomet, as handed down by tradition. They also recognize the title of the first three Caliphs, which the *Shie-as* (Shiyas) deny.

[2] The bigotry of the Persians appears mostly in matters of purification, remnants perhaps of their ancient faith. Baths and mosques are polluted by the presence of an infidel. Curious, also, that the Persians to this day curse Mamun as the poisoner of Aly Ridha, his son-in-law, and use his name as a term of abuse.

out of Europe altogether.   The Soonnie scorns the Shie-ite ;
and the Shie-ite in his turn spits on the graves of those
great Caliphs, Omar and Abu Bekr, to whom he owes it
that Islam spread thus marvellously, nay, even that it
survived the birth.

Islam stationary.   The Islam of to-day is substantially the Islam we have
seen throughout this history.   Swathed in the bands of the
Coran, the Moslem faith, unlike the Christian, is powerless
to adapt itself to varying time and place, keep pace with
the march of humanity, direct and purify the social life,
or elevate mankind.   Freedom, in the proper sense of
the word, is unknown ; and this apparently, because in the
body politic, the spiritual and the secular are hopelessly
confounded.   Hence we fail of finding anywhere the germ
of popular government or approach to free and liberal
institutions.   The nearest thing was the brotherhood of
Islam ; but that, as a controlling power, was confined to
the Arab race, and with its dominancy it disappeared.   The
type and exemplar of Moslem rule is the absolute and
autocratic monarch, alternating at times with the license of
lawless soldiery.   The only check upon the despot is the
law of the Coran, expounded by the learned, and enforced
by the sentiment, or it may be the uprising, of the nation.

Domestic institutions.   Nor has there been any change in the conditions of
social life.   Polygamy and servile concubinage are still as
ever the curse and blight of Islam.   By these may the unity
of the household at any time be broken ; the purity and
virtue weakened of the family tie ; the vigour of the upper
classes sapped ; and the throne itself liable to doubtful or
contested succession.   As to female slavery the Moslem
will not readily abandon an indulgence recognized by his
scripture.   Its influence on the master is really more to be
deprecated than on the wretched subject of the institution.
However much domestic slavery is ameliorated by the kindly
influences which in Moslem lands surround it, still the
license of servile concubinage fixes its withering grasp with
more damaging effect on the owner of the slave than on the
slave herself.

Divorce.   Hardly less evil is the one-sided power of divorce, at the mere word and will of the husband. Hanging over every household, like the sword of Damocles, it must affect the tone of society at large; for, even if seldom put in force, it cannot fail, as a potential influence, to weaken the marriage bond and lower the dignity and self-respect of woman.

Nor is it otherwise with the Veil, and such domestic The veil. injunctions of the Coran as exclude woman from her legitimate place and function in social life. The exclusion may, indeed, be little loss to her. But by this unreasonable law, mankind at large, beyond the harem's threshold, loses the grace and brightness of the sex, and purifying influence of its presence. Hence the cheerless aspect of Moslem outdoor life, and the drear austerity of their social gatherings. Opinion may differ as to the interdict on games of chance, and even the moderate use of wine. The double prohibition has no doubt tended to aggravate the gloom and gravity we speak of; but it may gladly be admitted that the absence of intemperance,— though with too frequent exception (as in this history we have seen) in the upper classes, is a spectacle in Mahometan lands much to be commended.

The institutions just noticed form an integral part of the Immobility teaching of Islam. They are bound up in the charter of of Islam. its existence. A reformed faith that should question the divine authority on which they rest, or attempt by rationalistic selection or abatement to effect a change, would be Islam no longer. That they tend to keep the Moslem nations in a backward, and in some respects barbarous, state cannot be doubted. It is still true that, as at Damascus, Bagdad, and Cordova, an era of great prosperity has at times prevailed. Commerce and speculation (the law of usury notwithstanding) were at such times advanced; the arts of peace were cultivated; travel and intercourse with other peoples to some extent broke down national prejudice and promoted liberality of sentiment; literature, science, and philosophy were prosecuted with marvellous success. But it was all short-lived, because civilization, not penetrating the family, was superficial. It failed to leaven domestic life. The canker-worm of polygamy, divorce, servile concubinage, and the veil, lay at the root. And society, withering under the influence of these, relapsed into semi-barbarism again.

Throughout this work we have often met with virtue and nobility, and acknowledged them gladly, whether in places high or low. But it has also been a duty, especially in the latter half of the volume, to thread our painful way in labyrinths of bloodshed and iniquity, and purlieus of Courts the sink of profligacy, treachery, and vice. It may be difficult to say how far the tree is here to be judged by the fruit; in other words, what of all this is due to the creed, and what to other causes, and even in spite of the creed. But, this difficulty notwithstanding, the conclusion can scarcely fail to force itself upon the impartial reader, that much of the dark retrospect is legitimate result of the laws and institutions just described. In one respect, indeed, there is no room for doubt; and that is in respect of intolerance and religious warfare. It is by direct command of his Master that the Moslem fights against the Jew and Christian 'until that they pay tribute with the hand, and are humbled;' and it is by a like command that he attacks the Heathen even to the bitter end. 'Fight against the Idolaters,' is the command which the Moslem holds divine,—' wheresoever ye find them; take them captive, besiege them, and lie in wait for them in every ambush.' If Christian nations have too often drawn the sword in propagation of their faith, it was in direct contravention of their Master's word,—'If My kingdom were of this world, then would My servants fight; ... but now is My kingdom not from hence.' Far different is the Moslem's case. Tribes and peoples for ages rushed into the battle-field, fulfilling what they believed their Maker's law 'to fight in the ways of the Lord;' and as its immediate effect, the world was drenched in blood from the Mediterranean to the Caspian Sea, and multitudes of men and women taken captive, and as such held in slavery. Yet with all this, how true has come the Saviour's other word,—' All they that take the sword shall perish with the sword.' At last the Crescent wanes before the Cross.

For now the political ascendency of the faith is doomed. Decline of political status. Every year witnesses a sensible degree of subsidence. In the close connection of the spiritual with the civil power, this cannot but affect the prestige of the religion itself; but nevertheless the religion maintains, and will no doubt long continue to maintain, its hold upon the people singularly unimpaired by the decline of its political supremacy.

As regards the spiritual, social, and dogmatic aspect of The Moslem world stationary. Islam, there has been neither progress nor material change. Such as we found it in the days of the Caliphate, such is it also at the present day. Christian nations may advance in civilization, freedom, and morality, in philosophy, science, and the arts, but Islam stands still. And thus stationary, so far as the lessons of the history avail, it will remain.

INDEX.

www.ingramcontent.com/pod-product-compliance
Ingram Content Group UK Ltd.
Pitfield, Milton Keynes, MK11 3LW, UK
UKHW020409010325
455677UK00029B/826